A HANDBOOK OF CULTURAL ECONOMICS, SECOND EDITION

A Handbook of Cultural Economics, Second Edition

Edited by

Ruth Towse

Professor of Economics of Creative Industries, CIPPM, Bournemouth University, UK and Professor Emerita, Erasmus University Rotterdam, The Netherlands

Edward Elgar
Cheltenham, UK • Northampton, MA, USA

Published by
Edward Elgar Publishing Limited
The Lypiatts
15 Lansdown Road
Cheltenham
Glos GL50 2JA
UK

Edward Elgar Publishing, Inc.
William Pratt House
9 Dewey Court
Northampton
Massachusetts 01060
USA

A catalogue record for this book
is available from the British Library

Library of Congress Control Number: 2010939205

Printed on elemental chlorine free (ECF)
recycled paper containing 30% Post-Consumer Waste

ISBN   978 1 84844 887 2 (cased)
          978 0 85793 103 0 (paperback)

Typeset by Servis Filmsetting Ltd, Stockport, Cheshire
Printed and bound in the USA

Contents

Contributors

Hans Abbing, University of Amsterdam, The Netherlands and a practising artist.

Keith Acheson, Carleton University, Canada.

Katrina Alford, Australian National University, Australia.

Orley Ashenfelter, Princeton University, USA.

William J. Baumol, New York University and Princeton University, USA.

Françoise Benhamou, Université Paris 13, France.

Mark Blaug, University of London and University of Buckingham, UK and University of Amsterdam, The Netherlands.

Lluís Bonet, University of Barcelona, Spain.

Andrew E. Burke, Cranfield University, UK.

Samuel Cameron, University of Bradford, UK.

Darlene C. Chisholm, Suffolk University, USA.

François Colbert, HEC-Montréal, Canada.

Tyler Cowen, George Mason University, USA.

Tiziana Cuccia, University of Catania, Italy.

Gillian Doyle, University of Glasgow, UK.

Joëlle Farchy, University of Paris 1 Panthéon Sorbonne, France.

Víctor Fernández-Blanco, Universidad de Oviedo, Spain.

Bruno S. Frey, University of Zurich, Switzerland and University of Warwick, UK.

Victor Ginsburgh, ECARES, Brussels and CORE, Louvain-la-Neuve, Belgium.

Kathryn Graddy, Brandeis University, USA.

Charles M. Gray, University of St Thomas, USA.

James Heilbrun (deceased), formerly Fordham University, USA.

Anders Henten, Aalborg University, Denmark.

Christian Hjorth-Andersen, University of Copenhagen, Denmark.

Michael Hutter, Social Science Research Centre Berlin, Germany.

William M. Landes, University of Chicago, USA.

Louis Lévy-Garboua, University of Paris 1, France.

William A. Luksetich, St. Cloud University, USA.

Christopher Maule, Carleton University, Canada.

Isidoro Mazza, University of Catania, Italy.

Claude Montmarquette, University of Montréal, Canada.

Dick Netzer (deceased), formerly New York University, USA.

John O'Hagan, Trinity College Dublin, Ireland.

Giacomo Pignataro, University of Catania, Italy.

Juan Prieto-Rodríguez, Universidad de Oviedo, Spain.

Ilde Rizzo, University of Catania, Italy.

Fabrice Rochelandet, Université de Paris Sud, France.

Michael Rushton, Indiana University, USA.

Dominique Sagot-Duvauroux, University of Angers, France.

Walter Santagata, University of Turin, Italy.

Günther G. Schulze, University of Freiburg, Germany.

Bruce A. Seaman, Georgia State University, USA.

Jen D. Snowball, Rhodes University, South Africa.

Mervi Taalas, Finnish National Gallery, Finland.

Reza Tadayoni, Aalborg University, Denmark.

David Throsby, Macquarie University, Australia.

Ruth Towse, Bournemouth University, UK and Erasmus University Rotterdam, The Netherlands.

Michele Trimarchi, University of Catanzaro, Italy.

Daniel Urrutiaguer, University of Paris 3, France.

Olav Velthuis, University of Amsterdam, The Netherlands.

Nachoem M. Wijnberg, University of Amsterdam, The Netherlands.

Glenn Withers, Australian National University, Australia.

Preface to the second edition

A Handbook of Cultural Economics has proved to be a useful source for students, teachers and many others wanting to find out about cultural economics. Its strength is that it is a compilation of chapters written by experts in their subject and I am indebted to them for their collaboration in producing this second edition. Many of the topics and authors in this edition are the same as those in the first edition, although a significant number of new ones are included and a few have been replaced. There are entirely new chapters that directly reflect developments in the subject, and almost every other chapter has been revised, more or less, depending upon recent research results, data and literature in the field and upon other factors, such as the impact of technological change. A few chapters remain as they were in the first edition for a variety of reasons – little new work has been done on the topic, the author was not available or even contactable and, sadly, two authors, James Heilbrun and Dick Netzer, both died in 2008. Rather than replace their chapters with ones written by other authors, their chapters (and those of some others whose authors could not be reached) have been retained from the first edition as they continue to make a contribution to cultural economics. In those cases, I have, as editor, added further reading. In a few cases, a chapter has been rewritten by a new author or authors. Inevitably, the addition of new chapters and revisions to former ones threatened to increase the length of the book, and in order to accommodate these improvements, several chapters from the first edition have not been retained.

Paul Stepan has ably and patiently assisted in the preparation of the second edition, and I am most grateful to him for that.

Introduction
Ruth Towse

Over the last 50 years, cultural economics has established itself as a field of study that is relevant to arts organizations, creative industries, cultural policy and, increasingly, to economic policy for growth and development. It began modestly in the 1960s with an interest in the economic analysis of the finance of museums and the live performing arts, and has spread and evolved into a broader analysis of the cultural or creative industries and their role in the creative economy. This 'new' economy is dominated by the digital revolution in the use of knowledge and information and its distribution via the Internet; it is shaped by the need to foster creativity and to understand the production and consumption of creative goods and services. While most economists hold that the new economy does not call for a new kind of economics, nevertheless new concepts have been adopted. Cultural economics has long wrestled with topics to which 'ordinary' economics did not seem fully applicable (for instance, understanding economic incentives for artists and other creators) and has accordingly developed an understanding of public policy issues concerning the development and support of the creative industries. Cultural economics now offers expertise in the analysis of markets for a wide range of creative products, ranging from art to digital television, and that is reflected in the topics covered in the second edition of this *Handbook*.

That said, a substantial part of this book reflects subjects that have been studied in cultural economics for many years, often under the heading 'economics of the arts'. Research on the economic characteristics of production and consumption of the performing arts, museums and built heritage on topics such as demand, elasticity, pricing, costs, market structure, finance and regulation continue to attract cultural economists. Some of these art forms – even the most traditional such as opera and museums – have been able to embrace new technologies, not so much on the production side (though that too) as in facilitating their ability to reach wider audiences. In addition, there has been an increase in economic research on the cultural industries (broadcasting, film, publishing and sound recording) and on the impact of the creative industries on economic development in cities and districts, including through festivals and cultural tourism. Besides the public finance of the arts, regulation by governments continues to play an important role in the creative economy in relation to heritage and the media, and through copyright law and artists' rights legislation. This book covers all these topics.

Economic characteristics of cultural goods and services
What all creative goods and services have in common is that they contain a creative or artistic element. Cultural goods may be capital or durable consumer goods – a picture in a museum, a DVD (digital video disk) – and they yield a flow of services over their lifetime; others, especially the performing arts, exist for only a particular time span. Cultural goods are tangible objects, like an artwork or a book; others are intangible services, like a musical performance or a visit to a museum. Some are final goods and services that

are supplied to consumers; others are intermediate goods and services that go into the production of other cultural products or into non-cultural output: a CD (compact disk) may be sold to the consumer, played on the radio as an input to a broadcast, played in a shopping mall or sports hall or split into tracks and downloaded on to an iPlayer or mobile phone.

Besides this cultural element, what creative goods have in common with all other goods and services is that their production utilizes resources of land, labour and capital and other inputs, particularly human ingenuity (entrepreneurship and human capital). These resources have other uses and therefore have an opportunity cost and a price. Even when they are supplied for free, the costs producing them have to be borne by someone: museum entry may be free for the visitor but the cost of the visit is paid by the funding organization – the state or other sponsor. When cultural products are supplied or financed by the government they are paid for out of taxes that are levied on all taxpayers, not just on those who visit cultural facilities, and therefore there is a redistribution of income from non-participants to those who participate (who are typically better off). Increasingly, services such as television and radio programmes and music are supplied for free to listeners and, as they are financed by advertising, they are ultimately paid for by sales to consumers who buy the advertised goods and services. These are the so-called 'two-sided' markets in which private for-profit firms finance the supply of creative services. This differs from sponsorship, where the firm finances a specific arts organization or project, often to publicize its brand name.

One more characteristic of cultural goods and services is that they typically require considerable investment in the fixed cost of producing the first unit, while the marginal cost of producing further units is relatively low. The ratio of fixed to marginal costs varies, however: in the performing arts, there is a high fixed cost of preparing and rehearsing a performance but then each live performance also requires the presence of the performers and back-stage support staff, thus making the marginal cost relatively. By contrast, if the performance is recorded, copies can be distributed for very little cost. In the case of digitally produced material, fixed costs are lower and distribution costs are virtually zero.

Economic theory and cultural economics

Cultural economics uses economic theory and empirical testing in order to explain these many aspects of the creative economy. Microeconomics, welfare economics, public choice economics and macroeconomics may be used and economists choose one or another of these bodies of theory as appropriate to analyse the topics they seek to explain. Sometimes this can seem confusing but in fact it is not inconsistent and the theories are not incompatible – they just tackle things in different ways. Microeconomics, as its name suggests, is concerned with individual decisions concerning the consumption and production of specific goods and services, and deals with their supply, demand and pricing at the level of the individual firm. So, for example, microeconomics can be applied to understanding how theatregoers respond to changes in prices.

By contrast, macroeconomics analyses broad aggregates at the level of the whole economy, looking at employment, economic growth and development: examples are the impact of a new cultural facility on a city or the contribution to national or regional income generated by the creative industries. Cultural economists also analyse the economics of sub-sectors of the creative economy and the term 'creative industries' is now widely used to cover the whole arts and cultural sector (the performing arts, including live music, theatre, opera and dance; heritage, including museums and built heritage; the cultural and media industries, including sound recording, film, software and games, publishing and broadcasting) as well as industries, such as fashion and advertising, that have not so far been part of the subject matter of cultural economics.

Welfare economics takes as its theme the economic well-being of a whole society and it offers an analytical framework for assessing the effect of changes due to technological developments, social attitudes on welfare and policy measures. It lays down theoretical criteria for increased social efficiency and it forms the basis for applying cost–benefit analysis, which is widely used by government to evaluate new projects. Although welfare economics looks at aggregate welfare, its analytical methods are founded in microeconomics. Cultural economics has made great use of welfare economics in evaluating government policies for financing and regulating cultural institutions. Less use has so far been made of public choice theory, which applies economic analysis to political decision-making and takes into account the self-interest of policy-makers and administrators.

Another area of economics that is widely used in cultural economics is public finance. Public finance is the term used for the study of taxation and expenditure at the national, regional and local levels of government. It analyses the efficiency and equity effects of taxes and subsidies: the former is concerned with incentives to consumers and taxpayers, and the latter deals with topics such as the redistribution of income and 'fairness'. Public finance is closely connected to government policy; however, although economists are frequently involved in the positive aspects of policy-making, for instance, estimating the costs and benefits of a particular programme or project, they have little professional competence in the normative side of policy formation. An important contribution by economists in analysing cultural policy-making has been the recognition that it often seeks to achieve multiple objectives that are in conflict (for example, raising quality and spreading access to the arts and heritage) and that require different policy measures and incentive structures. This is the case not only at the macro level but also at the level of individual arts organizations; a museum, for example is a multi-product firm, offering research and conservation services as well as education and entertainment for visitors. A lump-sum grant would not distinguish priorities of government policy, for instance, if a publicly funded museum is expected to target participation by new audiences, and such a grant, therefore, would not necessarily provide the right incentive to achieve the desired policy outcome. As almost all subsidy to the arts and heritage is channelled via the supply side, public expenditure given to arts organizations needs to be targeted and its success in achieving policy objectives monitored. There has been some limited experimentation with voucher schemes on the demand side but otherwise the focus of public finance is almost entirely on the supply of cultural goods and services by public and private organizations.

Applying the theories

An example of how different theories and economic research can be used in combination is presented by the well-known economic analysis of the performing arts by Baumol and Bowen (1966). Initially, the authors gathered a mass of microeconomic data on theatre, opera, ballet and orchestras on employment, prices, revenues and audiences in the USA and UK, and looked at trends over a period of time. They developed the theory that is now called Baumol's cost disease, using a macroeconomic framework to compare growth in two 'sectors' in the economy, manufacturing (the dynamic sector) and the performing arts (the stagnant sector) to explain why costs and prices were rising faster in the performing arts than in the manufacturing sector. They then employed micro-economic thinking about consumers' responses to price rises and predicted the possible consequences for arts organizations of a financial deficit. Evoking so-called 'market failure' arguments from welfare economics, they argued that external and unpriced ben-efits would be lost if the performing arts were left to market forces alone and that the presence of these externalities and spillover effects made the case for welfare-improving government intervention via direct subsidy or tax breaks.

In methodological terms, it can be seen that the cost disease theory is a mixture of posi-tive and normative approaches: data gathering and analysis is a 'positive' research activ-ity; measures of labour productivity and cost inflation utilize standard macroeconomic tools and are objective, while welfare economics is 'normative' in that it seeks to achieve the norm of social welfare improvement.

Positive and normative economics
The distinction between positive and normative is very important in economics because it is a way of legitimizing the scientific contribution of economic thinking and distin-guishing it from controversial opinion and belief. This distinction does not always hold water and there is even danger in being over-confident about the power of the distinction, but for economists, it is important to try to be objective and to respect individual choice. Thus to return to the example of Baumol's cost disease: establishing the 'real' increase in prices and costs (that is, increases after allowing for inflation) and audience figures is not controversial, although there may be some statistical errors in predicting future revenues. But we cannot go from those facts to argue that the government *ought* to sub-sidize the arts without making normative claims. That case had to be made in terms of the policy goal of maintaining a certain level of arts provision by showing that without financial support from other sources, revenues from ticket sales would be unlikely to cover costs of producing the same level and quality of performing arts, and those levels of output could not be achieved. Baumol and Bowen were very clear on this distinction.

So, if that is the case, you might reasonably ask why some economists did not accept the theory of the cost disease. The reason is that Baumol *assumed* that the arts are a stagnant sector unable to benefit from technological progress, whereas the manufacturing sector does benefit and as a result can produce goods more cheaply; second, he assumed that performing arts organizations, such as theatre companies and orchestras, cannot change their artistic labour component; third, he assumed that rates of pay in the performing arts would rise at the same rate as those in the economy as a whole (that the labour market is 'integrated'). It is these assumptions that have been criticized as unrealistic and incorrect, but not the logic of increasing costs. Moreover, it is not only the cultural sector that is prone to this 'disease': it has manifested itself in a range of public sector services.

Public finance
One of the earliest topics that concerned cultural economists was the case for public finance – either direct finance or subsidy, or tax measures to encourage private

donation – of the arts and heritage. The type of intervention adopted varies considerably from country to country, but it is possible to identify broad trends. In mainland Europe, many countries have what are tantamount to state-owned and -managed arts and heritage organizations: central, regional or local government owns the buildings and contents, employs the people working in them and is responsible for managing the organization. Arts organizations are therefore simply part of the public sector and are financed wholly out of taxation; revenues from ticket sales often revert to the government office responsible. At one time, broadcasting was also a state monopoly in most countries. Changes have been made to both ownership and management structures in some countries in all areas of the cultural sector but direct finance is still the norm in many instances. An exception to this model is built heritage, where many significant items are in private ownership and therefore regulation, often combined with subsidy, is used to achieve policy objectives.

By contrast, the model in the USA and other countries, for example Japan, has been of private finance through revenues from ticket sales and other enterprises and state encouragement of private giving through the tax system (such as the use of tax waivers) to privately constituted, typically non-profit, arts and heritage organizations. The 'intermediate' model adopted in the UK, Australia, New Zealand and Ireland, among others, is the so-called 'arm's-length' principle of public finance, whereby private, non-profit organizations (often constituted as charities) are granted sums of money from general taxation for a specific period of time and are expected to raise a considerable proportion of their incomes from sales and donations, increasingly helped to some degree by the tax system. In practice, these models overlap to some extent, but differing attitudes to the responsibility of the state and public finance still frame the debates and practices of cultural policy.

By contrast, the cultural industries are private, for-profit businesses that rarely receive public finance (the exception being public service broadcasting), although they are regulated by the state for monopoly (antitrust) abuses and, more significantly, by copyright and other intellectual property law.

Public goods

The main economic rationale for public finance for the arts is that they have public-good characteristics and so the extent to which that is the case has been debated for a long time in cultural economics. Pure public goods (of which there are almost no real-life examples) have the characteristics of being both non-rival and non-excludable, meaning that one person's consumption of them does not reduce what is available to others and, equally, they are available to all-comers. Over-the-air broadcasting is an example of a service with strong public-good characteristics. There are several implications of these features: an entrepreneur seeking to make a profit or a non-profit organization seeking to cover its costs with revenues from sales would not be able to fully capture those revenues as consumers would probably 'free-ride' on the expenditures of others – once a sufficient amount to get the good or service supplied were raised, everyone could 'cash in' and get access to the good or service. The result is that the good would not be supplied except through some form of collective finance – for instance, taxation – and the allocation of resources via the price mechanism would not produce the socially desirable output of goods and services.

Cultural goods and services vary as to the extent of their public goods characteristics: visits to the theatre or to a museum have a private benefit (utility) to the visitor for which they are prepared to pay and for which entry can be excluded for those who do not pay; however, visiting a beautiful city provides utility for which a price cannot be charged for by entry ticket. Even excludable goods and services may have some external (or 'spillover') benefits; an element of non-rivalry is present since consumption by paying audiences and visitors benefits the public good by reinforcing a sense of national or local identity and by increasing understanding of other people and cultures. The mere existence of a theatre or a museum in a city may also produce social benefits; contingent valuation studies have shown that people who do not participate in the arts and heritage are willing to pay something to provide these facilities either to ensure that they exist for others or as a option for their own future consumption. Markets therefore do not take their full value into account through prices, and this argues for some form of public intervention. A second argument for public finance of the arts and heritage is that consumer demand does not reflect the full value of these goods because they are 'experience' goods; consumers' tastes are not fully formed and they cannot have full information about cultural goods.

Information problems mean that expert judgement has to be relied on to ensure quality, and that leads to what is called 'supplier-induced' demand. This easily results in the domination of expert opinion, often supported by state finance, with consumers and taxpayers being unable to assert their preferences. An alternative but similar concept that is used to justify replacing consumer sovereignty with collective provision is that of 'merit' goods, the term used by economists for goods that are held, often by experts, to have inherent value for society. It is worth noting that the above arguments for government intervention are not confined to the arts but are also made in relation to health and education. The logic of these arguments has, however, not been extended to the creative goods and services produced by the private enterprise cultural industries, the exception being public service broadcasting.

Creative industries and the digital revolution
The growth of the service sector and the decline of manufacturing in developed economies have focused interest on the creative or knowledge economy, and this in turn has led to considerable interest in the creative industries, emphasizing their role as the main force for growth in the creative economy. The impact of this 'paradigm change' is reflected in the content of this second edition of the *Handbook*, with both new and some revised chapters demonstrating the significant impact of the digital revolution.

The digital technological revolution has had profound effects on the production, consumption, distribution and marketing of creative goods and services, on their costs and pricing and on their content. Digitalization has enabled producers to convert many cultural goods into intangible services for delivery via the Internet and to market other goods that way. It has transformed items that would have previously been classified as goods into services – books, newspapers and photographs are some examples. In electronic form, these items can be personalized, reused and retransmitted in ways that were not possible in the form of tangible goods. This transformation has meant that pricing policies have changed significantly: now, instead of buying a good that you can keep for as long as you like or give away to someone else for a fixed amount of money (the price), when you obtain them as electronic services, you pay a licence fee for a specific selection of services for a specific period of time and copyright law is likely to prohibit sharing them with others.

Digitalization has also meant that these services become akin to public goods since it is trivially easy to share digital files between users without payment, and that has produced an upheaval in the creative industries that produce digital material – recorded music, games, film and so on. Although copyright law exists to prevent such free-riding, digitalization has called into question its ability to enable creators and the creative industries to fully appropriate revenues in these markets. Although copyright law now includes technological protection measures and digital rights management is used to prevent unauthorized distribution, the scale of copying has made it an insuperable task to enforce it fully. Copyright law has to find a balance between the demands of producers and users in the digital world; this is fundamental to the success of the creative economy but, so far, the subject has attracted little interest in cultural economics, perhaps because it is too specialized a topic.

Empirical research on the creative industries

One of the main contributions economics can make to all the topics mentioned above is to provide empirical evidence. That can range from the collection of basic data (for example, the value-added of the creative industries) to testing theories of incentives. In the past, lack of data, especially of official statistics on the cultural sector, has been a barrier to good empirical research, but that is now changing in part due to the emphasis on the economic role of the creative industries in the creative economy as well as to past efforts by cultural economists. As with other branches of economics, good statistical analysis and theoretical development are vital to the success of cultural economics.

About this edition

This introduction has shown that cultural economics has a body of knowledge that provides common approaches to production and consumption in all the creative industries. The second edition of the *Handbook* shows how much the subject has progressed since 2003. As in the first edition, the titles of the chapters have been kept short to make the book easy to use, and chapters are cross-referenced to guide the reader to related topics and, as before, it is assumed that readers have a basic knowledge of economic theory. Several books listed at the end of this introduction explain the theories used in cultural economics. A new feature of this edition is the addition of suggestions for further reading, which in almost all cases have been provided by the chapter authors. Thus this second edition of the *Handbook* is significantly brought up to date and, I believe, improved.

References

Baumol, William J. and William G. Bowen (1966), *Performing Arts: The Economic Dilemma*, New York: Twentieth Century Fund.
Caves, Richard (2000), *Creative Industries: Contracts between Art and Commerce*, Cambridge, MA and London: Harvard University Press.
Frey, Bruno S. (2000) *Arts and Economics*, Berlin and Heidelberg: Springer.
Throsby, David (2010), *The Economics of Cultural Policy*, Cambridge: Cambridge University Press.
Towse, Ruth (2010), *A Textbook of Cultural Economics*, Cambridge: Cambridge University Press.

United Nations Conference on Trade and Development (UNCTAD) (2008), *Creative Economy Report 2008*, Geneva: UNCTAD. Available online at http://www.unctad.org/en/docs/ditc20082cer_en.pdf.

Further reading

Richard Caves's (2000) book is a detailed analysis of the structure of the creative industries based on the contracts between the artist or original creator and the firm; this provides a wealth of material covering the whole cultural sector. Bruno Frey is a leading writer on cultural economics (in addition to many other subjects) and his book *Arts and Economics* (Frey, 2000) contains essays on a range of topics; it has rightly been one of the most popular books on the subject. David Throsby's (2010) book demonstrates the relevance of economics to all aspects of cultural policy for the arts and cultural industries by an author who is one of the best-known cultural economists. My *Textbook of Cultural Economics* (Towse, 2010) provides an introductory account of the whole field of cultural economics, along with explanations of the economic theory necessary to understand it. The first part of the UNCTAD (2008) *Report* offers a brief overview of the concept of the creative economy and the role of the creative industries in economic growth and development.

1 Application of welfare economics
William J. Baumol

There are some very agreeable and beautiful talents of which the possession commands a certain sort of admiration; but of which the exercise for the sake of gain is considered, whether from reason or prejudice, as a sort of public prostitution. The pecuniary recompence, therefore, of those who exercise them in this manner, must be sufficient, not only to pay for the time, labour, and expence of acquiring the talents, but for the discredit which attends the employment of them as a means of subsistence. The exorbitant rewards of players, opera-singers, opera-dancers, &c. are founded upon those two principles; the rarity and beauty of the talents, and the discredit of employing them in this manner . . . Such talents, though far from being common, are by no means so rare as is imagined. Many people possess them in great perfection, who disdain to make this use of them; and many more are capable of acquiring them, if any thing could be made honourably by them. (Adam Smith, *The Wealth of Nations*, Bk I, Ch. X, Pt 1, ed. Cannan, pp. 108–9)

Welfare analysis and rationale for public funding of the arts

Welfare economists seem not to have devoted much systematic attention to the arts. The connection, rather, grew from the other direction – the arts seeking justification in the analysis of welfare theory, not for themselves, but for the public funding on which they often rely. The problem is that, for a number of reasons, the arts have found it difficult to support themselves in the marketplace. There are, of course, obvious exceptions, such as commercial theatre, and painters who have achieved popularity and wealth. However, much artistic activity historically has depended on the voluntary patronage of royal princes and, later, merchant princes. As democracy took over the world's wealthier economies, government support often replaced that of the patrons. But this gave rise to a troubling issue: why, in a society whose government ostensibly acted so as to contribute to the welfare of its citizens, should products such as paintings and services such as opera performances be singled out for financial support, when the bulk of the goods and services generated by the economy are left to their own devices to sink or swim in the marketplace?

The answer to some, few of them economists, seems obvious. The arts are among the most desirable products of civilization – indeed, they are among the most worthy of the outputs of the economy. But then, one is led to ask, if they are so worthy, why is this not matched by their demand? The answer is that their limited audience simply reflects inadequate education of the consuming public, and the consequently undeveloped ability to appreciate the finer things is all too easily attacked by those who question the credentials of the self-appointed arbiters of taste. The difficulties of those who advocate public support for the arts is compounded by the well-documented fact that their audience is typically composed of individuals whose incomes, wealth and education are well above those of the population as a whole. This means that devotion of general taxation to support of the arts invites condemnation as a reversal of 'Robin Hood' practice, taking from the poor to give to the rich.

Economists with interest in the arts have been led to employ the tools of welfare economics to construct a more solid foundation for public funding. They have proposed a number of arguments in support of this approach – among them: equality of opportunity, the external benefits of education, the public-good properties of the product, the infant-organization argument and investment for the future. In addition, economists have returned to the merit-goods argument the judgement that the arts merit public support simply because of the superiority of their inherent worthiness.[1]

Equality of opportunity
There can be little doubt that, on average, consumers of the arts have incomes above those of the members of society in aggregate. However, the other side of the coin is that the less affluent often do not get the opportunity to experience the arts and to discover the attraction of cultural activity for themselves. This problem is exacerbated by the high admission fees made necessary by high costs of live performance, museum operation and other cultural activities. So, if equality of opportunity is included in the calculation of social welfare, this can be taken as one justification for public support.

Beneficial externalities
It is, of course, a standard argument of welfare economics that, if an activity generates beneficial externalities, public subsidy of that enterprise may well enhance welfare. The externalities of artistic activity are, however, not entirely clear. There is the likelihood that one artistic undertaking can inspire others and, thereby, facilitate further creative endeavours. It has also been claimed that persons with interest in the arts are generally better members of society, increasing the benefits to others from their presence. However, these claims are not easy to prove or even to make explicit.

Culture as public good
There can be little doubt that cultural activities often possess public-good properties. A half-empty theatre or a sparsely attended museum is perfectly analogous to the uncrowded bridge (in the example provided by Dupuit (1844)) – since the true cost of an additional user is zero, if any non-zero price prevents anyone from using the facilities the result is a net social loss. This problem is particularly acute in the case of mass media, such as broadcasting, because there is no practical limit to the number of listeners who can be served without depletion of supply to others. Here too, however, a zero price is impossible without subsidy.

Infant cultural enterprise
The financial difficulties of new art forms and even new arts organizations are well known, and the starving unrecognized artist has become a cliché. The notion that new enterprises merit public assistance and that society benefits from such aid in the long run is an ancient argument, and one that has elicited much scepticism from economists.

Cultural reputation and investment for the future
It is often claimed that, even if a society does not value the arts for itself sufficiently to provide the requisite support through the market, it may want to do so for other reasons. For example, it may want to avoid the reputation of being a society of Philistines, or it may feel that future cultural activity justifies preservation of the arts in the present. This

attitude is parallel to that of that King of Naples, who reportedly supported the opera on condition that he never be asked to attend.

Merit goods

It seems generally to be felt among economists – even among those most personally supportive of the arts (see, for example, Peacock, 1969) – that, while these arguments have some validity, they do not by themselves constitute an overwhelming case for extensive support of the arts. The basic objection is that, while cultural activity undoubtedly offers such benefits, so do other human activities, and it is not clear on the grounds so far noted that the arts deserve to be singled out for special support. In response, it can be argued that subsidies *are* provided to many other activities, some with little in demonstrable benefits other than those they provide directly to their purchasers. However, few if any of these activities have made a convincing case for public support. Ultimately, then, at least some of the economists (and others) who advocate generous subvention to the arts fall back on Professor Musgrave's device: the merit-goods argument (see, for example, Scitovsky, 1976), which proposes that the arts deserve support simply because they are significantly worthy. In short, the arts deserve public funding because they are good. If asked why, or how one tests the proposition, the implied answer is that it is self-evident. Whether or not this is accepted as convincing, it must surely be recognized to be an honest reply.

This completes the brief survey of the issue that is surely central to the welfare economics of the arts. It must be admitted that its protracted investigation by analysts of the highest calibre has not carried the discussion much further from where it stood some decades ago. The discussion turns now to a second critical issue for which welfare theory is pertinent: the role of instruments, such as copyright, in ensuring compensation of the suppliers of cultural products. This issue is hardly new, but, as will be shown, recent economic developments have made the matter more acute, and analysis has contributed greatly to our insights on the subject.[2]

Cultural output: compensation, the need for repeated sunk costs, public-good properties and measures to protect intellectual property

The basic problems

Many art forms are characterized by public-good properties: they are not depletable, meaning that one can increase the number of consumers of a cultural product without having to reduce the consumption of anyone else, and exclusion may be difficult, meaning that individuals may be able to consume such a product without the permission of the supplier. These two attributes, in turn, raise two issues: how can the suppliers be compensated for their efforts (something desired not only as a matter of equity, but also in order to elicit their continued supply) and, if compensation is to be obtained through the market mechanism, what price, if any, should be charged for the products?

These are not new issues for the arts. As already noted, a half-empty theatre raises all these problems, but recent technological change has greatly increased their significance. The availability of the mass media and, especially, the Internet has magnified the size of the audience that can be provided for without depleting the provision to others. Moreover, these new transmission modes have made it more difficult to collect whatever compensation the supplier may consider appropriate.

As Dupuit (1844) and Samuelson (1954) made clear, a key dilemma here is the desirability of charging consumers anything at all. If the price mechanism is the means used to compensate suppliers, it is obvious that a zero price cannot be optimal socially because artistic activity is not costless, and, particularly where the activity is carried out for profit, a zero price will not elicit the socially optimal supply. Indeed, with such a product price, the output of commercial suppliers can be expected to be zero. On the other hand, zero output of such desirable products patently cannot be optimal.

But any non-zero price cannot be optimal either, for, if additional consumers can, for all practical purposes, be supplied at zero marginal cost, the exclusion of any consumer by a non-zero price must entail a social loss – preventing a benefit to a consumer whose cost to society would be zero.

This is only the beginning of the puzzles. Suppose that this dilemma is ignored as an unsolvable theoretical problem, and non-zero prices are the norm. What second-best price is consistent with maximal welfare benefits? The textbook conclusion does not suffice because price equal to marginal cost will generally not allow recoupment by the suppliers. The problem is traceable to the character of sunk cost that is common in artistic activity. Standard theory tells us that sunk costs do not matter, that their magnitude should not affect optimal price. As a piece of ancient history that cannot be changed by any current or future pricing decision, as these are simply irrelevant. But in the arts, sunk costs are not just historical data. The problem is that sunk outlays, characteristically, must be incurred again and again. For example, the production costs of a newly mounted drama are indeed a sunk cost, and if an acting company were to present that drama and no other for the indefinite future, the sunk cost would be irrelevant. It would not matter whether the future performances rewarded the investors handsomely or failed to return any of their outlays. But that is patently not how an acting company carries on its activities. New productions must be brought to the stage, normally at fairly frequent intervals, so that sunk outlays take the form of an intertemporal stream of periodic and relatively large expenditures, rather than a once-and-for-all occurrence. And future sunk costs are still variable, not sunk, in the present. To induce investors to keep providing the necessary resources, past recoupment history must be such as to promise the possibility or even the likelihood of recovery of future sunk investments. This is true not only of stage productions, but also of the training required for singers or dancers. Trained performers have a very limited working life, and the sunk outlays entailed in their training must be repeated constantly if the activities in their fields are not to come to an end.

These difficulties have a near perfect analogue in the 'new economy', in which innovation has become the prime weapon of competition in much of industry. The proprietary knowledge that emerges from inventive activity is well known to have significant public-good properties, and competition forces firms to repeat constantly the sunk outlays that are entailed in the innovation process. Not only are these problems in the performing arts and the innovation process the same, but it is arguable that the pricing principles that are applicable to either are also pertinent to the other.

Government buyout of intellectual property and the public-good problem
The analogy with the economics of innovation immediately offers one way of dealing with the problem that contributes further justification for government support. In the

case of innovation, patents constitute the most direct analogue to copyright in the case of the arts. Both of these raise the public-good problem: they are designed to reward the creator of intellectual property by enhancing that person's ability to exclude unauthorized users, thereby making it prospectively possible for the creator to extract a price for its use. But that non-zero price runs into the Dupuit–Samuelson dilemma: why exclude anyone from the benefit of costless usage of a product?

There is a considerable literature (see, for example, Kremer, 1998, for an excellent discussion and citations of other writings) that suggests a way to cut this Gordian knot: patent buyouts. This entails outright purchase of the property by government, with the creators thereby offered appropriate rewards, in return for which they give up any right to charge for use of their creations. Kremer provides a dramatic example:

> In 1839 the government of France combined elements of the patent system and of direct government support of research by buying out the patent for Daguerreotype photography and placing the technique in the public domain. After the patent was bought out, Daguerreotype photography was rapidly adopted worldwide and was subject to myriad technical improvements. (Ibid., p. 1138)

Obviously, this goes a good part of the way towards solving the problem, as it provides the desired incentive for creative activity, while not precluding socially costless access to others. Such an approach is possible in the arts, but it must be recognized that it does not solve the problem completely. First, as Ramsey analysis shows (see below), the government subvention, and the resources it provides to recipients, must come from somewhere. This, in turn, must entail non-zero taxes, which themselves unavoidably distort decisions and so entail welfare costs. Second, there remains the unsolved theoretical problem of determining an optimal buyout price, particularly in light of the fact that a patent or copyright is a (deliberate) grant of possible monopoly power to the creator of the intellectual property, who may well seek to extract a monopoly profit via the price. Finally, there is the problem of reality – while governments are often willing to supply part of such a subvention, they may not be prepared to provide enough to permit the activities to remain solvent with a non-zero price for their use, a problem exacerbated by the arts' ever-rising real costs.

Solvency generally requires price discrimination
Cultural products, then, are generally supplied at non-zero prices, even when they are produced with substantial government support. Moreover, the process is often characterized by considerable price discrimination – student and senior discounts, reduced subscription prices, lower group prices, arrangements with schools, churches and trade unions, and a variety of other such arrangements. This is done, at least in part, for reasons of equity – to prevent exclusion of the impecunious. Part of the purpose, however, as in the case of subscription pricing, is to help in dealing with the financial needs of the enterprise. Indeed, economics teaches us that the need for this approach may be more pressing than practitioners recognize. It has already been noted here that marginal cost pricing is incompatible with survival of firms that need to incur substantial sunk costs repeatedly. Nor will even absolute freedom of competitive entry at zero entry cost drive prices down to the uncompensatory marginal cost level in such circumstances. This is because entry can be expected to occur only if prices in the field

offer the prospect of enabling an entrant to cover all of its prospective sunk costs. So any prices above marginal costs, but insufficient to cover sunk costs, will elicit no entry. Entry will only occur and drive down prices if at least some of those prices are sufficiently above marginal costs to recoup the sunk outlays. But it has been known, at least since the writings of Dupuit in the mid-nineteenth century (see also the illuminating recent discussions by Hausman and Mackie-Mason, 1988, and Varian, 2000), that price discrimination helps the firm with fixed costs to recover its outlays. Indeed, recovery is sometimes unachievable without this. Here I shall go one step further and demonstrate that solvency generally is impossible without recourse to discriminatory prices – although this is not true in every case. Moreover, I shall show that effective competition in the form of totally unimpeded entry, at least into commercial cultural activity, not only does not prevent the adoption of such prices in those circumstances where it is required to prevent insolvency, but rather, such competitive pressures tend to make price discrimination mandatory.

Socially optimal discriminatory prices
The full story follows from the observation that full ease of entry not only ensures that the incumbent firm's profits will be driven down to the competitive level – it goes beyond that. In such a market, entry and the threat of entry ensure that the incumbent, in the long run, cannot expect to earn more than competitive returns, no matter what prices it chooses to adopt for its products. Then our result follows:

1. Among the prices more than very temporarily available to the incumbent, those that maximize its profit will yield exactly the competitive rate of return;
2. If that maximum is unique, any other prices adopted by the incumbent will yield a rate of return below the competitive level – that is, one that is not viable financially; and
3. Since differential prices are not subject to the constraint that all purchases must be provided at the same price, the profits attainable under discriminatory prices will generally be higher, and certainly no lower, than those offered by any uniform price. Consequently, the unique profit-maximizing prices that the firm is required to charge in order to break even normally will be discriminatory, with the firm that adopts them occupying the position of discriminatory price-taker.

The competitive model, as a guide to socially optimal pricing, then suggests that not only financial viability, but also static optimality, requires the prices for cultural products to be discriminatory. But there is a more direct way to see that. Ramsey theory, as is well known, addresses itself directly to the determination of second-best prices in the presence of recoupment shortfall if prices were set at marginal costs (see Ramsey, 1927, and, for a simpler description, Baumol and Bradford, 1970). Moreover, the well-known Ramsey formula clearly calls for discriminatory pricing, with the differences between prices and marginal costs determined by demand elasticities. Indeed, given the solvency constraint, the prices that emerge are precisely those that, in the past, were referred to as 'charging what the traffic will bear'. However, the zero economic profit constraint means that such prices constitute no exercise of monopoly power. This is one of the key implications of the discussion of this section.

Licensing of copyright for commercial reuse

Ramsey theory, then, constitutes the foundation of welfare analysis of the pricing of cultural products. In the world of mass media, however, this is not the end of the story. Once copyright becomes an instrument for the extraction of compensation, a new issue arises. Others engaged in cultural activities will want access to the material covered by copyright for its reuse in their own pursuit of profit. For example, films and recorded television programmes are often rebroadcast by others than their proprietors, and recordings of music are played by broadcasters. In some cases the users are direct competitors of the copyright owners. The question is whether or not there exists an economically efficient price for such access to the material covered by copyright. It will be shown next that there is such an efficient price.

It is clear that there are levels of such an access price that are materially too high or substantially too low for a social optimum. Prohibitively high licensing fees are equivalent to outright refusal to license to anyone, while inadequate fees, which can easily occur if licensing is compulsory, constitute a strong disincentive for investment in the creative activity that yielded the product. Fees that are excessively low can also lead to use of the product by some inefficient firms at the expense of others better qualified to do so.

The theory of price regulation provides a pricing principle that can be used in finding an efficient copyright-licensing fee. This principle has been referred to as 'the efficient component-pricing rule' (ECPR), or as 'the parity principle'. The efficiency property of the parity-pricing rule is the attribute that, when charged the parity licence fee, a renter of the copyrighted material will be able, viably, to charge consumers a lower price than the copyright owner's only if the former is the more efficient of the two in the process of transmitting the item to consumers.

The logic of the proof that the parity-pricing formula (given below) satisfies this requirement is not difficult to understand. For this purpose, it is helpful to think of the item covered by copyright as one of the inputs to the final product provided to consumers. Then, the purchaser of access to the material under copyright ('the renter') is engaged in the transmission of this material to customers. Thus the latter is clearly not placed under an inefficient competitive handicap by the licence fee if, when the renter's remaining input cost of supplying (transmitting) the final product to consumers is X pounds per unit of final-product output lower than the copyright owner's, the renter can just afford to provide the final product exactly X pounds cheaper than the copyright owner can. For obvious reasons, this has been called 'the level-playing-field theorem'.

All this can be described formally, giving an explicit formula for an efficient licence fee. We use the following notation:

$P_{f,i}$ = the copyright owner, I's, given price per unit of final product;

$\min P_{f,c}$ = the competitor, C's, minimum viable price of final product;

P_i = the price charged for a licence to use the copyright, per unit of final product;

$IC_{r,i}$ = the incremental cost to the copyright owner of the remaining final-product inputs, per unit of final product;

$IC_{r,c}$ = the corresponding figure for the competitor; and

IC_i = the incremental cost to the copyright owner of use of the copyright by itself or by others.

As will be demonstrated presently, ECPR requires that the licensing price satisfy the following rule:[3]

$$P_i = P_{f,i} - IC_{r,i} \quad \text{[licence price} = I\text{'s final-product price} - I\text{'s } IC \text{ of remaining inputs]}$$
(1.1)

Equation (1.1) tells us that ECPR establishes a tight link between the price, $P_{f,i}$, that the copyright owner charges for its final product and the price, P_i, it charges its rivals for the licence to use the copyright. If incremental production costs do not change, efficiency requires that a rise in one of these prices must be matched, pound for pound, by a rise in the other.

Then our task is to prove the level-playing-field theorem. The parity price, as given by (1.1), for use of material covered by copyright is both necessary and sufficient in order for the playing field to be level. This means that the maximum difference between the remunerative prices of the perfect substitute final products of the two firms, the copyright owner (I), and its final-product competitor (C), is exactly equal to the difference in the firms' remaining incremental costs (other than the licence fees).

Proof: The level playing field is defined by

$$\min P_{f,c} - P_{f,i} = IC_{r,c} - IC_{r,i}$$
(1.2)

That is, the lowest compensatory price the competitor can afford to charge should differ from the copyright owner's exactly by the amount (positive or negative) that the former's remaining costs are below the latter's. The lowest price that is financially viable for the competitor clearly is given by

$$\min P_{f,c} = P_i + IC_{r,c}$$
(1.3)

That is, the price must cover the copyright licensing cost plus the remaining cost of supplying the final product (of course, including the normal profit on the required capital).

Comparing the two equations, we see at once that the level-playing-field condition (1.2) will be satisfied if and only if

$$P_i = P_{f,i} - IC_{r,i}$$
(1.4)

But this is the parity-pricing formula (1.1). Thus parity pricing is both necessary and sufficient for a level playing field. QED.

This completes our proof that parity pricing of a copyright licence is necessary for economic efficiency in the provision of final product by its competing suppliers. For, if the rule is violated, a less efficient supplier of the remaining inputs can win the competition for the business of supplying those inputs, instead of the task going to its more efficient rival. That is, violation of (1.1) permits the less efficient supplier of the remaining inputs, such as transmission, to underprice its more efficient competitors.[4] The proof is readily extended to cases with three or more competing firms.

Other issues and concluding remarks

There seems, so far, to be no systematic literature that can be deemed to constitute a welfare economics of the arts and culture. Yet it has been possible to show here that these arenas do give rise to issues that clearly are within the scope of welfare theory and that require such theory for their analysis.

Indeed, I have noted some appropriate analytic methods, but the topics discussed here qualify primarily as illustrations. There are many other topics related to culture that appear to demand welfare analysis. For example, the issue of cultural heritage, and its valuation, is a significant and fascinating topic that calls for study in terms of welfare analysis. In addition, communication of the products of artistic activity naturally gives rise to such issues as network externalities and compatibility of the instruments of communication.

In sum, much remains to be done in the field. However, the promise of such an undertaking is underscored by the analytic tools already available in other areas of applied economics, which means that a good part of the requisite work has already been carried out.

Notes

1. For two excellent compendia of pertinent discussions, see Blaug (1992) and Towse (1997, vol. II, parts V–VII). For other discussions with significant additional insights, see Frey and Pommerehne (1989) and Throsby (1994). For a sceptical view, see Grampp (1986).
2. Much valuable information on the subject and much insight has been provided in Towse (2001).
3. This content was previously published in Baumol (2002, Chapter 13).
4. Here we should pause to admit that, where scale economies mean that marginal-cost pricing is not feasible, theory calls for adoption of a Ramsey price for the licence, as well as for final product, and that Ramsey price can violate ECPR. It should be noted, however, that a frequent complaint against ECPR in regulatory arenas, such as telecommunications and electricity, is that it yields bottleneck input prices that are disturbingly high. Yet the Ramsey-adjusted ECPR prices can be expected to be even higher. Specifically, so long as any rents are left to a competitor of the owner of an essential facility, such as a patent or a copyright, the rival's demand for the essential facility will be inelastic. Thus the Ramsey rule requires the price of access to the facility to be raised until all such rents accrue to the facility's owner, while ECPR leaves competitors' efficiency rents to them.

See also:

Chapter 49: Pricing the arts; Chapter 52: Public support; Chapter 60: Welfare economics.

References

Baumol, William J. (2002), *The Free-Market Innovation Machine: Analyzing the Growth Miracle of Capitalism*, Princeton, NJ: Princeton University Press.
Baumol, William J. (2005), 'Intellectual Property: How the Right to Keep It to Yourself Promotes Dissemination', *Review of Economic Research on Copyright Issues*, 2 (2), 17–23.
Baumol, William J. and David Bradford (1970), 'Optimal Departures From Marginal Cost Pricing', *American Economic Review*, 60, 265–83.
Blaug, Mark (ed.) (1992), *The Economics of the Arts*, Aldershot, UK: Gregg Revivals.
Dupuit, Jules (1844), 'De la Mesure de l'Utilité des Travaux Publics', *Annales des Ponts et Chaussées: Mémoires et Documents*, 2nd ser., 8 (2), 332–75. Reprinted in Marie de Bernardi (ed.) (1933), *De l'Utilité de la Mesure*, Torino; trans. R.H. Barback, *International Economic Papers* (1952, No. 2, 83–110).
Frey, Bruno S. and Werner W. Pommerehne (1989), *Muses and Markets: Explorations in the Economics of the Arts*, Oxford: Basil Blackwell.
Grampp, William D. (1986), 'Should the Arts Support Themselves?', *Economic Affairs*, December, 41–3. See also Towse (1997), 669–73.
Hausman, J.A. and J.K. Mackie-Mason (1988), 'Price Discrimination and Patent Policy', *RAND Journal of Economics*, 19 (summer), 253–65.

Kremer, Michael (1998), 'Patent Buyouts: A Mechanism for Encouraging Innovation', *Quarterly Journal of Economics*, November, 1137–67.

Musgrave, Richard (1959), *The Theory of Public Finance*, New York: McGraw-Hill.

Peacock, Alan T. (1969), 'Welfare Economics and Public Subsidies to the Arts', *Manchester School of Economic and Social Studies*, 37 (4), 323–35. Reprinted in Towse (1997), pp. 501–13.

Ramsey, Frank (1927), 'A Contribution to the Theory of Taxation', *Economic Journal*, 37, 47–61.

Samuelson, Paul A. (1954), 'The Pure Theory of Public Expenditure', *Review of Economics and Statistics*, 36, November, 387–9.

Scitovsky, Tibor (1976), 'What's Wrong With the Arts is What's Wrong with Society', in Mark Blaug (ed.), *The Economics of the Arts*, Aldershot, UK: Gregg Revivals, pp. 58–69.

Smith, Adam (1776), *An Inquiry Into the Nature and Causes of The Wealth of Nations*, London.

Throsby, David (1994), 'Production and Consumption of the Arts: a View of Cultural Economics', *Journal of Economic Literature*, XXXII (1), 1–20. See also Towse (1997, vol. I, pp. 51–85).

Towse, Ruth (1997), *Cultural Economics: The Arts, the Heritage and the Media Industries*, 2 vols, Cheltenham, UK and Lyme, USA: Edward Elgar.

Towse, Ruth (2001), *Creativity, Incentive and Reward*, Cheltenham, UK and Northampton, MA, USA: Edward Elgar.

Varian, Hal (2000), 'Differential Pricing and Efficiency', *First Monday*, 23 October, 1–16.

Further reading

For a general overview of the economic issues raised by the arts, there can be no better source than the superb collection put together by Ruth Towse (1997). Though an older volume, the work by Blaug (1992) lays out the subject very effectively. On the issue of public funding, opinions range from Scitovsky (1976), who was an enthusiastic supporter of government financing, to Grampp (1986), who is at the opposite end of the spectrum, with careful intermediate positions taken by Peacock (1969) and Frey and Pommerehne (1989). The classical exposition of the issues raised by public finance and the 'public-good' issue, in particular, can be found in Musgrave (1959). For more on the optimal pricing of permission to use material covered by copyright, see Baumol (2005).

2   Art auctions
Orley Ashenfelter and Kathryn Graddy

Works of art and culture are sold by many means. These include transactions between dealers and their customers, auctions with open outcry, and even, occasionally, sealed-bid auctions. However, the standard procedure for establishing art valuations is most commonly the English auction, where prices ascend in open bidding. (The primary, but not the only, alternative is the Dutch auction, where the auctioneer starts at a high price and reduces it until a bidder is found.)

How 'English auctions' really work

Many people think they understand the rules of an English auction because they are so commonly used.[1] Sotheby's, Christie's, Phillips and the other English auction houses have invented and refined these rules over two centuries, and they are now common in many other parts of the world. It is well known that in an English auction the bidding begins low and edges upward as bidders escalate their bids. When the bidding stops, the item for sale is said to be 'knocked down' or 'hammered down'. The price at which an item is knocked down or hammered down is called the 'hammer price'.

What is not so well understood is that the items knocked down have not necessarily been sold. Here is the reason. The seller will generally set a 'reserve price', and if the bidding does not reach this level the item will go unsold. Auctioneers say that an unsold item has been 'bought in'. (This terminology is somewhat misleading since the auction house rarely buys unsold items.) An item that has been bought in may be put up for sale at a later auction, sold elsewhere, or taken off the market. In auctions of Impressionist paintings, about one-third of the paintings put up for sale will not find buyers in a normal period. In wine auctions, on the other hand, the typical 'buy-in' rate ranges from 5 per cent to 10 per cent. The typical buy-in rates for other auction items – European paintings, silver, furniture and jewellery – usually, but not always, fall between these extremes. Table 2.1 shows sale rates (equal to one minus the buy-in rate) in different departments at Christie's in London in 1995 and 1996, along with average value of a lot sold. As can be seen from the table, 96 per cent of items put up for sale in auctions of arms and armour were sold, 89 per cent of wine at auction was sold, and 71 per cent of Impressionist and modern art items were sold.

Auctioneers are very secretive about whether and at what level a reserve price may have been set, and there is a real auctioneer's art in getting the bidding started on each item without revealing the reserve price. For example, the auctioneer may have to accept and announce fictitious bids 'off the wall' or 'from the chandelier' to start the 'real' bidding. Bids from off the wall are legally being placed on behalf of the seller. At the same time, sellers are forbidden by contract with the auctioneer from bidding in the auction. This is the protection that the auctioneer offers to the prospective buyers to ensure that they are not being artificially 'bid up'.

If you sit through an auction, you will find that every item is hammered down and treated as if it were sold.[2] Only after the auction does the auctioneer reveal whether and

Table 2.1   Average sale rates by department

Department	Average sold lot value, £		No. of auctions in sample	Sale rate (% of lots sold)		% sold by value	
	1996	1995		Mean (%)	Std dev.	Mean (%)	Std dev.
Impressionist	122820	135430	8	71	(0.11)	80	(0.10)
Old Master drawings	50670	29210	4	77	(0.09)	89	(0.08)
Contemporary	36820	36840	7	79	(0.04)	87	(0.06)
British pictures	29710	23560	7	78	(0.14)	83	(0.17)
Old Master pictures	29180	6560	11	73	(0.15)	82	(0.15)
Continental pictures	21810	10450	7	72	(0.11)	79	(0.10)
Clocks	14340	5130	4	88	(0.03)	89	(0.07)
Jewellery	12190	6750	8	86	(0.05)	89	(0.04)
Furniture	11670	8220	25	85	(0.09)	92	(0.06)
Silver	11080	5910	10	87	(0.11)	92	(0.07)
Sculpture	11070	6340	5	78	(0.21)	81	(0.20)
Modern British pictures	10340	7190	9	70	(0.05)	81	(0.05)
Victorian pictures	9460	8400	6	66	(0.13)	75	(0.11)
British drawings & watercolours	9160	3400	14	72	(0.14)	87	(0.10)
Rugs & carpets	9160	3700	8	80	(0.17)	85	(0.14)
Topographical pictures	8640	8010	2	68	(0.13)	81	(0.00)
Islamic	6670	6950	5	68	(0.22)	82	(0.12)
Cars	5750	7610	6	71	(0.16)	65	(0.22)
Chinese works of art	5640	6400	8	70	(0.19)	79	(0.16)
Books & manuscripts	5220	4270	15	81	(0.12)	86	(0.09)
Russian works of art	4490	5480	4	64	(0.14)	69	(0.15)
Japanese	4410	2840	5	72	(0.04)	76	(0.05)
Musical instruments	3960	4110	5	77	(0.05)	76	(0.16)
Watches	3870	2190	6	71	(0.09)	81	(0.11)
Prints – old, modern and contemporary	3850	4230	8	81	(0.12)	92	(0.09)
Miniatures	3350	3260	2	82	(0.05)	92	(0.07)
Antiquities	3260	3640	3	57	(0.08)	66	(0.13)
Porcelain and glass	2700	2600	14	76	(0.12)	85	(0.10)

Table 2.1   (continued)

Department	Average sold lot value, £		No. of auctions in sample	Sale rate (% of lots sold)		% sold by value	
	1996	1995		Mean (%)	Std dev.	Mean (%)	Std dev.
Tribal art	2 650	2 090	3	67	(0.08)	75	(0.19)
Photographica	2 580	1 660	3	61	(0.27)	79	(0.08)
Modern guns	2 510	3 620	5	93	(0.06)	94	(0.04)
Garden statuary	2 120	1 540	4	91	(0.10)	91	(0.11)
Arms & armour	1 890	2 400	4	96	(0.03)	99	(0.01)
Frames	1 800	2 260	4	81	(0.15)	85	(0.14)
Stamps	830	650	22	78	(0.13)	82	(0.12)
Wine	690	580	37	89	(0.09)	91	(0.08)

at what price an item may have actually been sold. In short, the auctioneers do not reveal the reserve price and they make it as difficult as they can for bidders to infer it.

Although the above description outlines commonly accepted practice in auctions, many people describe them differently. For example, Milgrom (1989) states: 'the auctioneer begins with the lowest acceptable price – the reserve price – and proceeds to solicit successively higher bids from the customers until no one will increase the bid. Then the item is '"knocked down" (sold) to the highest bidder.' As noted above, real auctioneers do not reveal the reserve price in this way, and many 'knocked-down' items may be unsold. In another example, Graham and Marshall (1987) state: 'When the bidding stops, the auctioneer will generate a false or phantom higher bid if he feels that the high bidder is "good for another bump"'. However, inventing fictitious bids above the reserve price is certainly unethical and probably illegal, too. Since the auctioneer's rules are known to an entire array of personnel who often move on to become bidders or their agents, it is difficult for an auction house to engage systematically in the generation of fictitious bids above the reserve price over long periods. Indeed, the recent litigation by the US Department of Justice over price fixing engaged in by Sotheby's and Christie's, where the chairman of Sotheby's was convicted, demonstrates how difficult it can be to avoid the detection of collusion. Any auction house that values its reputation – and the long-run profits its reputation secures – has an incentive to avoid this practice.[3]

Secret reserve prices and high 'buy-in' rates have some interesting implications for the theoretical study of auctions. In the optimal auctions model of Riley and Samuelson (1981), for example, the reserve price serves to extract a slightly higher price from the bidder with the highest valuation of the item on offer.[4] The reason is that in an English auction the seller receives only an amount equal to the second highest valuation placed on the object among the bidders. By setting a reserve price, the seller takes a chance on extracting part of the valuation gap between the two bidders with the highest valuations in exchange for the risk of losing the sale altogether.

However, this optimal auctions model is probably not much help in understanding how reserve prices are set in most auctions. First, since it is a dominant strategy for each bidder in an English auction to bid up to their true valuation of the object, the optimal reserve price is identical no matter whether it is kept secret or not. This model therefore offers no explanation of why the reserve price should be secret. Second, in the optimal auctions model the reserve price is independent of the number of bidders. It follows that the probability that an item will be sold increases with the number of bidders. In fact, however, as was noted above, buy-in rates are very high for some types of items despite a large number of bidders. Moreover, buy-in rates differ systematically across types of items in a manner that is almost certainly not related to the number of bidders in these auctions. It seems very unlikely that actual buy-in rates can be explained primarily by the considerations important in the optimal auctions literature.

One likely explanation for the secrecy surrounding reserve prices is that it serves to thwart 'rings'.[5] There is always random variation in the interest and turnout of bidders; when the turnout is low, some sellers may prefer that their goods be bought in and offered for sale at a later date rather than risk a collusive ring bidding to depress the item's price. The auctioneer may also engage in other practices that weaken rings. For example, the auctioneer typically does not reveal the identity of the purchaser, if there is one, and this creates strong incentives for the ring members to bid privately in opposition to the interests of the ring.

An explanation for the key determinants of the seller's reserve price may be found in models of search (Mortensen, 1970), where the seller may expect to offer the item at auction more than once, or even to sell it privately to a dealer as an alternative. The highest observed price in a particular auction may be thought of as a 'job offer' that will be accepted only if it exceeds the reserve price. In these models there is a 'natural rate of unemployment' that may well be related to the 'normal buy-in rate' that characterizes auction markets.

Competition among auction houses
It is sometimes said that the auctioneers at Christie's (now French-owned) are gentlemen who try to act like businessmen, while the auctioneers at Sotheby's (now American-owned!) are businessmen who try to act like gentlemen. There is no doubt an element of truth to this characterization of the style of these two auction houses. The competition among auctioneers is more than a matter of style, however. The auction business is an interesting example of an industry where the cost of building a reputation may act as a significant entry barrier to new competitors. Surprisingly little attention has been paid in the literature about auctions to the role of the auctioneer.

In principle the auctioneer acts on behalf of the seller, but the auction house typically receives compensation from both the buyer and the seller for items that are sold. The buyer's premium is a percentage of the sale price paid to the auctioneer by the buyer. In most auction houses, the buyer's premium varies from 10 to 25 per cent of the sale price, typically being a lower fraction of higher-valued sales. This use of a sliding scale by value for the buyer's premium is a fairly recent innovation. It seems likely that competitive pressures among the major auction houses resulted in this change in the scale, as it is more likely to represent the real selling costs of an item. However, it is almost certainly also due to the fact that more of the auction houses' revenues have, in recent years, derived from the buyer's side of the market. Table 2.2 lists the buyer's premium for Christie's and Sotheby's as of January 2010. These buyer's premiums had been in effect since June 2008. This amount is generally not negotiable.

Table 2.2 Buyer's commissions for selected locations at Christie's and Sotheby's auction houses (effective 1 June 2008 (Sotheby's); effective 2 June 2008 (Christie's))

	Amount of hammer price	Buyer's commission (%)
London	Up to £25 000	25
	Above £25 000–£500 000	20
	Above £500 000	12
[London wine]	All amounts	15
France	Up to €15 000*	25
	Above €15 000–€800 000*	20
	Above €800 000	12
New York	Up to US$50 000	25
	Above US$50 000–US$1 000 000	20
	Above US$1 000 000	12
[NY wine]	All amounts	21**
Hong Kong	Up to HK$400 000	25
	Above HK$400 000–HK$8 000 000	20
	Above HK$8 000 000	12

Notes:
*   The cut-off at Christie's is €20 000 rather than €15 000.
**   Commissions at Christie's are 20%; at Sotheby's, 21%.

The seller's commission is a percentage of the sale price paid to the auctioneer by the seller. It varies with the type – and importance – of the item being sold, ranging from 15 per cent for wine to as little as 5 per cent or less for certain kinds of paintings. Furthermore, auction houses operate a sliding scale for commission rates, based on total annual sales.

Thus, with a buyer's commission of 25 per cent and a seller's commission of 5 per cent, if a painting is sold at an auction for a hammer price of $100, the buyer will pay $125 to the auctioneer, and the seller will receive $95 from the auctioneer, giving the auctioneer a gross revenue of $30.

If an item goes unsold, the auctioneer will receive neither a buyer's premium nor a seller's commission. To make sure the seller bears some of the cost of auctioning but not selling an item, auctioneers usually charge the seller a fee on unsold items. This fee is often a percentage of the reserve price set by the seller, which obviously gives the seller an incentive to keep the reserve price low. In addition, some auction houses will not allow a seller to put up an easily recognized item for resale until some time has passed. Sometimes it is claimed that when an advertised item goes unsold its future value will be affected. Such items are said to have been 'burned'. Indeed, Beggs and Graddy (2008) find that paintings that have failed between sales return about 30 per cent less than other paintings.

Whether failure at auction actually causes the lower price is still open to debate. While paintings may sell for less after they fail at auction, it is not at all clear that the failure caused the lower price. Changes in the seller's reserve price – perhaps because of a previous failure – can cause final observed prices to be either higher or lower after an item fails to sell, in which case observed price changes are not caused directly by failure, but result from sample selection. Lower prices may also be observed because of downward price trends when an artist falls out of fashion, or for other idiosyncratic reasons.

When bidders have independent private valuations of the items on offer, as in Riley and Samuelson (1981), the failure of an item to sell should not influence its future saleability either at auction or privately. But in models where bidder valuations are correlated, as in Milgrom and Weber (1982), the failure of an item to sell is informative about the value it might achieve in another sale. If an object can be burned, the assumption of correlated valuations becomes more appropriate. However, it is not clear whether paintings really are burned – that is, whether their failure to sell has caused a price decrease – or whether this is a fiction invented to encourage sellers to be satisfied with lower reserve prices.

Most auction houses now collect a much larger part of their revenues from the buyer's premium than was the case in the past. The most commonly given reason is that auction houses have been increasingly forced to bargain down the size of the seller's commission when they deal with large consignors. Since it is far more difficult for a large number of small buyers to bargain effectively, the buyer's premium has provided a new source of revenue. This suggests that real bargaining costs have changed in recent years.

Since Christie's and Sotheby's operate much as a duopoly with respect to the sale of major works of art, there is a strong incentive for them to collude in the setting of sellers' commissions. Evidence of their collusion has recently emerged in the major criminal trial of Alfred Taubman, chairman of Sotheby's, in New York City, who was found guilty of price-fixing in 2001. (Price-fixing is a criminal offence in the USA, and penalties may include both incarceration and monetary fines.) Testimony in the trial by the former president of Sotheby's indicated that executives anticipated higher profits as a result of collusion that were in the tens of millions of dollars. Ashenfelter and Graddy (2005) provide an economic analysis of this price-fixing scandal.

The declining-price anomaly
The empirical study of auctions has led to some findings that have challenged some theories of auction behaviour and also led to new theoretical work. One of the most prominent examples is the discovery of what is now called the 'declining-price anomaly' in wine auctions by Ashenfelter (1989).

The existence of this anomaly has now been found in the sale of many other items, including paintings (Beggs and Graddy, 1997), condominiums (Ashenfelter and Genesove, 1992), and cattle (Englebrecht-Wiggans and Kahn, 1992)! Although not much discussed, it seems to be common knowledge among auctioneers that, when identical lots of wine are sold in a single auction, prices are more likely to decline than to increase with later lots. This does not mean that price declines always occur, but they are far more common than would be expected by chance alone. Most auctioneers are aware that later bidders on similar items are more likely to pay lower prices, but they are uncomfortable about revealing this information to uninformed bidders. Apparently most bidders, like economists, expect to see identical items sold at identical prices! When inexperienced bidders see exceptions to this rule they may think something unethical is going on. As a result, auctions are set up to disguise this regularity. For example, the auctioneer will usually offer smaller lots of the same item before larger lots. Since most bidders see nothing anomalous in quantity discounts, declining per unit prices seem more acceptable.

Auctioneers have another device for limiting the extent to which bidders are likely to see price declines for identical items. When a series of lots of identical items is offered, the winning bidder on the first lot has the option of immediately taking all the subsequent lots at the same price.[6] This rule has two effects. On one hand, for a bidder who wants some (but not all) of the items on offer, it increases the risk of waiting for the lower prices that may materialize with later lots. Risk-averse buyers are thus forced to pay a real price for any attempt to exploit the typical pattern of price declines: they may lose the opportunity to buy any of the lots they want. Thus this rule increases the seller's revenue so long as there are risk-averse buyers. In addition, since the option to purchase several lots is often exercised, bidders will in this case see a uniform price for all items.

These results suggest that risk aversion or quantity constraints play a significant role in real auction markets. Indeed, assuming bidders are risk averse may simply be a convenient analytical device for dealing with the fact that many bidders at auctions are buying to fill orders and are effectively quantity-constrained. In fact, the mechanism used in practice by the auctioneers that gives the first buyer the option to purchase subsequent lots at an identical price is clearly related to the optimal auction design suggested by Maskin and Riley (1984) when there are risk-averse bidders.

Since the first discussion of the declining price anomaly in Ashenfelter (1989), over 30 papers have been published on this subject, both trying to explain the anomaly, and documenting the anomaly in other auction markets.

The information in auction results: an externality

Some of the most fascinating stories about auctions involve the surprising 'discovery' of a highly valued artwork in an auction where prices were expected to be very low. This kind of story illustrates one way that regular auctions confer information benefits that are typically not captured by the profits of the auctioneer. In essence, the presence of an auction system provides a way for an uninformed seller to obtain approximately the market value for the items they own without the necessity of becoming informed. So long as there are two well-informed buyers in the room who do not collude, the price the object attains will be the same as if the seller were well informed in the first instance.

The value of a public auction system as protection for uninformed sellers has long been understood in Europe, but it is not widely appreciated in the USA. In both Sweden and Austria, for example, auction houses have sometimes been run as state-owned monopolies. The major auction houses in both the USA and England are certainly not state-owned, but they are watched with some care by institutions like the Metropolitan Museum of Art, which disposes of its property only through public auctions.

The basic problem is that the public auction system provides a method for setting values, but these values can be used for determining prices in transactions outside the auction system. In other words, the auction system allows traders to make private transactions outside the auction system, but if everyone traded in this way there would be no auctions in the first place. It is probable that the inability of auctioneers to capture a significant part of the benefits of the information they produce leads to less use of the auction system than is optimal for society.

Auctioneers and accurate information

The theoretical literature about auctions emphasizes that there are good reasons for auctioneers to provide truthful information about the items being sold (Milgrom and Weber, 1982). The basic idea is that revealing information tends to remove uncertainty and make low bidders more aggressive; this puts upward pressure on the bidding of the others, which is in the interest of the auctioneer. It may seem surprising to some, but auctioneers do appear to act consistently with this prediction. For example, auction houses typically go to considerable effort to estimate the price that an item offered for sale will fetch. Predicting the price at which a unique item will sell requires a high level of expertise, so it is of some interest to see just how good these predictions are. The usual practice is for the auctioneer to provide a high estimate and a low estimate in an auction catalogue.

Ashenfelter's (1989) results generally show that auction houses are truthful; the average of the auctioneer's high and low estimate is very highly correlated with the price actually received. Furthermore, Abowd and Ashenfelter (1988) find that auctioneers' price estimates are far better predictors of prices fetched than hedonic price functions.

The details of the arrangements for price-fixing revealed by Diana Brooks, the CEO of Sotheby's, during the Christie's–Sotheby's price-fixing trial provide further insight into the role of experts at auction houses. Brooks reported that at one point her boss, Chairman Alfred Taubman, proposed that the auction houses collude in providing clients with similar estimates of the value of their art. Brooks reported that this was impossible because she could not simply tell Christie's departmental experts, who produce the estimates, to do a dishonest job without causing a breakdown in the conspiracy.

Since Abowd and Ashenfelter (1988), many papers have looked at the issue of whether pre-sale estimates are truly unbiased. Some of this research has found systematic over- and undervaluation, based on various characteristics of the items being sold. However, in most of these papers the biases are small and appear unintentional. The one exception to this body of work is Mei and Moses (2005), who conclude that estimates for expensive paintings are intentionally biased upwards in order to increase revenue. Most recently, however, McAndrew *et al.* (forthcoming) have found that once unsold items are taken into account, the auction house estimates are unbiased.

In sum, auctioneers do seem to provide genuine expertise in predicting prices. Perhaps honesty is an auctioneer's most profitable policy rule.

Notes

1. What is called an English auction is, in fact, Roman. The word auction comes from the Latin 'auctio', which means 'to ascend'.
2. There are exceptions to this rule. In New York City the auctioneer is legally required to state whether an item has been sold at the conclusion of the bidding. When an item goes unsold, the auctioneer announces that the item has been 'passed by'. This rule was promulgated after it was revealed publicly that an auction in the early 1980s consisted primarily of unsold paintings and a lawsuit was filed by their owner against Christie's. The New York auctioneers did not reveal this information before this rule was promulgated, and they usually do not reveal this information in other locations except where required by law.
3. It should be appreciated that an auctioneer faces a real trade-off in deciding whether to follow the standard ethical auction practices. If the auctioneer gains a reputation for following these practices he receives the benefit that buyers will reveal their true valuations of the items put up for sale, and this results in higher prices for the buyers (and higher commissions for the auctioneers). Many sellers try to give the impression that they follow standard auction practices even when they do not, apparently because they believe that it increases their sale prices to uninformed buyers. Some of the most amusing examples of this practice are

depicted by the home shopping clubs broadcast on late-night cable television. This kind of cheating seems to be endemic to any kind of economic activity where reputations are valuable.

4. The term 'reserve price' is an unfortunate choice of words in this context. In reality virtually every seller has some price below which they would not agree to sell an object; the theory of optimal auctions indicates why, for strategic reasons, a seller should set a reserve price that is strictly higher than the minimum price for which they would sell the object.

5. Webster's Dictionary defines a 'ring' as 'An exclusive combination of persons for a selfish, and often corrupt, purpose, as to control the market.'

6. Since the buyer must exercise this option immediately, this rule does not establish an option value for risk-neutral traders that could be used to explain the price decline anomaly. Here is the reason. Since the option expires as soon as it is purchased, it is only of value if it is exercised. If it is exercised, however, there will be no price decline. Thus the existence of an option value is not consistent with the price declines.

See also:

Chapter 4: Art markets; Chapter 5: Art prices.

References

Abowd, John and Orley Ashenfelter (1988), 'Art Auctions: Price Indices and Sale Rates for Impressionist and Contemporary Pictures', mimeo, Department of Economics, Princeton University, NJ.

Ashenfelter, Orley (1989), 'How Auctions Work for Wine and Art', *Journal of Economic Perspectives*, 3 (3), 23–36.

Ashenfelter, Orley and David Genesove (1992), 'Testing for Price Anomalies in Real-Estate Auctions', *American Economic Review*, 82, 501–5.

Ashenfelter, Orley and Kathryn Graddy (2003), 'Auctions and the Price of Art, *Journal of Economic Literature*, September, 41 (3), 763–87.

Ashenfelter, Orley and Kathryn Graddy (2005), 'Anatomy of the Rise and Fall of a Price-Fixing Conspiracy: Auctions at Sotheby's and Christie's', *Journal of Competition Law and Economics*, 1, 3–20.

Beggs, Alan and Kathryn Graddy (1997), 'Declining Values and the Afternoon Effect: Evidence from Art Auctions', *Rand Journal of Economics*, 28, 544–65.

Beggs, Alan and Kathryn Graddy (2008), 'Failure to Meet the Reserve Price: The Impact on the Returns to Art', *Journal of Cultural Economics*, 32, 301–20.

Engelbrecht-Wiggans, Richard and Charles Kahn (1992), 'An Empirical Analysis of Dairy Cattle Auctions', mimeo, University of Illinois.

Graham, Daniel A. and Robert C. Marshall (1987), 'Collusive Bidder Behavior at Single-Object Second-Price and English Auctions', *Journal of Political Economy*, December, 95, 1217–39.

McAndrew, Clare, James L. Smith and Rex Thompson (forthcoming), 'The Impact of Reservation Prices on the Perceived Bias of Expert Appraisals of Fine Art', *Journal of Applied Econometrics*.

Maskin, Eric and John Riley (1984), 'Optimal Auction with Risk Averse Buyers', *Econometrica*, November, 52, 1473–518.

Mei, Jianping and Michael Moses (2005), 'Vested Interest and Biased Price Estimates: Evidence from an Auction Market', *Journal of Finance*, 60, 2409–36.

Milgrom, Paul R. (1989), 'Auctions and Bidding: A Primer', *Journal of Economic Perspectives*, 3 (3), 3–22.

Milgrom, Paul R. and Robert J. Weber (1982), 'A Theory of Auctions and Competitive Bidding', *Econometrica*, September, 50, 1089–122.

Mortensen, Dale T. (1970), 'Job Search, the Duration of Unemployment, and the Phillips Curve', *The American Economic Review*, December, 60, 847–62.

Riley, John C. and William F. Samuelson (1981), 'Optimal Auctions', *American Economic Review*, June, 71, 381–92.

Further reading

We recommend Ashenfelter (1989) and Ashenfelter and Graddy (2003) as further reading on how art auctions work, and their effect on prices.

3 Art dealers
Olav Velthuis

Art dealers mediate supply and demand on the primary and secondary markets for art. In doing so they compete with other intermediaries such as auction houses, or with artists themselves, who sell their work directly out of their studios. The work they sell may range from prints or other multiples worth several hundreds of dollars to multimillion-dollar works of art by old and modern masters or contemporary celebrity artists. At the high end of the market, some dealers predominantly sell to a small fixed club of wealthy collectors who have expressed loyalty to them over a long period of time. At the lower end, art dealers may cater to the demand of a relatively anonymous group of buyers who are interested in acquiring a piece for decorative reasons or as a souvenir of a tourist trip.

Almost invariably, dealers are small-scale enterprises employing only a few people, with a single owner who also operates as managing director. The rare exceptions are large art dealers in the centres of the global art market, New York and London, who run several exhibition spaces and may have over 50 employees. Apart from labour costs, the main expenses art dealers incur are rent and the inventory they may have in case they sell from stock (Shubik, 2003). Since banks are often reluctant to provide capital to what is considered to be a risky enterprise, many dealers attract capital, for instance to renovate their exhibition space or to add works of art to their inventory, from so-called backers. Frequently backers are loyal collectors who may have a stake in the dealership.

The dealers' market is relatively competitive. In major art capitals such as New York, London or Berlin, several hundreds of dealers are active. Barriers to entry tend to be low: in most countries, no special licences or diplomas need to be obtained for an art dealer to start a business, while start-up costs are relatively low as well. Given their private nature and the absence of public listings, little is known for sure regarding art dealers' revenue and profit rates. From surveys in some national markets, the average annual revenue seems to be several hundred thousands of dollars annually. For the world's largest and most prestigious galleries such as the Gagosian gallery and PaceWildenstein for contemporary art or Johnny van Haeften and Otto Naumann for Old Masters, revenues are estimated to be tens of millions of dollars.

Since dealers often need to establish new markets for artists who lack a solid reputation or whose reputation has deteriorated, they may start to make sales only after a long period of time. According to anecdotal estimates, more than 50 per cent of the dealers do not survive the first five years. Even when their enterprise fails to make money by then, a partner's income, pre-existing wealth or side jobs may allow art dealers to continue their business longer than would be the case with loss-leading firms in other markets. Indeed, for some art dealers their enterprise is more of a calling, a hobby or a social pastime than a rational means of making a living.

In spite of the strong competition, art dealers, especially on the primary art market, may in practice be engaged in monopolistic competition: they often represent artists on an exclusive basis, at least within a predefined geographical area.

Dealers on the primary and the secondary market

The way art dealers operate differs radically between the primary market where new works of art are sold for the first time, and the secondary or resale market. On the secondary or resale market, dealers take works on consignment from collectors or institutions who want to sell them. Once the work is sold, the dealer receives a commission, which may vary from 5 to 25 per cent. Alternatively, the dealer may buy pieces from collectors and institutions, from other dealers or at auction, and subsequently try to sell them at a profit. In all these cases, the dealer's profit ultimately relies on information asymmetries regarding the value of the work involved in a transaction, the willingness to pay of collectors interested in a specific piece of art or the need of other collectors to sell (parts of) their collection.

On the primary art market dealers tend to represent a limited number of artists (10–30 on average) on a long-term basis. The dealer tries to develop a market for these artists, for example by creating demand among collectors and by promoting their work among cultural experts. Once a market is established, a dealer may protect it, for instance, by bidding up prices at auction if a work by one of the artists s/he represents comes up there. Frequently, only a small number of artists a dealer represents are commercially successful. The profit s/he makes by selling the work of these artists tends to be invested in the careers of the others – a form of cross-subsidization.

Usually new artists are incorporated into the gallery's roster through recommendations by artists or by other experts whose judgement the art dealer trusts. Dealers represent these artists on a consignment basis: the artist does not sell his/her work to the gallery but consigns it for a solo or group exhibition. In the event that the work is sold, the proceeds are divided according to a pre-established ratio. For starting artists, this ratio tends to be 50–50, but once the artist manages to establish a firm market and reputation, s/he may command 60 or 70 per cent of the retail price. If the work remains unsold, the dealer can either keep it in the inventory, without transfer of property rights, or the artist can take the work back.

In these consignment relationships, risk, which is high given the uncertain economic value of contemporary art, is shared between artist and dealer. As Richard Caves puts it, the relationship between an artist and a dealer resembles a joint venture more than a principal–agent relationship (Caves, 2000, p. 39). A second advantage for a dealer to sell art on the basis of consignments is that the capital intensity of his enterprise remains low: since s/he does not need to buy the works he offers for sale, the dealer does not tie up capital in inventory.

Although standard, legally binding contracts exist for consignment relationships, they are often conducted without them. The reason is that complete terms cannot be stated in a contract. First of all, an artist cannot be contractually enforced to continue producing valuable works of art in the future. Second, if a contract were written up, it would be difficult for one party to monitor the other and ensure that all terms of the contract were complied with. Third, litigation is expensive in case of breach of contract and may damage the reputation of the artist and the gallery. Transaction costs involved in developing a contract, monitoring and litigation are, in other words, high in the case of consignments. Finally, it is questionable if a dealer can expect financial compensation from successful litigation. In the absence of complete contracts, dealers often try to engage in long-term trust relationship with their artists. As Caves argues: 'The infeasibility of explicit contracting leads the parties into the language of moral obligation, with reputation the insurance of reasonable performance in the absence of legally binding obligations' (Caves, 2000, p. 41).

In the past, economic exchange between artists and their dealers took other forms than consignment. In the pre-modern visual art world, dealers occasionally employed artists to make copies of a popular original image. Apart from dealers, courts and patrons frequently employed artists. In the present day, employment relationships are observed only at the lower end of the market, where art is sold by art gallery chains or art wholesalers. The artists they employ produce standardized artworks in semi-mass production.

Another type of exchange between artists and dealers is direct acquisitions. After property rights are transferred by the artist, the dealer can decide when and at what price the artworks will be sold to a collector. For instance, s/he may decide to keep artworks in the inventory if s/he wants to speculate on future rises in the price of an artist's work. Within this system, however, the dealer runs the risk that the economic value will never be realized. This system of direct acquisition has been referred to as the French system, since it was mainly used by French art dealers in the late nineteenth and early twentieth centuries. Nowadays, some dealers with extensive financial resources still buy works directly from artists if they consider the market for these works to be firmly established.

Gatekeepers to the art market
In order to be successful, a dealer needs to have a discriminating taste, a strong network within the art world to acquire information regarding promising artists or the whereabouts of valuable works of art, and clients who may be interested in them. Normally, dealers have developed both this taste and this network before opening their business, for instance, as art collectors or during a failed career as artists themselves.

On both the primary and on the secondary market, dealers actively need to convince collectors of the lasting economic and artistic value of the work they offer. On the primary market, dealers may invite them to the artist's studio, to public exhibitions featuring the artist, or to dinners with other collectors and artists whom the gallery represents. Dealers on the secondary market may, for instance, take collectors to museums in order to further develop their taste and to embed the works they sell in a wider art-historical context.

Especially on the primary market, art dealers play many other roles than just matching supply and demand and making sales. They also serve as one of the main gatekeepers to the art market: they make a selection of the many artists who seek to be represented after leaving the art academy. Dealers furthermore have a public role since most of them run exhibition spaces that are, without charge, open to the public. Art dealers who operate on the primary art market furthermore 'promote' the artists they represent. This means that they regularly organize exhibitions that usually last six to eight weeks. They bring the work of artists to the attention of cultural institutions and independent curators, and try to make sales to museums and stimulate museums to organize exhibitions involving the work of these artists. Art dealers also encourage art critics and art historians to review their exhibitions, or commission them to write catalogue texts.

These activities underscore on the one hand the cultural role of economic actors like art dealers, and on the other hand the economic role of cultural institutions like museums and the art press. Indeed, with their manifold relations to other economic actors in the visual arts, art dealers are the central nodes or the 'crucible' of the art world (Fitzgerald, 1995). The economic rationale of these promotional activities is that they enhance the economic value of the art sold in the gallery. For two reasons, however, these promotional activities may not be undertaken or take place to a lesser extent than would be optimal: first of all, if an artist is represented by more than one dealer, free-rider problems arise. One or more dealers may abstain from investing in costly promotional activities while profiting from the activities undertaken by others. This is one of the main reasons why dealers often insist on representing artists on an exclusive basis. Second, promotional activities are by and large specific to each artist. This means that once the consignment relationship between the artist and the dealer is terminated, the dealer's costs related to promotional activities need to be considered 'sunk'.

Relationships between dealers and artists may be terminated for various reasons, but the most frequent are that an artist does not sell, in which case a dealer may want to 'drop' him/her; or that the artist, once s/he becomes successful, moves on to or is 'stolen away from' the gallery by a more established, often more commercial dealer who offers to represent the artist on more favourable terms and who has the network of clients and cultural institutions to further develop the artist's career. In fact, a division of labour exists between explorer galleries, which start with young, new artists with no market whatsoever, and commercial galleries, which work only with artists whose markets are already firmly established (Bystryn, 1978). While the latter may outperform the former in terms of revenues and profits, the former's esteem within the art world tends to be higher.[1]

Note

1. When it comes to types of dealers, economists and sociologists have come up with similar distinctions between traditional and entrepreneurial dealers (Moulin, 1967), between dealers motivated by symbolic and those motivated by monetary rewards (Bystryn, 1978), or between dealers who sell popular and those who sell high art (Fitz Gibbon, 1987).

See also:

Chapter 4: Art markets; Chapter 5: Art prices; Chapter 48: Poverty and support for artists.

References

Bystryn, Marcia (1978), 'Art Galleries as Gatekeepers: The Case of the Abstract Expressionists', *Social Research*, 45 (2), 390–408.

Caves, Richard (2000), *Creative Industries: Contracts between Art and Commerce*, Cambridge, MA: Harvard University Press.

Coppet, Laura de and Alan Jones (2002), *The Art Dealers. The Powers Behind the Scene Tell How the Art World Really Works*, New York: Cooper Square Press.

Fitz Gibbon, Heather M. (1987), From Prints to Posters: The Production of Artistic Value in a Popular World', *Symbolic Interaction*, 10 (1), 111–28.

Fitzgerald, Michael C. (1995), *Making Modernism. Picasso and the Creation of the Market for Twentieth-Century Art*, New York: Farrar, Straus and Giroux.

Gimpel, René (1987), *Diary of an Art Dealer*, New York: Farrar, Straus and Giroux.

Goldstein, Malcolm (2000), *Landscape With Figures. A History of Art Dealing in the United States*, Oxford: Oxford University Press.

Klein, Ulrike (1994), *The Business of Art Unveiled. New York Art Dealers Speak up*, Frankfurt am Main: Peter Lang.

Moulin, Raymonde (1967 [1987]), *The French Art Market. A Sociological View*, New Brunswick, NJ: Rutgers University Press.

Plattner, Stuart (1996), *High Art Down Home. An Economic Ethnography of a Local Art Market*, Chicago, IL: Chicago University Press.

Rewald, John (1973 [1986]), 'Theo van Gogh as art dealer', in John Rewald (ed.), *Studies in Post-Impressionism*, New York: Harry N. Abrams, pp. 7–115.
Russell, John (1999), *Matisse. Father & Son*, New York: Harry N. Abrams.
Shubik, Martin (2003), 'Dealers in Art', in Ruth Towse (ed.), *A Handbook of Cultural Economics*, Cheltenham, UK and Northampton, MA, USA: Edward Elgar, pp. 194–200.
Thurn, Hans Peter (1994), *Der Kunsthändler. Wandlungen eines Berufes*, München: Hirmer.
Velthuis, Olav (2005), *Talking Prices. Symbolic Meanings of Prices on the Market for Contemporary Art*, Princeton, NJ: Princeton University Press.

Further reading

For sociological studies of art dealers, see Moulin (1967), Plattner (1996) and Velthuis (2005). For a history of the profession, see Thurn (1994) and Goldstein (2000). For studies of individual art dealers, see Russell (1999), Rewald (1973) and Gimpel (1967). For interviews with art dealers, see Klein (1994) and Coppet and Jones (2002).

4 Art markets
Olav Velthuis

On art markets, suppliers and buyers of works of art exchange cultural objects such as paintings, antiquities or sculptures. Within some market segments, such as the market for contemporary art, the objects are directly supplied by the artist, who sells them out of his studio or through a gallery. In other cases, for instance within the market for antiquities or for works of art by deceased artists, suppliers are private collectors or public institutions who want to part with these pieces. Often, intermediaries such as auction houses, art dealers or art consultants are involved to match supply and demand.

In 2007, the latest year for which figures are available, the size of the art market was estimated to be €48.1 billion worldwide. This figure, which includes both dealer and auction sales and comprises fine art as well as decorative arts and antiques, was the highest in the history of art markets. Geographically, the art market is dominated by the USA, with a market share of 41 per cent, followed by the UK with a market share of 30 per cent. After World War II, a division of labour emerged between the art capitals of these two countries: in New York the market for Impressionism, modern and contemporary art is concentrated, while London has developed a comparative advantage when it comes to Old Masters. France, until World War II the centre of the art market, has recently been surpassed by China as the third-largest art market (the latter's market share is 8 per cent). Between 2003 and 2007, the art market grew spectacularly by 311 per cent overall. This was partially caused by new demand from emerging economies, such as China, Russia and India, that gradually became part of global art markets (see below) and by the strong growth of high net worth individuals in Europe and the USA.

Within the auction market for fine arts, Impressionist and modern art has long been the most important category, but in 2006 it was surpassed by contemporary art, defined as art made by artists who were born after 1945. In 2007, contemporary art contributed more than 20 per cent of the annual turnover at both Sotheby's and Christie's. Between 2003 and 2007, the contemporary art market grew 851 per cent, more than double the average growth of the art market over that period. It is likely that following the financial crisis of 2007–08, the size of the market has shrunk. Indicatively, price levels for contemporary art at auction decreased by 27 per cent between January and December 2008 (McAndrew, 2009; Artprice, 2009). As in previous bust periods, auction houses have reported higher rates of lots that remain unsold.

Motives of buyers

Three different motivational categories can be distinguished for buyers within art markets. Some are primarily motivated by reasons directly related to the work of art itself: people may buy art because they find it aesthetically pleasing, because they seek to decorate their interior, or because they have a profound artistic interest and are building up a collection of artworks. A second set of reasons is financial: art may be bought as an investment, a store of wealth or as a hedge against inflation. The speculative motive is the one that cultural economics has focused on (for an early overview, see Frey and Eichenberger, 1995). Most research indicates that, compared with traditional asset classes such as stocks and bonds, rates of return on investment in art are lower and risks are much higher, both in the short and in the long run (see, for example, Ginsburgh, 2003). Only during brief boom periods, such as the second half of the 1980s or between 2003 and 2007, did art outperform traditional asset classes. The widely held belief that art is a safe investment may be caused by widespread media attention on a relatively small number of multimillion-dollar sales. The relative unattractiveness of art as an asset class is partially compensated by the low correlation of returns between art works and financial assets, which suggests that art may be used to diversify a traditional portfolio (Worthington and Higgs, 2004).

Finally, art may be bought for social reasons: by buying art, one buys oneself a ticket to a social circle, such as a group of collectors who regularly buy at the same art gallery and meet each other at art-world events. In emerging countries such as India and China, buying art may be a means of expressing membership of a rising middle class. Social reasons for buying art not only include group membership but also its very opposite: art can be used for what the early twentieth-century economist Thorstein Veblen has called 'conspicuous consumption' – works of art may enhance the status of their owners among their peers or within society. In this case, properties that are extrinsic to the work of art, such as its high price or the exclusive venue where it is bought, make a work of art all the more attractive for status-oriented buyers. Status-related reasons may also motivate companies to collect art. For instance, financial institutions may thus try to signal to clients that their interests are more encompassing than profit-making only, while directors of the company can enhance their reputation within their peer group by demonstrating their knowledge of art.

Although the three sets of motives may be distinguished in theory, in practice, a mixture of all three tends to motivate buyers to acquire art. Indeed, the lower return on paintings compared to other financial assets has been interpreted as evidence of the fact that other motives than merely financial ones are involved: the lesser financial return is compensated by the artistic, decorative, aesthetic or status value that buyers derive from buying a work of art.[1] For some parties in the art market, however, one motive may prevail: for instance, since the 1980s some banks and hedge funds have tried to set up art investment funds, albeit with different degrees of success. During the financial crisis, many of them had to close. The pieces owned by these funds are usually kept in storage, making it impossible for the owners to enjoy the artistic or decorative value of the paintings. These funds find their predecessors in investment groups such as the Parisian Peau de l'ours, which, early on, were buying works by Cubist painters such as Picasso and Braque, and made a handsome profit when they sold them in 1914 (Fitzgerald, 1995).

By contrast, a public institution such as a museum will focus solely on artistic value when buying a work of art. The rate of return that may be made on this acquisition will be disregarded, if only because deaccessioning, that is selling works of art from a public collection, is considered illegitimate in many museums in Europe and the USA. Only when it is considered a lesser piece, when the museum holds a more or less identical piece, when the museum is in dire straits, or when the work can be exchanged with another party for a more appropriate one, might deaccessioning be an option for a museum.

Structure of the market

Art markets present an extreme case of trade in heterogeneous goods. For some works of art, no substitutes may exist. Buyers may be interested solely in one particular piece of art made by an artist of their liking, executed in a specific style, and depicting a specific subject matter. The supply curve is in that case fully inelastic. This explains why, at auction, some works by the same artist fetch much higher prices than others. Thus, in theory, the art market may not be seen as a single market but instead as a large set of monopolistic or, in the case of a single interested buyer, monopsonistic markets (see, for example, Moulin, 1967).

In practice, however, almost invariably some substitutability does exist: a collector may for instance be interested in owning a work by the American pop artist Andy Warhol, without an absolute preference for one work in particular. But even then, when the artist is deceased, supply must be regarded as fixed. Moreover, within this fixed supply, many works of art by old or modern masters may no longer easily appear on the market, for instance because they are part of museum collections or because they are the property of collectors who are known to be extremely reluctant to sell parts of their holdings. At the very least, a price premium may have to be paid in order to persuade such a collector to sell.

Substitutability may be more extensive for a buyer who is interested in art merely for decorative reasons. Such a buyer will consider buying work by a variety of artists, as long as the subject matter is pleasing, and the colours go, so to say, with the couch. Likewise, a starting collector may not have a fully developed taste or may have decided only that s/he will be buying contemporary rather than modern or pre-modern art. Within those categories, his/her taste may be influenced by what artists, art dealers or other intermediaries are offering for sale. In that sense, all dealers operating within the same region are competing for the scarce resources of such collectors. Competition is not based on price, however, but on the capacity of dealers to convince the collector of the work's lasting artistic and economic value and on their ability to influence and shape the collector's taste.

Finally, substitutability may be almost perfect in a wholesale market for art where, by and large, mass-produced, anonymous paintings and multiples are exchanged between parties such as hotel chains or tourist retail stores and art production companies (Fitz Gibbon, 1987). In those companies, which frequently have their production facilities in China, art is produced in an assembly-line fashion, with many employees working on the same pieces of art, according to a strict division of labour in order to increase productivity. The wholesale trade of these paintings frequently takes place through the Internet or at specialized annual trade fairs.

Not only because of its lack of homogeneity, but also in other respects, the art market deviates radically from the textbook theory of perfect markets (Santagata, 1995). First of all, transaction costs are hardly negligible. For instance, at auction, buyers and sellers of works of art may have to pay up to 20 per cent of the sales price. These transaction costs render art even less attractive as a financial asset class (as do insurance and storage costs related to art investments). Second, if the art market is considered as a financial market, its lack of liquidity is striking. A collector who wants to sell his work because he urgently needs cash may need to wait several months before an auction will take place in which this work fits. For many artists, an active resale market may or may no longer exist. Some art dealers, such as the illustrious Paris and New York Wildenstein Gallery, are known to have had works for decades in inventory before they finally managed to sell them. Also, unlike assets on financial markets, works of art are hardly divisible. Although some pieces of art have been bought by consortia of investors and collectors, such as Damien Hirst's diamond-covered skull *For the Love of God*, it is generally impossible to buy, for example, a one-hundredth share in a painting by Rembrandt.

Third, the art market is characterized by a lack of transparency. Information regarding the quality of the art supplied or the willingness to pay on the side of buyers is incomplete, difficult and often expensive to gather. Prices for which art dealers sell works of art are frequently unknown. For instance, the most expensive painting ever was not sold at auction, but through a private deal (as are four other works in the top ten list): the abstract expressionist painting No. 5 by the American artist Jackson Pollock, which according to media reports was sold in 2006 for US$140 million by the Hollywood producer David Geffen. Since neither the buyer nor the seller ever confirmed the sale, we cannot know for sure which work of art is the most expensive ever and who owns it.

The lack of transparency is also striking when it comes to the identity of buyers and sellers, whose names are not usually disclosed. Take the extreme case of Vincent van Gogh's portrait of *Dr Gachet*, which sold in 1990 for US$82.5 million. The buyer at that time, the Japanese paper tycoon Ryoei Saito, said that he would have the work cremated with him. This did not happen, but after his death in 1996, the whereabouts of the work were unknown to the wider public for 11 years, when media reports said that the work had been sold after Saito's death to the Austrian fund manager Wolfgang Flöttl. Flöttl subsequently sold it, allegedly because of financial troubles. Its current owner remains unknown. The transparency of the art market has been improved considerably, however, by companies that have specialized in providing market information, for instance regarding the careers of living artists and the galleries that represent them (e.g. artfacts. net) and comprehensive art auction data (such as artprice.com or artnet.com). Because of this, buyers and sellers all over the world may now know instantly where particular pieces of art have been auctioned and for how much.

However, lack of transparency remains a problem, and information asymmetries abound on the art market. Some participants may, for instance, have better knowledge about the authorship, authenticity or provenance of a work of art than their competitors, which enables them to make excess returns. For instance, a work may be sold at auction as a work made by a member of Rembrandt's studio, while some parties may have information indicating that the work was made by Rembrandt himself. Likewise, the New York art dealer Duveen made handsome profits in the early twentieth century on the trade of Italian Renaissance artists through his famous partnership with the art historian Bernard Berenson. After Berenson had confirmed the authenticity of important Renaissance works or reattributed them to more famous masters, Duveen would sell them at high prices to the roster of wealthy American collectors whom he assisted in building up their collections.

The widespread existence of information asymmetries provides ample opportunities for fraud and deceit. Forgeries have been created of many Old and Modern Masters; moulds used for sculptures that were promised to be made in an edition of five or ten have been reused to make more copies; the same applies to other multiples such as etchings. In all these cases, the art market is akin to the market for 'lemons' discussed by

George Akerlof, where the quality of the work is known to the seller but not to the buyer (Akerlof, 1970). Realizing this, interested parties may refrain from buying works of art altogether. In order to prevent this, dealers award certificates of authenticity or hire the services of art experts who should assure buyers of the quality of the works involved. Other forms of fraud, albeit not related to the quality of the work, may occur if artists sell works out of their studio without paying a commission to a dealer who represents them and who is contractually entitled to a pre-negotiated percentage of each sale; or if a dealer sells a work at full price, tells the artist it went at a discount, and subsequently pockets the difference between the two. In order to handle these information asymmetries and the opportunities for deceit they entail, economic interaction on the art market is, unlike the economics textbook's assumptions, far from anonymous. Instead, participants develop long-term trust relationships that reduce the incentives for mutual deceit.

Finally, information asymmetries aside, what characterizes the art market is that it is a market for credence goods. Its value cannot be objectively and individually determined, but relies to a large extent on the credibility of the experts involved in the collective evaluation processes that take place within art worlds. Changing tastes and fashions, on which individual participants in art markets may have little influence, can radically increase or diminish the artistic and economic value of objects within art markets (Bonus and Ronte, 1997). To put it in sociological terms, the value of art is socially constructed, or, as the French sociologist Pierre Bourdieu put it, it is a market based on the production of belief. Not everybody can participate to the same extent in the process of credibility generation. This by and large involves cultural experts such as artists themselves, art dealers, museum curators and art critics, who possess the symbolic capital to bestow value on works of art. This symbolic capital is in turn generated by a mixture of factors such as a longstanding commitment to the art world, extensive cultural knowledge and personal charisma. As Bourdieu has argued, in accumulating this symbolic capital it is crucial that experts signal to the art world that they are not interested in short-run economic profits, but care genuinely about the art itself. In the long run, however, symbolic capital may be converted into economic capital: an art dealer who has become recognized for his selection of artists whose work has and maintains artistic value may in the long run make high profits on the sale of these works (Bourdieu, 1992, 1993).

This credence aspect of cultural objects means that the art market cannot be understood properly without taking the role of various cultural institutions into account, such as museums where artworks are exhibited and preserved, 'alternative' exhibition spaces like artists' cooperatives, and the art press (art magazines, newspapers and book publishers that devote considerable attention to the arts). In addition to their cultural functions of exhibiting and reviewing art, putting artworks in a historical or critical context, and educating artists and their audience, these institutions participate in the art market. Museums, for instance, are not only a source of demand on the art market. They also have an indirect economic impact on the art market: they, as well as the art press, are gatekeepers, which means that they make a selection out of the large 'pool' of oeuvres and individual artworks that have been made throughout history. Gatekeepers allocate scarce resources to this selection of artworks. In economic terms, this gatekeeping role of cultural institutions serves to reduce information and search costs for economic agents on the market: collectors may economize on these costs if they want to acquire art by taking the judgement of cultural institutions into account. By channelling resources to a limited group of visual artists, cultural institutions also enhance superstar phenomena within the visual arts. Finally, these cultural institutions generate 'credibility' or 'belief' in the artistic value of art among an audience of museum visitors and art collectors.

Several empirical studies indicate that the 'cultural judgement' of museum curators and art critics on the one hand, and the 'economic judgement' of the art market on the other hand, are correlated (see, for example, Frey and Pommerehne, 1989; Galenson, 2000). This can be interpreted in different ways: either collectors derive extra utility from consuming artworks that cultural institutions deem important; or the taste of collectors is directly influenced by the choices of cultural institutions. Traditionally, cultural economists have abstracted from the latter effect, however, since it violates a core assumption of neoclassical economic theory that tastes are constant.

Primary versus secondary markets

The art market consists of many segments, which can be categorized in different ways. The most important distinction is between the primary market, where contemporary artists sell their work for the first time, and the secondary or resale market. Since data on the primary market barely exist, this section of the visual arts has been largely ignored in cultural economics. Instead, most studies focus on auction sales on the secondary market. On the primary market, some artists sell their work directly from their studio. Others try to find intermediary institutions such as commercial art galleries. These galleries usually represent 10 to 30 artists, promote their work among art experts, and receive a predetermined percentage of each sale as a compensation for those efforts.

Since works of art appear on the market here for the first time, a consensus of art experts regarding their value is by and large absent, uniform standards of value are lacking, and the careers of their producers are frequently unstable, economic value on the primary art market is radically uncertain. In these circumstances, one might expect bidding as a preferred means of setting prices. In reality, auctions are hardly ever used on the primary market. One of the few exceptions was the case of the Impressionists, who in their early days auctioned their work with little success at the Paris auction house Hotel Drouot. More recently, in September 2008, the British celebrity artist Damien Hirst sold off 223 works out of his studio at auction house Sotheby's, much to the dismay of his dealers. The auction revenue totalled US$200 million, the highest amount ever for a single-artist auction. Although the art press was rife with speculation that his example might signal a watershed change in the primary art market because of the entry of auction houses as new competitors to art dealers, Hirst's example has not so far been followed.

In most Western European countries and the USA, only a small percentage of contemporary artists can make a living from selling their work on the market. Works made by an even smaller percentage of living artists are traded on the secondary market. On the secondary market it is predominantly works by deceased artists that are traded. This segment of the market is dominated by two auction houses – Christie's and Sotheby's. The two have historically been engaged in cut-throat competition for clients and works of art. In the 1990s, however, the two auction houses were accused of market collusion: according to prosecutors in the USA, they had divided important clients in order to prevent them from competing over these, and had made secret price-fixing deals over the commissions they ask their clients. After the suit had been partially settled and Sotheby's

CEO Alfred Taubman had been convicted to a jail sentence, competition resumed. In the first decade of the new millennium, financial guarantees appeared as one of the instruments to lure important sellers. With these guarantees, the seller receives a predetermined minimum price. If the work remains unsold at auction because it does not meet a reserve price, the auction house becomes the new owner. If the work is sold above the guaranteed price, the remainder is split between the seller and the auction house.

Apart from the auction houses, the secondary art market involves art dealers who either sell works on a consignment basis or buy works for inventory and subsequently try to sell them at a profit. Throughout the twentieth century, this inventory was by and large acquired by art dealers at auction houses, where they were the main customers, but in the last couple of decades, retail clients have started buying at auction as well.

Many interactions between the primary and the secondary markets occur. For the works made by a relatively small group of living artists, both markets may be active. While older pieces by the artist may come up on the secondary market, new works are sold by their galleries on the primary market. Some collectors may not be able to acquire pieces by very popular contemporary artists on the primary market because the galleries do not sell them to those buyers with the highest willingness to pay. Instead, they ration the output of these artists through a waiting list or sell the output exclusively to loyal clients, well-known collectors or important public institutions. Other collectors may then circumvent the waiting list by trying to buy the work on the secondary market, providing an incentive to collectors who already own the work to resell it. Another type of interaction between the two market segments relates to pricing. Customarily, art dealers on the primary market tend to adjust price levels to prices achieved at auction, although only in a piecemeal fashion. Vice versa, estimates that auction houses provide in their catalogues tend to be based on price levels on the primary market.

Local versus global markets

A different type of segmentation of art markets can be made based on their geographical scope. Some markets are by and large locally oriented, with local artists catering for the demand of local collectors. Regional art institutions such as small-scale county museums and the local art press may devote attention to the art that is exchanged here. What goes on within these markets in terms of schools or styles may be influenced by trends in national or global markets, but is hardly noticed or recognized by the latter. At the other extreme are global markets that are mostly concentrated in art capitals such as New York, Berlin or London. Galleries within these capitals often represent artists from many different countries while their clientele may likewise be dispersed geographically. The most important art auctions, which traditionally take place at Christie's and Sotheby's in New York in May and November, are likewise marketed globally.

To some extent, the art market has always crossed borders. In the sixteenth and seventeenth centuries, artists such as Peter Paul Rubens were travelling through Europe to cater for the demand at courts in France, England and Spain. In the early twentieth century, works made by Italian Renaissance painters and French Impressionists were sold to American collectors. In the 1980s, the newly rich Japanese middle class took an interest in Impressionism. Since the late 1990s, however, art markets have become global to an unprecedented extent: they now encompass many more regions than in the past. New collectors from Latin America, the former Soviet Union and Asia have entered the art market, while artists from, among others Mexico, India and China have had their work sold at international auctions and acquired by well-known Western museums and private collectors. Also, market participants now operate more widely than ever before. Auction houses, for instance, have started organizing sales in emerging markets such as Dubai and Hong Kong, while globally operating art dealers have opened up branches or organized exhibitions in those regions.

One of the most striking aspects of the globalization of art markets is the rise of the Chinese art market. Between 2003 and 2006, contemporary art sales at auction in China increased 100 times to $88 million, according to data provider Artprice.com. According to estimates, 2000 auction houses and 50000 art dealers are active within the country. And while in 2002 there was only one Chinese artist part of the list of the world's top 100 artists (computed on the basis of annual auction revenue), in 2008 this list contained 34 Chinese artists. By comparison, the list held just 20 American artists. In the same year, 44 Asian artists were represented in the list, as against 27 European (Artprice, 2009).

One of the most important institutions that has developed over the last decades as part of this globalized art market is art fairs (Quemin, 2008). Art fairs are organized on an annual basis. Participants are usually a hundred or several hundreds of art dealers, each of whom has a booth where they exhibit their highest-quality objects to the thousands of potential buyers who pass by over a period of a week or less. Although local fairs do exist, where participants generally have the same nationality, they tend to have an international character. Art fairs, which originated in the Cologne art fair of 1967, enable both buyers and collectors to economize on search and information costs: while it would be time-consuming and thus costly for a wealthy collector with high opportunity costs to regularly visit all art galleries in his home town, let alone in his home country or all over the world, the fair brings a large selection of these galleries together. For dealers, art fairs are an important venue for meeting new collectors. Some fairs also have an important reputational component: the most prestigious fairs, such as Art Basel, Art Basel Miami Beach and the London Frieze on the primary art market or the Maastricht Tefaf on the secondary market, attract many more applications from dealers than they allow to exhibit. As a result, getting accepted at these fairs functions as a sign of quality or approval that may facilitate sales. Participation in these fairs is costly, however, with admission fees of several thousands to several tens of thousands of dollars, as well as high transportation and insurance costs for the works of art that are exhibited. With their many parties, talk shows and busy crowds that allow for celebrity spotting, art fairs are part of the experience economy, where not only the objects themselves, but also the experience that is generated is valued by consumers.

Cultural/economic circuit

A final way of segmenting the art market has been developed by the French sociologist Pierre Bourdieu (and similar taxonomies are proposed by various other sociologists and economists). His taxonomy consists of two types of hierarchy. First of all there is the opposition between large-scale production directed at catering the pre-existing demands of a larger audience, and small-scale production meant for an audience that consists mainly of fellow artists, experts, critics and a limited number of other insiders; on different occasions Bourdieu has referred to this opposition as that between the commercial and the non-commercial, between traditional and avant-garde or between bourgeois and intellectual art, between the 'immediate, temporary success of best-sellers' and the 'deferred, lasting success of "classics"' (Bourdieu, 1993, p. 82; 1992 [1996]). The second hierarchy concerns the circuit of small-scale, avant-garde production, in particular; it is a hierarchy between a young, still unrecognized fraction and a 'consecrated', well-to-do fraction of the cultural field, whose work has already been incorporated in the canon. As a result, the avant-garde circuit harbours a wide variety of galleries, from small, idealistic enterprises that try to help beginning artists to show their work, to large, global corporations with offices around the world; within the traditional circuit some dealers represent the expensive and painstakingly realist work of artists who have a waiting list of collectors willing to buy their work, while others sell a wide variety of low-priced works made by artists with no reputation whatsoever.

Note

1. Since this artistic and social value is hard to measure, no empirical evidence exists for this interpretation. It is based on the assumption of market equilibrium, which is not fulfilled if total returns on art differ from total returns on other financial assets.

See also:

Chapter 2: Art auctions; Chapter 3: Art dealers; Chapter 5: Art prices.

References

Akerlof, George A. (1970), 'The Market for "Lemons": Quality Uncertainty and the Market Mechanism', *The Quarterly Journal of Economics*, 84 (3), 488–500.

Artprice (2009), *The Contemporary Art Market 2008/2009. The Artprice Annual Report*, Lyon: Artprice.

Baumol, William J. (1986), 'Unnatural Value: or Art Investment as Floating Crap Game', *American Economic Review*, 76 (2), 10–15.

Bonus, Holger and Dieter Ronte (1997), 'Credibility and Economic Value in the Visual Arts', *Journal of Cultural Economics*, 21, 103–18.

Bourdieu, Pierre (1992 [1996]), *The Rules of Art*, Stanford, CA: Stanford University Press.

Bourdieu, Pierre (1993), *The Field of Cultural Production. Essays on Art and Literature*, Cambridge: Polity Press.

Buelens, Nathalie and Victor Ginsburgh (1993), 'Revisiting Baumol's "art as a floating crap game"', *European Economic Review*, 37, 1351–71.

Bystryn, Marcia (1978), 'Art Galleries as Gatekeepers: The Case of the Abstract Expressionists', *Social Research*, 45 (2), 390–408.

Candela, Guido and Antonello E. Scorcu (2001), 'In Search of Stylized Facts on Art Market Prices: Evidence from the Secondary Market for Prints and Drawings in Italy', *Journal of Cultural Economics*, 25, 219–31.

De Marchi, Neil and Hans J. Van Miegroet (1994), 'Art, Value, and Market Practices in the Netherlands in the Seventeenth Century', *Art Bulletin*, 76 (3), 451–64.

Fitzgerald, Michael C. (1995), *Making Modernism. Picasso and the Creation of the Market for Twentieth-Century Art*, New York: Farrar, Straus and Giroux.

Fitz Gibbon, Heather M. (1987), 'From Prints to Posters: The Production of Artstic Value in a Popular World', *Symbolic Interaction*, 10 (1), 111–28.

Frey, Bruno S. and Reiner Eichenberger (1995), 'On the Return of Art Investment Return Analyses', *Journal of Cultural Economics*, 19, 207–20.

Frey, Bruno S. and Werner W. Pommerehne (1989), *Muses and Markets: Explorations in the Economics of the Arts*, Oxford: Blackwell.

Galenson, David W. (2000), 'The Careers of Modern Artists', *Journal of Cultural Economics*, 24, 87–112.

Ginsburgh, Victor (2003), 'Art Markets', in Ruth Towse (ed.), *A Handbook of Cultural Economics*, Cheltenham, UK and Northampton, MA, USA: Edward Elgar, pp. 40–56.

Goetzmann, William N. (1993), 'Accounting for Taste: Art and the Financial Markets Over Three Centuries', *American Economic Review*, 83 (5), 1370–76.

Hutter, Michael, Christian Knebel, Gunnar Pietzner and Maren Schäfer (2007), 'Two Games in Town: A Comparison of Dealer and Auction Prices in Contemporary Visual Arts Markets', *Journal of Cultural Economics*, 31 (4), 247–61.

McAndrew, Clare (2009), *Globalisation and the Art Market. Emerging Economies and the Art Trade in 2008*, Helvoirt: Tefaf.

Montias, J. Michael (1987), 'Cost and Value in Seventeenth-Century Dutch Art', *Art History*, 10 (4), 453–66.

Moulin, Raymonde (1967 [1987]), *The French Art Market. A Sociological View*, New Brunswick, NJ: Rutgers University Press.

North, Michael (1992), *Art and Commerce in the Dutch Golden Age*, New Haven, CT: Yale University Press.

Pesando, James E. and Pauline M. Shum (1996), 'Price Anomalies at Auction: Evidence from the Market for Modern Prints', in Victor A. Ginsburgh and Pierre M. Menger, *Economics of the Arts. Selected Essays*, Amsterdam: Elsevier, pp. 113–34.

Plattner, Stuart (1996), *High Art Down Home. An Economic Ethnography of a Local Art Market*, Chicago, IL: Chicago University Press.

Quemin, Alain (2006), 'Globalization and Mixing in the Visual Arts. An Empirical Survey of "High Culture" and Globalization', *International Sociology*, 21, 522–50.

Quemin, Alain (2008), 'International Contemporary Art Fairs and Galleries: An Exclusive Overview', in *The Contemporary Art Market. Annual Report*, Paris: Artprice.

Santagata, Walter (1995), 'Institutional Anomalies in the Contemporary Art Market', *Journal of Cultural Economics*, 19, 187–97.

Schulze, Günther G (1999), 'International Trade in Art', *Journal of Cultural Economics*, 23, 109–36.

Velthuis, Olav (2005), *Talking Prices. Symbolic Meanings of Prices on the Market for Contemporary Art*, Princeton, NJ: Princeton University Press.

Watson, Peter (1992), *From Manet to Manhattan*, New York: Random House.

Worthington, Andrew C. and Helen Higgs (2004), 'Art as an Investment: Risk, Return and Portfolio Diversification in Major Painting Markets', *Accounting and Finance*, 44 (2), 257–72.

Further reading

For studies of art as an investment, see e.g. Baumol (1986), Frey and Eichenberger (1995), Ginsburgh (2003), Worthington and Higgs (2004), Goetzmann (1993), Buelens and Ginsburgh (1993), Pesando and Shum (1996), Candela and Scorcu (2001). On the relationship between the primary and the secondary market, see Hutter *et al.* (2007). For historical studies, see North (1992), Montias (1987), De Marchi and Van Miegroet (1994), Watson (1992). For sociological studies and anthropological studies of art markets, see Moulin (1967), Bystryn (1978), Plattner (1996), Velthuis (2005). For globalization of art markets, see Quemin (2006, 2008), Schulze (1999).

5 Art prices
Dominique Sagot-Duvauroux

One can characterize a commodity by its physical properties, the date at which it will be available, and the location at which it will be available. This definition underlines the three types of variables to be taken into account in understanding the prices of the works of art. In the first instance, the price of a work of art depends on its physical properties: size, materials used, date of creation, and of course the name of the creator. However, the same painting or print will have different prices depending on the date and place of sale.

Prices depend on the physical properties of the works of art
A work of art can be described by a set of properties that include the support, the subject matter and the signature. By support, we mean the size and the raw materials used (canvas, paper, oil, water colour, pastels, pencil, pigments and so on). The subjects depicted are mainly historical scenes, portraits, still lifes, landscapes, abstracts and the like. The artist's signature to the work acts as a trademark.

The relevant properties change over time
The history of art shows that the properties relevant to determining the price of a painting change over time (Moureau and Sagot-Duvauroux, 2010). For example, during the Italian quattrocento, the price on the art market was determined mainly by the support. The painter's greatest asset was his ability. The price was usually fixed before the painting was begun and depended on the cost of production. The order specified the colours to be used, the subject, the number of people and so on.

During the academic period in France (from the mid-seventeenth century to the end of the nineteenth century), the price of works of art depended mainly on the choice of subject. Historical paintings, because they revealed the knowledge of the artist–scientist, and his ability to draw from life, were more highly regarded than portraits, which, in turn, were more highly considered than still lifes or landscapes (Heinich, 1993).

Since the end of the nineteenth century, the relevant property has been the artist's signature. The value of an art work depends on the originality of the thought process of the artist, and the signature is the guarantee of this originality. The skilled craftsman with a knowledge of history is replaced by an artist with inspiration. It becomes impossible to price a work of art without the name of the artist.

Constructing a reputation
The construction of the artist's reputation was first studied by sociologists. Howard Becker (1982) described the process of the construction of a reputation in different 'art worlds', defined by conventions to which the members of each world adhered and by which the criteria of recognition were listed. Each art world has its own rules of price-fixing and has few links with the others. Moulin (1992) provides a stimulating framework for the study of networks and value for contemporary works of art. She shows that a

considerable proportion of the value of works of art is the outcome of the interaction between the different actors involved in the art market (in particular, galleries and curators, but also collectors and critics). She distinguishes between market-oriented art and museum-oriented art. In the latter, works are created specifically for museum exhibitions. Similarly, Jyrämä (1999) compares contemporary art networks in four countries (Finland, Sweden, France, the UK) and shows that the respective weight of the leading actors depends on the country. The analysis concentrates on the similarities and differences between each country in terms of market structure and management. Moureau and Sagot-Duvauroux (2010) underline the consequences of the uncertainty that surrounds the quality of contemporary artworks on the functioning of the market. They show that in the face of this uncertainty, poorly informed collectors may be rationally led to adopt copy-cat forms of behaviour that consist in following the opinion of a few agents who are believed to be in the know concerning the value of the works (dealers, curators or collectors). These informational cascades may be strategic when the opinion's leaders are interested in the result of the cascade. The outcome is a spate of information that can lead to speculation on some artists. Similarly, Bonus and Ronte (1997) have studied the role played by experts in legitimizing the creation of some artists in the eyes of the public; they defend the idea that this process is an example of 'path dependent institutional change'. They show how, over and above the talent of the artist, recognition depends on small-scale events and/or luck (meeting with a curator, for example).

All these studies underline the focus on the signature in evaluating the price of a work of art. Authenticity plays a major role in the price. Should there be any doubt as to the origin of the work, it will inevitably fall in value. Certificates from painters, names of former owners and bibliographies are all elements that contribute to raising the price. This is why auction houses use very precise terms to describe the works on sale.[1]

The price of works of art of equal artistic value varies according to the size, the technique used, the style or the subject matter. The price of a painting increases at a decreasing marginal rate with size. Similarly, a drawing is cheaper than a gouache, which in turn is cheaper than an oil or an acrylic painting, and a work on paper is cheaper than a work on wood or canvas.[2]

Prices depend on the date and the place of sale
While, at any given moment, the price depends mainly on the name of the artist and the physical properties of the work, the price of the same piece can vary in time and space. The price of works of art changes over time as a function of macroeconomic variables such as inflation, income per capita, or the quotations on the stock exchange, but also as a function of events that are specific to the life of the artist (his/her death, for example). However, the evaluation of the evolution of the price of a work over time and its comparison with that of other assets involves considerable methodological problems linked to the specificity of the work of art as an asset.

The work of art: a specific asset
The work of art is an object that can be stocked and that cannot be reproduced. It may be the object of a demand for an investment whose profitability is assessed in relation to that of other assets. However, there are many differences that set the art market apart from the financial markets (Baumol, 1986):

- On the financial markets, a high number of homogenous, substitutable stocks and shares are bought and sold, whereas the degree of substitutability is almost nil in the case of artistic products given the fact that they are unique.
- The owner of a work of art has a monopoly, whereas any given stock or share is owned by a great number of individuals who, theoretically, act independently of one another.
- The transactions relative to a specific stock or share take place in time almost continuously, whereas transactions concerning a single work of art may be several decades apart.
- The fundamental value of a financial asset is known; it is the present-day value of the expected flow of income; on the contrary, the work of art has no long-term equilibrium price.
- The costs of holding and transacting are much higher for works of art than for stocks and shares: insurance costs are high; there are charges borne by the seller and the buyer at auction, although on the other hand the taxes incurred by these goods may be more advantageous.
- Finally, art, unlike stocks and shares, does not provide any positive monetary dividends; its ownership may imply negative dividends in the form of insurance and restoration costs; it does, however, afford psychological dividends in the form of cultural consumption and services throughout its lifespan; the intensity of these services determines the value of its use, subjectively assessed by each consumer.

The rate of return on works of art

The question that economists have found by far the most interesting is that of the profitability of investments in artworks.[3] Given that works of art are assets that are unique, the calculation of their profitability raises considerable methodological difficulties. Two main methods have been used (Ginsburgh *et al.*, 2006). The first is to pool data from repeat sales and run a repeat-sales regression. The second method of deriving a price index is to run a hedonic regression in which the price of an item is regressed on its various properties, including age or purchase prices. In all cases, the prices used are the prices at auction, which, however, represent only about 25 per cent of the transactions on the art market.

Profitability varies with the method used. As a general rule, the rates obtained by studies using repeated sales are found to be appreciably lower that those using hedonic prices. The findings are also weakened by the choice of dates for the beginning and end of the period in a very volatile market. Finally, they vary considerably in function of the artistic trends taken into consideration (Impressionists, contemporary art and so on) (Worthington and Higgs, 2004).

However, all the studies note the degree of risk inherent to this type of investment. Nevertheless, this risk can be limited if the capacity of the buyer to select his or her purchases is introduced. Landes (2000), in his attempt to understand the record prices fetched at the 1997 Christie's auction of twentieth-century artworks from the estate of Victor and Sally Ganz, concluded that the high levels of profitability achieved were explained not so much by the reputation of the Ganz, which was superimposed on that of the artists, as on the acuity of their choices. The investment in knowledge thus enables the risks inherent to this type of investment to be appreciably limited.

The variation in price of works of art over time is in part explained by macroeconomic variables. Other things being equal, the average prices of artworks rise with per capita income. Similarly, inflation tends to enhance the rise in demand for artworks and therefore the increase in prices (Pommerehne and Frey, 1989). Finally, Gerard-Varet *et al.* (1993) establish a link between the evolution of quotations on the stock exchange and the evolution of prices for artworks, but with a time lag.

Price and place of sale
The price of works also varies with place. The prices in art galleries do not always tally with those in auction rooms. The latter vary depending on the auction house and the country in which the sale takes place.

Prices in art galleries versus prices at auction
Qualitative studies on the art market reveal the differences between prices in art galleries and the prices at auction. As a general rule, galleries hesitate to lower prices. As a result, the variations in price in galleries are smaller than those observed at auction. When prices are rising, the galleries limit their increase in prices by stressing quality, while in times of falling prices they put higher-quality artworks on the market. By comparing data collected by the Capital Kunstkompass (CKK) and their correlates generated by auctions over the course of 30 years, Hutter *et al.* (2007) show that the level of dealer prices is generally higher than auction prices and stickier in their downward movements. Candela and Scorcu (2001) have tested this hypothesis on the market for drawings and prints by comparing prices at auction with those listed in the catalogues of the Prandi gallery, which is well known for drawings and prints. Since 1977, they have published the prices and descriptions of the drawings and prints sold. Nevertheless, the authors do show the close link between the evolution of the prices at auction and those in private galleries.

Prices in New York versus prices in London and Paris
Within the auction world, there are systematic differences across international markets. De la Barre *et al.* (1994) thus demonstrate that the prices fetched for the same type of work (great masters, or other painters) are higher in New York than in London, and higher in London than in Paris. Pesando and Shum (1996) go further and show that the same item fetches appreciably different prices depending on the auction house that sells it, even if the sale takes place in the same town at the same time. Beggs and Graddy (2009) verify the existence of a strong anchoring effect of actual prices on previous prices reached by a work of art, involving a path-dependent process linked with the economic situation of the first sale (a 'hot' or 'cold' market). These findings do seem to invalidate the hypothesis of the efficiency of an art market of which the final outcome should be 'the law of one price'. However, auction theory teaches us that auction prices are heavily dependent on the number and quality of bidders. This is why Sotheby's and Christie's organize their sales at the same time in the same town, so as to benefit mutually from the presence of collectors. This strategy tends to inflate the prices when compared with sales of auction rooms that are not organized. Findings of this sort emphasize the uniqueness of each sale in time and space, the characteristics being the variation in number of different bidders and an order of numbering of the lots, which is equally specific. Moreover, several studies

stress 'the declining price anomaly', whereby the lots sold towards the end of the sale tend to fetch lower prices than those sold at the beginning (see, for example, Beggs and Graddy, 1997); this sort of finding can be explained by the fall in number of bidders as the sale takes place. Finally, prices strongly depend on previous and estimated prices.

Concluding remarks

Over the past 20 years, numerous studies have been published on the prices of artworks. This research has enabled the identification of the main determinants of the prices of artworks, the evaluation of the profitability of investment in artworks and the identification of various anomalies in the art market in determining prices. But little economic consideration has been given to the formation of and trends in taste in artistic matters. This seems to be the most promising direction for research today.

Notes

1. 'Attributed to': work of the period of the artist that may be in whole, or in part, the work of the artist. There is a warranty that the work was executed during the production period of the artist; 'studio of', 'workshop of': a work possibly executed under the supervision of the artist. It certifies that the work was made in his/her workshop or under his/her direction. The workshop name must be followed by a date when it was a family workshop. 'School of': work by a pupil or a follower of the artist. The painter was influenced by, or benefited from, the master referred to. This term can be used up to 50 years after the master's death. 'Work by', 'signature of': certifies the work was painted by the artist. 'In the style of', 'in the manner of', and so on: this is no warranty of the artist's identity, the date or the school.
2. For an econometric evaluation of the influence of these characteristics on price, see Gerard-Varet *et al.* (1993) or Agnello and Pierce (1996).
3. For a survey, see Ashenfelter and Graddy (2003), Mandel (2009), Burton and Jacobsen (1999), Agnello and Pierce (1996), Frey and Eichenberger (1995).

See also:

Chapter 2: Art auctions; Chapter 3: Art dealers; Chapter 4: Art markets.

References

Agnello, R.J. and R.K. Pierce (1996), 'Financial Returns, Price Determinants, and Genre Effects', *Journal of Cultural Economics*, 20, 359–83.

Ashenfelter, Orley and Kathryn Graddy (2003), 'Auctions and the Price of Art', *Journal of Economic Literature*, 41 (3), 763–87.

Barre, N. de la, S. Docclo and V. Ginsburgh (1994), 'Returns of Impressionist, Modern and Contemporary European Paintings 1962–1991', *Annales d'économie et de statistique*, 35, July–September, 143–81.

Baumol, W.J. (1986), 'Unnatural Value: or Art as a Floating Crap Game', *American Economic Review*, 76 (2), 10–14.

Becker, H.S. (1982), *Art Worlds*, Berkeley, Los Angeles and London: University of California Press.

Beggs, Alan and Kathryn Graddy (1997), 'Declining Values and the Afternoon Effect: Evidence from Art Auctions', *Rand Journal of Economics*, 28, 544–65.

Beggs, Alan and Kathryn Graddy (2009), 'Anchoring Effects: Evidence from Art Auctions', *American Economic Review*, 99 (3), 1027–39.

Bonus, H. and D. Ronte (1997), 'Credibility and Economic Value in the Visual Arts', *Journal of Cultural Economics*, 21, 103–18.

Burton, B.J. and J.P. Jacobsen (1999), 'Measuring Returns on Investments in Collectibles', *Journal of Economic Perspectives*, 13 (4), 193–212.

Candela, G. and A.E. Scorcu (2001), 'In Search of Stylized Facts on Art Market Prices: Evidence from the Secondary Market for Prints and Drawings in Italy', *Journal of Cultural Economics*, 25, 219–31.

Frey, B.S. and R. Eichenberger (1995), 'On the Return of Art. Investment Return Analyses, Survey and Evaluation', *European Economic Review*, 39, 528–37.

Gerard-Varet, L.A., O. Chanel, S. Docclo and V. Ginsburgh (1993), 'Rentabilité des Placements sur le Marché de l'Art de 1957 à 1988', *Risques*, 13, January–March, 133–67.

Ginsburgh, Victor A., Jianping Mei and Michael Moses (2006), 'The Computation of Price Indices', in Victor A. Ginsburgh and David Throsby (eds), *Handbook of the Economics of Art and Culture*, Amsterdam: Elsevier, pp. 947–79.

Heinich, N. (1993) *Du Peintre à l'Artiste, Artisans et Académiciens à l'Age Classique*, Paris: Les éditions de minuit.

Hutter, Michael, Christian Knebel, Gunnar Pietzner and Maren Schäfer (2007), 'Two Games in Town: A Comparison of Dealer and Auction Prices in Contemporary Visual Arts Markets', *Journal of Cultural Economics*, 31 (4), 247–61.

Jirämä, A. (1999), *Contemporary Art Markets, Structure and Practices: A Study of Art Galleries in Finland, Sweden, France and Great Britain*, Helsinki School of Economics and Business Administration.

Landes, W.M. (2000), 'Winning the Art Lottery: The Economic Returns to the Ganz Collection', *Recherches Economiques de Louvain*, 66 (2), 111–30.

Mandel, B.R. (2009), 'Art as an Investment and Conspicuous Consumption Goods', *American Economic Review*, 99 (4), 1653–63.

Moulin, R. (1992), *L'Artiste, l'Institution, le Marché*, Paris: Flammarion.

Moureau, N. and D. Sagot-Duvauroux (2003, 2010), *Le Marché de l'Art Contemporain*, Paris: La Découverte.

Pesando, J.E. and M. Shum (1996), 'Price Anomalies at Auction: Evidence from the Market for Modern Prints', in V. Ginsburgh and P.-M. Menger (eds), *Economics of the Arts: Selected Essays*, Amsterdam: Elsevier, pp. 113–34.

Pommerehne, W.W. and B.S. Frey (1989), *Muses and Markets: Explorations in the Economics of the Arts*, Oxford: Blackwell.

Velthuis, O. (2005), *Talking Prices*, Princeton, NJ and Oxford: Princeton University Press.

Worthington, A. and H. Higgs (2004), 'Art as an Investment: Risk, Return and Portfolio Diversification in Major Painting Markets', *Accounting and Finance*, 44 (2), 257–71.

Further reading

General analyses of art markets from the point of view of cultural economics are provided in Velthuis (2005) and Moureau and Sagot-Duvauroux (2010). For a survey on auction prices, see Ashenfelter and Graddy (2003) or Mandel (2009). Stimulating sociological approaches to art markets are provided by Becker (1982) and Moulin (1992).

6 Artistic freedom
Michael Rushton

The economic analysis of freedom of expression has primarily developed through the 'law and economics' tradition that plays down any consideration of abstract rights ('nonsense upon stilts') and instead looks for legal frameworks that maximize aggregate wealth, broadly defined. Richard Posner (1986) provides a systematic approach to freedom of expression based on a cost–benefit framework first articulated by Judge Learned Hand in *United States v. Dennis* (183 F.2d 201 (2d Cir. 1950)). By this model restriction of freedom of expression is justified when

$$V + E < PL / (1+i)^n$$

where V is the social loss from suppressing valuable information, E is the legal-error cost of trying to distinguish which expression is valuable and which is not, P is the probability that harm will occur if the expression is allowed, L is the cost if the harm occurs, i is the discount rate, and n is the amount of time between potentially harmful expression and the occurrence of the loss resulting from it. The left-hand side of the inequality is the cost of suppressing expression, and the right-hand side is the probable cost if the expression is allowed.

We can observe Posner's application of the economic approach in his rulings as Judge on the United States Court of Appeals for the Seventh Circuit. In *Miller v. Civil City of South Bend* (904 F.2d 1081 (7th Cir. 1990)), Posner ruled that a municipal ordinance banning nude dancing should not be allowed, on the grounds that the harm of the dancing could not be demonstrated. In *Piarowski v. Illinois Community College District 515* (759 F.2d 625 (7th Cir. 1985)), he held that the shutting down by a college administration of an art exhibition by a faculty artist was justified on the grounds that the exhibition, placed in a prominent location on campus, and containing works with racial and sexual themes that many unwilling viewers found offensive, could easily have been relocated to a place where the only viewers would have been those actually wanting to see the art. In this case the result reminds us of the Coasean solution to externalities where transaction costs are high: assign the rights to the party (in this case the college community at large) who would face the highest costs in avoiding the externality. Eric Rasmusen (1998) takes the economic approach to what is perhaps its limit, arguing that whether an expressive activity should be allowed should be determined entirely by comparing the willingness to pay for prohibition by those harmed by the expression with the willingness to pay for the right to expression by the expressor.

One complication is a common one from cost–benefit analysis: willingness to pay depends upon ability to pay, and although many cost–benefit decisions might have negligible distributional consequences, economists will appropriately be wary of making recommendations on artistic freedom where those in favour of censorship are rich and the artist is poor (see Nussbaum, 2000, for a critique of applying cost–benefit analysis to the case of freedom of expression). A second complication is whether political expression deserves special protection. If government represents a particularly dangerous place to have a monopoly, it might make sense to give an especially wide allowance for artistic works that contain political criticism, as hard as this might be to define. The question of whether and how to restrict political expression raises an issue relatively unexplored by economists, namely why in most Western political systems there is *constitutional* protection of freedom of expression, especially if economists are correct in treating the regulation of expression as simply a cost–benefit matter (see Mackaay, 1997; Cooter, 2000).

Artistic freedom can arise as an issue in the realm of copyright, especially in conflicts over the appropriate scope of 'fair use', which defines the allowable use of copyrighted materials without the permission of the original author. The economic approach to copyright seeks a level of copyright protection, and an associated definition of fair use, that maximize aggregate net value. Increased protection should provide higher monetary returns for creators, and so induce greater creative production, but it comes with two costs: consumer access to works is restricted, even though the intellectual property itself, once created, has a marginal cost of zero; and the cost of creating new works is increased, as all artists to some degree draw ideas and inspiration from what has come before (Landes and Posner, 1989). Although it might often be the case that an artist who wishes to use as an input a part of a previous creation could simply contact the original creator and discuss a mutually agreeable price for authorized use, this is quite unlikely when the artist wishes to make a parody of the first work. Posner (1992) suggests that fair use should be allowed where the parodied object is the target of the parody, since a voluntary agreement is unlikely even though it may be wealth maximizing in aggregate to allow the parody, but that fair use should not be allowed when the parodied work is being used as an instrument in the critique or ridicule of something else. But this is a difficult distinction to make. For example, is a comic book that takes Walt Disney's Mickey and Minnie Mouse and has them engage in various anti-establishment activities attacking Disney or American culture? (*Walt Disney Prods. v. Air Pirates 581* (F.2d 751 (9th Cir. 1978))).

The parody issue highlights an unresolved issue among economists studying copyright: is the purpose of fair use to balance the costs and benefits of increased copyright protection, or is it a means of solving a transaction cost/market failure problem, where the formation and monitoring of contracts between original creators and subsequent users is difficult? Posner's solution to the parody problem is based on the transaction cost rationale, but his solution is questionable if fair use is not the result of market failure but is instead based on the balancing approach. See Rushton (2002) for further discussion of the copyright/artistic freedom trade-off.

In most Western nations the general restrictions on artistic freedom are nearly non-existent, with the exception of the copyright issues noted above. However, an unresolved issue is whether stipulations attached to the granting procedures of publicly funded arts agencies constitute a violation of artistic freedom. Less controversial are granting procedures that require geographical balance, or the promotion of multiculturalism or the preservation of the culture of aboriginal peoples. More controversial are stipulations on the content of works by individual artists and whether some may find them offensive. In the USA, the issue reached the Supreme Court in *National Endowment for the Arts v. Karen Finley* (118 S.Ct. 2168 (1998)), which revolved around the issue of whether the amendment to the legislation governing the NEA requiring the chair of the NEA to ensure that 'artistic excellence and artistic merit are the criteria by which [grant] applications are judged, taking into consideration general standards of decency and respect for the diverse beliefs of the American public' violated the constitutional rights of the artist. The case was discussed intensively in the popular media, and was undoubtedly one of the contributing factors to the ultimate demise of NEA grants to individual visual artists.

Without delving into the complex world of US constitutional law, cultural economists will be interested in this important aspect of public funding for the arts. The economic justification for public spending lies, not in the desire to subsidize the expression of self-declared artists, but to correct the perceived underprovision of cultural goods that would arise under *laissez-faire*. The efficient level of cultural production is a function of the technology of production and of consumer preferences. If a significant number of consumers would find certain works of art utility reducing rather than enhancing, should those works of art be awarded public funding? Rushton (2000) argues that restrictions on the content of publicly funded works along the lines of the NEA provisions can be justified, whether the rationale for public funding is based on economic analysis or on other considerations such as liberal theory or communitarian/nation-building reasons.

Written guidelines for government grants to artists are not the sole determinant of what gets funding. There are always more proposals from artists than there is funding available, so some individuals must be in the position to choose who is funded and who is not. Is the need for artists to satisfy the government-appointed decision-makers for public funding a restriction on their artistic freedom? Hamilton (1996) argues that it is a restriction that necessarily distorts what artists do, and so we are left with a bureaucratic art whether or not the granting agency stipluates that 'excellence' is the only criterion in its adjudication process.

Political scientists using the methods of economists, with models of rational actors in the political bureaucratic process faced with transaction costs, have attempted to model the delegation decision by elected representatives when they have only imperfect ability to monitor the behaviour of the bureaucracy (Calvert *et al.* 1989; Spence, 1997; Epstein and O'Halloran, 1999). These models of 'transaction cost politics' (North, 1990; Dixit, 1996) suggest a potentially fruitful method of enquiry for cultural economists studying the public funding of art, allowing the modelling of the optimal degree of statutory control politicians should place on publicly finded arts councils, and uniting the literatures on the justification of public funding and the problem of artistic freedom. While there is significant evidence in the cultural economics literature that citizens favour at least some degree of public support for the arts, the problem remains of translating what kind of art the public wants to be funded into the actual works produced through the funding. The economic problem of organizational design in terms of the discretion to be given to arts agencies and the methods of political oversight of the agencies warrants further research.

If there is a consistent theme running through the cultural economics analysis of artistic freedom, whether on questions of censorship, copyright or public funding, it is that artistic freedom of expression is not a 'holy of holies' (Posner, 1986, p. 6) that must be protected at any cost. There will be occasions when, for reasons of the harm caused by the expression, or the need to preserve some amount of copyright protection, or to ensure that taxpayers are not being asked to provide funding for an activity over which their elected representatives can exercise no control, some limits can be justified. This is not to imply that economists lean towards censorship; their scepticism of the government's ability to intervene in commercial markets in a beneficial way is surely also present when it comes to government's ability to regulate expression. But artisitic freedom is still as appropriate a subject for the 'acid bath' of economic analysis as any other.

See also:

Chapter 8: Artists' rights; Chapter 14: Copyright.

References

Calvert, Randall L., Matthew D. McCubbins and Barry R. Weingast (1989), 'A Theory of Political Control and Agency Discretion', *American Journal of Political Science*, 33, 588–611.

Coase, R.H. (1974), 'The Market for Goods and the Market for Ideas', *American Economic Review Papers and Proceedings*, 64, 384–91.

Cooter, Robert D. (2000), *The Strategic Constitution*, Princeton, NJ: Princeton University Press.

Dixit, Avinash K. (1996), *The Making of Economic Policy: A Transaction Cost Politics Perspective*, Cambridge, MA: MIT Press.

Epstein, David and Sharyn O'Halloran (1999), *Delegating Powers: A Transaction Cost Politics Approach to Policy Making Under Separate Powers*, Cambridge, UK: Cambridge University Press.

Farber, Daniel A. (1991), 'Free Speech Without Romance: Public Choice and the First Amendment', *Harvard Law Review*, 105, 554–83.

Hamilton, Marci (1996), 'Art Speech', *Vanderbilt Law Review*, 49, 73–122.

Hammer, Peter J. (1988), 'Free Speech and the "Acid Bath": An Evaluation and Critique of Judge Richard Posner's Economic Interpretation of the First Amendment', *Michigan Law Review*, 87, 499–536.

Kammen, Michael (2006), *Visual Shock: A History of Art Controversies in American Culture*, New York: Random House.

Landes, William M. and Richard A. Posner (1989), 'An Economic Analysis of Copyright Law', *Journal of Legal Studies*, 18, 325–63.

Lewis, Anthony (2007), *Freedom for the Thought We Hate: A Biography of the First Amendment*, New York: Basic Books.

Mackaay, Ejan (1997), 'The Emergence of Constitutional Rights', *Constitutional Political Economy*, 8, 15–36.

North, Douglass C. (1990), 'A Transaction Cost Theory of Politics', *Journal of Theoretical Politics*, 2, 355–67.

Nussbaum, Martha (2000), 'The Costs of Tragedy: Some Moral Limits on Cost–Benefit Analysis', *Journal of Legal Studies*, 29, 1005–36.

Posner, Richard A. (1986), 'Free Speech in an Economic Perspective', *Suffolk University Law Review*, 20, 1–54.

Posner, Richard A. (1992), 'When is Parody Fair Use?', *Journal of Legal Studies*, 21, 67–78.

Rasmusen, Eric (1998). 'The Economics of Desecration: Flag Burning and Related Activities', *Journal of Legal Studies*, 27, 245–69.

Rushton, Michael (2000), 'Public Funding of Controversial Art', *Journal of Cultural Economics*, 24, 267–82.

Rushton, Michael (2002), 'Copyright and Freedom of Expression: An Economic Analysis', in Ruth Towse (ed.), *Copyright in the Cultural Industries*, Cheltenham, UK and Northampton, MA, USA: Edward Elgar, pp. 51–62.

Spence, David B. (1997), 'Agency Policy Making and Political Control: Modeling Away the Delegation Problem', *Journal of Public Administration Research and Theory*, 7, 199–219.

Strauss, David A. (2001), 'The False Promise of the First Amendment', in Lawrence Rothfield (ed.), *Unsettling 'Sensation'*, New Brunswick, NJ: Rutgers University Press, pp. 44–51.

Sullivan, Kathleen (1992), 'Are Content Restrictions Constitutional?', *Journal of Arts Management and Law*, 21, 323–7.

Sullivan, Kathleen (1995), 'Free Speech and Unfree Markets', *UCLA Law Review*, 42, 949–65.

Further reading

A concise history of freedom of expression in the USA is Lewis (2007), and Kammen (2006) deals with US controversies over art and censorship. On whether we ought to assess regulation of expression with the same methods we would apply to the regulation of markets for goods and services, see Coase (1974) and Sullivan (1995). A detailed critique of the economic approach to freedom of expression is given by Hammer (1988). For a public choice approach, see Farber (1991). On content restrictions on publicly funded art, see Sullivan (1992) and Strauss (2001).

7   Artists' labour markets
Françoise Benhamou

Artists and cultural workers constitute a very heterogeneous and *a priori* non-standard population. Everyone keeps in mind a long list of starving artists, and a series of artists who died unknown before becoming superstars on the modern art and cultural markets. This chapter examines two questions: how can we describe cultural employment (and who should be considered as an artist) and are there some characteristics of employment in the cultural field that might justify a unique and unconventional theoretical framework for its analysis? Since decisions on labour markets play a major role for the crucial question of the selection of talent, this chapter also emphasizes the question of developing labour market policies towards supporting cultural employment.

Cultural employment: a wide spectrum of jobs
There are many methodological questions. The conclusions of empirical testing of hypotheses about the characteristics of employment vary according to sources of data. Censuses are most reliable for well-known reasons (exhaustiveness and possibility of comparisons over time). In Europe, they generally rely on what the individuals declare as their main job. Since individuals often engage in several occupations inside or outside the cultural sphere, they are considered as artists in accordance with their own reporting of their main income sources during the Census period. The US Census identifies artists on a controversial criterion: the job in the previous week. Nevertheless, many studies use Census data (among them Santos, 1976; Filer, 1986; O'Brien and Feist, 1995).

Researchers also use surveys. Despite their more limited scope, they provide qualitative information, especially on the nature of multiple-job holding, which is probably the most distinctive aspect of artists' labour market involvement.

It is not easy to determine the perimeter of cultural activities and to define professional criteria. A census does not distinguish between non-profit and for-profit institutions where artists are involved; recreational services and the performing arts are generally included. Some countries – especially Germany – include craft jobs in the field of cultural employment, leading to an overvaluation compared with other countries. In this chapter, we emphasize artistic jobs that represent a part of cultural employment (which also includes administrative jobs, professors and so on). The definition of artists is often rather wide and blurred (except in Finland, where a strict definition was adopted): this point is a source of debate, since expanding the definition may change average artist earnings.

Many studies argue that artists behave like anyone else, and that the characteristics of cultural employment are close to those of the general workforce. For example, the regional distribution of cultural employment in the UK reflects the regional distribution of cultural activities, generally concentrated in urban centres. Contrary to preconceptions, there is no evidence of a more frequent gender discrimination in the arts than elsewhere; Cowen (1996) shows that women facing incentives meet with success in their artistic endeavours. Although the rate of unemployment among artists is comparable to that of all workers, artistic jobs seem more unstable in France and in the UK, but less so in the USA (Filer, 1986; Gouyon, 2010; Oakley, 2009). But part-time, temporary and fixed-term contracts, second-job holding and self-employment are much more frequent than in the general workforce. They can be considered as non-standard forms of employment (Benhamou, 2000). Wetzels (2008) points out that workers in the entertainment industries are less covered by permanent contracts, more often employed part time and paid less than elsewhere in North Holland in 2000.

These flexible working patterns are frequent and even unavoidable because of a twofold set of factors. First, there is the discontinuity of activity. Individuals undertake several jobs at the same time; they also switch from one job to another, since projects are limited in time (seasonal jobs in festivals, artists involved in a series of concerts, photographers working for a short-term project and so on). This characteristic implies that the building of a strong reputation from job to job is the best source of employability in artistic labour markets: 'reputational' competition is central for employees. Reputation and eligibility are not identified with being kept on in a firm. In many respects the contrary applies. The more numerous the job contracts, the higher the reputation. This issue relies on a paradox: in spite of a higher percentage of graduates in this field, one can observe the weak importance of a diploma for careers: experience and reputation are much more central. Since diplomas have a low signalling capacity, people enjoy ease of entry to careers, especially those in the visual artists (Throsby and Thompson, 1995), and this is a source of oversupply.

Second, flexibility is a consequence of the specific qualifications required for projects, resulting from the property of 'infinite diversity' (Caves, 2000) of cultural goods, which are often produced on a project-by-project basis.

One of the consequences of flexibility is the multiplication of short-term contracts, leading to an illusory growth rate of employment of artists: even if cultural employment increased more rapidly than general employment in most European countries during the 1980s and the beginning of the 1990s (Greffe, 1999), the rate is overstated by the shorter duration of the contract.

Can we consider artists as utility maximizers? For some researchers, they seek the optimal set of pecuniary and non-monetary rewards (as what Adam Smith calls 'public admiration') for their efforts. But hard training, low rate of success stories, risky careers and short-term contracts seem to be inherent to artistic choices: these general characteristics of artistic employment could lead a rational individual to choose other careers.

A theoretical framework

Among the clichés concerning artists, one of the strongest is their low average earnings, including the juxtaposition between two labour markets: one for the superstars and the other for all the more or less starving artists.

Filer (1989) analyses the 1980 US Census data and concludes that the 'starving artist' is a myth: for individuals having similar educational levels and personal characteristics, the average artist earned about 10 per cent less than he would have earned in a non-artistic job. Moreover, when lifetime differences are taken into account, Filer shows that the gap becomes almost negligible: the lifetime earnings are less than 2.9 per cent greater for non-artists. Filer concludes that artistic labour markets are not different from others.

Nevertheless, the analysis is compatible with the existence of a dual labour market, in which the level of the average income hides very contrasting situations.

Other studies argue that, although they are not poor, artists suffer an earnings penalty (Wassall and Alper, 1992). The sources of the divergence rely on the data basis (a strict or broad definition of artists), the country and the period. If there is such a penalty, one should consider that conventional theories of labour market are inappropriate in the case of artists. An original contribution is provided by Throsby (1994), who constructs a model of labour supply of multiple-job-holding artists. If the alternative consists in spending time in artistic or non-artistic jobs, when relative wages increase for non-artistic jobs, individuals spend less time on the latter activity, since they have obtained the amount of earnings that they need in order to pursue what they consider as their main job. This behaviour reflects the strength of their preferences for creative labour. This does not conform to conventional theories and favours a specific treatment of art labour markets. As Throsby notes, 'arts work tends to be less sensitive to financial considerations because of its nature as compared to non-arts work' (ibid., 264). Throsby also emphasizes the changes in behaviour between different three categories of artists (initial creative artists, performing artists and others). Nevertheless, he underlines that a mere human capital theoretical framework can explain the distribution of earnings in artistic professions. Towse (2006) discusses this point of view. She argues that human capital theory does not help understanding artists' decisions about investment in schooling and about occupational choice. Talent and creativity remain rather puzzling for economists.

Many studies focus on the distribution of earnings rather than on their average level. In Hollywood, artists are classified in two categories, A and B, A artists belonging to the happy few successful artists who earn much more and dominate their segment of the market.

Thus labour is considered as heterogeneous, and this leads to artists' labour markets being analysed as atypical and non-competitive. Artists are imperfect substitutes for each other. Rosen (1986) offers an explanation for the uneven distribution of rewards among artists, his superstar theory. He observes that whereas a few artists receive enormous amounts of money and dominate their activity, others remain poorly paid. This gap is disproportionately large, compared with the differences in talent. He offers two reasons for this: first, in a context of a consensus about talent (artists offer vertically differentiated services) and, with a hypothesis that talent is observable without any cost, he considers that there is no substitute for any particular talent. Therefore prices can increase without leading to a decrease in demand. Second, the increasing size of markets, due to new media, allows joint consumption.

As long-term contracts are rare, one can observe the quasi-absence of internal job markets. This high degree of flexibility may be interpreted as an argument in favour of the validity of standard theories for artist labour market analysis. The search-theoretic approach provides a framework for understanding the succession of employment and non-employment experiences. Since it hypothesizes that search costs would be compensated for by long-time commitments, it is unfortunately inappropriate in the case of artists, in spite of its hypothesis of labour heterogeneity: firms do not expect to be in business with the same artists indefinitely, but only on a temporary project basis.

Thus, for many researchers, artistic labour markets act as lotteries. As Adam Smith recognized in *The Wealth of Nations*, despite the risk linked to professions where 'twenty fail for one that succeeds', one can observe the growing number of aspirants. Many factors explain such a paradox: people try to enter artistic professions when they are rather young and can face a high degree of uncertainty. And, as in the case of lotteries, winners may earn a lot of money and artists overestimate their chances of fame and success. High rewards attract risk-seeking individuals:

> Since the probability of rising to the top group is so uncertain, entry into these fields has many aspects of a lottery in which only a few obtain the big prizes. This lottery is tempered and made less costly by considerable turnover, especially among young entrants. As new entrants gain information that their prospects are dim, they turn to other, less risky adventures. (Rosen, 1986, p. 681)

A simple explanation of behaviours relies on the age distribution of artists, they tend to be younger than the general workforce: hope of success and a propensity to assume risk are higher at a younger age. The accumulation of experience is the only way to determine one's chances of success. For MacDonald (1988), young artists study the critics and public reactions to evaluate their probability of succeeding. At each stage of a sequential process, they decide to go on or to abandon their career. Anyway, the span of careers varies with the type of activity: dancers in particular have very short career schedules and have to develop alternative skills in order to extend their career span (Rannou and Roharik, 2006).

Creative activity is fertilized by uncertainty. For Menger (2009), success and rewards depend on the way artistic activity remains surprising for the public and for the artist as well. Professionals, critics and the public make comparisons to identify the qualities of artists, as they ignore their absolute value. Overproduction results from the quest for originality.

Excess of supply is accentuated by the policy developed by art schools, which offer too many programmes compared to future prospects, especially for classical musicians and singers. Towse (1993) estimates an order of magnitude of private and social rate of return to training as a singer. She concludes that human capital investment is less efficient for arts occupations. Moreover, with public funding for training artists, if support leads to a decrease in the cost of artistic training, the number of artists will increase and the wages will fall.

Regulation of labour markets

Artists represent a small percentage of the total workforce (1.8 per cent in France in 2005, Lacroix, 2009; 1.4 per cent in the USA in 2000, Alper and Wassall, 2006), but are a very vociferous group; moreover, their living and working conditions may determine the level and quality of the production of culture. Some studies show that the information process for selecting consumption leads not only to a superstar phenomenon, but also to a totally random selection of talent. For Adler (1985), information costs lead consumers to choose what other people have already selected, according to a mimetic process. Market forces alone do not select naturally the most talented: selected performers may be untalented, and the inertia of consumers' behaviour leads them to dominate an increasing share of the market.

One can consider this issue as a justification for regulation, aiming to counteract the natural tendency of the market to eliminate in the short run talented but unknown artists. Three sources of regulation emerge: unions' negotiations, specific status provided by social security schemes, and artists' rights.

Unionization is more frequent among musicians, actors and technicians than among writers and visual artists. Situations vary considerably, from isolated artists dealing with gallery owners to the case of scriptwriters and actors in Hollywood (with a long-lasting strike of the US Writers' Guild in 2007–08). Caves emphasizes the propensity of unions to act in favour of the level of wages, and to erect entry barriers to newcomers. From this point of view, unions do not help the search for talent.

Do artists need specific social security schemes that would allow them to spend more time in trying to enter the market? In France a specific scheme for the performing arts and the film industry called 'intermittency status' compensates for unemployment periods for artists and technicians who have worked a minimum of 507 hours during the last 10 months for technicians and 10.5 months for artists. This aims to compensate for the precarious characteristic of artistic life, and to help artists to stay free to build their careers. A similar scheme exists in the Netherlands. Gurgand and Menger (1996) emphasize the perverse effect of such a scheme, which leads to moral-hazard incidences: oversupply and also overuse of the system. But this scheme can be viewed as supporting the arts by supporting the artists. Withers (1985) examines the hypothesis of artists subsidizing the arts by accepting low incomes in Australia. Intermittency of employment can be analysed in the same framework as a hidden subsidy that reduces work costs. It has led to a learning process: firms use it in order to diminish the risk linked to the discontinuity of their activity and to the 'nobody-knows property' (Caves, 2000), and also in order to avoid long-term employment commitments. For their part, artists facing a change in labour contracts, with a growing propensity to sign short-term ones, try to optimize their chances of being eligible by reaching the threshold required by the legislation.

Policies may also stimulate self-employment as an alternative to dependent employment for the unemployed, as in the case of the UK. But most countries do not provide specific protection for artists.

A third source of regulation is provided by the artists' property rights. The simple fact is that the appreciation of artists' works often needs a long period of time (McNertney and Waits, 1984). This characteristic may legitimate a system of payment that takes time into account, through royalties, intellectual property payments or artists' resale rights. Contracts naturally take the time factor into account through optional clauses and other advantages, as in the case of the cinema industry (Weinstein, 1998), but such advantages are reserved for well-known and powerful artists.

Concluding remarks

Labour market economics provides a powerful theoretical framework for analysing art labour markets. Nevertheless the specific features of artistic labour supply certainly require more empirical surveys, and also some research into the demand side and the different forms of earnings, including optional recurrent contracts, that link a creative artist to the few regular producers.

See also:

Chapter 56: Superstars; Chapter 48: Poverty and support for artists.

References

Adler, M. (1985), 'Stardom and Talent', *American Economic Review*, 75, 208–12.

Alper, N.O. and G.H. Wassall (2006), 'Artists' Careers and their Labor Markets', in V.A. Ginsburgh and D. Throsby (eds), *Handbook of the Economics of Art and Culture*, Amsterdam: Elsevier, pp. 813–64.

Benhamou, F. (2000), 'The Opposition of Two Models of Labour Market Adjustment. The Case of the Audiovisual and Performing Arts in France and in the United Kingdom', *Journal of Cultural Economics*, 24, 301–19.

Caves, R.E. (2000), *Creative Industries: Contracts between Art and Commerce*, Cambridge, MA: Harvard University Press.

Cowen, T. (1996), 'Why Women Succeed, and Fail in the Arts', *Journal of Cultural Economics*, 20 (2), 93–113.

Filer, R.K. (1986), 'The 'Starving Artist' – Myth or Reality? Earnings of Artists in the United States', *Journal of Political Economy*, 94 (1), 56–75.

Filer, R.K. (1989), 'The Economic Condition of Artists in America', in D.V. Shaw *et al.* (eds), *Cultural Economics 88: An American Perspective*, Akron, OH: Association for Cultural Economics.

Galenson, D. (2002), 'Quantifying Artistic Success: Ranking French Painters – and Paintings – From Impressionism to Cubism', *Historical Methods*, 35 (1), 5–19.

Ginsburgh, V. and S. Weyers (2006), 'Creativity and Life Cycle of Artists', *Journal of Cultural Economics*, 30, 91–107.

Gouyon, M. (2010), 'Une typologie de l'emploi salarié dans le secteur culturel en 2007', *Culture Chiffres* 3, March, available at: http://www2.culture.gouv.fr/culture/deps/2008/pdf/cc-2010-03.pdf.

Greffe, X. (1999), *L'emploi culturel à l'âge du numérique*, Paris: Anthropos.

Gurgand, M. and P.M. Menger (1996), 'Work and Compensated Unemployment in the Performing Arts. Exogenous and Endogenous Uncertainty in Artistic Labour Markets', in V. Ginsburgh and P.M. Menger (ed.), *Economics of the Arts*, Amsterdam: Elsevier, pp. 347–81.

MacDonald, G.M. (1988), 'The Economics of Rising Stars', *American Economic Review*, 78, 155–66.

McNertney, E.M. and C.R. Waits (1984), 'An Economic Model of Artistic Behavior', *Journal of Cultural Economics*, 8, 49–60.

Menger, P.M. (2009), *Le travail créateur. S'accomplir dans l'incertain*, Paris: Hautes Etudes–Gallimard–Seuil.

O'Brien, J. and A. Feist (1995), *Employment in the Arts and Cultural Industries: an Analysis of the 1991 Census*, London: Arts Council of England.

Oakley, K. (2009), 'Art Works – Cultural Labour Markets: a Literature Review', Hillprint Media, October (http://www.creativitycultureeducation.org/research-impact/literature-reviews/).

Lacroix, C. (2009), *Chiffres clés 2009. Statistiques de la culture*, Paris: La Documentation française.

Rannou, J. and I. Roharik (2006), *Les Danseurs. Un Métier d'Engagement*, Paris: La Documentation française.

Rosen, S. (1986), 'The Theory of Equalizing Differences', in O. Ashenfelter and R. Layard (eds), *Handbook of Labour Economics*, Vol. 2, Amsterdam: North-Holland, pp. 641–92.

Santos, F.P. (1976) 'Risk, Uncertainty and the Performing Arts', in M. Blaug (ed.), *The Economics of Arts*, Boulder, CO: Westview, pp. 248–59.

Throsby, D. (1994), 'A Work-Preference Model of Artist Behaviour', in A. Peacock and I. Rizzo (eds), *Cultural Economics and Cultural Policies*, Dordrecht: Kluwer Academic, pp. 69–80.

Throsby, D. and B. Thompson (1995), *The Artists at Work: Some Further Results for the 1988 Survey of Individual Artists*, Redfern, Australia: Australia Council.

Towse, R. (1993), *Singers in the Marketplace: the Economics of the Singing Profession*, Oxford: Clarendon Press.

Towse, R. (2006), 'Human Capital and Artists' Labour Markets', in V.A. Ginsburgh and D. Throsby (eds), *Handbook of the Economics of Art and Culture*, Amsterdam: Elsevier, pp. 865–94.

Wassall, G.H. and N.O. Alper (1992), 'Toward a Unified Theory of the Determinants of the Earnings of Artists', in R. Towse and A. Khakee (eds), *Cultural Economics*, Berlin: Springer-Verlag: pp. 187–200.

Weinstein M. (1998), 'Profit-Sharing Contracts in Hollywood: Evolution and Analysis', *Journal of Legal Studies*, 27, 67–112.

Wetzels, C. (2008), 'Are Workers in the Cultural Industries Paid Differently?', *Journal of Cultural Economics*, 32 (1), 58–77.

Withers G. (1985), 'Artists' Subsidy of the Arts', *Australian Economic Papers*, 24, 290–95.

Further reading

General analyses of artists' careers and their labour markets are provided in Alper and Wassall (2006). For recent data, the best reference remains national censuses. The relationship between careers and creativity is discussed in Galenson (2002) and Ginsburgh and Weyers (2006).

8 Artists' rights
Michael Rushton

At the foundation of the economic analysis of property and contract is the hypothesis that the common law, and other institutions, evolve to ensure that rights will be exchanged between individuals so that in the end the rights are held by those who value them the highest. The Coase (1960) theorem holds that, as long as property rights are clearly defined, and there are no transaction costs associated with their exchange, the resulting allocation of rights will be efficient and will be independent of their initial allocation. Of course, it is the existence of transaction costs that makes things interesting.

When transaction costs are high, so that rights will be difficult to exchange, efficiency will be obtained only when the law awards rights initially to those who will value them most highly. In this sense the law 'mimics' the market. And so, in cultural economics, we look to see whether the various property rights granted to artists represent an efficient allocation.

An application of this principle is in the economic analysis of the law of copyright, where efficiency dictates awards of limited rights to creators (the copyright) and users (fair use) so that aggregate wealth is maximized (Landes and Posner, 1989). For a more specific case, consider an artist creating a parody of a work. Landes (2002) and Posner (1992) claim that a transaction cost analysis would allow unlicensed use of works for parody if the target of the parody were the original work itself, since a bargain between the two creators is unlikely even though society at large would receive a net benefit from the parody. In other words, in such cases it makes sense to grant the right of parody to the parodist rather than to grant the right to prevent parody to the creator of the first work. However, Landes and Posner would not grant fair use when the original work is used by the parodist to attack something else, say the banality of consumer behaviour, since 'if the defendant uses the parodied work as a weapon to comment on society, he should have little trouble licensing the work' (Landes, 2002, p. 15).

The allocation of 'moral rights' to creators within the law of copyright – rights that the creator retains in the integrity, attribution, disclosure and withdrawal of a work even after the physical object and/or its reproduction rights have been transferred – can also be assessed within the efficiency framework (Hansmann and Santilli, 1997; Rushton, 1998). In general, with variations between countries, artists hold the moral rights in their works, and if they so choose can waive those rights in specific instances by using a contract with the owner of the work. A justification can be found in the potential harm that a current owner of a work of art might do to the reputation of the artist and to other owners of the artist's work.

Once a creator's rights in his/her work have been established, the question arises as to the best means of protecting those rights. The canonical essay on the means of enforcing rights is Calabresi and Melamed (1972), who begin by noting that 'property rules', which stipulate that a right can only be transferred by mutual agreement between buyer and seller, are the best means of protecting rights in a situation of low transaction costs.

However, there may be circumstances where the superior way to protect a right is a 'liability rule', where a potential user of a right owned by somebody else need not obtain the owner's agreement, but instead may use the good as long as a fee, set by some other agency, is paid to the owner. In the cultural sector compulsory licensing is an example of a right protected by a liability rule. Transaction costs would be prohibitively high in setting the terms for each public broadcast of each song, and so royalty schemes are established. However, Merges (1994) claims that statutory compulsory licence discourages players in the market from developing technologies that could reduce the costs of a property rights system, and so the industry may be locked into a 'suboptimal liability rule'.

The third way ownership rights can be protected is through an 'inalienability rule'. A narrow definition of inalienability is that there are restrictions on whether and how the ownership of a right may be transferred to someone else, although Rose-Akerman (1985) would broaden the definition to include restrictions on who may own the entitlement and whether there are duties or restrictions on the owner in his/her relationship to the property (on this last point, see Sax, 1999, who considers cases where there is private ownership of cultural works of great social significance, and where there should be restrictions on those owners). Calabresi and Melamed (1972) suggest that inalienability could be efficient in circumstances of high transaction costs and externalities, in other words where only a restriction on transfer could prevent an externality from occurring, since bargaining between the potentially harmed parties and the buyer and seller contemplating the sale would be prohibitively costly. Laws prohibiting the sale for export of cultural goods of national importance would be an example of an inalienability rule justified (possibly) by efficiency considerations (on this topic, see Kearns, 1998).

Even though inalienability can, in some circumstances, be justified for efficiency reasons, when artists' rights are restricted by inalienability it is often on distributional grounds, to 'protect' the naïve and possibly starving artist from unscrupulous dealers. A form of inalienability, occurs for example, when contracts that *ex post* are regrettable from the perspective of the artist (consider for example a songwriter who accepted an up-front payment in exchange for accepting low royalty rates on future earnings, and the work turned out to generate much more in royalties than anyone would have predicted) are invalidated by the courts on the grounds that they are 'unconscionable'. Do such rulings benefit all songwriters? If such judgments became routine, the law would be imposing an inalienability restriction on the human capital of songwriters; the terms under which they could rent their songwriting potential on a long-term basis would be limited, since publishers would not be willing to enter contracts that might be overturned by the courts. The expected outcome is that publishers would be less willing to deal with unknowns, and so would offer them less favourable terms. Care must be taken in restricting artists' ability to contract and exchange that efforts to protect the artist are not in fact making her/him worse off.

Rushton (2001) discusses inalienability restrictions on artists that are often, and wrongly, justified on distributional grounds. Consider again the example of moral rights. Most countries stipulate that moral rights may be waived only with the written consent of the artist in a particular circumstance; blank waivers are frowned upon. This is a rather slight restriction on alienability of rights, but some commentators hold that waiver should not be permitted at all, on the grounds that the presumably superior bargaining power of the purchaser of the copyright will force artists to waive their moral rights even when it is against their interest: 'making moral rights freely assignable and waivable will in practice eliminate them entirely' (Vaver, 1987, p. 774).

A second case of inalienability, in some jurisdictions, is 'droit de suite', an entitlement that artists maintain in works of art after initial sale that provides them with a royalty on subsequent resales (Perloff, 1998). While artists are certainly the intended beneficiaries of such an entitlement, if the right is inalienable it has the effect of forcing artists to be investors in their own works, which is inefficient if they are, as is quite likely, inferior owners of risk. However, Solow (1998) notes that investors in art are willing to pay a higher price for works if there is a greater probability that the artist will continue to build his/her reputation through valuable new works. No artist can guarantee to a potential buyer that s/he will in future take steps that lead to appreciation in the value of the works; an inalienable 'droit de suite' could be a useful way to convince buyers that the artist will continue to produce; the artist now has an inalienable financial stake in his/her own works.

Another example of inalienable rights comes from the USA, where constitutional freedoms cannot be forgone in exchange for payments from the government; the doctrine is called 'unconstitutional conditions' (Sullivan, 1989). For example, the government cannot ask a social assistance recipient to refrain from criticism of the government in exchange for continued receipt of assistance to which s/he would normally be entitled. The issue is important in the public funding of art: what conditions may government place on publicly funded arts-granting councils and the content of the art they fund before creating unconstitutional conditions that ask artists to trade their rights to free expression for government funding? Rushton (2000) argues that the rationales traditionally put forward to justify state support of the arts generally allow for some restrictions on what is funded. But that does not imply that these restrictions are compatible with a nation's constitutional rights and their inalienability. Again, this is a case of what superficially seems like a protection for artists being a double-edged sword; artists might win the right to remove any restrictions on publicly funded art, only to find that legislators cease to be interested in funding such agencies at all.

See also:

Chapter 6: Artistic freedom; Chapter 14: Copyright; Chapter 55: Resale rights.

References

Adler, Amy (2009), 'Against Moral Rights', *California Law Review*, 97, 263–300.
Boyle, Melissa, Stacy Nazzaro and Debra O'Connor (2010), 'Moral Rights Protection for the Visual Arts', *Journal of Cultural Economics*, 34, 27–44.
Calabresi, Guido and Douglas A. Melamed (1972), 'Property Rules, Liability Rules, and Inalienability: One View of the Cathedral', *Harvard Law Review*, 85 (6), 1089–128.
Coase, R.H. (1960), 'The Problem of Social Cost', *Journal of Law and Economics*, 3 (1), 1–44.
Epstein, Richard (1975), 'Unconscionability: A Critical Reappraisal', *Journal of Law and Economics*, 18, 293–315.
Ginsburgh, Victor (2005), 'The Economic Consequences of *Droit de Suite* in the European Union', *Economic Analysis and Policy*, 35, 61–71.
Graddy, Kathryn and Chanont Banternghansa (2011), 'The Impact of *Droit de Suite* in the UK: An Empirical Analysis', *Journal of Cultural Economics*, 35, forthcoming.
Hansmann, Henry and Marina Santilli (1997), 'Authors' and Artists' Moral Rights: A Comparative Legal and Economic Analysis', *Journal of Legal Studies*, 26 (1), 95–143.
Kearns, Paul (1998), *The Legal Concept of Art*, Oxford: Hart.
Landes, William M. (2001), 'What has the Visual Artists' Rights Act of 1990 Accomplished?', *Journal of Cultural Economics*, 25, 283–306.

Landes, William M. (2002), 'Copyright, Borrowed Images and Appropriation Art: An Economic Approach', in R. Towse (ed.), *Copyright in the Cultural Industries*, Cheltenham, UK and Northampton, MA, USA: Edward Elgar, pp. 9–31.

Landes, William M. and Richard A. Posner (1989), 'An Economic Analysis of Copyright Law', *Journal of Legal Studies*, 18 (2), 325–63.

Masiyakurima, Patrick (2005), 'The Trouble with Moral Rights', *Modern Law Review*, 68, 411–34.

Merges, Robert P. (1994), 'Of Property Rules, Coase, and Intellectual Property', *Columbia Law Review*, 94, 2655–73.

Perloff, Jeffrey (1998), 'Droit de Suite', in P. Newman (ed.), *The New Palgrave Dictionary of Economics and the Law*, London: Macmillan.

Posner, Richard A. (1992), 'When is Parody Fair Use?', *Journal of Legal Studies*, 21 (1), 67–78.

Rose-Akerman, Susan (1985), 'Inalienability and the Theory of Property Rights', *Columbia Law Review*, 85, 931–69.

Rushton, Michael (1998), 'The Moral Rights of Artists: Droit Moral ou Droit Pecuniaire?', *Journal of Cultural Economics*, 22 (1), 15–32.

Rushton, Michael (2000), 'Public Funding of Controversial Art', *Journal of Cultural Economics*, 24 (4), 267–82.

Rushton, Michael (2001), 'The Law and Economics of Artists' Inalienable Rights', *Journal of Cultural Economics*, 25 (4), 243–57.

Sax, Joseph L. (1999), *Playing Darts with a Rembrandt: Public and Private Rights in Cultural Treasures*, Ann Arbor, MI: University of Michigan Press.

Solow, John L. (1998), 'An Economic Analysis of Droit de Suite', *Journal of Cultural Economics*, 22, 209–26.

Sullivan, Kathleen M. (1989), 'Unconstitutional Conditions', *Harvard Law Review*, 102, 1413–506.

Trebilcock, Michael (1976), 'The Doctrine of Inequality of Bargaining Power: Post Benthamite Economics in the House of Lords', *University of Toronto Law Journal*, 26, 359–85.

Vaver, David (1987), 'Authors' Moral Rights – Reform Proposals in Canada: Charter or Barter of Rights for Creators?', *Osgoode Hall Law Journal*, 25, 749–86.

Further reading

For economic analysis of the effects of moral rights legislation on artists, in particular the Visual Artists' Rights Act of the USA, see Landes (2001) and Boyle *et al.* (2010). Recent critiques of the granting of moral rights include Masiyakurima (2005) and Adler (2009). On the economic analysis of 'unconscionable' contracts, see Epstein (1975) and Trebilcock (1976). Evidence on the effects of droit de suite is provided by Graddy and Banternghansa (2011); also see Ginsburgh (2005).

9 Awards
Nachoem M. Wijnberg

The cultural industries are home to an apparent contradiction: competition is denied and glorified at the same time. On the one hand, artists are loath to consider themselves in open competition with each other, like salesmen of second-hand cars; on the other hand, there are few industries in which the phrase 'and the winner is . . .' is pronounced more often than in the cultural industries. Awards are the most prominent signs of competition in the cultural industries and, as such, objects of desire, as well as of derision.

All the cultural industries have their own awards, and these awards often receive considerable public attention, in itself providing a kind of multiplier to the original effects of the award. Among the best-known examples are the Oscars or the prizes of the Cannes Festival for films, the Booker Prize or the Prix Goncourt for books, the prizes of the Venice Biennale for painting, and the World Press Photo prize for (journalistic) photos. In fact, cultural awards have a long pedigree, in which figure awards with great historical and economic significance, such as the prize of the Athenian Festival of Dionysos for theatre (Aylen, 1985) and the Prix de Rome for painting (White and White, 1993).

A partial explanation for the popularity of awards in the cultural industries can be found in the fact that it is one of the salient characteristics of cultural goods that product quality is relatively difficult to establish before or even after consumption. To the majority of consumers, most cultural goods are credence goods, in the terminology of Darby and Karni (1973). This means that consumers, and even other selectors, look to surrogate measures of quality, and in some cases rank these higher than their own judgement. The award serves as such a measure of quality and this explains its popularity in the cultural industries. However, for a better and more complete understanding of the role of awards (or prizes; here the term 'awards' will be used) from the point of view of cultural economics it is necessary to analyse more closely what an award is.

At least three types of economic agent are involved with an award. The first is the one setting up the award, making the institutional arrangements to enable the award to be conferred and providing the substance of the award – be it money or other benefits, such as a statuette. The second is the one – this is usually a jury or a commission – empowered to designate the winner. The third is the one on whom the award is conferred. The award can be conferred on the person or on something the person has produced. All three types of agent can be either individuals or organizations, or groups of individuals or organizations.

Awards are conferred on the basis of a judgement by the jury about the qualities of the contestant or his/her product by comparison with the others in the same category.

There is a category of potential award winners, not just one potential winner. If someone has an aunt who confers an award upon her lovable nephew, this does not count as an award, at least not as one that can be sensibly compared, in an economic analysis, to an Oscar. Although not all awards are bestowed in public, secret awards do not count either. Third parties, and also unsuccessful potential award winners, must at least have the possibility to find out on whom the award is conferred and why. The award has to be conferred more than once. Finally, a prize is not a price. The award is not conferred as payment, as if the first or the second party were the customer of the award winner.

This sketch of the essential actors and relations involved with an award allows us to see that, whatever may be the private considerations of those setting up, conferring or receiving awards, every award by definition performs three basic functions: (a) making explicit the boundaries of the category of potential winners; (b) making explicit which characteristics of the members of this category are considered significant enough to be included in a quality judgement; and (c) providing an exemplar of the category and of a member of the category displaying a qualitatively excellent set of the most significant (in the opinion of the agent conferring the award) characteristics.

All specific effects of awards derive from these three basic functions. For the purpose of a more detailed analysis, it is possible to distinguish the economic effects, especially the possible benefits, of these basic functions for the three types of agents. The first type, the one who creates the conditions to award the award, benefits from the fact that the award allows the agent to publicize the jury's judgements, at least with respect to function (a) and, sometimes, to function (b). By doing so, the award organizer has a chance to influence the way other people look at the industry or activity for which the award is conferred. Classification systems are always ambiguous (Bowker and Leigh Star, 1999) and even small interventions in the classification system can have significant effects on the development of an industry. One can think of the effects of the speed of recognition of, for instance, rock and roll or rap music as separate categories of the Grammy or MTV awards for recorded music (Frith, 1996).

The second type of agent, the one who participates in choosing the winner, usually receives payment, often not more than expenses but sometimes a significant financial reward, from the organizers for assisting them in achieving the benefits described above. He or she also has the opportunity to publicize his/her judgements, especially by way of function (c). Being invited to be a member of a prestigious jury and choosing winners who prove to have been worthy choices increases the status of the jury member, and this can bring additional economic benefits, especially if the juror is also a professional expert in the field in which the award is conferred.

Most attention is given, in the literature on awards, to the effects of the award on the agent of the third type, the winner. Three main types of effects can be distinguished. First, the award in itself may represent important benefits such as a significant amount of money, valuable objects, such as statuettes or plaques, specific privileges, such as lifelong memberships or even the right to enter other competitions, and the very explicit recognition that the award winner or his/her work belongs to the category for which awards are given. Also belonging to the first type of direct benefits may be secondary benefits, such as the increase in longevity that winning an Oscar seems to bring (Redelmeier and Singh, 2001).

Second, an award may function as a signal to competitors, making clear that the award winner belongs to a particular sub-group of competitors, should be treated as such and can be expected to behave as such.Where the award is a passport to enter a specific network of competitors and membership of this network brings, for instance, privileged access to flows of information (Stuart, 1998; Kogut, 2000), the second type of benefit to the winner automatically leads to additional benefits of the first type. The award can also have an impact on competitive dynamics by reinforcing existing governance systems determining what kinds of competitive behaviour are allowed or are attractive. Winning an award may, for example, deter competitive imitation as the award and the related publicity enhance the chance of an imitator also being quickly discovered as an imitator (Gemser and Wijnberg, 2001).

A third benefit of awards is that winning one may function as a means of certification. The signal is directed towards other actors in the value system, such as distributors and, of course, final consumers, and also to other certifiers. The importance of certificate providers in competitive dynamics is more evident in cultural industries than in most others (Eliashberg and Shugan, 1997; Mossetto, 1993; Smith and Smith, 1986), again because of the credence-good characteristics of many cultural products and especially in those industries where the selection system is dominated by expert selection (Wijnberg and Gemser, 2000). Cultural industries are well known for exhibiting bandwagon effects, where there is a 'winner-takes-all' phenomenon, further adding to the significance of being certified as a winner.

A relatively well-researched example is the Oscar. The Oscar seems to have a huge impact on future earnings of prize-winning directors, actors and other participants, an impact that has increased in the last decade (Levy, 1987; Holden, 1993; Nelson *et al.*, 2001). The impact of the Oscar on box office results seems to be more variable (Smith and Smith, 1986; Dodds and Holbrook, 1986), although anecdotal evidence (Holden, 1993; Biskind, 1998) and quantitative evidence (Nelson *et al.*, 2001) again point towards an increasing impact in recent years.

See also:

Chapter 19: Criticism; Chapter 56: Superstars.

References

Anand, N. and M.R. Watson (2004), 'Tournament Rituals in the Evolution of Fields: The case of the Grammy Awards', *Academy of Management Journal*, 47, 59–80.

Aylen, L. (1985), *The Greek Theater*, Cranbury, NJ: Associated University Presses.

Biskind, P. (1998), *Easy Riders, Raging Bulls: How the Sex-Drugs-and-Rock'n'Roll Generation Saved Hollywood*, New York: Simon & Schuster.

Bowker, G.C. and S. Leigh Star (1999), *Sorting Things Out: Classification and its Consequences*, Cambridge, MA: MIT Press.

Darby, M.R. and E. Karni (1973), 'Free Competition and the Optimal Amount of Fraud', *Journal of Law and Economics*, 16, 67–89.

Deuchert, E., K. Adjamah and F. Pauly (2005), 'For Oscar Glory or Oscar Money?', *Journal of Cultural Economics*, 29, 159–76.

Dodds, J.C. and M.C. Holbrook (1986), 'What's an Oscar Worth? An Empirical Estimation of the Effect of Nominations and Awards on Movie Distribution and Revenues', in B.A. Austin (ed.), *Current Research in Film: Audiences, Economics and Law*, Vol. 4, Norwood, NJ: Ablex Publishing, pp. 72–88.

Eliashberg, J. and S.M. Shugan (1997), 'Film Critics: Influencers or Predictors?', *Journal of Marketing*, 61, 68–78.

Frith, S. (1996), *Performing Rites*, Oxford: Oxford University Press.

Gemser, G. and N.M. Wijnberg (2001), 'Effects of Reputational Sanctions and Inter-Firm Linkages on Competitive Imitation', *Organization Studies*, 22 (4), 563–91.

Gemser, G., A. Mark, A.M. Leenders and N.M. Wijnberg (2008), 'Why Some Awards are More Effective Signals of Quality than Others: A Study of Movie Awards', *Journal of Management*, 34 (1), 25–54.

Holden, A. (1993), *The Oscars: The Secret History of Hollywood's Academy Awards*, London: Little, Brown.

Kogut, B. (2000), 'The Network as Knowledge: Generative Rules and the Emergence of Structure', *Strategic Management Journal*, 21, 405–25.

Levy, E. (1987), *And The Winner Is . . .: The History and Politics of the Oscar Awards*, New York: Ungar.

Mossetto, G. (1993), *Aesthetics and Economics*, Dordrecht: Kluwer Academic.

Nelson, R.A., M.R. Donihue, D.M. Waldman and C. Wheaton (2001), 'What's an Oscar Worth?', *Economic Inquiry*, 39 (1), 1–16.

Redelmeier, D.A. and S.M. Singh (2001), 'Survival in Academy Award-Winning Actors and Actresses', *Annals of Internal Medicine*, 134 (10), 955–62.

Smith, S.P. and V.K. Smith (1986), 'Successful Movies: A Preliminary Empirical Analysis', *Applied Economics*, 18, 501–7.

Stuart, T.E. (1998), 'Network Positions and Propensities to Collaborate: An Investigation of Strategic Alliance Formation in a High-Technology Industry', *Administrative Science Quarterly*, 43, 668–98.

Wijnberg, N.M. and G. Gemser (2000), 'Adding Value to Innovation: Impressionism and the Transformation of the Selection System in Visual Arts', *Organization Science*, 11 (3), 323–9.

White, C. and H.C. White (1993), *Canvases and Careers: Institutional Change in the French Painting World*, 2nd edn, New York: John Wiley.

Further reading

For recent work on this topic, see Anand and Watson (2004), Deuchert *et al.* (2005) and Gemser *et al.* (2008).

10 Baumol's cost disease
James Heilbrun

In 1966, William J. Baumol and William G. Bowen published *Performing Arts: The Economic Dilemma*. Their book was extraordinarily influential and it is generally agreed that analysis of the economics of the arts had its origin in that work.

The economic dilemma Baumol and Bowen referred to was the problem of financing the performing arts in the face of ineluctably rising unit costs. These, they argued, are the result of 'productivity lag'. The resulting cost pressure has come to be known as 'Baumol's cost disease'. Productivity is defined by economists as physical output per work hour. Increases in productivity over time may occur for the following reasons: (1) increased capital per worker, (2) improved technology, (3) increased labour skill, (4) better management, and (5) economies of scale as output rises.

As this list suggests, increases in productivity are most readily achieved in industries that use of a lot of machinery and equipment. In such industries output per worker can be increased either by using more machinery or by investing in new equipment that embodies improved technology. As a result, in the typical manufacturing industry the amount of labour time needed to produce a physical unit of output declines dramatically decade after decade. The live performing arts are at the other end of the spectrum. Machinery, equipment and technology play only a small role in their production process and, in any case, change very little over time.

That is not to say that technological improvements are entirely absent. For example, stage lighting has been revolutionized by the development of electronic controls and audience comfort greatly enhanced by air conditioning, which also facilitates longer seasons and more flexible scheduling. But these improvements are not central to the business at hand. As Baumol and Bowen point out, the conditions of production themselves preclude any substantial change in productivity because 'the work of the performer is an end in itself, not a means for the production of some good' (ibid., p. 164). Since the performer's labour *is* the output – the singer singing, the dancer dancing, the pianist playing – there is really no way to increase output per hour. It takes four musicians as much playing time to perform a Beethoven string quartet today as it did in 1800.

The productivity lag argument

The productivity lag argument can be summarized as follows. Costs in the live performing arts will rise relative to costs in the economy as a whole because wage increases in the arts have to keep up with those in the general economy even though productivity improvements in the arts lag behind. It is not suggested that artists must be paid the same hourly wage as workers in other jobs, since working conditions and the non-monetary satisfaction obtained from employment differ across occupations. Rather, the argument is that all industries, including the arts, compete to hire workers in a nationally integrated labour market and that artists' wages must therefore rise over time by the

Table 10.1   Hypothetical illustration of productivity lag

	1990	2000	Change (%)
Widget industry			
Output in widgets per work hour (opw)	20	24	+20
Wage per hour (w)	$10	$12	+20
Unit labour cost (ulc) per widget = w/opw	$0.50	$0.50	0
Symphony orchestra			
Output, measured by admissions per work hour (opw)	2	2	0
Wage per hour (w)	$20	$24	+20
Unit labour cost (ulc) per admission = w/opw	$10	$12	+20

same proportion as wages in the general economy to enable the arts industry to hire the workers it needs to carry on.

Of the five sources of increased productivity cited above, only economies of scale as a result of longer seasons is really effective in the live performing arts. With only that factor to rely on, the live performing arts, as Baumol and Bowen emphasized, 'cannot hope to match the remarkable record of productivity growth achieved by the economy as a whole' (1966, p. 165). As a result, cost per unit of output in the live performing arts is fated to rise continuously relative to costs in the economy as a whole. That, in brief, is the unavoidable consequence of productivity lag.

A hypothetical example
In Table 10.1 we compare two industries, the widget manufacturing industry in which productivity rises steadily, and the symphony concert industry in which it is stagnant.

The widget manufacturer
Output per work hour (opw) is measured by widgets produced per worker per hour. We assume that it rises from 20 widgets in 1990 to 24 in 2000, an increase of 20 per cent. Wages rise at the same rate as productivity, going from $10 per hour in 1990 to $12 per hour in 2000. Unit labour cost (ulc) equals wages per work hour divided by output per work hour. In 1990, ulc equals $10/20 widgets, or 50 cents per widget. In 2000, unit labour cost is unchanged. Though wages have risen 20 per cent, so has output per work hour, leaving ulc still at 50 cents per widget. Thus wages in a progressive industry can rise as fast as productivity without causing any increase in costs.

The symphony orchestra
To explain and quantify output per work hour for a symphony orchestra, we make the following assumptions:

Capacity of concert hall = 1600
Concerts per week = 5
Potential admissions per week = 5 × 1600 = 8000
Number of musicians = 100

Musicians' work hours per week = 40
Orchestra hours per week = 100 × 40 = 4000
Orchestra output per work hour (opw) = admissions per week divided by orchestra hours per week = 8000 divided by 4000 = 2.

As to wages, we assume musicians are paid $20 per hour in 1990. By the year 2000 musician wages have risen 20 per cent, to $24 per hour, in order to keep pace with rising wages in the general economy. Unit labour costs, which equal wages per hour divided by output per work hour, therefore rise from $10 to $12. Thus unit labour cost rises by the same proportion as productivity lags.

Historical evidence on costs

The historical record strongly supports the hypothesis that, because of productivity lag, unit costs in the live performing arts have increased substantially faster than the general price level. Baumol and Bowen (1966) provide abundant examples, pieced together from remarkable historical sources.

Using a set of account books for the Drury Lane and Covent Garden theatres in London covering the years 1740–75, Baumol and Bowen calculate that the average cost per performance came to an estimated £157 in the five-year period 1771–2 to 1775–6. For the sake of comparison, they estimated that the average cost per performance at the Royal Shakespeare Theatre in 1963–4 stood at £2139, or 13.6 times its eighteenth-century level. Over the same period (1771–2 to 1963–4) the general price level in England rose to about 6.2 times its initial level. Thus 'the cost per performance over the period as a whole went up more than twice as much as the price level' (ibid., p. 183).

The above conclusion is based on the comparison of costs of two different organizations at two points in time. Baumol and Bowen were also able to measure the change in costs within a single organization over a long period. For the New York Philharmonic Orchestra they put together a nearly continuous cost history covering 1843 to 1964. Over that period cost per concert rose at a compound annual rate of 2.5 per cent while the US index of wholesale prices rose an average of only 1.0 per cent per year (ibid., p. 186).

For the years after World War II, they analysed data on 23 major US orchestras, three opera companies, one dance company, and a sample of Broadway, regional and summer theatres. Table 10.2 shows that in every group the results were the same: cost per performance rose far faster than the general price level.

An international comparison

Baumol and Bowen also found that their evidence, although rather sketchy, did support a conclusion that the problem of productivity lag is international in scope. In the theatres they investigated in the UK in the 1950s and 1960s, 'cost per performance rose at a rate of 7 to 10 percent while prices went up at about a 4 percent rate' (1966, p. 201). In the USA, 'Costs rose during the postwar period at an annual rate close to 4 percent while prices went up between 1 and 2 percent'. Thus the ratio was roughly 2 to 1 in both countries, suggesting to the authors that the problem of productivity lag 'knows no national boundaries' (ibid., p. 201).

Table 10.2   Growth in expenditure per performance and in the wholesale price index, postwar period, USA

Organization	Period	Average annual percentage increase (compound rate)	
		Expenditure per performance	Wholesale price index
23 major orchestras	1947–64	3.1	1.3
Metropolitan Opera	1951–64	4.4	0.3
City Center Opera	1958–63	2.0	0
New York City Ballet	1958–63	2.3	0
Theatres:			
Broadway sample	1950–61	6.0	1.4
Regional theatre A	1958–63	11.2	0
Regional theatre B	1958–63	6.0	0
Regional theatre C	1955–63	2.5	0.9
Summer theatre	1954–63	3.6	0

Source: Baumol and Bowen (1966, Table VIII-3, p. 199).

The earnings gap

From the beginning, Baumol and Bowen were concerned about the financial implications of productivity lag for performing arts firms. The principal implication, as they saw it, was that, because of productivity lag, costs would rise ineluctably. Revenues, having no built-in growth mechanism, would necessarily lag behind, and the earnings gap would grow continuously.

At this point we must define some terms. The absolute size of the earnings gap equals expenditures less earned income. Its relative size equals that amount as a percentage of earned income. Since non-profit firms generally cannot run an operating deficit, the gap must be approximately covered by unearned income. The amount of unearned income is therefore another measure of the gap.

In the foreword to Baumol and Bowen's book, August Heckscher, director of The Twentieth Century Fund, which had financed its publication, wrote: 'It is not only that the live performing arts do not pay for themselves, but that, within the developing economic system, they will show deficits of increasing size' (1966, p. vii). Indeed, a whole chapter of the book is devoted to 'Trends in the Income Gap' and the final chapter, entitled 'Prospects', deals with little else. Moreover, the authors found evidence of a growing earnings gap not only in the USA and the UK, but also in Italy and Sweden.

On the basis of postwar experience, Baumol and Bowen estimated that, from the mid-1960s to the mid-1970s, expenditures of performing arts firms would rise between 5 and 7 per cent per year while earned income would rise only 3.5 to 5.5 per cent yearly, resulting in continued relative (as well as absolute) growth of the gap. Fortunately, that did not happen. Expenditures continued to increase rapidly, but in some art forms earned income rose as fast or faster, so that the gap in some areas declined in relative size. Data from a Ford Foundation study (for which Baumol was a consultant) show that, from 1965–6 to 1970–71, the gap as a percentage of total expenditures rose for symphony

Table 10.3 The earnings gap: contributed income as percentage of total revenue

	Sample size	Beginning year	(%)	Ending year	(%)	Change
Symphony orchestras	39	1972	36.4	1992	35.4	−1.0
Opera[a]	24	1981	48.7	1991	46.2	−2.5
Ballet	7	1983	36.6	1992	34.2	−2.4
Modern dance	6	1983	43.0	1992	56.1	13.1
Non-profit theatres	39	1980	38.0	1992	38.1	0.1

Note: [a] Excluding the Metropolitan Opera.

Source: Felton (1994).

orchestras and non-profit theatres, but fell for opera, ballet and modern dance companies (Ford Foundation, 1974, pp. 388–93). A study by Samuel Schwarz and Mary G. Peters (1983) indicated that, in the 1970s, the relative size of the gap fell substantially in ballet, modern dance and non-profit theatre, declined slightly for symphony orchestras, and was approximately stable for opera.

More recent data gathered by Marianne Felton (1994), indicate that the gap continued to decline into the early 1990s, except in the field of modern dance (see Table 10.3). It should be noted that in the UK a study by Peacock, Shoesmith and Millner of the performing arts in the 1970s found no evidence of the cost disease in that decade. Apparently, the extremely high rate of inflation in those years induced performing arts companies to adopt cost-reducing policies that temporarily halted the operation of the cost disease (see Towse, 1997b, p. 351).

On the whole, then, dire predictions that productivity lag would lead to a relentlessly increasing earnings gap proved to be incorrect. A number of factors can work to offset the effects of productivity lag. In this instance expenses of performing arts companies did increase more or less as predicted, but earned income rose at an equal or slightly higher rate, so the relative size of the gap began to decline. What explains the rise in earned income? Apparently, ticket prices rose much faster than the general price level without causing a drop in attendance. (I say 'apparently' because we have no summary measure of ticket price movements.) As a result, box office revenues, adjusted for inflation, rose substantially. Thus productivity lag in the arts persisted, but so did some of its potential offsets.

Interpreting the earnings gap

Something more must be said by way of interpretation. Schwarz and Peters point out that, since performing arts firms in the non-profit sector cannot normally operate with a cash deficit, an earnings gap cannot exist unless unearned income is available to cover it. Emphasis on the earnings gap as the starting point in a financial analysis leads one to think of unearned income as a passive factor that responds after the fact to the financial needs of the company. But one could just as well look at it the other way around and argue that the existence of unearned income makes it possible for a performing arts firm to finance expenditures in excess of earned income. A very large earnings gap for a given firm might indicate, not that the firm is in serious financial trouble, but rather that it has succeeded in finding generous outside support, probably in response to its very high quality of operation.

Is there an 'artistic deficit'?

Faced with the continual upward pressure on costs generated by productivity lag, firms in the live performing arts might be expected to seek ways of economizing by gradually altering their choice of repertory or their production process. For example, theatrical producers might look for plays with smaller casts or plays that could be mounted with a single rather than multiple stage sets. Or they might try to compensate for higher costs by shunning artistically innovative plays that do not draw well at the box office and so have to be 'carried' by revenues from more conventional offerings. Orchestras and opera companies, too, might be driven away from innovative or 'difficult' material by box office considerations. Or, operating on the cost side, they might select programmes with an eye to reducing rehearsal time or hire fewer outside soloists or other high-priced guest artists.

Although experience clearly teaches us that firms will respond to rising input costs by economizing in the use of the offending inputs, economists interested in the arts are likely to be disturbed when they find firms in the performing arts doing just that. They are offended at the notion that *Hamlet* is no longer viable because its cast is too large, or that piano concertos will be less frequently heard because soloists have become too expensive. When that occurs it has been said that performing arts firms are reducing their fiscal deficit by incurring an 'artistic deficit'.

It is worth noting that this problem is peculiar to the performing arts. In the fine arts – for example, in architecture – we fully expect practitioners to adapt their 'products' to changes over time in the relative prices of alternative inputs. We are not surprised to find that modern buildings are devoid of the elaborate hand-carved stonework that decorated important buildings in earlier times. Indeed, the aesthetic rationale of the modern movement in architecture was precisely to design buildings that could use machine-finished materials in place of the increasingly costly hand-finished ones. In this instance it is not too strong to say that the necessity of adapting was the challenge that gave rise to a whole new school of design.

What makes the performing arts different is that the past provides much of the substance that we want to see performed. We do not want *Hamlet* with half the characters omitted because of the high cost of labour. Nor do we wish to give up symphony concerts in favour of chamber music recitals simply because symphonies employ too many musicians. We want the range of 'artistic options' to include the option of hearing or seeing performances of great works that were invented under very different economic circumstances from our own. There would indeed be an artistic deficit if today's companies became financially unable to present for us the great works of the past.

Have our performing arts institutions, responding to financial pressure, already begun cutting back along some dimensions of quality? Are we even now the victims of an artistic deficit? Some of the evidence is what social scientists call 'anecdotal', but there is systematic evidence, as well. Table 10.4 reproduces data from a study by the Baumols showing that average cast size for all non-musicals produced on Broadway fell from 15.8 in 1946–7 to 8.1 in 1977–8. More recently, I have shown that, from 1983 to 1998, com-

Table 10.4   Cast size of Broadway plays

Broadway season	Average cast size
1946–7	15.8
1953–4	14.4
1957–8	13.4
1962–3	12.4
1967–8	8.9
1972–3	10.2
1977–8	8.1

Note: As a result of printing/editing errors, table 11 did not actually appear in the cited source. It is used here with the permission of the authors.

Source: Baumol and Baumol (1985).

panies have produced popular operas at the expense of new or less well-known works, which could be interpreted as evidence of a growing artistic deficit in the field of opera (Heilbrun, 2001, pp. 63–72).

Income from the mass media in the USA

Some years ago it was suggested that performing arts firms might be able to earn income from the mass media to help relieve the financial pressure generated by productivity lag. Symphony orchestras, to pick the most obvious example, might be able to earn royalties from the sale of recordings. Theatre, ballet, and opera companies, in addition to earning royalties from the sale of pre-recorded tapes or videodiscs, might be paid for performances on broadcast or cable TV. After all, in the analogous case of professional sports, earnings from television far outweigh income from ticket sales.

Unfortunately, this potential revenue never materialized. Royalties are trivial for most US symphony orchestras, and the trend has been down. (See the evidence cited in Heilbrun and Gray, 2001, pp. 148–50.) Nor did performing arts companies ever earn significant income from television performances. In the early days of commercial television, the networks made a modest effort to present high culture on the tube. But as time went by and public television became increasingly important, the commercial networks virtually abandoned cultural programming to the public stations. A commercial market for culture on TV no longer exists.

In assessing the prospect that the mass media might at some future date become heavy purchasers of performing arts material, there is further bad news: Hilda and William Baumol have shown that programme production costs on television are subject to inflation on account of productivity lag for exactly the same reasons as costs in the live sector are (Towse, 1997a). Thus the same cost problem that bedevils live production of the performing arts reappears to limit the prospect of substantial sales to the mass media.

Baumol's good news

The problem of productivity lag exists only because there is persistent technological progress in the general economy that causes a rise in output per work hour and in real wages, in other words a rise in per capita income, which, in turn, increases the demand for the arts. In the case of the live performing arts, that means the demand for tickets increases: at any given price level the public will be willing to buy more tickets than it did previously. Thus, while productivity lag causes ticket prices to rise, which will lead to a decline in quantity demanded, rising income to some extent offsets that effect by stimulating ticket purchases. This does not mean that productivity lag causes no problems, but only that rising living standards work to mitigate them. Perhaps an analogy is in order. Because of productivity lag in the business of high-quality food preparation, the price of a meal in a gourmet restaurant has risen sharply in recent years. That probably causes a good deal of anguish to both customers and owners, but it has not prevented the gourmet restaurant business from growing. A similar effect is likely in the live performing arts. Baumol and Bowen were criticized for failing to emphasize that possibility, but Baumol has corrected that failure in a more recent paper (Baumol, 1996, pp. 183–206).

Productivity lag does not justify subsidies

The hypothesis that productivity lag is bound to cause a long-run increase in the real cost of the performing arts was often cited by arts advocates as a justification for public subsidies. Without subsidies, it was asserted, either ticket prices would have to rise continuously, which would end all hope of reaching new audiences, or else performing arts companies would face increasingly large deficits that would force many of them out of business. Leaving aside the fact that there are some alternatives to these gloomy predictions, it must now be emphasized that productivity lag *per se* does not provide justification for government subsidy. Productivity lag is a market process that would cause unit cost to rise in any technologically unprogressive industry. But there is no reason to subsidize an industry simply because it is technologically unprogressive. On the contrary, given that its real costs are rising relative to those in more progressive industries, it is best to let its prices increase to reflect the rise in real costs. As long as markets are operating efficiently, those higher costs will be absorbed optimally by the economy. We would all be better off if there were no technologically unprogressive industries, but, since there are, matters are made worse, not better, if we use subsidies to prevent market prices from reflecting their true costs. Lag or no lag, subsidies can be justified only by some form of market failure.

Indeed, economists have written extensively about market failure, and Baumol and Bowen discuss the rationale for public support of the performing arts in Chapter XVI of their book. But this is not the place to enter into that large and complicated subject.

See also:

Chapter 15: Costs of production; Chapter 43: Opera and ballet; Chapter 44: Orchestras; Chapter 47: Performing arts.

References

Baumol, Hilda and W.J. Baumol (1985), 'The Future of the Theater and the Cost Disease of the Arts', in Mary Ann Hendon, James F. Richardson and William S. Hendon (eds), *Bach and the Box*, a special supplement to the *Journal of Cultural Economics*, Akron: Association for Cultural Economics, table 11. As a result of printing/editing errors, table 11 did not actually appear in the cited source. It is used here with the permission of the authors.

Baumol, William J. (1996), 'Children of Performing Arts, the Economic Dilemma: The Climbing Costs of Health Care and Education', *Journal of Cultural Economics,* 20, 183–206.

Baumol, William J. and William G. Bowen (1966), *Performing Arts: The Economic Dilemma,* New York: The Twentieth Century Fund.

Felton, Marianne V. (1994), 'Historical Funding Patterns in Symphony Orchestras, Dance, and Opera Companies, 1972–1992', *Journal of Arts Management, Law, and Society,* 24, 8–31, table 11 and 'Historical Funding Patterns in Nonprofit Theaters, 1980–1992', unpublished manuscript, table I.

The Ford Foundation (1974), *The Finances of the Performing Arts, Volume I,* New York: The Ford Foundation.

Heilbrun, James (2001), 'Empirical Evidence of a Decline in Repertory Diversity among American Opera Companies 1991/1992 to 1997/1998', *Journal of Cultural Economics,* 25 (1), 63–72.

Heilbrun, James and Charles M. Gray (2001), *The Economics of Art and Culture,* 2nd edn, New York: Cambridge University Press.

Schwarz, Samuel and Mary G. Peters (1983), 'Growth of Arts and Cultural Organizations in the Decade of the 1970s', a study prepared for the Research Division, National Endowment for the Arts, Rockville, MD, Informatics General Corporation.

Towse, Ruth (ed.) (1997a), *Baumol's Cost Disease: The Arts and Other Victims,* Cheltenham, UK and Lyme, USA: Edward Elgar.

Towse, Ruth (ed.) (1997b), *Cultural Economics: The Arts, the Heritage and the Media Industries,* Vol. II, Cheltenham, UK and Lyme, USA: Edward Elgar.

Further reading

Heilbrun and Gray (2001), Chapter 8 is a somewhat expanded version of this chapter. Baumol and Bowen (1966) is, of course, the *Ur*text on this topic and Towse (1997a) is a nearly complete collection of Baumol's writings on the subject.

11 Broadcasting

Glenn Withers and Katrina Alford

There have been substantial ongoing technology-induced changes in broadcasting over the past decade and more. The broadcasting market has been transformed and boundaries between traditional broadcast media and the new digital media blurred. Digitalization, satellite transmission, broadband networks, online programme downloading and forums, mobile broadcasting and other developments have challenged the traditional definition of broadcasting as the television and radio component in a set of four neat and distinct media market pigeon-holes – free-to-air television, pay television, radio and print.

This chapter defines broadcasting as the range of television and radio services for entertainment, educational and informational purposes, while recognizing that 'broadcasting . . . [has become] a portmanteau bursting at the seams as more and more activities [are] stuffed into it' (Inglis, 2006, p. 582). It reviews the changing broadcasting landscape in the late twentieth and early twenty-first century, and the analytic and policy responses to this.

Technological change and broadcasting

From the introduction of radio and television, the dominant technology for broadcasting programme delivery has been terrestrial transmission via an airwave signal sent from a broadcasting station transmitter to receivers owned by listeners and viewers. The technical quality of the transmission has depended on the frequency spectrum occupied, strength of signal transmitted, and topography and distance to the receiver. A second delivery platform emerged with the advent of the space age. Satellite technology enabled powerful transmitters ('transponders') in geostationary orbit above the earth to distribute signals over a very wide 'footprint' on the earth's surface. A third delivery platform of increasing use and power, cable networks, uses telephone lines or dedicated separate cable networks. With cable, geography does not affect signals, multi-channel capacity is immense and two-way transmission is possible.

In the past 20 years, the digitalization of television and radio has particularly enabled increasing levels of broadband access, online programming and an increasing range and modes of service delivery. Broadband technology has enabled development of a wide band of frequencies to transmit information, thereby overcoming frequency spectrum limits on terrestrial service supply, increasing opportunities for substitute and/or complementary service provision including programmes and content on demand, and increasing direct user charging.

Particular features of the new broadcasting environment that have emerged from the evolution of delivery platform technology have been the dramatic increase in each of: user-pay television's share of the overall television market; Internet downloading of broadcasts and other media, either freely or by subscription; the emergence of a mobile broadcasting sector in many countries; and the growth of new interactive media applications and activities.

This in turn has had major implications for the previously dominant models in national broadcasting systems, namely the commercial and the public. The former model is based on commercial or profit-oriented stations deriving revenue from advertiser funding. The latter model is based on government funding of state-owned public broadcasting organizations. Individual countries have adopted different blends of private and public provision and extent of regulation, and the accommodation of new technology has proceeded at different rates across countries. Common to both models, however, is dominance of centralized structures for control of programming decisions, whether through commercial networks or state authorities. This enables significant economies of scale and scope. Common to both national structures is an extensive system of regulation.

For traditional private media corporations, great reliance on mass advertising revenues has come under increasing challenge, leading to wholesale reviews of relying on this revenue base. For public broadcasters the emergence of numerous new outlets for news and current affairs and for minority tastes has also provided a challenge. Globalization under new technology has challenged all national broadcasting, public and private.

Overall, the speed and array of technological changes have massive implications for the cost, quality and control of transmission, the extent of the market, the degree of direct competition and the efficiency and public value of the resulting broadcasting. The role of government intervention in these changing markets has also been reviewed.

Key economic and policy issues include: have consumer choices and accessibility increased? Have the changes led to greater competition between broadcasters, and to increasing diversity or quality in broadcasting? What is or should be the government regulatory role in these rapidly changing circumstances? Have they made public broadcasting residual, or even unnecessary?

To answer these questions using economics involves looking at how financing of broadcasting, including public financing, has operated, how regulation has evolved, and what the changes in technology mean for governments in all countries.

Funding and regulating broadcasting

The three conventional sources of financing for broadcasting are advertiser payment, audience payment and government or community subvention. In the case of advertiser support, programmes are supplied free of direct charge to the audience. The audience in turn is sold wholesale to advertisers who seek, by attaching their messages to the programmes, to inform or persuade consumers in regard to their products and services. The ultimate incidence of payment depends on the extent to which advertising costs can be passed on in product prices to consumers of the advertised goods and services.

Indeed it was this distinctive reliance at the time on advertiser funding rather than on listener/viewer direct payments that, along with the idiosyncrasies of a limited frequency spectrum for transmission, produced analysis of broadcasting as a distinct field of economics.

In the case of direct payment by audiences, as this emerged, the analysis then recognized that the incidence would lie with individual viewers or listeners who determine for themselves their willingness to pay for programmes or programme services, including under subscription arrangements. In this instance, broadcasting purchase is closest to purchase arrangements for standard commodities. The growth of pay television in recent years indicates a willingness of audiences to pay for an expanded menu of choices as technology has increasingly made this option accessible and convenient.

Subvention occurs with voluntary donations by community members, as is common in community broadcasting, or subsidy by governments based on their taxation power. Tax payments for broadcasting may be from general taxation, as in Australia, or from 'hypothecated' taxes or charges enforced by government, such as earmarked state lottery revenues, or broadcasting licence fees as in the UK.

In many countries, state broadcasters are funded through a mix of advertising and public money, either through a licence fee or directly from the government. In most European countries and Australia, public broadcasting is regarded as a public good. State revenues often support public and community broadcasting, but can subsidize commercial activities too. The incidence of funding in this case depends on the incidence of the taxation source used.

Analysts have sometimes looked at the comparative incidence of the finance options, recognizing that tax-based funding under progressive income taxation has quite differing implications from advertiser funding where incidence may be more regressive, with direct purchase somewhere in between. But equity concerns in this area have never been a major focus.

Whatever the source and incidence of financing, broadcasting has also been a highly regulated sector. This has derived in the past especially from the need to allocate limited frequency spectrum under terrestrial transmission, the presence of economies of scale, scope and networks, and from the pervasive and persuasive nature of the broadcasting product.

Regulation covers rules rather than incentives. Such rules may be backed by penalties such as fines but they are distinctive in that they are enforceable under law rather than depending on the choices made voluntarily by agents. Regulatory law for broadcasting relates to the structure, behaviour and performance of participants in the sector's activities. The principal focus has traditionally been on providers, but also extends to consumers and users.

A mix of the following specific instruments of public intervention is commonly observed across countries: access controls to existing technology and controls over introduction of new technology for broadcasting; government award or auction of spectrum licences; fiscal subsidy for community and public broadcasting (as discussed earlier); regulation of ownership (vertical, horizontal and foreign); and regulation of programme content, particularly advertising time, local content, children's programming and offensive content. The assignment of instruments to particular objectives is not strict. Some may affect multiple objectives. For example, foreign ownership restrictions may affect both anti-monopoly objectives and local content objectives.

Analysis of this broadcasting intervention can be positive or normative in approach. The former seeks to explain what governments actually do. The latter reviews what governments should do. Political science has been the principal source of positivist studies of government regulatory behaviour and of state-owned enterprises, while management science has focused on the behaviour of individual private broadcasting companies. Public choice economics has also offered some complementary insights.

Positivist analysis recognizes that there is a significant capacity for media interests to influence public decision-makers so as to provide media subvention and/or regulation that may reflect the media's interests as much as the public interest. It also observes that the scope and scale of government intervention in the broadcasting market is influenced by the political complexion of national governments. For example, the deregulatory emphasis of conservative or 'neoliberal' governments in the English-speaking world has eased or abolished a number of regulatory controls, including in relation to media ownership and foreign ownership and control restrictions in national broadcasting legislation. At the same time, in the European Union, deregulation of cross-border television broadcasting is said to have led to a high level of investment flight and to resistance to further deregulation by many governments of member states.

Economic science (and law) has nevertheless focused more on the normative approach to regulation, specifying what government should be doing if it is to serve the public interest.

Welfare economics of broadcasting

The normative approach has long been at the heart of the economic approach to broadcasting. Broadcasting policy analysis starts from the First Fundamental Theorem of Welfare Economics, which states that market competition is Pareto efficient. That is, competitive market processes will ensure that individual preferences, as expressed through the market, will be met at least resource cost to society. Qualifications to this conclusion include recognizing that competitive markets sometimes fail to operate, or that preferences beyond those of individuals and beyond those based on the existing distribution of income and wealth may be crucial but not reflected well in market processes.

Problems with the operation of competition in markets have been emphasized in broadcasting economics. In particular, market failure has been seen as arising from technologically imposed supply limitations and associated funding requirements. In free-to-air broadcasting, this has led to concern not only over any monopoly pricing that occurs but also to concern over reduced programme diversity that results from a limited number of channels being available in the dominant frequencies (medium wave for sound and very high frequency for television).

In this situation profit maximization is predicted to result in a 'lowest common denominator' approach in commercial broadcasting, whereby competition for market share favours mainstream generic programmes, currently such as crime dramas and 'reality TV', rather than audience targeted and special interest programmes based on age, ethnicity or minority tastes, for example, such as arts and culture. Duplication of similar programmes will occur as long as the audience share obtained is greater than that from programme diversity (Steiner, 1952).

There is no mechanism in free-to-air broadcasting for the viewer or listener to express the intensity of their particular programme preferences, unlike the case in conventional markets where preferences are indicated by willingness to pay the market price. The result is a reinforcement of programme duplication and 'lowest common denominator' programmes, with advertisers who fund programmes assumed to be motivated by maximization of audience.

Beyond competition concerns, the second focus of past welfare economics in broadcasting has been the separate market failure issue of externalities, where externalities refer to non-market effects on people other than those contracting for the supply of broadcasting services. Free markets deal badly with externalities as they have no market price, and hence tend to be underproduced when beneficial and overproduced where damaging.

There have been two concerns about externalities in broadcasting: the particular issue of congestion or signal interference from competitive access to limited spectrum, and the wider issue of cultural, social and political effects of broadcasting.

The former externality problem has been dealt with through government determining spectrum allocation in a form that prevents signal interference. This raises the question of what criteria are used for this allocation. This question has long been discussed by economists since Ronald Coase's economic analysis of spectrum allocation, which criticized spectrum licensing by government and suggested auctions be used to create property rights as a more efficient method of allocating spectrum to users (Coase, 1959). Proponents of competitive auctions say that they are generally an efficient tool for assigning exclusive rights, eliminate many costs of alternative methods and bring transparency to government awards.

But what of social, cultural and political externalities? These are potentially important given the extensive penetration of broadcasting in modern society and its influence on social and political behaviour and national culture. Examples include positive effects from quality news and current affairs in improving national political decision-making and from education programming enhancing children's development, or negative social effects including those from programmes containing explicit sex and violence that may debase family relationships and encourage greater crime. The presumed positive role of broadcasting in enhancing national culture through local content is also highlighted.

It is hard to quantify or value these effects, given the diversity of probable views about the value of different programmes and their actual effect on behaviour. By definition, the market provides no direct measure (Snowball, 2008).

There is also a threshold conceptual issue, which is how much such notions are truly externalities, which thereby possess certain public-good characteristics, as opposed to their being instead merit goods. Merit goods refer to the denial of the value of individual preferences in favour of a notion of non-individualist values informing judgements about what should be provided. In broadcasting, the difference would be between wanting to prevent people from watching programmes with explicit violence because they induce actual violence from some viewers (an externality), and wanting to restrict such programmes because they are inherently immoral even if they do not affect behaviour (merit good).

The distinction between externality and merit goods can be a fine one, and both are hard to measure. What is clear, however, is that if either externalities or merit goods are present, such social, cultural or political characteristics will only be taken into account in commercial broadcasting decisions if they are consistent with profit imperatives or are required by regulation.

Similarly in the case of monopolistic broadcasters, exercising public responsibility is less likely and monopoly pricing is more likely in the absence of regulation.

Technological change and broadcasting

Some commentators see the technology changes as so great that market failure considerations lose their weight and any special status accorded government funding or regulation of broadcasting by 'administrative fiat' (Murdoch, 2009) has disappeared.

In particular, the new diversity and charging options provided by ongoing technological change promise reduced supply delivery limitations and allow direct user payment systems – muting two distinctive features of traditional broadcasting, and rendering the industry more like other user-pay, supply-responsive industries. In these circumstances greater deregulation or liberalization is an appropriate policy response, proponents argue.

However, seeing broadcasting as now simply analogous to conventional markets is flawed. In the competition area, for example, considerable problems remain with limits to competition imposed by economies of scope and scale, and especially so through network effects. Distribution networks can reduce costs substantially to incumbents, making new entry difficult, even in the absence of regulatory impediments. Indeed the term 'networks' is quite commonly attached to television distribution arrangements, more than in most markets.

This became a national concern in the USA in the late twentieth century, where the giants of the industry engaged in a wave of communications industry mergers and acquisitions. One result of such worries has been the emergence of new challenges to the definition of the broadcasting market for legal and policy purposes. Along with more traditional distinctions between electronic media and print media, the question is now asked: where does broadcasting end and information technology begin?

The market definition issue is further complicated by increasing globalization under modern technology. On the plus side, authoritarian regimes find it even harder to restrict access to information about abuse of rights and corruption under the new technology. Equally, on the downside, concerns have been expressed that global corporate giants could swamp legitimate national and local cultures. In getting the balance right, further complications have been introduced by the increased engagement in this area by non-national forms of governance, for example the European Commission. Similarly, while some governments support the further liberalization of audiovisual services under the umbrella of the General Agreement on Trade in Services (GATS) and the World Trade Organization (WTO), other countries see this as undermining national media and broadcasting governance and culture and the United Nations 2001 Declaration on Cultural Diversity.

In addition, as regards competition and the new technologies, private ownership or control of new common carrier delivery platforms and of new products that serve as industry standards remains a concern. Common carriage refers to the fact that cable delivery has certain natural monopoly characteristics, such as substantial economies of scale in the rollout of cable, that make it difficult to establish competition, or, where a big enough market does exist for duplication, such duplication is an inefficient use of resources given the capacity of modern cable.

With product standards, the continuing problem is that, in the absence of government regulation, first-mover advantage may go to those who first develop new systems that then become locked in as industry standards for followers and for complementary products. In the absence of some form of external product regulation or standardization there may be substantial consumer losses. This occurred with the early adoption of the NTSC (National Television Standards Committee) colour system in the USA, versus the PAL (Phase Alternate Line) standard from Europe, later adopted elsewhere.

Equally, a traditional public-good market failure problem in broadcasting first identified by Samuelson (1964) arises when user-pay systems are adopted. While user-pays technology may reduce the principal–agent information problem arising under advertiser funding, direct pricing applies to what is still typically a non-rival commodity with low marginal cost. That is, once a programme has been produced and transmitted, extra viewers and listeners can be accommodated at almost zero additional resource cost. Pricing above such zero cost (as with pay TV) then excludes consumers who would have been quite willing to cover the costs (zero) of their receipt of the service. This is a fundamental allocative inefficiency usually ignored by proponents of liberalization.

Beyond the competition arena, the new technologies have not eliminated concerns over the social, political and cultural effects of broadcasting. In many cases they have accentuated these concerns, and in others they enable new solutions for responding to these externalities. In relation to negative social externalities, for example, one significant component of Internet use is pornography, and governments are seeking new technologies and forms of regulation to protect children in this area.

Moreover, the new technologies may necessitate new government policy responses. Television local content regulations, for example, have been designed for a channelized one-way medium and are unworkable in the Internet environment. This has led critics of a 'heavy-handed' government approach to regulation to suggest that a vertical sector approach may no longer be tenable, and to advocate a horizontal approach of government policy across different media.

A further concern is reflected in an ongoing debate over 'quality' of broadcasting under the imperatives of the new technologies. The expansion of broadcasting content and delivery forms means that revenue is spread over increasingly fragmented audiences, leading to strains on higher-cost quality programmes and services in television and radio, and perhaps to lower standards of journalism and broadcasting. This has led to what is variously described as a 'dumbing down' of broadcasting or a 'crisis in journalism'.

Similarly there are arguments that where two competing products, online and print news, for example, are substitutes, a price rise in one, say online news, will lead to a decline in demand and loss of profit for its producers.

In an attempt to pull together these aspects of external effects, a new notion of 'public value' adopted from Mark Moore's analysis has been increasingly employed to provide more strategic guidance for government and public broadcasters (Moore, 1995). The term is the equivalent of 'shareholder value' in corporate management but seeks to embrace the full value of public-value-based investments, including both the internal value to government operations and the broader political and social returns to the public at large.

Creating and demonstrating net economic and broader social value in the cultural, social and political arena is, as emphasized, inherently difficult, although it has been embraced with enthusiasm by some broadcasters, such as the BBC and Australia's ABC. This enthusiasm has helped kindle greater research into measurement of the components of such value via market impact analysis, industry modelling and contingent valuation analysis, and perhaps also greater recognition of the essentially non-economic argument that in culture and the arts there is 'value beyond price' (Hutter and Throsby, 2008).

Finally, there is in response to the new technologies a new willingness in broadcasting economics to interrogate the extent to which underlying assumptions about market coherence may need qualification in this market. One reason for this is that the technology changes themselves have introduced new market characteristics. Behavioural economists have also questioned conventional economic assumptions about markets and consumer behaviour, including in broadcasting markets specifically. Further, the existence of unique competitive equilibria under the First Fundamental Theorem of Welfare Economics depends heavily on independence of consumer and producer decisions. The new interactivity between broadcasters and their audiences increasingly challenges this independence assumption. The nature of the new 'citizen journalism' facilitated by new telephony facilities (for example, digital cameras) and the explosive growth of Facebook, Linked-In, Twitter and the like is leading to reassessment of consumer behaviour and its implications for market operation.

Public broadcasting and policy objectives
Just as new technology has challenged the welfare economics of broadcasting and the nature of regulatory responses to market failure, there is much interest in the public funding response too, especially public broadcasting.

Many governments have responded to the limitations on competition and the problems of externalities under traditional technology by extensive use of public broadcasting. Public broadcasters can provide competition for private media and can pursue complementary or minority taste broadcasting to enhance programme diversity. They can also be directed to take account of the social, cultural and political effects of broadcasting in their style of programming, for example emphasis on current affairs or children's programming. The latter could also, in principle, be supported by direct subsidy of such programmes on commercial media. But important economies of scale and scope would then be lost to public broadcasters retained for other purposes, so that such direct commercial subsidy tends to be limited (Withers, 1997).

This case for public broadcasting has been re-examined in economics and the wider social sciences in view of the profound changes that have occurred in broadcasting (and media) markets in recent years, and the rationale for public broadcasting has been questioned in view of the expansion of consumer choices in the digital and broadband era.

An alternative argument is that public broadcasting still fulfils important functions. It is a light-handed intervention primarily based on transparent public subsidy rather than regulatory mechanisms. It can continue to provide countervailing power in situations of concern over monopolization, concentration, programme quality and diversity, and over alternative funding arrangements to both advertiser and user-pay methods, each of which has inefficiency properties. It provides an alternative to programming that allows for divergence of social from private costs and benefits, and it can promote recognized 'merit' objectives.

Alternative subsidy of commercial broadcasters again cannot for the most part provide equivalent achievement of these objectives, irrespective of technology. In this case, public ownership matters precisely because it can produce diversity, pricing and socially responsive programming divergent from commercial imperatives. No matter how much programming the new abundance of technology produces for the broadcasting market, its private provision remains profit derived, and its community provision remains unable to acquire economies of scale, scope and networks because of the free-rider problem.

Criticism is made that such public broadcasting will be provided inefficiently compared to commercial providers. And theoretical 'property rights' critiques may have merit in many applications. For broadcasting, though, there is strong empirical evidence that public broadcasting can and does operate at lower unit costs of production than commercial broadcasting, partly because it avoids the high transaction costs of private revenue raising whether through advertising or by subscriptions and user payments.

A basic problem with public broadcasting itself, though, is another 'principal–agent' problem. Viewers and listeners (the principals) are unable to transmit their preferences easily to the public broadcaster (the agent), with a consequent ability for public broadcasting management and staff to substitute their own preferences for those of the public. Direct accountability to government may allow voters' preferences to constrain broadcasters more, but this raises the issue of political control for partisan purposes in crucial areas such as news and current affairs.

In many countries arm's-length arrangements are devised that seek to limit short-term political interference in editorial functions while retaining public accountability for use of taxpayers' monies. Guaranteeing public broadcasters' independence, for example by statute, allows content creators a measure of independence from management and from government, and arguably more creative risk-taking than is the case in 'bottom-line', profit maximization oriented commercial broadcasting.

Public broadcasters ultimately remain vulnerable, though, to government for ongoing subvention, especially in times of straitened government budgets. For this reason there are proponents of allowing advertising and other commercial revenue raising by public corporations. But this raises competitive neutrality issues *vis à vis* private providers and, more importantly, it compromises the core not-for-profit distinction that justifies the very establishment of public broadcasters.

In sum, there is market failure and there can be collective failure. For these reasons a mixed system of broadcasting allowing for the divergent strengths and weaknesses of each principal approach is a sensible application of the 'balanced portfolio' principle that has been adopted in many countries. The question is, in a world of contending principles, divergent histories, cultures and stages of development and ceaselessly changing technology, just what is the right balance? The challenges in answering this question ensure that broadcasting economics will remain a lively and relevant field in the future.

See also:

Chapter 1: Application of welfare economics; Chapter 38: Media economics and regulation; Chapter 58: Television; Chapter 60: Welfare economics.

References

Alexander, A., J. Owers and R. Carbeth (eds) (1998), *Media Economics: Theory and Practice*, 2nd edn, Mahwah, NJ: Lawrence Erlbaum & Associates.

Cave, M. and A. Brown (1992), 'The Economics of Television Regulation: A Survey with Application to Australia', *Economic Record*, 68, 377–95.

Coase, R.H. (1959), 'The Federal Communications Commission', *Journal of Law and Economics*, 2, 1–40.

Cowen, T. (2002), *Creative Destruction: How Globalisation is Changing the World's Cultures*, Princeton, NJ: Princeton, NJ: Princeton University Press.

Doyle, G. (ed.) (2006), *The Economics of the Mass Media*, Cheltenham, UK and Northampton, MA, USA: Edward Elgar.

Hutter, M. and D. Throsby (eds) (2008), *Beyond Price: Value in Culture, Economics and the Arts*, Cambridge: Cambridge University Press.

Inglis, K. (2006), *Whose ABC? The Australian Broadcasting Corporation 1983–2006*, Melbourne: Black.

Lieurouw, L. and S. Livingstone (2002), *Handbook of New Media*, London: Sage.

Moore, M. (1995), *Creating Public Value: Strategic Management in Government*, Cambridge, MA: Harvard University Press.

Murdoch, J. (2009), MacTaggart Lecture at the Edinburgh International Television Festival.

Noam, E. (ed.) (1985), *Video Media Competition: Regulation, Economics and Technology*, New York: Columbia University Press.

Noll, R.G., M.J. Peck and J.J. McGowan (1973), *Economic Aspects of Television Regulation*, Washington, DC: Brookings.

Owen, B. and S. Wildman (1992), *Video Economics*, Cambridge, MA: Harvard University Press.

Picard, R.G. (1989), *Media Economics: Concepts and Issues*, Newbury Park, CA: Sage.

Samuelson, P.A. (1964), 'Public Goods and Subscription Television', *Journal of Law and Economics*, 7 (1), 81–4.

Snowball, J.D. (2008), *Measuring the Value of Culture: Methodology and Examples in Cultural Economics*, Berlin and New York: Springer.

Spence, M. and B. Owen (1977), 'Television Programming, Monopolistic Competition and Welfare', *Quarterly Journal of Economics*, 91 (1), 103–26.

Steiner, P.O. (1952), 'Program Patterns and Preferences and the Workability of Competition in Radio Broadcasting', *Quarterly Journal of Economics*, 66 (2), 194–223.

Withers, G. (1997), 'The Cultural Influence of Public Television: an Economic Analysis', in R. Towse (ed.), *Cultural Economics: The Arts the Heritage and the Media Industries*, Cheltenham, UK and Lyme, USA: Edward Elgar, pp. 449–64.

Further reading

The foundations of broadcasting economics were laid in seminal contributions by Steiner (1952), Coase (1959), Samuelson (1964) and Spence and Owen (1977). Development in the literature as analysis and technology evolved is summarized for the 1960s in Noll *et al.* (1973), for the 1970s in Noam (1985), the 1980s in Picard (1989), the 1990s in Owen and Wildman (1992), Cave and Brown (1992) and Alexander *et al.* (1998) and, most recently, Lieurouw and Livingstone (2002) and Cowen (2002). A compendium of major contributions is Doyle (2006).

12 Cinema
Samuel Cameron

There is still a tendency among economists to write of film and cinema as synonymous. Articles submitted to the *Journal of Cultural Economics* frequently display this trait. Clearly they are not the same thing. The cinema is an economic and social space where films are watched (in consumer speak) and exhibited (in industry speak). Although the distinction is simple, it is muddied by the use of terms like 'home cinema' to describe the experience of watching DVDs (digital video disks), or other file formats, on surround-system speakers with (usually) large screens. This brings up the issue of the home versus the cinema film-watching experience. This may be substitute or complement. Substitution comes from the relative price of cinema-going versus the price of home viewing. Complementarity would arise from mutual linkages. Greater enjoyment of cinema may increase home cinema consumption through an interest in movies *per se*. The DVD (or film download) experience may increase interest through repeat viewing, enjoyment of extras and so on. There may be an element of so-called 'rational addiction' in cinema-going in that consumption in the past influences consumption in the future. This would suggest that the long-run impact of price cuts would potentially be much bigger than the short-run impact. The pricing decision in the cinema industry is one of its most unusual features and is dealt with below.

Cinema-going is a complex commodity in which the purchase of a ticket to view a film is one element. Historically other features have accompanied it, such as socializing with friends, or for romance, eating food not so often consumed elsewhere (popcorn) and so on. Modern cinemas are functionally utilitarian. They increasingly tend to be sited in leisure complexes where restaurants, cafés, shopping and other options are on offer in the same space. Many cinemas in the golden age of Hollywood movies were designed to be grandiose places of escapism from mundane households. This is depicted, for example, in Brian Moore's novel *The Lonely Passion of Judith Hearne*, later made into a film. The cost of transport plus paid baby-sitters may be added to the ticket price to give the full or hedonic price of cinema (which would be discounted if the building did give additional aesthetic pleasure).

Attendance

Attendance at cinema has shown marked aggregate trends. From the 1950s until the 1980s, in the UK sales declined rapidly. Cinemas closed in large numbers. These two factors may be interrelated. A fall in attendance leads to closures due to falling profits. Closures of cinemas increase the hedonic price of getting to a cinema and may also reduce the variety of choice on offer. Even with the pick-up of attendances following the growth of multiplexes, the ratio of UK attendances declined to about one-fourteenth of their historic peak (MacMillan and Smith, 2001). Attendance at cinema has always been heavily weighted towards the teenage and younger adult viewer. This has made it susceptible to rising availability of alternative leisure-time activities in forms such as sport, music, gambling and computer gaming. Periods of increased demand for cinema tend to be due to the arrival of major (often franchise) movies aimed at this segment of the audience, not least because these may excite repeat viewing with friends, families and significant others.

Independent cinemas

The cinema originated in magic lantern and slide shows, which would be exhibited in a general-purpose building. The dominant form became dedicated single-screen buildings where the projection equipment was permanently installed. Economists have paid seemingly no attention at all to the major sub-market of 'drive-ins'. According to Fox (2011), at their peak (in the late 1950s) drive-ins comprised one-third of cinemas, yet by 2008 there were only 393 drive-ins in the USA, comprising only 6.6 per cent of all cinemas. The drive-in offered characteristics that were absent in the movie theatre experience. Its niche, however, is even more susceptible than that of the movie theatre to competition from the home cinema market as the living room takes the place of the car as the consumption enclave.

The drive-in was an independent film exhibition sector in which the majors did not participate. It has proven progressively difficult for independent distributors to survive in the mainstream film market. It is even harder for new firms to enter it. Outside of art-house niche markets, they have been forced to charge low prices and show old films due to the refusal of suppliers to supply them with current-issue movies. This in textbook economics would seem to be a case of monopolistic abuse arising from vertical integration in the industry, which is to the detriment of consumers. No major attempts to challenge this took place until 2005 (see http://news.bbc.co.uk/1/hi/programmes/working_lunch/2932232.stm), when entrepreneur Stelios Haji-Ioannou, the entrepreneur behind the 'Easy' brand of Internet Cafés and flights, opened his 'Easy Cinema' in one town in the UK. There was no box office. Booking was on line or by phone, and the earlier you reserved your seats the less you paid. There was no popcorn or drinks. Customers could bring their own as long as they took their litter home. For the opening shows, Easy Cinema agreed to pay Sony, one of the main suppliers, £1.30 for each customer; it still charged only 20p entry, but Stelios and his team asked people to donate to a fund to challenge the Hollywood monopoly. The price of 20p was about 4 or 5 per cent of the regular ticket price at the time.

The original plan was for scores of Easy Cinemas across Europe within five years. The venture proved ill fated. The cinema was sold next year and the project was abandoned. Easy Cinema attempted to both undercut the core industry and exercise flexible price discrimination. It could be seen as attempting to 'spoil the market' where customers are still charged high prices even when the movie theatre is poorly sold, indicating a lack of demand.

Pricing

The cinema industry has been characterized by long-established price maintenance, which Easy Cinema was unable to break. This has also withstood anti-trust pressures. Along with maintaining the first-run feature price, cinemas have also shown very limited price flexibility. Within a given circuit this tends to be restricted to some matinée discounts. It would generally be argued that, by forgoing profitable price discrimination opportunities, cinema chains tend to underperform for their owners (Orbach, 2004). Orbach claims, from contemporary US data, that weekend audiences are typically 3.4 times those for weekdays, yet this is not used to leverage profits by price discrimination.

The base level of prices is governed by the licence agreements made for the showing of films, which have four elements (Orbach, 2004):

1. The house nut, which sets exhibitor expenses, including rent and other types of overhead costs and would typically provide the exhibitor with something like textbook 'normal profits'.
2. The formula. During the first week or two, the distributor receives 70–90 per cent of the box office receipts net of the house nut. Afterwards the exhibitor's share increases.
3. The floor, which is the minimum share of gross box office receipts remitted to the distributor before subtracting the house nut. This declines over time.
4. The per capita requirement sets a minimum dollar amount to be paid to the distributor for every ticket.

These terms are supposed to be negotiated on a movie-by-movie and venue-by-venue basis, so that exhibitors' costs vary across movies. This is a peculiarly labyrinthine contract that has attracted surprisingly little attention from economists in terms of analysing its efficiency. Given the absence of price flexibility, the major impact of the contract will be on determining when a film is pulled from screening due to the time-variable elements interacting with the pattern of demand.

Influence of home viewing

Cinema has faced, and increasingly faces, more problematic competition from outside its immediate sphere. The spread of television in the 1950s and 1960s was combated by distribution restrictions and product innovation. The product innovation was mainly to change the shape of screen to emphasize the bigness of theatre viewing versus home viewing. Other product innovations include sound development and gimmicks that have come and gone, such as 3-D glasses and devices placed in the seats to simulate shocking events on screen. The key distributive restriction was to prevent recent films from being shown on television. In the early days of analogue television the barring period was quite long. The advent of satellite and cable hastened the reduction of the bar to extremely short times.

There has also been a collapse in the tightness of product differentiation. Home-viewing screens now use the aspect ratio that became favoured in cinemas. In terms of production values and content, the distinction between a cinematic and a television film has become blurred. This began when major film studios moved into 'TV movies'. The advent of DVD has also brought scope for a 'literary' mode of consumption for the viewer who can buy multi-episode box sets of television dramas, that did not necessarily score massive ratings.

Price competition as a strategy has not been used much by cinemas. Relative prices of cinema have not, in any case, been unduly high, compared with other goods of similar duration such as live theatre, popular music concerts or team sports events. The shift to multiplex cinemas offered more choice and effectively tended to improve the travel costs situation. Multiplexes probably served to hasten the death of independent cinemas, which struggled to replicate the strategy not least due to small size. In extreme cases, a small independent cinema would give consumers the problem that the sound of a film in one screening room would leak into the adjacent screening room.

The ultimate competitive advantage of cinema has always been the quality of the experience, some of which depends on 'bigness', that is, the sheer volume of sight and sound on offer. The more distinct quality improvement aspect is the definition and clarity of the screen image. Innovations have been made in this arena with 'Cinerama' and the IMAX film format. This offers larger-than-life-size images in enhanced definition. However, this is not remotely threatening to enter the mainstream market. There are no commercial cinemas of this type. The number of titles is still very small, being largely restricted to a few nature documentaries and a Rolling Stones 'live' show.

In contrast, the home cinema market now faces a period of quality-based growth due to the resolution of the HD (high-definition) versus Blu-Ray format war. This offers the 'bigger is better' inducement to consumers and may create a small window against piracy during which only leading-edge copyists find duplication easy or cheap enough. As the number of television broadcasts using the new higher-file formats increases, the incentive to visit a cinema theatre will weaken.

We then come to the ultimate problem that is discussed in film and media studies of the 'death of cinema'. As home cinema consumption (which now must be expanded to include TV and Internet delivery) increases its technical quality level, consumers may come to expect that the same item will be delivered in the cinema. Historically there has been a dichotomy in home and theatre consumption of films, in that theatres would be exhibiting a costly 'print' on celluloid that is distinctly different from the exhibiting source used in the home or delivered to it by broadcasters. However, if cinemas shift to delivering digital content, then the wedge between home and theatre content shrinks greatly. There are still some factors maintaining it. One of these is censorship, but Internet delivery will tend to erode this also.

See also:

Chapter 17: Creative industries; Chapter 39: Motion pictures; Chapter 49: Pricing the arts.

References

Cameron, S (1999), 'Rational Addiction and the Demand for Cinema', *Applied Economics Letters*, 6, 617–20.
Fox, M. (2011), 'The Rise and Decline of Drive-in Cinemas', in S. Cameron (ed.), *Handbook of the Economics of Leisure*, Cheltenham, UK and Northampton, MA, USA: Edward Elgar.
MacMillan, P. and I. Smith (2001), 'Explaining Post-War Cinema Attendance in Great Britain', *Journal of Cultural Economics*, 25, 91–108.
Orbach, Barak Y. (2004), 'Antitrust and Pricing in the Motion Picture Industry', American Law and Economics Association Annual Meetings Paper 40, at http://law.bepress.com/alea/14th/art40.
Spraos, J. (1962), *The Decline of the Cinema: An Economist's Report*, London: Allen & Unwin.

Further reading

Although it is now a very old book, Spraos (1962) still provides an incisive commentary on the factors determining cinema attendance. The historical evolution of pricing in the industry is explored by Orbach (2004). Cameron (1999) provides the first attempt to apply Becker's model of rational addiction to cinema attendance.

13 Contingent valuation
Tiziana Cuccia

Contingent valuation (CV) is a method of estimating the value that individuals attribute to non-market goods (for example, public goods) or to some non-market values of market goods that the price cannot reveal (for example, externalities). CV basically consists in asking selected samples of population directly, in survey or experimental settings, what are they willing to pay (WTP) for qualitative and quantitative increments in non-market goods or values, or what are they willing to accept (WTA) to tolerate qualitative and quantitative decrements. Both WTP and WTA can be used as measures of the individual's demand of the non-market goods, services, or values.[1] The main goal of CV is to estimate the individual preferences for the policy alternatives proposed in the survey.

CV studies started in environmental economics, where their use is widespread. Later, in the 1980s, and mainly in the following decades, CV studies have been applied in eliciting the individual preferences for a wide range of cultural goods. Heritage, historical and archaeological sites are still the main objects of analysis (Navrud and Ready, 2002); they are typical examples of goods that in different degrees display the two characteristics of public goods – non-rivalry and non-excludability in consumption – that make them unprofitable for an enterprise to supply in the market. However, CV has also been applied to the evaluation of the benefits of other cultural institutions (theatres, museums, libraries and public broadcasting) and to questions of urban design.[2]

The increasing use of CV, compared to the other methods of eliciting individual preferences, depends on its extreme flexibility, which makes it easily adaptable to different objects of analysis, and on its capability to estimate all the different aspects that contribute to the economic value of goods: use values and, above all, non-use values or passive use values (Arrow *et al.*, 1993). These characteristics also justify the increasing interest of international organizations, such as the World Bank, that consider CV a useful informative tool to use in the evaluation of the development plans of underdeveloped and developed countries where the natural and cultural capital is significant.

This does not mean that the debate on the theoretical significance and the applicability of this method is over. There are many weak points economists have to take into account when they carry out a CV survey. Theoretical studies on CV aim at improving the structure of a CV survey in order to strengthen the validity of the results.

Adopting CV studies in public project appraisal represents a significant innovation from the political point of view. It means that decision-makers do not adopt a paternalistic approach but try to base their decisions on individual preferences. This is particularly relevant in the case of public decisions that concern cultural goods and services.

In what follows, we describe this method in more detail and the reasons why it is preferable to other methods in the valuation of cultural assets; we present the theoretical debate on the pros and cons of CV, and the role it can play in cultural policy planning, considering the CV studies in the cultural sector already carried on; finally, we trace what are the main fields of interest of the theoretical and applied research on CV.

The structure of a CV study

According to the taxonomy of the economic valuation methods of non-market goods (Mitchell and Carson, 1990), CV is a direct stated-preference method. The peculiar characteristic of CV that makes it different from the other classes of valuation methods – the direct and indirect revealed-preferences methods[3] and the indirect stated-preference methods[4] – is that individuals directly state their preferences for a non-market good or service by completing a structured questionnaire that is specifically prepared by the analyst to reproduce a hypothetical market situation where the good or the service can be exchanged.

The structure of CV could seem very simple. The main steps of CV analysis are: the sample selection, the description of the contingent market; and the choice of technique for eliciting willingness to pay. However, under its apparently simple structure many problems having to do with aspects of economics, psychology and political theory must be solved to obtain reliable information on the individual WTP and/or the individual WTA. Many of these problems have been discussed by the NOOA panel,[5] who suggested that a large number of stringent requirements must be satisfied in order to obtain reliable WTP estimates in CV studies.

The first problem concerns what has to be measured. The choice between WTA and WTP could be relevant in the case of cultural assets for two main reasons: first, because they have no substitutes; second, because of the loss aversion, or endowment effect, of the individuals who enjoy it.[6] However, the NOAA guidelines suggest a preference for WTP estimates.

The second critical point of a CV study concerns the stratification of the sample. In the case of cultural assets that have international historical and artistic recognition, the size and the stratification of the sample should be very large and should include people from everywhere. Obviously, the cost of the study increases with the sample size. Cost considerations can also influence the choice of how to submit the questionnaire (through in-person, telephone or mail interviews): this choice can have effects on the response rates (usually lower in mail surveys). Cost considerations have sometimes led to the use of 'convenience' samples but the WTP values obtained cannot be generalized in a larger population (Cropper and Alberini, 1998).

The third key point of the CV method is the design of the questionnaire. The increasing use of CV studies in policy decision-making and litigation (Natural Resource Damage Assessment) make the definition of a common design questionnaire inevitable. The NOOA panel focused its guidelines on survey and questionnaire design (Kerry Smith, 2006).

The main sections of the questionnaire are the following (Whitehead, 2006):

- an introductory section that includes attitudinal questions to find out what is the opinion and the behaviour of the respondents about cultural goods or services in general;
- a valuation section with the key questions on the WTP for the specific cultural good or service that is the object of the study. It must include: a plausible description of the hypothetical scenario to be valued, supported, if possible, by visual aids; the payment vehicle, to make respondents aware of the budget constraints; and the question on the WTP for the scenario described. Some follow-up questions

on the WTP questions should also be included to validate the primary valuation
estimates;
- a final section that includes questions on the sociodemographic characteristics of
  the respondents (age, income, profession, education etc.). This allows researchers
  to analyse the possible determinants of the price and the income elasticity of the
  demand.

The choice of questioning format for eliciting WTP in the valuation section is the most
critical aspect of the questionnaire design. Different biases would be present, depending
on the WTP elicitation question adopted. The two main formats are: the open-ended and
the close-ended or dichotomous-choice format.

The open-ended format that consists in the simple question 'What is the most you
would pay [for the cultural good or services]?' could prove difficult. Respondents have no
reference amount and may prefer not to answer the question or to give such a different
amount as to produce a high dispersion in the answers (Carson *et al.*, 2001).

The NOOA guidelines suggest adopting the dichotomous-choice format that requires
only a yes or no answer from the respondents on a stated amount for the item. This
format reproduces the situation consumers face every day in the market and in a referendum setting, and it has been shown to be incentive compatible, that is, it helps to
reduce the free-rider problem. The main weakness in this elicitation format, however,
is its statistical inefficiency. The double-bounded format (Hanemann *et al.*, 1991) helps
to improve the statistical efficiency of the dichotomous-choice format. In the double-
bounded format, after the 'yes' answer, a follow-up question with a higher bid (usually
the double of the earlier WTP) is asked; after the 'no' answer, a follow-up question with
a lower bid (usually half of the earlier WTP) is asked. This format, with its follow-up
questions, aims to find out in which interval the WTP of each respondent lies. A key
point is how to define the bid vector from which to choose at random the bid to insert
in the questionnaire. An open-ended or a payment-card CV survey is usually used as
a pre-test to determine the possible distribution of WTP. The double-bounded format
avoids 'starting-point' bias. This bias is connected to respondents' weariness, anchoring
and yea-saying. In the case of a double-bounded approach we do not have respondents'
weariness because there is only a single follow-up bid. Neither do we have an anchoring
factor because the second bid is very different from the first one. The yea-saying in the
second bid is less likely because the respondents in the second bid are a censored sample
with a WTP equal to or higher than the first bid. However, the double-bounded format
could suffer incentive incompatibility: the second WTP question can have a negative
effect on the respondents that, regardless of their true WTP, answer 'no' to the second
WTP question (Whitehead and Finney, 2003).

The questionnaire design is an essential step in CV studies. It enables the researcher
to minimize the bias and zero WTP values and increases the validity and reliability of
the estimates. The validity of the CV estimates depends on the consistency of the WTP
estimates with theoretical expectations about them (construct validity) and on the comparison of the WTP estimates with the results of actual or simulated market transactions
and with the estimates produced by other indirect revealed-valuation methods, such
as hedonic pricing, travel cost studies[7] and referenda[8] (convergent validity). Reliability
would require the possibility of replicating the study either in a different context or at a

different time (temporal reliability).[9] The validity and reliability of this method are still controversial, and the debate concerns both technical and theoretical aspects.

Theoretical debate on CV methods

The main positive aspects of the CV method are: (i) the opportunity to recover all the components of the total economic value (TEV), that is use and non-use values of a good or service;[10] (ii) its flexibility, which allows for analysing new policy options for cases in which data are not available (Hanemann, 1994).

The negative aspects concern the validity and reliability of the CV estimates (Diamond and Hausman, 1994). The main theoretical criticisms that make decision-makers suspicious of the use of the outcome of this method are:

- hypothetical markets and free-rider behaviour: asking respondents for a hypothetical payment is different from asking for a real payment, and they can act strategically;
- the embedding effect and 'warm-glow' hypothesis: CV results could be inconsistent with the economic theory. The WTP value for some specific goods is found to be similar to the WTP value for more inclusive goods; that is, the WTP to restore a single monument could be found to be roughly equal to the WTP for restoring two or more monuments (the embedding effect). In this case the normal economic assumption 'more will always be better' is not applicable. The hypothetical nature of the market investigated by CV studies and the positive attitude and moral satisfaction ('warm glow') that respondents derive from declaring a high WTP more for a worthy cause than for a specific good or service are the main causes of this effect, also known as 'scope insensitivity'.[11] These problems can be overcome by a careful design of the survey, which includes the use of focus groups and pre-testing. However, Kahnemann *et al.* (1999) argue that CV responses generally reflect attitudes and not preferences.

Further criticisms based on technical aspects concerning the questionnaire design are:

- *information bias*: information on the vehicle of payments (tax, entry fee, voluntary contributions etc.), on the current tax burden[12] and on other categories of goods, that can be in trade-off with cultural goods (e.g. health care, education etc.) influence the WTP responses. If respondents are not directly aware of the value of the cultural good that is the object of the study, the information provided can even determine the WTP responses. A low level of information increases the number of non-responses and zero WTP bids. Providing the right level of unbiased information and avoiding the cognitive overload of the respondents are important to correct design of the questionnaire;
- *positive valuation bias*: the common assumption of CV studies is that the cultural goods or projects always have a positive value. We do not usually consider the possible negative externalities of the goods or projects in view (Epstein, 2003).

Even the most optimistic experts on CV studies advocate caution in the adoption of the outcomes obtained in CV studies and suggest checking the quality (peer review) of the specific CV study: the review process must focus on each step of the study, from the design of the questionnaire to the analysis of data and presentation of results.

Why is CV useful for cultural economics?

The characteristics of CV make it particularly suited to estimate cultural goods (CG) that are not tradable on the market because of their non-rivalry and/or non-excludability in consumption. If the cultural content of a good or service is a 'common good', two kinds of rivalry can arise: an intratemporal rivalry in consumption due to an over-exploitation of this content that can cause its irreversible depletion, and an intertemporal rivalry because future generations cannot have access to this cultural asset.

The quantification in monetary terms of the TEV of cultural assets leads to the justification, on the basis of welfare economics principles, for public intervention in favour of CG and avoids the over-exploitation or the abandon of non-market cultural assets.

Some components of the non-use value, such as aesthetic and authenticity value of a good, are a significant component of the economic value of CG but can only be appreciated and ranked in qualitative terms by a restricted group of experts. Adopting a paternalistic approach in cultural policies may seem more appropriate. However, experts represent an elite and, in the economic valuation of the cultural policy, public decision-makers should mitigate experts' opinions with the preferences for the non-use values expressed by individuals that can be based on other components of the non-use value, such as a good's identity and symbolic value.

In particular, when decision-makers plan measures to preserve cultural assets, quantification of these assets in monetary terms allows them to rank possible means to preserve cultural heritage (CH) by taking into account the different motivations and to assign priorities when a conservation programme has to be planned within a limited conservation budget. CV surveys have the great advantage of allowing every individual – expert and non-expert – to express their different motivations for WTP in the same language and in monetary terms.

Moreover, a central cultural policy based on general taxation collects funds from everyone but gives benefits to only a very limited segment of the population who can afford to pay for cultural goods and services. A pricing mechanism, where it is technically possible, can be a more efficient and equitable funding scheme: if the price can be discriminated, public cultural goods suppliers can capture a larger part of the consumers' surplus and, at the same time, provide the incentive for cultural consumption of some low-income segments of the population (the young, senior citizens, students, teachers etc.).

CV is a useful test for policy-makers in assessing the likelihood of success of a pricing policy to manage cultural assets, to design the appropriate – compulsory or voluntary – private funds collection structure and compute the total revenue-capture potential, in addition to ranking cultural public projects appraisals.

Even if it is controversial whether the non-use or existence value has to be considered in the public project appraisal, a large body of literature shows that the non-use values of cultural assets have to be estimated: the values obtained are usually significant and sometimes exceed use values by a considerable margin (see Mourato and Pearce, 1999).

The application of CV in cultural economics

Compared to the large amount of literature that has been published about the evaluation of environmental goods and the damage they suffer from pollution, the empirical studies on the valuation of CG are still few in number. This could be just a question of time, as the increasing number of CV surveys on a large range of CG in most recent years shows. However, other reasons are possible: a stronger resistance on the part of cultural experts, a higher level of opposing and subjective opinions, a high degree of ignorance of ordinary people about cultural goods, the 'addiction' factor in the consumption of cultural goods, whereby the more people consume cultural goods, the more they can appreciate them, but if they do not have this opportunity their demand will be underestimated.

At present, CV studies concern a large variety of CG and situations, and this makes them difficult to classify and compare. We can distinguish CV studies by the type of cultural good or service observed and the type of the benefit estimated.[13]

In CV surveys on CH, which still represent the largest section of CV studies on CG, the valuation of individuals' WTP concerns different kinds of benefits: protection from air pollution, protection from abandonment/neglect, protection from urban development/ infrastructure, gaining access, maintaining the present level.

The objects of CV studies on CH are single goods (e.g., a cathedral) or multiple goods and services (such as a group of monuments, a group of buildings, an archaeological site and related services). Studies of multiple cultural goods should minimize the part–whole bias, that is, the overestimation of the WTP for a single item, which also includes the preferences for CH in general. Despite this classification, it is difficult to compare the findings obtained by different CV studies because they rarely follow all the NOAA guidelines and can differ in many aspects that influence the WTP estimation, such as the different format of the elicitation question (payment-card, double- or single-bounded dichotomous choice, open ended), the instrument of payment chosen (tax, entry fee, donations etc.) and the survey mode chosen (mail, telephone, and door-to-door). This is why the different WTP estimates as a percentage of per capita GNP cannot be used to rank CH and to define priorities for preserving them.

Nevertheless, some interesting observations emerge from the meta-analysis by Noonan (2003) aimed at verifying the consistency of the findings with expectations, and trying to extrapolate the estimate values to other cultural resources (benefit transfers). This study, based on the data from 65 studies on more than 100 citations reviewed, provides the regression of average WTP values on survey characteristics, goods features and information bias. It finds that door-to-door surveys, small sample size, archaeological sites and aggregated goods, and observance of NOOA guidelines such as on dichotomous choice are associated with larger WTP. Larger sample size and cost information are associated with lower WTP. A time trend is evident: WTP estimates seem to fall over time. Surprisingly, the payment vehicle does not seem to influence WTP estimates.[14]

A common characteristic of CV studies is the large proportion of non-responses and zero WTP bids.[15] This can be partially interpreted as a form of protest or a lack of interest of respondents in the survey. Some of them, however, could be expressing their real preferences or do not have sufficient information on the cultural good or service. A lack of information seems to be related to a high number of non-responses and zero WTP bids. The real problem is what to do with these protest bids: do we have to take account of them in the data processing?

Another common aspect concerns the different WTP expressed by users and non-users: the WTP expressed by users is higher than that expressed by non-users. Therefore the recreational and educational aspects of CG seem to be more appreciated than the non-use benefits that produce smaller but nevertheless positive values.

All these aspects can have economic policy implications. They can support the introduction of a pricing policy to discriminate among different categories of consumers. In the case of cultural tourism destinations, foreigners, national visitors and residents could have a different WTP for the conservation of the cultural items under investigation (Signorello and Cuccia, 2002).

Alternatively, voluntary contribution schemes can play a significant role in financing cultural initiatives, as the pioneering CV study on Durham Cathedral by Willis and Garrod (1998) and the CV survey on Napoli Musei Aperti by Santagata and Signorello (2000) demonstrate.

Further developments on CV in cultural economics

Further developments on CV studies may arise in both the empirical and theoretical aspects. The empirical aspects concern the design of the CV studies and the elaboration of data. Much work has been done on this, borrowing from other social sciences such as marketing research and psychology. Nowadays, using pre-tests, focus groups or other forms of interview (Delphi technique) that mainly involve experts with different backgrounds in defining the range of values to submit to the full sample selected for the survey is routine. It attests the importance of experts avoiding any paternalistic setting of priorities. The increasing adoption of the NOAA procedure in CV studies should help to get results that could also be generalized and transferred to other similar sites for which few or no data exist. However, much work remains to be done to better assess the validity and reliability of the estimates produced by CV studies and for benefit transfers.

Some lines of research are devoted to the refinement of the discrete and other types of selected responses to survey questions to reduce the overestimation of WTP that seems to be related to the adoption of the dichotomous-choice model. Other lines are interested in comparisons between estimates obtained by a CV study and estimates on the same cultural good or service obtained by other revealed-preference methods or experimental settings (Carson *et al.*, 2001).

As the number of comparable CV studies on CG increases, other meta-analyses should be carried out that overcome the present limitations in data availability and provide reliable estimates for benefit transfers. Research is also involved in improving the reliability of the data, and the stability and reproducibility of the results, with repeated surveys and tests over different periods of time.

One weakness of a CV survey is the radical choice it imposes (all or nothing). Fortunately, there are the indirect stated-preference methods (conjoint analysis and contingent ranking), which can be considered an evolution of CV simply because they simulate the real process of formation of individual preferences, which usually compare different goods and level of consumption. This is particularly relevant in CV studies that aim to investigate the WTP for different combinations of price and outcomes (for instance, more or less congested museums) or attributes of a cultural tourism destination (such as, accommodation facilities and local attractions; see Cuccia and Cellini, 2007; Cuccia, 2009).

The theoretical developments concern both positive and normative points. From the positive point of view, the CV method of estimating demand for public and partially public goods can be a useful instrument to test what psychological findings could be relevant to economics. Some aspects of the non-use values of CG can be easily reduced to psychological foundations (the sense of identity and cultural memories). CV surveys can also help to explain the motivations on which social preferences are based. It has been demonstrated that self-interested behaviour may not be the only determinant of individual preferences for the provision of public goods (Throsby and Withers, 1986). Rational free-rider behaviour is frequently contradicted by empirical research. The role of social preferences and altruistic behaviours can be tested in CV studies on CG.

From the normative point of view, the empirical aspects and positive findings mentioned above may be useful indications for policy. On the basis of welfare economics, policy-makers should choose the economic allocation of public funds that maximizes social welfare, resulting from the aggregation of individual preferences. Cultural policies are justified only if social welfare increases. In a context of increasingly limited public economic resources, cultural policies have to compete with other social policies that promote public health, social security, education, job opportunities and so on. To value the net social effect of alternative public investment projects, decision-makers adopt cost–benefit analysis (CBA), based on the comparison of the social benefits and costs of each project. The consumers' surplus estimated by CV surveys on a specific cultural good (e.g. a historical building, museum or site) is a measure of the benefit individuals attribute to that good; including this benefit in the CBA can increase the probability that a policy to intervene on behalf of that cultural good is preferred to other public policies.

Cultural policies based on general taxation have inequitable distribution effects: they benefit a very limited niche of consumers who, in most of the surveys conducted, show a WTP or willingness to donate higher than the access price or tax they pay. Therefore, where it is technically possible, pricing schemes should be designed to apply the efficient rule that the marginal cost has to be paid by those who really benefit from the CG. Greater use of reliable CV studies can help to pursue this possibility. The risk of underestimating the demand by individuals for cultural goods and services, because they can be appreciated only by educated people, can be overcome. The public authority, following this approach, should not supply CG as merit goods, but should provide individuals with the cultural instruments to appreciate CG and the technical instruments to express their own preferences for the arts.

Notes

1. To be more precise, the estimated demand function is the Hicksian (or compensated) demand, which tells us what is the minimum expenditure to acquire a good or to compensate the loss of a good that individuals are willing to pay (WTP) or to accept (WTA) and maintain their utility constant.
2. For recent reviews of CV studies, see Noonan (2003) and Snowball (2008).
3. The direct revealed-preference methods infer the WTP for a non-market good from the individuals' preferences revealed in associated markets (simulated markets, parallel private markets, replacement costs) or in a different context (referenda). The indirect revealed-preference methods infer the WTP for a non-market good from the consumers' behaviour in related markets: the housing market in the hedonic pricing method; the expenditure for defensive activities in the averting costs approach; the demand for outdoor recreational goods in the travel cost method.
4. The indirect stated-preference methods (conjoint analysis) refer to surveys where people are asked to respond as in a hypothetical market and indirectly infer the WTP for a non-market good from the individuals' responses.

5. The special panel of economists appointed by the US National Oceanic and Atmospheric Administration in 1993 following the *Exxon Valdez* oil spill in Alaska in 1989 (Arrow *et al.*, 1993).
6. The endowment effect has been developed and tested by Kahneman *et al.* (1990).
7. See note 3.
8. A referendum has been proposed as a good alternative to CV (Frey, 1997). The two instruments have different aims, however. Referenda allow you to overcome the obstacles inside the political economic process. CV studies can be used in different cases: litigation, introduction of new cultural services and planning a more efficient cultural policy design based on information about the consumers' surplus of different classes of respondents.
9. See Snowball (2008, pp. 163-4).
10. For instance, the TEV in the case of cultural heritage includes the actual use, the vicarious use (through pictures and/or films) and the indirect benefits deriving from the use revealed or not revealed by the market mechanism (e.g. higher hotel and restaurant prices in the area around the cultural asset). Connected to the use value, there is the option value, that is the value attributed to the possibility of using the cultural asset in the future for their own utility and/or the utility of future generations. The non-use or existence value has many components (aesthetic, historical, symbolic) that are linked by the fact that they do not refer to the use of the cultural asset.
11. More precisely, scope insensitivity exists if WTP estimates for a public good and a public good of greater quality or quantity are not significantly different (Whitehead and Finney, 2003, p. 232).
12. Information about current tax burdens can bias respondents' answers towards that amount (Throsby and Withers, 1986).
13. For a more detailed classification of CV studies on CG see Noonan (2003) and Snowball (2008).
14. Noonan (2003) himself suggests taking the results of his analysis with caution, taking into account the sign and the significance of coefficients rather than their quantitative dimension.
15. For further details see Snowball (2008, pp. 155-7).

See also:

Chapter 25: Cultural value; Chapter 28: Economic Impact of the arts; Chapter 32: Heritage; Chapter 52: Public support; Chapter 60: Welfare economics.

References

Alberini, A. and J.R. Kahn (2006), *Handbook on Contingent Valuation*, Cheltenham, UK and Northampton, MA, USA: Edward Elgar.
Arrow, K. *et al.* (1993), *Report of the NOOA Panel on Contingent Valuation*, National Oceanic and Atmospheric Administration, US Department of Commerce, Washington, DC.
Carson, R., N. Flores and N. Meade (2001), 'Contingent Valuation: Controversies and Evidence', *Environmental and Resource Economics*, 19, 173–210.
Cropper, M.L. and A. Alberini (1998), 'Contingent Valuation', in P. Newman (ed.), *The New Palgrave Dictionary of Economics and the Law*, London: Macmillan.
Cuccia, T. (2009), 'A Contingent Ranking Study on the Preferences of Tourists across Seasons', *Estudios de Economia Aplicada*, 27 (1), 161–76.
Cuccia, T. and R. Cellini (2007), 'Is Cultural Heritage Really Important for Tourists? A Contingent Rating Study', *Applied Economics*, 39, 261–71.
Cuccia, T. and G. Signorello (2002), 'A Contingent Valuation Study of Willingness to Pay for Heritage Visits: Case Study of Noto', in I. Rizzo and R. Towse (eds), *The Economics of Heritage: A Study in the Political Economy of Culture in Sicily*, Cheltenham, UK and Northampton, MA, USA: Edward Elgar, pp. 147–63.
Diamond, P.A. and J.A. Hausman (1994), 'Contingent Valuation: Is Some Number Better than No Number?', *Journal of Economic Perspectives*, 8 (4), 45–64.
Epstein, R.A. (2003), 'The Regrettable Necessity of Contingent Valuation', *Journal of Cultural Economics*, 27, 259–74.
Frey, B.S. (1997), 'Evaluating Cultural Property: The Economic Approach', *International Journal of Cultural Property*, 6, 231–46.
Hanemann, M.W. (1994), 'Valuing the Environment through Contingent Valuation', *Journal of Economic Perspectives*, 8 (4), 19–43.
Hanemann, M.W., J. Loomis and B. Kanninen (1991), 'Statistical Efficiency of Double-bounded Dichotomous Choice Contingent Valuation', *American Journal of Agricultural Economics*, 73, 1255–63.
Kahnemann, D., J. Knetsch and R. Thaler (1990), 'Experimental Tests of the Endowment Effect and the Coase Theorem', *Journal of Political Economy*, 98 (6), 1325–48.

Kahnemann, D., I. Ritov and D. Sckade (1999), 'Economic Preferences or Attitude Expressions: An Analysis of Dollar Responses to Public Issues', *Journal of Risk and Uncertainty*, 19 (1–3), 203–35.

Kerry Smith, V. (2006), 'Fifty Years of Contingent Valuation', in A. Alberini and J.R. Kahn (eds), *Handbook on Contingent Valuation*, Cheltenham, UK and Northampton, MA, USA: Edward Elgar, pp. 7–65.

Mitchell, R.C. and R.T. Carson (1990), *Using Surveys to Value Public Goods: The Contingent Valuation Method*, Washington, DC: Resources for the Future.

Mourato, S. and D. Pearce (1999), *Dealing with Low Willingness to Pay for Cultural Heritage: Statistical and Policy Implications*, London: CSERGE.

Navrud, S. and R.C. Ready (eds) (2002), *Valuing Cultural Heritage: Applying Environmental Valuation Techniques to Historic Buildings, Monuments and Artefacts*, Cheltenham, UK and Northampton, MA, USA: Edward Elgar.

Noonan, D.S. (2003), 'Contingent Valuation and Cultural Resources: a Meta-Analytic Review of the Literature', *Journal of Cultural Economics*, 27, 159–76.

Santagata, W. and G. Signorello (2000), 'Contingent Valuation and Cultural Policy: The Case of "Napoli Musei Aperti"', *Journal of Cultural Economics*, 24, 181–204.

Snowball, J.D. (2008), *Measuring the Value of Culture*, Berlin and Heidelberg: Springer-Verlag.

Throsby, C.D. and G.A. Withers (1986), 'Strategic Bias and Demand for Public Goods', *Journal of Public Economics*, 31, 307–27.

Whitehead, J.C. (2006), 'A practitioner's Primer on the Contingent Valuation Method', in A. Alberini and J.R. Kahn (eds), *Handbook on Contingent Valuation*, Cheltenham, UK and Northampton, MA, USA: Edward Elgar, pp. 66–91.

Whitehead, J.C. and S. Finney (2003), 'Willingness to Pay for Submerged Maritime Cultural Resources', *Journal of Cultural Economics*, 27, 231–40.

Willis, K.G. and G.D. Garrod (1998), 'Estimating the Demand for Cultural Heritage: Artefacts of Historical and Architectural Interest', in *Heritage, the Arts and the Environment: Pricing the Priceless*, Hume Papers on Public Policy, 6 (3), 1–16.

Further reading

For more on the economic value of culture, see Snowball (2008). For a review of different CV studies on cultural goods, see the monographic volume of the *Journal of Cultural Economics* (vol. 27, 2003); for CV studies on cultural heritage in particular, see Navrud and Ready (2002). A more general analysis on the state of the art in CV is provided by Alberini and Kahn (2006).

14 Copyright
William M. Landes

This chapter sets out the economic rationale for copyright protection and describes the basic structure of copyright law.[1] It shows that copyright law has an implicit economic logic. Its doctrines can be best explained as efforts to create rights in intangible property in order to promote economic efficiency.

The benefits of copyright protection

Copyright protects original works of authorship that are fixed in a tangible form. A copyright covers not just unauthorized copying but also rights over the distribution of copies, derivative works and public performances and displays. As we shall see, however, property rights in copyrightable goods are subject to significant limitations. 'Original' does *not* mean novel or creative but simply that the work originates with the author: that is, the author did not copy it from another person. Originality is a threshold question. Its purpose is to save administrative and enforcement costs by screening out low-value works that probably would be created even without copyright protection. 'Fixation' also saves enforcement costs because it would be more burdensome for a court to decide, for example, if an alleged infringer had copied the plaintiff's live jazz performance than one that had been taped or recorded (and, therefore, fixed).[2]

Original works include, among others, books, photographs, paintings, sculpture, musical compositions, technical drawings, computer software, sitcoms, movies, maps and business directories. These works all have in common what economists call a 'public-goods aspect' to them. Creating these works involves a good deal of money, time and effort (sometimes called the 'cost of expression'). Once created, however, the cost of reproducing the work is so low that additional users can be added at a negligible or even zero cost.

To illustrate, suppose the marginal cost of manufacturing and distributing a copy of a novel is one dollar, there are no fixed production costs (for example, typesetting and editing costs are nil) and the author incurs a $1000 cost (mainly his time) in writing the book. Once the $1000 cost of expression has been incurred, it can be incorporated into additional copies of the book at zero cost. Put differently, once expression is created it is not diminished by one or one million uses. In the absence of copyright protection, competition among publishers would drive down the price of a book to one dollar. Publishers would just cover their full costs, with nothing left over to compensate the author for his efforts. As a result, the incentive for authors to write books will diminish, as will the supply of new books. Copyright protection enables the publisher to charge a price above one dollar without worrying about competition from unauthorized copies. A price of, say, two dollars would more than cover the costs of publishing and provide compensation to the author, encouraging him to write new books.[3]

To be sure, some original works will still be created even in the absence of copyright protection. There may be substantial benefits from being recognized as the creator or from being first in the market, or the copies may be of 'inferior' quality. Creators may also use contract law or other private enforcement means to discourage unauthorized copying. For example, a software manufacturer could license the software subject to a contract term that prohibits the licensee from making unauthorized copies or derivative works. But a contract, unlike a copyright, would be difficult to enforce against third parties or subsequent purchasers of the original work. There is also the possibility that the creator will be able to capture some of the value of copies made by others by charging a higher price for the copies he makes. For example, the publisher of an academic journal may be able to charge a higher price to libraries to capture some of the value that individuals receive from copying articles in the journal.

In short, given the speed and low cost of copying as well as the difficulty of employing private measures to prevent copying, we would expect a decrease in the number of new works created in the absence of copyright protection. This leaves open the question of how extensive copyright protection should be. The answer depends on the costs as well as on the benefits of protection.

The costs of copyright protection

Unlike most ordinary goods, copyright protection generates access costs related to the public-goods aspect of copyrighted works. Access costs fall on both consumers and creators of subsequent works who substitute other inputs that cost society more to produce or are of lower quality, assuming (realistically) that copyright holders cannot perfectly price discriminate. In the numerical example above, consumers who value the work by more than the one dollar, the cost of making additional copies, but less than the two-dollar price being charged, will be deterred from using the work. This generates a social loss. Similarly, some creators will be deterred from building upon prior works because they are unwilling to pay the price the copyright holder demands. In this case, copyright protection raises society's cost of creating some new works. Paradoxically, too much copyright protection can reduce the number of new works created. To be sure, the copyright owner has an incentive to lower prices to potential customers initially denied access. But information costs and arbitrage may make price discrimination infeasible. In contrast, access costs are not a significant problem for most tangible goods. In a competitive industry, the price of a tangible good equals its marginal cost. Only individuals who value the good at less than its price (equal to marginal cost) are denied access.

The second major cost of a copyright system is administrative and enforcement costs. These include the costs of setting up boundaries or erecting imaginary fences that separate protected and unprotected elements of a work. They also include the costs of excluding trespassers, proving infringement and sanctioning copyright violators. Moreover, the public-goods character of copyrightable works also raises enforcement costs because it makes detecting 'theft' a greater problem. One may be able to copy a copyrighted work without the author knowing it. One cannot steal a car or house without the owner discovering it. Overall, the administrative and enforcement costs tend to be greater for intangible than for tangible property.

Separation of ownership

A fundamental feature of copyright law separates ownership of the copyright from the good it embodies. From an economic standpoint, this separation might appear puzzling because, normally, concentrating in a single owner all rights to a good will minimize transaction costs and promote economic efficiency. For a copyrighted work, however, the opposite is often the case.

First, consider a work that has many copies. Imagine that each purchaser of a copy of a Batman comic book also acquired the copyright as well. Then someone wanting to make a movie, television series or clothing collection based on the comic book might have to obtain permission from millions of individual copyright holders in order to avoid infringement. This would create potential hold-out problems and add to transaction costs, compared to the alternative of separating ownership of the copyright from the physical good. Then a potential licensee need only negotiate a single transaction with the sole copyright owner.

A related reason for separation is that it enables the original creator to earn a return to cover the cost of creating the work. Although each owner of a copy of the comic book might be willing to pay a little more if he also owned the copyright, this amount is likely to be trivial because the high transaction costs of dealing with millions of copyright holders will make it uneconomical for a potential user to license the copyright in the first place. Alternatively, if each owner of a copy had the right to license the copyright, transaction costs would fall but the price of the comic book would not reflect any premium for the copyright. Competition among holders of copies would drive the licensing fee to zero and, thereby, reduce the incentive to create the original work.

To be sure, the efficiency explanation for separating ownership of the good from the copyright is less clear for a unique work such as a painting or sculpture where copying is likely to be very limited or not to occur at all.[4] To illustrate, suppose *A* sells a unique work to *B* but retains the copyright. If *C* wants to reproduce *A*'s work, he must obtain access from *B* and a licence to copy from *A*. Typically, this will involve greater transaction costs than if *B* owned both the copyright and the work. But even here there are offsetting benefits from divided ownership. In the painting example, it will be more difficult for the artist to return to earlier themes because he risks infringing the copyright on his earlier work. Similarly, the author of a detective novel might be barred from writing sequels by the copyright owner. These problems will tend to multiply if the artist or author builds upon several of his earlier works in which he no longer holds copyrights. Or take the case of letters in which the copyright is held by the letter writer while the recipient owns the letter. The circumstances in which one desires to publish a single letter will be rare. Typically, the letter writer (say, a famous author) will have corresponded with many individuals. If a publisher desires to publish the collected letters, transaction costs will be lower if the author holds the copyrights (and retains copies of his letters) rather than numerous recipients who may be scattered throughout the world. A related problem concerns joint authorship such as a composer and lyricist who create a copyrighted song. Transaction costs are minimized because either the composer or the lyricist without the other's consent can license the song provided he shares equally the licensing revenues with the other party.

Doctrines that limit copyright protection
Because copyright tends to be a costly system of property, economics predicts that property rights in copyrighted works will be more limited than for tangible or physical property. Positive economic analysis of copyright law aims to show that various copy-

right doctrines that limit protection can be best explained as rough efforts to achieve the optimal balance between incentive benefits and access and other costs in order to promote economic efficiency. Consider the following important copyright doctrines.

Protection of expression

Copyright protects expression but not ideas, concepts, principles, techniques or processes ('ideas' for short). Protecting original ideas would involve substantial administrative and enforcement costs. From an evidentiary standpoint, it is far simpler to determine if *B* has copied *A*'s original expression rather than *A*'s original idea. In addition, most original ideas in copyrighted works are trivial and involve small expenditures of time and effort relative to the cost of expressing them. Hence the added incentive benefits from protecting ideas would probably be swamped by the resulting access and administrative costs.

Closely related to the idea/expression dichotomy is the merger doctrine. If we suppose that there are only a few ways of expressing an idea, protecting expression will, as a practical matter, protect the idea. Here copyright protection will be denied. Merger might occur, for example, in the case of instructions explaining a paint-by-numbers game. The game itself is an unprotected idea and the instructions are the expression. Since there is only a handful of ways of writing the instructions and the costs involved are probably small, the absence of copyright will reduce administrative, enforcement and access costs without having a significant effect on the incentive of firms to produce these games. A related explanation is that, since competitors are bound to produce substantially similar instructions whether or not they copied, it would not be worth the evidentiary costs to figure out whether copying took place.[5]

Protection against copying

Copyright protects against copying but not independent duplication.[6] Here 'free-riding' is missing, so independent duplication will not significantly undermine the incentives to create new works. Two other points reinforce this result. First, independent duplication should be rare for most works. Second, if independent duplication were actionable, authors would spend less time creating new works and more time checking earlier works to avoid copyright liability. This would lead society to expend greater resources on administering the copyright system in order to facilitate searching old records.[7] In short, since independent duplication is probably rare, it is unlikely that the added incentive benefits from making independent duplication actionable would be worth the extra costs it would entail.

Right of adaptation

Copyright gives the creator adaptation rights on his work. This right, called the derivative works right, is broader than the right to prevent unauthorized copying, for it covers 'any other form in which a work may be recast, transformed or adapted'.[8] Examples of derivative works include the musical *My Fair Lady*, based on George Bernard Shaw's play *Pygmalion*, mechanical dolls based on the Walt Disney characters, the movie *Clueless* based on Jane Austen's *Emma*, or a dance performance based on a Jackson Pollock painting. If the underlying work is not in the public domain, the party creating the derivative work must get the copyright owner's permission.

The economic rationale for giving the original copyright holder rights over derivative works depends both on the added incentives to create original works and on the savings in transaction and enforcement costs that result from concentrating property rights in a single party. Consider first the incentive argument. One might reason that the added incentive benefits will be negligible if only a few copyrighted works will generate income from derivative works. Moreover, there is likely to be a substantial time lag between the date of the original work and the later derivative works. This, however, confuses *ex ante* and *ex post* returns. Even if the number of copyright holders who receive substantial income from adaptations is small, the *ex ante* return, which depends on both the small probability and the potentially large income, could be relatively large.

Turning to transaction and enforcement costs, consider derivative works based on a Walt Disney character. Many ancillary products, ranging from umbrellas to lunch boxes, incorporate Disney images. By concentrating the copyrights in Disney rather than having each creator of a derivative work hold a separate copyright, the court avoids potentially burdensome lawsuits involving multiple plaintiffs. For example, how would a court decide, among many similar and widely accessible works, which one the defendant copied from? Licensing costs would also rise because a potential licensee would be advised to seek licences from many parties to avoid the risk of being sued by one of them. Finally, the copyright on the original Disney character will be sufficient to prevent unauthorized copying of the various derivative works since a party copying from a derivative work will still infringe the copyright on the original work.

Fair use
Fair use limits the rights of the copyright holder by allowing unauthorized copying in circumstances that are roughly consistent with promoting economic efficiency. One such circumstance involves high transaction costs. For example, copying a few pages from a book probably does not harm the copyright holder because the copier would not have bought the book. Here A might be willing to pay B, the copyright holder, a sum that B would be happy to accept for the use of the work, but the cost of locating and negotiating with B may be prohibitive if all A wants to do is quote brief passages from B's work. A fair-use privilege creates a clear benefit to A but does no harm to B, whereas, if copying were prohibited, transactions costs would prevent an otherwise beneficial exchange from taking place. Here fair use creates a net social gain. The copier benefits, and the copyright holder is not harmed.[9]

Another circumstance that justifies fair use may be termed 'implied consent'. Take a book review that quotes brief passages from the book. A book is an experience good so that accurate pre-use information about its quality is likely on average to enlarge the demand for it and benefit authors. A critical review may destroy the market for a particular work but on balance reviews will provide information to potential customers and thereby benefit authors. Moreover, if the law required the reviewer to obtain the author's consent to reproduce these passages, readers would have less confidence in the objectivity of the review, fearing that consent might well be conditioned on the reviewer's deleting critical parts of the review. And the more valuable the information, the greater on average should be the demand for the underlying works. In these circumstances, fair use can produce beneficial incentive effects and reduce access costs as well.

The final category of fair use involves some harm to the copyright holder that is more than offset by lower access costs and possible benefits to third parties. Here the courts are more likely to find fair use for a productive than for a reproductive use of a borrowed work. The former transforms the original work into a new work and reduces the cost of creating the transformative work since transaction and licensing costs are avoided. Still, deeming a productive use a fair use may result in lost licensing revenues to the author of the copied work. This loss, however, would have little effect on the incentive to create the copied work since the prospect of such revenues was largely unanticipated at the time the work was created. A reproductive use, on the other hand, is more likely to substitute for the original work and, therefore, have significant negative effects on the incentives to create that work in the first place.

The well-known 'veil of ignorance' concept provides a helpful way to explain why the law treats productive uses more leniently than reproductive uses. Behind a veil of ignorance, authors would be more likely to favour a rule allowing productive fair use because it would enable an author to borrow some expression from others and lower his costs, while his expected revenues would not change much when others borrowed from him. In contrast, a reproductive use risks substantially reducing the profits of the original author and hence his incentives to create the work in the first place.

Parody is often protected as a fair use. Parody can involve high transaction costs because of the difficulty of negotiating with someone you want to poke fun at. It provides information or critical comment like a review. Finally, it is a transformative use of the original work. Still, calling something a parody is not a blanket licence to copy the parodied work. Parody is limited in two ways. One is that the parody can only take what is necessary to conjure up the original work. It cannot take so much of the original work that it effectively substitutes for that work. The other is that the parody must be aimed at the work it parodies.[10] Here the economic rationale is that a voluntary transaction is less likely when the parody attacks a particular work than when it uses the work to comment on or criticize society at large.

Other copyright issues

Infringement

Evidence that the defendant copied from the plaintiff is usually circumstantial because the public-goods aspect of intellectual property makes it rare to catch a copier in the act.[11] The two key evidentiary factors that support an inference of copying are a 'reasonable probability of access' to the plaintiff's work (for one cannot copy without access) and 'substantial similarity' between the works. In some cases, striking similarity alone may support an inference of access. If the plaintiff's work is unique and complex, and nothing similar exists in the public domain, its appearance in the defendant's work is strong evidence of access, eliminating the possibility of independent creation. Once the plaintiff shows access and substantial similarity, the burden then shifts to the defendant to rebut the evidence. From an economic standpoint, this tends to minimize dispute resolution costs because the defendant possesses the information on how he created the work and, therefore, has the lowest cost of proving independent creation.

Finally, even if the defendant copied, his copying may not be illicit. The plaintiff must show that the substantial similarities between the two works relate to what the law protects: expression not ideas, the non-utilitarian parts of useful works, what was original in the plaintiff's work, and that the copied material was not a fair use.

Authorship and work-for-hire

Authorship conveys a bundle of rights because copyright vests initially in the author of the work. But since most works are the product of numerous parties, how does the law decide the question of authorship? One possibility is that the author is the person who physically executes the work. But that might mean that the Copyright Act would deem a typist or research assistant the author or joint author. From an economic standpoint this would be inefficient for it would lead to added contracting and transaction costs as the party responsible for creating the work would require that his assistants assign the copyright to him. Consistent with efficiency considerations, the copyright statute provides that the author may be someone other than the person who actually fixes the work in a tangible form, although it leaves undefined the term 'author'. A more modern view of authorship is that it lies with the person who conceives of the work and arranges for its execution. Thus the market regards a conceptual artist as the author even though he hires other individuals to execute the work.

Coase's theorem is helpful in both deciding which party or parties should be deemed the author and in showing the futility of legal rules that are inconsistent with promoting efficiency. Recall that the Coase theorem states that, in the absence of transaction costs, the initial assignment of property rights will not affect the efficient allocation of resources. Suppose A and B are involved in creating a copyrighted work, A values the copyright more than B does, and the law regards B as the author because B has fixed the work. Then the initial contract between A and B will include a term that transfers the copyright to A or, if the contract is silent on this point, A will buy the copyright from B in a subsequent transaction. If the law had deemed A the author at the outset, contracting or transaction costs would be saved. This suggests that the law would promote efficiency if it assigned authorship and hence the copyright to the party who values it more: that is, the party who would wind up with the copyright if transaction costs were negligible.

There is another conception of authorship that is worth mentioning. Here, the author is the party who finances the work and bears the financial risks, although he may delegate the creative decisions to the party who actually executes the work. The 'work for-hire' doctrine is based on this conception. A work created pursuant to an employment relationship (such as when Disney hires an animation artist who is paid a regular wage, receives fringe benefits and can be assigned to work on different projects) is unambiguously a work-for-hire. But a commissioned work executed by an independent artist may also be a work-for-hire if the commissioning party pays a monthly stipend, health and other fringe benefits during the time the artist works on the project, covers the cost of materials and exercises overall but not day-to-day supervision. Consistent with the Coase theorem, the work-for-hire doctrine lowers transaction and contracting costs by assigning the copyright to the party in the best position to exploit it. In the Disney example, transaction costs would be very high if each artist employed by Disney owned the copyright to his work. Then, each artist/employee would be in a position to hold up and delay projects (for example, publication of a comic book) that require Disney to coordinate the efforts of many employees. Knowing this in advance, Disney would acquire the separate copyrights before embarking on a project. By assigning the copyrights to Disney at the outset, the work-for-hire doctrine saves contracting and potential hold-up costs.

Copyright duration

It is worth mentioning a major economic puzzle about copyright – its long duration. Today, a copyright lasts for the life of the author plus 70 years. In the case of a work-for-hire, the term is 95 years. But from an incentive standpoint, the present value of $1000 in say 80 or 90 years is trivial given any reasonable discount rate. On the other hand, life plus 70 years can create substantial access costs (including the cost of tracking down the copyright owner and licensing the work) because a smaller amount of public-domain material will be available at any point in time.[12] Thus a shorter copyright term would reduce access costs without significantly reducing the incentives to create new works.

There are several possible explanations for a long copyright term. These include the possibility that the returns from copyrighted works occur mainly in the last few years, that the value of an author's earlier works will be enhanced by his later efforts and that a near-perpetual term avoids the 'tragedy of the commons'. The first argument appears factually wrong, based on an analysis of US data showing that copyrights were rarely renewed (for an additional 28 and later 47 years of protection at the end of the initial 28-year term) for works created before the 1978 Copyright Act.[13] The second argument might account for a copyright term that extends 20 or so years after the author's death, but not 70 years. The third argument appears to overlook the widespread belief that copyrighted expression is not exhaustible, so the tragedy of the commons does not apply. We called this the public-goods aspect of copyright works. Unlike natural resources that can be used up by overexploitation, previous editions of Shakespeare's works do not preclude publishers from bringing out new editions. This objection to a lengthy copyright term, however, is overstated. It overlooks the possibility that unlimited use of a still valuable copyright that was dumped into the public domain (even many years after the work was created) could create negative externalities that might reduce the overall value of the work compared to extending the copyright term. A related economic argument against limiting the duration of copyright is that it reduces the incentive to invest resources in developing markets for works that have fallen into the public domain.[14]

Indirect liability

An important question in copyright today is: under what circumstances can *C* be held liable for *B*'s infringement of *A*'s copyright? Since *B* is the actual infringer, *C*'s liability would be indirect. There are two long-standing common-law doctrines of indirect liability: contributory infringement and vicarious liability.[15]

Contributory infringement

Contributory infringement applies when *C* induces, causes, or otherwise materially contributes to the infringing conduct of *B*. Consider the following example: suppose *C* manufactures a decoder box that enables any purchaser *B* to unscramble premium and pay-per-view cable programmes without paying for them. *A* is the injured copyright holder who owns those programmes and *B* is the direct infringer. Should the equipment-maker *C* be held liable for *B*'s infringement of *A*'s copyright?

Two considerations are worth noting. First, there are probably substantial enforcement and administrative savings if *A* is allowed to sue *C* rather than pursuing each *B* individually. The costs of tracking down many *B*s, gathering evidence as to the specific activities of each, and then litigating many separate lawsuits involving small damages would probably make it uneconomical for *A* to enforce its copyright. Because *B* knows this in advance, *B* has little incentive to comply with the law. By contrast, if the law holds *C* liable for the total damages caused by the many *B*'s, the savings in enforcement costs are likely to be sufficiently large for *A* to enforce its copyright. In turn, the prospect of liability will most likely put *C* out of business and lead some or most *B*s to pay for cable rather than infringe *A*'s copyright.

Second, if there are lawful uses of *C*'s product, the case for liability is weakened. The 'lawful use' question does not arise in the decoder example because the decoder's only use involves violating the law. But consider a firm that makes photocopiers or personal computers. Such a firm knows that some of its customers will infringe copyright, but the firm does not have specific knowledge about any particular customer. Thus, even though substantial savings in enforcement costs might still arise in these cases were courts to impose liability, it is unlikely that any court would be willing to do so. The benefits in terms of increased copyright enforcement come at too high a cost in terms of possible interference with the sale of a legitimate product.

In some cases it may be possible for the equipment-maker *C* to redesign its product in a way that would eliminate or greatly reduce the level of infringement without significantly cutting down on the quantity and quality of lawful uses. In such cases, liability is again attractive. Often, however, these sorts of solutions are out of reach. For instance, it is hard to imagine a redesigned photocopier that would make infringement less attractive without substantially interfering with lawful duplication. As a result, holding the equipment manufacturer liable would be equivalent to imposing a tax on the offending product. The 'tax' would reduce overall purchases of photocopiers and it would redistribute income to copyright holders, but it would not in any way encourage users to substitute non-infringing for infringing uses.

The examples of the decoder box and the photocopier mark two extremes and serve to delineate the key issues. Holding all else equal, contributory liability is more attractive: (a) the greater the harm from direct copyright infringement; (b) the less the benefit from lawful use of the indirect infringer's product; (c) the lower the costs of modifying the product in ways that cut down infringing activities without substantially interfering with legal ones; and (d) the greater the extent to which indirect liability reduces the costs of copyright enforcement as compared to a system that allows only direct liability.

Vicarious liability

Vicarious liability applies in situations where one party – often an employer – has control over another and also enjoys a direct financial benefit from that other's infringing activities. A typical case arises where an employer hires an employee for a lawful purpose, but the employee's actions on behalf of the employer lead to copyright infringement. One rationale for imposing liability is to encourage the employer to exercise care in hiring, supervising, controlling and monitoring its employees so as to make copyright infringement less likely. Another is the cost savings from suing an employer rather than multiple infringing employees. A final rationale is that liability helps to minimize the implications of an infringing employee who lacks financial resources to pay damages by putting the employer's resources on the line.[16]

Consider the example of a dance-hall operator who hires bands and other performers who sometimes violate copyright law by performing copyrighted work without permission. It is probably less expensive for a copyright holder to sue the dance-hall operator than it is for him to sue each performer individually, both because there are many performers and because the dance-hall operator is probably easier to identify and to serve with legal process. Putting litigation costs to one side, it is also the case that dance-hall operators are typically in a position to monitor the behaviour of direct infringers at a relatively low cost. Finally, because performers are more likely than dance-hall owners to lack the resources to pay copyright damages, vicarious liability prevents the externalization of copyright harm.

It is worth pointing out that the threat of vicarious liability has encouraged dance halls, concert halls, stadiums, radio stations, television stations and other similar entities to look for an inexpensive way to acquire performance rights. For the most part, they do this by purchasing blanket licences from performing rights societies, the two largest of which in the USA are Broadcast Music International (BMI) and the American Society of Composers, Authors, and Publishers (ASCAP). The blanket licence gives licensees the right to perform publicly all the songs in the performing rights society's repertoire for as many times as the licensee likes during the term of the licence. The blanket licence saves enormous transaction costs by eliminating the need for thousands of licences with individual copyright holders and by eliminating the need for performers to notify copyright holders in advance with respect to music they intend to perform. In addition, the blanket licence solves the marginal use problem because each licensee will act as if the cost of an additional performance is zero – which is, in fact, the social cost for music already created.

Current controversies

Probably the most significant legal decision in recent years was the 1984 Supreme Court decision in *Sony v. Universal City Studios.*[17] The plaintiffs were firms that produced programmes for television; the defendants manufactured an early version of the videocassette recorder (VCR). The plaintiffs' legal claim was that VCRs enabled viewers to make unauthorized copies of copyrighted television programmes. This allowed viewers more easily to skip commercials, which diminishes the value of the associated copyrighted programming. Suing viewers directly would have been both infeasible and unpopular, so the programme suppliers sued the VCR manufacturers on grounds of both contributory infringement and vicarious liability.

The Supreme Court rejected vicarious liability because it did not believe that VCR manufacturers had sufficient control over their infringing customers. The only contact between VCR manufacturers and their customers occurred 'at the moment of sale', a time far too removed from any infringement for the manufacturers to be rightly compared to controlling employers.[18] The Court rejected contributory infringement because the VCR is 'capable of substantial non-infringing uses' – legitimate uses that in the Court's view left manufacturers powerless to distinguish lawful from unlawful behaviour.

Importantly, the main concern in *Sony* was a fear that indirect liability would have given copyright holders control over what was then a new and still-developing technology. The analogous modern situation would be a lawsuit attempting to hold Internet service providers liable for online copyright infringement. It is easy to see why courts would be reluctant to enforce such liability. Copyright law is important, but at some point copyright incentives must take a back seat to other societal interests, including an interest in promoting the development of new technologies and an interest in experimenting with new business opportunities and market structures.

Congress became involved with indirect liability again in 1998 when it passed the Digital Millennium Copyright Act.[19] One provision immunizes from indirect liability a broad class of Internet access providers, telecommunications companies and Internet search engines, so long as these entities satisfy certain specific requirements designed to safeguard copyright holders' interests. The Digital Millennium Copyright Act established a safe harbour: if these Internet entities follow the requirements laid out by the statute – requirements that typically require the entity to act when a specific instance of infringement is either readily apparent or called to the entity's attention by a copyright owner – they are immune from charges of vicarious liability and contributory infringement.

Probably the most talked-about litigation on indirect copyright liability is the music industry's successful lawsuits against Internet startups Napster and Grokster.[20] Napster provided software that allowed a user to identify any song he was willing to share with others, and it provided a website where that information was made public so that an individual looking for a particular song would be able to find a willing donor. Napster had the ability to limit copyright infringement in ways that VCR manufacturers do not. Napster knew that specific infringing material was available using its system, and it could have used that knowledge to identify and block at least some of the infringing material. With respect to vicarious liability, Napster could have refused service to users who were violating copyright law. Grokster provided software for peer-to-peer sharing but did not index the songs that users were willing to share, nor did it monitor what songs were being downloaded. Still, the Supreme Court held Grokster liable because (unlike in *Sony*) its product was mainly used to enable consumers to infringe copyrights in music.

Notes

1. Although I focus on copyright law in the USA, the principal copyright doctrines are similar throughout most of the world. For a more complete analysis, see Landes and Posner (1989).
2. See Lichtman (2001).
3. In the case of unique works, such as a painting, the case for copyright protection is weaker because the main source of income typically comes from the sale of the work itself, not from copies. Still, unauthorized copying or 'free-riding' on unique artworks will reduce the income an artist receives from posters, note cards, puzzles, coffee mugs, mouse pads, t-shirts and other derivative works that incorporate images from the original work.
4. Of course, *A* may explicitly transfer ownership of the copyright to *B* or to anyone else. Our illustrations concern default rules in which there is no explicit contract governing ownership of the copyright.
5. See Lichtman (2001).
6. In *Sheldon* v. *Metro-Goldwyn Pictures*, 81 F.2d 49, 54 (2d Cir. 1936), Judge Learned Hand stated that 'if by some magic a man who had never known it were to compose anew Keats's Ode on a Grecian Urn, he would be an "author" and, if he copyrighted it, others might not copy that poem, though they might of course copy Keats's. But though a copyright is, for this reason, less vulnerable than a patent, the owner's protection is more limited, for just as he is no less an "author" because others have preceded him, so another who follows him, is not a tort-feasor unless he pirates his work.'
7. It is worth noting that the copyright registration system involves minimal cost. Registration creates a public record of the basic facts of the copyright. An applicant seeking to register his work submits a

$30 filing fee and fills out a short form listing the work's title, author, year of creation, and date and place of publication (if published). The applicant must also deposit a copy of the work (or, in cases where this is not feasible, a photograph of the work). Registration is optional and is not a condition for copyright protection, though it is a prerequisite to an infringement action in the USA (but not in most countries outside the USA). The Copyright Office makes no effort to search prior copyrighted works for similarities with the applicant's work before registering the copyright. Registration information and forms are available online from the US Copyright Office website (http://www.loc.gov/copyright).

8. See 17 U.S.C.A. § 106(2) (2000) and the definition of a derivative work in 17 U.S.C.A. § 101 (2000).
9. The high transaction cost rationale should be narrowly construed. Otherwise, it would reduce the incentive to develop innovative market mechanisms that reduce transaction costs. These include performing rights societies like ASCAP and BMI, the Copyright Clearance Center for journals, and two arts organizations (Visual Artists' and Galleries Association and The Artists' Rights Society) that license reproduction rights to the works of many artists.
10. See Posner (1992).
11. In the case of maps, directories, software and information-type works, the copyright holder often deliberately includes a few errors. If the errors show up in the alleged copier's work, this is pretty good evidence that he has copied from the original copyright holder. This is known as the common error doctrine. It is useful in discovering unauthorized copying because of a special feature of the copyright as distinct from the patent system. Under the patent system, the patentee must point out and distinctly claim what he regards as his invention. In copyright, you do not have to identify beforehand the elements for which you claim protection. Thus, if you publish a book based on public-domain material plus your own material, you do not have to point out which is which.
12. I add, however, that, just as potential future revenues from a longer copyright term must be discounted, so must future access or deadweight losses.
13. See Landes and Posner (2003).
14. Both the negative externality and investment arguments in favour of an unlimited copyright term (more correctly, permitting copyrights to be renewed if they are sufficiently valuable to cover the costs of renewal) are developed in Landes and Posner (2003).
15. This section is taken from Landes and Lichtman (2003).
16. Note that employers are held responsible only for infringements that occur within the scope of employment. Infringement committed by an employee on his own time and for personal reasons would not trigger vicarious liability. See Sykes (1998).
17. *Sony Corp. of Am. v. Universal City Studios, Inc.*, 464 U.S. 417 (1984).
18. The Court took a restrictive view of what it means for a manufacturer to 'control' its purchasers. For example, the Court did not consider whether a relatively simple technology solution – say, making the fast-forward button imprecise and thus diminishing the ease with which purchasers can skip commercials – might have gone a long way toward protecting copyright holders without interfering unduly with legitimate uses.
19. Pub. L. No. 105-304, 112 Stat. 2860 (1998) (codified in scattered sections of 17 U.S.C.).
20. See *A&M Records, Inc. v. Napster, Inc.*, 239 F.3d 1004 (9th Cir. 2001) and *MGM Studios, Inc. v. Grokster, Ltd.*, 545 U.S. 913 (2005).

See also:

Chapter 8: Artists' rights; Chapter 17: Creative industries; Chapter 35: The Internet: economics; Chapter 55: Resale rights.

References

Landes, William and Douglas Lichtman (2003), 'Indirect Liability for Copyright Infringement: Napster and Beyond', *Journal of Economic Perspectives*, 17, 113–24.
Landes, William M. and R.A. Posner (1989), 'An Economic Analysis of Copyright Law', *Journal of Legal Studies*, 18, 325–66.
Landes, William M. and Richard A. Posner (2002), 'Indefinitely Renewable Copyright', University of Chicago Law School Working Paper in Law and Economics No. 154.
Landes, William M. and Richard A. Posner (2003), 'Indefinitely Renewable Copyright', *University of Chicago Law Review*, 70, 471–518.
Lichtman, Douglas (2001), 'Copyright as a Rule of Evidence', University of Chicago Law School Working Paper in Law and Economics No. 151.
Posner, Richard A. (1992), 'When Is Parody Fair Use?', *Journal of Legal Studies*, 21 (2), 67–78.

Sykes, Alan O. (1998), 'Vicarious Liability', in Peter Newman (ed.), *The New Palgrave Dictionary of Economics and the Law*, Vol. 3, Basingstoke: Palgrave Macmillan, p. 673.
Towse, Ruth, Christian Handke and Paul Stepan (2008), 'The Economics of Copyright Law: A Stocktake of the Literature', *Review of Economic Research in Copyright Issues*, 5 (1), 1–22. Available on line.

Further reading

Towse *et al.* (2008) is an accessible survey of the literature. Landes and Posner (1989) is the seminal article on the law and economics of copyright.

15 Costs of production
Mervi Taalas

The seminal study by Baumol and Bowen (1966) introduced the theory of production to cultural economics. Since then there has been continued interest in applying the framework of production theory in analyses of cultural services. However, compared to the proliferation of other approaches, the interest in production theory has remained relatively limited among cultural economists.

As to theoretical modelling, there is very little tradition of analysing production of cultural services in particular. The likely reason for this is the similarity of production of cultural services to production of other types of services: at the level of theoretical modelling, production of cultural services is difficult to differentiate from other types of services. For example, information asymmetries, monopolistic provision and difficulties of defining the quality of production riddle most analyses of the production of services.

The limited interest in empirical analysis of production stems mainly from two factors. First, there are fewer high-quality data sets available on production of cultural services than, let us say, banking or production of energy. The other problem is related to finding appropriate measures for analysis. Selecting measures for output and inputs in cultural services is often a complex problem.

In sum, analyses based on the theory of production have remained relatively marginal in cultural economics. Given the insights the analyses could provide into characteristics of production, this is surprising, particularly as the analyses could cast light on to topical policy questions related, for example, to efficiency, optimal input utilization and optimal output mix.

This chapter aims at establishing the basic tenets for analysing cultural production in the framework of production theory. It first introduces some basic concepts utilized in the theory of production that are relevant to studies on production of cultural services. Second, it surveys some examples of both theoretical and empirical studies that apply production theory to cultural services. Finally, the chapter points out possible avenues for future research.

Basic concepts

Production of cultural services by different types of cultural institutions can be described in the framework of the theory of production in which representation of production presupposes an *input* bundle, an *output* bundle and an illustration of the input and output correspondences, that is *production technology,* that indicate how inputs are turned into output(s). The production technology can be approached from the perspective of either inputs or output(s). The former perspective defines production technology in terms of minimization of inputs at a given output level, while the latter determines production technology in terms of maximization of output(s) with given inputs. Moreover, the production technology, either input- or output-oriented, can be modelled in either a quantity or price space. This means that input and output bundles can be defined in terms of either quantities or prices and, hence, the production technology (correspondence between input and output) can be defined in terms of quantities, prices or a combination thereof.

Traditionally, the correspondence between inputs and output has been modelled as a production function. The production function is an output-oriented representation of technology: production technology is modelled in a quantity space as a transformation of an **n**-dimensional vector of non-negative inputs x into an **(m-n)**-dimensional vector of non-negative output; that is, $y = f(x)$. The production function is generally assumed to represent the maximum output for given inputs, and some additional properties are generally posed in order for $f(x)$ to represent a well-behaved production function that depicts the economic behaviour presupposed in neoclassical economic theory.

A cost function, in turn, is an input-oriented representation of technology in a quantity–price space that represents the minimum inputs required to produce a given output or outputs. Assuming a vector of strictly positive input prices **p**, the cost function $c(p, y)$ can be written as the following minimization problem:

$$c(p, y) = \min x[p \cdot x: x \in V(y)],$$

in which $V(y)$ is the input requirement set that has to be non-empty and closed. In this definition the input requirement set $V(y)$ and the producible output set Y^* define the input–output correspondence: the input requirement set $V(y)$ contains all the input bundles x that can produce output level y; that is, $V(y) = \{x: (x, y) \in Y\}$, whereas Y^* includes all output bundles that appear in the production possibility set Y, which includes those pairs of input and output bundles (x, y) with which y can be produced by using x; that is, $Y^* = \{y|(x, y) \in Y\}$. Furthermore, a well-behaved cost function has the properties of (1) non-negativity, (2) non-decreasingness in p, (3) non-decreasingness in y, (4) positive linear homogeneity p, (5) concavity and continuousness p, and (6) differentiability (Chambers, 1989).

Shephard demonstrated in the early 1950s that cost and production functions can be used instead to represent the same input–output correspondence. This feature is captured in the theory of production *duality* which implies that, under certain conditions, it is possible to derive from the cost function the underlying dual production technology (Färe *et al.*, 1985).

Whether the input–output correspondences are represented in quantity or quantity–price space, the most frequently analysed characteristic of technology has traditionally been the scale economies. The *elasticity of scale* $\in (y, x)$ that can be derived from the production function is a measure of output variation associated with a simultaneous change in all inputs in the same proportion. Formally, the elasticity of scale can be written as $\in \equiv \partial \ln f(x)/\partial \ln | = 1$. The alternative measures – *elasticity of size* and *cost flexibility* – are derived from the cost function and measure the effect of output change on costs. The elasticity of size is the reciprocal of the cost flexibility that is defined as the first derivative of the cost function with respect to output. In fact, the concept of cost flexibility $n(p, y)$ measures the elasticity of cost with respect to output, and it can be written as $n(p, y) = [\partial c(p, y)/\partial y] y/c(p, y) = \partial \ln c(p, y)/\partial \ln y$. The interpretation of this is that, if $n(p, y) > 1$, smaller size production is more cost-effective, and if $n(p, y) < 1$, there are cost advantages in larger-sized production. As noted, the elasticity of size $\in^*(p, y)$ is the reciprocal of cost flexibility; that is, $\in^*(p, y) = 1/n(p, y)$.[1] According to this, an enterprise exhibits decreasing economies of size if $\in *(p, y) < 1$, and increasing returns to size if $\in *(p, y) > 1$.

Besides the scale properties of production, the performance of a producer in turning inputs into outputs is generally assessed using the notion of *productivity*. Productivity depicts how well inputs are transformed into outputs: the higher the productivity, the less inputs are required to produce a given output. Usually, productivity is determined in terms of *total factor productivity* (TFP), defined as a ratio of an index of outputs to an index of inputs. The variations of productivity between producers and over time have been of particular interest. Traditionally, productivity has been assumed to vary, solely owing to *technical change* that refers to a change in production technology. Recently, productivity has been interpreted as a result of a net change in output due to technical change, changes in *efficiency* and the environment in which production takes place. The change of productivity in time – *productivity growth* – has generally been defined as a change in TFP in time.

Efficiency can be defined by comparing observed and optimal values of output produced and inputs utilized. This comparison can be either output-or input-oriented and efficiency can be defined as the ratio of observed to maximum potential output obtainable from the given input, or as the ratio of minimum potential to observed inputs required to produce a given output level (Fare *et al.*, 1985). In both of these comparisons, optimum is defined in terms of the difference between the actual production and optimal feasible production possibilities determined by the production technology. Hence this type of efficiency is called *technical efficiency*, defined in terms of either Koopmans efficiency or Debreu–Farrell efficiency.

In addition to technical efficiency, efficiency also includes the notion of *allocative* (or price) *efficiency*. Allocative efficiency, introduced by Farrell in the late 1950s, implies that inputs are employed in optimal proportions in terms of prevailing market prices, and that the production process is economically efficient. In more detail, production is allocatively efficient where the ratios of market prices for inputs are equal to corresponding marginal rates of technical substitution: allocative efficiency is often defined residually as the ratio of cost efficiency to the Debreu–Farrell input-oriented measure of technical efficiency. *Cost efficiency*, in turn, is generally defined as the ratio of minimum feasible cost, given technical and allocative efficiency, to the observed actual cost. Hence a producer is cost-efficient if and only if it is technically and allocatively efficient.

Applications of production theory

Recent attempts to model economic behaviour of cultural institutions rely on models of monopolistic behaviour. The pioneering study by Brito and Oakland (1980), with reference to museums, looks at the properties of private market provision under conditions of monopoly. The analysis is based on a model assuming that museums produce excludable public goods, that the underlying production technology exhibits scale economies, and that production is unique owing to locational considerations. Brito and Oakland conclude that a museum, a local and private monopoly, will produce a suboptimal level of goods and exclude some consumers from part of the output actually produced, irrespective of whether the producer is constrained to a single uniform price. Moreover, the model emphasizes that it is profitable for the monopoly to apply price discrimination.

Hansmann (1981) portrays performing arts institutions as monopolistic non-profit producers that maximize their attendance, quality or budget. Moreover, the institutions charge an admission fee for their services, the production of which requires relatively high fixed costs. The performing arts institutions, however, are not able to set the fee high enough to cover the production costs owing to relatively high demand elasticity and restricted demand for 'high culture'. As a result, producers of performing arts must acquire private donations, depicted in the model as voluntary relinquishing of a part of consumer surplus, as well as being entitled to public subsidies because of an evident 'free-rider' problem connected to private donations.

Holtman (1983), in turn, depicts performing arts institutions by using a public utility pricing model, in which demand is assumed to be stochastic, implying that producers decide both capacity and price prior to knowing the level of actual demand. Non-profit producers operating in the markets are assumed to pursue a social objective that maximizes the expected consumers' willingness to pay minus total costs. This leads the non-profit producers to set a socially optimal price that covers operating costs, but no capital costs. The resulting low price of admission calls for rationing: different types of non-profits apply different rationing rules that reflect their ethical norms. In addition to a host of different non-profits, for-profit enterprises may also enter the market. The for-profits set prices and capacity in order to maximize profit and they remain in the industry only if the consumers are ready to pay a higher price for the assured availability of the service. Thus the main contribution of the model is to explain coexistence of non-profit and for-profit producers in the same market.

Taalas (1995) applied a mixed oligopoly model based on Bester and Petrakis (1993) to analyse incentives for cost reduction in a differentiated industry production of cultural services. The numerical simulation suggests that, with the simulated parameter values, the profitability of a cost reduction in the social optimum is always higher than in a private oligopoly or a mixed oligopoly. This means that both private and mixed oligopolies lead to underinvestment in a cost reduction relative to the social optimum. Besides this, the profitability of a cost reduction for the private firm is higher in a private duopoly than in a mixed one. In the mixed oligopoly there is a higher incentive for a cost reduction for the private firm if the public agency resembles a for-profit firm than when the public agency pursues mainly the consumer surplus. In all these cases the profitability of the cost reduction decreases when the degree of product differentiation increases.

The empirical analyses, for their part, have looked at the economic behaviour of different types of performing art institutions – orchestras, theatres, dance companies and opera – as well as institutions connected to visual arts: museums and galleries. These empirical analyses fall into three main categories. First, several studies stem directly from the Baumol and Bowen (B–B) thesis and focus on the growth of costs and stagnant productivity. Second, a multitude of studies look at features of production technology and particularly the scale properties of production. Finally, some recent studies examine efficiency of production.

Most of the empirical studies that assess the B–B thesis focus on comparisons between growth rates of costs in production of cultural services and general price level. This line of inquiry has been followed, for example, by Netzer (1978), Throsby and Withers (1979), Peacock *et al.* (1982), Baumol and Baumol (1980, 1984) and Schwartz (1986). They all suggest that costs in performing arts rise at a faster rate than in the rest of the economy, thus implying a continuously widening earnings gap. The underlying assumptions of the B–B thesis have attracted less attention. Felton (1994) addressed the assumption of stagnant productivity by constructing a rudimentary measure for labour input productivity in US orchestras. The study gives, contrary to the B–B thesis, preliminary evidence that productivity of labour input may fluctuate considerably in performing arts institutions. Taalas (2000) revisited the issue by using a panel data set (1978–95) on 19 Finnish symphony orchestras and concluded that production in orchestras is characterized by stagnant productivity that is the result of economies or diseconomies of scale cancelling out technical change.

Studies on production technology have generally employed the cost function approach. Globerman and Book (1974), who examined scale properties of US symphony orchestras and theatre groups, were the first to apply single-output cost functions. Throsby (1977) followed suit and assessed Australian performing arts institutions in the context of cost functions. More theoretically rigorous estimations have been carried out by Lange *et al.* (1985), who estimated cost flexibilities for different sizes of US symphony orchestras, by Jackson (1988), who compared cost flexibilities of different types of US museums, and by Paulus (1993), who examined scale economies of French museums. All these applications found different degrees of increasing scale economies, notwithstanding the producer type. Taalas (1997) was the first to allow allocative inefficiencies in a framework of single-output generalized cost functions. The results suggested the existence of moderate allocative inefficiencies and economies of scale in Finnish theatres. Taalas (2000) ventured to assess the underlying assumption of single-output production and tested different output measures by using cost functions together with structural equation models. The results called for multi-output analyses and pointed out the sensitivity of results as to the choice of output measure.

The trail of efficiency analysis was blazed by Gapinski (1979), who already in the late 1970s estimated, for US performing arts institutions, time-series transcendental production functions that allowed a variety of configurations for marginal products of inputs. The estimated production functions, which capture both technical change and divergences from the doctrine of positive but declining marginal products of inputs (technical efficiency), suggested, first, that performing arts institutions generally exhibit decreasing scale economies, and second, that both artistic personnel and capital input are over-utilized. The subsequent studies on efficiency employed non-parametric mathematical programming methods. The pioneering application is by Ek (1991a, 1991b, 1994), who assessed technical efficiency of Swedish theatres by using data envelopment analysis (DEA). Similarly, Paulus (1995) examined technical efficiency of French museums and Mairesse (1997) assessed efficiency of Belgian museums. All these applications found substantial technical inefficiencies in cultural institutions.[2] The results were confirmed by Taalas (2000), who applied the non-parametric Free Disposable Hull (FDH) method to cross-sectional data on Finnish museums and found out that a quarter of producers were cost-inefficient.

Conclusions

By and large, the previous studies on economic behaviour of cultural institutions have two distinctive characteristics. First, the studies have a tendency to treat different types of producers similarly. The theoretical studies assume economic behaviour of different types of performing arts institutions to be of the same kind, whereas the empirical applications have employed similar approaches even to performing arts institutions and museums: for example, Jackson (1988) and Lange *et al.* (1985) use similar single-output cost functions with similar functional form for museums and symphony orchestras, respectively.

The results of the empirical analyses appear, moreover, to be relatively similar across different institution types. Cost disease, it is argued, plagues similarly both performing arts institutions and museums: performing arts institutions and museums are found to exhibit scale economies, and production seems to be technically inefficient in both. Notwithstanding this, there are grounds for suspecting that production technology varies significantly between different kinds of producers: staging an opera piece by Wagner is likely to differ radically from setting up an exhibition of watercolours by Turner. This dissimilarity is strongly supported by Taalas (2000).

The previous empirical studies also fail to discuss the methodological issues or explicitly argue for methodological choices. This is partly due to the fact that the research has been to a great extent driven by policy concerns: the research topics, rather than methodologies, have dominated the discussion. Proliferation of methodological tools has, however, revealed a need to discuss applicability and relative performance of different econometric methods in more detail. Generally, the methodological choices should be based on the assessment of the objectives of the analysis, maintained hypotheses of the methods, computational ease and ease of interpretation. In the case of cultural institutions these four criteria are of interest particularly since caveats are derived from available data sets as well as conceptual and measurement problems related to inputs, output(s) and quality. Furthermore, the level of *a priori* knowledge on the production technology is often limited. The theory of production provides ample instruments for more flexible approaches that have lately increased in popularity.

Notes

1. In general, the latter concept, elasticity of size, is used rather than the concept of cost flexibility. This is because the interpretation of the elasticity of size is analogous to the elasticities of scale, whereas interpretation of cost flexibility is vice versa.
2. Since the non-parametric methods provide information on relative performance as well as level of excess spending, they are clearly public policy-oriented. This is reflected in the fact that all applications on production of cultural services have been done in European countries in which public subsidies are of great importance. The new tradition appears as the first European-driven line of inquiry.

See also:

Chapter 10: Baumol's cost disease; Chapter 44: Orchestras; Chapter 47: Performance indicators.

References

Baumol, W.J. and H. Baumol (1980), 'On Finances of the Performing Arts During Stagflation: Some Recent Data', *Journal of Cultural Economics*, 4 (2), 1–14.
Baumol, W.J. and H. Baumol (1984), *Inflation and the Performing Arts*, New York: New York University Press.
Baumol, W.J. and W. Bowen (1966), *Performing Arts – The Economic Dilemma: A Study of Problems Common to Theater, Opera, Music and Dance*, Cambridge, MA: MIT Press.
Bester, H. and E. Petrakis (1993), 'The Incentives for Cost Reduction in a Differentiated Industry', *International Journal of Industrial Organisation*, 11, 519–34.
Brito, D.L. and W.H. Oakland (1980), 'On the Monopolistic Provision of Excludable Public Goods', *American Economic Review*, 70 (4), 691–704.
Chambers, R.G. (1989), *Applied Production Analysis – A Dual Approach*, Cambridge: Cambridge University Press.

Ek, G. (1991a), *Jamforelser as teatrarnas produktivitet – en matning av institutionsteatrarnas 'inre effektivitet' via icke-parametriska produktionsfronter*, Stockholm: PM Statskontoret.

Ek, G. (1991b), *Produktivitetsutvecklingen vid institutionsteatrarna i Sverige – icke-parametriska produktions-fronter och Malmquist-index*, Stockholm: PM Statskontoret.

Ek, G. (1994), Att vara (produktiv) eller inte vara? – En matning av institutionteatrarnas produktivitets-forandringar med icke-parametriska produktionsfronter och Malmqvist-index', in *Den Offentliga Sektorns Produktivitetsutveckling 1980–1992*, Finansdepartment DS, vol. 71, Norstens Tryggeri AB, Stockholm.

Färe, R., S. Grosskopf and C.A.K. Lovell (1985), *The Measurement of Efficiency of Production*, Boston, MA: Kluwer.

Felton, M.V. (1994), 'Evidence of the Existence of the Cost Disease in the Performing Arts', *Journal of Cultural Economics*, 18, 301–12.

Gapinski, J.H (1979), 'The Production of Culture', *The Review of Economics and Statistics*, 2, 578–86.

Globerman, S. and S. Book (1974), 'Statistical Cost Functions for Performing Arts Organizations', *Southern Economic Journal*, 40, 668–71.

Hansmann, H. (1981), 'Nonprofit enterprise in the performing arts', *The Bell Journal of Economics*, 12, 341–61.

Holtman, A.G (1983), A Theory of Nonprofit Firms', *Economica*, 50, 439–19.

Jackson, R. (1988), A Museum Cost Function', *Journal of Cultural Economics*, 12, 41–50.

Lange M., J. Bullard, W. Luksetich and P. Jacobs (1985), 'Cost Functions for Symphony Orchestras', *Journal of Cultural Economics*, 9, 71–85.

Mairesse, P. (1997), 'Les limites d'analyse d'efficacité dans le secteur des musées. Actes', paper presented at the fourth AIMAC conference, San Francisco.

Netzer, D. (1978), *The Subsidized Muse. Public Support for the Arts in the United States*, A Twentieth Century Fund Study, New York: Cambridge University Press.

Paulus, O. (1993), Approche des coûts des musées', paper presented at the second AIMAC conference, Jouy-en-Josas, France.

Paulus, O. (1995), 'Museums' Efficiency', paper presented at the fourth European Workshop on Efficiency and Productivity Analysis, CORE, Université Catholique de Louvain.

Peacock A., E. Shoesmith and G. Millner (1982), *Inflation and the Performed Arts*, London: Arts Council of Great Britain.

Schwartz, S. (1986), 'Long Term Adjustments in Performing Arts Expenditures', *Journal of Cultural Economics*, 10 (2), 57–66.

Taalas, M. (1995), 'Does it Matter Who Stages King Lear? A Duopoly Model of Not-for-Profit and For-Profit Theatres and Numerical Simulations of Welfare Consequences', IGREG – ADDEC, ed. F. Benhamou, J. Farchy and D. Sagot-Duvaroux, Ministre de la Culture, Paris.

Taalas, M. (2000), 'Four Essays on Efficiency and Productivity of Cultural Institutions – Empirical Analyses of Orchestras, Theatres and Museums', PhD thesis, Department of Economics, University of Warwick.

Throsby, D. (1977), 'Production and Cost Relationships in the Supply of Performing Arts Services', in K. Tucker (ed.), *Economics of the Australian Services Sector*, London: Croom Helm, pp. 414–32.

Throsby, D. and G.A. Withers (1979), *The Economics of the Performing Arts*, New York: St Martin's Press.

Towse, R. (2010), *A Textbook of Cultural Economics*, Cambridge: Cambridge University Press.

Further reading

An introduction to the theory of costs of production is to be found in Towse (2010), Chapter 5 (editor).

16 Creative economy
Tyler Cowen

Over the years 2000–05, international trade in creative goods and services grew at the strong rate of 8.7 per cent per year; cross-country trade in such goods amounts to over $400 billion per year, according to one recent estimate (UNCTAD, 2008, pp. 4–5). Since this time, the concept of the 'creative economy' has taken on a central role in discussions of policy and in positive analyses of cultural economics.

The phrase 'creative economy' is used loosely to encompass a variety of concepts; UNCTAD's *Creative Economy Report* defines the creative economy as follows:

The creative economy is an evolving concept based on creative assets potentially generating economic growth and development;

- It can foster income generation, job creation and export earnings while promoting social inclusion, cultural diversity and human development;
- It embraces economic, cultural and social aspects interacting with technology, intellectual property and tourism objectives;
- It is a set of knowledge-based economic activities with a development dimension and cross-cutting linkages at macro and micro levels to the overall economy;
- It is a feasible development option calling for innovative multidisciplinary policy responses and interministerial action;
- At the heart of the creative economy are the creative industries.(UNCTAD, 2008, p. 4)

This concept of creative economy revises some of the central issues in cultural economics. Perhaps most importantly, the notion of a creative economy suggests that the difference between cultural sectors and non-cultural sectors is one of degree rather than of kind. Cultural economics has not traditionally focused much on sectors such as software, design, advertising, marketing and services more generally, but these activities appear to be increasingly integrated with the arts in the narrower sense of that word. Cultural economics is also moving toward a microeconomics with an emphasis on institutions, learning and local increasing returns to scale from creative activity. In fact at the same time that the creative economy concept took off in cultural economics, standard microeconomics underwent a series of revolutions in broadly similar directions. Krugman (1992) and others emphasized the concept of local increasing returns in explaining patterns of trade and the location and growth of cities. International economics and urban economics became more closely tied together and now cultural economics is joining this mix.

To offer a simple example, a disproportionate percentage of US carpets are produced in Dalton, Georgia, a city that has no obvious geographic or natural resource advantage in carpet production. Instead, once some carpet producers located in Dalton, others followed, attracted by the trained supply of labour and the infrastructure of complementary carpet production inputs. The growing population also helped the town finance amenities and thus it made Dalton a more attractive place to live. Dalton is now a leading 'exporter' of carpets (mostly non-artistic), both to other parts of the USA and abroad (Porter, 1998).

This parable has become illustrative of many forms of cultural production more generally. Hollywood is an obvious example of such a cultural clustering, even if most of the movies are shot on other locations. Applying the important inputs of project evaluation and assembly of the talent usually takes place in southern California. Most developing countries have similar talent clusters, whether in specific forms of music (reggae in Jamaica), indigenous arts (textile traditions), or fashion, design and advertising in the Indian economy. In each of these cases, and many more, cultural production seems marked by learning externalities and local increasing returns to scale. The cultural outputs of these regions are also closely tied to the more general cultural traits; the Indian design tradition, for instance, draws on a long tradition of iconography in Indian religion, temples, chromolithographs and so on.

Implications for cultural economics

The creative economy concept suggests some revisions to the standard approach to cultural policy and the issue of government subsidies. In particular, cultural policy is now seen as less separate from economic policy more generally, including urban policy, educational policy, transport economics and related inputs that help to shape creative clusters. For instance, good urban policies may be some of the best cultural policies we can institute. Economist and cultural analyst Richard Florida (2003) has turned this analysis on its head. He claims that cultural amenities are critical in driving the success of growing cities or clustered suburban areas. Older approaches suggest a greater role for the more traditional factors of quality schools, jobs, housing stock, weather and favourable commute times.

In any case, subsidy policy for the arts is less likely to be discussed in 'stand-alone' terms. In previous times, some analyses in cultural economics might have taken a single activity, such as an opera house, and asked whether it is a merit good or connected to social externalities. Today the inclination is to think more in terms of local cultural networks in an area, their robustness, and what can be done to support and nourish them. It's less of a top-down planning approach and more like a loose and indirect form of industrial policy, focusing on preconditions for creativity, rather than on any single or prespecified venture *per se*. Precisely because the analysis has become looser and wider ranging, it is harder to specify a very exact menu of policy recommendations. Still, there is an increasing recognition that what is done, or not done, in terms of policy is extremely important. The looseness of the topic has been taken as recognition of multidisciplinarity, rather than a suggestion of analytic nihilism. Cultural economics is now more closely connected to the sociology of science, the history of artistic movements, and cultural anthropology.

Cultural economics has also focused more on analysing the production and generation of ideas. Analytically speaking, production of ideas differs from the production of widgets. Ideas are more likely non-rival in consumption, as one person can borrow an idea without restricting the ability of others to use that same idea. It is also the case that idea production stems from favourable preconditions and that many important ideas fall out of good creative processes more or less by accident (Schelling, 1996). Finally, ideas beget more ideas and so creative clusters are often self-sustaining and self-enhancing, as has been the case with carpets in Dalton, Georgia. In other words, the production process for ideas is more social than firm-specific and it is harder for any single entity to manage, steer, or control it. Successful idea production for creative clusters is a mix of planned and evolutionary forces and as a result breakthroughs are often easier to identify *ex post* rather than to replicate *ex ante* according to any simple formula.

Nations, regions and localities know that if they nourish successful cultural clusters, those clusters can produce an enduring source of economic and creative value. They will produce outputs with values above their marginal costs for many years to come. It is the same difficulty of analysing and replicating such creative clusters that makes them hard to copy and for this reason they can be enduring sources of market power.

Innovative ideas also depend on the creative ethos surrounding individuals, and this is produced collectively and is not easily planned (Cowen, 2002). The worldviews and experiences of the eighteenth century gave rise to the styles of Haydn and Mozart, and it is probably impossible to replicate these styles today on any large scale; in other words some of the inputs we can no longer produce and thus some of the outputs we can no longer produce at high levels of quality. This insight helps us account for the classic notion, emphasized by the English literary critic William Hazlitt, that aesthetic 'progress' in the arts is not automatic.

The arts and development

The creative arts are now viewed as a possible engine of development for many poorer countries in the world. Precisely because these countries still have a unique background ethos, they are well situated to offer unique styles, moods and creative inspirations in their arts, even if they cannot compete technologically with the wealthiest countries in every manner. A stereo system produced in the USA is unambiguously better than one produced in Senegal, but when it comes to the music it is more a matter of taste and thus a Senegalese producer has some chance of gaining a market foothold, even in the USA. For this reason poorer countries often develop their cultural sectors by expressing their histories and identities rather than by abandoning or denying them.

Impact on productivity

The notion of increasing returns to scale from clustered production alters the portrait of cultural production suggested by the 'cost disease' of Baumol and Bowen (1966). The classic Baumol and Bowen example represents a string quartet that plays a Mozart quartet in 40 minutes, whether the year be 1780 or 2010. In this example it is hard to see where the productivity increase comes from, over time. Yet productivity increases in the service sectors have been frequent over the last several decades, and this includes many of the arts, including the live performing arts. The contemporary world offers new and varied ways of generating and trading ideas; this includes the Internet, social software, advanced database techniques, and new methods of training and feedback. The end result is that many forms of human labour are much more productive. If you read about a new play on your Twitter account, buy the ticket on line, and use your cell phone to meet a friend at the door, those are productivity advances for the arts, even if they do not look like such at first glance. The creators of the performance may well have used similar technology to discover each other's existence and coordinate their production and marketing.

Role of intellectual property law

As more economic value is embodied in intellectual property rights, copyright and patent law have become more contentious. To the critics it is obvious that current laws favour corporate interests rather than consumer interests or the desire to maximize the value of historic heritage. For instance, the USA repeatedly extends copyright terms to protect corporate profits, even when this would not appear to do much to increase the incentive for valuable current production. The traditional doctrine in US law of 'fair use' is interpreted fairly strictly, when arguably cultural borrowing should be made easier rather than harder. Many free trade agreements are as much about intellectual property rights as anything else. Technological developments, namely the ease of digital copying, have raised the question of how well intellectual property rights can be protected for music and movies at all. The number of illegal music downloads, for instance, far exceeds the number of paid, legal music purchases, and that is likely to remain the case for the foreseeable future.

Times change

The fragility of creative clusters has not received full research attention. World War II, for instance, appears to have destroyed many European cultural clusters. Paris is no longer the world centre for painting and the Germanic lands have lost their commanding lead in producing first-rate classical composers. Italy is no longer pre-eminent in the composition and production of new operas. Preventing human capital from fleeing seems to be of critical importance, as New York City received a great deal of artistic talent from Europe and shortly thereafter assumed a dominant cultural role for decades. Today, with the spread of the Internet, it is an open question whether urbanized cultural clusters will retain their previous importance. It is today much easier to learn, work and sell one's cultural products at a distance and so the relationship between the creative economy and spatial economics is changing rapidly.

In sum, the notion of 'creative economy' is driving a good deal of research in cultural economics. It is an important topic, and commonly regarded as such, even though firm and definite answers are not likely to be forthcoming in the foreseeable future.

See also:

Chapter 18: Creativity; Chapter 21; Cultural districts; Chapter 27: Digitalization.

References

Baumol, William J. and William G. Bowen (1966), *Performing Arts – The Economic Dilemma*, New York: Twentieth Century Fund.
Cowen, Tyler (2002), *Creative Destruction: How Globalization is Changing the World's Cultures*, Princeton, NJ: Princeton University Press.
Cowen, Tyler (2008), 'Why Everything has Changed: The Recent Revolution in Cultural Economics', *Journal of Cultural Economics*, 32 (4), 261–73.
Florida, Richard (2003), *The Rise of the Creative Class: How It's Transforming Work, Leisure, Community, and Everyday Life*, New York: Basic Books.
Krugman, Paul (1992), *Geography and Trade*, Cambridge, MA: MIT Press.
Porter, Michael E. (1998), *The Competitive Advantage of Nations*, New York: Free Press.
Potts, Jason, Stuart Cunningham, John Hartley, and Paul Ormerod (2008) 'Social Network Markets: A New Definition of the Creative Industries', *Journal of Cultural Economics*, 32 (3), 167–85.
Schelling, Thomas C. (1996), 'Research by Accident', *Technological Forecasting and Social Change*, 53, 15–20.

Towse, Ruth (2008), 'Why Has Cultural Economics Ignored Copyright?', *Journal of Cultural Economics*, 32, 4, 243–59.
UNCTAD (2008), *Creative Economy Report 2008*, Geneva, UNCTAD, on line at http://www.unctad.org/en/docs/ditc20082cer_en.pdf.

Further reading

See also Cowen (2008), Potts *et al.* (2008) and Towse (2008).

17 Creative industries
Ruth Towse

By the end of the twentieth century, the term 'creative industries' had been adopted by the UK government, whose 1998 *Creative Industries Mapping Document* triggered a wider interest in the topic, while Richard Caves's influential book *Creative Industries* (Caves, 2000) brought mainstream economics into the analysis of these industries. A decade later 'creative industries' had become an established concept, although the previous term, 'cultural industries', is also in use and still preferred by some. 'Creative industries' seems to chime with the creative economy 'paradigm'[1] that has been adopted by many national governments and by international organizations, notably in the *Creative Economy Report 2008*, produced by a consortium of United Nations agencies (UNCTAD, 2008). In essence, the term 'creative industries' puts together the creative and performing arts with cultural industries, which variously include advertising, architecture, the art and antiques market, crafts, design, fashion, film, games, heritage services/museums and libraries, the Internet, publishing, software, television and radio, and video. This list is a compendium of those industries mentioned under different classification systems discussed in the *Report* (UNCTAD, 2008, p. 13). Other classifications involve ordering the industries or part of their activities as 'core' and 'peripheral' or 'wider' in terms of the degree of creativity entailed in their output or, as discussed below, in terms of the engagement with copyright.

The cultural industries have been defined as consisting of firms that mass-produce goods and services with sufficient artistic content to be considered creative and culturally significant. The essential features are the combination of industrial-scale production with creative content. The creative content mostly results from work by trained artists, or 'creators', as they are now often known – creative artists, performers, craftspeople, designers – people who may be self-employed freelancers or employees of firms in the creative industries. That is the first stage in the production of goods and services that are supplied to the market by both for-profit commercial enterprises and non-profit organizations. Mass production, however, is not routinely a feature of the live performing arts or visual arts, and so the overlap between the creative industries and the cultural industries is not complete. Although digitalization is altering even those activities, it will probably not erode the artisanal qualities of those (and other) arts for some time to come.

Commercialization
The possibility of commercial mass production is due to the development of technologies – printing, sound recording, photography, film, video, the Internet, digitalization – and the growth of the cultural industries gathered force during the twentieth century. Reproduction techniques, such as printing and lithography, had, of course, existed for several centuries, but did not permit large-scale output of modern technologies. The term 'cultural industry' (in the singular) was first introduced by Adorno and Horkheimer to disparage 'low' culture, which they believed necessarily resulted from repeated output,

distinguishing it from 'high' culture produced by 'true artists' whom they believed would not repeat a work of art and who would have no concern with commercialization. The theme of the commercialization of art and culture dominated the literature on cultural industries that was written almost entirely by sociologists or political economists until the 1990s. By contrast, the contemporary notion of creative industries clearly includes both high and low culture, and makes no distinction between them on artistic grounds. This is in keeping with a world in which there is a great deal of cross-over activity on the part of both producers and consumers of cultural goods and services.

Over the last 20 years or so, there has been a burst of interest by cultural economists in the creative industries, especially in television, film and music, in addition to a long-term interest in the economics of the arts and heritage; economists are also active in media economics and in the economics of copyright in these industries (Towse, 2008). The shift in policy circles, though, is what is responsible for the now-dominant view that the future generation of wealth and economic growth relies on creativity and the creative industries in the world of the creative economy. Rather than the view that it is wealth that drives creativity (held among others by John Maynard Keynes), that position is reversed and creativity is viewed as the engine of wealth creation.

There is also concern in policy circles, though, that commercialization of culture via international trade in creative goods and services (globalization) has led to homogeneity. To some, free trade needs to be curbed by interventionist policies to protect national cultures, while others welcome the effect of unregulated market forces as stimulating creativity and diversity. Cultural economics has accordingly been involved with the question of cultural diversity; Acheson and Maule (2006) review these arguments.

Work by cultural economists on the creative industries can be basically classified as, on the one hand, macroeconomic measurement of the economic contribution of the creative industries to national income or gross domestic product (GDP), and, on the other, the application of microeconomic theory of production and supply that utilizes the neoclassical theory of the firm, contract theory and transaction cost economics to analyse the economic organization of the creative industries.

Measuring the creative industries

In the 1980s, when systematic collection of data on the arts and cultural industries began, the question arose of how to define the 'low-culture' commercial cultural industries in order to distinguish them from 'high' culture produced by non-profit organizations. The presence or absence of state subsidy seemed a likely criterion. International comparisons, however, revealed that for-profit firms were in receipt of subsidy for some purposes (for example, publishing contemporary music or poetry) and that industries that were subsidized in one country were successful profit-making enterprises in another (for example, the press). Moreover, even if the cultural industries in a country do not receive subsidy, they are often regulated either by copyright law or by specific cultural policy measures, such as those in the audiovisual sector.

It is frequently said that the arts economy is ill served by standard national statistics. That applies particularly to the cultural industries, whose products appear under many different industry classifications. The guiding principle that is increasingly adopted for unifying the creative industries is their reliance upon copyright law to protect the creative or cultural content, that is, the intellectual property. Thus 'industries protected by copyright' have become virtually synonymous with the creative industries and they have been measured in those terms for their contribution to GDP in a number of countries (reviewed in *RERCI*, 2004).

There are many problems with the figures that have been produced for the creative industries. Because they are only now becoming recognized as a sector in national income accounting by countries' statistical authorities, early data were gathered from a multitude of sources and measured in different ways (value-added, market size, turnover); in some cases, data were used (and still may be) from industry-led bodies or organizations with some sort of axe to grind (as with data on copyright piracy, for example); moreover, the way the industries are classified varies considerably (UNCTAD, 2008). Data therefore may not be internally compatible or comparable across countries. The creative industries 'paradigm' has led to considerable improvement in data collection and statistical analysis within countries, although not yet for international comparison (Towse, 2010b).

In most developed countries in which the size of the 'creative sector' has been measured, its contribution to GDP exceeds that of manufacturing (which is a declining sector); individual industries may also be higher-than-average exporters (film in the USA, music in the UK, publishing in the Netherlands). In those countries where measures have been made over several years, their growth rate is therefore higher than that of the whole economy. It is also believed that the creative industries offer good employment prospects, but the measurement of cultural employment and earnings in this sector is so fraught with difficulties that such claims are hard to verify (Towse, 2010a).

It is worth stressing, however, that what is of more interest to cultural economists than size (and so-called 'economic importance' is not an economic concept!) is the organization and other economic features of the cultural industries.

Economic characteristics

'Are the cultural industries different?' is a question that has been very important in cultural economics. After all, if cultural industries or organizations are no different from those in the rest of the economy, why do we need a special field to study them? The same question applies to artists' labour markets. A quick answer is that what makes them different are the economic characteristics of cultural content production or 'creativity'. This theme is developed below.

The creative industries share features of other knowledge or information goods producers. First, the fixed cost of producing the original master copy is high, whereas the marginal cost of making copies is very low, even approaching zero – the classic characteristics of a natural monopoly – which suggests that either subsidy or price regulation is in order. This feature has become even more marked with digitalization. Second, their products are risky and subject to radically uncertain reception by consumers, which results in a very high failure rate (ratio of financial successes to flops) that adds to firms' fixed costs and exacerbates barriers to entry due to high initial capital requirements for production and global marketing. It is generally held by cultural economists that success of individual titles in the publishing, film and record industries cannot be predicted from any specific characteristic, such as star participation or the amount of financial outlay. Barriers to entry are also present because products are protected by intellectual property law (patents, copyright, trademarks, design rights). These characteristics offer at least a partial explanation for the observed concentration of ownership and control. There seem to be not only economies of scale but also economies of scope and network economies, enabling a few large corporations to dominate the production of all types of cultural goods. It is this tendency to market concentration that has led political economists in particular to the view that culture is being increasingly homogenized worldwide by global capitalism.

Industrial organization and contracting

Industrial organization is the field of economics that analyses the structure of firms, industries and markets, dealing with questions such as competition and price-setting. Caves (2000) applies this analysis to the creative industries, taking the stance that they differ from other industries in significant ways.

It is useful to think of cultural production as consisting of two distinct aspects, content creation and its delivery – the former is the province of the artist and the latter that of the businessman. Caves calls this second element of the combination of art and commerce 'humdrum' inputs – a memorable tag. Humdrum inputs, in fact, constitute a substantial portion of the outlay of firms in the creative industries – think of the promotion and distribution costs of a film or of a new pop CD or game. These products have particular characteristics that led Caves to an overarching analysis: they require sequential (often large) outlays of sunk capital on the humdrum side and considerable coordination of creative workers with different skills for content creation. At every stage in this entrepreneurial activity, contracts need to be made to enable delivery of the final output at a specific date (the 'opening'). Because of uncertainty ('nobody knows') about the quality and novelty of creative input, however, contracts cannot stipulate fully all details or envisage all contingencies and therefore cannot provide optimal incentives to input suppliers. Contracts are therefore 'incomplete'. Caves's analysis of the creative industries has at its core organizational structures that overcome, or at least minimize, the potential losses of capital outlay to entrepreneurs in the whole production process from content creation to delivery in the marketplace in conditions of radical uncertainty. That is what determines the economic organization of markets in the creative industries. Moreover, the individual artist/creator of the creative content also faces uncertainty and is typically in a weak bargaining position in contracting with the commercial entrepreneur over payments and the transfer of rights.

According to Caves's analysis, the simple hand-shake contract between a visual artist and his or her dealer is subject to the same economic problems as a contract between all the different participants in movie production, the only difference being the complexity of the creation and delivery process and the sheer number of people and amount of money involved in the latter. The movie industry, in fact, offers a particularly interesting case study because its structure was changed dramatically by the coincidence of a single institutional change, the anti-trust ruling of the 'Paramount case' with the swift adoption of a new medium – television. The Paramount case destroyed the control movie producers had had over cinema. The so-called 'Hollywood studio' system, in which artists were hired on salary with exclusive long-term contracts, broke down and was replaced by what is called 'flexible specialization'. With flexible specialization, content creators freelance on short-term contracts, thereby sharing risk with the cultural industry entrepreneurs, who no longer have the incentive to invest in their training and development

(Storper, 1989). This is a striking example of the unintended consequences of a legal ruling exaggerating the effects of technological progress that can give rise to profound effects on labour markets. The creative industries are all subject to such changes, whether from policy, such as legal changes, or from technical progress, notably home copying technologies, digitalization and the Internet.

The gatekeeper role

Caves (2000) also notes the important intermediary or 'market-making' function of 'gatekeeping', a concept adopted from sociology. Sociologists see markets as forms of mediation between buyers and sellers that are social, even power, relationships, forming the fabric of society. In economics, the supplier of a good or service is thought of as simply putting on the market something that buyers are prepared to pay for; the profit motive ensures that consumer sovereignty rules, more or less, depending upon the degree of competition in the market. Producers will not, at least in the medium to long run, produce goods no one wants, and they cannot force or even persuade them to pay for goods they do not wish to buy. Gatekeeping is an interim process that takes place within the chain of production and effectively determines the nature of cultural supply.

Firms in the creative industries perform the task of selecting which items to produce and market from an abundant (even excess) supply of creative content and therefore they decide what cultural goods and services are offered to consumers – which music or books are on offer, or whether poetry is available at all. The desire to maximize profits and/or to ensure the long-run growth of the firm does not, however, have a neutral effect upon cultural production, and that in turn affects cultural development. Thus, if record companies believe hip hop or heavy metal will be commercially successful, they can influence youth culture; or if publishers think their women readers can cope only with love stories with happy endings, they commission works of authors producing those stories and do not publish others of greater literary merit or social significance, thereby perpetuating a female stereotype. Firms in the creative industries, whether for profit or non-profit organizations, act as filters or mediate between artists and the consumer, with the power to influence artists' careers and cultural output.

Copyright and creative industries

Copyright has become almost synonymous with the creative industries, and nowhere more so than in the World Intellectual Property Organization's (WIPO) 2003 *Guide on Surveying the Economic Contribution of the Copyright-Based Industries*, which classifies activities in these industries and ranks them in terms of their 'dependence' on copyright. The production of cultural content is the so-called 'core copyright' activity and the classification fans out to those activities concerned with its distribution as being more or less dependent upon copyright. WIPO is only one of the UN agencies that brackets together copyright and creative industries, however, as the *Creative Economy Report 2008* demonstrates. In fact, many national policy documents and those of the EU do the same – some going further with the claim that copyright is essential for creativity itself. It is all too easy therefore to believe that there is a causal relation between the two and that copyright is the driver of the creative industries and hence of the creative economy. There is no economic evidence to date, however, of the responsiveness of cultural production to changes in copyright, for instance that strengthening copyright increases creative output, a claim that is frequently made by creative industry lobbyists (Towse, 2010a). Even the economic effects of unauthorized copying ('piracy') on production have proved difficult to evaluate.

The economic case for copyright is that without statutory property rights for authors and publishers, the production and dissemination of new works would be less than that which is socially desirable. This evokes the 'public-goods' characteristics of information and knowledge that point to underinvestment in them for the reason that, without the ability to control their use, sufficient revenues from their sale cannot be appropriated to make it worthwhile to produce them. So, copyright is a solution to the financing of cultural production and it works through market forces: by being able to control the rights to a work in copyright, the rights holder can set a price for a copy that is above the cost of producing it and that provides 'extra' revenue that can be used to finance the initial outlay on the creation of the work – the economic incentive that copyright law offers. Copyright has costs and benefits, however, and overly strong copyright protection of one generation of authors and publishers imposes higher costs on the next due to search and information costs. The economics of copyright tells us that costs and benefits must be balanced in order to find the optimal strength of copyright, meaning its term, scope and degree of enforcement, but they are very difficult to calculate, especially as technological development is altering them all the time. The law always lags behind technical change and risks being out of date; new rights have had to be introduced to deal with digital material and satellite dissemination, for instance. Markets adapt more quickly and that leads to the view that the law should be technologically neutral so as not to impede technological progress.

Digitalization has presented interesting questions for the economics of copyright. On balance, economists see it as just another technological change like photocopying, sound recording, radio and so on, that have in turn fundamentally affected the production and consumption of cultural goods and services. Different entrepreneurs benefit and those well established in a business are often slow to adapt, but that is the price of innovation – the Schumpeterian concept of 'creative destruction'. Adapting is not just a matter of producing goods in a different way but of adopting new business models. We live at a time in which those are fast changing, along with the exploitation of new technologies. Advertiser-based free distribution is a viable way of financing delivery of creative goods and services but causes problems for contracting with and paying the creators, who have individual rights. Some economists would go further and argue that business models alone can provide sufficient incentive for the creation of new works and the production of cultural products, and that copyright law is not needed.

Conclusion

The creative industries 'paradigm' has been a very successful rhetorical device for the promotion of this 'sector', but it has had a mixed reception: cultural analysts have objected to the economic slant on cultural production while economists ask themselves what difference rearranging national income accounts makes to economic growth. Yet Caves's analysis has demonstrated that indeed the term has meaning in terms of the economic structure of the producers in these industries. There are, though, some major weaknesses in the creative industries paradigm, in particular that it overuses the term creativity and renders it devoid of meaning. It remains to be seen if the creative industries paradigm survives the next conceptual shift to the 'knowledge economy', which appears to be well under way in policy circles.

Note
1. By paradigm in this context is meant the notion of a shift in the way of thinking about the arts and cultural production.

See also:
Chapter 7: Artists' labour markets; Chapter 14: Copyright; Chapter 18: Creativity; Chapter 22: Cultural entrepreneurship; Chapter 23: Cultural statistics; Chapter 27: Digitalization; Chapter 31: Globalization; Chapter 34: The Internet: culture; Chapter 35: The Internet: economics.

References

Acheson, K. and C. Maule (2006), 'Culture in International Trade', in V. Ginsburgh and D. Throsby (eds), *Handbook of the Economics of Art and Culture*, Amsterdam: North-Holland, pp. 1141–82.

Caves, R. (2000), *Creative Industries: Contracts between Art and Commerce*, Cambridge, MA: Harvard University Press.

RERCI (*Review of Economic Research in Copyright Issues*) (2004), 1 (1).

Storper, Michael (1989), 'The Transition to Flexible Specialisation in the US Film Industry: External Economies, the Division of Labour and the Crossing of Industrial Divides', *Cambridge Journal of Economics*, 13, 273–305.

Towse, R. (2001) 'Richard Caves *Creative Industries: Contracts between Art and Commerce*', *Journal of Political Economy*, 110, (1), 234–7.

Towse, R. (2008) 'Why has Cultural Economics Ignored Copyright?', *Journal of Cultural Economics*, 32 (4), 243–59.

Towse, Ruth (2010a) 'Creativity, Copyright and the Creative Industries Paradigm', *Kyklos*, 3, 483–500.

Towse, Ruth (2010b), *A Textbook of Cultural Economics*, Cambridge: Cambridge University Press.

UNCTAD (2008) *Creative Economy Report 2008*, Geneva: UNCTAD.

World Intellectual Property Organisation (WIPO) (2003), *Guide on Surveying the Economic Contribution of the Copyright-Based Industries*, Geneva: WIPO.

Further reading
UNCTAD (2008) is a non-specialist summary of the subject. Caves's book should be required reading for anyone interested in the economics of creative industries (and those with a special interest might like to read my review of the book when it first appeared – Towse, 2001). Acheson and Maule (2006) deal particularly well with international trade and its wider implications for cultural development. Towse (2010b) is a textbook treatment of all these issues.

18 Creativity
Ruth Towse

Creativity is nowadays routinely invoked as having economic as well as cultural value, especially in the context of the creative industries, but it is an elusive concept for economists and there have been few attempts to develop an economic analysis of creativity. This is needed for two reasons: first, because the well-attested growth of the creative industries relies to a considerable extent on novel content supplied by creative and performing artists (hereafter 'creators'); and second, because one of the main justifications for copyright law is that it stimulates creativity. Attempting to understand the motivation for individual creativity and, especially, whether it is amenable to economic incentives has barely been tackled directly in the cultural economics literature. Studies of artists' labour markets, however, have thrown light on artists' supply decisions in respect of their time allocation to creative and other income-earning work.

Defining creativity

A joint publication by several UN agencies concerned with the creative industries, *Creative Economy Report 2008* (UNCTAD, 2008), adopts a broad (one might say too broad) view of creativity: it applies the term 'creative' to the creative economy, creative industries, creative cities, creative clusters and a range of creative goods and services. It offers this definition:

> 'Creativity' . . . refers to the formulation of new ideas and to the application of these ideas to produce original works of art and cultural products, functional creations, scientific inventions and technological innovations. There is thus an economic aspect to creativity, observable in the way it contributes to entrepreneurship, fosters innovation, enhances productivity and promotes economic growth. . . . 'creativity' is associated with originality, imagination, inspiration, ingenuity and inventiveness. It is an inner characteristic of individuals to be imaginative and to express ideas; associated with knowledge, these ideas are the essence of intellectual capital . . . [T]he twenty-first century has seen a growing understanding of the interface between creativity, culture and economics, the rationale behind the emerging concept of the 'creative economy'. (UNCTAD, 2008, p. 3).

This would seem to be far too broad a concept for meaningful research on individual artistic creativity, embracing as it does scientific invention and entrepreneurship under the one blanket term and apparently assuming that the motivation for each is the same.

Individual and institutional creativity

The essay by Bruno Frey, 'State Support and Creativity in the Arts', distinguishes between institutional and personal creativity, where institutional creativity is related to publicly funded arts organizations (in Frey, 2000). Frey regards these institutions (which in many European countries are directly managed and financed by the state authorities) as stifling creativity one way or another by bureaucratic rules and regulations. For personal (or individual) creativity, Frey acknowledges the influence of the work on the social psychology of creativity by Teresa Amabile, and links it to his theories of intrinsic and extrinsic motivation.

Artistic motivation

Frey (1997) makes the distinction between intrinsic motivation, whereby a person does something from inner conviction, such as artistic drive or social conscience, and extrinsic motivation, when people respond to 'outside' stimuli; he also makes the distinction between intrinsic reward, such as recognition or satisfaction, and extrinsic reward, for example payment or promotion. Frey's contribution is his 'crowding' theory. 'Crowding out' takes place when intrinsically motivated people are given extrinsic rewards, such as monetary payment, which has the unintended consequence that that which is supposed to act as an incentive acts instead as a disincentive or could even elicit the opposite response. Expressed as a moral-hazard problem, the classic example of an unwanted response is that paying blood donors encourages people like drug addicts to sell blood while crowding out the gift of it that would be made by intrinsically motivated and healthier people. Frey (2000) applies crowding out to personal creativity, suggesting that extrinsic motivation leads to an increase in quantity of lower-quality works of art, but he also discusses the opposite possibility, 'crowding in', whereby intrinsic motivation can be fostered by extrinsic reward if this is presented in such a way as to be acceptable to artists. One such way is to give 'unconditional' grants; another is to leave expert panels consisting of peers to distribute the money. The main point Frey makes is that institutional arrangements matter in offering a stimulus to creativity; in Towse (2010), the argument is developed that copyright law is one of these institutions.

Creativity and artists' labour market behaviour

The other area of research in cultural economics that throws light on creativity by individual creators is that on artists' labour markets. The results of this research can be related to intrinsic motivation as they show that maximizing pecuniary reward is far from what is sought by creators and performers. Literature going back to the 1980s recognizes the non-pecuniary 'psychic' reward of artists and even measures its value in terms of the opportunity cost of working as an artist by comparing artists' alternative earnings to those of other workers with equivalent education and years of experience.

In *Economics and Culture*, Throsby devotes a chapter to the economics of creativity, for the most part considering whether the creative process is capable of being interpreted in terms of rational decision-making (Throsby, 2001). He has tested models of artists' economic decisions about their allocation of labour time to working in the arts, where the decision is cast in terms of how much time to allocate between arts and non-arts work, using data from his surveys of artists' labour markets in Australia. Allocating time to working in their chosen artistic occupation is subject to the constraints of the need to earn sufficient income for the household, not as the loss of leisure time as it is perceived in 'ordinary' labour economics – hence Throsby's 'work preference' model. He finds that when rates of pay rise, creators spend more time on their preferred creative work. This and other work on artists' labour markets is reviewed in Alper and Wassall (2006).

In later work, Throsby (2006) models the artist's decision to devote effort to 'commercial' rather than 'creative' work. He views creative arts work as 'intrinsically satisfying' and commercial work as 'extrinsically rewarding' using a production function rather than a work preference model. Bryant and Throsby (2006) extend the production function by introducing an index of creativity or talent to explain artists' decisions to supply 'commercial' rather than 'creative' work. That trade-off is also to be found in Cowen and Tabarrock (2000), which considers the artist's decision between pursuing aesthetic satisfaction, the desire for fame, and the need for income from market sales. Cellini and Cuccia (2003) approach the question as a repeated game between a private for-profit 'financier' and an artist choosing between 'experimental' and 'conservative' work, in which the artist learns to adapt the extent of his/her creativity to the expectation of obtaining finance.

One of the inescapable and universal conclusions of studies of artists' labour markets is that there is excess supply of artistic labour even at low rates of pay. This ties in with Frey's analysis of artistic motivation – 'art for art's sake' is unconcerned with financial gain – and it has been associated with a very high elasticity of supply with respect to subsidized training of artists and even with grants and other financial support for artists – unintended consequences of policies designed to support artists.[1] This uncomfortable fact underlies many of the problems that artists and other primary creators experience in bargaining for rates of payment, particularly as individuals but in collectively bargained situations as well. Another uncomfortable fact is that studies of artists' earnings repeatedly show that length of training and experience have no influence on earnings from creative work (though they do for non-arts work). It has to be concluded therefore that individual creativity cannot be increased by investment in training, despite the frequent but unsubstantiated claims made for it (Towse, 2006b).

The above summarizes the work that has been done specifically on the economic aspects of the motivation of individuals to create, and it shows that economic factors play a role in influencing the creator's decision about how 'creative' they choose to be. The underlying model is that of utility maximization of inner satisfaction with a budget constraint that consists of extrinsic reward and 'crowded-in' financial payments. This is in contrast to the motivation of firms in the creative industries: that is simply assumed to be profit maximization in for-profit enterprises and a mixture of motives (revenue maximization, reaching new audiences, and so on) for non-profit organizations. Furthermore, research on artists' labour markets models the use of time, whose value is measured in earnings, while the measure for firms is the value and quantity of output. Finally, research has concentrated on earnings from sales of work, fees and wages, but recently there has been additional interest in earnings from copyright royalties and other remuneration from the use of copyright works. As might be expected from other research on artists' earnings, the distribution of income from royalties is greatly skewed – those of the superstars are high and the majority's royalties are trivial.[2]

Creativity and copyright

Creativity is frequently evoked in the debates about copyright that have taken place over the last century; claims that strengthening copyright increases creativity are frequently made nowadays by lobby groups and also by policy-makers. Copyright law, however, is not concerned with creativity *per se*. In economic terms, copyright is supposed to finance creativity by providing an incentive to the creation and dissemination of literary and artistic works. By granting statutory property rights to creators that make it illegal to copy someone's copyright works without their permission, authors are able to control and to charge for the use of their work. Without such rights, creative works that are non-rival and non-exclusive (which is the case with all digital works and many others) would become public goods. Copyright finances the creation of works of art by charging users for the use they make of those works: the more popular the work, and the higher the price, the greater the income it generates for the copyright holders. Thus the economic rationale for copyright is that it provides an incentive for the creation of works of art, literature, music, drama and so on, financed via the market.

Copyright, or authors' rights as they are in many countries, applies only to authors of 'original' works. Therefore performers do not have copyright proper but 'rights related to copyright' or 'neighbouring rights' that allow them, for example, to control recording of live performances, and they also have rights to remuneration for the use of their work, which are typically administered by copyright collecting societies, or rights management organizations, as they are also called.[3] Where a copyrightable work is created in the course of employment, the employer, and not the employee, is considered the creator and therefore the copyright attaches to the employer rather than to the person(s) who took part in creating it. This is known as a 'work made for hire' in US copyright law.

The incentive to the creator or the performer is, however, mediated through two channels: first, the creative content is typically combined with a medium of delivery and with the creative work of others to form a good or service as a product for the market; second, this process is undertaken by an enterprise that requires the transfer of rights conferred by copyright in exchange for a contract for royalties. As copyright is an individual right and individual creators generally have low bargaining power with firms in the creative industries, as Caves (2000) amply demonstrates, it is not hard to conclude that copyright in practice has a limited impact on creativity by individual creators and is more valuable to creative industries.

Copyright's view of creativity

Copyright law does not take a stance on creativity – it merely defines the scope of works that attract protection and requires that they be original; in UK copyright law, for instance, 'originality' means the employment of 'labour, skill and judgement', while in European law on authors' rights the concept of originality requires that a work be its author's 'own intellectual creation'. Copyright law offers no standard of quality, and no distinction exists in copyright between artistic creativeness and banality that falls in the scope of the law – so great poetry and the ditties in greetings cards are equally protected. It is not difficult to see that the law does not wish to get involved in the question of what constitutes worthwhile creativity!

Moral rights

The rights discussed above are known as economic rights. Copyright law and especially authors' rights also include moral rights, which protect the integrity and attribution of the author's work. Artists value these rights greatly and it may be argued that they provide intrinsic motivation that is important as an incentive to artists even if the extrinsic financial reward is low. Although moral rights are differentiated from economic rights, the question has been raised about the extent to which they have an economic dimension and so act as an extrinsic incentive to create (see Towse, 2006b, for a review of work on this subject).

Conclusion

This chapter has briefly reviewed two literatures in cultural economics that show how economists have approached the question of creativity. They deal in different ways with incentives to creators to create works of art of all kinds and suggest, in the language of Frey, that the institutional arrangements by which intrinsic and extrinsic rewards reach creators are central to creativity. The emphasis placed on stimulating creativity for reasons of economic growth in the context of the creative industries, creative clusters and the like needs therefore to consider how much can be achieved by economic policies, including copyright law, and whether it is quantity or quality of creative output that is the objective. What is clear is that there is a great deal of work to be done on this topic, which is fundamental to many aspects of cultural economics.

Notes

1. See Abbing (2002) and Towse (2001).
2. See Kretschmer and Hardwick (2007) for a review and the results of their survey of authors in the UK and Germany.
3. See Towse (2006a) for more details.

See also:

Chapter 7: Artists' labour markets; Chapter 9: Awards; Chapter 14: Copyright; Chapter 17: Creative industries; Chapter 50: Poverty and support for artists.

References

Abbing, Hans (2002), *Why are Artists Poor? The Exceptional Economy of the Arts*, Amsterdam: Amsterdam University Press.
Alper, Neil and Gregory Wassall (2006), 'Artists' Careers and their Labour Markets', in Victor Ginsburgh and David Throsby (eds), *Handbook of the Economics of Art and Culture*, Amsterdam: North Holland, pp. 815–64.
Bryant, William and David Throsby (2006), 'Creativity and the Behaviour of Artists', in Victor Ginsburgh and David Throsby (eds), *Handbook of the Economics of Art and Culture*, Amsterdam: North Holland, pp. 507–28.
Caves, Richard (2000), *Creative Industries: Contracts between Art and Commerce*, Cambridge, MA: Harvard University Press.
Cellini, Roberto and Tiziana Cuccia (2003), 'Incomplete Information and Experimentation in the Arts: A Game Theory Approach', *Economia Politica*, 20, 21–34.
Cowen, Tyler and Alexander Tabarrock (2000), 'An Economic Theory of Avant-Garde and Popular Art, or High and Low Culture', *Southern Economic Journal*, 67 (2), 232–53.
Frey, Bruno S. (1997), *Not Just for the Money*, Cheltenham, UK and Lyme, USA: Edward Elgar.
Frey, Bruno S. (2000), *Arts and Economics*, Heidelberg: Springer-Verlag.
Kretschmer, Martin and Philip Hardwick (2007), 'Authors' Earnings from Copyright and Non-Copyright Sources: From a Survey of 25,000 British and German Writers, available at www.cippm.org.uk/publications/alcs/ACLS%20Full%20report.pdf.
Throsby, David (2001), *Economics and Culture*, Cambridge: Cambridge University Press.
Throsby, David (2006), 'An Artistic Production Function: Theory and an Application to Australian Visual Artists', *Journal of Cultural Economics*, 30, 1–14.
Towse, Ruth (2001), *Creativity, Incentive and Reward*, Cheltenham, UK and Northampton, MA, USA: Edward Elgar.
Towse, Ruth (2006a), 'Copyright and Artists: a View from Cultural Economics', *Journal of Economic Surveys*, 20 (4), 567–85.
Towse, Ruth (2006b), 'Human Capital and Artists' Labour Markets', in Victor Ginsburgh and David Throsby (eds), *Handbook of the Economics of Art and Culture*, Amsterdam: North-Holland, pp. 867–94.

Towse, Ruth (2010), 'Creativity, Copyright and the Creative Industries Paradigm', *Kyklos*, 3, 483–500.
UNCTAD (2008), *Creative Economy Report 2008*, Geneva: UNCTAD.

Further reading

Chapter 8 in Bruno Frey's collection *Arts and Economics* (2000) is a good introduction to his crowding theory applied to the motivation of creativity. Chapter 6 in David Throsby's (2001) *Economics and Culture* clearly lays out his view on creativity in the context of artists' labour markets, and my survey (Towse, 2006b) covers the economic literature on copyright and artists. Much of the analysis of artists' supply behaviour is based on the human capital paradigm in labour economics that is relevant to the question whether creativity can be invested in through arts training courses; this is surveyed in Towse (2006b).

19 Criticism
Samuel Cameron

Criticism is an enduring feature of arts and entertainment. This does not necessarily mean that it is important, although a strictly neoclassical economics perspective implies that anything that persists must be serving some socially useful function unless it is a manifestation of market failure from use of power by a dominant group. Criticism is a service that yields utility to consumers. The person who performs criticism is called a critic if they earn their living from such activity and/or have attained some acclaim for the status of their proclamations. Little empirical evidence exists on the labour market for critics. There do not seem to be any statistics on how many critics there are and what they earn. One also needs to distinguish between criticism and reviewing. Taken literally, reviewing simply means reporting on what has been consumed; indeed, some economics journals instruct book reviewers not to embark on criticism. One might envisage a distinction between the review as being 'positive' (factual) and criticism as 'normative' (value judgemental). In practice, the distinction is hard to maintain: for example, the reviewer of a production of Shakespeare may still pass some comment on whether or not it is one of the better productions of his plays. Such a remark might influence consumer demand. This takes us to the role of critics in terms of economic models of culture markets. If markets approximated to idealized perfect competition there would be no need for critics other than the possibility that their opinions might be a source of utility *per se*, in which case they become additional cultural products.[1] This has become prominent in television talent shows, where people are entertained by the extreme abusive opinions of 'Mr Nasty' figures who may be more significant than the performers.

Critics and taste formation

If cultural products are to circulate, then criticism can play a role in determining market size through information provision and taste formation. Admittedly, some markets can emerge independently of critical awareness, but their subsequent development will be influenced by the presence of criticism. The simplest theoretical approach is to assume that all people have identical tastes, but knowledge of products is limited and costly to acquire. Knowledge is a major problem in the culture sector due to the uniqueness of many products. The principal–agent model is the relevant tool for this topic. Specialized critics are agents who consume plays, soap operas, music, films and books on behalf of the principals in order to try them out. Specialization might bring benefits from scale economies in studying the genre of work, although it could be argued that producers-cum-critics are superior as they bring to bear more understanding of the creative process. Generally, those creators who move into doing some criticism are on a mission to promote a vanguard in which they reside, with Debussy being an example of this. Few critics move into the form of which they are established critics. The modern English composer Michael Nyman is a noted exception to this rule.

The potential output generated has often been signalled by critics using a 'star' system, where five stars is excellent, one poor and so on. Problems arise because tastes are not identical. Nevertheless, if markets were efficient, consumers would be able to identify critics whose tastes were similar to their own or different, in a stable way, in a manner that could be reliably mapped to their own preferences. The critic may also operate as the 'voice' of the consumer, which can be welfare enhancing as many arts consumers are locked in by loyalty. If the creator changed their style, it might still lead to purchases by loyal consumers; hence there would be no indication of exit until disappointment began to affect future products.

Historically, criticism has been jointly supplied with other things in a newspaper or magazine; for example it is supplied at zero marginal production cost to the consumer. A magazine that has an identifiable cultural stance is likely to employ critics with similar preferences. A corporate critical identity is an instance of the use of reputation as a signal of product quality. Reputation imparts public-good characteristics to critical output. That is, people who have not read Mr. X or publication Y's review may be persuaded by hearsay reports of its favourability or otherwise. The advantage of this is that criticism is cross-subsidized, with attendant benefits to the culture market. Given that zero-priced criticism is of benefit to the culture industry, there would seem to be gains to the culture industry of subsidizing critical publications in some way that does not undermine their credibility. The main obstacle is the difficulty of capturing the gains, as many of these would go to rivals. This problem will diminish as the degree of monopolization of a market segment increases. Examples of this can be found in the music and print industries, where a small number of retail distributors have considerable market power. These issue magazines, covering all forms of music, which look like independent productions but never contain any negative views on the artists/works covered.

Critics have a potentially important role in taste formation. One might argue that critics have been the guardians of aesthetic values. Aesthetics involves some absolute notions of what is 'good' and 'bad' in art and culture. This argument has been around much longer than formal economics: in 1777, a writer believed to be Nicolas Etienne Framery wrote:

> Music, painting, all the arts which depend on taste are everywhere subject to the errors of ignorance, to the blind whims of the masses, and, what is worse, to the false judgments of those would-be amateurs, who, without truly liking the arts or ever having cultivated them, join a party, pass judgment without knowledge, speak without understanding, applaud with a yawn, and thrive on destroying performer's reputations. (Framery, cited in Haskell, 1995, 43–4).

Critics and quality

Here we have the fear of some kind of 'Gresham's Law of Philistinism' where the tastes of the lowest common denominator drive out more worthy productions in the arts sector. This kind of thinking has been formalized in recent papers such as Frank (2008), which see the TV talent show of the 'Idol' kind of presentation as competition that lowers quality rather than increasing it. It is clearly problematic to define 'quality' as something other than just one's own tastes. This leads back to the argument that critics are needed as some kind of qualified judges of output. Rent-seeking activity by supporters of a cultural form, which may include critics, could capture government subsidies to maintain the market. Rent-seeking in this area could involve an attempt to mould audience preferences to a particular pattern. The social pressure required for this is initiated and/or maintained by critical output. The implicit critical patent of 'originality' may be exploited by dealers and artists through a deliberate restriction of output (see Singer, 1988). Originality where something new is done to no meaningful end other than novelty may be deemed 'useless originality'. Consumers thus run the risk of being sold a 'lemon' by the critics. If we are seeking guidance on how to develop our tastes and originality, then we might find ourselves sitting through a play or looking at a painting that is the equivalent of a chocolate tea-pot (highly original but not much use). It might seem that a lexicographic form of assessment could be used to circumvent the 'useless originality' problem. That is, one could put some baseline content of meaning that an art product must contain before its originality content can be admitted as an added value that might be traded off against other features like ease of access, instant gratification and so on. This is limited by the very nature of originality. Aspects of a work of culture that are seen, by the majority, as ridiculous when it is first produced may come to be seen as breathtakingly beautiful or insightful when the decoding of the work has been popularized.

Empirical studies

There are many legends surrounding the influence of critics, especially Broadway critics. Many of these tales are asymmetric in that negative reviews are seen as capable of killing a product while favourable ones are less capable of vaunting it to success. Cultural economists have carried out some empirical work on the influence of critics on demand. Hirschman and Pieros (1985) found, surprisingly, that a positive review may have a negative impact on attendance. This may indicate a rational use of critics' judgements, as a favourable review may be seen as revelation of elitist preferences that an audience maps back into their own preferences as negative values. A wider use of criticism is in the area of prizes. Prizes do not tend to give content feedback in the main but they reflect a critical ranking, with the outright winner usually gaining. There are prizes voted for by established critics (sometimes themselves performers/writers etc.) and those voted for by the general public only (typically in television and popular music). In the UK comedy market, the Perrier award at the Edinburgh festival seems to have contributed greatly to the careers of all its winners. It may of course simply be rank ordering those who would succeed anyway, but it does provide a boost in terms of word of mouth and publicity. The sponsorship of this award has been lost, leading to anxiety in the performing community about its future. Boyle and Chiou (2009) show that the Tony awards have a statistically significant positive impact on New York's Broadway theatre.

Most of the work of economists is on the performance of movies/films. The empirical work on films has reflected the shift away from reliance on specialist professional critics to the use of general opinion or 'citizen criticism'. Online shopping websites, particularly Amazon, effectively allow all buyers to become critics by posting reviews of books, videos and DVDs. These reviews are even averaged by the vendors into a summary statistic. The effort and cost of accessing this information is very small. That was also true of the television movie preview shows or the reviews of all arts in newspapers, but those critical fora exhibited a high degree of monopoly power for the individual critic with an established reputation. Beyond shopping outlets we have websites such as 'Rotten Tomatoes', which collate citizen criticism. The term 'word of mouth' has been used to describe informally circulating opinions on the merits of a cultural product. This is now largely embodied in the blogosphere and twittering, which have come to displace the message-board type of website. These recent developments are placing a downward pressure on the demand for the specialized critic. In 2001, mainstream Hollywood movies began to be trailed using exclusively audience reactions, thereby usurping the reputation function of the critics.

Citizen criticism potentially shifts the nature of cultural production somewhat. Internet rumours (such as 'who is going to play Wonder Woman in the film?') and leaked portions of future products mean that criticism of the product made *before* it is even completed will influence its contents. This has always been true to some extent, due to the use of 'test screenings' in the film industry, but it is now able to become a more widespread and powerful factor.

Note

1. In the early nineteenth century a flourishing market in literary magazines allowed the criticism of such writers as de Quincey, Hazlitt and Lamb to function in this way.

See also:

Chapter 9: Awards; Chapter 26: Demand; Chapter 29: Experience goods; Chapter 50: Principal–agent analysis; Chapter 56: Superstars.

References

Basuroy, S., S. Chatterjee and S.A. Ravid (2003), 'How Critical are Critical Reviews? The Box Office Effects of Film Critics, Star Power and Budgets', *Journal of Marketing*, 67, 103–17.
Boor, M. (1992), 'Relationships Amongst Ratings of Motion Pictures by Viewers and Six Professional Movie Critics', *Psychological Reports*, 70, 1011–021.
Boyle, M. and L. Chiou (2009), 'Broadway Productions and the Value of a Tony Award', *Journal of Cultural Economics*, 33, 49–68.
Cameron, S. (1995), 'On the Role of Critics in the Culture Industry', *Journal of Cultural Economics*, 19, 321–31.
Framery, N.F. (attributed) (1777), 'On the Best Means for Naturalizing a Taste for Good Music in France', *Journal de Musique*, 5, reprinted in H. Haskell (ed.) (1995), *The Attentive Listener: Three Centuries of Music Criticism*, London and Boston, MA: Faber and Faber, pp. 43–5.
Frank, J. (2008), 'Perverse Outcomes of Intense Competition in the Popular Arts and its Implications for Product Quality', *Journal of Cultural Economics*, 32 (3), 215–24.
Hirschman, E. and A. Pieros (1985), 'Relationships Among Indicators of Success in Broadway Plays and Motion Pictures', *Journal of Cultural Economics*, 9, 35–63.
Singer, L. (1988), 'Phenomenology and Economics of Art Markets: An Art Historical Perspective', *Journal of Cultural Economics*, 12, 27–40.

Further reading

A more detailed consideration of the issues discussed here can be found in Cameron (1995). Empirical studies of the influence of professional critics can be found in Basuroy *et al.* (2003), Hirschman and Pieros (1995) and Boyle and Chiou (2009). The comparative ratings of professional critics and non-critics are examined in Boor (1992).

20 Cultural capital
David Throsby

The concept of capital has been fundamental to the interpretation of production processes in economics for more than 200 years. Capital can be defined as durable goods that give rise to a flow of services over time that may be combined with other inputs such as labour to produce further goods and services. The original and longest-serving interpretation of capital arising from this definition has been *physical* or *manufactured capital*, meaning plant and equipment, machines, buildings and so on. In the second half of the twentieth century a further form of capital was identified, namely *human capital*, being the inherent characteristics of people that make them productive. Subsequently, the idea of *natural capital* was developed, allowing the designation of renewable and non-renewable resources as capital assets. More recently still, the concept of capital has been extended into the field of art and culture, in an effort to recognize the distinctive features of artworks and other cultural goods as capital assets, and to capture the ways in which such assets contribute, in combination with other inputs, to the production of further cultural goods and services. Thus the economic concept of *cultural capital* has taken shape.

What is distinctive about cultural capital, allowing it to be set apart from the other forms of capital described above? Two possibilities have been suggested. First, it could be proposed that items of cultural capital are simply cultural goods that happen to be capital goods (in the sense defined in the previous paragraph) rather than consumption goods. Such a definition presupposes a definition of a cultural good. Although there has been some debate among economists as to whether cultural goods and services can be differentiated from 'ordinary' economic goods and services, and if so how, it is reasonable to suggest that a cultural good is one that has involved human creativity in its making, conveys symbolic meaning (or multiple meanings), and is identifiable, at least in principle, as embodying some intellectual property. Accepting these characteristics of a cultural good would allow us to substantiate the definition of cultural capital given above.

Second, an alternative approach to defining cultural capital can be couched in terms of the types of value to which cultural assets give rise. Consider a historic church building. It may have a potential sale price as real estate, and a non-market value measured, for example, by the willingness of people to pay to see it preserved. But these measures of its *economic value* may be incapable of representing the full range and complexity of the cultural worth of the building: it may have religious significance unable to be expressed in monetary terms; it may have had an influence over time on architectural styles, it may act as a symbol of identity or place, and so on. All these things and many more are elements of what might be termed the building's *cultural value*, a multidimensional representation of the building's cultural worth assessed in quantitative and/or qualitative terms against a variety of attributes such as its aesthetic quality, its spiritual meaning, its social function, its symbolic significance, its historical importance, its uniqueness and so on. Many of these characteristics will influence the economic value of the building, but there is no reason to suppose a perfect correlation between economic and cultural value as defined. If this concept of cultural value is accepted (notwithstanding the formidable problems of identifying and measuring it in practice), it can be used in the formulation of a definition of cultural capital. That is, following this route, cultural capital can be defined as an asset that embodies, stores or gives rise to cultural value independently of whatever economic value it may possess.

Whichever of these two definitions is accepted, we can proceed to consider the characteristics of cultural capital in comparison with the other types of capital we have mentioned. Cultural capital may exist in two forms, tangible and intangible. Tangible cultural capital occurs in the form of artworks and artefacts such as paintings and sculptures, and heritage buildings, locations and sites. Intangible cultural capital comprises artworks that exist in their pure form as public goods, such as music and literature, and the stock of inherited traditions, values, beliefs and so on that constitute the culture of a group, whether the group is defined in national, regional, religious, political, ethnic or other terms. Furthermore, intangible cultural capital also exists in the cultural networks and relationships that support human activity, and in the variety of cultural manifestations within communities – that is, in cultural 'ecosystems' and cultural diversity, phenomena that we discuss further below.

Both tangible and intangible forms of cultural capital exist as a capital stock held by a country, a region, a city or an individual economic agent. This capital stock could be assigned an asset value in both economic and cultural terms at a given point in time. The net effect of additions to and subtractions from the capital stock within a given time period indicates the net investment/disinvestment in cultural capital during the period, measurable in both economic and cultural terms, and determines the opening value of the stock at the beginning of the next period.

Any holding of cultural capital stock gives rise to a flow of capital services over time that may enter final consumption directly, or that may be combined with other inputs to produce further cultural goods and services. So, for example, the services of artworks held as capital items by an art museum may be combined with materials, labour and other inputs to yield consumption experiences for visitors to the museum; in addition, the artworks may stimulate the production of further works through their influence on creative artists who view them, thus leading to further capital formation.

Like any other type of asset, cultural capital may deteriorate over time, necessitating investment in its maintenance or refurbishment. Economic evaluation of such expenditure can call upon standard investment appraisal techniques used in economics such as cost–benefit analysis or cost-effectiveness analysis. In the case of a heritage restoration project, for example, the discounted net present value of the time stream of benefits yielded by the project could be calculated using these techniques and set against the project's capital cost; the internal rate of return on this project could then be compared with the returns on alternative investment opportunities. It is possible to imagine in principle that, in addition to this sort of financial assessment, an appraisal could also be carried out in terms of the expected flow of *cultural* value to be derived from the project, although, as noted above, the measurement of cultural value in such an exercise is likely to be difficult, to say the least.

The economic benefits derived from cultural capital are likely to have a significant externality or public-good component similar in kind to the sorts of benefits generated by the natural environment. Indeed there are close parallels in both theoretical and applied terms between the concepts of cultural and natural capital: both have been inherited from the past, both yield use and non-use benefits, and both impose a duty of care. As a result, methods for assessment of the value of environmental amenities, including the measurement of non-use values by means of such methods as contingent valuation, discrete choice modelling and hedonic analysis, have been able to be applied in the cultural arena.

Two aspects of the congruence between cultural and natural capital are particularly significant, namely diversity and sustainability.

Cultural diversity

A similarity can be observed between biodiversity as an element of natural capital and cultural diversity as a key component of cultural capital. The sources of value that have been articulated in explaining why biodiversity is important have their counterparts in the valuation of cultural diversity, as follows:

- Both biodiversity and cultural diversity generate existence value for individuals, deriving from the knowledge that the richness of the natural world and the variety of cultures and cultural expressions are simply there.
- Both natural and cultural 'ecosystems' are necessary to support economic activity; the invisible networks and relationships that hold cultures together and give meaning to people's lives are as essential in underpinning the functioning of the economy as are the ecosystems of air, land and water that make up the natural environment.
- Biodiversity is valued because some species may have economic value as yet unrecognized; likewise certain cultural manifestations may have economic and cultural value that is not yet evident, such that their loss could incur economic costs or forgone opportunities in the future.

Cultural diversity has emerged from the shadows in recent years to become an important focus for international cultural policy-making, exemplified in a new standard-setting instrument – the Convention on the Protection and Promotion of the Diversity of Cultural Expressions – which was adopted by UNESCO member states in 2005 and which entered into force in 2007. A significant motivation for the establishment of this treaty was the hope in a number of countries that it would provide protection for local cultural expressions such as film and television programmes, whose diversity was threatened by imported cultural product. In fact the Convention ranges over a much wider scope than simply international cultural trade, setting out the rights of parties to adopt a variety of policy measures in relation to culture and encouraging intercultural dialogue within and between countries.

Cultural sustainability

The second aspect of the parallel between natural and cultural capital lies in the fact that both have long-lasting properties requiring management over time. An appropriate framework within which to consider these long-term aspects is that of sustainability, a concept most often encountered in the phrase 'sustainable development'.

This proposition, first enunciated by the World Commission on Environment and Development (the Brundtland Commission) in the 1980s, refers to development that meets the needs of the present generation without compromising the capacity of future generations to meet their own needs. When applied to cultural capital, it can be given substance by reference to the idea of *culturally sustainable development*. No single definition of this phenomenon is adequate on its own; instead, a better indication of the meaning of this term can be obtained by articulating a set of principles by which the sustainable management of cultural capital might be judged. Six such principles can be identified, as follows:

- *Material and non-material well-being*: This criterion relates to the generation of both tangible and intangible benefits to individuals and to society from the use of cultural resources and the production and consumption of cultural goods and services.
- *Intergenerational equity* or *intertemporal distributive justice*: This principle refers to fairness in the distribution of welfare, utility or resources between generations, in particular between the present and future generations; it applies to the management of cultural capital, both tangible and intangible, because such capital embodies the culture we have inherited from our forebears and which we hand on to future generations.
- *Intragenerational equity*: This principle asserts the rights of the present generation to fairness in access to cultural resources and to the benefits flowing from cultural capital, viewed across social classes, income groups, locational categories and so on.
- *Maintenance of diversity*: Here we refer to the reasons why the diversity element in cultural capital is of value to individuals and to society, as discussed above.
- *Precautionary principle*: This states that decisions that may lead to irreversible change should be approached with extreme caution and from a strongly risk-averse position; the precautionary principle could be invoked in the management of cultural capital if, for example, a historic building were threatened with demolition, or if an indigenous language were in danger of extinction.
- *Maintenance of cultural systems and recognition of interdependence*: An overarching principle of sustainability is the proposition that no part of any system exists independently of other parts – in this respect it can be suggested that cultural capital makes a contribution to long-term sustainability that is similar in principle to that of natural capital: neglect of cultural capital by allowing heritage to deteriorate, by failing to sustain the cultural values that provide people with a sense of identity, and by not undertaking the investment needed to maintain the stock of tangible and intangible cultural capital or to increase it (for example, by the production of new artworks) will likewise place cultural systems in jeopardy and may cause them to break down, with consequent loss of welfare and economic output.

The final principle listed above essentially draws together the entire concept of sustainability when applied to culture. Taken together, the principles define the concept of culturally sustainable development, which has the same significance for cultural capital theory as ecologically sustainable development has for the theory of natural capital.

Conclusion

The economic theory of cultural capital is now established, at least in conceptual terms, but empirically the picture is less clear. The financial valuation of individual items of cultural capital stock is reasonably straightforward, and measurement of the economic value of the flow of services that a given item of capital stock produces is also well advanced in terms of both use and non-use components. But replicable means for measuring the cultural value of an item of cultural capital in either stock or flow terms remain elusive; the most promising prospects appearing to lie in assessment according to multiple criteria, with some weighted aggregation as the end result. At a macro level the difficulties of all types of valuation are compounded, particularly because of problems in defining the extent of cultural capital stock held in any given macro setting.

Finally, it should be noted that the term cultural capital is used in other disciplines to mean something different from its interpretation in economics. In sociology, cultural capital is used, following Pierre Bourdieu, to mean an individual's competence in high-status culture. In economic terms this characteristic of people can be construed as an aspect of their human capital, and not as cultural capital as defined above. It might be noted that sociologists and some economists also speak of 'social capital', meaning the social networks and relationships that exist within communities. This concept overlaps significantly with one of the forms of intangible cultural capital mentioned above, namely the idea of cultural ecosystems as shared cultural networks and relationships that facilitate cultural, social and economic interaction between members of a group.

See also:

Chapter 21: Cultural districts; Chapter 25: Cultural value; Chapter 32: Heritage; Chapter 31: Globalization.

References

Cheng, Sao-Wen (2006), 'Cultural Goods Production, Cultural Capital Formation and the Provision of Cultural Services', *Journal of Cultural Economics*, 30, 263–86.

Rizzo, Ilde and David Throsby (2006), 'Cultural Heritage: Economic Analysis and Public Policy', in Victor Ginsburgh and David Throsby (eds), *Handbook of the Economics of Art and Culture*, Amsterdam: Elsevier/North-Holland, pp. 983–1016.

Shockley, Gordon E. (2004), 'Government Investment in Cultural Capital: A Methodology for Comparing Direct Government Support for the Arts in the US and the UK', *Public Finance and Management*, 4, 75–102.

Throsby, David (1999), 'Cultural Capital', *Journal of Cultural Economics*, 23, 3–12.

Throsby, David (2001), *Economics and Culture,* Cambridge: Cambridge University Press.

Ulibarri, Carlos A. (2000), 'Rational Philanthropy and Cultural Capital', *Journal of Cultural Economics*, 24, 135–46.

Wang, Xiaohui (2007), 'An Analysis of Optimal Allocation and Accumulation of Cultural Capital', *Doshisha University Policy and Management*, 9, 197–213.

Further reading

A fuller account of cultural capital and sustainability is contained in Rizzo and Throsby (2006). The original article defining cultural capital in economic terms is Throsby (1999). Developments of the theory and some applications are contained in Ulibarri (2000), Throsby (2001), Shockley (2004), Cheng (2006) and Wang (2007).

21 Cultural districts
Walter Santagata

Creating cultural districts is an example of an economic policy that has been extremely successful in bringing together culture, managerial creativity and industrial design. These special industrial and artisan agglomerations are the subject of this chapter, as they are an example of how culture and creativity can be the moving force in sustainable local economic development (OECD, 2005).

Developing systems of micro and small enterprises or concentrating business activities whose products and aims are similar are phenomena that are generally well situated in time and space, as they depend on the birth and evolution of material culture and the production of goods and services that have delineated an environmental and cultural habitat in a geographical area. The ancient writings of Mediterranean, Oriental and Asian civilizations, and the chronicles of medieval Europe, provide a wealth of examples of concentrations of micro enterprises that over time evolved into potential or real industrial districts. Some types of cultural district in fact correspond to industrial systems where small firms produce material culture's traditional goods (textiles, ceramics, jewellery, designer objects and so on), while in others the emphasis is on offering services rather than goods (museum districts, production systems for the performing arts and folklore) and on a less cohesive form of agglomeration between the participating firms (historical heritage and cultural tourism networks, archaeological sites).

Cultural district

A cultural district or cluster is a social and economic experience at the confluence of two phenomena: that of localization, as first identified by Alfred Marshall (Marshall, 1890 [1920]), and that of the idiosyncratic (peculiar, unique) nature of culture and cultural goods. Many case studies confirm the powerful role of cultural districts in local economic development (Santagata 2002, 2004, 2006; Scott, 2000; Cuccia and Santagata, 2003; Cellini *et al.*, 2007; Cuccia *et al.*, 2008).

Marshall's theory of localized industries

Marshall's original idea was rich with potential for development, yet for Marshall, industrial districts were a thing of the Middle Ages. They were understood as nothing more than a specific phase resulting from the effects of the division of labour upon technological innovation, processes and organization. In this perspective, the shift to mass-produced goods was one of the factors that ushered in the decline of some old districts such as Sheffield or St-Étienne.

One of the most meaningful characteristics of a district is the interdependence of its firms, its 'industrial atmosphere'. Frequent contacts favour the exchange of specialized inputs; continuous and repeated transactions cause information to circulate. Within the districts it is easier to find contractors, to verify the quality of goods and services and to sign standardized contracts. Mutual trust and the accumulation of social capital are pervasive traits of local society and culture. When most of the economic and human resources are local, the economic process becomes endogenous. Art markets, the performing arts, museums and cultural heritage, design-based goods and cultural industries can all be articulated in chains of creation of value that assume the form of, and are governed in the logic of, *industrial districts and clusters.*

Culture as an idiosyncratic good
Culture-based goods are among the most specialized goods. Indeed, culture has two profound anthropological roots: time and space. The production of a culture is indissolubly linked to a place, or in a social sense, to a community and its history.

Since efficient economic behaviour is mainly grounded on timeless and spaceless goods, the market becomes an imperfect institution as and when it must regulate creativity and idiosyncratic goods, like fashion, design and art. The more time-specific and space-specific a commodity, the less the market mechanism is able to efficiently regulate its production and consumption. The more specialized and exceptional a good, the less the price system provides the relevant information and the less the competition rule reaches its expected results (Salais and Storper, 1993). Cultural districts are defined by the production of idiosyncratic goods based on creativity and intellectual property. The movie industry, the audiovisual sector, the extensive domain of industrial design and the production of arts and crafts, museum services and the enogastronomic complex all draw their inspiration from some cultural link with their original local community. 'Place, culture, and economy are symbiotic with one another' (Scott, 2000, p. 4).

Finally, a cultural district is characterized by strong district-based presence of personal knowledge and what Polanyi (1953) called *tacit knowledge.* The concept involves an information system that is a local public good, which is non-excludable and is circumscribed within a communal space defined by the personal experience of each individual in it. Technological and cultural information circulates freely: it is transmitted via tacit systems of communication, since there is a gap between technology, art, culture and the essential facts of personal experience. Cultural commodities are idiosyncratic not only because tacit knowledge is needed to create and produce them but also because this knowledge is based on people's prior idiosyncratic experience: personal and collective history count.

Industrial cultural districts

The *industrial cultural district* belongs to the endogenous growth models based on the presence of small firms, basic social and cultural conditions, and of specific forms of social local regulation (Pyke *et al.*, 1990).

The basic components of this peculiar strategy of district building are based on:

- a local community, which is cohesive in its cultural traditions and in the accumulation of technical knowledge and social capital (trust and cooperation);
- a significant development of increasing returns to scale and increasing returns to scope;
- accumulation of savings; strongly entrepreneurial cooperative local banking;
- a bent towards open international markets;

- public financial support along the entire chain of the creation of value;
- a high rate of birth of new firms, often of household size, as a result of social capability and interactive learning; the ability to be district-minded, to become a system, and to produce positive externalities.

In a cultural district or cluster the costs of the *use of the market* are lower than anywhere else because of the very intense reduction of transaction costs and the creation of positive externalities.

From industrial cultural districts to institutional cultural district

While the culture-based goods are in a better position to develop the agglomeration of an industrial cultural district, due to their idiosyncratic nature and to the embodiment of a high degree of intellectual property and a relatively low level of standardization, their variety leads to a large typology, according to the presence of high-tech or handicraft production, horizontal industrial integration or independent vertically integrated firms. Regarding the last point, it is worth distinguishing between two types of cultural district: those in developed and those in developing economies. They involve the same economic players, namely artisans, artists and entrepreneurs. Localized micro and small firms run by artisans and small entrepreneurs exist everywhere, but because a higher rate of technology is employed in developed countries, vertical and horizontal integration of these companies is the pattern found there, while the agglomeration of a large number of identical, horizontally integrated micro companies is the norm in developing ones (Santagata, 2006).

Using the industrial cultural district and cluster as a policy instrument for local economic development is complicated because the crucial requirements and necessary conditions for establishing an industrial cultural district are, in fact, difficult to find anywhere. It is not possible to follow a rational constructivist approach. The industrial cultural district is the result of a long and often socially painful incubation. During that time, the process of advancement is spontaneous, market-oriented and subject to 'trial and error' feedback. In other words, we are witnessing a process of long duration. There is no one specific factor that causes or assists the appearance of entrepreneurial spirit.

One potential solution is to focus on the function of intellectual and collective property rights in promoting market-oriented incentives sustaining local development. This is the class of *institutional cultural districts* (Santagata, 2006). Its essential characteristic is its grounding in formal institutions that allocate property rights and trademarks to a restricted area of production. These rights take on the meaning of *community* or *collective* property rights. In this sense, they legally protect the cultural capital of a community in a given area.

The enforcement of a sign-of distinction carries out many economic effects, as with a trademark: it reduces the probability of unauthorized copy and gives rise to individual efficient incentives to create and produce. Signalling the general characteristics of the product, the intellectual property rights reduce the asymmetric information pertaining to the agents involved in an exchange of goods of hidden quality. The assignment of property rights yields a set of interesting issues. As they create a monopolistic privilege through product differentiation, they allow a substantial accumulation of capital. The legal protection generates incentives so that producers invest in reputation and high quality of products. But it should even be considered that legal protection and economic incentives lead to better control of the productive and distributive process, with a notable increase in the quality of the products.

Remarkable cases of potential cultural districts

(i) Industrial cultural districts of material culture
There is a surprising number of potential cultural districts in the world: from Sigchos in Ecuador, where artistic ceramics are produced, to Aleppo in Syria, where micro enterprises produce soap using traditional, three-millennia-old methods, to Lucknow in India's Uttar Pradesh, where artisans embroider *chikan* fabric (Moreno *et al.*, 2004–05; Santagata, 2006).

(ii) Districts and museum-based cultural systems
Museum districts are situated in cities' historical centres. Their density in itself creates systemic effects that attract visitors and tourists. The museum cultural district in general is the outcome of public policies, whose success factors are the existence of a localized culture, incorporated in human capital and in museum collections, and institutional startup, represented by the local authorities' decision to create a museum district. Interesting examples include the museum island (*Museeninsel*) in Berlin, the museum district (MuseumsQuartier) in Vienna, with 40 structures devoted to modern art and culture, and the system of the Savoy Collections in Turin.

(iii) Tourist cultural districts
In many developed and developing countries, the types of district described above are being transformed into cultural-tourism districts. These are represented by concentrations comprising activities related to accommodation and hospitality (hotels, bed-and-breakfast establishments, restaurants, tour operators, transportation services), the offer of traditional cultural services (historic heritage, museums, folklore, traditional medicine, spas) and the production of craft goods and material culture. The aim is to valorize all local activities, generating maximum synergy and contributing to establishing an image and international reputation as a tourist destination.

(iv) Cultural-heritage systems
These potential districts include a wide variety of cases and take the form of a circuit or a network connecting individual sites or monuments. Their economic value is strengthened by the production of collective services and the offer of a common identity. Impressive examples are Egyptian tombs (the pyramids, the Saqqara necropolis), the Khmer temples in Cambodia and the ancient cities of Sri Lanka.

(v) The USA's urban cultural districts
Urban cultural districts are injecting new blood into their local communities, using artistic and cultural services to attract people, fight economic industrial decline and create a new image for the cities where they are located. An urban cultural district is a spatial conglomerate of buildings devoted to the figurative arts – museums and organizations

that produce culture and goods connected to it; correlated services and structures. The majority of the world's cultural districts are found in US cities and in the UK, where the idea of the cultural district has been studied in theory and applied in practice starting from the first experiment in Glasgow in the 1980s (Frost-Kumpf, 1998).

(vi) Districts for contemporary art

The Dashanzi Art District in Beijing is an outstanding example of a cultural district specializing in the production of contemporary art. It is a locality with artists' studios, galleries of Chinese and international art, and small businesses for developing an art market that has skyrocketed in recent years. The Dashanzi Art District is a system of abandoned factories leased to artists and art dealers. Designed in Bauhaus style, it occupies 230 000 square metres with streets, buildings, squares, boulevards, galleries and restaurants daily filled with visitors, collectors, artists, art curators and cultural intermediaries.

Conclusions

Cultural districts are now a worldwide phenomenon, creating endogenous growth at a local level. Based on the local cultural capital, they generate income and create jobs.

See also:

Chapter 16: Creative economy; Chapter 28: Economic impact of the arts; Chapter 30: Festivals.

References

Cellini R., T. Cuccia and W. Santagata (2007), 'Policy Decisions on Collective Property Rights in Cultural Districts: A Positive Model', in R. Cellini and G. Cozzi (eds), *Intellectual Property, Competition and Growth*, New York: Palgrave Macmillan, pp. 25–40.

Cuccia T. and W. Santagata (2003), 'Collective Property Rights and Sustainable Development: The Case of the Pottery Cultural District in Caltagirone, Sicily', in E. Colombatto (ed.), *Companion to Property Rights Economics*, Cheltenham, UK and Northampton, MA, USA: Edward Elgar, pp. 473–88.

Cuccia T., M. Marrelli and W. Santagata (2008), 'Collective Trademarks and Cultural Districts: The Case of San Gregorio Armeno, Naples', in P. Cook and L. Lazzeretti (eds), *Creative Cities, Cultural Clusters and Local Economic Development*, Cheltenham, UK and Northampton, MA, USA, Edward Elgar, pp. 121–36.

Frost-Kumpf, H.A. (1998), *Cultural Districts Handbook: The Arts as a Strategy for Revitalizing Our Cities*, Durham, NC: Duke University Press.

Marshall, A. (1890 [1920]), *Principles of Economics*, London: Macmillan.

Moreno, Y.J., W. Santagata and A. Tabassum (2004–05), 'Cultura materiale e sviluppo economico sostenibile', *Sviluppo locale*, 26, 31–50.

OECD (2005), *Culture and Local Development*, Paris: OECD.

Polanyi, M. (1953), *Personal Knowledge*, Chicago, IL: University of Chicago Press.

Pyke, F., G. Becattini and W. Sengenberg (1990), *Industrial Districts and Inter-Firm Co-operation in Italy*, Geneva: International Institute for Labour Studies.

Salais, R. and M. Storper (1993), *Les mondes de production*, Paris: Ecole des hautes études en sciences sociales.

Santagata, W. (2002), 'Cultural Districts, Property Rights and Sustainable Economic Growth', *International Journal of Urban and Regional Research*, 26, 181–204.

Santagata, W. (2004), 'Some Effect of Creativity on Fashion Market Behaviour', in D. Power and A.J. Scott, *The Cultural Industries and the Production of Culture*, London and New York: Routledge, pp. 75–90.

Santagata, W. (2006), 'Cultural Districts and Their Role in Economic Development', in V. Ginsburgh and D. Throsby (eds), *Handbook on the Economics of Art and Culture*, Amsterdam: Elsevier Science North-Holland, pp. 1100–19.

Santagata, W. (ed.) (2009), 'White Paper on Creativity in Italy. Towards an Italian Model of Development', downloadable from www.css-ebla.it.

Scott, A.J. (2000), *The Cultural Economy of Cities*, London: Sage.

Scott, A.J. (2005), *Hollywood. The Place, The Industry*, Princeton, NJ: Princeton University Press.

Further reading

The collection edited by Santagata (2009) demonstrates, in the case of Italy, how creativity may be harnessed for economic development. The book by Scott (2005) applies the idea of the cultural district to Hollywood.

22 Cultural entrepreneurship
Mark Blaug and Ruth Towse

Entrepreneurship is one of the most elusive and misunderstood concepts in modern economics; ironically, it has been largely ignored by many business economists, while the word is bandied about, often mistakenly, by others. Before discussing cultural entrepreneurship, therefore, it is worth considering the meaning and role of entrepreneurship as understood by economists.

A brief history
Richard Cantillon, that enigmatic Irishman with a Spanish name who spent much of his life in France, was the first to use the term in the modern sense in his *Essai Sur la Nature du Commerce en Général*, written around 1730. Writing in French (hence the term *entrepreneur*), he held entrepreneurs to be responsible for bringing about competition in markets through risk-taking – they 'buy at a certain price and sell at an uncertain one'. His contribution was to make it clear that the functions of the entrepreneur and the capitalist are distinct. The capitalist is the owner of capital and employs labour with the intention of obtaining a return on capital; the entrepreneur can ply his trade without either.

In this perception, he was far in advance of Adam Smith. Smith did not make that distinction and he used the English terms 'projector' and 'undertaker' for the business proprietor, who combined the role of capitalist and manager. John Stuart Mill popularized the term 'entrepreneur' in his *Principles of Economics* but retained the Smithian concept of his role. That view prevailed until the early twentieth century with the writing of Schumpeter.

The Schumpeterian view
Joseph Schumpeter was concerned with the ability of the capitalist system to develop through innovation and he identified the innovator as the entrepreneur in his book *The Theory of Economic Development* (Schumpeter, 1934). 'Innovations' in Schumpeter, as distinct from 'inventions', were the discovery of new technical methods, new products, new sources of raw materials and new forms of industrial organization. He perceived innovation to be an inevitable force for the 'creative destruction' of the status quo that enabled economic development to take place. Entrepreneurship was therefore the source of dynamic change and growth, and its reward was profit. The entrepreneur might also be a capitalist or a corporate manager, obtaining reward for those activities too; indeed, Schumpeter realized that once a new undertaking was established, the business might settle down and lose its entrepreneurial thrust, with the entrepreneur transformed into a mere capitalist or manager. The business would in the first place have a monopoly due to the entrepreneurial factor, and it would take further entrepreneurial effort to defend that monopoly.

Modern developments

It took some time before the Schumpeterian view was adopted into modern econom-ics. The neoclassical theory of the firm left no place for either the entrepreneur or the manager, and so it was left to those who did not subscribe to that theory to develop the notion of entrepreneurship. The so-called neo-Austrians debated the nature of entrepre-neurial profit, whether it was an income waiting to be serendipitously discovered through 'alertness' to opportunities for Schumpeterian innovation, or whether it was the reward of positive action to create new sources of profit opportunities. Some economists questioned whether entrepreneurship is always beneficial innovation and whether at times it is in fact not just rent-seeking in the form of activities, such as company takeovers, tax-evasion efforts, patent litigation and the like. Baumol (1990) distinguishes between productive and unproductive entrepreneurial activity, the latter being capable of reducing rather than increasing the social product, and argues that it is the overall 'rules of the game' of a capitalist society that determine the precise nature of entrepreneurial behaviour.

Nor is entrepreneurship confined to economic activity: in principle, it is performed in all societies by individuals whose judgement differs from the norm, and the political and military arena may provide as much scope for entrepreneurship as the economy.

Cultural entrepreneurship

With these issues in mind, it is interesting to consider cultural entrepreneurship. Skimming through literature on creative industries that mentions cultural entrepre-neurship (and there is a considerable volume of it) shows that many authors and organizations see it simply as an aspect of management. The Global Center for Cultural Entrepreneurship, an international network of cultural entrepreneurs, has a view that is close to the economists' concept, though. According to its website:

> Cultural Enterprise Entrepreneurs are cultural change agents and resourceful visionaries who generate revenue from a cultural activity. Their innovative solutions result in economically sus-tainable cultural enterprises that enhance livelihoods and create cultural value for both creative producers and consumers of cultural services and products.

Cultural enterprises large and small include for-profit or non-profit enterprises that adopt a 'business approach' and operate in the arts, heritage and cultural industries. Cultural entrepreneurs have specific attributes: passion, vision, leadership, resourceful-ness and 'market savvy' (Global Center for Cultural Entrepreneurship, accessed June 2010).

Motivation for cultural entrepreneurship

Although many entrepreneurs, including cultural entrepreneurs, as we see below, have become wealthy, profit is not the motivation that drives them. Swedberg (2006) points out that, according to Schumpeter, the entrepreneur is driven primarily by non-monetary motivation, such as building an empire, and struggles with outside and inner resistance to seize on novelty and carry projects through to their completion. In the spirit of Schumpeter, Swedberg sees cultural entrepreneurship as the creation of something new and appreciated in the cultural sphere (ibid., p. 260); inner, intrinsic motivation is the driving force. But is that sufficient to explain the application of the term to every cultural enterprise?

For-profit and non-profit enterprises
Many of the creative industries, such as advertising, design, fashion, film, sound recording, broadcasting and publishing, consist of for-profit enterprises, often large international corporations, whose measure of success is profitability. Even small for-profit firms need to pursue sufficient revenues to cover their costs, although they may not be under the same pressure to maximize profits. Individual artists, who are highly innovative and entrepreneurial in their art, may not be seeking profit at all but may become wealthy, and indeed some have.

In terms of non-profit enterprises, there is considerable variation in the adoption of business-like behaviour. In the USA and the UK, non-profit cultural enterprises, such as museums and performing arts organizations, are more or less reliant on their ability to appeal to consumers; in their 'mixed economy' model of private non-profit organizations, being 'entrepreneurial' means a combination of artistic innovation and other strategies to attract more paying audiences and private donors and sponsors. In many countries in Europe, though, such organizations are state-owned and -managed bureaucracies, and cultural economists have frequently inveighed against their lack of response to consumers, let alone their tendency to create new ways of doing things. There is a big difference between exhorting cultural organizations to be less dependent upon state finance and to be entrepreneurial. As Minister of State for Culture in the Netherlands, the economist Rick van der Ploeg urged cultural entrepreneurship on the state-run cultural organizations, which at the time received 85 per cent of their revenues from subsidies (van der Ploeg, 2006); thus Baumol's rent-seeking would seem more appropriate here. Acheson *et al.* (1996), however, claim that the non-profit status is no barrier to being entrepreneurial, even where subsidy is involved.

Role of the individual
Schumpeter clearly identified the entrepreneur as an individual, a man of action, and, indeed, the characteristics of cultural entrepreneurs presented above – problem-solving leaders with passion and vision, alertness and energy, imagination and commitment – seem to stress the importance of individuality. Case studies of cultural entrepreneurs suggest that they were founders of cultural enterprises – builders of their own empires, with a strong personal and individual imprint.

Case studies of cultural entrepreneurs
Any list of famous cultural entrepreneurs should include, for theatre: William Shakespeare, one of the group of Elizabethan playwrights and actors who owned, built and managed theatres in London; in our own day, Andrew Lloyd Webber (Baron Lloyd-Webber of Sydmonton, listed as the 87th richest Briton in 2006) is the composer of a number of hit musicals and founder of The Really Useful Theatre Company, which owns a number of West End theatres in London, as well as companies holding the musical rights, publishing, making recordings and films of his theatrical productions.

In art, Rembrandt van Rijn dealt in art, ran a studio and made and sold etchings of his works but nevertheless became bankrupt; by contrast, Peter Paul Rubens, who in addition to his prodigious income from commissions as an artist, ran a paid-entry workshop, dealt in art and pioneered print-making of his works, for which he trained a number of engravers, became very rich; similarly, in the twentieth century, Andy Warhol produced silkscreen prints on a commercial scale in his Factory, in addition to producing original works of art and other undertakings, from all of which he became very rich.

In music, the Italian opera *impresarii* (taken from the word *impresa* meaning enterprise or undertaking) commissioned new works (*opera*) from librettists (often well-known poets) and composers such as Bellini, Donizetti and Rossini (to name only a few that are still well known), made all the arrangements for producing them, including hiring the singers, musicians, the costumes and sets, for which they had to put up considerable sums of money, and toured them all around Italy and Europe from Moscow to New York; this form of organization carried on from around the mid-eighteenth century for well over one hundred years until they were more or less put out of business by the music publisher Giulio Ricordi, another superb cultural entrepreneur. Richard Wagner, who besides writing the libretti and music for his operas, revolutionized the production of opera through theatre design, conducting and dramaturgy. Richard D'Oyly Carte not only founded an opera company and commissioned Gilbert and Sullivan to write operettas for it, he also ran a concert agency (representing the singer Adelina Patti and the author Oscar Wilde among others), and with the profits financed the building of the Savoy Theatre and the Savoy Hotel in London. Sergei Diaghilev created the company Ballet Russes, organized its tours, commissioned a roster of composers – Debussy, Ravel, Satie, Prokofiev and most famously Stravinsky, hired Fokine as choreographer, legendary dancers Nijinsky and Pavlova (to mention just two) and kept the company going until his death in 1929.

Turning to the cultural industries: Walt Disney was an actor (the original voice of Mickey Mouse), animator, screen writer and probably the best-known film producer and director in the world; in 2008, the Walt Disney Company had gross revenues of just under US$40 billion. In the Netherlands, Joop van den Ende, the Dutch billionaire theatre producer and media tycoon, was co-founder of Endemol (and owner of the TV rights to *Batman*, among others); John de Mol, his partner in the enterprise, has the distinction of having invented the *Big Brother* and *Deal or No Deal* reality TV formats and has become very rich as a result. And let us not forget Steven Spielberg, film director and producer and master of the modern blockbuster movie.

Some of these people were artists who supplemented their own artistic work with other entrepreneurial activities; they were individuals and innovators in their arts. Others were mainly in the cultural business. They are all very well known and some, though not all, became rich. We could mention many, many more.

But where do we stop? Is Bill Gates a cultural entrepreneur because he created a software business? or Richard Branson because he started record companies and radio stations?

Conclusions

To sum up and to reiterate: an entrepreneur is not just a manager, although he or she may do a great deal of managing, since management may be hired in the labour market; nor is he or she a coordinator of production, because again industrial engineering is available for hire in the marketplace; nor is he or she a capitalist, because capital funds can be borrowed at the going rate of interest in the credit market. Entrepreneurship, though, cannot be bought. Thus what characterizes any form of entrepreneurship is the very quality that is the *modus vivendi* of dynamic change in an economy. Unless we empty the word 'entrepreneurial' of all meaning, we must hang on to its distinguishing characteristics, namely novelty of action, leadership in the sense of being ahead of the pack, wealth-creating and individuality. It is difficult to see how large institutions and mammoth corporate entities can be both innovative and trail-blazing.

A *cultural* entrepreneur is an innovator, usually but not necessarily an individual, who generates revenue from a novel cultural activity. Cultural entrepreneurs do much more than manage the activity; typically they discover it and exploit its revenue potentialities. They have the one quality that cannot be bought or hired, namely alertness to revenue-generating arbitrage, involving either new products, new materials, new processes or all of these in some combination.

See also:

Chapter 18: Creativity; Chapter 41: The music industry.

References

Acheson, Keith, Christopher Maule and Elizabeth-Filleul (1996), 'Cultural Entrepreneurship and the Banff Television Festival', *Journal of Cultural Economics*, 4, 321–39.

Baumol, William J. (1990), 'Entrepreneurship: Productive, Unproductive, and Destructive', *Journal of Political Economy*, 98 (5), 893–921.

Baumol, W. (2010), *The Microtheory of Innovative Entrepreneurship*, Princeton, NJ and Oxford: Princeton University Press.

Blaug, Mark (1998), 'Entrepreneurship in the History of Economic Thought', in P. Boetke, I. Kirzner and M. Rizzo (eds), *Advances in Austrian Economics*, London: JAI Press, pp. 217–39.

van der Ploeg, F. (2006), 'The Making of Cultural Policy: A European Perspective', in Victor Ginsburgh and David Throsby (2006), *Handbook of the Economics of Art and Culture*, Amsterdam: North-Holland, pp. 1183–221.

Global Center for Cultural Entrepreneurship (2010), www.culturalentrepreneur.org.

Schumpeter, Joseph (1934), *The Theory of Economic Development*, Cambridge, MA: Harvard University Press.

Swedberg, Richard (2006), 'The Cultural Entrepreneur and the Creative Industries: Beginning in Vienna', *Journal of Cultural Economics*, 30, 243–62.

Further reading

Blaug (1998) provides a detailed account and analysis of the development of entrepreneurship in the history of economic thought and the website of the Global Center for Cultural Entrepreneurship spells out the features and tasks of cultural entrepreneurship. For those readers interested in the theory of entrepreneurship, Baumol (2010) provides a thorough and up-to-date treatment.

23 Cultural statistics
David Throsby

Statistics covering the volume and value of cultural output, levels of employment, cultural consumption and participation, public and private funding and so on are required for purposes such as:

- describing the size of the cultural sector, its place in the economy and society, and the nature and extent of its functioning;
- underpinning evidence-based policy formation, which depends both on raw data and on relevant analysis of those data;
- monitoring and evaluation of the success or otherwise of cultural policies and programmes while they are being implemented or after they have been completed; and
- comparing various items of data using intra- or internationally comparable statistics to assist, for example, in the benchmarking of performance standards.

Cultural statistics that are useful for these purposes can be derived from three sources. First, official government statistical agencies routinely gather and publish data on the economy and society and are a major source of information about the arts and culture. The data they provide may occur as a subset of more general statistical collections such as censuses, national accounts or workforce surveys, or they may be put together specifically for the arts and culture sector, perhaps by specialized units devoted to cultural statistics. Second, a number of independent bodies collect data of various sorts that may be relevant for policy purposes; for example, cultural observatories, university research institutes and private consultants carry out surveys, while industry bodies and NGOs gather data from their members. Third, a number of international organizations publish data of relevance to the arts and culture, most notably the UNESCO Institute of Statistics, which has a primary responsibility to collate and publish cultural statistics from the member states of its parent body.

The range of data types covered by the overarching term 'cultural statistics' is very wide. This chapter discusses these various types and areas of application, paying particular attention to matters of definition and classification.

Cultural industries
Statistical compilations for the cultural industries face two problems. The first is a definitional problem, raising questions such as: 'Are they "creative" or "cultural" industries?', 'Which industries are included?', 'What product classifications are used?' and so on. The specific industries regarded as either cultural or creative that are identified within national systems vary between countries, although there is broad agreement that the cultural industries include the arts and heritage, film, broadcasting and print media, audiovisual industries, publishing, design and so on. Nevertheless countries differ in their interpretation of how far the terms 'cultural' or 'creative' extend, and as a result

international comparisons of, for example, the cultural industries' contribution to GDP can be problematical.

The second problem is to define the data series of interest for policy or other purposes. Conventional economic data that are routinely collected for all industries include gross value of production, contribution to GDP or GNP, value added, fixed capital formation, wholesale and retail prices, and so on, as well as trade and employment statistics (to be considered further below). Data on these variables for the cultural industries can be extracted from the economy-wide statistics by imposing whatever cultural industry classification scheme is in use. It may then be possible to carry out inter-industry analyses that examine the relationships between the cultural sector and the rest of the economy using methods such as input–output analysis or computable general equilibrium models.

International trade in cultural goods and services

Statistics on cultural trade have to rely on a workable product classification system rather than on industrial or other classifications, since the concern is with the actual movement of identifiable goods and services across national borders. Generally speaking, the product classification systems in use do not display cultural goods or services as separate categories. Hence compilation of statistics on cultural trade has to rely on extracting the relevant numbers according to the particular definitions of cultural goods and services in use, just as was the case with the industry data discussed above.

The audiovisual industries give rise to a particular difficulty in measuring cultural trade. In earlier years international transactions relating to films or music, for example, could be readily observed since they involved the export and import of physical commodities – reels of film, cassette tapes, compact discs and so on. With the advent of the Internet, trade in audiovisual product occurs increasingly across the World Wide Web – the material is transmitted in electronic form and so also is payment for rights, royalties and the like. Systematic tracking of these flows by statistical agencies is generally not possible, so estimates of the volume and value of such trade have to be assembled from other sources, for example from data provided by collecting societies responsible for the collection and distribution of copyright revenues. These data vary in their quality and coverage. Thus compiling a fully comprehensive and accurate statistical picture of cultural trade in all its various forms is well-nigh impossible.

Cultural employment

Once again, issues of definition are raised when labour force statistics for the cultural sector are being derived. Questions arise such as: 'What is a cultural occupation?' and 'How is the creative workforce to be delineated?' The answers to these questions are not as straightforward as may appear. For example, a cultural worker could be defined as one who works in a cultural industry, whether the work that person does is 'cultural' (producing cultural output such as writing poetry or acting) or 'non-cultural' (such as selling tickets for a theatre company). Alternatively a cultural worker could be more narrowly defined, for example by limiting this category to artists or other creative workers.

Thus a cultural occupation can be defined by reference not to the industry of employment but to the nature of the work that occupation entails. But in this case it may make for clearer definition to identify *creative* occupations instead, since this terminology is related to an easily recognizable input (creativity) rather than to a less easily observed output (culture). Even so, the designation of a set of creative occupations from ISCO (the overall International Standard Classification of Occupations) is not a simple matter, since it depends on how far the adjective 'creative' is deemed to extend. As a result, different countries use different approaches to measuring cultural employment, the creative workforce and so on.

Artists

Data about artists can be derived from two main sources. First, a population or labour force census provides the most accurate information available on the size and characteristics of the population of workers within specific occupational categories. Given that in most countries' censuses, standard occupational classifications are adopted that include various identifiable types of artists, in some cases down to quite a fine level of occupational disaggregation, these statistics have been useful in studying the extent and nature of the artistic workforce. However, they suffer from several important drawbacks. First, in most cases the allocation of an individual respondent to a job category is based on his or her main job at the moment of the census or survey; it is well understood that this procedure will overlook many genuine artists who are forced to take other work as a means of supporting their artistic practice, and who are therefore working at some other 'main job' at the time of the data collection. Second, the categorization of artist in such statistical collections does not distinguish professional from amateur; whilst it may be reasonable to assume that professional status attaches to someone who declares their 'main job' as artist, there is no way of knowing if such individuals would meet more refined criteria for professionalism. Third, there may be problems in understanding what 'artist' means as a job category when the data collection is based on self-evaluation. Finally, the descriptive data collected via censuses may be very limited in their capacity to enable analysis of the sorts of issues of interest to economic and sociological researchers. For example, economists are usually concerned to identify time allocation and corresponding earnings from arts work and from non-arts work, and indeed even this two-way classification does not go far enough for many purposes. Income statistics for artists derived from census returns are thus problematical for economic analysis, and researchers who use census data to analyse the income position of artists are inevitably limited in the conclusions they can draw.

The second main data source is special-purpose surveys. Targeted surveys of artists can pick up part-time as well as full-time workers, including those temporarily not working, and hence more accurate estimates of the size of artist populations can be obtained than are usually possible from the general census. If the category of interest in a particular study is professional artists, filters can be used to screen out amateurs from the sample or, in a broader study aimed at covering a range of types of practice, appropriate questions can be included to establish precisely the occupational status of respondents. The definition of 'artist' is controllable by the researcher instead of being provided by census requirements or by self-evaluation. Finally, and of course most significantly, the quality and extent of data obtainable can be expected to be much richer in a specially targeted survey than in a general data collection, since the survey instrument is custom-designed to answer the precise questions of interest to the researcher.

Nevertheless, there are some problems with sample surveys. They are generally costly to administer. Furthermore, the usefulness of their results for purposes of inference depends critically on the researcher's capacity to identify the artist population of interest and to draw a statistically valid random sample from it. For some occupations, identifying the artist population may be relatively straightforward. For example, in many countries actors or musicians are highly unionized; in such cases, with the cooperation of the union concerned, a researcher may be able to obtain a reasonably complete list of professional practitioners, together with contact details, from which to draw a sample. In other artistic occupations, however, such centralized lists may not exist, and a researcher may have to rely on building up a database by putting together lists from various sources and eliminating duplication. Even so, it may still be difficult to establish the overall size of the relevant artist population by these means, since the extent of those not included in the population list may not be readily estimable. In these circumstances, the use of techniques such as network sampling or respondent-driven sampling may enable extension of the sample to those groups not on the original list.

Demand for cultural goods
The volume and value of consumers' purchases of tangible cultural commodities are recorded in a variety of ways. They may be accessed via household expenditure data (see below) or collected for specific categories of goods by commercial firms or by trade or industry associations and the like. Examples of the latter include:

- art market data collected and made available (usually at a price) by sales monitoring organizations; for instance a wealth of data is available on the prices of artworks sold at auction by the major auction houses;
- record industry data on sales of music in various formats collected by the International Federation of the Phonographic Industry (IFPI); these data include estimates of levels of piracy (sales of illegally copied music) in various countries;
- data collected by publishers' associations in various countries on the numbers and prices of different categories of books, magazines and newspapers sold.

In some cases special-purpose surveys of cultural consumption are undertaken by statistical agencies that provide a wide range of statistics on the artistic and cultural goods purchased by consumers.

Cultural consumption can also be tracked via household expenditure surveys, either carried out across all types of expenditure of which cultural spending is a part, or focused specifically on consumption of the arts and culture. Either way, such surveys – a standard means of regular data collection employed by most official statistical agencies – can yield a great deal of information about individual and household spending on culture in all its forms. Nevertheless international comparisons of such statistics may be problematical; whilst data for particular items of expenditure may be compared, aggregate concepts such as 'total cultural spending' and so on will depend on the classification schemes for cultural goods and services that may or may not be comparable between countries.

Attendance and participation
The generic terms 'participation' and 'involvement' of people in the arts and culture cover a range of activities from passive attendance as an audience at a concert or a

theatrical performance to active engagement in acting, dancing, creative writing, musical performance, film-making and so on. In surveys concerned with these latter activities, it is assumed that they are undertaken voluntarily and on a non-professional basis for pleasure rather than for reward. Despite the apparent clarity of a definition of participation along these lines, it remains a concept of some fuzziness, especially if international comparisons are involved. Nevertheless, sidestepping questions such as how 'active' are apparently 'passive' cultural pursuits like reading or going to the opera, we can draw a pragmatic distinction between:

- *attendance* as measured by surveys of cultural institutions or tabulated by the institutions themselves;
- *readership* as indicated by surveys of book, magazine and newspaper purchases, library borrowings and so on;
- *viewing* and *listening* as assessed by television and radio ratings and so on;
- *access* to online cultural consumption either streamed or downloaded and consumed subsequently, as measured by Internet tracking and other services; and
- *creative involvement* in active artistic and cultural activities of any type, such as writing a novel, singing in a choir or painting landscapes, as documented in special-purpose surveys.

All these types of data and more can be gathered together under the generic heading of participation studies, of which there are many in existence.

Cultural funding
The implementation of cultural policy in all its many guises entails direct and indirect expenditure by government, the levels of which are reported in various ways in national accounting data. Although standardized formats exist according to which national governments present their accounts, there are many variations in detail between countries as to what is counted as 'cultural', if indeed that adjective is used at all. Moreover, it is not just at the national level that public funding of the arts and culture is important. Subnational levels of government (states, counties, municipalities, cities and so forth) also provide funds to support the arts and culture through subsidies, grants, capital and operating allocations to cultural institutions, investment allowances, tax breaks and so on. The formality and rigour by which these expenditures are recorded and published differ widely between jurisdictions, such that in some countries it is difficult or impossible to aggregate cultural funding statistics across all tiers of government to obtain a comprehensive national picture.

These variations both within and between countries make international comparisons of cultural funding extremely hazardous. Yet comparing the level of cultural funding per head is a favourite pastime in many quarters, even to the extent of constructing 'league tables' of countries ranked in order of their apparent commitment to arts and cultural support. Such comparative statistics suffer from three particular problems. First, as noted repeatedly in this chapter, different countries use different classification systems to assemble their data. Second, comparative statistics generally fail to account for the cost to the public purse of indirect support measures such as tax concessions. Finally, in concentrating on public sector outlays they neglect to account for direct private support for the arts and culture that is necessary to complete the picture.

Cultural indicators

Indicators are statistics that go beyond simply describing some phenomenon; they are intended to imply something more – for example, to be used in conjunction with other data to monitor or evaluate some circumstance or process. As such, they occupy an intermediate position between raw data on the one hand and analysis on the other, in other words between the supply of information in the form of primary statistics and the demand for information for purposes of analysis and policy-making. Indicators can be either quantitative or qualitative in nature. Examples include:

- a suite of statistics gathered together to indicate levels of cultural participation or enjoyment;
- performance indicators for cultural institutions to indicate their success or otherwise in achieving certain designated goals;
- 'quality of life' indicators to demonstrate the artistic or cultural ambience of a city or region or the cultural vitality of communities;
- various data that can be taken as indicators of cultural development in a developing country; and
- indicators of cultural value for some artistic or cultural phenomenon, to be used when direct measures of cultural value are not available.

Much effort has gone into devising workable procedures for constructing and utilizing indicators of various sorts, including cultural indicators. There is general agreement that good indicators should be firmly grounded in theory, linked to policy practice, and relevant, unambiguous, measurable and easily understood.

Satellite accounts for culture

Satellite accounts provide a representation of national accounting data for a particular field that is more detailed than that available from the normal national accounts. They essentially expand the System of National Accounts (SNA) that is used as a basis in most countries for the construction of statistics measuring aggregate economic activity such as national income and GDP. Since their construction entails data, expertise and resources that are not generally available, such accounts are relatively rare; to date the main areas for which satellite accounts have been put together are tourism and the environment.

Following these leads, it is possible to imagine developing procedures for identifying satellite accounts for culture. If so, they could provide information on a range of macroeconomic data for the cultural sector with greater product and industry specificity than would otherwise be available. In addition a system of cultural satellite accounts would be expected to cover various social and cultural dimensions of the operations of the cultural sector. At present, however, the development of satellite accounts for culture is in its infancy. Only two systematic efforts have been made to date in this direction, one in Colombia under the auspices of the Convenio Andrés Bello, the other by Statistics Finland. These two initiatives seem certain to illuminate the path towards a wider development of this form of cultural statistics in the future.

Conclusion: towards a new framework for cultural statistics

Several international standard classifications exist that provide individual countries with a template for the design of their own classification systems for statistics covering a range of economic variables, including industry, occupation and commodity classifications. In the specialized field of cultural statistics, a framework was put forward in 1986 by UNESCO that was intended to provide some consistency across jurisdictions in national statistical collections for the arts and culture. The framework has guided the development of cultural statistics collections in many countries over the intervening years. However, the social, economic and technological changes that have occurred since the 1980s have rendered the original framework increasingly out of date, prompting the initiation of a process designed to produce a new framework for cultural statistics by the end of the first decade of the new millennium. This deadline was met by UNESCO's Institute for Statistics, which produced a revised Framework for Cultural Statistics in 2009.

The new framework provides a basis for classifying the cultural industries that can be integrated with broader standard industrial classifications both internationally and at the national or subnational level. It also allows the specification of an updated system for classifying cultural occupations and for measuring cultural participation. The revised framework is not intended to be a blueprint that every country will follow, since different aspects of cultural statistics are of different importance in different countries. Rather, it provides a coherent and consistent basis on which national systems of cultural statistics can be developed. To the extent that the framework is utilized in different jurisdictions, we can hope that stronger, more reliable and more internationally comparable cultural statistics will result in future.

Finally, in any discussion of cultural statistics, it must be borne in mind that data are not collected just for their own sake, but to inform discussion and to enable analysis of the size, structure, interrelationships, causal connections and so on that characterize the cultural sector. The validity of such discussions and the strength of such analyses will depend critically on the quality of the statistics on which they are based, imposing a major responsibility on collection agencies to provide consistent, comprehensive and reliable statistics for the variety of users that they serve.

See also:

Chapter 7: Artists' labour markets; Chapter 17: Creative industries; Chapter 33: International trade; Chapter 46: Performance indicators.

References

Madden, Christopher (2005a), 'Indicators for Arts and Cultural Policy: A Global Perspective', *Cultural Trends*, 14, 217–47.

Madden, Christopher (2005b), 'Cross-country Comparisons of Cultural Statistics: Issues and Good Practice', *Cultural Trends*, 14, 299–316.

McCaughey, Claire (2005), *Comparisons of Arts Funding in Selected Countries: Preliminary Findings*, Ottawa: Canada Council for the Arts.

Pattanaik, Prasanta (1998), 'Cultural Indicators of Well-being, Some Conceptual Issues', in UNESCO, *World Culture Report: Culture, Creativity and Markets*, Paris: UNESCO, pp. 333–40.

Schuster, J. Mark (1996), 'The Performance of Performance Indicators in the Arts', *Nonprofit Management and Leadership*, 7, 253–69.

Schuster, J. Mark (2003), 'Informing Cultural Policy – Data, Statistics, and Meaning', in Serge Bernier and Denise Lievesley (eds), *Proceedings of the International Symposium on Culture Statistics: Montréal, 21 to 23 October 2002*, Montréal: Government of Québec, pp. 41–61.

Schuster, J. Mark (2007), 'Participation Studies and Cross-national Comparison: Proliferation, Prudence, and Possibility', *Cultural Trends*, 16, 99–196.

Throsby, David (2010), *The Economics of Cultural Policy*, Cambridge: Cambridge University Press.

Further reading

This chapter is an abridged and edited version of Chapter 14, 'Cultural Statistics', in Throsby (2010). For discussions of cultural indicators, see Schuster (1996, 2003), Pattanaik (1998), and Madden (2005a). The perils and possibilities in making cross-national comparisons of cultural statistics are discussed in Madden (2005b), McCaughey (2005) and Schuster (2007).

24 Cultural tourism
Lluís Bonet

Introduction

The phenomenon of cultural tourism, despite not having attained any special recognition from the tourism industry itself or from the field of cultural promotion as a whole, existed long before tourism was even structured into a particular sector of the economy. A large number of the travellers who for various reasons moved throughout Italy, Greece, Egypt and the Holy Land centuries ago can be seen as pioneers of the present-day concept of cultural tourism. Beyond excitement and adventure, these intellectuals and artists, who often left a trail of texts, drawings and music behind them, were propelled onward by a curiosity about different cultures and a desire to be inspired by the classic landmarks of history and art. Not until the second half of the twentieth century, as increased income and free time became widespread among developed countries, would these journeys begin to acquire a significant following. The main destinations of these travels would be those grand monuments and cities with an established richness in cultural heritage and, to a lesser degree, exotic places made fashionable by great discoveries or by alternative movements (many hippies, for example, made pilgrimages to India during the 1960s).

Nevertheless, the current reality of cultural tourism, while sharing a curiosity and awakened longing for exploring diverse cultures, has little to do with either romantic notions of adventure or with scientific interest. It has ceased to be an unusual request by a minority of travellers who had to resolve their own transport and accommodation needs, becoming instead an additional product of the tourist trade with all of its corresponding services. It has emerged as a consequence of the very development of the tourist market and its need for diversification. Cultural tourism can also be attributed to the growing importance of the new urban middle class with a high level of education, an interest in experiencing something different from the usual tourist traps, and a desire to learn something rich in cultural, symbolic, spiritual or historical content. In line with the definition used by the European Association for Tourism and Leisure Education (ATLAS), cultural tourism is 'the movement of persons to cultural attractions away from their normal place of residence with the intention to gather new information and experiences to satisfy their cultural needs' (Richards and Bonink, 1995, p. 174). Therefore, thanks to the new contacts made between cultural institutions and tourist intermediaries, it is now possible to speak of a structured programming within the field of cultural tourism, which includes newly designed products and services as well as cultural tourist attractions previously in existence.

In the present chapter, first, the emergence of cultural tourism and its defining characteristics will be studied in the context of the development of the contemporary tourist sector. Next, the motivation and strategies of the public sector for developing cultural tourism will be analysed. Following this, an examination of some of the paradoxical characteristics of the field will be presented. The chapter will conclude with a review of the analyses conducted to determine the impact made by cultural tourism on the economy.

The emergence of cultural tourism and its defining characteristics within the contemporary tourist sector

In the last 30 years, the number of tourist visits to European heritage establishments has more than doubled. Nevertheless, it is not easy to quantify the volume of people and businesses associated with the practice of cultural tourism or what this means with regard to the tourism industry as a whole. In the first place, it is difficult to define what is included in the practice of cultural tourism. If the term 'culture' is considered in a wider sense (as interest in the objects and lifestyles of other peoples), then the vast majority of tourists consume cultural products and services at one time or another (whether relatively authentic or largely commercialized in the style of theme parks). From a traditional standpoint, it is appropriate to limit the analysis of cultural tourism to the supply and demand of heritage services associated with visits to museums, monuments, historic buildings, archaeological sites and natural parks. However, along with these elements, cultural tourism also includes participation in any manifestation of a cultural tradition (such as folkloric celebrations and local festivals), fairs displaying art, crafts, recordings or books; and festivals presenting cinema, theatre, dance or opera; as well as the wide array of regular programming of exhibits and performances.

Faced with such a diverse and heterogeneous picture, it is not unusual for cultural tourism to be confused with urban tourism or limited solely to heritage tourism. This is a logical occurrence since a great deal of the cultural products and services available are usually concentrated in either a large metropolis or a city's historic centre. Furthermore, according to a survey conducted by ATLAS in 1997, in a sample of 8000 visitors to 20 different cultural locations in Europe, more than 50 per cent claimed to have toured a museum during their trip, 40 per cent had visited a monument, and 30 per cent had seen an exhibit. Meanwhile, admission to a live performance, for example, was reduced to just 23 per cent of those surveyed (Richards, 1997).

Similarly, the profile of the typical cultural tourist is quite varied. A small part corresponds to the tourist who chooses a destination with the primary objective of enjoying a cultural activity or product in mind and who identifies himself as a cultural tourist (between 20 and 30 per cent of those surveyed at these 20 locations). This profile usually describes a young person with a high level of education, a professional connection to cultural activities and an increased capacity for interpreting the cultural activity at hand within its proper context. Yet, while the rest of the tourists surveyed did not consider cultural tourism the main motive of their trip, the vast majority still admitted to having visited a museum during their travels. In this case, the profile also corresponds to a well-educated but significantly older tourist, between 40 and 60 years of age.

As mentioned earlier, cultural tourism has recently developed as a consequence of the evolution of the tourist industry. As the market following the traditional model of tourism development became saturated, the industry itself looked for alternative ways to respond to the ever-increasing, fragmented and changing demand. The previous model, stimulated by increased life expectancy, vacation time and income levels, was based on the heavy exploitation of a limited number of tourist attractions (sunny beaches or big cities) and was no guarantee of growth or profitability. In contrast, tourist agents now work in an increasingly global and competitive marketplace, which obliges them to continue to look for new attractions and special offers. This new setting can be characterized as more dynamic and competitive, taking into account improved transport conditions, lower living expenses associated with several of the new destinations, and increased information available thanks to new communication technologies. Thus cultural attractions become an excellent way to respond to the need for alternative options, new experiences and diversification. They can serve as either primary or complementary features of a tour, helping to convince the tourist of where to spend his vacation time.

Public policy and strategies for development

Additionally, the discovery made by many government and business officials of the potential of cultural tourism as a strategic factor in developing the local economy and generating jobs has encouraged its growth. The European Commission advocates harnessing the potential of cultural tourism as a means of reducing tourist congestion and rigid seasonal cycles while expanding the positive effects of tourism development on a regional and timely basis (European Commission, 1995). According to this argument, locations far from principal tourist routes or those without the classic resources to attract visitors in this regard (sun and surf, monuments and other attractions of symbolic value) see an element of tourist attraction and economic development in the restoration and preservation of their cultural patrimony and heritage. Thus these places must simply adapt or redesign specific products for this new market and gather together a sufficient supply of available products and services in order to attract travel agents and tourists with cultural interests towards new destinations.

However, merely offering hospitality and attractive cultural itineraries does not guarantee tourists or stable economic development. In fact, the number of cultural tourist resources in Europe has grown in the last two decades far beyond the demand for cultural tourism (Richards, 1996). The subjective and often unpredictable tendencies of this sector can partially be explained by the intangible and symbolic values – learned beliefs that are passed on by society over time – that each package tour represents to the potential buyer. For many cultured Westerners, a tour of ancient Europe holds a higher level of recognition (greater capacity for interpreting and appreciating its value) than does a tour of the Buddhist and Shinto temples of Eastern culture. Similarly, this learnt value can be overshadowed or complemented by the powerful influences of a great discovery (for example, what Machu Picchu meant in its time) or by the promotion of prestigious cultural events (as often is the case with large, international arts festivals or fairs).

For this reason, it is necessary to keep in mind the appropriateness of each of the possible development strategies. An isolated attraction within a largely unknown or remote region has little hope of standing out in a dense market of tourist products and services. This is why it can be beneficial to associate oneself with a larger campaign of regional tourist itineraries, a network of events based on a particular theme, or other tourist attractions that in turn seek out complementary activities. Strategies for promoting cultural tourism that assume that generic tourist interest will automatically embrace any new cultural itinerary must be discarded. It is precisely the interest in the unusual, the experimental and the exceptional associated with the phenomenon of cultural tourism that explains the high level of selectivity used in choosing destinations for package tours. Therefore the traditional focal points of cultural attraction, with their infinite number of possible itineraries (capital cities such as Paris, London or New York), or the main historical centres of cultural heritage (Rome, Athens, Florence, Granada or Venice) have a considerable advantage over any new proposals. For example, very few foreigners interested in cultural tourism in Catalonia would visit a Romanesque church in the Pyrenees, no matter how spectacular it might be, if they had not previously heard of its beautiful murals, architecture and surrounding scenery; and even fewer would visit the industrial park at the Llobregat River. They would be more inclined to tour the Dalí Museum in Figueres or the Modernist architecture in Barcelona first.

Paradoxes surrounding cultural tourism

Contact and openness between cultures has repeatedly generated a multitude of exchanges and mutually influential effects throughout history. However, when the authenticity and original value, in anthropological and social terms, of a culture turn into mythical legend, the external projection of its own image tends to become simplified or frozen in time. Maintaining this stereotypical image helps facilitate the promotion of tourism, even though it may falsify or contradict the unstoppable transformation, through cross-cultural mixing or through natural evolution, of all human experience. It is important to add that tourism (tourists and tourism professionals) often tends to trivialize, socially marginalize and segregate the expression of native cultures from their own environment. The commercialization generated by the development of cultural tourism frequently leads to making a spectacle out of cultural identities (García Canclini, 1989): natives who dress up in their folkloric costumes, often a flashy or exaggerated reproduction of those traditionally worn, only when tourists come onto the scene. Hence it is no surprise that tourism has been identified as the principal culprit in the commercialization and falsification of numerous cultural traditions and even the natural environment (Croall, 1995). An effort to preserve the quality of cultural and patrimonial resources and to avoid triviality must therefore be made alongside the sustainable development of tourism.

On another note, the rise in the number of visitors implied by the operation of cultural tourism as a whole presents a risk in exposing communities, monuments or areas of special scenic, cultural or ecological sensitivity to pressures incompatible with their maintenance and preservation. For example, patrimonial treasures such as Pasqua Island, the Alhambra of Granada, or the cave paintings of Altamira have had to adopt protective measures that do not exclude tourism, acquiring the respective economic resources needed to make their public enjoyment and promotion compatible with their preservation. Thus strategies such as limiting the number of annual visitors or constructing a replica located next to the original assist in resolving the dilemma.

Nevertheless, one must not forget that one of the economic impacts associated with the tourist exploitation of a cultural, patrimonial or natural resource is the consequent increase in social sensitivity, economic resources and efforts on behalf of local citizens to maintain and preserve it.

Economic analysis of cultural tourism

The large-scale development of cultural tourism has had a direct positive effect not just on the financial outlook of the cultural entities themselves but also on the local economy as a whole. With the objective of measuring this relationship, several studies over the last 25 years have been conducted to analyse the economic impact of cultural activities. The greater part of these are centred upon the economic consequences of expenditure on culture and only laterally look at the impact of cultural tourism. One must keep in mind, however, that often the criteria for determining the scope of the budgets and procedures followed for obtaining the relevant data are neither explicit nor clear, which does not help to legitimize the results obtained. For example, the lack of an exact distinction between 'solely cultural-motivated' visitors (or tourists) and those who are 'combined-motivated' could carry an important extra dimension in the form of effects of indirect spending on culture (Puffelen, 1996). Another possible source of exaggeration lies in the overestimate of the complementary expenses incurred by the consumption of the cultural goods themselves (such as transport and lodging expenses). In this way, unlike cost–benefit breakdowns (or similar models) or any perfectly legitimate political justification, the results obtained from these studies do not allow one to compare different projects and evaluate the allocation of resources for different objectives; nor do they leave room for justifying political support for public expenditure on culture (Baró and Bonet, 1997).

Beyond these studies, further economic research is needed in the analysis of the supply and demand of cultural tourism. A significant portion of the existing research on the subject stems from the economic analysis of urban tourism (Ashworth and Tunbridge, 1990; Law, 1996; Page, 1995). Only the few papers that have focused on the economics of heritage have paid any attention to the phenomenon of cultural tourism (Agnus, 1985; Greffe, 1990; Dupuis and Desjardins, 1994). Also the research conducted on the impact of museums and festivals has on occasion alluded to the economic implications of cultural tourism or to the activity of the various agents involved in the organization and financing of 'superstar' museums and arts festivals (Frey, 1998). Still, there is a great need for a deeper understanding of organizational behaviour, the services sector of the economy, the patterns of demand for cultural tourism and the cost–benefit breakdown of projects, a challenge left to be faced by a new generation of cultural economists.

See also:

Chapter 30: Festivals.

References

Agnus, J.M. (1985), *Ressources économiques engendrées par le patrimoine monumental en France*, Paris: Ministère de la Culture.

Ashworth, G.J. and J.E. Tunbridge (1990), *The Tourist-Historic City*, London: Belhaven Press.

Baró, E. and L. Bonet (1997), 'Els problemes d'avaluació de l'impacte econòmic de la despesa cultural', *Revista Econòmica de Catalunya*, 31, 76–83.

Croall, J (1995), *Preserve or Destroy: Tourism and the Environment*, London: Calouste Gulbenkian Foundation.

Dupuis, X. and C. Desjardins (1994), *Éléments de synthèse sur l'économie du patrimoine*, Paris: Ministère de la Culture et de la Francophonie.

European Commission (1995), *The Role of the European Union in the Promotion of Tourism*, Brussels: EC.

Frey, B. (1998), 'Superstar Museums: An Economic Analysis', *Journal of Cultural Economics*, 22, 113–25.

García Canclini, N. (1989), *Culturas híbridas: Estrategias para entrar y salir de la modernidad*, Grijalbo, Mexico: Consejo Nacional para la Cultura y las Artes.

Greffe, X. (1990), *La valeur économique du patrimoine: La demande et l'offre de monuments*, Paris: Anthropos-Economica.

Law, C.M. (1996), *Urban Tourism: Attracting Visitors to Large Cities*, London: Mansell.

Page, S. (1995), *Urban Tourism*, London: Routledge.

Puffelen, F. van (1996), 'Abuses of Conventional Impact Studies in the Arts', *Cultural Policy*, 2, 241–54.

Richards, G. (1996), 'Production and Consumption of European Cultural Tourism', *Annals of Tourism Research*, 23, 261–83.

Richards, G. (1997), 'From Cultivated Tourists to a Culture of Tourism?', paper presented at the VTB-VAB Conference on Cultural Tourism, Brussels, 27 November.

Richards, G. (2007), *Cultural Tourism: Global and Local Perspectives*, New York: Haworth Press.

Richards, G. and C.A.M. Bonink (1995), 'European Cultural Tourism Markets', *Journal of Vacation Marketing*, 1, 173–80.

Further reading

The collection edited by Greg Richards (2007) (editor).

25 Cultural value
Jen D. Snowball

While most people accept that the arts have value to society, not all would agree that this value is measurable, or indeed, that it should be measured. This chapter describes the kinds of value that the arts can provide and also how at least some aspects of their value might be quantified.

Why quantify the value of the arts at all?

One of the questions often asked of cultural economists is why one needs to put a monetary value on the arts at all. Is it not possible to accept that the arts *are* valuable and so just agree to fund them publicly? If governments had unlimited funds, then this would certainly be enough, but in reality, limited public resources have to be allocated to all kinds of competing, and equally valid, needs, like education and healthcare. All funding decisions thus have an opportunity cost – the next-best alternative forgone. That is, money spent on culture is money not available to be spent on anything else. In this scenario, the question is not simply one of whether to fund the arts or not, but of whether to fund the arts or something else.

A related issue is *which* arts to fund. Thirty years ago, there was a general consensus that what should be funded was 'high' culture – largely represented by European art forms, like opera and ballet and fine art forms identified by experts – while 'popular' culture was funded through the market by ticket sales and merchandising. Today, there is much less agreement on what constitutes 'culture' or 'art'. Puppet shows, street theatre and installations are considered just as valid as more traditional art forms. Expert valuations can help, but since publicly funded arts are, after all, paid for by the public, there is a growing need to take into account public sentiment about what makes up 'culture and the arts' and how they should be funded.

Policy-makers are obliged to make funding decisions with the information at hand, whether it is quantitative or qualitative. The advantage of quantitative information is that it can be used to compare the benefits to society of various projects in order to make a socially efficient choice between them. Qualitative valuations are more difficult to compare, but may also have a role to play in measuring longer-term, socially constructed cultural values. The problem is how one quantifies the benefits of culture to society so that the best decisions possible can be made.

Instrumental and intrinsic values

The arts have broadly two kinds of values: instrumental and intrinsic. Intrinsic value is the unique value of the arts themselves – it reflects the purpose of producing art in the first place. Instrumental values are those things that arise as side effects of the arts – not the main aim of the artistic endeavour, but nevertheless valuable. For example, the aim of a performing arts festival may be to celebrate the art and culture of a particular region and to encourage artistic collaboration between local and international performers, to entertain, delight and inform audiences and to lead to more and better-quality productions – this is the *intrinsic* value of the festival. Side effects might include visitors coming to the region and spending on things like accommodation and food, job creation for providers of such services, spending to improve infrastructure and so on – these would be regarded as *instrumental* values.

Many artists, scholars and policy-makers suggest that the value of the arts should not be quantified. This largely stems from a tendency of some studies to focus on the instrumental values of the arts and not on the intrinsic values. Instrumental values are often captured by some market transaction, with its value measured in terms of price, and are thus much easier to quantify than intrinsic values. By using well-tested methods, like economic impact studies, a monetary value could be put on something like an arts festival, or a museum, or a library, or a cultural heritage site.

Such measurements of impact became popular because of their ability to produce a single monetary amount that could be used, often effectively, for the promotion of a particular event or institution and to argue for public or private funds. Not surprisingly, however, there were vehement objections to such studies because the intrinsic value of the arts, their reason for existence in the first place, was completely excluded:

> Mozart is Mozart because of his music and not because he created a tourist industry in Salzburg or gave his name to decadent chocolate and marzipan Salzburg Kugel. Picasso is important because he taught a century new ways of looking at objects and not because his paintings in the Guggenheim Museum are regenerating an otherwise derelict northern Spanish port . . . Absolute quality is paramount in attempting a valuation of the arts; all other factors are interesting, useful but secondary. (Tusa, 1999; cited in Reeves, 2002, p. 36)

A danger of representing the value of culture using only instrumental values is that these same effects might be equally well provided by other, non-cultural industries. If opening a local supermarket creates more jobs than an arts festival, should the government subsidize the supermarket instead? If the mining sector has a greater effect on economic growth than the cultural industries, should public spending be focused on mining instead of on culture? The answer in both cases is clearly no: culture and the arts are not primarily about creating jobs or economic growth. If they ceased to be funded and no longer existed, not only the jobs and growth would be lost, but also their unique intrinsic values that could not be provided by other industries. Yet it is often through the measurement of instrumental benefits that the value of the arts is represented, which could lead to such dangerous comparisons.

On these grounds, several interest groups argued that the value of the arts should not be quantified – that they are a unique case and should thus be exempt from market valuations. However, it is not true that there is no possible way of measuring intrinsic value: economics offers effective non-market valuation methods that can go some way towards capturing this value. Contingent valuation (CV) methods use surveys to ask large samples of people about their consumption of cultural activities and whether they would be willing to pay (usually through an increase in taxes) to support them. While initially regarded with some scepticism, CV has become an accepted and widely used valuation technique that has been applied, not only to just about any cultural product one can think of, but also in other fields, like environmental economics.

A surprising finding of many of these studies is that it is not only those people who actually attend arts events, or museums, or heritage sites who are willing to pay to preserve or expand them – quite a lot of non-users are willing to do so as well. This is because, in addition to the private benefits that the arts provide to people who have bought a ticket, they also provide public benefits to society at large.

Culture as a public good with longer-term, socially constructed value

One of the most compelling arguments for the use of government funds to support the arts is their 'public-good' nature. Public goods are special because, once they have been provided, they benefit not only their purchaser, but also the whole society. It has been argued that the arts can enhance national identity and pride and international prestige, they provide ongoing education for children and adults, they offer a critique of social policy, foster personal development, integrate individuals into society and encourage experimentation and the entrepreneurship that drives economic growth.

It is thus not only those who purchase tickets to cultural events or who visit museums and heritage sites who benefit through their direct use values, but also people who do not consume the arts directly. While this is a positive thing for society, it may lead to market failure and the underprovision of cultural goods because those who provide such goods are not able to recoup their value completely through market sales. A characteristic of public goods is that they are not completely appropriable by their supplier or by their purchaser. As such, the supply of cultural goods is likely to be below the socially optimal level, and the argument is that public (government) funds should be used to correct this by providing support to suppliers.

A potential problem with even the non-market valuation methods suggested above is that they are based on random utility theory (RUT), which is essentially about perceptions of value *by individuals*. While RUT can take into account intrinsic values, it does so by creating an imaginary market in which individual people signal their value through their willingness to pay. Klamer (2003), as well as many other economists, finds this approach problematic for cultural goods. He argues that individual ownership and valuation of culture makes little sense, since such values are constructed by society and can be changed:

> If foreigners point out to indigenous people that their piles of old stones are actually cultural treasures and that they are willing to pay to conserve them, the indigenous people change their perception of those stones and may even begin to value them. Get a cultural good listed on the UNESCO world heritage list, and people will value that good more. (Klamer, 2003, p. 11)

Throsby (1999, 2001) first introduced the idea of 'cultural capital' defined as a 'long lasting store of value', providing a stream of benefits to individuals and groups (Throsby, 2001, p. 44). The concept is closely related to the intrinsic value of the arts – unique values provided by the art form itself. While economic or 'ordinary' capital generated by arts and culture (the instrumental benefits) could also be supplied by other industries, cultural capital is that part of the value of culture that can be provided only by culture itself. Just like other forms of capital, cultural capital can decay if it is not protected and enhanced, thus also eroding the stream of benefits it might have provided to future generations.

Klamer (2002) argues that 'cultural capital' should be included as part of a nation's or individual's wealth. Cultural capital may impact positively on (or underpin) other parts of the economy through, for example, developing creativity and experimentation, helping to develop a sense of identity and encouraging social cohesion. In modern econo-mies, creativity and entrepreneurship are highly prized and often conceived as drivers of growth, as suggested by Florida (2002).

Another form of capital that can arise from the arts and culture is social capital, related to the generation of social values, like friendship and trust. This kind of capital is finding more acceptance with the recent revitalization of institutional economics, which gives renewed importance to the role of socio-institutional networks in stimulating eco-nomic growth. Holden (2009, p. 453) gives an example of how culture can impact on foreign relations:

> The way that a museum deals with objects from another country; or the fact that Israeli and Palestinian musicians can play together . . . become significant way beyond questions of aesthet-ics or artistic quality.

These reasons for providing public support for the arts and culture are perhaps more compelling than those provided by individual non-market valuation methods (contin-gent valuation) or short-term financial impacts (economic impact studies). However, they are much more difficult to measure, and any attempt at measurement is likely to be qualitative and thus not directly comparable to other projects. But does this mean that they should not be measured?

Take, for example, the National Arts Festival in South Africa. The Festival was started in 1974 as an annual event, originally to celebrate the English culture of British settlers who came to South Africa in 1820. However, it quickly developed into a much more multicultural, African festival and, during the dark days of apartheid, played a sig-nificant role in resistance to government policies that deliberately sought to exclude and undermine the culture and art of black South Africans. The Festival helped to maintain diverse cultural capital, build new cultural capital, provided a platform for political and social resistance and awareness, and was a forum for the judging (valuation) of South African art and culture by artists, agents and audiences. These values are unlikely to be captured by any market or non-market valuation method.

To conclude, culture provides many forms of value, some of which are fairly easily measured in the market (the instrumental values) and some of which (intrinsic values) are much more of a challenge to quantify. However, it is not true that economic valua-tion of culture includes only instrumental values and is unaware of, or entirely unable to measure, intrinsic worth. The important thing to remember is that any one valuation method will only ever capture part of the value of culture, and a completely quantitative valuation is probably not possible. However, when difficult decisions about public (and private) funding allocations have to be made, some measures of the value of culture to individuals and society may be a very useful and powerful tool.

See also:

References

Bakhshi, H., A. Freeman and G. Hitchen (2009), 'Measuring Intrinsic Value – How to Stop Worrying and Love Economics', *Munich Personal RePEc Archive (MPRA)*, Paper number 14902, available at http//mpra. ub.uni-muenchen.de/14902.

Bohm, S. and C. Land (2010), 'No Measure for Culture? Value in the New Economy', *Capital and Class*, 33, 75–98.

Florida, R. (2002), *The Rise of the Creative Class: And How It's Transforming Work, Leisure, Community and Everyday Life*, New York: Basic Books.

Holden, J. (2009), 'How We Value Arts and Culture', *Asia Pacific Journal of Arts and Cultural Management*, 6, 447–56.

Klamer, A. (2002), 'Accounting for Social and Cultural Values', *De Economist* 150, 453–73.

Klamer, A. (2003), 'A Pragmatic View on Values in Economics', *Journal of Economic Methodology*, 10, 1–24.

McCarthy, K., E. Ondaatje, L. Zakarus and A. Brooks (2004), *Gifts of the Muse: Reframing the Debate About the Benefits of the Arts*, The Rand Corporation for the Wallace Foundation, available at http://www.culture.gov.uk/images/publications/supportingexcellenceinthearts.pdf.

Reeves, M. (2002), 'Measuring the Economic and Social Impact of the Arts', London: Arts Council of England.

Snowball, J. (2008), M*easuring the Value of Culture: Methods and Examples in Cultural Economics*, Berlin and Heidelberg: Springer-Verlag.

Throsby, D. (1999), 'Cultural Capital', *Journal of Cultural Economics*, 23, 3–12.

Throsby, D. (2001), *Economics and Culture*, Cambridge: Cambridge University Press.

Further reading

For further discussion of intrinsic and instrumental cultural values, see McCarthy *et al.* (2004), Klamer (2002, 2003), Throsby (1999, 2001), Bakhshi *et al.* (2009) and Bohm and Land (2010). Snowball (2008) discusses the various ways in which such values can be measured, with examples of applications to cultural goods.

26 Demand
*Louis Lévy-Garboua and Claude Montmarquette**

If you gotta ask, you ain't never going to know. (Louis Armstrong[1])

An economist being asked to specify and estimate demand for the arts might begin to say that it is not essentially different from the demand for more down-to-earth consumer goods and services. Then, and only then, he or she would want to consider the specificity of 'art'. This short story summarizes the lines of research followed by art and cultural economics so far in the field of demand. By and large, the first economic studies were concerned with income and price elasticities, which they drew from scanty data, basic consumer theory and crude econometric models. The literature is still groping towards firm answers to simple questions, such as: is art a luxury good? Is it price-elastic or inelastic? Do art goods have close substitutes? However, the consumption of art challenges the conventional assumptions of homogeneous goods and services, completed learning of tastes, independence of choice among individuals and so forth. How do we deal with aesthetic quality and the heterogeneity of tastes? How do consumers who do not have full knowledge of their own taste decide and rely on others? Indeed, if you are going to ask why you like the theatre of Shakespeare, the operas of Puccini, and the paintings of Manet, you are never going to know. The subtle alchemy of individual taste for the arts ultimately relies on experience.

Following the lead of Baumol and Bowen (1966) and the availability of data, a majority of studies have dealt with live performing arts (theatre, music, opera, dance) and the cinema, which is a good substitute (see, for instance, the early works of Moore, 1968, and Throsby and Withers, 1979). A growing number of studies (see, for instance, Frey and Pommerehne, 1989; Agnello and Pierce, 1996; Pesando and Shum, 1999; Flôres *et al.*, 1999; Locatelli-Biey and Zanola, 1999) are now investigating the pricing and choice of artworks (paintings, pieces of sculpture and other artefacts). Since these have distinctive features of financial assets, public goods and uniqueness, we find it impossible to do justice in a short chapter to the expanding literature on artwork. We focus our discussion on the demand for live performing arts and the cinema because these have been more extensively studied so far and raise interesting questions for demand theory. Readers who are especially interested by artworks should consult the more extensive survey of Throsby (1994) and the additional references listed above. The aim of this chapter is to bring some clarification to the theories that can be used to understand the cultivation of taste and estimate the demand for the arts. This exercise is followed by a brief summary of the empirical evidence.

The cultivation of taste
The merit-good nature of the classical arts is attested by the permanence of public policies to enhance and preserve their production and consumption. The learned people, who are generally lovers of the classical arts, think that very many others would eventually

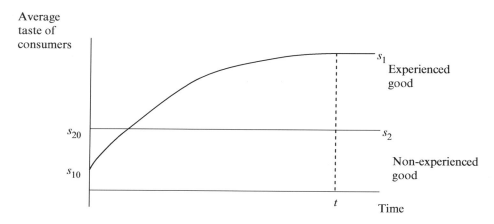

Figure 26.1   The cultivation of taste

feel like themselves if they were better exposed to them. This remark, which needs to be taken seriously, implies that the taste for arts is acquired or discovered, and the rate of art consumption increases over time with exposure. It may well be the case that the taste for popular culture, and even vegetables, is acquired or discovered too, but we would expect that most children have a broad exposure to such goods. Therefore the difference between classical arts and popular culture or vegetables would seem to be that the former are far less widespread in the consumption of parents than the latter. This might occur if classical arts were a strongly inferior good, but we would then run into a contradiction because they are disproportionately consumed by the rich and the educated. A more plausible assumption is that the classical arts are luxury goods[2] the consumption of which should relatively increase with economic growth. However, they run into the danger of getting lost over the generations because of lack of sufficient early exposure to them. Subsidizing the classical arts in order to give the new generations equal opportunities to invest in the acquisition of taste or discover their unknown taste for them would be a Pareto-improving policy.[3] The relative price increase of classical arts due to a lack of technical innovation in their production (Baumol and Bowen, 1966) would limit rather than legitimate the use of subsidization.

Figure 26.1 will help to visualize this argument. It depicts the average variation of taste over time. The taste for good 1 (say, popular music) increases and eventually levels off because additional taste has been acquired through repeated exposure and experience. By contrast, the taste for a non-experienced good (say, classical music) remains stable. Even though the average individual might have initially more taste for classical music than for popular music, she would end up liking popular music better after a while because she was not exposed to classical music. A statistical confirmation of this story is given by Kurabayashi and Ito (1992), who show a positive correlation of preferences for different types of music of the same genre (either classical or popular) but a negative correlation between genres. Prieto-Rodríguez and Fernández-Blanco (2000) suggest, from a bivariate probit model, that both groups of popular and classical music lovers have a common 'innate' taste for music. However, they also show that age has a negative and non-linear effect on popular music listening. Favaro and Frateschi (2007) further demonstrate with Italian survey data that persons actively taking part in musical activities listen to all kinds of music while non-musicians listen selectively to popular music.

The above intuition is borne by theories of specific consumption capital and rational addiction (Stigler and Becker, 1977; Becker and Murphy, 1988), and learning by consuming (Lévy-Garboua and Montmarquette, 1996). These two classes of theories can predict the dependence of current consumption of art goods upon past behaviour. However, they have different implications for the shape of demand. The issues of quality and risk are also discussed. We hope to bring some clarification in the theoretical discussion by presenting the alternative hypotheses in a common framework that will facilitate comparison and permit the derivation of closed-form equations of demand. To make the addiction model tractable, a simple version of these two models is derived in the technical appendix.

A common feature of these models is suggested by Figure 26.1: tastes for art and culture develop over long periods of time, through repeated exposure and consumption of cultural goods. This is captured by distinguishing the 'quantity' x_t of cultural experiences in period t from their 'quality' s_t, which has the nature of a stock of habit. Thus the true argument of period utility for art and cultural goods is not the quantity consumed but the quality-adjusted quantity of art or cultural appreciation X_t:

$$X_t = s_t x_t \qquad (26.1)$$

Throsby (1990) defines objective quality for the live performing arts by a vector of characteristics including the repertoire classification, standards of performance, production and design, standards of comfort, seating, acoustics and so on. Hamlen (1991, 1994) even used the vibrato of pop singers as an index of their objective talent. Objective characteristics have been extensively used as regressors in hedonic price functions (Rosen, 1974) but they fall short in the prediction of superstars *à la* Rosen (1981) and MacDonald (1988). In an interesting study, De Vany and Walls (1999) show that movie box-office revenues are asymptotically Pareto-distributed and have infinite variance. Superstar movies are not determined by awards and totally unpredictable because the informational cascade among filmgoers leads to a great many paths. The models of rational addiction or learning by consuming under review endogenize s_t in equation (26.1). They describe two processes for the cultivation of taste by assuming distinct ways of updating s_t to past (before t) behaviour. The latter is the endogenous determinant of taste in both models and we call it the 'subjective quality' or, briefly, the individual's *taste* for art.

Specific consumption capital and rational addiction
This is the model developed by Stigler and Becker (1977) to account for musical appreciation and consumption, and further elaborated by Becker and Murphy (1988) under an assumption of consistent forward-looking behaviour. Brito and Barros (2005) have recently proposed an adaptation of this model of rational addiction (which they designate as 'learning by consuming') to cultural goods. These models define rational addiction (first introduced by Spinnewyn, 1981) as opposed to myopic habit formation, which was a common assumption for estimating 'dynamic' consumer demand equations

(Pollak, 1970). The taste for music is generated by a music-specific capital that raises musical appreciation in the future. We write this simply[4] (for $t \geq 1$):

$$s_t = s_{t-1} + r x_{t-1} \tag{26.2}$$

with $r > 0$.[5] Since the arguments of the individual's utility function are quality-adjusted, the natural concept of price here is a quality-adjusted price, the 'price of art appreciation'. Art appreciation is not exchanged directly on the market, but it has a shadow price. It is shown in the appendix that, if the shadow price of art appreciation declines over time, the demand for art appreciation will certainly rise over time when the discount rate does not exceed the interest rate. The more impatient consumers, however, that is those with a high discount rate, may diminish their demand for art appreciation over time even if the shadow price of the latter commodity declines. Moreover, an increase of the demand for art *appreciation* over time does not necessarily entail that the demand for *consumption* also rise because the cultivation of taste allows consumers of art to maintain their level of appreciation by a diminishing level of consumption. Once again, the consumption is the more likely to rise, the lower is the discount rate and the higher is the interest rate. The choice of a quadratic utility function implies that demand be linear negative in the marginal utility of wealth. Since the latter is normally decreasing in wealth, the consumption of art is the more likely to be a luxury, the lower the levels of wealth. The demand functions are linear negative functions of the shadow prices of art appreciation. However, demand studies have not measured the shadow price elasticity of art appreciation but the market price elasticity of art consumption ($e_{11} = \partial x_1/\partial p : x_1/p$). It is possible to show that the shadow price elasticity is always lower than the market price elasticity on the negative scale because they differ by a term that is negative when addiction takes place. Hence, a shadow-price-elastic demand for art appreciation is not inconsistent with a market price inelastic demand for art consumption.

The model enables the researcher to calculate the current taste elasticity of art consumption $e_1 = \partial x_1/\partial s_1 : x_1/s_1$, which indicates the influence of cultivated taste on the consumption of art. The latter relates to the market price elasticity and it can be shown that $e_1 > -(1 + e_{11})$. The last condition corroborates Stigler and Becker's (1977, p. 80) claim that 'the time (or other inputs) spent on music appreciation is more likely to be addictive – that is, to rise with exposure to music – the more, not less, elastic is the demand curve for music appreciation.

Learning by consuming

A different approach is taken by the theory of learning by consuming[6] (Lévy-Garboua and Montmarquette, 1996). Consumers are supposed to be unaware of their true taste and to discover it through repeated experiences in a sequential process of unsystematic learning by consuming. Tastes are given but unknown. Every new experience of a given art form reveals to the consumer an unexpected positive or negative increment in her taste for it. Instead of assuming a deterministic increase in taste, as equation (26.2) does, the shift is now stochastic and may take negative as well as positive values with an expected value of zero. It is certainly more realistic to assume that individuals differ widely in their taste for specific art forms than is implied by the pharmacological force of addiction. Some like attending concerts, while others definitely prefer the opera. Recognition of the vast heterogeneity of tastes does not preclude the study of taste formation, as Stigler and Becker once feared (see, for instance, Becker, 1996). Furthermore, it allows for the great differentiation of art and cultural goods. Keeping the notations defined above, the experienced taste for the art consumption of period t is:

$$s_t = E_{t-1}(s_t) + \varepsilon_t, \text{ if } x_t > 0 \tag{26.3}$$

where E_{t-1} designates the expectation operator before period t's choice and ε_t is the taste surprise experienced in period t (that is, $E_{t-1}(\varepsilon_t) = 0$). Someone who discovers that she has a taste for music will normally experience over time repeated pleasant surprises by listening to music and will revise her expectations upward. Since consumers base their expectation of taste solely on their own past experience of the specific art form, the expectation of taste one period ahead is no different from its expectation in the more distant future. This feature of the model, which obtains whether expectations are rational or not, preserves the intertemporal separability of the utility function conditional on past consumption, contrary to what occurs in the rational addiction model. Consequently, the shadow price of art appreciation is p_t/s_t, so that the shadow price elasticity is equal to the market price elasticity (e_{11}) and the taste elasticity (e_1) is simply related to the own-price elasticity by: $e_1 = -(1 + e_{11})$. If the price elasticity is greater than unity (in absolute value), the experience of consuming a good will have a positive effect on current consumption when the good was enjoyable overall, and a negative effect when it was not enjoyable overall. These effects of experience are reversed if demand for the good is inelastic, and are non-existent if the elasticity is equal to unity. This implication provides a useful way of measuring the price elasticity of art consumption from survey data yielding proxies for accumulated experience and taste for a specific art form. If rational addiction also takes place, the latter measures still provide an upper bound for the absolute value of the market price elasticity. The demand equation (26A.11 in the appendix) also describes the dynamics of consumption. Since the dynamic elements of the model are the shadow prices rather than the parameters defining the utility function, the long-term equilibrium is achieved when all the subjective qualities have stabilized at path-dependent stationary values determined at the end of the learning period. The 'true' price and income elasticities are the same in the short run and the long run. The learning-by-consuming model is thus a case where the addition of a stochastic process does greatly simplify, not complicate, the analysis.

Rational addiction and learning by consuming describe distinct processes of taste formation that may both be present at successive stages of consumption. West and McKee (1983) have suggested a threshold in the demand for the arts, with art consumption climbing slowly for some time and then rising quite rapidly as the effect strengthens. Moreover, rationality has a different meaning in the two theories. It describes forward-looking behaviour (which is no longer a controversial issue among economists) in one case; and it describes rational expectations in another. Besides, the sole and perhaps excessive reliance of expectations on past own experience introduces a special sort of 'myopia', long recognized by habit formation models (e.g. Pollak, 1970), which has in fact more to do with ignorance and uncertainty than with irrationality. Part of the ignorance and uncertainty that surrounds the demand for arts is resolved by repeated exposure and experience.[7] However, an element of short-run uncertainty is inevitable for live performances whose subjective quality cannot be assessed prior to own experience.[8] Abbé-Decarroux and Grin (1992) and Abbé-Decarroux (1994) suggest that potential spectators of live performances must bet on the latter's quality. If the coefficient of relative risk aversion is smaller than one, the more risk-averse the consumer, the less risky the performances attended. The presence of risk also helps to explain the role of critics and herd behaviour in the consumption of arts.

The empirical evidence

A growing body of empirical research is devoted to estimating the demand for the arts. The demand for live performing arts (theatre, dance, opera, music) and cinema has been estimated from aggregate time-series data, cross-section surveys on the audience of live performing companies, and individual survey data on specific groups or on the general population. The difficulty of gathering good data is obvious to account for own price, cross price, human capital accumulation, learning experience, quality and time costs. Thus the results are often partial and the methodology varies considerably from one study to another (see also the extensive review by Seaman, 2006). Since attendance at live performances is typically an infrequent event, the use of aggregate data requires caution in interpreting the price and income elasticities of demand when the frequency rate changes over time. The estimation of micro demand equations for the arts requires large samples in order to obtain a sufficient number of participants and be able to correct for a potential selectivity bias. Until recently, these sources of bias have not been largely discussed in the empirical literature devoted to the demand for arts. Moreover, few empirical studies have relied on a structural model. Without specific theoretical references, our previous discussion points to the difficulty of correctly interpreting the empirical results.

Most of the empirical work on the demand for the arts is concerned with price and income elasticities and the tracking of who is the audience of performing arts. The characteristics of audience are often similar, whether for classical music, theatre or museums: the audience, which includes a number of tourists (Gapinski, 1988), is predominantly female, well educated, from upper and middle class and with well-paying jobs (Dickenson, 1992; Kurabayashi and Ito, 1992; Towse, 1994; Donnat, 1998; Prieto-Rodríguez and Fernández-Blanco, 2000; Favaro and Frateschi, 2007; Ateca-Amestoy, 2008). For live performances with the conventional demand equation, own price elasticity estimates (short-term) are negative, relatively low but statistically significant (see, for example, Moore, 1966 and Gapinski, 1984, 1986). Price-inelastic demand was observed in studies for group of companies and Felton (1992) has confirmed this result even in restricting the econometric regressions to a sample of subscribers (long-term demand). She found an exception for metro orchestras and stressed that elasticities vary widely among companies (this is the well-known Le Châtelier principle). Throsby and Withers (1979) observe that elasticities are unequal between genres. Cameron (1990), Fernández-Blanco and Banos-Pino (1997), McMillan and Smith (2001) found that the demand for cinema is price elastic. Few studies (see Krebs and Pommerehne, 1995) have estimated cross-price elasticities, but Gapinski (1986) showed that price interdependencies with close substitutes do matter. Income elasticity estimates are positive, not always statistically significant, and in many studies less than one (see Gapinski, 1986). This finding, which runs counter to the impression that art goods are luxuries, may be a consequence of the cost of time (Becker, 1965). Attending live performances is a time-intensive consumption and Withers (1980) has shown that a large full-income effect may be partially offset by a negative leisure-price effect. He found a 'pure' income elasticity of about unity. Zieba (2009) confirms these findings with a large dataset for 178 German public theatres over 40 years (1965–2004). By adding the value of leisure time to disposable income, she finds that the disposable income elasticity is approximately one and the full-income elasticity is well above one, indicating that the performing arts are a luxury good.

Do these elasticity estimates differ when quality is taken into account? Quality matters to explain attendance to performing arts. Most of the studies that find a low price elasticity of demand measure prices by dividing revenues by the number of seats and, thus, don't adjust prices by the objective quality of seats[9] and performances. The resulting elasticity captures the offsetting effects of price and quality and tends therefore to be low. Indeed, Abbé-Decarroux (1994), observing the paid attendance at 64 productions by one theatre company in Geneva over seven years, showed that the demand for full-price seats is inelastic but the demand for reduced-price seats has a unit price elasticity. Schimmelpfennig (1997) also estimated that for three out of five categories of seats, the demand for ballet is significantly downward sloping. Survey data are generally rich in quality variables, but do not normally allow for the variation of quality-adjusted prices. However, Lévy-Garboua and Montmarquette's (1996) learning-by-consuming model enabled them to recover the own-price elasticity from survey data that provided adequate measures of art experience and taste. After controlling for many variables including indexes of the cost of time and information, the cost of transportation and babysitting and the price of substitutes, they conclude that the demand for theatre is price-elastic, holding the marginal utility of wealth constant. The elasticity of price does not significantly differ from unity in absolute value and reaches a peak of 1.47 for the most experienced category of theatregoers. Their results also indicated a significant effect of the marginal utility of wealth on theatregoing.

The idea that early exposure to arts or investment in human capital increases interest in art consumption has been supported by various studies (Ekelund and Ritenour, 1999; Smith, 1998; Dobson and West, 1997; McCain, 1995; Lévy-Garboua and Montmarquette, 1996). Smith (1998) concluded that culture or art is at the very least habit forming rather than addictive. Results by Cameron (1999) and Dewenter and Westerman (2005) mildly support the rational addiction model on the demand for cinema in the UK and Germany, while stronger support was obtained by Sisto and Zanola (2004) on pooled cross-section time-series data for 13 European countries over the period 1989–2002.

Abbé-Decarroux and Grin (1992) have related risk with age and concluded that risk-free ventures will attract relatively older audiences (opera and symphony), while more risky venues will attract younger audiences (theatre). But the latter results may also be interpreted somewhat differently: older people are more likely to gain experience with the given stock of classical operas and symphonies, but less so with more innovative theatre shows.

Several studies have examined the consumer's decision to attend a specific live performance. The latter depends on the alternatives one has. The set of alternatives may differ from one individual to another. For example, the set of alternatives of a theatre critic consists exclusively of the plays that are being currently produced while an occasional theatregoer might consider a movie or a television show as viable alternatives. This might help explain why the evaluation of plays appearing in press reviews has a strong influence on attendance on a by-performance basis, according to Abbé-Decarroux (1994) and Urrutiaguer (2002), but, according to the second author, has no influence on the average attendance of theatre companies, which often seek to attract a stable public to their theatre and away from alternative activities.

Conclusion

It is likely that the demand for the arts is price-elastic and art is a luxury good. But this prediction stems more, as yet, from a theoretical conjecture than from well-replicated empirical estimates. Careful econometric work, the increased use of large data sets, and a more intensive use of explicit models of the cultivation of taste are certainly needed before definite answers to these basic questions can be given. Price, income, education and learning experiences are important factors in the demand for the arts, but art is also associated with emotions and feelings. The extent to which aesthetic emotions are amenable to economic analysis and measurement remains to be shown. However, we believe that this is perhaps not an impossible task. For instance, aesthetic emotions may be simply approached by the reported satisfaction for an experienced art event (Lévy-Garboua and Montmarquette, 1996), which is an easily observable variable. Thus the endogenization and cultivation of taste, the role of emotions and the many distinguishing features of demand for the arts are important fields for future research.

Notes

*   We thank Claire Owen for excellent research assistance.
1. Quoted by Throsby (1994).
2. Browning and Crossley (2000) show, under a few technical assumptions, that luxury goods are easier to postpone. Indeed, the consumption of classical arts seems to be easier to postpone than the consumption of vegetables.
3. Champarnaud *et al.* (2008) have recently argued, based on an overlapping-generations model, that it is preferable to subsidize public education of art than the consumption of art if the intergenerational transmission of art generates a positive externality. Using a model calibrated on French data, they even show that art consumption should then be taxed rather than subsidized. This corroborates our analysis that what should be subsidized is the investment in taste rather than the consumption of art goods.
4. Smith (1998) substitutes music-specific training (in the form of piano lessons, for instance) for music consumption (like listening to recorded music or attending concerts) to characterize the investment effort. This does not alter the main qualitative conclusions that we wish to draw here. Moreover, it is often difficult to distinguish empirically between training and consumption of music.
5. Becker and Murphy (1988) deal with harmful addictions, like heroin, by assuming $r < 0$. Therefore their model cannot be applied to the cultivation of musical taste without the appropriate adaptations.
6. McCain (1979) coined the term 'learning by consuming' in a study on wine. McCain (1995) used this idea in the context of a simulated model of bounded rationality to explain discontinuities in the consumption of art events.
7. Art and cultural goods are essentially experience goods in the sense of Nelson (1970). Attendance is obviously required for a full appreciation of live performances. However, even though objects of art like paintings can be inspected in art galleries before purchase, their full appreciation requires extensive comparisons with many alternative paintings that are not commonly exhibited in the same place.
8. Price appreciation of an art object also contains a random component. Anderson (1974) showed that paintings are not very attractive investments when risk has been adjusted for. Similar findings are reported in Throsby (1994) for investments in the secondary and tertiary art markets and in Pesando and Shum (1999) for the return to Picasso's prints. However, Locatelli-Biey and Zanola (1999) find that, from 1987 to 1991, an investment in paintings (with repeat sales) performs well compared to US stocks, US 30-year government bonds and gold.

9. It is worth noticing that movie theatres usually sell all tickets for the same price, in contrast with most theatres. Interestingly, higher price elasticities have been found for the demand for cinema (see Cameron, 1990; Fernández-Blanco and Banos-Pino, 1997; McMillan and Smith, 2001 cited above).

See also:

Chapter 37: Marketing the arts; Chapter 49: Pricing the arts; Chapter 56: Superstars.

References

Abbé-Decarroux, F. (1994), 'The Perception of Quality and the Demand for Services: Empirical Application to the Performing Arts', *Journal of Economic Behavior and Organization*, 23, 99–107.

Abbé-Decarroux, F. and F. Grin (1992), 'Risk, Risk Aversion and the Demand for Performing Arts', in R. Towse and A. Khakee (eds), *Cultural Economics*, Berlin: Springer Verlag, pp. 125–40.

Agnello, R.J. and R.K. Pierce (1996), 'Financial Returns, Price Determinants, and Genre Effects in American Art Investment', *Journal of Cultural Economics*, 20, 359–83.

Anderson, B.C. (1974), 'Painting as an Investment', *Economic Inquiry*, 12, 13–26.

Andersson, Ake E. and David Emanuel Andersson (2006), *The Economics of Experiences, the Arts and Entertainment*, Cheltenham, UK and Northampton, MA, USA: Edward Elgar.

Ateca-Amestoy, V. (2008), 'Determining Heterogeneous Behaviour for Theatre Attendance', *Journal of Cultural Economics*, 32, 127–51.

Baumol, W.J. and W.G. Bowen (1966), *Performing Arts: The Economic Dilemma*, New York: Twentieth Century Fund.

Becker, G.S. (1965), 'A Theory of the Allocation of Time', *Economic Journal*, 75, 209–27.

Becker, G.S. (1996), *Accounting for Tastes*, Boston, MA: Harvard University Press.

Becker, G.S. and K. Murphy (1988), 'A Theory of Rational Addiction', *Journal of Political Economy*, 96, 675–700.

Brito, P. and C. Barros (2005), 'Learning-by-Consuming and the Dynamics of the Demand and Prices of Cultural Goods', *Journal of Cultural Economics*, 29, 83–106.

Browning, M. and T.F. Crossley (2000), 'Luxuries Are Easier to Postpone: A Proof', *Journal of Political Economy*, 108, 1022–26.

Cameron, S. (1990), 'The Demand for Cinema in the United Kingdom', *Journal of Cultural Economics*, 14, 35–47.

Cameron, S. (1999), 'Rational Addiction and the Demand for Cinema', *Applied Economics Letters*, 6, 617–20.

Champarnaud, L., V.A. Ginsburgh and P. Michel (2008), 'Can Public Arts Education Replace Art Subsidization?', *Journal of Cultural Economics*, 32, 109–26.

De Vany, A. and W.D. Walls (1999), 'Uncertainty in the Movie Industry: Does Star Power Reduce the Terror of the Box Office?', *Journal of Cultural Economics*, 23, 285–318.

Dewenter, R. and M. Westerman (2005), 'Cinema Demand in Germany', *Journal of Cultural Economics*, 29, 213–31.

Dickenson, V. (1992), 'Museum Visitors Surveys: An Overview, 1930–1990', in R. Towse and A. Khakee (eds), *Cultural Economics*, Berlin and Heidelberg: Springer-Verlag, pp. 141–50.

Dobson, L.C. and E.G. West (1997), 'Performing Arts Subsidies and Future Generations', in R. Towse (ed.), *Cultural Economics: The Arts, the Heritage and the Media Industries*, vol. I, Cheltenham, UK and Lyme, USA: Edward Elgar, pp. 108–16.

Donnat, O. (1998), *Les Pratiques Culturelles des Français. Enquête 1997*, Paris: La Documentation Française.

Ekelund, Jr, R.B. and S. Ritenour (1999), 'An Exploratory of the Beckerian Theory of Time Costs: Symphony Concert Demand', *American Journal of Economics and Sociology*, 58, 887–99.

Favaro, D. and C. Frateschi (2007) 'A Discrete Choice Model of Consumption of Cultural Goods: The Case of Music', *Journal of Cultural Economics*, 31, 205–34.

Felton, M.V. (1992), 'On the Assumed Inelasticity of Demand for the Performing Arts', *Journal of Cultural Economics*, 16, 1–12.

Fernández-Blanco, V. and J.F. Banos-Pino (1997), 'Cinema Demand in Spain: A Cointegration Analysis', *Journal of Cultural Economics*, 21, 57–75.

Flôres Jr, R., R.G. Gôres Jr, V. Ginsburgh and P. Jeanfils (1999), 'Long- and Short-Term Portfolio Choices of Paintings', *Journal of Cultural Economics*, 23, 191–208.

Frey, B.S. and W.W. Pommerehne (1989) *Muses and Markets*, Oxford: Basic Blackwell.

Gapinski, J.H. (1984), 'The Economics of Performing Shakespeare', *American Economic Review*, 74, 458–66.

Gapinski, J.H. (1986), 'The Lively Arts as Substitutes for the Lively Arts', *American Economic Review*, 75, 20–25.

Gapinski, J.H. (1988), 'Tourism's Contribution for the Demand for London's Lively Arts', *Applied Economics*, 20, 957–68.

Hamlen, W.A. (1991), 'Superstardom in Popular Music: Empirical Evidence', *Review of Economics and Statistics*, 73, 729–33.

Hamlen, W.A. (1994), 'Variety and Superstardom', *Economic Enquiry*, 32, 395–406.

Krebs, S. and W.W. Pommerehne (1995), 'Politico-Economic Interactions of German Public Performing Arts Institutions', *Journal of Cultural Economics*, 19, 17–32.

Kurabayashi, Y. and T. Ito (1992), 'Socio-economic Characteristics of Audiences for Western Classical Music in Japan', in R. Towse and A. Khakee (eds), *Cultural Economics*, Berlin and Heidelberg: Springer-Verlag, pp. 275–87.

Lévy-Garboua, L. and C. Montmarquette (1996), 'A Microeconometric Study of Theatre Demand', *Journal of Cultural Economics*, 20, 25–50.

Locatelli-Biey, M. and R. Zanola (1999) 'Investment in Paintings: A Short-Run Price Index', *Journal of Cultural Economics*, 23, 209–19.

MacDonald, G.M. (1988), 'The Economics of Rising Stars', *American Economic Review*, 78, 155–67.

McCain, R.A. (1979), 'Reflections on the Cultivation of Taste', *Journal of Cultural Economics*, 3, 30–52.

McCain, R.A. (1995), 'Cultivation of Taste and Bounded Rationality: Some Computer Simulations', *Journal of Cultural Economics*, 19, 1–15.

McMillan, P. and I. Smith (2001), 'Explaining Post-War Cinema Attendance in Great Britain', *Journal of Cultural Economics*, 25, 91–108.

Moore, T.G. (1966), 'The Demand for Broadway Theater Tickets', *Review of Economics and Statistics*, 48, 79–87.

Moore, T.G. (1968), *The Economics of American Theater*, Durham, NC: Duke University Press.

Nelson, P. (1970), 'Information and Consumer Behavior', *Journal of Political Economy*, 78, 311–29.

Pesando, J.E. and P.M. Shum (1999), 'The Returns to Picasso's Prints and to Traditional Financial Assets, 1977 to 1996', *Journal of Cultural Economics*, 23, 181–90.

Pollak, R.A. (1970), 'Habit Formation and Dynamic Demand Functions', *Journal of Political Economy*, 78, 745–63.

Prieto-Rodríguez, J. and V. Fernández-Blanco (2000), 'Are Popular and Classical Music Listeners the Same People?', *Journal of Cultural Economics*, 24, 147–64.

Rosen, S. (1974), 'Hedonic Prices and Implicit Markets: Product Differentiation in Pure Competition', *Journal of Political Economy*, 82, 34–55.

Rosen, S. (1981), 'The Economics of Superstars', *American Economic Review*, 71, 845–58.

Schimmelpfennig, J. (1997), 'Demand for Ballet: A Non-parametric Analysis of the 1995 Royal Ballet Summer Season', *Journal of Cultural Economics*, 21, 119–27.

Seaman, B.A. (2006), 'Empirical Studies of Demand for the Arts', in V.A. Ginsburgh and D. Throsby (eds), *Handbook of the Economics of Art and Culture*, Amsterdam: Elsevier (North Holland), pp. 415–72.

Sisto, A. and R. Zanola (2004), 'Rational Addiction to Cinema? A Dynamic Panel Analysis of European Countries', Universita Del Piemonte Orientale, Working Paper No. 41.

Smith, T.M. (1998), 'Two Essays on the Economics of the Arts: The Demand for Culture and the Occupational Mobility of Artists', unpublished PhD thesis, University of Illinois, Chicago.

Spinnewyn, F. (1981), 'Rational Habit Formation', *European Economic Review*, 15, 91–109.

Stigler, G.J. and G.S. Becker (1977), 'De Gustibus Non Est Disputandum', *American Economic Review*, 67, 76–90.

Throsby, D. (1990), 'Perception of Quality in Demand for the Theatre', *Journal of Cultural Economics*, 14(1), 65–82.

Throsby, D. (1994), 'The Production and Consumption of the Arts: A View of Cultural Economics', *Journal of Economic Literature*, 32, 1–29.

Throsby, D. and G.A. Withers (1979), *The Economics of the Performing Arts*, London: Edward Arnold.

Towse, R. (1994), 'Achieving Public Policy Objectives in the Arts and Heritage', in A. Peacock and I. Rizzo (eds), *Cultural Economics and Cultural Policies*, Dordrecht: Kluwer Academic Publishers, pp. 143–65.

Urrutiaguer, D. (2002), 'Quality Judgements and Demand for French Public Theatre', *Journal of Cultural Economics*, 26, 185–202.

West, E.G. and M. McKee (1983), 'De Gustibus Est Disputandum: The Phenomenon of "Merit Wants" Revisited', *American Economic Review*, 73, 1110–21.

Withers, G.A. (1980), 'Unbalanced Growth and the Demand for Performing Arts: An Econometric Analysis', *Southern Economic Journal*, 46, 735–42.

Zieba, M. (2009), 'Full-Income and Price Elasticities of Demand for German Public Theatre', *Journal of Cultural Economics*, 33, 85–108.

Further reading

Extensive surveys on the demand for the arts can be found in Seaman (2006) and in Chapter 3 of a recent book by Ake E. Andersson and David Emanuel Andersson (2006). Victoria Ateca-Amestoy (2007) derives the market demand for cultural goods from a two-period version of the rational addiction model presented here.

Appendix: simple models of demand for cultural goods

We assume simply two goods ($i = x, y$) and three periods ($t = 1, 2, 3$), and the time-additive utility function

$$U(X_1, y_1) + \beta U(X_2, y_2) + \beta^2 U(X_3, y_3) \tag{26A.1}$$

where X_t designates 'art appreciation', that is the subutility associated with the art good x in period t and β is the discount factor. The arguments of the utility function are the values expected at the time of decision, that is, the beginning of period 1. To illustrate the properties of these models, we assume

$$X_t = s_t x_t, \text{ for } t = (1, 2, 3) \tag{26A.2}$$

For comparison purposes, we specify everywhere a quadratic period utility function

$$U(X, y) = X - \frac{1}{2}aX^2 + by - \frac{1}{2}cy^2 + dXy \tag{26A.3}$$

with $a, b, c, d > 0$ and $ac - d^2 > 0$ to ensure the second-order conditions. The individual maximizes her utility function (26A.1) under (26A.2), (26A.3), and her wealth constraint

$$\sum_{t=1}^{3}\rho^{t-1}(p x_t + y_t) = W \tag{26A.4}$$

The interest factor (ρ) and the price of art (p) are assumed constant because we focus on the role of tastes. With positive consumption of the two goods, the first-order conditions yield the relative shadow prices of art appreciation in the three periods. However, the expression of these shadow prices crucially depends upon the formation of taste. Two alternative assumptions are explored.

(a) Rational addiction

If taste follows a deterministic process depicted by the recurrence equation (26.2), the first-order conditions can be written as:

$$\frac{MU_{X_3}}{MU_{y_3}} = \frac{p}{s_3} \equiv \Pi_3 \tag{26A.5}$$

$$\frac{MU_{X_2}}{MU_{y_2}} = \frac{p}{s_2}[1 - \rho\alpha_3] \equiv \Pi_2 \tag{26A.6}$$

$$\frac{MU_{X_1}}{MU_{y_1}} = \frac{p}{s_1}[1 - \rho\alpha_2(1 - \alpha_3) - \rho^2\alpha_3] \equiv \Pi_1, \tag{26A.7}$$

with $\alpha_t = rx_t/s_t, t = (1, 2, 3)$

The *rate of addiction* (α_t), that is the rate at which the taste for art increases with the consumption of art, is always positive. It might rise at young ages and eventually decrease. Under the assumptions that $\alpha_1 > \alpha_2 > \alpha_3$ and that they are small, we can neglect terms of the second order – like $\alpha_2 \alpha_3$ in (26A.7) – and show that the relative shadow price of art appreciation declines over time.[1]

We can then derive the *taste-constant Frisch* (marginal utility of wealth constant) *demand functions* for art[2]

$$s_1 x_1 = D[c + bd - d\lambda - \lambda\Pi_1]$$ (26A.8)

$$s_2 x_2 = D[c + bd - \sigma d\lambda - \sigma\lambda\Pi_2]$$ (26A.9)

$$s_3 x_3 = D[c + bd - \sigma^2 d\lambda - \sigma^2\lambda\Pi_3]$$ (26A.10)

with λ (> 0) for the marginal utility of wealth, $\sigma = \rho/\beta$ and $D = \dfrac{1}{ac - d^2} > 0$.

(b) Learning by consuming

If taste follows a stochastic process described by (26.3), the intertemporal separability of the utility function (26A.1) is preserved conditional on past consumption, contrary to what occurs in the rational addiction model. Consequently, the demand function for art in period 1, as any other period, keeps the simple form:

$$s_1 x_1 = D\left[c + bd - d\lambda - \lambda\frac{p}{s_1}\right]$$ (26A.11)

and the shadow price of art appreciation is simply $\dfrac{p}{s_1}$.

Notes
1. By (26.3), (26A.5) and (26A.6),

$$\frac{MU_{X_3}}{MU_{y_3}} - \frac{MU_{X_2}}{MU_{y_2}} < 0 \text{ if } (1 + \alpha_2)(1 - \rho\alpha_3) > 1.$$

This inequality is certainly verified if $\alpha_2 > \alpha_3$ since $\rho \le 1$. Similarly, by (26.4), (26A.6) and (26A.7),

$$\frac{MU_{X_2}}{MU_{y_1}} - \frac{MU_{X_1}}{MU_{y_1}} < 0$$

yields, if terms of the second order can be neglected: $\alpha_1 - \rho\alpha_2 - \rho(1 - \rho)\alpha_3 > 0$. This inequality holds because the left-hand expression exceeds $(1 - \rho)(\alpha_1 - \rho\alpha_3) \ge 0$ *if* $\alpha_1 > \alpha_3$.
2. The Frisch demand function is natural in the time-additive framework. It is also convenient because the marginal utility of wealth is invariant over the life cycle and this non-observable factor can easily be captured through socioeconomic variables when current income is not known, as is often the case in survey data.

27 Digitalization
Anders Henten and Reza Tadayoni

The aim of this chapter is to describe the digitalization of the cultural industries from a technology perspective by providing an overview of the processes of digitalization and the use of digital technologies in those industries.

The technology focus, however, does not imply any technology determinism. We do not intend to discuss any basic cause-and-effect issues. But it can easily be established as a fact that new technological possibilities will be used by industries and society at large if they fit the workings of these entities. And digital technologies have certainly 'fitted the workings' of large segments of the cultural industries and have had, and continue to have, huge implications for the developments of these industries. Sometimes changes come fast and in other cases implications of technology change and use take much longer than expected.

The digitalization of information and communication technologies (ICTs) has been used in the processes of transformation of almost all industries and areas of life. ICTs are pervasive technologies. There is, however, a special affinity between ICTs and large segments of the cultural industries. The obvious reason is that the cultural industries are concerned with communications and that ICTs are communication technologies.

There are clearly differences between different parts of the cultural industries. The art of painting is not much affected, apart from the advertisement of exhibitions and the selling of paintings, although admittedly digital technologies are increasingly used in creating works of art. The same applies to the theatre. However, the cultural industries in the areas of audio, video and text have vastly changed because of the new possibilities offered by digital technologies. This is why these industries are the focus of this chapter.

Digitalization affects each segment of the cultural industries separately. But it also changes the boundaries between the different segments. It provides a common technology platform, which is, however, not a sufficient platform for changing the boundaries between the separate industries. One can easily imagine digitalization of the different industries without any changes in the boundaries. This has actually been the case, to a large extent, until recently. What has been required to initiate the processes of convergence (and new divergences) that are witnessed at present is a common transportation platform. Packet-switched technology and the Internet have provided this. Digitalization and packet-switched technology offer the basis for technology convergence and constitute the technology platform for the developments of industrial and market convergence.

For the segments of the cultural industries most affected, there are implications not only for the means by which cultural products/expressions are transported and communicated but also for the products/expressions themselves and, furthermore, for the relations between the producers and the users. The Internet has become a common means of transportation for audio, video and text; cultural products have converged and new products involving novel combinations of audio, video and text have developed; and

Internet applications have contributed to blurring the formerly clear lines of demarcation between producers and users.

In this chapter, we first offer an overview of technology developments followed by examples of implications of digital technologies in the audiovisual area and the text media respectively. As the Internet is the common communication platform, its main characteristics are then described, and broadband developments outlined before the concluding summary. In addition, there is a short literature review on the digitalization of the cultural industries.

Technology developments

Digitalization is the technological foundation for the modern convergence process. At first, the concept of digitalization was used synonymously with the simple conversion of an analogue signal to a digital one. However, even though the analogue/digital conversion is the precondition for digitalization, the concept of digitalization, as it is used at present, goes beyond this and encompasses the whole system of digital platforms and standards. Five main technological developments have been important to make ICT digitalization a reality: (1) modulation, (2) compression, (3) forward error correction, (4) computerization, and (5) packet switching.

Modulation

Modulation technology is used for transmitting information, including audio and video signals, on different transmission media. The information is modulated on the carrier waves when transmitted and demodulated at the reception point. In principle, the technology is used for both analogue and digital transmission, although the techniques used in digital modulation – where a stream of binary numbers is transmitted – are different from those used in analogue modulation.

Developments of modulation technologies are based on the characteristics of the transmission medium so that data are transmitted in the most efficient manner (Schiller, 2003). Modulation efficiency in digital transmission can be measured in bit per symbol or bit per second per Hertz (bit/s/Hz). The modulation efficiency depends on the deployed modulation technology, which, furthermore, depends on the type of the deployed delivery network. There is always a trade-off between the error performance required and the minimum data payload needed, which makes some modulations more attractive to a particular broadcast media.

Compression

Compression denotes the techniques and protocols that reduce the bandwidth necessary for the transmission of a given signal. There is a huge amount of redundant information in the analogue audio and video signals. This redundancy can be removed and, consequently, the amount of bits per second transmitted will be reduced substantially. Compression technologies determine the digital bandwidth by making a trade-off between the level of much capacity available and the quality of service needed.

Compression standards have been a vital factor for enabling the distribution of audio/video services on the Internet Protocol (IP) networks. Furthermore, compression techniques are the main pillars in the digital broadcast standards. A number of different standards are defined for audio/video compression. The International Telecommunication

Union (ITU), the European Telecommunications Standards Institute (ETSI) and a number of other standardization organizations have been involved in the development of compression standards. Moving Pictures Expert Group (MPEG) has developed three audio/video compression standards, widely deployed in the development of audio/video services:

- MPEG-1: primarily intended for applications such as computer images and graphics.
- MPEG-2 is used in digital broadcasting. It is intended to be generic in the sense that it serves a wide range of applications, bit rates, resolutions and services. MPEG-2 covers different picture resolutions from low-level (352×288) pixels to a very high resolution of 1920×1152 pixels, also called high-definition TV (HDTV) resolution.
- MPEG-4: contrary to MPEG-1 and MPEG-2, which are frame-based, MPEG-4 is object-based. MPEG-4 supports two-dimensional arbitrarily shaped natural video objects as well as synthetic data. Synthetic data include text, generic 2D/3D graphics, and animated faces, enabling content-based interaction and manipulation. MPEG-4 is an important standard for the distribution of digital TV to handheld devices and also for broadband IPTV and video on demand (VoD).

Forward error correction

Especially in the wireless environment, due to noise and multi-path interference in the transmission medium, among other things, the signals that are received at the end-users' sites are often erroneous. These errors are experienced by the end-user as signal degradation and consequently degradation of the quality of service. In two-way communication networks, the error problem is often solved by retransmission of the signal. Another technology that can be used, when there is no return path to send commands up stream and ask the source to retransmit the signal, or the timing requirements of the signal do not permit retransmission, is forward error correction (FEC).

FEC is implemented so that overhead information is calculated and added to the signal before transmission. The FEC overhead information is then used in the decoder to detect and, if possible, correct the errors in the signal. An important issue regarding FEC is that a part of the transmission capacity is 'sacrificed' to reduce errors and increase quality. The more capacity 'sacrificed' for the FEC overhead, the more secure the transmission. In practice, the level of FEC is determined by the characteristic of the transmission medium.

Computerization

The development of computers has had a vital influence on the effective organization and operation of network infrastructures. As end-devices, computers act as intelligent terminals. Using computers in the network nodes has reduced the cost of technology, network management, operation and maintenance.

The processing power of computers and the new applications have had radical impacts on the ICT sectors. On the one hand, the expensive and complex functions in the network, such as switching, intelligent network services and so on are done, to a large extent, by computers. On the other hand, computers have diffused in practically every function necessary for the operation of an ICT network, such as billing, human resource management and the like.

Packet switching

The development from the circuit-switched to the packet-switched paradigm is another important technological development. In a circuit-switched network, a dedicated connection (circuit or channel) is set up between two parties for the duration of the communication. The connection and, therefore, the network resources are occupied during the whole session. The plain old telephone network is an example of a circuit-switched network. The problem with circuit-switched networks is that the network resources are occupied even when they are not in use.

Packet-switched technologies, on the other hand, are designed to use the network resources only when meaningful data are subject to transport. Hence packet-switched networks utilize network resources more efficiently through bandwidth sharing. Another aspect of packet-switched networks is their ability to carry different types of services. Many modern packet-based technologies like IP are designed to be able to carry different types of services. However, specific technologies/protocols must be implemented for different services.

Different packet-switched networks are designed to support variable or fixed packet sizes and to operate in connection-oriented or connection-less modes. The most important packet technology with the widest spread and use in the ICT platforms is the Internet Protocol (IP), which is used in the general Internet.

Digitalization of broadcast media

Digital broadcasting denotes a broadcast system in which the broadcast signal is digitalized. The digital signal at the end-user's site can be fed directly into the integrated digital receivers or, in a transition period, for example, regarding TV, through a set-top box to a regular analogue TV receiver.

Using digital technology for the transmission of digital broadcasting has become relevant in recent years due to the extensive development of audio/video compression and modulation of digital signals, making it possible to 'compress' the digital signal and drastically reduce the required transmission capacity. The frequency capacity needed for a transmitter to distribute an analogue TV programme can be shared by several digital TV and radio services and other data services. Exactly how many services sharing the capacity for one traditional TV channel depends on the quality requirements.

For the users, digital broadcast offers many advantages such as better technical quality, more programmes and services on a given set of frequencies, and the option of multimedia and interactive services (O'Leary, 2000). This development is an expression of the convergence of media: digital broadcast platforms integrate elements from several different media, computers, telecommunications and broadcasting.

Mobile digital broadcast

Mobile broadcast platforms are essentially broadcast TV/radio infrastructures optimized for mobile reception. The services are viewed using mobile terminals, which are enabled for one of these standards, and there can be a return path for interactivity and on-demand services through an IP network based on Wi-Fi, 3G or beyond.

Broadcast networks are characterized by one-to-many transmission and high capacity. By combining broadcast and a return channel (offered by a mobile operator), the service provider can split the services into different elements and transmit the elements with high capacity requirements and mass appeal within the broadcast networks. This combined platform enables service providers to develop new services including high-quality video/audio components and interactive services.

On-demand aspects, furthermore, will be integrated in these platforms, as the return channel offered by mobile operators also can be used as a forward path to deliver on-demand services to the users. Therefore the same content, which is transmitted 'live' over the broadcast channel, can also be delivered to individual users at other times. This creates several possibilities for packaging the content in different forms and delivering it to the users in specific contexts using different business models.

The main advantage of the mobile broadcast platform is that one person's use of video/audio services doesn't influence the use of others by taking up capacity. This is a very important advantage for the video/audio services with mass appeal. A notable drawback of these platforms is that they need specific mobile terminals that can connect to broadcast networks.

Digitalization of text media

The computerization and digitalization of the print media have long affected the production processes in these industries. In the newspaper area, for instance, this resulted in vast redundancies among printers in the 1980s when their job functions became obsolete. However, it was not until the spread of the Web from the mid-1990s that readers were fundamentally affected. And now, the implications of digitalization and the Internet are felt everywhere in the text-based media: newspapers on the Internet, alternative Internet news sites, blogs, the project of scanning of all printed material by Google, e-books, hyperlinking, search machines, and so on and so forth.

Most newspapers have had websites since the second half of the 1990s. The business models differ: in some cases, websites are smaller or substantial add-ons to the paper-based editions; in other cases, most or all of the articles in the paper edition can be found on the net or two parallel but different editions (one on paper and one on the Web) are published. The Web also provides the possibility for combining text-based news with audio and video elements. In all cases, there is an issue regarding complementarity and substitution. Paper-based newspapers for sale have almost all witnessed decreasing numbers of buyers and readers. However, most newspapers seek to follow a strategy where a paper-based newspaper and a presence on the Web supplement one another.

News readers can also access news and information from alternative news sites on the Web. This may, for instance, be web-based news sites and/or blogs. The attraction of these forms of news and information access is that they can be very specialized, they can be very fast, and one can easily link to sources and complementary links. The whole hyperlink structure of the Web constitutes an enormously powerful tool for accessing specialized information and for serving the specific needs of individuals. Search engines on top of this enable users to find specific information and news among the billions of websites available. And, by means of automatic or self-administered recommendation systems, users can build their own news profiles. They can, furthermore, get access via mobile devices, with the Internet increasingly going mobile. A recent example of these new possibilities is Twitter, where users get information from other users they 'follow'.

In the area of weeklies and magazines, the look and feel of the printed material plays a greater role than in the news area. Websites, therefore, mostly play a supplementary role in addition to the paper-based versions. In the book industry, digital products have been on their way for a long time. CDs with mp3 files of books read aloud are becoming increasingly popular, and at the beginning of the second decennium of the 2000s, e-books are starting to appear on the market. New books, which are 'set' digitally from the beginning, can be read as e-books, and with the projects of scanning books that exist only on paper, the whole text-based cultural heritage can be accessed via electronic devices.

The text-based media are thus subject to fundamental alterations. This applies to all aspects, from the production of text-based material to the products themselves, to their spread and diffusion, and to the relations between producers and users. The financial aspects and the business models are also changing, but it should be acknowledged that changes take time in industries where the products are as culturally embedded as in the media and where there are strong business interests seeking to avoid or lower the speed of change.

The Internet

The emergence of the Internet is considered one of the most radical innovations in the communication field in recent years, driven by the digitalization of communication technologies. The Internet Protocol (IP) is designed in a way that enables a radically different environment for service development, innovation and competition when it comes to infrastructure platforms as well as service development platforms. Apart from digitalization and packet-based technologies, a number of design issues have been instrumental in the development of the Internet. These are briefly presented in the following:

- Separation of network technology and services
- End-to-end architecture, and the extension of intelligence from the core to the edge of a network
- Scalability
- Distributed design and decentralized control.

The separation of the underlying network technology and the services that are provided on the IP networks removes entry barriers for the service providers when entering the network. The only precondition for service provision is access to the network. This has created huge dynamics in service developments on the Internet.

End-to-end architecture is another factor that moves the development and innovation activities to the edge of network. The concept was first introduced in a paper entitled: 'End-to-end argument in system design' (Saltzer *et al.*, 1981). The authors' main argument was that an efficient network design can be based on a 'dumb core network', where processing is moved to the edge of the network.

Scalability is yet another main feature of the IP design. One of the barriers to further scalability is the shortage of addressing space in the current version of IP (IPv4). This has been dealt with in the new version IPv6 (see below).

Distributed design and decentralized control is an additional characteristic feature that has obviously improved conditions for the development of services, innovations and the creation of new business possibilities. Different networks can easily connect to other IP networks, including the Internet.

The general Internet is the major IP network, but it is far from the only IP network. In recent years, several private IP networks have been established and utilized for corporate as well as for residential services, and the future of communication platforms, like the core of the Next Generation Network (NGN) architecture, is based mainly on IP technology.

Two recent developments have been important for the Internet: (1) the development of the IP from IPv4 to IPv6, and (2) the development towards WEB 2.0. In the following these developments are introduced.

IP version 6

The current IP is primarily based on IPv4 (IP version 4). IPv4 suffers from major weaknesses due to the rapid growth in the number of devices connected to the Internet and the new applications and services. This has resulted in the standardization of a new version of the IP, IPv6, to cope with the shortcomings of IPv4.

One of the main weaknesses of IPv4 is the amount of IP addresses available globally. An IPv4 address consists of 32 bits, meaning that there are about 4 billion addresses available, which is obviously not enough in a world where still more devices and terminals become IP-enabled. IPv6 extends the address room to 128 bits, which means that the number of IP addresses will not be a problem in the foreseeable future.

The other issues dealt with in IPv6 are related to the applications and services. The main issues here are quality of service (QoS) and security. QoS is important in relation to real-time services like VoIP, IPTV, interactive TV and so on, and security at the IP level will generally be required by a number of services in the future.

WEB 2.0

WEB 2.0 is defined as a set of technologies and applications that enable interaction and user participation rather than static viewing and consumption, which characterizes the WEB 1.0 paradigm (O'Reilly, 2005; Anderson, 2007; Hoegg *et al.*, 2008). This distinction has been challenged by some of the pioneers in Web development, arguing that the original Web was meant to be interactive and the reason for the development of 'static Web' in the beginning was that 'during a series of ports to other machines from the original development computer, the ability to edit through the web client was not included in order to speed up the adoption process . . .' (Berners-Lee, 2000).

A number of different technologies have driven the shaping and development of WEB 2.0 developments. These technological drivers are partly at the hardware/infrastructure side, that is the development of broadband networks, server technologies, storage capacity and the end terminals, and partly on the software, that is the service infrastructure side, including semantic web technologies, which enable the computers to interpret the contents of the web, the content storage and transport technologies like XML (Extensible Markup Language) and RDF (Resource Description Framework), the presentation technologies like XSLT (Extensible Stylesheet Language Transformations) and the GUI (Graphical User Interface) technologies like the new widget and widget-handler technologies. The new technologies enable and ease the implementation of user participation when it comes to both user-generated content and user tagging/voting. Furthermore, these technologies enable sharing and exchange of the content, for example the exchange of user profiles or sharing of other content such as pictures, weblogs and so on.

Social networking and user participation in the production have been important contributions to the value proposition in WEB 2.0 applications and have enabled a number of new actors to take part in the development and innovation process. With respect to the extent of newcomers getting involved in the market, almost half of the mobile content and application startups were aimed at social networking areas as early as 2007, according to Feijoo *et al.* (2009).

In recent years, a number of different social networking sites have been created with different scope and extent. Among the most famous sites are: Facebook, MySpace, LinkedIn, Twitter and Orkut. Social networking sites have different targets. LinkedIn is intended for business professionals and Facebook, MySpace and Orkut are intended for finding new friends and dating.

With the emergence of smartphones and the development of mobile broadband, the social networking applications are becoming increasingly mobile. The mobile dimension creates a number of new possibilities like 'flexibility of use', 'mobility' and 'always on', but also creates a number of challenges that are connected to, among others, the limited resources in the mobile devices and the fragmentation of standards and device platforms.

Broadband infrastructures

The development of broadband has been an important factor in the development of the Internet and, consequently, the ongoing digitalization of the cultural industries. Many services and applications driving the development of the Internet, in particular audio and video services, are highly dependent on the bandwidth capacity of the network infrastructures. A number of different broadband technologies are available on the market.

xDSL

xDSL (Digital Subscriber Line) denotes different technologies deployed to deliver broadband over telephone networks. Due to the widespread installed base of the physical telephone infrastructure, xDSL has been the basis for a fast and efficient development and penetration of the Internet. The main xDSL standards presently on the market are ADSL, ADSL2, ADSL2+ and VDSL (Aware, 2002).

Cable TV

The cable TV infrastructure is another infrastructure with a relatively high installed base and with great potential for delivering broadband access. A cable TV system is a distributive system, where the resources are organized as a number of 8 MHz channels for broadcast TV distribution. Cable TV systems have a huge capacity. However, the total capacity depends on how modern the system is and the degree of utilization of the frequency bandwidth of the coax cables (Rohrer *et al.*, 2004).

To enlarge the IP/broadband capacity in the cable TV system, several solutions can be used:

- Use new standards with more efficient modulations technology
- Modernize the cable TV system and utilize more frequencies (channels) in the system

- Reallocate more channels from TV to broadband
- Digitalize the cable TV distribution system.

Optical fibre technology and FTTx

Optical fibre infrastructures are implemented using different architectures, which are denoted commonly as Fibre-To-The-x, FTTx (FTTHome, FTTArea, FTTCabinet, FTTCurb etc.), depending on how close to the user the fibre is brought. Optical fibres are broadband infrastructures with huge potentials. The physical capacity is not indicated in Mbps (megabits per second) but in Gbps (gigabits per second) and with regard to coverage we talk about distances of around 10 km from the central points to the user. Cost of deployment of the optical infrastructures is higher than for other broadband technologies (Andersson *et al.*, 2001) but the broadband product is substantially better than traditional broadband.

Mobile and wireless

Mobile broadband technologies are increasingly contributing to the development of broadband infrastructures. In particular the developments beyond 3G (HSPA) and 4G (LTE and WiMAX) are important. Compared to the fixed networks, mobile broadband has the advantage of not being bound to a fixed location and giving the users huge flexibility in use. The drawback is that the bandwidth capacity at the user site is still lower than the fixed networks, and indoor coverage is a challenge.

Conclusion

The processes of digitalization affect all parts of the cultural industries – some parts more than others. The strongest implications are related to the audiovisual and the text media. In these media areas, digitalization has not only contributed to changing the communication channels; the media products/expressions themselves have also changed, and so have the relations between the formerly clearly separate categories of users and producers.

Digitalization alone is, however, not sufficient to effect these changes. Other and related technologies are also important, such as modulation, compression and packet switching. In particular, packet switching is the basic technology of the Internet and, as such, constitutes the basis for the processes of convergence technologically, market-wise and with respect to media genres. Convergences are expressed in new and combined media products and in the blurring of formerly stricter bounds between the different media areas.

The Internet is the central network facility in these changes. The core technology of the Internet is the Internet Protocol (IP). However, the Internet is much more than this. It is e-mail, peer to peer, steaming technology, search engines, and so on. To most users, the Internet is primarily the Web. This was the technology that from the mid-1990s revolutionized the Internet and made it spread wide beyond its former primary user groups at universities. Another important technology area is broadband. Many different technologies are applied in order to deliver broadband, and broadband is essential for the development of the Internet. The Internet is thus a continuously developing set of technologies.

The term WEB 2.0 does not denote a set of entirely new and radical technologies. It mainly means new ways of using existing technologies. However, future generations of the Internet and the Web will be based on incremental as well as more radical innovations. As these innovations will be a combination of new technologies and new ways of using existing technologies, it is essential, in order to understand the evolving relationships between the Internet and the media, to combine knowledge of a technological character in an interdisciplinary manner with knowledge on the usage and market aspects, as well as the developments in genres and media content.

See also:

Chapter 16: Creative economy; Chapter 17: Creative industries; Chapter 34: The Internet: culture; Chapter 35: The Internet economics; Chapter 38: Media economics and regulation.

References

Anderson, Paul (2007), 'What is Web 2.0? Ideas, Technologies and Implications for Education', *JISC Technology & Standards Watch*, February.

Andersson, Per O., Ingvar Fröroth and Stefan Nilsson-Gistvik (2001), 'Building a Reliable, Cost-effective and Future-proof Fiber Optical Access Network', *Ericsson Review*, 4, 196–203.

Aware (2002), *White Paper: ADSL2 and ADSL2+, the New ADSL Standards*, http://whitepapers.techrepublic.com.com, viewed 12 February 2010.

Berners-Lee, Timothy (2000), *Weaving the Web*, New York: Harper Paperbacks.

Feijoo, Claudio, Corina Pascu, Gianluca Misuraca and Wainer Lusoli (2009), 'The Next Paradigm Shift in the Mobile Ecosystem: Mobile Social Computing and the Increasing Relevance of Users', *Communications & Strategies*, 75 (3rd quarter), 57–78.

Garnham, Nicholas (2000) *Emancipation, the Media, and Modernity*, Oxford: Oxford University Press.

Hesmondhalgh, David (2007), *The Cultural Industries*, London: Sage.

Hoegg, Roman, Robert Martignoni, Miriam Meckel and Katarina Stanoevska-Slabeva (2008), *Overview of Business Models for Web 2.0 Communities*, St Gallen University, Institute of Media and Communication Management.

Jenkins, Henry (2006), *Convergence Culture – Where Old and New Media Collide*, New York: New York University Press.

Küng, Lucy, Robert Picard and Ruth Towse (eds) (2008), *The Internet and the Mass Media*, London: Sage.

Lievrouw, Leah and Sonia Livingstone (eds) (2006), *The Handbook of New Media*, London: Sage.

Mansell, Robin (2004), 'Political Economy, Power and New Media', *New Media & Society*, 6 (1), 74–83.

Melody, William H. (2007), 'Markets and Policies in New Knowledge Economies', in Robin Mansell, Chrisanthi Avgerou, Danny Quah and Roger Silverstone (eds), *The Oxford Handbook of Information and Communication Technologies*, Oxford: Oxford University Press, pp. 55–74.

Noam, Eli, Jo Groebel and Darcy Gerbarg (eds) (2003), *Internet Television*, Mahwah, NJ: Lawrence Erlbaum.

O'Leary, Seamus (2000), *Understanding Digital Terrestrial Broadcasting*, Boston, MA: Artech House Inc.

O'Reilly, Tim (2005), *What is Web 2.0? Design Patterns and Business Models for the Next Generation of Software*. Available on line at: http://oreilly.com/web2/archive/what-is-web-20.html, viewed 12 February 2010.

Rohrer, Chris and Douglas C. Sicker (2004), 'Implications of DOCSIS-QoS on Cable Broadband Service', paper presented at TPRC, 1–3 October.

Saltzer, Jerome H., David P. Reed and David D. Clark (1981), 'End-to-End Argument in System Design', *2nd International Conference on Distributed Systems*, Paris, France, 8–10 April, pp. 509–12.

Schiller, Jochen (2003), *Mobile Communications*, Singapore: Pearson Education.

Literature review and further reading

There is an extensive literature in the separate fields relating to the digitalization of the cultural industries. The degree of extensiveness obviously differs between the different areas of study under the umbrella heading of the digitalization of the cultural industries. However, the point is that when examining the different areas of study separately there is already a track record, while the overlaps between the areas of study are relatively weak. The different areas of work are reaching out to each other, but there is presently little actual synergy.

A case in point is that while different areas of study are concerned with ICT and media convergence, they do not converge in their understanding of what ICT and media convergence means. The humanistic tradition focuses on the convergence of genres; the social science tradition gives emphasis to industrial and market convergences; and the technical sciences concentrate on the technology aspects of convergence based on digitalization and packet-switching technologies. These differences in emphasis are not problematic in themselves. They reflect the strengths of different scientific traditions. The problem is that there is too little interdisciplinarity among the different traditions.

Three of the most relevant areas of study for the topic of the digitalization of the cultural industries are (1) technology studies on the digitalization of audio, video and text respectively and technology studies on the development of Internet applications, (2) media studies, which is a broad field encompassing humanistic as well as social science approaches and where the study of new media is especially relevant in our context, and (3) politico-economic studies of ICT networks and services.

In the technology field, there is a wide array of literature of a more general character presenting digital technologies and Internet and media developments. The relevant and cutting-edge literature is primarily developed and provided by specific research projects, specific industries, and standardization and industry forums. The whole Internet technology development, for instance, is documented by IETF (Internet Engineering Task Force) in a number of RFCs (Request For Comments). The new mobile standards are developed and documented by the UMTS (Universal Mobile Telecommunications System) Forum, the GSM (Global System for Mobile communications) Association, OMA (Open Mobile Alliance) and so on. Media technologies are standardized and documented by interest organizations and industry forums, as in the cases of Digital Audio Broadcast (DAB), Digital Video Broadcasting (DVD), Advanced Television Systems Committee (ATSC) and the like.

Regarding media studies, Henry Jenkins's *Convergence Culture* (Jenkins, 2006) and David Hesmondhalgh's *Cultural Industries* (Hesmondhalgh, 2007) need mentioning alongside *The Handbook of New Media* edited by Leah Lievrouw and Sonia Livingstone (Lievrouw and Livingstone, 2006) and *The Internet and the Mass Media* edited by Lucy Küng, Robert Picard and Ruth Towse (Küng *et al.*, 2008). With respect to the politico-economic studies of ICT networks and services, the contributions by William Melody, for instance 'Markets and Policies in New Knowledge Economies' in *The Oxford Handbook of Information and Communication Technologies* (Melody, 2007), and Nicholas Garnham, for example *Emancipation, the Media, and Modernity* (Garnham, 2000), are among the most prominent. Few authors have managed to cross or merge the different approaches. Some of the most outstanding contributions managing to cross the barriers are those by Robin Mansell, for instance 'Political Economy, Power and New Media' (Mansell, 2004), and Eli Noam, for example *Internet Television* (Noam *et al.*, 2003).

On the journal side, the following journals are among the more prominent presenting contributions to the topic of the digitalization of cultural industries: *Media, Culture & Society*; *New Media & Society*; *INFO – The Journal of Policy, Regulation and Strategy for Telecommunications, Information and Media*; *Convergence – The International Journal of Research into New Media Technologies*; and *Telecommunications Policy*.

28 Economic impact of the arts
Bruce A. Seaman

How might one answer the question: 'What is the economic value of the Chicago Symphony Orchestra to the city of Chicago?' This type of question has many variations. The cultural asset need not be a single organization but may be an entire sector, such as the arts industry in Chicago. The geographical area in which to measure this economic impact need not be a city boundary, but may be an entire metropolitan area, several counties, a state or an entire region (or nation). The focus of the enquiry can also be a single event or series of events, such as the Mozart Festival in Salzburg, the Boston Pops summer concert series in Tanglewood, or Mardi Gras in Rio de Janeiro. Nearly identical issues are raised when the concept of a cultural asset is expanded to include sports- rather than arts-related subjects, and the comparison of those two sectors continues to be of great interest to both practitioners and academicians (see Crompton, 1995; Seaman, 2006b).

Special challenges exist in the case of cultural assets that are non-market goods, for which the exclusion of non-payers is largely infeasible or impractical (e.g. icons such as the French language, the kiwi as the symbol of New Zealand, the Brandenburg Gate, or the Grand Canyon). While almost all cultural assets have non-market features, these cultural icons generate especially limited market data that can be used in the valuation process.

But economics does have analytical options in even the most problematic cases. An important 'revealed-preference' approach to this dilemma measures travel costs incurred to specific locations, while the 'hedonic-price approach' attempts to isolate the value of living near cultural amenities as capitalized into housing prices. 'Stated-preference' approaches include contingent valuation, willingness to pay, and choice experiments, and share the essential feature of exploring how various hypothetical attributes of the object of study are valued via direct questioning of individuals under controlled experimental conditions (see Snowball, 2008).

The methodology followed in economic impact studies is essentially a revealed-preference approach that attempts to identify the incremental output, income, employment and tax revenues generated in a specified region by new spending stimulated by the existence or expansion of an organization or an event. However, since the preponderance of such studies are *ex ante* predictions of such impacts rather than *ex post* examinations of the evidence for such impacts, elements of stated-preference theory are present in the attempt to identify what visitors are willing to spend and whether their visit to a region was primarily due to the existence of event *X* or institution *Y*.

Regardless of specific methodology, an overriding tension remains between 'instrumentalist' and 'intrinsic' impacts of the arts. Much of the past 50 years has seen the relentless rise of instrumentalist thinking, with economic impact studies being a prime and controversial example due to their potential for abuse and misinterpretation (see Seaman, 1987; Crompton, 1995). Due in part to those controversies, there has been a notable backlash against instrumentalism despite the continued popularity of economic impact studies.[1]

This backlash has taken several especially noteworthy forms. McCarthy *et al.* (2004) attempt to 'reframe the debate' and plead for arts advocates to move away from an emphasis on economic growth (and even on improved student test scores) and to return to their original passion for stressing more fundamental rewards (some potentially measurable) such as pleasure, captivation, cognitive growth, creation of social bonds and expression of communal meaning. The Arts Council of England launched a 2006 public inquiry that led to a call for a more balanced approach between a return on investment (public value) standard to tax financed arts funding and one that recognized also the importance of enriching arts experiences (see Bunting, 2008). And when the Museum of Modern Art (MoMA) commissioned a study claiming that its reopening would create a two-year $2 billion spending impact, $650 million in New York City incomes, $50 million in local tax revenue and more than 4000 jobs, two economists called this 'creative accounting' (Hassett and Swagel, 2006). Yet, as supporters of MoMA's contributions to 'culture and enlightenment', those economists defended the notion that the average New York resident was willing to pay the $11.25 per capita required to fund the $90 million annual tax-financed direct and indirect subsidies bestowed upon that museum, based upon its ability to create 'joy' and make New York 'a special place'.[2]

Types of economic impact

There are three broad categories of economic impact of a cultural asset. First, there is the consumption value, including the value received by both users (those who actually attend events or performances) and non-users. The most observable use value is total expenditure on tickets. But there are other consumption values that are not easily captured by suppliers, such as consumer surplus (the difference between the maximum that someone would pay for a given quantity of the good and the actual amount that they pay to suppliers), and any necessary travel and related expenditure directly related to the consumption of the good. Even those who never attend cultural events or visit cultural institutions can derive non-use consumption value as reflected in their potential willingness to pay for the option of being a direct future consumer, through the indirect prestige or quality-of-life benefits they receive from the existence of cultural assets in their community, or through their interest in preserving such assets for their heirs (bequest value).

Second, there are potential long-run increases in productivity and economic development linked to the cultural asset. As noted, these might be measured by hedonic values, reflected in increases in property values and rents in a community with desirable cultural amenities (which also generate additional local tax revenues used to enhance local public services important for development), or reduced business labour expenses resulting from workers willing to accept lower wages in locations having such cultural amenities (hence encouraging business expansion). More direct productivity benefits resulting from the educational value of cultural goods are frequently mentioned, but difficult to verify. While these types of longer-run effects are linked to the consumption value of the assets, they can generate potentially measurable economic impacts on the real economy in the form of expanded population and economic growth. Richard Florida (2002) argues that firms and jobs follow the relocation of highly mobile 'creative' people (rather than people relocating to jobs and industries) who are initially attracted to tolerant and creative cities. While this argument has been enthusiastically adopted by arts advocates eager to claim the arts as vital to a city becoming creative and hence an engine of long-term economic growth, the Florida argument has been subject to considerable criticism. The connection between the arts and the Florida indicia for a creative city are tenuous, the definition of creativity seems most closely linked to high income regardless of occupation, and the empirical relationship between highly ranked creative cities and rapid economic (or population) growth has not been consistently established, and at times has been strongly negative (for example, see MacGillis, 2010).

Finally, there are the primarily short-run net increases in economic activity (as measured in output, income, jobs and tax revenues) related to the net injections of new spending into the region as a direct consequence of the cultural asset. The total impact includes the longer-run multiplier effects of such new spending.

These economic impacts can be summarized as in equation (28.1):

$$\text{Total impact (TI)} = \text{Consumption impact (C)} + \text{Long-run growth impact (LRG)} \\ + \text{Short-run spending impact (SRS)} \qquad (28.1)$$

Methodological approaches related to types of impact
It is useful to think of each of these three impacts as being addressed by particular methodologies. The term 'economic impact study' is most commonly reserved for the conventional approach that focuses on the third type of impact – the short-run effects of spending generated by the cultural asset. To many casual observers, and almost all arts advocates, this is the only imaginable type of economic impact, and the term 'economic' is uniquely reserved for what they believe to be the highly measurable jobs, income and tax revenues linked to their organization or event.

The non-survey (revealed-preference) willingness-to-pay methods such as the hedonic market approach that estimates the complex market values linked to housing, land and labour market compensating differentials is most applicable to measuring the long-term economic growth impacts, the second of the three impacts. And the contingent valuation (stated-preference) survey methodology (CVM) attempts to capture the non-market consumption benefits linked to use value (consumer surplus) and non-use value (option, existence, prestige and bequest benefits), while the travel cost method is a more traditional approach to measuring that part of consumption (use) value not captured by the suppliers of the attraction being visited.

Each of these approaches has strengths and weaknesses. The use of the results of any of these valuation approaches to justify expanded government support for the cultural sector (a frequent claim of arts proponents) is limited by the inherently partial equilibrium nature of such studies, which generally fail to consider the costs as well as the benefits, and cannot provide a ranking of all the possible public sector investment projects that could make competing claims upon the public purse. Hence the finding that a cultural asset generates significant economic benefits is, at best, a necessary but not a sufficient condition for justifying tax-financed support. Furthermore, to the extent that such benefits confirm the potential for additional earned income (by expanded use of price discrimination strategies to capture more user consumer surplus), or reveal the magnitude of public benefits that would motivate more business and individual nonprofit contributions, the case for tax-financing could actually be weakened.

Conventional economic impact models (EIM): background and variations

The EIM approach remains the most common valuation method in the arts (although the CVM approach and its variants are more academically respectable and have exploded in popularity among arts economists). The intellectual foundations for economic impact models can be traced to the work done in the 1930s by Wassily Leontief and John Maynard Keynes. Leontief's inter-industry analysis generated input–output tables designed to reflect the relationships among the various sectors of the economy. His work is the inspiration for both the Regional Input–Output Modeling System (RIMS II), developed by the US Bureau of Economic Analysis, and the 'IMPLAN' software and databases supplied by the Minnesota IMPLAN Group (MIG, Inc.), which are the primary sources of the state- and industry-specific multipliers used in most USA-based EIM studies, and the multipliers developed for other countries such as the Australian Bureau of Statistics *Multipliers for Culture-related Industries* (distributed by the Cultural Ministers Council), and industry multipliers from *Input–Output Analytical Tables for the United Kingdom* (Office for National Statistics).

Keynes's emphasis on income and expenditure flows as key determinants of at least short-run real output variations also popularized the concept of multiplier analysis and the search for demand-based sources of economic vitality, which is fundamental to the export-base orientation of the EIM approach. As with the broader macroeconomic debate regarding demand-focused Keynesian models, fluctuations in outside demand will affect local economic activity, even if more fundamental determinants of long-term growth are often linked to labour productivity, infrastructure quality, the effect of industry structure on innovation and other more supply-oriented factors. So even if the arts can be portrayed as a basic export industry (usually a significant challenge), their role in long-run economic growth would not be established via conventional economic impact studies (see Seaman, 1987).

Conceptually, a sophisticated economic impact model (SEIM) of '*X*' should attempt to answer the question: 'How much would short-run economic activity decline in a specific region if *X* were no longer to exist?' A thorough input–output model combined with a scrupulous analysis of the data designed to identify the accurate direct economic impact would ideally be used to address this question since it could (1) distinguish between net injections into the region from tourists or other external sources (typically called the 'primary direct impact') and diversions of local spending; (2) identify immediate leakages from the local region by carefully identifying all vendors and spending flows (with the amount of spending retained locally through at least one round sometimes termed the 'capture rate'); (3) properly identify any ancillary spending by those tourists or other external sources that are uniquely the result of the existence of *X* (often but not always called the 'induced direct impact'); and (4) utilize multipliers that reflect the actual interdependencies among specific economic sectors and the size and degree of self-sufficiency of the target region so that all of the subsequent indirect impacts can be properly measured (both the primary indirect and the induced indirect impacts).[3]

In short, such an economic impact study would measure the total impact (whether in terms of output, earnings or employment, and there are distinct multipliers for each) as in equation (28.2):

$$\text{Total impact} = \text{Direct impacts} + \text{Indirect impacts}$$
$$= \text{Direct impacts} \times \text{Multiplier} \qquad (28.2)$$

But this is a difficult standard to meet, is costly to produce, and must be distinguished from more modest economic impact studies that do little more than document the financial magnitudes of some sector or activity in the spirit of 'national income accounting'. Such sector size studies are in the same spirit as other 'naïve' economic impact models (NEIM) such as the census method, which simply uses the aggregate budget of an organization, its total ticket revenues and possible capital expenditures without any adjustments to separate net injections from diversions of spending, and then typically applies average multipliers that do not adjust for the nature of the asset being evaluated or for the size and degree of self-sufficiency of the relevant region.

A third low-cost EIM alternative has emerged that seems inexplicably limited to the USA: the online economic impact calculator. While not always focused on the arts (airports, boating, animal agriculture, public libraries and general tourism are particular variations), the first one originally extrapolated from the findings of the unprecedented 1992 effort by the National Association of Local Arts Agencies (NALAA) to study the impact of diverse arts organizations in 33 different communities in 22 states (in cooperation with economists at Davidson-Peterson Associates). This has evolved into the *Arts & Economic Prosperity* calculator, and a third companion national report (1994, 2002 and 2007) based most recently on 156 US communities and regions across all states (Americans for the Arts, 2007, with project economists from the Georgia Institute of Technology). Other arts-focused and more regionally specific online calculators are the Greater Philadelphia Cultural Alliance economic impact calculator (in cooperation with local economists), and the GAARTS (Georgia Arts) impact calculator focused on cultural organizations created by the current author for the Georgia Council for the Arts (2010).[4]

Despite the relative technical and analytical sophistication of some of those online calculators, they cannot substitute for case-by-case detailed studies (and there is always such a warning to users). Everitt (2009) provides a critical review of *The Arts & Prosperity III* (2007) study, and there is one particular feature of the related Americans for the Arts online calculator that is especially troubling: the direct translation of an organization's 'total expenses' into a component of the expenditure impact on the community without any apparent adjustment for the origin of those funds (local or non-local) and the uses of those funds (the degree of local capture). This naturally gives user organizations the entirely false impression that their own budgets are the minimum relevant local economic impacts, and dangerously focuses their attention on how big a multiplier effect can mechanically be applied to their budgets rather than on whether they are having any net incremental impact at all.[5] Also, compared to more state-specific online calculators, the *Arts & Economic Prosperity* calculator has the natural disadvantage (despite its link to underlying carefully done surveys of target organizations and regions) of not being able to fully incorporate county-specific multipliers, local options sales tax rates, the relevant state sales tax rate, and the relative populations of counties versus municipalities that are usually important in dividing sales tax revenues among local jurisdictions.

Further evaluation and recent developments

The residents of any local region will annually be exposed to numerous economic impact claims. It is unsurprising that general scepticism (or total indifference) will meet the simultaneous assertion that non-profit arts and cultural organizations have added $765 million per year to the local economy, the local sports sector has added another $1.25 billion, while other industries (or organizations) from A to Z weigh in with their own impact claims. Is it correct to presume that these claims are always systematic overstatements?

It is important to realize that in terms of equation (28.1), the short run spending impact (SRS), which is the focus of conventional economic impact studies, is only one of the three components of the total impact (TI). Therefore, assuming away interdependencies among those three components (including the consumption and long-run growth impacts), a correct derivation of the short-run spending impact would itself be an *understatement* of the total impact. Thus, even if a naïve study overstates the true short-run economic impact, that overstatement can conceivably be a more accurate measure of the true total impact than a more sophisticated impact study. Seaman (2006a) examines the specific circumstances under which a naïve economic impact model (NEIM) might consequently be right for the wrong reasons.

Seaman (2006a) also poses the question: 'When more than one methodology is used to measure economic impact, are those separate results complements or substitutes?' That is, if a contingent valuation study is performed along with an economic impact study, should those separate results be summed to obtain the relevant total economic impact? The answer depends critically on whether those two methods are measuring entirely different aspects of economic impact. That would be the case if, for example, contingent valuation only was capturing the user and non-user consumption impacts in equation (28.1) above, while economic impact was exclusively measuring the short-term spending impacts in that equation. But as one alternative possibility, people's stated willingness to pay for the expansion of an arts organization, or the sponsorship of a local arts event, may in fact not be independent of their expectations regarding the resulting increases in output, incomes, employment and tax revenues (even if small in magnitude). This creates the distinct possibility of double counting if the CVM impact is added to the EIM since those two approaches are likely to be at least partial substitutes.[6] Snowball (2008, p. 223) reports finding just this kind of substitution effect between willingness-to-pay results in at least one of her South African case studies, especially among low-income residents. Alberini and Longo (2006) combine a travel cost approach with contingent valuation methods in their study of the value of heritage sites, but those two methods are purely complementary inasmuch as they utilize travel cost to measure the value of sites based on actual observed visitor trips given existing attributes of those sites, and by contrast they use contingent valuation to estimate expected future trips under hypothetical conditions linked to changes in those attributes (ibid., pp. 288–9). They also observe that the travel cost method is capable of measuring only use values for those who actually visit a site and cannot measure non-use values of the site to those who wish to conserve them but do not or cannot visit them. To the extent that contingent valuation methods can estimate those non-use values, the results from the travel cost method and the contingent valuation method would again not be overlapping.

But ignoring those complications and returning to our focus solely on the short-run spending impacts as measured by economic impact studies, the aggregate of all EIM studies will invariably be an overstatement of the net additional regional economic activity that would not otherwise occur since (1) the mix of all reported EIM results will include some combination of inflated naïve models (NEIM) such as 'size' or 'census' studies and sophisticated economic impact models (SEIM), and (2) those cases in which the actual local economic impact in terms of net increased output, earnings and employment is actually $0 (as would be the case if the local arts sector had *no* export component and only served local residents, or did have external funding sources but a 0 per cent 'capture rate', hence changing at best the composition but not the size of the local economy) will never be reported publicly (at least not by industry sponsors).

Regarding any individual study, what are the critical types of errors, and to what extent have modern SEIM studies succeeded in avoiding them? Seven broad types of errors are identified, and where applicable, selected examples of studies that provide noteworthy improvements in study design to limit those errors are briefly identified:

1. Direct base (spending diversion) error: the failure to subtract local *sources* of funds and non-local *uses* of funds from the budgets of the subject entities.
2. Induced (ancillary spending) base error: the erroneous attribution of all hotel, restaurant, retail and other spending by non-local arts consumers to the existence of those arts organizations or arts events.
3. Multiplier (indirect impact) error: the failure to adapt the multiplier to the specific region, including the failure to recognize that smaller less self-sufficient regions that are more likely to have more net injections of non-local spending also have smaller multipliers due to more extensive spending leakages.
4. Supply constraint (crowding-out) error: especially relevant to large tourist events rather than arts organizations, the failure to consider whether the local transportation and hospitality infrastructure could simultaneously absorb the influx of arts event visitors as well as the normal flow of local tourists.
5. Aggregation error: the simple summation of incremental impacts from smaller jurisdictions, such as counties, into a total statewide economic impact without adjusting for the fact that what was a net injection of new activity into a smaller region by 'non-local visitors' may not be a net injection into the larger region when those same visitors to a smaller region are in fact residents of the larger region.
6. *Ex post* verification error: the failure to verify whether any observed closures of local arts organizations or temporary interruptions of activity due to labour disputes have had any adverse economic effects consistent with prior economic impact claims, or whether econometric testing can isolate the beneficial effects on taxable sales, employment or incomes in relevant time periods linked to an event.
7. Policy interpretation (partial versus general equilibrium) error: the incorrect presumption that a positive economic impact is a sufficient condition to make a claim for government support without considering the opportunity costs of diverting such support from other potentially higher rate of return public sector investments.

Economic impact studies done by professional economists generally limit the first three of these technical errors, and sometimes can limit most of them. A study of the 1999 Eurovision Song Contest in Israel (Fleischer and Felsenstein, 2002) conceptually ties the usual short-run spending effects to theoretically important economic surplus concepts (consumer, producer and government) and also uses a balance-of-payments approach to provide a more complete cost–benefit analysis. Two studies that do an especially good job in avoiding the induced base error are the Kentucky study (cited in endnote 6) and the Renoir and Barnes Art Exhibit study by Stanley *et al.* (2000), which documents with special clarity the importance of carefully adjusting visitor spending for the 'primary purpose of visiting a local region' (in that case Ontario and Quebec). From a total base of $67 million (Canadian) in spending by visitors to the Renoir Exhibit in 1995, various downward adjustments eventually yielded only $8 million (11.9 per cent) in 'new money brought into the province which would not otherwise have been spent there'.

The policy interpretation error is primarily committed by sponsors of such studies and other arts advocates, despite warnings by economists, and this error is not limited to EIM studies, but is also equally common in CVM and other methodologies. The two issues that are frequently addressed by economists in sports contexts, but rarely in arts impact studies, are the potential supply constraint and the *ex post* verification errors (see Seaman, 2006b). Sports economists often come close to arguing that the incremental economic impact of a city hosting a major sporting event, or an entire professional sports team, approaches zero. This is generally linked to extreme scepticism that a normal-sized city (e.g. Tampa Bay) could absorb the claimed 100 000 additional visitors to a mega-event like the Super Bowl without fully displacing all other tourists over that time period, essentially stressing supply constraints and crowding out. These arguments can some-times be shown to be overstated since the significant advance notices of major events of this type should allow normal events and visits to be rescheduled rather than perma-nently cancelled. Normally 'time switching' is cited by critics of economic impact studies when no adjustment is made for those who would have visited city *X* in September, but shift that visit to March to correspond to some scheduled arts or sporting event (see Crompton, 1995, p. 27). But in this case, the ability to delay visits to less crowded periods weakens the supply constraint criticism.

But the most notable analytical advances are the increasingly sophisticated econo-metric studies done primarily by sports economists regarding *ex post* verification of *ex ante* impact claims. For example, Baade *et al.* (2008) provide a useful survey as well as new results focused on taxable sales, while Porter and Fletcher (2008) examine the 1996 Summer Olympics and the 2002 Winter Olympics. There are increasing numbers of such studies alleging that past historical experience has failed to reveal significant changes in the level of local economic activity in years (weeks or months) in which a city has hosted various mega-events. While technical issues can always be raised about such estimations, and at least one alternative study found lingering beneficial employment effects from the 1996 Olympics in some geographical areas, these recent *ex post* sports studies are gener-ally consistent with earlier empirical studies finding that work stoppages in professional football and baseball had no notable impact on the economies of cities with those sports franchises, and that the departure of professional basketball had no discernible impact on the economies of host cities in the following years. This is not to deny that fans of those teams were not upset, or did not lose consumption or other economic value, but that the traditional measures of economic impact were not registering those effects.

Similar systematic *ex post* attempts to verify any of the *ex ante* claims made in arts economic impact studies are rare (but see Skinner, 2006), although the threat of actor and other television and movie industry strikes always generates fearful claims as to the dire consequences on the economy of Southern California (with similar claims made regarding Broadway and New York City). Also, there are sometimes non-econometric *ex post* verifications focused on seeing whether pre-opening predictions about attendance, or where zip code or other location-tracing data are available, whether the geographic distribution of visitors was as expected. But more *ex post* econometric testing is certainly a major area for further research into the conventional economic impact of the arts, and the sports studies provide useful methodological guides as to the strengths and weaknesses of such efforts.

Notes

1. In the USA alone, the National Assembly of State Arts Agencies identifies 45 economic impact studies between 2005 and 2009. Previous surveys identified as many as 250 such US studies between 1973 and 1993, but their popularity is hardly limited to the USA.
2. When interviewed for his opinion, William Baumol took the diplomatic route by essentially conceding to doubts that any one of the numerous outstanding New York arts organizations could itself generate such impacts, but defending the general instrumentalist point that 'taken together, the cultural institutions . . . are really the key attraction of visitors to the city' and 'together with the financial center, are among the primary ingredients in the city's prosperity' (*The New York Sun*, 26 July 2006). Schwester (2007) provides an excellent example regarding sports stadiums where he finds support for public subsidies only stemming from 'nonpecuniary, public good externalities' rather than their insignificant effects on local jobs or incomes.
3. Inconsistent terminology regarding indirect and induced effects (with both combined sometimes called secondary effects) can be frustrating. For example, the multiplier effects are sometimes called the induced effects, and some popular regional accounting system models like IMPLAN generate 'Type I' multipliers to refer to 'indirect' inter-industry supply relationships and 'Type III' multipliers to refer to multiple rounds of 'induced' re-spending of household incomes linked to increases in both direct and indirect spending. In that case, the Type III multiplier would be the 'final' multiplier to apply to the direct impact (see equation (28.2) in the text).
4. The author has also created a more complicated but still user-friendly four-worksheet spreadsheet economic impact model focused on cultural events and festivals as distinct from established organizations. It is called GEMODE (Georgia Economic Model of Developmental Events), and the user is asked to input data in a limited number of cells of the spreadsheet, and the formulas in the model generate the results.
5. For example, a recently completed statewide study of the economic impact of the arts to the state of Georgia that inserted survey data from arts organizations into the GAARTS calculator generated a result that while the combined annual revenues of the surveyed organizations was $722 million, the incremental economic impact on the state was $387 million. This disparity is often very difficult to explain to arts personnel. See *Atlanta Business Chronicle* (22 January 2010, article by Maria Saporta).
6. One of the few studies to report valuation results using both economic impact and contingent valuation methods is *Arts and the Kentucky Economy*, Eric C. Thompson *et al.* (1998). They added their contingent valuation result to their economic impact result to get a total impact result, hence implicitly assuming that those two methods were purely complementary.

See also:

Chapter 13: Contingent valuation; Chapter 25: Cultural value; Chapter 24: Cultural tourism; Chapter 60: Welfare economics.

References

Alberini, Anna and Alberto Longo (2006), 'Combining the Travel Cost and Contingent Behavior Methods to Value Cultural Heritage Sites: Evidence from Armenia', *Journal of Cultural Economics*, 30, 287–304.

Americans for the Arts (2007), *Arts & Economic Prosperity III: The Economic Impact of Nonprofit Arts and Culture Organizations and their Audiences*, Washington, DC: Americans for the Arts.

Baade, Robert A., Robert Baumann and Victor A. Matheson (2008), 'Selling the Game: Estimating the Economic Impact of Professional Sports through Taxable Sales', *Southern Economic Journal*, 74, 794–810.

Bunting, Catherine (2008), 'What Instrumentalism? A Public Perception of Value', *Cultural Trends*, 17, 323–8.

Crompton, John L. (1995), 'Economic Impact Analysis of Sports Facilities and Events: Eleven Sources of Misapplication', *Journal of Sports Management*, 9, 14–35.

Everitt, Sian (2009), 'Arts and Economic Prosperity III: A Review', *Cultural Trends*, 18: 315–21.

Fleischer, Aliza and Daniel Felsenstein (2002), 'Cost–Benefit Analysis Using Economic Surpluses: A Case Study of a Televised Event', *Journal of Cultural Economics*, 26, 139–56.

Florida, Richard (2002), *The Rise of the Creative Class*, New York: Basic Books.

Georgia Council for the Arts (2010), Georgia Council for the Arts Economic Impact Calculator (SM), Georgia Council for the Arts in cooperation with Bruce A. Seaman, available at http://gaartsimpact.org/.

Hassett, Kevin and Phillip Swagel (2006), 'Creative Accounting: MoMA's Economic Impact Study: A Museum's Value to the City', *Wall Street Journal* (30 August).

MacGillis, Alec (2010), 'The Ruse of the Creative Class', *American Prospect* (4 January).

McCarthy, Kevin F., Elizabeth H. Ondaatje, Laura Zakaras and Arthur Brooks (2004), *Gifts of the Muse: Reframing the Debate About the Benefits of the Arts*, Santa Monica, CA: RAND Corporation.

Porter, Philip K. and Deborah Fletcher (2008), 'The Economic Impact of the Olympic Games: Ex Ante Predictions and Ex Post Reality', *Journal of Sport Management*, 22, 470–86.

Schwester, Richard W. (2007), 'An Examination of the Public Good Externalities of Professional Athletic Venues: Justifications for Public Financing?', *Public Budgeting & Finance*, Fall, 89–109.

Seaman, Bruce A. (1987), 'Arts Impact Studies: A Fashionable Excess', in *Economic Impact of the Arts: A Sourcebook*, Washington, DC: National Conference of State Legislatures. Reprinted in Ruth Towse (ed.) (1997), *Cultural Economics: The Arts, the Heritage and the Media Industries, Vol. 2*, Cheltenham, UK and Lyme, USA: Edward Elgar, pp. 224–31.

Seaman, Bruce A. (2006a), 'The Relationship Among Regional Economic Impact Models: Contingent Valuation versus Economic Impact in the Case of Cultural Assets', Andrew Young School of Policy Studies Research Paper Series No. 07-05, available at SSRN: http://ssrn.com/abstract=975773.

Seaman, Bruce A. (2006b). 'The Supply Constraint Problem in Economic Impact Analysis: An Arts/Sports Disparity', Andrew Young School of Policy Studies Research Paper Series No. 07-04, available at SSRN: http://ssrn.com/abstract=975770.

Skinner, Sarah. J. (2006), 'Estimating the Real Growth Effects of Blockbuster Art Exhibits: A Time Series Approach', *Journal of Cultural Economics*, 30, 109–25.

Snowball, Jeanette D. (2008), *Measuring the Value of Culture: Methods and Examples in Cultural Economics*, Berlin and Heidelberg: Springer-Verlag.

Stanley, Dick, Judy Rogers, Sandra Smeltzer and Luc Perron (2000), 'Win, Place or Show: Gauging the Economic Success of the Renoir and Barnes Art Exhibits', *Journal of Cultural Economics*, 24, 243–55.

Thompson, Eric, Mark C. Berger and Steven N. Allen (1998), 'Arts and the Kentucky Economy', Center for Business and Economic Research, University of Kentucky, February.

Further reading

Snowball (2008) provides a readable and technically enlightening description and comparative evaluation of economic impact, contingent valuation, willingness to pay, and choice experiment methods. Alberini and Longo (2006) combine travel cost (measuring actual use value) and contingent valuation (measuring hypothetical future use value) methods in valuing heritage sites, while Seaman (2006a) explores the theoretical relationships between contingent valuation and economic impact methodologies. Seaman (1987) and Crompton (1995) provide detailed descriptions of the potential abuse of economic analysis in economic impact studies. Baade *et al.* (2008) address the gap between the 'optimistic' results generated by *ex ante* economic impact studies in sports and the dismal findings from *ex post* econometric studies, while Skinner (2006) provides a rare arts-based econometric *ex post* analysis (of blockbuster art exhibits) and suggests some consistency with what might have been a simplified *ex ante* set of predictions. Seaman (2006b) documents the substantially greater emphasis on community supply constraints in sports impact studies compared to arts studies (consistent with *ex post* sports studies finding *de minimis* regional impacts).

29 Experience goods
Michael Hutter

The notion of 'experience goods' appears in two strands of literature. The first one originates with Nelson (1970) and links consumer behaviour to information: in order to estimate the utility of an unknown good, the consumer has a choice of searching for information about the good or experiencing the good. Experience goods, in this theoretical tradition, are goods with high search costs. The second strand of literature was triggered by attempts to redefine the set of sectors that make up the economy by introducing a 'creative sector' whose branches or industries are characterized by unusually high rates of product change, by high growth rates and by contributions to productivity in the rest of the economy (DCMS, 1998; UNCTAD, 2008). The common feature of these branches is seen in individual 'creative acts', but it has also been argued that the consumer's experience (Bille and Lorenzen, 2008; Bille, 2009) is the decisive feature. The notion of 'experience goods' appears to be of increasing theoretical and practical relevance.

Experience as a means to an end
According to Nelson (1970), consumers who are in the market for goods, but have incomplete information about the benefits obtained from consuming them, have two alternatives to find such information: they can search for available external signals regarding the expected benefits, or they can experience the good and thus generate their own internal information. Experiences in this model are experiments to discover something about the true state of the world that, once attained, will lead to stable choices. Three categories of goods are distinguished: (1) goods with easy search characteristics, whose quality attributes can be *inspected* before buying, like nails; (2) goods with high search costs which lead the buyer to *experience* the good in order to determine the quality, like movies and wine; (3) goods whose effects depend on *credence* even after the experience, like health services and spiritual services (Benz, 2006; Darbi and Karni, 1973).

Nelson (1974) pointed to a particular branch of services that provides additional information to uninformed buyers, namely advertising. In the case of goods with experience qualities, advertising can only state and repeat the claim, any further information about the good must be gathered by the consumer. But there are other sources of additional information, and the issue widens to a new look at transaction behaviour: 'How are additional information sources like a signal or a third opinion introduced in the actors' decision problem?' asks Benz (2006, p. 1). Bergemann and Välimäki (2006) not only distinguish between 'informed' and 'uninformed' buyers; they also attribute 'sophistication' to the search process:

> The demand curve in the part of the population that has already learned its preferences is similar to the standard textbook case. Those buyers who are uncertain about the true quality of the product behave in a more sophisticated manner. Each purchase incorporates an element of information acquisition that is relevant for future decisions. The value of this information is endogenously determined in the market. (Ibid., p. 3)

The recognition of search sophistication links the literature to earlier models that integrated the 'consumption skills' of buyers. Scitovsky (1976) distinguished between goods that evoke comfort and goods that evoke a sensation of novelty and discovery. The novel experiences have 'beneficial accompanying effects' for the entire economy. Becker and Stigler (1977) interpreted knowledge and competence in consuming cultural experiences as a capital asset: consumers invest in such capital in order to develop the 'taste' that allows them to choose the most effective experiences (see Hutter and Shusterman, 2006).

Very recent contributions demonstrate that experience characteristics are applicable in a wide product spectrum, ranging from the selection of automobiles (Paredes, 2006) to online-dating experiences (Frost *et al.*, 2008). In these more recent contributions, the distinction between experiences as experiments and experiences as goals in themselves becomes blurred.

Experience as an end in itself

During the 1990s, experiences began to attract economists' attention for their own contribution to aggregate production. Business scholars suggested that experiences accompany every consumption act, and that the provision of pure experiences constitutes a profitable new business field. Pine and Gilmore (1999) distinguish four 'realms', namely entertaining, educational, aesthetic and escapist experience goods. They focus on instructing the reader how to set up or improve commercial performances that generate more valuable experiences, rather than exploring the wider implications of the phenomenon. A similar interest in instructing entrepreneurs how to produce the most effective experience goods motivates Boswijk *et al.* (2007) and Sundbo and Darmer (2008). Andersson and Andersson (2006, p. 83) focus on product characteristics: they emphasize the intangiblity, inseparability, heterogeneity and perishability of experience goods.

The wider implications of distinct experience goods emerged in the context of a policy-driven debate on expanding the notion of the 'cultural sector' to a 'creative sector'. Particularly in the UK, it was claimed that branches of industry that produce goods and services with a high degree of novelty show above-average growth rates, and that they lead to a higher rate of product change in many other branches (Smith, 1998). Such positive externalities are arguments for public support. The arguments are strengthened by technological properties. Experience goods frequently consist of information symbols stored on some carrier medium, like paper or computer file. Because of the public-good properties of information, there are low marginal costs of technical reproduction and high economies of scale in efficient distribution.[1] In 1998, the UK's newly founded Department of Culture, Media and Sports published a *Creative Industries Mapping Document* that identifies 11 branches as parts of a sector named 'creative industries'. The common feature is the 'creative act', which generates products with new content and new features. An enhanced version of the DCMS definition, which has found worldwide attention and triggered policy decisions in many countries, was suggested by UNCTAD (2008) in a report that explored the growth of exports and imports in creative industries products. According to this definition, the sector combines four subsectors, namely heritage, arts, media and creative services, which include design, fashion, advertising and architectural services.

The approach of identifying a common feature in the production of creative industries products, namely the 'creative act' of the author–producer, has its counterpart in identifying a corresponding feature on the consumption side, namely the 'experience' of the consumer–user (Power, 2009). Such an approach is more in line with neoclassical theory which considers the preferences of buyers to be the driving force of economic value creation. It is most intensely discussed and tested in the Northern European countries. According to Bille and Lorenzen (2008), the approach was triggered by Pine and Gilmore's 'discovery' of experiences as value creations in their own right.[2] The notion of experience applies to the set of industrial branches identified by the DCMS or the UNCTAD report, but it also applies to branches for touristic experiences and for experiences in watching and participating in sports and games. Bille and Lorenzen (2008) suggest that the experience economy creates value in (1) branches that have experience as the primary goal and where artistic creativity is essential to its production as in theatre, music, visual arts, literature, film, computer games (*creative experience areas*), (2) branches that have experience as the primary goal, but where artistic creativity is not essential, as in museums, libraries, cultural heritage sites, natural and green areas, restaurants, the pornography industry, spectator sports (*experience areas*), and (3) areas where artistic creativity is essential but which do not have experience as a primary goal, as in design, architecture and advertising (*creative areas*) (see Bille, 2009). The sector includes legal as well as illegal services; it includes pure information goods, like books, as well as all kinds of combinations with physical impact, from pornography to hiking tours. Bille and Lorenzen (2008) criticize the notion of experience goods because of its potential pervasiveness and immeasurability: just about every good consumed has some experience content. This critique corresponds to the charge that 'creative acts' are part of the most humdrum production processes. The indeterminacy can be reduced by applying both criteria at the same time: experience goods are mainly demanded for their direct mental effects on the user, rather than their instrumental effects, and the value added in their production lies mainly in the creativity of their authors, irrespective of the media used up in the process.

The search for experience goods

The shift toward goods that contain experiences in their own right brings renewed attention to the consumer's search phase. Experience goods, in order to remain attractive, are continuously changed. Novels, music pieces or TV shows are varied on a yearly, monthly or even daily basis in order to appear at the same time familiar and mildly surprising to their prospective buyers.[3] In consequence, it is not enough to try out the good once in order to appreciate its properties because the next movie, song or news item consumed will be different, even if it uses the same media format.

Under such conditions, the difficulty consists in finding out something about a good that cannot be consumed on an experimental basis because to experience it once would exhaust total consumption. The producers, therefore, will provide signals about the qualities of new detective stories, videogames and music albums without enabling the interested consumer to actually enjoy the desired experience. The methods for doing so operate on three levels: (1) advertising messages make claims about the features of novel experience goods; (2) the consumer gets limited access to the good, constrained by trial periods, by providing excerpts of the experience, or simplified demonstration versions. Such experimental experiences seem to be an effective tool. They are increasingly offered since digital technology permits a sophisticated management of such limited access rights; (3) publicly stated preferences, based on reputation, are used as predictors for one's own experience.[4] The reputation of 'experts' is gained in institutions that specialize in quality comparisons between very specific types of experience goods, be they opera performances, hiking tours or sculptures.

The generation of expert networks is enforced by the growth of creative industries branches (see Potts *et al.*, 2008). One of the subsectors of the creative industries, the mass media, provides opinions that are perceived as independent of producers: media companies, mainly newspapers and TV networks, employ experts to make their judgements about a particular novel product known. They also report on public recognitions of quality, like the awarding of prizes or the success of events and tours. From the multiplicity of messages, weighed with the degree of reputation attributed to the sender of the message, consumers derive the information that then prompts them to spend a portion of their disposable income on experiences that are new to them.

In addition, there is a benefit that draws not only on numbers, but on mutual exchange of signals: everyone who has already seen a new movie or played a new game can also talk about it, and rate their own experience. The well-known impact of 'word-of-mouth' signals stems from such reciprocal interaction between past and potential users within differentiated peer groups and may lead to 'social contagion'.[5] As the user offers information to prospective users, s/he generates future credit if the actual experience is rated positively, or is discounted if the experience was disappointing. This effect is multiplied in the quality signals of external experts: their judgements add to the enjoyment of an experience. The total utility for the consumer increases.

Conclusions

Experiences, first introduced as a limited extension of the standard rational choice model, appear to be destined for a larger role. In contemporary information-intensive economies, 'experience industries' constitute an economic subsector in its own right. Experience goods, interpreted as products that contain regularly varied information inducing new mental experiences in their users, pose interesting theoretical challenges. Information is needed to enable informed choices by future consumers, and such information draws its effectiveness from consistent value rankings within networks of experts, which are perceived as independent of commercial interests. The expert valuations gain a marketable value in themselves as they are experienced by the consumers and their communication networks. Both notions, scales of quality and networks of communication, pose new challenges to economic theory.

Notes

1. See Hutter (2003) on the characteristics of 'information goods'.
2. A short English version is provided in Bille (2009).
3. The relevance of surprise is already noted in Pine and Gilmore (1999). See also Hutter (2011).
4. Andersson and Andersson (2006, p. 108) see the reputation of 'professional certifiers' as most relevant for reducing consumers' expectation uncertainty.
5. See Kretschmer *et al.* (1999). Empirical evidence for the effect of word of mouth is presented in De Vany (2004).

See also:

Chapter 9: Awards; Chapter 16: Creative economy; Chapter 19: Criticism.

References

Andersson, A.E. and D.E. Andersson (2006), *The Economics of Experiences, the Arts and Entertainment*, Cheltenham, UK and Northampton, MA, USA: Edward Elgar.

Becker, G. and G. Stigler (1977), 'De Gustibus Non Est disputandum', *American Economic Review*, 67 (2), 76–90.

Benz, M.-A. (2006), *Strategies in Markets for Experience and Credence Goods*, Wiesbaden: Deutscher Universitäts-Verlag.

Bergemann, D. and J. Välimäki (2006), 'Dynamic Pricing of New Experience Goods', *Journal of Political Economy*, 114 (4), 713–43.

Bille, T. (2009), 'The Nordic Approach to the Experience Economy', Copenhagen: Creative Encounters Working Papers.

Bille, T. and M. Lorenzen (2008), *Den danske oplevelsesøkonomi*, Frederiksburg: Samfundslitteratur.

Boswijk, A., T. Thijssen *et al.* (2007), *The Experience Economy – A New Perspective*, Amsterdam: European Centre for the Experience Economy.

Darbi, M.R. and E. Karni (1973), 'Free Competition and the Optimal Amount of Fraud', *Journal of Law and Economics*, 16, 67–68.

DCMS (1998), *Creative Industries Mapping Document*, London, Department of Culture, Media and Sports.

De Vany, A. (2004), *Hollywood Economics. How Extreme Uncertainty Shapes the Film Industry*, London: Routledge.

Frost, J., Z. Chance *et al.* (2008), 'People are Experience Goods: Improving Online Dating with Virtual Dates', *Journal of Interactive Marketing*, 22 (1), 51–61.

Hutter, M. (2003), 'Information Goods', in Ruth Towse (ed) *A Handbook of Cultural Economics*, Cheltenham, UK and Northampton, MA, USA: Edward Elgar, pp. 263–8.

Hutter, M. (2011), 'Infinite Surprises. Value in the Creative Industries', in P. Aspers and J. Beckert (eds), *The Worth of Goods: Valuation and Pricing in the Economy*, Cambridge: Cambridge University Press.

Hutter, M. and R. Shusterman (2006), 'Value and the Valuation of Art in Economic and Aesthetic Theory', in Victor Ginsburgh and David Throsby (eds), *Handbook of the Economics of Art and Culture*, Amsterdam: North-Holland, pp. 169–210.

Kretschmer, M.K., George Michael Klimis and Chong Ju Choi (1999), 'Increasing Returns and Social Contagion in Cultural Industries', *British Journal of Management*, 10, 61–72.

Nelson, P. (1970), 'Information and Consumer Behavior', *Journal of Political Economy*, 78, 311–29.

Nelson, P. (1974), 'Advertising as Information', *Journal of Political Economy*, 82 (4), 729–54.

Paredes, G.M. (2006), 'Consumer Behavior in Markets of Durable Experience Goods', mimeo, New York: New York University.

Pine, B.J.I. and J.H. Gilmore (1999), *The Experience Economy. Work is Theatre and Every Business a Stage*, Boston, MA: Harvard Business School Press.

Potts, J., S. Cunningham *et al.* (2008), 'Social Network Markets: A New Definition of the Creative Industries', *Journal of Cultural Economics*, 32 (3), 167–85.

Power, D. (2009), 'Culture, creativity and experience in Nordic and Scandinavian cultural policy', *International Journal of Cultural Policy*, 15 (4), 445–60.

Scitovsky, T. (1976), *The Joyless Economy: An Inquiry into Human Satisfaction and Consumer Dissatisfaction*, New York: Oxford University Press.

Smith, C. (1998), *Creative Britain*, London: Faber & Faber.

Sundbo, J. and P. Darmer (eds) (2008), *Creating Experiences in the Experience Economy*, Cheltenham, UK and Northampton, MA, USA: Edward Elgar.

UNCTAD (2008), *Creative Economy Report 2008*, Geneva: United Nations.

Further reading

I recommend for further reading: Boswijk *et al.* (2007), Power (2009) and Scitovsky (1976).

30 Festivals
Bruno S. Frey

Most cities or regions today have a festival of opera, theatre, cinema or some other form of art. The oldest contemporary music festival is the Three Choirs Festival in Gloucester, Hereford and Worcester, dating back to 1724, followed by the Handel festivals in Westminster Abbey. Among the most acclaimed European music festivals are the Bayreuther Festspiele (since 1876), the Glyndebourne Festival, the Salzburger Festspiele and the Spoleto Festival of the Two Worlds. Some other famous festivals take place, for instance, in Edinburgh, Avignon, Aix-en-Provence, Würzburg, Lucerne, Verona and Bregenz.

It is difficult to define which cultural activity is a festival and which is not. A particular festival may embody a number of quite different types of performances and may take place in various locations. It has nevertheless been estimated that there are between one and two thousand music festivals per year in Europe alone.

This chapter concentrates on music festivals, but most arguments also apply to other kinds of festivals. The emphasis is on Europe, where most festivals are located; the situation in the USA is somewhat different, because a larger part of established artistic supply is privately organized and therefore the need for festivals is smaller.

Much of the literature on festivals in cultural economics has been devoted to calculating the 'impact effects', that is, the multiplier effects generated by festivals on regional economic activity. In contrast, this text looks at the function of festivals themselves. It is useful to distinguish the various factors on the demand side from those on the supply side.

Demand for festivals

Five determinants are crucial:

1. *Growth of income.* The large increase in real disposable income since the war has made it possible to spend more money on vacation and cultural entertainment. In line with other cultural events, festivals benefit from an income elasticity of demand larger than one.
2. *Lower cost of attendance.* Many festival performances take place during the holiday season, so that attending provides a welcome chance for entertainment at little or no time opportunity cost. At the same time, travel costs have decreased. As a result, the incentive for individuals to take advantage of the economies of scope provided by combining holidays and culture has steadily increased.
3. *Lower transaction costs.* One of the great handicaps of attending an artistic performance in a traditional venue is the trouble involved in getting the tickets and in committing oneself to a particular evening. In contrast, festival tickets are often provided by the same travel agency as makes the holiday bookings, and hence no additional effort is needed on the part of the visitors.

4. *Groups deriving monetary advantages.* The recording industry finds festivals an excellent opportunity to market discs, tapes and videos. The same holds for artists under contract, who can be placed in the limelight of an often very large crowd of spectators. Corporate sponsors can advertise their products and brand-name more prominently than they can in the case of regular concerts and opera performances.

5. *Politicians seeking popularity.* Politicians can project themselves as patrons of the arts (with taxpayers' money). They profit from the high media attention associated with the opening nights and gala performances of well-known festivals.

Supply of festivals

There are four major incentives for organizing festivals.

1. *Lower cost of hiring.* Musical festivals can supply performances more cheaply than regular concert halls and opera houses. Most employees (administrative, technical and artistic staff) have their main and permanent occupation at a concert hall or opera house paying their fixed costs (old age pension, health insurance, holidays and the like). Festivals can often be run with a small number of permanently employed staff. Most participants (in particular the artists and the technical personnel) are employed for a limited period only and can be hired at relatively low cost. This does not mean that a festival's artists and employees are badly paid; quite the opposite may be true.

2. *Lower cost of venues.* Festivals normally use existing structures and the production technology of a permanent concert hall or opera house, since they are not used during the festival, or they take place in the open (often historic sites) or in churches. In any case, they can often be rented at a low price or free of charge.

3. *Avoiding restrictions.* Established music venues have increasingly been burdened by a straitjacket of regulations, making it difficult, if not impossible, for enterprising conductors and other musicians to reach their artistic and personal goals. One type of restriction is imposed by government. In Europe, most venues are either under close scrutiny, or are even part of the public administration, with all the consequences of very restricted flexibility and muted incentives. Festivals, in contrast, are usually privately organized. The directors are freer to pursue a policy suitable to their own artistic ideas. As market wages can be paid, it is easier to hire superstars, who in turn attract many visitors and allow high entrance fees. As festivals run only for a short season (often only one or two weeks), there is practically no permanent employment, so that restrictions on hiring and firing are less relevant. The organizers may choose the form of collaboration with sponsors and recording companies that best suits their needs. They can use the revenue as they see fit, for instance to engage in new artistic endeavours.

   Other types of restrictions on established venues are imposed by trade unions. In addition to closely regulating salaries, they strongly restrict working hours. As festivals hire people to perform specific services over a limited period of time, trade union restrictions apply to a lesser extent, if at all. Their influence is further reduced by the possibility of substituting volunteers for professionals to a certain extent.

4. *Overcoming artistic ossification.* Many established concert and opera venues have lost their flexibility over time. The taste, particularly of the season ticket holders in

these establishments, is normally quite conservative. By specializing in particular types of music, festivals offer the possibility of breaking new artistic ground – by performing more modern programmes.

The future of festivals

Some of the determinants identified for the growth of music festivals also apply to other kinds of festivals, and even beyond to the visual arts. Art museums have also benefited from the rise in the demand for culture, and they too have been subject to government and trade union restrictions. Indeed, some of the major museums have become ossified, as the collection presented may not be changed in any way for historical reasons (this even applies to the hanging of paintings in a collection). Moreover, many such museums are not given the necessary funds to acquire additional art objects. In order to overcome these restrictions, enterprising museum directors arrange special exhibitions, with which they can pursue their artistic goals, gain prominence in the art world and attract large crowds. 'Blockbuster' exhibitions are similar to festivals, as they have become major tourist attractions.

Music festivals are an art form in constant flux. One may even speak of a 'festival cycle'. To begin with, festivals are typically created as the result of private initiative without government intervention, and often against the official, publicly subsidized and regulated concert and opera activities. The temptation for the organizers to accept subsidies from official sources is strong, however, so that over time, governmental involvement increases. As subsidies are given only if official regulations are observed, the festivals tend to become ossified. This provides incentives to arts entrepreneurs to create spin-offs to the established festivals in an attempt to regain discretionary power. After some time, these festivals acquire a life of their own, thus restarting the 'festival cycle'.

Festivals may be interpreted as an effort to overcome the 'cost disease', according to which live cultural performances face increasing deficits because their wage costs constantly rise, while there is little scope for increase in productivity. Switching to festivals with lower wage and capital cost and higher income from recording firms and corporate sponsors constitutes a discontinuous shift towards live performances with better chances of survival. The steadily increasing number of festivals suggests that they are alive and well.

See also:

Chapter 10: Baumol's cost disease; Chapter 28: Economic impact of the arts; Chapter 24: Cultural tourism.

References

Baumol, William J. and William G. Bowen (1966), *Performing Arts – The Economic Dilemma*, Cambridge, MA: Twentieth Century Fund.
Frey, Bruno S. (1986), 'The Salzburg Festival from the Economic Point of View', *Journal of Cultural Economics*, 10, 27–44. Reprinted in Bruno S. Frey and Werner W. Pommerehne (1989), *Muses and Markets*, Oxford: Blackwell, pp. 49–60.
Frey, Bruno S. (1994), 'The Economics of Musical Festivals', *Journal of Cultural Economics*, 18, 29–39.
Frey, Bruno S. (1996), 'Has Baumol's Cost Disease Disappeared in the Performing Arts?', *Ricerche Economiche*, 50, 173–82.
Frey, Bruno S. and Isabelle Vautravers-Busenhart (2000), 'Special Exhibitions and Festivals: Culture's Booming Path to Glory', in Bruno S. Frey (ed.), *Arts & Economics*, Berlin: Springer-Verlag, pp. 67–93.
Galeotti, Gianluigi (1992), 'Riflettori sull'iposcenio: elementi per un' analisi economica del Festival di Spoleto', in Giorgio Brosio and Walter Santagata (eds), *Rapporto sull'economia delle arti e dello spettacolo in Italia*, Torino: Fondazione Agnelli, pp. 125–47.

Kyrer, Alfred (1987), *Der wirtschaftliche Nutzen von Festspielen, Fachmessen und Flughäfen am Beispiel der Region Salzburg*, Regensburg: Transfer-Verlag.

O'Hagan, John W. (1992), 'The Wexford Opera Festival: A Case for Public Funding?', in Ruth Towse and Abdul Khakee (eds), *Cultural Economics*, Berlin: Springer-Verlag, pp. 61–6.

Towse, Ruth (1997), *Baumol's Cost Disease: The Arts and Other Victims*, Cheltenham, UK and Lyme, USA: Edward Elgar.

Vaughan, David Roger (1980), 'Does a Festival Pay?', in James L. Shanahan, William S. Hendon and Alice J. McDonald (eds), *Economic Policy for the Arts*, Cambridge, MA: Abt Books, pp. 319–31.

Further reading

General analyses of festivals from the point of view of cultural economics are provided in Frey (1994). Specific festivals are discussed in Galeotti (1992) and in Frey (1986). Impact effects of festivals are calculated in Vaughan (1980), Kyrer (1987) and O'Hagan (1992). The relationship of festivals to special exhibitions is the subject of Frey and Vautravers-Busenhart (2000). For the cost disease, see Baumol and Bowen (1996), Towse (1997) and Frey (1996).

31 Globalization
Keith Acheson

Thomas Friedman (2005) believes that we are now in the third period of globalization in which the individual is being directly integrated into a world setting. In his framework, countries became globalized in the first period and organizations in the second. Friedman concludes *The World is Flat* by contrasting the positive of globalization, represented by the peaceful and almost spontaneous dismantling of the Berlin Wall on 9 November 1989 (11/9) with the negative, represented by the carefully planned destruction of the World Trade Center on 11 September 2001 (9/11). This chapter focuses more narrowly on the globalization of cultural industries and activities in the past quarter-century.

Currently, individuals have unprecedented scope to distribute among themselves music, images, stories and videos through the Internet and have similarly wide opportunities to buy traditional books, CDs and DVDs on line. In addition they can access a wide range of films and television programmes from cable and satellite services and stream radio stations, television programming and recorded music from Internet sites. The impact of this globalization on cultural activities depends on the quality of national communications grids and their links to the Internet, and national policies governing copyright, spectrum allocations, subsidies, taxes, foreign investment controls, privacy and censorship. In particular, within Friedman's second and third periods of globalization, a set of cultural policies subsidizing and protecting national companies and non-profits producing and distributing traditional media was introduced and has evolved.

National cultural policies have been typically mercantilist. They have protected traditional media – magazine and book publishing, film production, distribution and exhibition, broadcasting, and cable or satellite distributors – from foreign competition and subsidized the creation, production, distribution and export of content by national companies. The post-World War II progressive liberalization of trade and investment in manufacturing and service sectors of the economy under the GATT (General Agreement on Tariffs and Trade) and its successor the WTO (World Trade Organization) were intended to reduce the effects of borders and discriminatory national tariffs and non-tariff barriers on trade in goods and services. In contrast, national cultural policies are designed to restrain the impact of globalization on culture and restore cultural 'contour' to the world.

To maintain this difference, many countries agreed not to further liberalize barriers to trade or constrain national subsidy and preference policies affecting their cultural industries and activities in the Uruguay Round of trade negotiations and to shift the international forum for future discussions of international cultural policy issues from the WTO to UNESCO. The WTO has a tribunal system for adjudicating a complaint by one member that another is not complying with its commitments and a mechanism for requiring a member to comply if the complaint is valid. UNESCO in comparison operates through discussion and moral suasion. Exceptions to this separation, which resembles in a broad way the distinction between law and religion in some countries, are commitments affecting cultural policy agreed to in past GATT or future WTO negotiations.

Despite the prevalence of mercantilist industrial policies in cultural activities, many outward-looking initiatives by individuals and national institutions have been instigated. Theatre and music festivals, art galleries, museums and traditional performing arts centres have arranged foreign tours of exhibits, musical ensembles and theatrical performances, and some have established branches abroad. Visitors to the Guggenheim Museum in Bilbao, for example, enjoy its exhibitions and the cultural distinctiveness of the Basque culture. As this complex in Spain expands and matures, the construction of a second Frank Gehry designed Guggenheim museum in Abu Dhabi (the GAD) nears completion in the late autumn of 2009. Religious cultures are typically global in reach and sometimes in conflict. It would be surprising if the cultural and political cross-currents of a joint venture with critical contributions from an American-Jewish family's foundation, a Canadian-born and -raised Jewish architect who lives in the USA, and the government of the capital city of the Islamic Gulf Emirates, did not create difficult operational challenges. Among the many culturally sensitive issues to face the curators of the GAD is whether or not to exhibit nude works from the Guggenheim's collection that might offend conservative Muslims.[1]

Cultural economics

Cultural economics integrates the impact of cultures into an analysis of individual economic activity and government policy. It has a broader, more nuanced and less precise structure than traditional economics. From this perspective, a culture establishes values, obligations and beliefs about the responsibility of members to each other and to non-members. Each individual chooses some cultures; is a member by mutual agreement in others; and still others are imposed by governments, family, time and place. Some cultures depend on birthplace, residence and gender. Religion, schools and residence of children are typically chosen by parents or kin. Associations are cultures that are held together by common interest, achievement or the discretionary choice of others. Sports enthusiast, Internet hacker and music lover, for example, are associations. Country of residence and nationality are cultures that determine laws and regulations governing access to other cultures. Many, if not most, of the cultures and associations *chosen* by an individual do not conform to national boundaries. Membership in cultures affects the consumption and investment choices of individuals and what they chat about.

Consumption choices among films, television series or stories in books and magazines also differ in some key aspects from the economic textbook example of choosing between two goods, say apples and oranges. When making the apples or oranges decision, the consumer is typically assumed to know what the net impact on satisfaction (utility) is of spending a bit more on one of these fruits and the same amount less on the other. In contrast, each reader or viewer does not want to know the details of how the story in a book or a film develops but hopes to be pleasantly surprised by the twists and turns of the plot. A buzz by friends and critics about different books or films is a welcome influence on decisions to enjoy one and not another, but prospective book buyers or moviegoers will cover their ears if a friend threatens to disclose the details of the plot.[2] In addition, a person's cultural allegiances may provide dissonant explicit or implicit signals about what to read or watch.

The regulation of traditional media

Social influences on individuals are often disseminated through the cultures and cultural affiliations of an individual. Many of these paths of influence, such as daily conversations in coffee shops, defy government control or oversight. The media extend the reach of interactions and influence. They are almost universally subject to regulation, which varies with their characteristics. Border towns often have more over-the-air radio and television signal choices than towns distant from borders because blocking foreign signals at the border is costly. Cable systems, in contrast, typically deliver programming through coaxial cable. Governments are able to impose uniform regulations on the foreign and domestic television and cable services that can be carried, often in tiered packages, and sold to the public. As a result of each government's protection of domestic signals, the signals carried in the cable systems in towns on either side of an international border can and usually do differ from the over-the-air menus.

Satellite technology is competitive with cable systems for delivering audiovisual programming to the home or entertainment centres while creating jurisdictional spillover problems. Packages of signals are encrypted and sold legally with decoders in the areas in which they are licensed. These services are also received and decoded illegally in neighbouring jurisdictions or bought clandestinely by some who prefer the foreign offerings with billing addresses in that country. If ideological differences are significant, national governments may engage in a mutually impoverishing media competition, such as the lengthy and wasteful ideological battle of the radio and television airwaves between Cuba and the Cuban community in Florida, USA.

The rendering global of cultural ideas and influences

Ideas and cultural influences are potent and almost impossible for a government to confine to its own borders. For example, Dr José Antonio Abreu of Venezuela, who has a Ph.D. in economics, developed Venezuela's El Sistema (Fundación del Estado para el Sistema Nacional de las Orquestas Juveniles e Infantiles de Venezuela) for training and inspiring young musicians. El Sistema has flourished in Venezuela under a variety of governments and variations have been adopted in over 20 countries.

Like the books and other holdings in local, national and university libraries, the Internet contains a prodigious amount of information, some misinformation, and a range of interpretations and commentaries. Unlike the information in those venerable libraries, it is accessible to an extraordinary number of people. The Internet has also made the legal framework supporting the traditional cultural industries and activities, in particular copyright law, outdated while playing a significant role in conveying to the public the debate about reforming national copyright laws.

Before the Internet, an individual received information about cultural events and issues from reviews in local media and conversations with friends. The ownership of the media in many countries was often restricted to nationals and local newspapers linked with particular political parties in a democracy, influential factions in an oligopoly, the Church in a theocracy, or owned by the government in a dictatorship. In a dictatorship, government broadcasting and film monopolies produced or supervised the production of entertainment with a social purpose. Information was often predictably 'shaped'. The public management of information provided by local media, controlled media or powerful cartels allied with local groups has become more difficult because of the proliferation of video cameras, cell phones, instant messaging, social networking sites, blogs open to comment, and information sites on the Internet.

Many of the cultures that one embraces on the Internet are partial commitments that one can enter and exit at will. These cultures are either communally or cause-supported, dependent on advertising revenues, or commercial. Some commercial sites are locally oriented and provide information about opening hours, location, and what is available at stores or cinemas in the neighbourhood. Other sites are available internationally but widely used locally. For example, Google Maps or Bing Maps provide directions for driving from one address to another wherever one might be, or will show one's house through satellite photography wherever that house is. Many portals gather links to news from different sources by topic tailored to the interests of each registered user.

Newspapers and magazines have traditionally managed two sources of net revenue – advertising and circulation. Some local newspapers, for example, are free to the reader. Their managers choose to depend only on advertising revenue. On the web, there is more customization than in print, as past choices or submitted interests may result in tailored content guides for each visitor. Specialized sports news, classified ads, business news and job search websites compete very effectively with the sections offering these services in traditional newspapers. Information can be constantly updated at low cost. Social interaction sites with their own rules and mores have also become popular vehicles for the spontaneous exchanging of information. E-commerce sites can be programmed to make further purchasing suggestions of complementary goods based on current and past purchases and automatically update a user on the status of existing orders. None of these new Internet cultures yet has the history, breadth and conforming valences of traditional ethnic, national and religious affiliations.

Linguistic minorities of a country were penalized in older technologies. The Internet transforms their situation. The choices of, say, Spanish literature, journals or magazines available to Spanish-speaking individuals in a majority English-speaking country's book or magazine stores are limited. The Internet gives this minority language community the same access to Spanish-speaking sites as they would have anywhere else in the world. This shift from scarcity to abundance may delay the learning of the majority language and absorption of information about a host country by older immigrants and alter their attitudes to national issues. The subtle impact of the integration of language groups in the Internet on national cohesion will keep sociology researchers busy for some time.

Creative influences flow back and forth with imitation being followed by innovation across cultures. Literature, for example, travels exceptionally well in a language market and less quickly but more widely through translation. In winning the third awarding of the UK's Man Booker International prize in 2009, Canadian short story writer Alice Munro commented that the prize 'celebrates the writing of fiction as a world-wide phenomenon.'[3] Her international success reveals the universal elements in parochial life. A typical Munro story describes a slice of life in a small Ontario (a central Canadian province) town through the eyes of a woman. Foreign magazines, such as *The New Yorker*, *The Paris Review* and *The Atlantic Monthly*, were instrumental in bringing her work to the attention of an international English-reading audience. 'The View from Castle Rock', which originally appeared in *The New Yorker,* remains available to the public at no charge on its website four years after its publication.[4]

The decentralized structure of the international publishing industry and its development of rights through subsidiaries and printers in many countries reflect the costs of transporting, storing, distributing, retailing, returning, managing inventories and disposing of remaindered stock in the book trade. The recent introduction of several sophisticated and relatively inexpensive e-book readers, the negotiation of copyright arrangements for e-books with publishers, and the development of distribution networks for e-books are likely to alter significantly the organizational structure of publishing, distribution and customer reading habits. This transformation has begun.

The size of the relevant language market at home *and* in the world affects a national book or audiovisual product's sales. Translation of a literary work, written in a widely spoken language, to a language spoken by few people is expensive relative to potential sales. The cost per expected sale is much lower for translations into a major language. As a result, the relative breadth of offerings in large language markets becomes more pronounced after translations are added. In the large language markets, there is competition between quickly put together sequentially crafted 'crowd-sourced' translations posted on collaborative translation websites and the later appearance of an authorized translation.

Foreign-language films or television programmes can be adapted for domestic airing by either dubbing or subtitling. The latter is cheaper but its effectiveness decreases as the illiteracy rate rises. Some poorer countries with high rates of illiteracy like Egypt incur the additional costs of dubbing in order to serve a wider audience and protect the native language. Subtitling has an advantage in also making dialogue available to the hearing-impaired. For example, automatic speech recognition is being combined with caption generation on the Internet service YouTube to make the soundtrack of videos posted on the site available to the hearing-impaired. Films of multilingual stories such as *The Kite Runner* are also currently shot in the languages of the story and translated to an English-language audience through subtitles.

A multiplicity of languages makes it more costly but not impossible for cross-national cultural overlays to facilitate communication and deeper understandings. The European Union, for example, has 27 states as members and recognizes 23 official and working languages[5] in its deliberations and policy formulation. Individual countries within the EU may recognize official languages nationally that are not recognized by the union. The European Commission conducts business in English, French and German, but communicates publicly or officially to each member in its official languages. About 700 translators are required to allow each member of the EU's Parliament to speak in any EU official language. Fidrmuc and Ginsburgh (2007, p. 3) report that before the most recent expansion of the official and working languages, 'the cost of translation and interpreting for the various EU institutions is envisaged to reach 1045 million euros per year, including 807 million for translation of written documents and 238 million for interpretation of oral statements'.[6]

UNESCO estimates that there are about 2500 languages around the world that are likely not to survive. Its Director-General Koïchiro Matsuura warns that

[t]he death of a language leads to the disappearance of many forms of intangible cultural heritage, especially the invaluable heritage of traditions and oral expressions of the community that spoke it – from poems and legends to proverbs and jokes. The loss of languages is also detrimental to humanity's grasp of biodiversity, as they transmit much knowledge about the nature and the universe.[7]

National censorship, security and copyright laws determine illegal postings on the Internet within a country. Copyright owners monitor postings on popular video sites in many countries, and their associations take legal actions designed to protect their interests. In China, the State Administration of Radio, Film and Television closed 25 online video sites and reprimanded others for hosting illegal content in the spring of 2008. The Chinese regulator had previously announced that any new video posting sites would be government-owned and run.[8]

In addition to varying degrees of censorship, national cultural industry policy includes a blend of grants, export promotion and tax benefits or subsidies to firms and individuals producing and distributing 'national' cultural content to cinemas, television broadcasters, cable systems and satellite direct-to-the-home services. Over time, these national cultural support policies tend to become more 'industrially' oriented, rules-based and generous. The bulk of government funding is granted to nationally owned companies, such as book publishers, film and television production companies, or large non-profit organizations such as a symphony orchestra, rather than to individual creators.

There has also been an increasing emphasis on formulaic refundable tax credit funding in comparison to discretionary funding for individual projects. The tax credits are generally greater for national films or television programmes. With team-produced cultural products like movies, the 'nationality' of a film or a television programme is typically assessed by a formula or points system based in large part on the nationality, but usually not the residence, of key personnel and the production company and on spending within the country. The subject matter of the television programme or film receives little or no weight in qualifying as national in many countries.

An increasing number of countries also provide generous tax incentives or grants for foreign film and television producers to locate their films' production and the associated 'spend' within their borders. Refundable tax credit and grant competition among countries to attract foreign film and television production projects hiring national skilled professional and other workers has intensified. Given the nationalistic rhetoric of cultural policies, these programmes appear to be the equivalent of subsidizing the military budgets of a hostile country. The public political rationale for these subsidies is that local production spending by television or film production companies making 'foreign' content increases the skills of national workers and develops supporting infrastructure.

Policy favours national production much more than widening the choices of national readers, music lovers, movie buffs and television watchers. The equivalent in the food industry would be to ignore what people in the country eat and label as national only what it produced. In Canada, for example, films that are classified as Canadian typically account for 5 per cent or less of Canadian box-office revenue. The Canadian public are much more outward looking than national policy-makers think they ought to be. The rhetoric supporting inward-looking cultural policies continues to stress the danger of US cultural dominance as its relative influence declines because of globalization. National cultural policy discourse is also disconnected from the growing importance of the Internet, video posting, computer images and graphics, blogs, social networking and other manifestations of a significant deindustrialization and dispersion of content provision and distribution. No Hollywood film in recent memory has generated the international attention and debate that was seeded on the Internet by 12 culturally insensitive cartoons published in the Danish *Jyllands-Posten* newspaper.

The many dimensions of cultural globalization

Technological innovations have continuously generated new media and distribution channels while improving the quality and reducing the cost of existing ones. Digitalization, satellite transmission, fibre cables, compression, 'intelligent' flexible routing on broadband networks and high-definition television have reduced the costs and increased viewers' satisfaction from watching a movie at home. Specialized cinema complexes feature 'live' (simultaneous to the performance on stage) performances of operas from major venues as well as an array of 'art-house' films from around the world. The Internet has also become a rapidly expanding way of delivering films and television programming to the home. For example, Joost, which uses the Bit Torrent architecture, is a successful P2P site for films, videos and television programmes. Hulu, which is owned by NBC Universal, News Corp. (Fox) and Disney, distributes content produced by or from the libraries of its owners. This vertical integration increases the bargaining power of these studios over terms of carriage of their shows on US and foreign cable and satellite services.

The new technologies have been particularly disruptive of traditional production and distribution channels in the recording industry while creating new opportunities for aspiring musicians to reach local and distant music listeners. Change has been rapid. Digital encoding and Internet distribution have resulted in songs being sold individually and in a number of combinations rather than being bundled in CDs. Apple, for example, introduced its iTunes store in early 2003 and served customers in 22 countries by the end of 2008. Hard-drive-based music players dominate the portable market and high-end streaming players. The CD appears to be on its way to joining 8-track tapes and cassettes as discarded music technologies.

Similarly, the book, magazine and newspaper publishing industries are experiencing rapid changes from the local and global effects of the Internet and are anticipating more. Locally, want ads and personal commentaries have migrated from newspapers to Internet sites. Globally, large newspapers or broadcasters in each major language have attracted readers from all over the world to their Internet news sites. Some, like the *New York Times* and the BBC have adopted a free access policy to their sites and rely on advertising revenues or government support to finance their operations. Others, such as the *Financial Times* and the *Wall Street Journal* in business news, generate both electronic subscription and advertising revenue. Many newspapers in smaller cities have been adversely affected by this competition from major players. A number have shut down. Search engines have also become important competitors to newspapers, magazines and broadcasters for advertising by selling 'space' for promotional blurbs and links that are placed beside search results.

In addition to their impact on the book trade, digital readers are likely to revolutionize how newspaper and magazine content is delivered and consumed. Libraries may replace books on shelves with electronic hard disk storage and lend 'self-destruct' files to readers with computers or specialized display devices solving the 'failure to return borrowed books' problem. People who live in small towns would have similar reading options to those in large cities and expanded opportunities to work collaboratively with others. The resulting decline in demand for paper and the associated rise in value of the spectrum would have significant economic effects.

Cultural homogeneity, openness and protection

Some observers consider that increased trade in cultural goods and services has increased cultural homogeneity, while others conclude the opposite. These apparently conflicting views can be reconciled. Consider a small country that chose cultural autarky. The smaller the country, the fewer economies of scale will be realized within its borders and the more costly is achieving diversity in cultural production. A small isolated economy can afford only a few cultural experiments and will have fewer successes and less choice. Autarky generates a hierarchical diversity in opportunities among countries, depending on size. If national cultural policies are open to exchange, each country, large or small, can gain access to the world menu and contribute to its composition. Opportunities are more homogeneous but the scope for individual and communal diversity remains broad. If trading opportunities do not impose, but allow, choice, patterns of consumption are not coerced. The gains from having broader options are larger for small countries. Symmetrically, small countries have the most to lose if they have to adjust to a collapse of a liberal trading regime in cultural goods and services and return to autarchy.

If trade is voluntary, the argument for economic liberalization is persuasive, but what is the right amount? Economists often support free trade based on the first welfare theorem, but that argument is inapplicable because of the cost conditions and informational problems faced by the cultural industries. There is no scarcity of applicable models, each with different policy implications that could be applied, but economists cannot effectively distinguish empirically among them. As a result, the case for openness rests on a time-tested theme – open borders counter the adverse effects of concentrated production at home, provide alternative interpretations of events and possibilities, increase choice for consumers, and stimulate business, professional and artistic creativity and performance – rather than on a particular model of imperfect competition.

Those that support protection stress that the cultural industries differ from other economic activities in shaping individual and community development. Unfortunately, there is no consensus on how this process operates and what are its implications for policy, except for the responsibility to protect children from detrimental content. This linkage is effectively mobilized to support discrimination against foreign content. In particular, the dominance of international trade in mass media of the USA disseminates an American 'spin' to viewers around the world. Americans wondering why their country is not better liked abroad might question the efficacy of Hollywood's or international publishers' fare as national propaganda. Viewers, listeners and readers abroad seem quite capable of putting a counter-spin on what they choose to see, hear and remember.

Notes

1. Published in *Jerusalem Post*, 9 July 2006, posted at http://www.jpost.com/servlet/Satellite?cid=115088595 3739&pagename=JPArticle%2FShowFull.
2. This feature of a cultural consumption decision is not resolved by introducing uncertainty in the conventional manner into the analysis. A risk-averse investor, for example, will not cover his or her ears to avoid hearing more detailed and accurate information about the prospects of companies before making an investment decision.
3. http://www.themanbookerprize.com/news/release/1242/.
4. http://www.newyorker.com/archive/2005/08/29/050829fi_fiction?currentPage=all. Her story will particularly resonate for those with roots in the Scottish Diaspora.
5. Bulgarian, Czech, Danish, Dutch, English, Estonian, Finnish, French, German, Greek, Hungarian, Irish, Italian, Latvian, Lithuanian, Maltese, Polish, Portuguese, Romanian, Slovak, Slovene, Spanish and Swedish.

6. Statistics and details of language policy in the EU are from http://ec.europa.eu/public_opinion/archives/ebs/ebs_243_en.pdf. The cost estimate is from Fidrmuc and Ginsburgh (2007).
7. http://portal.unesco.org/en/ev.php-URL_ID=44605&URL_DO=DO_TOPIC&URL_SECTION=201.html.
8. See Loretta Chao, 'China Cracks Down on Online Video', *Wall Street Journal*, 22 March 2008

See also:

Chapter 27: Digitalization; Chapter 33: International trade; Chapter 34: The Internet: culture; Chapter 35: The Internet: economics; Chapter 38: Media economics and regulation; Chapter 53: Publishing.

References

Acheson, Keith and Chris Maule (1999), *Much Ado about Culture: North American Trade Disputes*, Ann Arbor MI: University of Michigan Press.
Acheson, Keith and Chris Maule (2006), 'Culture in International Trade', in V.A. Ginsburgh and D. Throsby (eds), *Handbook of the Economics of Art and Culture*, Amsterdam: Elsevier, pp. 1141–82.
Fidrmuc, Jan and Victor Ginsburgh (2007), 'Languages in the European Union: The Quest for Equality and its Cost', *European Economic Review*, 51 (6), 1351–69.
Friedman, Thomas L. (2005), *The World is Flat: A Brief History of the Twenty-first Century*, New York: Farrar, Straus and Giroux.
Guerrieri, Paolo, Lelio Iapadre and Georg Koopman (2005), *Cultural Diversity and International Economic Integration: The Global Governance of the Audio-Visual Sector*, Cheltenham, UK and Northampton, MA, USA: Edward Elgar.
Robertson, Roland (1992), *Globalization: Social Theory and Global Culture*, London: Sage.
Throsby, David (2001), *Economics and Culture*, Cambridge: Cambridge University Press.

Further reading

The references provide some guideposts for an interested reader. Robertson's interdisciplinary study of globalization complements Friedman's book. Throsby's broad study integrates economic, cultural and heritage considerations. The approach to incorporating the impact of cultural allegiances and associations on economic decisions used in this chapter has its roots in Acheson and Maule's chapter in the Ginsburgh and Throsby *Handbook*. That chapter also discusses related international heritage issues, distinguishes between the international dimensions of visual and performance arts as compared to the cultural industries and outlines some of the many difficulties of measuring cultural 'trade'. The *Much Ado* book discusses the unique economic characteristics of cultural policies as a background to case studies of the frequent cultural trade disputes between Canada and the USA. The volume edited by Guerrieri *et al.* provides seven different country studies of the impact of economic integration and cultural differences on international trade and investment in the audiovisual sector.

32 Heritage
Françoise Benhamou

The economics of the built cultural heritage has a particular status in the field of cultural economics. Heritage goods share some characteristics with other cultural goods, especially uniqueness and their perception as merit goods. They also differ from other cultural goods because of durability and irreversibility: if a historical building is transformed or destroyed, it cannot be recreated or restored in its initial shape. From this point of view, heritage economics is close to environmental economics. They share the preoccupation with sustainability, and the existence of an international demand linked to tourism.

Heritage goods generate mixed feelings among researchers. Publications are not very numerous, probably because of many methodological difficulties: empirical issues lack data, and comparative studies are limited by the very specificity of national situations. Moreover, there is a kind of soft consensus in favour of public regulation, while at the same time subsidization is criticized for its inefficiency.

Definition

Heritage includes different forms of cultural capital 'which embodies the community's value of its social, historical, or cultural dimension' (Throsby, 1997, p. 15). In this chapter we emphasize only the question of built heritage, in the restrictive sense of immovable heritage, including archaeological sites, historic buildings and historic urban centres (or some part of them). A minimal definition would identify the built heritage as the buildings and monuments inherited from the past, with a cultural or historical dimension justifying their preservation for next generations, but also contemporary monuments whose symbolic or cultural value is high, such as houses or buildings designed by a kind of international elite architects. Even in this sense, heritage includes a large range of goods, whose definition changes over time and space, and depends on the variety of dimensions (symbolic, cultural, national identity oriented, social) included in the concept (Chastel, 1986). Therefore heritage is a social construction whose boundaries are unstable and blurred, with a threefold source of extensions: historical additions, enlarging the concept of heritage towards additional items (gardens, industrial buildings and so on) and to the intangible value of tangible assets. This last aspect can be considered as capital value (Rizzo and Throsby, 2006). It also deals with trademarks and property rights that derive from heritage.

Peacock (1997, p. 195) argues in favour of a Beckerian definition of heritage as 'an intangible service increasing the utility of consumers, in which historic buildings and artefacts are inputs'. Such a definition recognizes the existence of substitutes for goods that share some characteristics. This conception presents the advantage of including services offered through new technologies, provided that the consumer considers a visit through the Internet as a satisfying substitute for a 'real' use.

An institutional definition (the official listing of historic buildings) is the opposite of a more informal definition (what art historians or mere citizens think should be kept up and preserved). Different institutional definitions of heritage also may be distinguished, depending on the level of the administration in charge of them: from a small-city mayor deciding to undertake restoration of a little rural church, to an international organization like UNESCO providing lists of artefacts that it considers as the basis of an international human patrimony. In 2010, the World Heritage list includes 890 properties that UNESCO considers as having outstanding universal value. Those goods share some characteristics of global public goods: decision-making involves many countries in the process of conserving. Their symbolic value reaches beyond one country and one generation (Frey and Pamini, 2009).

Local or national authorities may be in opposition to international demand. Contrary to Klamer and Throsby (2000), preservation is never obvious, as we have seen in 2001 with the Taliban's destruction of Afghanistan's giant sculptures, but also with the recurrent debate about the spoliation and restitution of parts of monuments, as in the case of the Parthenon friezes and their display in the British Museum, or with the controversial question of destroying or preserving urban centres built in the 1950s (Hoffman, 2006).

Characteristics of cultural heritage

Cultural monuments and buildings may be privately or publicly owned. Whatever their status, they have public-good characteristics. First, indivisibility generally prevails: the consumption of publicly owned goods is potentially identical for all consumers provided that the monuments – especially their façades – represent joint, non-rival goods. Nevertheless, congestion may occur for overcrowded monuments, putting them at risk: degradation, especially for 'superstar' sites or monuments (such as Venice, Mont Saint-Michel, the Statue of Liberty, the Leaning Tower of Pisa, Angkor Wat), threatens buildings that attract too many visitors. Reputation increases with the number of users, creating network externalities.

Second, externalities are a source of market failure: heritage constitutes a legacy to be passed on to future generations (bequest value); heritage also confers benefits to individual citizens who have not contributed to their production or preservation; in addition, many economists emphasize the spillover effects of historical monuments for local activities and tourism.

Moreover, excludability is not always possible or desirable. Greffe (2003) addresses the question of whether or not to price (when possible). He analyses the management of sites and buildings, and price discrimination policies emphasizing the lack of clarity that results from the large variety of policies.

Those characteristics constitute a strong argument for public funding in order to correct market failure, and for the impossibility of grounding the choice of preservation solely on market forces (Mossetto, 1994; Koboldt, 1997).

The market value of historic buildings: some methodological questions

One of the greatest methodological difficulties is the evaluation of demand and supply. Tools are available to evaluate heritage demand and willingness to pay. Contingent valuation methods value consumer preferences that people place on heritage. Different biases are inherent to this survey-based methodology, especially 'free-riding', that can be explained by the collectively owned nature of certain goods, as described above. Referenda have the advantage of combining the evaluation of competing alternatives with democratic decisions. They are routinely undertaken in Switzerland (Frey, 1997).

The travel cost method is based on the hypothesis that the cost of travel (including time opportunity cost) to heritage sites is a satisfactory proxy for the visitors' willingness to pay. Such a method underestimates demand by excluding non-users, however.

A proxy of the market value of historic buildings is the property rental. It may differ greatly from their scientific value (as the object of study) and communication value (the social significance of heritage, its aesthetic and commercial value); a property with zero market value, except that of the land, can have very great heritage value (such as a country church). Heritage goods have both option and existence value. Option value is defined by what the non-user is willing to pay in order to preserve the possibility of benefit from an asset in the future. Existence value is obvious when individuals gain utility from the mere existence of cultural goods that they do not directly consume.

The hedonic pricing method is theoretically much more convincing. According to this method, a building is considered as a bundle of characteristics. It estimates the differences in value of buildings with a set of identical characteristics, but located in two different areas (listed and non-listed), considering that the price of a property can be viewed as the sum of the shadow prices of its characteristics. Unfortunately, many difficulties arise for the estimation of hedonic prices (Stabler, 1995).

It has been suggested that the utility of preserving the past increases with the age of consumers, especially during rapid social and economic change, when national identities seem threatened by changes. Therefore the intensity of demand varies according to a series of factors – access, revenues, price, age.

Costs of restoration and upkeep are high since listing implies the hiring of skilled labour and the use of rare and hence expensive building materials (Benhamou, 1996). Those costs increase with the stock of heritage. One can argue that nobody can anticipate the test of time. This uncertainty implies the broadest preservation policy possible, taking into account that present-day preferences of consumers may differ markedly from future preferences. But the vast financial burden of preservation imposes the need to select a set of buildings from among the large variety of possibilities and claims. Two kinds of criteria coexist: objective criteria, like the age of the building, its state of conservation and the emergency, and subjective criteria, like the definition of experts, who give the *imprimatur* to heritage goods. With subjective criteria, there is a risk of a conventional and self-referential process (Throsby, 2001), given that criteria are not well established and may be imposed by experts for their own benefit: regulators have their own preference functions that they impose on the public; in such a case, regulatory capture, as for other public utilities, leads to an oversupply of heritage.

Regulations

When the stock of cultural items is large, the marginal value of a specific item is low (Hutter, 1997; Netzer, 1998); this is an explanation of the low level of preservation in Italy. The problem is probably merely due to the huge costs of preservation in this country. Throsby (2001) makes the contrast between 'soft' and 'hard' regulations. Soft regulations open up the possibility of relatively large tax incentives and subsidization, or simple agreements, while hard regulations include enforceable legal restrictions on use, exchange and transformation.

Listing requires owners to conform to a series of constraints that range from restrictions on alteration and demolition, and supervision of works by public experts, to the requirement that the work be done by approved contractors. Moreover, in many countries, inheritance tax deductions are submitted on the opening to the public of the property during a defined period. Therefore regulation creates an incentive to reveal the existence of heritage goods and to provide services to the public. But regulation also creates an incentive to apply for subsidies: moral hazard occurs, creating a collective propensity to produce more heritage than would be preserved in a free market situation (Benhamou, 1996). Individuals asymmetrically weight losses and gains in the case of heritage, and therefore have a natural propensity to apply for preservation. Social costs of preservation may be much higher than is socially desirable.

Theoretically, bestowing on a monument a mark of architectural quality has a contradictory effect on its market value. But a study conducted in the UK in 1993 does not find any substantial change in the commercial value. Creigh-Tyte (2000) compares returns of listed and unlisted office properties over the period 1980–95. He concludes that the value of listed properties built before 1974 matches or exceeds their unlisted equivalents. Moreover, the oldest (pre-1945) listed properties slightly exceed the return on all property. Unfortunately, data collected in this survey only concern offices and not residential buildings.

Listing gives birth to a twofold contrasted effect on value: higher value because of symbolic significance versus lower value because of a loss resulting from the opportunity costs of constraints and delays. Subsidies may compensate for this.

An alternative way of analysing the question of the effects of listing on market value consists in taking into account property rights allocation. Different individuals may own distinct attributes of the same commodity (Barzel, 1997). Thus, among the multiple attributes of a historic building, some belong to the private owner, and others have to be shared with others, because they are a part of the national collective heritage. Therefore restrictions are imposed on the owner's behaviour in order to protect the rights of the other citizens, and public authorities capture a part of the property rights because of the inherent heritage quality of the property. The state and the owners share the responsibility for restoring registered monuments, as is observed in most countries.

Sable and Kling (2001) identify a double public-good feature: historic assets enter into household utility functions *and* contribute to the public externality of 'shared experience'. This 'shared experience' leads to a public concern and may legitimate regulations. The twofold nature argument applies better to façades than to interiors; the idea of preserving only the façades gave birth to a very questionable preservation choice called 'façadism', consisting in preserving the integrity of façades and freely reorganizing the interiors, with owners free to adapt their properties to modern life. Art historians generally criticize such an exercise, considering that it implies a loss of cultural value. This question of quality is emphasized by Mossetto and Vecco (2001), who show that people wish to keep heritage almost unchanged for centuries, as in the case of Venice, in such a way that conservation costs grow almost continuously. Reuse responds to cost concerns but it is always susceptible to threatening the historic quality of a site. As in Baumol's cost disease case for the performing arts, economizing on costs may lead to a decrease in quality.

An interesting debate concerns the degree of restoration. Do identical reproductions of the past stimulate solutions, or should we leave unchanged the architectural transformations made at different periods? The well-known architectural theory of Viollet Le

Duc relies on the idea of mixing history with modernity (Leniaud, 1994). This question is close to that of inalienability. When historic buildings are publicly owned, are there any possibilities of applying market forces in order to diminish the burden of preservation for taxpayers? The same issue concerns some works of art in the storage of public museums (de-accessioning). From this point of view the question of the preservation of non-moveable heritage (providing fixed-location services) shares many aspects with moveable artefacts.

Peacock (1997, 1998) denies the existence of inalienable rights for the preservation of buildings that would lead each generation to preserve a stock of heritage equivalent to that which it has inherited. This intertemporal redistribution issue relies on the assumption that future consumers will cover the costs of such an accumulation. He adds that there are no grounds that justify

> [forcing] present generations, especially in poor countries, to make the implied sacrifices in terms of the alternative use of resources in the expectation – which could be falsified – that future generations will perceive extra benefits from a bequest of historical artefacts at the expense of other forms of physical capital. (Peacock, 1997, p. 229)

The question is more complicated when taking into account the international concern for the preservation of other countries' heritage. According to Netzer (1998), there are cases in which foreigners are ready to contribute to preservation because of option, existence or bequest values. International demand for heritage services in many poor countries is undersupplied when financing preservation depends only on the national decision-making process.

Private versus public; local versus central

A large part of cultural heritage remains in private hands. Mossetto (1994) notes the existence of three different levels for the extent of preservation: reuse, (partial) restoration and preservation. In the two first cases the market works adequately, while public regulation is unavoidable in the third case. One of the specific problems is the risk linked to the two first cases: without any intervention, heritage may be radically transformed and its long-term value reduced by the loss of its historical characteristics.

Privatization is often presented as a solution in order to limit public expenditure. Whatever the case, public funding may be in addition to private financing. Public funding helps listed buildings' owners to undertake work and preserve the property as a whole. Therefore private and public financing do not conflict. There are private altruistic solutions, in the case of non-profit institutions in charge of heritage (like the National Trust in England and in Scotland) and friends' associations. Another form of private altruism relies on the proportion of voluntary labour in this field. The National Lottery, mainly developed in the UK, which contributes to heritage financing, with the burden on taxpayers being reduced by people who like to gamble, leading to a regressive effect (Peacock, 1997). The final structure of financing depends on the context, on the nature and extent of externalities.

Some debates emphasize a second opposition between local and central support. For Peacock, devolution towards funding by regional and local authorities would increase the individual involvement in the decision-making process. But the legitimacy of devolution depends on the type of monument concerned. A case study of Sicily shows that devolution does not diminish the gap between local voter preferences and those of policy-makers: while administrative responsibility relies on local authorities, funds still come from central authorities (Rizzo, 2002).

Final remarks

The economics of built heritage does not exist in a ghetto concerned only with the question of preserving the past. Economists help policy-makers to find appropriate solutions when intellectual property rights intervene in the decision process. For example, they discuss the fact that every image of the 'Pyramide du Louvre' designed by Pei provides royalties to its architect. Economists value the way digitalization increases the market value of monuments by enlarging the circle of their potential users (as in the case of the record industry for the performing arts). Economists should undertake more studies on the impact of regulation on supply and demand behaviours in relation to heritage. Many stimulating avenues for further research are still open in this field.

See also:

Chapter 13: Contingent valuation; Chapter 20: Cultural capital; Chapter 54: Regulation.

References

Barzel, Y. (1997), *Economic Analysis of Property Rights*, Cambridge: Cambridge University Press.
Benhamou, Francoise (1996), 'Is Increased Public Spending for the Preservation of Historic Monuments Inevitable? The French Case', *Journal of Cultural Economics*, 20 (2), 115–31.
Chastel, André (1986), *La notion de patrimoine*, in Pierre Nora (ed.), *Les Lieux de Mémoire*, 2, Paris: Gallimard, pp. 405–50.
Creigh-Tyte, Stephen W. (2000), 'The Built Heritage: Some British Experience', *Recherches Economiques de Louvain*, 66 (2), 213–30.
Frey, Bruno S. (1997), 'The Evaluation of Cultural Heritage. Some Critical Issues', in Michael Hutter and Ilde Rizzo (eds), *Economic Perspectives on Cultural Heritage*, London: Macmillan, pp. 31–49.
Frey, Bruno S. and Paolo Pamini (2009), 'Making World Heritage Truly Global: The Culture Certificate Scheme', Working Paper No. 419, Zurich: Institute for Empirical Research in Economics.
Greffe, Xavier (2003), *La Valorisation Economique du Patrimoine*, Paris: La Documentation Française.
Hoffman, Barbara T. (ed.) (2006), *Art and Cultural Heritage: Law, Policy, and Practice*, Cambridge: Cambridge University Press.
Hutter, Michael (1997), 'Economic Perspectives on Cultural Heritage: An Introduction', in Michael Hutter and I. Rizzo (eds), *Economic Perspectives on Cultural Heritage*, London: Macmillan, pp. 3–10.
Klamer, Arjo and David Throsby (2000), 'Paying for the Past: The Economics of Cultural Heritage', *World Culture Report*, UNESCO, pp. 130–45.
Koboldt, C. (1997), 'Optimizing the Use of Cultural Heritage', in M. Hutter and I. Rizzo (eds), *Economic Perspectives on Cultural Heritage*, New York: St Martin's Press, pp.50–73.
Leniaud, Jean-Michel (1994), *Viollet-le-Duc ou les Délires du Système*, Paris: Mengès.
Mossetto, Gianfranco (1994), 'The Economic Dilemma of Heritage Preservation', in Alan Peacock and Ilde Rizzo (eds), *Cultural Economics and Cultural Policies*, Dordrecht: Kluwer Academic Publishers, pp. 81–96.
Mossetto, Gianfranco and Marilena Vecco (2001), *Economia del Patrimonio Monumentale*, Venice: ICARE, Universita Ca' Foscari.
Netzer, Dick (1998), 'International Aspects of Heritage Policies', in A. Peacock (ed.) (1998), *Does The Past Have a Future? The Political Economy of Heritage*, London: Institute of Economic Affairs, pp. 135–54.
Peacock, Alan (1997), 'A Future for the Past: the Political Economy of Heritage', *Proceedings of the British Academy*, 87, reprinted in Ruth Towse (ed.), *Cultural Economics: the Arts, the Heritage and the Media Industries*, vol. I, Cheltenham, UK and Lyme, USA: Edward Elgar, pp. 189–243.
Peacock, Alan (ed.) (1998), *Does The Past Have A Future? The Political Economy of Heritage*, London: Institute of Economic Affairs.
Rizzo, Ilde (2002), 'Heritage Conservation. The Role of Heritage Authorities', in Ilde Rizzo and Ruth Towse, *The Economics of Heritage. A Study in the Political Economy of Culture in Sicily*, Cheltenham, UK and Northampton, MA, USA: Edward Elgar, pp. 31–47.

Rizzo, Ilde and David Throsby (2006), 'Cultural Heritage: Economic Analysis and Public Policy', in Victor Ginsburgh and David Throsby (eds), *Handbook of the Economics of Art and Culture*, Amsterdam: North-Holland, pp. 983–1016.

Rizzo, Idle and Ruth Towse (2002), *The Economics of Heritage. A study in the Political Economy of Culture in Sicily*, Cheltenham, UK and Northampton, MA, USA: Edward Elgar.

Sable, Karin A. and Robert W. King (2001), 'The Double Public Good: A Conceptual Framework for "Shared Experience" Values Associated with Heritage Conservation', *Journal of Cultural Economics*, 25 (2), 75–89.

Stabler, Mike (1995), 'Research in Progress on the Economic and Social Value of Conservation', in P. Burman (ed.), *The Economics of Architectural Conservation*, York: Institute of Advanced Architectural Studies, pp. 33–50.

Throsby, David (1997), 'Seven Questions in the Economics of Cultural Heritage', in Michael Hutter and Ilde Rizzo, *Economic Perspectives on Cultural Heritage*, London: Macmillan, pp. 13–30.

Throsby, David (2001), *Economics and Culture*, Cambridge: Cambridge University Press.

Further reading

General analyses of heritage from the point of view of cultural economics are provided in Rizzo and Throsby (2006). Specific analyses are discussed in Rizzo and Towse (2002) and in Hoffman (2005). For contingent valuation studies, see volume 27 of the *Journal of Cultural Economics*, 2003.

33 International trade
Günther G. Schulze

The market for cultural goods is arguably one of the most internationalized – Van Gogh's paintings can be admired in New York, a large collection of Egyptian art is on display in Berlin, Isabel Allende's and Thomas Mann's books are popular in Europe and the Americas alike, the Beatles' and Madonna's CDs are sold throughout the world, and Hollywood movies have global coverage. Yet this phenomenon is not uniform: the market share of American films in Europe is much higher than that of European films in the USA and it's fair to say that Pop Art had a larger influence on the European culture than traditional Javanese paintings. Why is that? What determines the pattern of trade in cultural goods?

Trade theory explains why sellers (mostly producers) of certain goods reside in different jurisdictions from the buyers/consumers of these products. In order to understand the trade pattern we need to know what determines the demand for foreign art and its supply, that is, what determines consumption for foreign art and under which conditions are the respective cultural goods produced. In both dimensions cultural goods are distinctively different from most other goods.[1]

The demand for cultural goods in the international market

The demand for cultural goods is characterized by the positive addiction in consumption of cultural goods. The idea goes back to Alfred Marshall, who wrote: 'It is therefore no exception to the law [of diminishing marginal utility] that the more good music a man hears, the stronger is his taste for it likely to become . . .' (Marshall, [1891] 1962, p. 94). Marginal utility from cultural consumption increases with the ability to appreciate (a particular form of) cultural goods, which is a function of past consumption (Stigler and Becker, 1977). In the course of consuming cultural goods, such as enjoying Flemish painters or French *film noir*, art-specific 'consumption capital' is built up. Marginal utility from cultural consumption increases with the accumulation of consumption capital and therefore rises over time. This leads to an actual shift in the demand for the specific cultural goods without a change in prices or income. Empirical evidence for such an addictive effect of art consumption is ample (for example, Smith, 1998). Becker (1996) distinguishes two components of consumption capital: personal capital, which is formed out of past consumption and other relevant individual experience,[2] and social capital, which represents the influence of others on a person's utility, namely the influence of peers or relevant others. Social capital can be influenced by the individuals only to a limited degree by the choice of the social milieu they live in. Part of social capital is cultural capital (cf. Throsby, 1999), which is given for the individual.

In the international context this notion of positive addiction has two implications: first, people value cultural goods from abroad less as long as they have not accumulated enough personal consumption capital for this unfamiliar art; social capital is likewise underdeveloped as their peers have not either. This *cultural discount vis-à-vis* domestic art limits the degree of trade – the closer (national) cultures are, the smaller the difference in the relevant consumption capital and, thus, the larger bilateral trade in art. This cultural discount can be asymmetric. One country can accumulate consumption capital for the other country's culture, but the opposite need not be true (to the same extent). The more consumption capital is built up, the easier its further accumulation until foreign-originated cultural goods become part of the national culture (see below). Trade levels go up and remain high. This describes the hysteresis effect in trade in cultural goods. These arguments imply that trade in art is a positive function of cultural proximity and that current trade is a positive function of past trade. Still, this does not predict the pattern of trade in art; we need to look at the supply side in the international market for cultural goods.

The supply of cultural goods: a classification
Cultural goods comprise very heterogeneous products such as sculptures and statues, original paintings, CDs and DVDs, books, films for cinema and TV, prints and so on. From an economic perspective they fall into two categories:[3] unique cultural goods (for instance, original paintings and sculptures, antiques) and reproducible cultural goods (recorded music and films, literature, and so on).

Reproducible cultural goods are produced in two steps, the creative step in which the artist creates the blueprint (that is, the manuscript, the original recording, the master copy of the film) and the reproduction step in which the master copy is industrially copied under strongly increasing returns to scale and marketed.[4] Artists (musicians, authors, actors) and the companies that reproduce the original work (music labels, publishers, film producers) need not reside in the same country, so that there may be a first international transaction, an international art service, which is paid for in royalties or fees. The second international transaction takes place between the companies that industrially reproduce the original work and the consumers ('primary market').[5] As these cultural goods are differentiated goods and are produced under strong scale economies, (international) trade can be explained by a Dixit–Stiglitz type model of monopolistic competition (cf. Wong, 1995, ch. 6).

In contrast, original paintings, sculptures, drawings and so on are produced in a single – creative – step without scale economies. They are unique and highly durable, and thus precious, which makes them a store of value and creates a strong 'secondary market', that is, a market between former and future consumers. The observable substantial price increases for these goods demonstrate that additions of the primary market to the secondary market's stock are insufficient to satisfy rising demand for these collectors' items and thus the secondary market dominates the primary market, partly also due to low substitutability between the stock of old art objects and the new products. This makes international trade in works of art demand-determined, as both sellers and buyers are consumers, and this distinguishes it from trade in most other products.

Before we turn to the characteristics of trade in these two types of cultural goods, a remark on the magnitude of international trade in cultural goods is in order. It is very hard to measure the actual trade in cultural goods and services, not only because these groups are not easily defined, but also because many of the international transactions are reflected in trans-border royalty payments, for which consistent data are hard to find, and not in cross-border movements of physical goods.[6] Table 33.1 shows the average trade in 1990–94 for 154 countries and selected categories of cultural goods.

*Table 33.1   Average trade in selected groups of cultural goods as defined by SITC,
1990–94*

	Works of art (SITC 8960)	Sound recordings (SITC 8983)	Books etc. (SITC 8921)	Total manufacturing trade
Volume of trade (billion US$)	10.569	18.27	8.441	3586.802
As percentage of total trade in manufactures	0.30	0.51	0.24	100

Source: Schulze (1999), based on IMF Direction of Trade Statistics.

More recently, the *Creative Economy Report 2008* published by UNCTAD (2008) provides international trade figures for the *creative* industries, a wider concept than cultural industries. According to this report, the value of world exports of creative industry goods and services reached US$424.4 billion in 2005, accounting for 3.4 per cent of world trade (UNCTAD, 2008, p. 106). They have been growing very dynamically at a rate of 8.7 per cent per annum in the period 2000–05. Creative industries' exports comprise the groups design (share of 65 per cent in 2005), arts and crafts (7 per cent), audiovisuals (0.2 per cent), music (4 per cent), new media (4 per cent), publishing (13 per cent) and visual arts (7 per cent) (ibid., p. 108). Yet the data have major shortcomings beyond the usual deficiencies of international trade data by product group as (1) fewer than half of the 192 UN member states report trade in creative industries services, (2) data for royalties that pertain exclusively to creative industries are unavailable due to the non-availability of copyright statistics, and (3) digitalized creative content traded via the Internet (music, films, books) is not recorded. Thus the above data will highly underestimate 'and do not reflect the vibrant reality of global markets for phonographic, audiovisual and digital products' (ibid., p. 102). Thus even though the report is the most comprehensive and most recent one, its statistics are flawed as they include many activities that are not linked to *cultural*, but *creative* industries and contain important gaps for very dynamically developing submarkets as movies, music and literature.[7]

Trade in unique art
Trade in unique art is demand-driven and this demand in turn is a function of the income level as works of art are luxury goods. Demand also depends on cultural proximity, which should have a substantially stronger impact on the trade of works in art than on total trade. Schulze (2002) compares the pattern of trade in works of art with the total manufacturing trade pattern in a gravity model that links gross bilateral trade flows to the country sizes of both countries as measured by GDP, the geographical distance between the two countries, the income levels (GPD per capita) and dummies for a common border, a common language, and for countries that are members of the same trade bloc.

His findings are consistent with the theoretical predictions: the effect of GDP per capita of the importing country is significantly stronger for works of art than for total trade, pointing towards a higher income elasticity of demand. Also the variables that capture cultural proximity – distance and a common language – exert a much stronger influence on trade in unique art than on total trade. People have closer ties to and have built up more consumption capital for nearby cultures; likewise a common language not only facilitates cultural exchange but is often tied to a common (mostly colonial) history. It turns out that people trade five times as many works of art if they have a language in common, which is 2.5 times the factor for total trade.[8]

Trade in reproducible cultural goods

While trade in unique art establishes a particularity not only because of the special demand characteristics and therefore the importance of cultural proximity, but also because works of art are the only group of products where the secondary market dominates the primary one,[9] the latter does not apply to reproducible art. For these goods cultural discounts are likewise important, and this refers to the different cultures of the artists (first production step) and the consumers, not the country of reproduction. Reproduction is characterized by strong scale economies – once a manuscript is written, it is cheap to reproduce additional copies of the book. This explains why (re-)production of a particular cultural good is often concentrated in one location. At the same time production of many cultural goods is characterized by strong economies of scope at the firm level, as a substantial part of fixed costs is not tied to the production process of one particular product (a certain CD) only, but to producing similar products as such (CDs in general): production facilities (CD production plants) and distribution networks are efficiently used only if used for many similar products. This explains the existence of labels, film studios and publishing houses. In addition there may be economies of scale at the industry level, which may be local, national or international, depending on the industry.

Recently, theoretical papers have analysed the effect of trade in cultural goods on welfare and preference formation. In particular, they have called into question whether the commonly accepted free trade postulate carries over to trade in (industrially produced) cultural products without qualifications. Francois and van Ypersele (2002) show that a tariff for cultural products *may* be welfare-improving if the good is produced under strong scale economies and there is strong heterogeneity of preferences in the countries involved in the trade. For instance, if France imposes a tariff on Hollywood movies, the market share of Hollywood movies declines, their prices rise and French films as well as independent American (*auteur*) movies gain a larger market share or become viable at all in their respective country. This may increase overall welfare in both countries if a number of consumers in France value French films much more highly than the rest of their fellow citizens and in the USA a number of consumers value non-Hollywood American films much more highly than Hollywood movies, while Hollywood movies are valued relatively similarly. The overall consumer rent goes up.

Instead of assuming scale economies, Janeba (2007) analyses trade effects in a standard Ricardian trade model with constant returns to scale, but assumes positive network externalities in the consumption of the cultural good: people are better off if more people consume the same cultural good as they do.[10] He shows that under certain constellations trade may reduce welfare of a country compared to autarky: since trade changes the relative price of the network good, people may switch to the imported network good, thereby making the consumers of the domestically produced cultural good worse off as price and user base of this good have deteriorated. A country's welfare may (or may not) go down with free trade in cultural goods. Rauch and Trindade (2009) combine network externalities in consumption with scale economies in production. They show in a two-country model of differentiated cultural products that if the cultural discount is not too large and the difference in size is sufficiently great, the cultural products of the smaller country may disappear. Cultural globalization thus reinforces the home market effect of standard Helpman–Krugman type trade models. Increased cultural globalization – a reduction in the cultural discount – reduces the number of varieties of cultural goods leading to higher network externalities; at the same time the quality of future cultural products decreases as it is modelled to depend on the present number of varieties in the two countries, which are imperfect substitutes. Thus the welfare effects of globalization are ambiguous.

Bala and Van Long (2005) use an evolutionary approach to analyse how preferences are shaped through generations as a consequence of relative scarcity or abundance of cultural goods and their resulting price level. They show that free trade between a large and a small country with different stable preferences in autarky can lead to the extinction of the preferences of the small country. The small country will gradually lose its cultural identity – trade may bring about the demise of cultural diversity. Olivier *et al.* (2008) introduce a dynamic approach to the evolution of preferences that is based on a socialization mechanism and incorporates cultural identity as group externality – people meet randomly and derive utility from meeting someone from the same culture. They assume constant-returns-to-scale production and thus their transmission channel is not characterized by the dominant economy/culture being able to offer its cultural product more cheaply after market integration, which would provide a tendency for corner solutions. Olivier *et al.* show that factor endowments drive the preferences for cultural goods in the long run – people will have a preference for the good that is produced in abundance. They show that trade integration leads to cultures becoming more dissimilar across countries, but more homogeneous within the country, leading to cultural tensions within the countries. Social integration, on the contrary, leading to increased interactions between individuals of different countries, gives rise to cultural convergence in that the distribution of cultures becomes more similar across countries.[11]

Thus there is no general presumption that free trade in cultural goods is welfare-deteriorating – gains from trade may occur also with trade in cultural products – but the literature identifies a number of distinct situations in which unrestricted trade may actually reduce welfare compared to a situation that limits the trade in cultural products.[12]

Trade in movies

The movie industry may serve as an important example for reproducible art (cf. De Vany, 2006). Obviously, *re*production is characterized by economies of scale as it is easy to copy film rolls. Production and marketing are characterized by scope economies, as studios, marketing departments and distribution networks can serve for production and especially financing and sale of many films at rapidly decreasing unit costs. Another reason is the high risk involved in film-making – studios pool the risk and thus serve as an insurance device, a function that capital markets may not fulfil equally well as knowledge is highly industry-specific. This explains the existence of the big studios. The making of the film itself requires highly specialized labour – actors, stuntmen, cameramen, stylists and the rest – for a very limited period of time. These workers make a living by working consecutively or even simultaneously in many movie productions, and also for different studios. As flexibility and short-term availability are important, this creates a specialized localized labour market and thus local economies of scale at the industry level. This explains the existence of Hollywood or 'Bollywood' (Bombay), the concentration of the movies industry in one place in a country.

The dominance of American films in the Western world is explained by the concurrence of scale economies and the demand characteristics for cultural goods. Since initially the cultural discount works both ways, and domestic films are preferred to foreign films, the film industry in the larger home market will have larger total sales as they face cultural discounts in the demand for their films for a smaller portion of the world market (Wildman and Siwek, 1988; Frank, 1993). Given strong scale economies in film production, this effect allows the larger country's film industry to lower its prices or to increase its fixed costs and thereby to try to enhance the quality of its products. Either way it gains a competitive edge and enjoys a higher market penetration in the foreign countries than foreign films in its home country. Market penetration in the foreign markets will build up consumption capital and reduce the cultural discount until eventually American films have become part of the European culture. The opposite does not hold to the same degree – trade in films may become a one-way road. Although this phenomenon is not uniform for all countries, empirical evidence is consistent with this theory.

In 2008 the market shares for domestic films (in terms of visitors) were: 92 per cent in the USA, 27 per cent in Germany, 30 per cent in Italy, 45 per cent in France, 11 per cent in Hungary, 6 per cent in Austria, and an average of 35 per cent for the EU-27. The market sizes in terms of movie attendances were 1364 million for the USA compared to 924 million for the EU-27 (Germany 129 million, Italy 112 million, France 190 million, Austria 16 million, Hungary 10 million). The market shares in the EU-27 market by country of origin of the film were 63 per cent for the US films (including 10 percentage points US–EU co-productions, but excluding the 7 percentage points EU–US co-productions), 13 per cent for French films, 4 per cent each for German and Italian films, and 2 per cent for UK films (Berauer, 2009). These figures underline the importance of the size of the home market, scale economies and the endogenous nature of the cultural discounts.

Marvasti and Canterbery (2005) estimate a specific gravity equation of US movie exports that conflates the role of national GDPs and distance, and studies the effect of language and trade barriers for which they construct two different measures. They show that the demand for protection of domestic films rises with cultural and geographic proximity. The effect of these trade barriers on motion picture trade is significant. Hanson and Xiang (2009) show the dominance of US films in Europe – over the period 1992 to 2002 they averaged a share of 69 per cent of total box-office receipts in Europe. They use a gravity type of equation to explain the relative dominance of US films in 19 European countries and find that dominance is larger for smaller countries, countries with lower linguistic distance and lower relative wages and with higher trade barriers. Disdier *et al.* (2007) study trade in reproducible cultural products in general and find in a gravity approach that common language and colonial history matter significantly more for cultural trade.

Government intervention in the international trade in cultural goods

The observed trade patterns for both types of cultural goods are also partly a result of various government interventions. For instance, according to Article 36 of the Treaty of Rome, the EU member states have the right to protect their national patrimony through export restrictions (embargos, export licensing, pre-emptive rights to purchase works of art to be exported) and they are free to define what they regard as their national patrimony. VAT regulations may distort trade as well: within the EU, works of art are taxed at the margin (on the difference between purchasing and selling price) according to the origin principle, which disfavours high-VAT countries. On imports of works of art into the EU, the import VAT is levied mostly at reduced rates, which differ substantially between countries, favouring low-tax countries such as the UK. The *droit de suite* entitles artists to a fraction of the gross selling price each time their works of art are resold. This right functions like a turnover tax and thus may divert trade away from countries that enforce these resale royalty rights. The EU has decided on introducing a uniform *droit de suite* on a sliding scale with a derogation period between five and ten years for some countries, whereas the important art markets Switzerland and the USA do not have resale royalty rights. Lastly, direct subsidies to art museums or indirect subsidies to art institutions and private individuals in the form of tax incentives (wealth and inheritance tax exemptions, income tax deductions for donations to art institutions, acceptance of art objects in lieu of tax payments) increase the incentive for residents to acquire or to hold art and thus distort trade.

Government intervention in the movie industries is also frequent. This refers not only to direct subsidization of the domestic film industry (also in the form of lucrative awards), but also to local content requirements for national TV.[13] These measures increase the supply of and the demand for domestically produced films and therefore reduce imports and increase exports. To what extent government interventions actually distort trade is of course an empirical matter that to date remains largely unresolved.

Notes

1. The following two sections draw on Schulze (1999). For normative issues of trade in cultural goods, see, for example, van Hemel *et al.* (1996) and O'Hagan (1998, chs 4 and 6).
2. This includes the interaction with others and it helps to explain the emergence of superstars; cf. Chapter 56 in this volume.
3. We disregard live performances like concerts, plays and so on, which are internationally tradable services if bands or theatre companies tour abroad. We also disregard international cultural tourism, which is international trade in services as well.
4. The second step can be divided into functionally defined substeps (production, financing, marketing, distribution), see below 'Trade in reproducible cultural goods'.
5. This does not exclude possible intermediaries such as foreign publishers, so that the international trade can also take place between the producer and the foreign intermediary and the subsequent sales are between this intermediary and a consumer.
6. One example is the case of a domestic publisher who sells the right for a foreign edition of a book to a foreign publisher.
7. UNESCO (2005) is the most comprehensive report on trade in *cultural* goods and services.
8. The other results are: art trade rises more than proportionally with GDP, a common trade bloc increases trade significantly and a common border does not increase trade in addition to the proximity as measured by geographical distance.
9. The only other exception is antiques and scientific collections, which are in the same SITC category.
10. Cf. also the chapter on 'superstars' in this book (Chapter 56) for network externalities in art and culture.
11. In a related vein, Melitz (2007) shows how, in an integrated world, market forces tend to privilege transla-

tions from the dominant English into other languages, with the consequence of reduced world literature production negative welfare effects for all countries involved.
12. See also Suranovic and Winthrop (2005).
13. For the Canadian case see Acheson and Maule (1992); for Germany see Perino and Schulze (2005).

See also:

Chapter 31: Globalization; Chapter 38: Media economics and regulation; Chapter 55: Resale rights.

References

Acheson, Keith and Christopher Maule (1992), 'Canadian Content Rules for Television: Misleading Lessons for Europe', *Journal of Cultural Economics*, 16, 13–23.

Bala, Venkatesh and Ngo Van Long (2005), 'International Trade and Cultural Diversity with Preference Selection', *European Journal of Political Economy*, 21, 143–62.

Becker, Gary (1996), *Accounting for Tastes*, Cambridge, MA: Harvard University Press.

Berauer, Wilfried (2009), *Filmstatistisches Jahrbuch 2001*, Spitzenorganisation der Filmwirtschaft, Baden-Baden: Nomos.

De Vany, Arthur (2006), 'The Movies', in Victor Ginsburgh and David Throsby (eds), *Handbook of the Economics of Art and Culture*, Amsterdam: North-Holland, pp.615–66.

Disdier, Anne-Célia, Silvio Tai, Lionel Fontagné and Thierry Mayer (2007), 'Bilateral Trade of Cultural Goods', Centre d'Etudes Prospectives et d'Informations Internationales, CEPII, Working Paper No. 2007-20, Paris.

Francois, Patrik and Tanguy van Ypersele (2002), 'On the Protection of Cultural Goods', *Journal of International Economics*, 56, 424–40.

Frank, Björn (1993), *Zur Ökonomik der Filmindustrie*, Hamburg: Steuer- und Wirtschaftsverlag.

Hanson, Gordon and Chong Xiang (2009), 'International Trade in Motion Picture Services', in M. Reinsdorf and M. Slaughter (eds), *International Trade in Services and Intangibles in the Era of Globalization*, National Bureau of Economic Research, Chicago: Chicago University Press, pp. 203–22.

Janeba, Eckart (2007), 'International Trade and Consumption Network Externalities', *European Economic Review*, 51, 781–803.

Marshall, Alfred ([1891] 1962), *Principles of Economics*, 8th edn, London: Macmillan.

Marvasti, Akbar and E. Ray Canterbery (2005), 'Cultural and Other Barriers to Motion Pictures Trade', *Economic Inquiry*, 43 (1), 39–54.

Melitz, Jacques (2007), 'The Impact of English Dominance on Literature and Welfare', *Journal of Economic Behavior & Organization*, 64, 193–215.

O'Hagan, John (1998), *The State and the Arts*, Cheltenham, UK and Lyme, NH, USA: Edward Elgar.

Olivier, Jacques, Mathias Thoenig and Thierry Verdier (2008), 'Globalization and the Dynamics of Cultural Identity', *Journal of International Economics*, 76, 356–70.

Perino, Grischa and Günther G. Schulze (2005), 'Competition, Cultural Autonomy and Global Governanace: The Audio-Visual Sector in Germany', in Paolo Guerrieri, Lelio Iapadre and Georg Koopmann (eds), *Cultural Diversity and International Economic Integration: The Global Governance of the Audio-Visual Sector*, Cheltenham, UK and Northampton, MA, USA: Edward Elgar, pp. 52–95.

Rauch, James E. and Vitor Trindade (2009), 'Neckties in the Tropics: A Model of International Trade and Cultural Diversity', *Canadian Journal of Economics*, 42, 809–43.

Schulze, Günther (1999), 'International Trade in Art', *Journal of Cultural Economics*, 23, 109–36.

Schulze, Günther (2002), 'International Trade in Art – A Tale of Cultural Proximity and Secondary Markets', University of Freiburg, rev. manuscript.

Smith, Thomas (1998), 'The Addiction to Culture', paper presented on the biannual meeting of the Association for Cultural Economics International in Barcelona, 14–17 June 1998; also part of 'Two Essays on the Economics of the Arts: The Demand for Culture and the Occupational Mobility of Artists', unpublished doctoral dissertation, University of Chicago, September 1998.

Stigler, George and Gary Becker (1977), 'De Gustibus Non Est Disputandum', *American Economic Review*, 67, 76–90.

Suranovic, Steve and Robert Winthrop (2005), 'Cultural Effects of Trade Liberalization', George Washington University, unpublished manuscript, EconWPA series International Trade with number 0511003, http://ideas.repec.org/p/wpa/wuwpit/0511003.html.

Throsby, David (1999), 'Cultural Capital', *Journal of Cultural Economics*, 23, 3–12.

UNCTAD (2008) *Creative Economy Report 2008*, Geneva: UNCTAD, available at http://www.unctad.org/en/docs/ditc20082cer_en.pdf (accessed 15 May 2010)

UNESCO (2005), *International Flows of Selected Cultural Goods and Services, 1994–2003*, Montreal: UNESCO

Institute for Statistics, available at http://www.uis.unesco.org/template/pdf/cscl/IntlFlows_EN.pdf (accessed 15 May 2010).
Van Hemel, Annemoon, Hans Mommaas and Cas Smithuijsen (1996), *Trading Culture*, Amsterdam: Boekman Foundation.
Wildman, Steven and Stephen Siwek (1988), *International Trade in Films and Television Programs*, Cambridge, MA: Ballinger.
Wong, Kar-yiu (1995), *International Trade in Goods and Factor Mobility*, Cambridge, MA: MIT Press.

Further reading

Bala and Long (2005), Francois and van Ypersele (2002), Rauch and Trindade (2009), Schulze (1999) and UNCTAD (2008).

34 The Internet: culture for free
Joëlle Farchy

By emphasizing both the specific features of a sector (in this case, that of live perform-ance) and the role of public authorities, Baumol and Bowen's groundbreaking work (1966) paved the way for work on the economics of culture in a rather unusual per-spective. The economics of culture – having long ignored the cultural industries that, ironically, are its principal source of employment and value added – has to a great extent structured itself not around concern for the industrial economy but rather around matters relating to public economics and non-profit organizations. As such, 'free' culture – in reality, financed by the taxpayer for purposes of public interest (democratization or the demand for diversity, for example) – in essence correspond to the public model, the goal being to organize culture in a way that is free of the demands of the market.

The Internet has very much revived the debate on free culture, bringing with it both confusion and paradoxes, as evidenced by the many conflicting viewpoints on the subject. In France, for example, the Ministry of Culture decided to make certain museums free of charge in order to attract a broader audience; almost simultaneously, it passed a rather controversial law banning free downloads – that notorious cultural assassin.

One paradox is: that at the same time as traditionally non-profit cultural institutions such as museums have taken a commercial stance by developing their own financial resources in recent years, private companies such as Google are offering more free serv-ices than ever. Yet another paradox is that while theories on zero pricing – as it has come to be known – pervade the Web, the Internet economy is among those – with the excep-tion of the bursting of the late 1990s bubble – with the greatest growth rate. Google, that symbol of the dynamism of these services that saw its turnover multiply by a factor of nearly 40 between 2002 and 2007, all the while maintained its original motto 'Don't be evil' – a simplistic digest of the place the company would ideally like to occupy in the social space. Various large-scale takeovers attest the confidence economic players have in the potential value of Internet trade. In 2006 Google bought YouTube for $1.6 billion and agreed to pay Fox Interactive $900 million over three years to become the exclusive supplier of sponsored links on search pages for the MySpace social network; for its part, Yahoo! bought the photo-sharing site Flickr to the tune of $35 million.

Since 1998 – which now seems like another epoch – when an American student created the site Napster, never has so great a profusion of free content been so readily available to the world's consumers. And yet behind the appearance of zero price for users hides a variety of economic models in which public subsidies occupy only a marginal place. Cooperative models, on the other hand – be they encyclopaedias like Wikipedia, user-generated or other amateur content, social networks that allow users to share opinions and ideas, or cultural works under free licence – occupy an important place, and the making available of content for free (with the author's consent) is a cooperative logic that has attracted a great deal of attention – even if such logic maintains complex links with the market (Farchy, 2009a).

New forms of free – a far cry from what the cultural realm has seen until now – have appeared over the past few years. Chris Anderson's (creator of the 'Long Tail') 2008 article eloquently entitled 'Free! Why $0.00 is the future of business' exemplifies this mutation. The analysis, in which 'free' paradoxically serves no other purpose than to enable companies to increase their profits, was taken up again by the author in a 2009 publication. Anderson's work lacks scientific rigour; the question of free's purpose in terms of social well-being above and beyond the business interests of the audience to whom he speaks is not addressed at all. And yet, despite these obvious failings, the work brilliantly captures the spirit of the times, indisputably illustrating the fact that the debate on free culture has changed.

Throughout this chapter we shall use 'free' to mean free of charge for users. We shall examine a form of free that is neither public nor cooperative, which we shall call 'for-profit free', meaning profitable zero-pricing business models. After analysing both the historical and economic conditions of this mutation, we shall explore forms of for-profit free on the Web in detail, as well as the respective limits of the different economic models.

The Internet and digital free: a twofold explanation
Far from curbing new practices, the closing of Napster for failure to comply with copyright laws only accelerated the flight of many users towards more ingenious competitors that were even less easy to control because they were decentralized: the P2P (peer to peer) networks. Subsequently, new practices for free access to digital content developed (automatic copying of music from Web radio stations, podcasting etc.). The success of a wide variety of WEB 2.0 services (community portals, video or photo-sharing sites, e-commerce platforms, collaborative online encyclopaedias etc.) has marked the emergence of intermediaries that give users themselves the means to access creative content quickly, thus reviving the cooperative tradition of universities use of the Internet in its early years – this time, for the general public.

Historical heritage of a cooperative and public world
The unusual history of the Internet – long protected from the realities of the market – provides an initial explanation for the persistence of the logic of free. In 1958 the Pentagon created an agency to coordinate its federal research contracts; ten years later, in order to better facilitate exchanges between the contracting teams, this agency financed a first network – ARPAnet – the predecessor of which was to become the Internet. Two entirely different professional realms (that of the military and that of academic computing research) contributed to the building of ARPAnet. The gradual success of ARPAnet led them to envisage building networks for all universities, the bulk of whose financing came under the charge of another public institution in the USA, the National Science Foundation. Thus the development of the Internet did not take place within a market framework but rather as the result of a long period of public financing that greatly stimulated its startup phase, with universities fashioning the system according to their own scientific needs and practices. Cooperation and free, needless to say, played a key role here. These principles, however, gradually became blurred, leaving only traces of the way users imagined access to its many services. Moreover, experience shows that users' relationship to the price of goods and services does not follow a simple logic; rather, it is their perception of them that, formed over time, enables them to accept the reality of paying

widely differentiated costs for different goods (opera versus television, to use examples from the cultural domain). Through a historical 'lock-in' effect, the culture of free has permeated the minds of users, giving rise to the dream of free, direct and unlimited access to the dissemination of culture now and in the future.

The economics of information

The specific characteristics of the economics of information offer a second explanation for free services offered on the Internet. As early as 1962, Arrow underlined the specific qualities and paradoxes of the economic good that is information: as it is an experiential good (meaning the buyer does not know the value of the information before having acquired it), giving it a value and setting a market price become difficult. Likewise it is difficult for a seller wishing to sell a piece of information to take full advantage of its associated value as the information – costly to produce but relatively inexpensive to *re*produce and distribute – can easily be passed on for little to no cost once known by another seller. In the tradition developed by economists following Arrow, informational goods have the specific properties associated with public goods, meaning those of non-rivalry and non-excludability. With the marginal cost being zero and the economic optimum implying that in a competitive business economy the prices of goods and services tend towards their marginal cost, the price of information should theoretically be zero.

Because it is a public good, we could consider placing the production of information under the jurisdiction of the state, or even giving consumers free access to additional information while imposing a flat-rate subscription to cover fixed costs. These are not, however, the models of free services financed by public subsidies that are used on the Internet. The economic and commercial argument that latched on to the Internet beginning in the mid-1990s likewise moved away from the vision of a cooperative approach, of which many a purist dreamed. To understand just how the Web has opened new spaces of for-profit free, we must emphasize not only the drop in the marginal costs of distribution and reproduction of the *supply* but also another fundamental characteristic of the economics of information: a major transformation in the *demand*, made possible by the consequences of network effects in the digital economy (Bomsel, 2007).

On the one hand, informational goods in circulation on the Web, notably cultural content, which are non-rival, and non-excludable, have repercussions in terms of cost:

- Using digital means, a consumer can – by copying – dispose of his own unit of good X equal (or nearly equal) in quality to that of the original in almost real time and at little or no cost. The gap between production costs and other costs incurred in order to put a good on the information market widens. Digital hyper-reproducibility tends to wipe out all rivalry.
- Access to information is always possible via another consumer. No longer is it only a few isolated economic agents that have the means to reproduce and distribute information for next to nothing; nowadays, potentially millions of users worldwide have the ability to do so, with no truly effective technological means for excluding non-payers.

On the other hand, in respect of demand, the digital revolution has caused us to shift from a distributor model (founded on controlled access) to a network economy model (based on the abundance of available information and the ever-growing number of users). It is the users' attention (Simon, 1971; Lanham, 2006) that is becoming a rare and vital resource amidst this sea of information. This model, which favours a more direct relationship between producers and consumers, nevertheless does not mean the end of all intermediation: on the contrary, it is inextricably linked to emergence of new inter-mediaries whose primary function is to grab users' attention and guide them through this economy of abundance. It is not the information itself that counts in this economy of audience and traffic, but rather the management of information flows and control of the interfaces through which users enter the network. Thus it is no longer the informa-tion or content itself whose abundance depreciates the value of the demand and allows companies to make a profit, but the services – potentially useful to the mass of users on the Web – associated with it.

Forms of for-profit free

Online content combines diverse logics of reception (downloading and streaming), financing (payment per unit consumed by the user, subscription, advertising) and mar-keting (for rent, for sale, for free). The Internet did not invent these forms of free: it did, however, significantly amplify their development potential. In a very schematic way, the models of free – financed by private companies for profit-making purposes and brought to the consumer – fall into three major categories.

The sale of complementary products: an inter-product logic
Since Gillette began almost giving away razors in the 1950s – making money instead on the sale of blades – there is nothing new in the idea that companies can actually make money by distributing certain products for free. In the digital world, promotional giveaways – offering the consumer a product for free in the hope that the offer will lead to the sale of related goods and services in the future – take on a another dimension. The fact that content is inherently non-rivalrous can be an opportunity for producers to indirectly appropriate the combined value of copycat works many times over; content that circulates on the Internet can then be 'consumed' by thousands of users (principle of non-rivalry), even if only a single copy is sold. Thus producers are tempted to indirectly appropriate the value of these multiple uses without making the user pay.

In the case of copying, this strategy results in pricing discrimination (see Liebowitz's 1985 pioneer article using the example of academic journals), grouped sales and the bundling of goods likely to be copied with another item – one that is much more dif-ficult to copy (the selling of hardware *and* copiable software, for example, even if the two goods are not sold in a single sale). The item can then be copied and distributed for free or at a loss once the consumer is forced to use a hardware item – whose production is profitable – in conjunction with it. The company then includes the price of the copied item in the price of the material, which in turn goes up. In 2007, for example, Apple made $10.8 billion from the sales of music and video players (45 per cent of its turnover), while iTunes brought in only $1.8 million that same year. Ipods – which we assumed would accompany this new model of pay for use – in reality became the Trojan Horse of free downloads. Apple made a profit by selling its hardware, all the while allowing copycat material to spread freely; the main problem here was that the works were produced *not* by Apple but by other companies that made no profit whatsoever from the sale of iPods.

Two-sided markets: an inter-consumer logic

While it applies to a former state of the world, analysis of so-called 'two-sided' markets appeared in theoretical economics at the beginning of the new millennium. A two-sided (or multi-sided) market is one whose organization requires the existence of two (or more) very different but interdependent user groups that rely on one another for web benefits. A platform – a meeting point – such as a radio station, newspaper or website serves as an intermediary for the two groups, to whom it offers a joint product. As it allows economic players to maximize the profits of their transactions, this platform is not economically neutral; left to their own devices, the players would be incapable of internalizing the impact of the benefits to other users of their use of the platform. The presence of an inter-group network effect, characteristic of two-sided markets, has had surprising economic consequences for the formation of prices as well as price level and structure (for a survey, see Rochet and Tirole, 2003). The optimal pricing system involves subsidizing one side of the market to attract users from the other side; when the subsidy is completed, the other side of the market becomes accessible for free.

This is the classic model used by the media (TV, radio, free newspapers and so on) for funding advertising: on one side of the market, the media company offers the public free programmes; on the other, it sells advertisers an audience. Advertisers obviously place greater value on companies that capture a large audience; the company, which receives payment from the advertisers, turns around and puts the money back into new programming. Thus the media serve as a platform for the joint product: media content for the audience and the audience's attention for advertisers. The platform is able to appropriate the benefits to advertisers and viewers by its intermediation, with free enabling platforms to create the logic for developing the audience towards advertisers.

The model whereby services – financed by advertisers' monetization of the audience – are given away for free is also used by the majority of Internet intermediaries, from video-sharing platforms like YouTube to search engines, or to portals open to the general public (for a study of different audience models, see Hamilton, 2004). Here again we see how a difference in size contrasts the two-sided model of a video-sharing site with that of a private television channel financed by advertising; in the latter case, the diffusion of content is negotiated with the rightful owner; in the former, the sharing site – in a logic of developing its audience – leaves productions protected by intellectual property for public use, with no return for the rightful owner (Farchy, 2009b). For example, YouTube, after having had strictly discordant relations with beneficiaries, developed reconnaissance tools for works in order to cooperate and combat this problem.

Offering free products to increase future market share: an intertemporal logic

Distributing goods or their digital copy at time T is a business strategy that allows the supplier, company or artist to increase its future market share, either by locking in new entrants' access (supply) or by propagating product awareness with consumers (demand).

The strategy of locking in the supply is subject to prices and technology. Bill Gates, the head of Microsoft, officially allows for the development of pirated copies of his company's software in China in order for it to become the standard for an emerging market in the future. Predation by price, which for a company consists in offering a good or service at little or no fee in order to eliminate potential competitors and then raising prices once the coast is clear (Carlton and Perloff, 1998), completes the technological lock-in. Strategies of commercial supply for free – extreme strategies of predatory pricing normally suppressed by the law of competition – arouse fears. Thus Google, by offering a great many of the services associated with its search engine for free, imposes a standard – a way of obtaining information. If it wishes, it can raise the price of certain services once its monopoly has been successfully established, thereby imposing its conditions on its interlocutors (the rightful owners, for example, in the case of Google Book).

At the same time, new forms of marketing based on the user's role as influencer and his sharing capacity are developing. The exposure effect goes hand in hand with the idea of a free version of a work that familiarizes the public with a previously unknown production, thus creating a learning effect and encouraging a purchase at a later date. Experiments with voluntary payment systems by artists like Radiohead, Nine Inch Nails and Jane Siberry, or even Paulo Coelho's experiment distributing online versions of his books for free, likewise attest to the possible links between reputation and market demands. For cultural goods – also experience goods, whose satisfaction is known only once the product has been consumed – gaining popularity with users becomes a formidable promotional and reputation-building tool thanks to the power of digital technology.

The limitations of for-profit free models

What with the abundance of free content available to consumers and companies continuing to develop new models of for-profit free, cultural industries are fretting over what this new El Dorado heralds. While interest in music and information has never been greater, the CD and paper press markets – to name only those most affected by the phenomenon – seem indeed to be dying breeds.

The problem is not so much that of free but that of the transfer of economic profitability within the value chain between the industries and creators that finance content, and firms (telecommunications, technical industries and so on), which are often strangers to the world of culture and take advantage of this content to sell anything and everything. Whether it is the sale of mp3 players, Internet plans, advertising or other products, the logic of using cultural productions as loss leaders is the same.

The fact remains that the creators and cultural industries that play a role in capturing the audience on behalf of the many free service providers do not appropriate the associated financial benefits – a classic problem of externality. And yet, despite problems for creators and consumers (supposedly the first to benefit from free works) alike, the need to rethink the sharing of value added and the financing of cultural works is real. To better understand this point, let us look again at the three models examined above.

Reputation: the adverse consequences of monopolies and the star system
The biggest winners of for-profit free are not the consumers – who often pay more for other associated products – but the companies creating new markets for this occasion. As the state does not guarantee public redistribution, free is organized by private companies teetering on the brink of potentially abusive, monopoly-like domination. Moreover, a good reputation on the Internet allows some artists to market more than just the standard industry products such as CDs, for example a special moment with the audience during a concert. For consumers, however, this is in no way free; concert ticket prices have skyrocketed in France in the last five years. Establishing a reputation on the

Internet (or anywhere else, for that matter) favours the adverse effects of the star system, the risks of which are all too well known in the cultural sector (Benhamou, 2002).

Complementary goods: the domination of technical industries
The commercial world that seems to be taking shape currently relies on the coexistence of an economy of restricted access supported by technology – reserved for products with a high value added – and an economy of enlarged access, in which the outputs of cultural industries are loss leaders used to sell just about anything. In both cases, the centre of gravity of marketable creation shifts in favour of international actors that, economically speaking, are infinitely more powerful than cultural industries and control the increasingly costly downstream market for product access and visibility. These actors also handle negotiations for the sharing of new sources of value with content producers under their own terms. Thus, for example, the price of €0.99 ($0.99 in the USA) set by Apple – whose core business is *not* music distribution but the sale of hardware – has weakened classic distributors and become *the* global psychological price ceiling for downloads almost overnight.

Moreover, so-called 'free' consumption is largely an illusion; for users, it implies a considerable investment in high-speed connection plans and multimedia equipment – from computers to iPods to mobile phones. The non-freeness of hardware items – the material results of the rapidity of technological development – is the 'price to pay' for free, non-material content.

Advertising: low yields and improved methods for surveillance
Internet advertising, although quite recent, has become the driving force for growth in the advertising market, with a dividend rate increase of approximately 30 per cent in the past three years. Expenditure in this sector – which accounted for 4.6 per cent of global advertising expenditure in 2005 – is likely to reach 11.5 per cent in 2010 (Zenith Optimedia agency estimates the global market for advertising on the Internet at US$44.6 billion in 2008). While the Internet advertising market is growing rapidly, it nonetheless remains small. What is more, its growth – despite the gloominess of the global advertising market as a whole – simply means we are witnessing an increase in the Internet's overall market share. The Internet, then, has not contributed to an increase in the size of the global advertising market as yet; rather, substitution effects between different forms of media have taken place, much to the detriment of radio and newspapers in particular, which depend largely on advertising in order to function. Classical forms of media suffer this competition from new operators in two ways: first, because they share the same global advertising market and, second, because they must compete with news content aggregators for the diffusion of their *own* content. Thus, after having invested in making their presence on the Internet felt, newspapers are seeing competition from press reviews like Google News and Yahoo News that aggregate editorial content from multiple news sources. By allowing users to directly access the pages that interest them (without going through an online newspaper's portal), news aggregation providers have given rise to a loss of advertising revenue for newspapers.

Considering the stringency of expected real earnings, the profitability of the advertising model has not proved more viable for the economic agents concerned. Many 2.0 websites have yet to see a profit. Companies' reputations have indeed been converted into audience attention and success, but the monetization phase (that is, earning the advertisers' attention) remains difficult. The video-sharing site Daily Motion – the second most visited site in France – is looking to raise funds for the third time since 2005. YouTube – bought for millions by Google – is a giant as far as audience is concerned, but even though it sees nearly 100 million visits worldwide per month, it has announced losses. The only formats sold on Daily Motion's non-professional video pages – 80 per cent to 90 per cent of the site's offers – are classic, rotating formats, which are also the least lucrative. The most lucrative formats are those on the home page or those shown right before the start of a video, on which the user clicks in return for a certain 'quality assurance' for limited-time-only, 'star' product offers. The presence of amateur content – often of low quality but that nonetheless captures the spirit of sharing sites – keeps advertisers, who prefer to have their ads associated with professional content, from buying space, thus maintaining control over the brand image linked to certain content. The economic viability of video-sharing sites thus seems to have to do with their level of professionalism, contracts negotiated with content providers and their integration into powerful groups with multiple lucrative activities, with no thought for their autonomous profit-earning capacity – a huge paradox indeed.

Content owners, for their part, are asking themselves what kind of modes of collaboration they should establish with these 2.0 websites. Television channels do not necessarily see any interest in broadcasting content – to which they hold the rights – on sites in return for paltry, shared advertising earnings; they prefer instead to develop their own brand of services or websites. The advertising market indeed appears to be too narrow to finance the bulk of creation. The website Deezer, which since 2007 has offered unlimited free access to streamed music titles, earns its revenue through advertising. According to Sacem (the French collective management company for composers and music publishers to protect copyright and royalties), the most listened-to song on Deezer (240 000 times) generated only €147 worth of royalties in 2008. Hulu, a video-sharing site, also relies on an advertising-based model that, because it uses professional content, could prove more profitable. The site, created in 2007 by NBC-Universal and Newscorp – which offers viewing access to numerous Fox/NBC films, series and programmes in free streaming – has been highly successful in the USA. Although its audience is infinitely smaller than that of YouTube, the presence of strictly official content attracts advertisers to a much greater extent according to a classic, two-sided media system.

For the consumer – other than the risk of saturation by the many formats of advertising to which s/he is subjected – free content likewise demands compensation, as advertising has an impact on the price of goods and services bought by the consumer *and* because free content (financed by advertising) is always coupled with an invasion of privacy by widespread mechanisms for surveying the tastes and practices of Internet users.

See also:

Chapter 1: Application of welfare economics; Chapter 11: Broadcasting; Chapter 27: Digitalization; Chapter 35: The Internet: economics; Chapter 38: Media economics and regulation; Chapter 49: Pricing the arts; Chapter 59: Television.

References

Anderson, C. (2008), 'Free! Why $0.00 is the Future of Business', *Wired* magazine, February.
Anderson, C. (2009), *Free, The Future of a Radical Price*, New York: Hyperion.

Arrow, K. (1962), 'Economic Welfare and the Allocation of Resources for Invention', in R. Nelson (ed.), *The Rate and Direction of Inventive Activity : Economic and Social Factors*, Princeton, NJ: Princeton University Press, pp. 609–26.

Baumol, W. and W. Bowen (1966), *Performing Arts, the Economic Dilemma*, Cambridge, MA: Twentieth Century Fund.

Benhamou, F (2002), *L'économie du Star System*, Paris: Odile Jacob.

Bomsel, O. (2007), *Gratuit! Du déploiement de l'économie numérique*, Paris: Folio.

Carlton, D. and J.M. Perloff (1998), *Modern Industrial Organization*, 3rd edn, New York: Addison Wesley Longman.

Farchy, J. (2009a), 'Are Free Licences Suitable for Cultural Works?', *European Intellectual Property Peview*, April, 255–64.

Farchy, J. (2009b), 'Economics of Sharing Platforms', in Pelle Snickars and Patrick Vondereau, *The YouTube Reader*, Stockholm: National Library of Sweden, pp. 360–61.

Hamilton, J. (2004), *All the News That's Fit to Sell: How the Market Transforms Information into News*, Princeton, NJ: Princeton University Press.

Lanham, R. (2006), *The Economics of Attention: Style and Substance in the Age of Information*, Chicago, IL: University of Chicago Press.

Liebowitz, S. (1985), 'Copying and Indirect Appropriability: Photocopying of Journals', *Journal of Political Economy*, 93 (5), 945–56.

Rochet, J.C. and J. Tirole (2003), 'Platform Competition in Two-sided Markets', *Journal of the European Economic Association*, 1 (4), 990–1029.

Simon, H.A. (1971), 'Designing Organizations for an Information Rich World', in Martin Greenberger (ed.), *Computers, Communication and the Public Interest*, Baltimore, MD: The Johns Hopkins Press, pp. 37–72.

Snickars, Pelle and Patrick Vondereau (2009), *The YouTube Reader*, Stockholm: National Library of Sweden.

Further reading

I recommend as further reading Anderson (2008), whose title 'Free! Why $0.00 is the Future of Business' eloquently summarizes, in a non-academic perspective, business models in a digital free world. The classical Arrow (1962) and Simon (1971) provided the first important discussions on the economics of information on the one hand, and the economics of attention on the other. For a theorical approach to two-sided markets, see Rochet and Tirole (2003) and for an explanation of the economics of sharing platforms, see Snickars and Vondereau (2009). For a specific analysis of free licences for cultural works, see Farchy (2009a).

35 The Internet: economics
Fabrice Rochelandet

The Internet has emerged as a new worldwide medium for communications, social networking, dissemination of informational goods and electronic commerce. The 'network of networks' is, in fact, a set of basic standards and interconnected networks enabling remote computers and mobile devices to interoperate universally as 'clients' and 'servers'. It constitutes the latest step of a technological revolution starting in the USA with the military and academic network ARPAnet (1969–74), followed by the development of the inter-universities' NSFnet (1981–86) and finally resulting in the creation of the worldwide Internet hypertextual application: the Web (1989–95).

In contrast to private networks, information flows are not oriented by a central authority (the network organizer who designs standards and protocols) on the basis of circuit-switched end-to-end services. Instead, the Internet is made up of decentralized, universal and unspecialized open networks that use connectionless packet-switching communications technology and interoperate through 'Transmission Control Protocol over Internet Protocol' (TCP/IP) languages. These common protocols are combined with various applications that process information exchanges and thereby allow the interconnection of heterogeneous computers through private and public networks. Accordingly, the use of the Internet infrastructure amounts to consuming numerous complementary goods from the terminal to the backbone wires through common standards.

The regulation and standardization of the Internet prove to be a decentralized process too. Three main organizations provide standards and basic services enabling the Internet to run: the Internet Corporation for Assigned Names and Numbers (ICANN) in charge of Internet Protocol (IP) address space allocation; the Internet Engineering Task Force (IETF), which builds and promotes Internet standards; and the World Wide Web Consortium (W3C) that develops compatibility standards for the World Wide Web.

All these technologies and organizations have major implications for the pricing, the coordination of agents and the efficient use of network resources. Moreover, the strict separation between infrastructure facilities and services using these facilities permits a high pace of innovation because each of them can develop independently. After all, although it would prove to be less efficient than private networks, the Internet represents much more a 'social innovation' than a technological one: it has quickly turned into an important place where individuals and organizations valorize and exchange information, goods and services.

Many ways of tackling the Internet economy

A first analysis consists of dividing it into two categories of services: use services (communication services such as e-mails; information services; transaction services such as e-commerce; networking services such as virtual communities) and infrastructure services (transportation and routing of data, networks access, software, e-payment). A second method is to define and quantify the fields of activities involving the use of the Internet. The idea here is that the Internet economy is not grounded in innovations resulting in new raw materials, but rather on high-speed networks based on new norms and applications, as well as on new business models and electronic intermediaries. For instance, the CREC (University of Texas) has developed a specific methodology in order to measure the Internet economy by dividing it into four layers: firms whose production is oriented towards an IP-based networks infrastructure such as Internet backbone and service providers, networking software and hardware producers, PC manufacturers and so on); companies producing Internet applications oriented towards online business activities such as search engines; Internet intermediaries whose activities increase the efficiency of markets by facilitating online commercial interaction (e.g. portals); and finally, Internet commerce such as online entertainment and 'e-tailers'.

Beyond e-commerce and IT industries, the Internet economy has been increasingly dominated by end-user services, such as infomediation, content aggregation, file-sharing and social networking. For instance, all these services are deeply based on a 'two-sided market' approach rather than requiring Internet users to pay whenever they want to get something by this means. This duality between paying and free online services is crucial to understanding the current difficulties met by cultural industries.

A third (more ambitious) way is to study the consequences of the Internet on markets, organizations, behaviour and regulations. The extent of the Internet economy, as well as the pervasiveness of IT, has turned the technical question of managing this network into a research topic for economists. Thus the purpose of Internet economics is to highlight the impact of IT on the process of production and on pricing policy, as well as on inter-individual coordination and regulation. Just as the pricing policy deregulation of telecommunications in the 1980s gave rise to new economic tools such as contestable markets, the Internet constitutes a new field of research that leads to a renewal of economic thought, in particular in relation to network economics, pricing models and antitrust policy.

Internet economics divided into 'theoretical layers'

The first layer: quality
The first layer deals with the essential question of the quality of the Internet. From the outset, network economics has supposed that any network is owned by a single firm and thus the task of economists is to highlight the optimal allocation and use of resources on this network. However, because the Internet is composed of heterogeneous networks, other crucial parameters must be taken into account: compatibility, interoperability, interconnectivity and coordination of services. So higher quality of Internet infrastructure and applications requires two complementary goals to be fulfilled; to reduce the time for information delivery and to ensure the interconnection of networks.

As a composite network, the Internet exhibits the feature of positive network effects. However, every firm operating a network has a great incentive to prevent compatibility with other networks in order to ensure profits higher than would be achieved in the case of perfect compatibility. Until now, this strategy has not prevailed and Internet service providers (ISPs) have agreed to interconnect because the Internet is characterized by high growth rates of interconnected networks, insufficient market concentration, relative homogeneity of users and cooperative behaviours. Nevertheless, this situation is likely to change rapidly as ISPs provide competitive services and increasingly serve a great variety of differentiated markets. Thus industrial and antitrust policies will have an important role to play in reducing opportunities for the major firms to control essential network structures (backbones) in order to get the power to block universal interconnection.

This issue relates to the now-famous debate on 'net neutrality'. However, it is not confined to the interconnection but refers to other questions in terms of standards and pricing.

Individuals and firms agree on common standards to communicate and exchange data. What is specific to the Internet is that the various institutions that produce technical norms are private and their activities do not rely on the support of all participants. These small committees adopt most of the technological standards for network interoperability. As a result, both public (open) and private standards emerge over the Internet. Furthermore, some are hybrid, such as, the Java technology: Sun protects the integrity of this language while keeping some components under patent to prevent other firms from threatening its universal nature by adding incompatible components for their sole benefit.

The challenge is not only to preserve the benefits of interoperability and positive network effects, but also to develop effective Internet pricing mechanisms. The economics of networks makes it possible to determine the conditions for an efficient use of networks by eliminating congestion costs as the Internet expands (that is, time spent by users waiting for data transfers). Two solutions exist in order to overcome these social costs: either firms and governments invest in order to adjust facilities by increasing the size of Internet infrastructure, or they try to improve the management of digital data flows, for example by shifting priorities for their routing, removing inefficient intermediaries or implementing new pricing models.

Because of the specific features of the Internet, the first solution is very costly. Economists therefore generally favour new pricing models to achieve efficient allocation of networks flows between users (for example, the bidding model of MacKie-Mason and Varian, 1995). According to McKnight and Bailey (1997), three types of pricing are to be found on the Internet. The first is flat-rate pricing: a uniform price is fixed whatever actual use, transmitted flow of data or kind of connection. In fact, such pricing is rare and users have the option of lump-sum pricing according to the quality of connection. The second type is capacity-based pricing: a price is fixed according to the speed of transmission and whatever the actual transmitted flow of data is. Finally, there is usage-sensitive pricing, which is based on the actual transmitted flow of data.

More generally, the 'net neutrality' issue refers to all factors that can challenge the neutral, non-specialized, innovation-promoting architecture of the Internet mostly based on the end-to-end principle. Net neutrality consists in not favouring excessively certain ISP and content providers to the detriment of others, for example by blocking access to the network, charging excessive price discrimination and prioritizing systematically the routing of certain kinds of contents and services. This principle is currently challenged by ISP according to which there is a trade-off between quality of service – harmed by the exponential development and diversification of flows and services using the Internet – and universal non-discriminatory access. Data discrimination could in fact improve the quality of service by prohibiting specific data flows, such as P2P and online gaming, that might cause negative externalities to ISPs and final users (higher costs to ISPs, reduced network performance, and so on. . .). According to the advocates of net neutrality, any kind of discrimination might in fact reduce competition and pace of innovation by preventing new entrants from benefiting from the same quantity and quality of service.

The second layer: facilitating economic exchange

Beyond technical and pricing problems, the second 'theoretical layer' of Internet economics poses two essential questions: does this innovation facilitate economic exchanges; and, how are online transactions made possible? Digitalization applies to all or part of the components of economic exchange: identification of relevant partners, matching, contract negotiation, security, e-payment, enforcement and so on. Electronic intermediation and marketplaces allow not only 'Business-to-consumers commerce' but also 'business-to-business commerce' and 'consumer-to-consumer exchanges'. Various economic tools are mobilized to characterize these evolutions, such as transaction costs, intermediation, (collective) reputation, opportunism and so on.

According to earlier analysis, digital technologies make both perfect competition and disintermediation more likely by allowing consumers easily to compare product information and prices. Digital technologies would decrease information and transaction costs to such an extent that online markets would tend to the world of zero transaction costs and perfect rationality described by microeconomic textbooks. It was frequently argued that digital technologies and Internet infrastructure would permit online suppliers to reach online consumers directly and to leap over all intermediaries. Such direct interactions would thereby cause the elimination of intermediaries' margins and a decrease in price.

In the area of electronic commerce, some even speak of a 'retailing revolution'. Traditionally, producers make supply decisions before they have accurate data on consumer preferences and consumers act as price-takers. New software tools would offer producers the possibility of a 'dynamic pricing' in which more flexible retail prices reflect the current state of supply and demand and they enable consumers to become 'product designers' on the basis of a menu of product options offered by suppliers. Meanwhile, potential buyers can compare prices by using specialized websites ('shopbots') in order to select the cheapest provider. Finally, the Internet permits the emergence of communities of buyers with similar needs who increase their bargaining power by obtaining lower prices and better product quality.

However, many studies provide evidence that actual business practices and consumers' behaviour over the Internet contradict this kind of analysis. Instead, price dispersion prevails. Because of the frequent boycotting of major producers as well as their (over) differentiation strategies preventing any price comparison, the shopbots do not work efficiently. In fact, the condition for homogeneous products is far from being fulfilled and factors such as reputation, brands and trust prevail and explain price dispersion on the Internet by determining consumers' choices by reducing their price sensitivity. Furthermore, consumers are not likely to spend their time learning and using these new tools and websites. And even if they are willing to, their information would be limited because shopbots generally index only a small portion of the web. Furthermore, even though digital technologies would be efficient, other questions emerge about electronic transaction, for instance, how to assure consumers and producers that their economic partners do not try to defraud them? Some institutions are needed somewhere in the process of exchange.

In fact, electronic transaction and e-marketplaces have emerged essentially in the area of interfirm exchange and were supposed to enhance the production process in various areas, such as the car industry. Indeed, because of the small number of traders and their continuing relationship, the condition of costless exchange of information is more likely to prevail: (collective) reputation more easily ensures greater confidence and so information technologies would have played an essential role in economic coordination by facilitating the gathering and management of information.

By contrast, in addition to generating B2C e-commerce, the Internet has facilitated direct connections between individuals and thereby online social interactions. The success of social networking platforms – from peer-to-peer to online communities – suggests that most of the digital revolution might reside here. In particular, in the field of cultural goods, many new opportunities will enable even small producers to reach consumers. According to the emblematic argument of the 'long tail', physical limitations that constraint the distribution of contents might be abolished due to the unlimited capacity of digital storage and exhibition over the Internet. Power law in the distribution of sales might be challenged.

However, many questions have not been answered, in particular, that of cultural diversity. If more people access more works, nothing is said about (1) how consumers make their choice and (2) how the model of the 'long tail' could finance these small productions. In other words, what kind of 'prescription' would prevail? In fact, nothing will change radically if huge promotional strategies prevail. By contrast, the role played by social networking, such as the case of MySpace.com, is more convincing. It can be conceived as a new way not only to reduce search costs incurred by individuals when looking for new works, but also and more fundamentally to find diversified works thanks to the cognitive and cultural links built among artists through this network. Online sellers and artists could find here a solution to replicate the face-to-face relation that prevailed in the past between small record dealers/booksellers and consumers.

The third layer: profitability and the Internet
Lastly, the third 'theoretical layer' focuses on the question of how to make profitable investments and to implement successful business models on the Internet, given that it has so far proved to be a place where non-profit and free-riding behaviours have prevailed since its creation. In fact, digital technologies give rise to new kinds of exchange and behaviour, such as those from peer to peer. Is it always possible and socially preferable to lead web users to make online purchases while preventing them from free-riding?

Cultural goods are good examples to illustrate this problem. They are non-rival and non-excludable when no specific measure prevents free-riding. Their production entails high fixed costs, whereas their reproduction costs nothing on the Internet. Thus, if e-markets are somewhat competitive and prices reflect marginal costs, are there some arrangements allowing appropriation of at least some revenue over the Internet? At first glance, intellectual property law appears to provide a general solution for overcoming this failure by prohibiting unauthorized uses, but are these rights still enforceable on the Internet? Of course, the same technologies that permit circumvention of copyrights can be used to enforce them, such as anti-copying devices or electronic traceability. For example, steganography and fingerprinting are used as dissuasive devices in order to organize the circulation of content on the Internet. However, if alternative arrangements are found and prove to be more efficient, should copyright be implemented? Given the uncertain technological competition between content producers and hackers, trying to protect copyright is often conceived as a wasteful effort.

So, which profitable business models could be designed and set up on the Internet? Generally, the opponents of copyright suggest cross-subsidizing (multi-sided market). Because they freely distribute content to final users, business models such as advertising and tied sales take into account the fact that the Internet economy is characterized by non-profit behaviour. However, these models of 'free distribution' are now largely outdated because most of the time they do not sufficiently generate income. Another point of view emphasizes that digital technologies could replace copyright and do the same work at a lower social cost, for example by enabling price discrimination. Producers of valuable content could single out individual consumers thanks to those technologies. Pricing models such as *versioning* or *bundling* would be more efficient by using accurate information about consumer preferences, but monopolistic rents, informational problems and risks of privacy intrusion may hinder such models.

Beyond the sole case of cultural goods, this potential movement towards price discrimination and the diversity of business models reveals the capabilities and threats of the Internet, even in its nascent stages. However, those who suggest a progressive shift towards a purely commercial Internet should take into account the inherently non-profit nature of individual interactions that may hinder such an evolution. Accordingly, business people and scholars must keep in mind that the Internet proves more oriented towards intermediation ('infomediation') than towards commercial transaction.

See also:

Chapter 1: Application of welfare economics; Chapter 16: Creative economy; Chapter 27: Digitalization; Chapter 35: The Internet: economics; Chapter 38: Media economics and regulation; Chapter 49: Pricing the arts.

References

Bakos, Y. and E. Brynjolfsson, (1999), 'Bundling Information Goods: Pricing, Profits and Efficiency', *Management Science*, 45 (12), 1613–30.
Brousseau, E. and N. Curien (eds) (2007), *Internet and Digital Economics. Principle, Methods and Applications*, Cambridge: Cambridge University Press.
Brynjolfsson, E. and M. Smith (2000), 'Frictionless Commerce? A Comparison of Internet and Conventional Retailers', *Management Science*, 46 (4), 563–85.
DeLong, J.B. and A.M. Froomkin (2000), 'Speculative Microeconomics for Tomorrow's Economy', *First Monday*, 5 (2), available at firstmonday.org.
Economides, Nicholas (2005), 'The Economics of the Internet Backbone', in B. Kahin and H.R. Varian (eds) (2000), *Internet Publishing and Beyond – The Economics of Digital Information and Intellectual Property*, Cambridge, MA and London: MIT Press.
Leiner, B.M., V.G. Cerf, D.D. Clark, R.E. Kahn, L. Kleinrock, D.C. Lynch, J. Postel, L.G. Roberts and S. Wolff (2000), 'A Brief History of the Internet', http://www.isoc.org/internet/history/brief.html.
MacKie-Mason, J.K. and H.R. Varian (1995), *Economic FAQs About the Internet*, http://www.press.umich.edu/jep/econTOC.html.
Majumdar, S.K., I. Vogelsang and M.E. Cave (eds) (2005), *Handbook of Telecommunications*, Vol. 2, 'Technology, Evolution and the Internet', Amsterdam: Elsevier Publishers.
Shapiro, C. and H.R. Varian, (1998), *Information Rules: A Strategic Guide to the Network Economy*, Boston, MA: Harvard Business School Press (http://www.inforules.com).

Online resources

http://ebusiness.mit.edu/ (Center for eBusiness@MIT)
http://www.sims.berkeley.edu/resources/infoecon/ (website maintained by Hal Varian)

http://www.stern.nyu.edu/networks/site.html (website maintained by Nicholas Economides)
http://www.utdallas.edu/~liebowit/netpage.html (website maintained by Stan Liebowitz).

Further reading

Articles by Bakos and Brynjolfsson (1999), Brynjolfsson and Smith (2000), DeLong and Froomkin (2000), Leiner *et al.* (2000), the chapter by Economides (2005) and volumes by Brousseau and Curien (2007), Majumdar *et al.* (2005) and Shapiro and Varian (1998).

36 Management of the arts
François Colbert

Management is a relatively new discipline, and the management of arts and culture an even more recent off-shoot. The non-profit status of many arts and cultural organizations not only means that they must be managed in a particular way; it also imposes a specific set of professional requirements on the manager and the board of directors. In this chapter, we shall examine these two aspects of cultural management. But let us begin with some background information.

The discipline of management

Management is a new discipline compared with age-old sciences such as physics, geometry and philosophy. The phenomena associated with organizational management were not examined in any systematic way until the very end of the nineteenth century, and the first treatises on this topic were not published until the early twentieth century, with Taylor contributing one of the seminal texts in 1911. The establishment of the general discipline of management eventually led to the emergence of other disciplines such as financial management, operational management and human resources management, which in turn gave rise to various subdisciplines. As they have developed, these various management disciplines have borrowed theories, concepts and knowledge from other fields, including economics, psychology, sociology, anthropology, mathematics and, more recently, information technology.

In the early 1960s, interest in the study of management increased significantly among both researchers and students. The number of academics in the field grew, as did the number of scientific publications. The body of management knowledge expanded considerably and was applied in an increasingly broad range of sectors. Researchers thus began to publish studies on the management of particular types of entities such as non-profit organizations, providers of financial services, hospitals and, in the early 1970s, arts and cultural organizations.

That being said, arts and cultural management is hampered by a twofold legitimacy problem. On the one hand, it is viewed with suspicion by the arts world, and, on the other, it is often taken less than seriously by management scholars. To counter this indifference, particularly among the scientific community, it is possible to adopt a proactive attitude by highlighting the contributions of arts and cultural management in general (Évrard and Colbert, 2000).

Specific characteristics of the arts sector

In the arts world, discontinuous modes of production are the norm. Since many arts activities assume the form of individual projects (a show, a film), the organizations that produce them must be extraordinarily flexible. The task at hand is to manage, not continuous flow production, but rather the sequential production of new products. In fact, this continuing effort to market prototypes is one of the distinguishing features of the arts sector (Colbert *et al.*, 2007).

These discontinuous production modes also affect the management of human resources. The use of freelance workers requires a particular kind of human resources management. A small staff of permanent employees is responsible for the basic continuity of the organization, while its creative resources remain outside the organizational framework. This work structure has led to the emergence of charismatic leaders with highly personal motivational styles.

Another distinctive feature of arts production also affects human resources management. Indeed, the mode of project-based creation has made dual management possible, with artistic and administrative directors sharing tasks. Since these two administrators generally have the same status within an organization, potential conflicts are resolved by the board of directors. Though not universal, this form of organizational structure has become quite widespread in the arts and cultural milieu.

The manner in which arts organizations operate is remarkably consistent with Mintzberg's theory about the way organizations are structured. The organization is managed by a strategic apex comprising the board of directors, the artistic director and the administrative director. This strategic apex defines the mission of the organization and oversees its development. In the case of a theatre company, for example, each individual production is entrusted to a director, who assumes sole responsibility once the reins are handed over. From this point on, the strategic apex does not intervene in the production process. The success of the organization thus rests entirely on the shoulders of an external party. Functions such as marketing, human resources and accounting play only supporting roles and are dependent on artistic decisions. And the success of the organization is by no means certain, because when it comes to artistic endeavours the unknown is the rule and success almost entirely unpredictable.

Lastly, two characteristics of arts products complicate the task of accounting or financial analysis, namely, the immateriality of the product and its heritage value. A work of art is by definition an immaterial product whose value depends on the evolution of public tastes (heritage value). These characteristics make it more difficult to determine the value of organizational assets (rights portfolio, market value of assets and so on).

These characteristics are not necessarily common to all cultural organizations. In fact, it is appropriate to distinguish between organizations based on individual sectors. Generally speaking, cultural organizations belong to one of three major sectors: the arts, cultural industries and the media. The defining characteristic of organizations in the arts sector is the production of prototypes, while cultural industries market reproductions of prototypes and the media rely on powerful tools that make it possible to deliver cultural products directly to consumers. Each of these sectors has a distinct logic, but all three offer products with a high degree of creative content. However, while most companies in the arts sector are product- rather than market-oriented, the reverse is true for cultural industries and the media. In fact, one of the defining characteristics of the arts sector is that artistic vision takes precedence over market considerations. Rather than selling a product that satisfies the needs and desires of consumers, these organizations offer an artistic vision likely to be of interest to a certain audience. In practice, the job of the marketing staff is to identify a market segment interested in the product being offered, not to provide consumers with what they want to see.

The board of directors: a fundamental entity

Non-profit arts and heritage organizations are not managed in the same way as for-profit organizations in other sectors, for the simple reason that their social missions are different; and the role of the board of directors must of course reflect these different management styles. Since cultural organizations do not modify their products to please consumers, they obviously incur greater risks. It is to allow these custodians of heritage and creators of culture to fulfil their missions that governments provide them with funding. This money, which comes directly out of the pockets of taxpayers, is meant to serve the greater good and to allow the entire population to benefit from past and present intellectual advances. This unique mandate of cultural organizations, along with their product orientation, means that a suitable set of criteria must be used to assess their performance. The success of such organizations cannot be measured in the same way as that of companies seeking to maximize profits. Concepts such as profit, per-share profit and market share have no relevance for a non-profit organization with a social and educational mission. Rather, the appropriate performance-measurement criteria must be centred on the achievement of the organizational mission.

The roles and functions of the board of directors thus extend well beyond financial considerations. Since a cultural organization is an institution with a social and educational mission and is financially supported by society as a whole, the primary responsibility of the board of directors is to ensure that this mission is fulfilled. As a non-profit organization, it has no actual shareholders to hold it accountable. However, the society that provides the organization with funding can be regarded as its principal shareholder. The board of directors is thus responsible for safeguarding the organizational mission on behalf of this collective shareholder.

The most important decision that the board has to make is the selection of the executive director, or the artistic and administrative directors, of the institution, after which it is responsible for assessing the performance of the individual or individuals chosen. Safeguarding the organizational mission, and choosing and evaluating the performance of the director – these are the key tasks of the board of directors of an institution resolutely focused on its product rather than on the market. It also bears the task of long-term sustainability of the artistic organization.

So how does the board of directors fulfil its role? By selecting new board members very carefully and by equipping itself with strict rules of governance. The application of these rules is very much at odds with the unfortunately widespread notion that the role of a board member of a cultural organization can be summed up by the phrase 'give, get or get out'. Organizational governance can be defined as follows: the process and monitoring structure employed by the management of an organization to ensure that it can effectively fulfil its mission. Governance thus involves monitoring the organizational mission. Monitoring entails relations with management, and relations entail rules of conduct and the clear definition of roles. These various elements must be clearly set forth in a governance document.

Rules of governance must be established in collaboration with the executive personnel of the organization, because they are directly affected by this process. Although the role of the board is to establish the organizational objectives and to assess the extent to which they are achieved, its actions must be based on a strategic plan formulated in collaboration with those responsible for managing the organization. This plan must outline the short- and long-term objectives of the organization and the means by which these objectives will be met, as well as the performance criteria. At this stage, the role of the board members is to guide and advise management with regard to the strategic planning process, and then approve the resultant plan. From this point on, it must regularly review the assumptions underlying the plan and ensure that appropriate corrective action is taken, based on the results obtained. Of course, to ensure that relations between the board and management are harmonious, it is essential that the board allow management to manage the institution on a daily basis and not interfere in day-to-day matters. The distinction between the respective roles of the board and management is a key and sensitive element of the governance document, and as such merits careful consideration.

To be in a position to assess compliance with the strategic plan, the board must ensure that the main risks associated with the finances and physical assets of the organization are identified and that the appropriate risk management systems are put in place. A non-profit cultural organization does, of course, face financial risks, but the primary risks are associated with its organizational mission; and these are the aspects of the organization that new board members must ensure they thoroughly understand. One of the key tasks of a board of directors is to select new members, but it must also ensure that they receive the appropriate training. This task is facilitated by the formation of a governance committee responsible for advising the board with regard to all matters associated with governance problems. This committee should be the mechanism of choice for assessing the skills that board members require and should also be responsible for assessing the effectiveness of the board as a whole, including each of its committees and the contribution of each director. It is important for the organization to embrace the notion that even a board of directors can be evaluated – just as volunteers can, and should, be subject to an evaluation process.

To be able to fulfil its role effectively, the board must be made up of a group of people who are capable of understanding the various aspects of the operations of the institution. Not all board members can or should be expected to have expertise in all these aspects at the same time – hence the importance of having a well-rounded group of members. The organization must be able to rely on a complementary and comprehensive set of skills, as must non-profit organizations in other economic sectors. It is of course important to find people who can assess the financial performance of the organization and others who have sound knowledge of the target markets, but what is most important is to ensure that there are people on the board who can objectively and effectively assess the extent to which the institution is achieving the fundamental objectives associated with its mission. Lastly, the board must include members who can ask the appropriate questions and who will not settle for less-than-adequate responses.

Conclusion

By virtue of their mission and product orientation, cultural organizations are risky ventures. The risks they face have to do with both the quality of the works presented and the balancing of budgets. The board of such an organization always operates amidst uncertainty and must account for its performance to the shareholders, namely, the taxpayers who fund the organization via the governments they elect. An effective board of directors and equally effective management are the markers by which such an organization must gauge its success. A carefully considered governance structure, accepted and monitored by all concerned, will help the organization engaged in managing prototypes and discontinuous operations to fulfil its difficult and demanding mission.

See also:

Chapter 22: Cultural entrepreneurship; Chapter 42: Non-profit organizations; Chapter 46: Performance indicators.

References

Colbert, François *et al.* (2007), *Marketing Culture and the Arts*, 3rd edn, Montreal: Chair in Arts Management/ HEC-Montréal.

Évrard, Yves and François Colbert (2000), 'Arts Management: A New Discipline Entering the Millennium', *International Journal of Arts Management*, 2 (2), 4–14.

Guillet de Monthoux, Pierre (2004), *The Art Firm*, Stanford, CA: Stanford University Press.

Hagoort, Giep (2000), *Art Management: Entrepreneurial Style*, Utrecht: Eburon.

Lapierre, Laurent (2005), 'Managing as Creating', *International Journal of Arts Management*, 7 (3), 4–11.

Rentschler, Ruth (2002), *The Entrepreneurial Arts Leader*, St Lucia, Queensland: The University of Queensland Press.

Further reading

Recommended further reading: Évrard and Colbert (2000), Hagoort (2000), Lapierre (2005), Guillet de Monthoux (2004) and Rentschler (2002).

37 Marketing the arts
François Colbert

Traditional marketing theory maintains that a company seeks to fulfil an existing need among consumers in order to be successful. In the traditional model, the marketing components of the model must be considered a sequence that starts in the 'market'. The market is thus both the starting and the finishing point for this process.

Although the marketing model for cultural enterprises contains the same components as the traditional marketing model, the marketing process for product-centred cultural enterprises is different. As Figure 37.1 shows, the process starts within the enterprise, in the product itself, as stated in the definition below. The enterprise tries to decide which part of the market is likely to be interested in its product. Once potential customers are identified, the company will decide on the other three elements – price, place and promotion – for this clientele. In this type of company, the process order would be company (product)–information system–market–information system–company–residual marketing mix–market. The starting point is the product and the destination is the market. This 'product-to-client' approach is truly typical of the not-for-profit arts sector.

Therefore we can define cultural marketing as:

> the art of reaching those market segments likely to be interested in the product while adjusting to the product the commercial variables – price, place and promotion – to put the product in contact with a sufficient number of consumers and to reach the objectives consistent with the mission of the cultural enterprise. (Colbert *et al.*, 2007, p. 14)

Let us briefly examine the different components of this model.

The market

A market is a group of consumers expressing desires and needs for products, services or ideas. The notions of need and desire are the cornerstone of marketing and the key to any marketing strategy. Thus a consumer expresses needs, and a cultural enterprise will seek out consumers with needs likely to be met by the works produced. These consumers could be either individuals or other organizations.

A cultural company may serve four different markets: state, sponsor, partners (distribution intermediaries, co-producers, distribution partners or presenters, media people) and, of course, the ultimate consumer. These are, in effect, distinct markets responding to different motivations.

State

'State' is used here to denote the different levels of government, federal, provincial and municipal (and the European Union), that support cultural enterprises in various ways. The state plays a dominant role in the cultural sector in most industrialized countries. Sometimes it acts as a consumer, or it may intervene to varying degrees, in different guises – from simple partner to patron controlling the entire cultural sector of a nation.

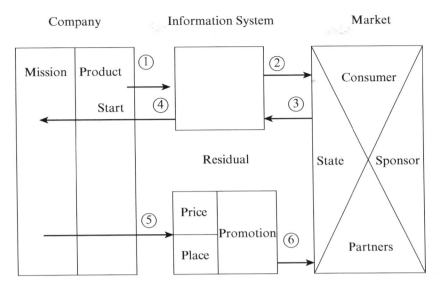

Figure 37.1   The marketing model for cultural enterprises

The level of state involvement is quite different depending on countries; the two extremes may be exemplified by countries such as the USA, where a small percentage of the companies' budgets in the performing arts comes from the different levels of government (from 0 to 10 per cent), while in Europe, some countries, such as France or Germany, will see their respective governments represent as much as 80 per cent of the total budget of symphonies or theatres.

Sponsor
The sponsor's support may take two forms: contributions and sponsored events or products. Contributions may be made by individuals, foundations or companies; however, sponsorships come mainly from companies. A contribution is normally a philanthropic act, whereas sponsorship is a promotional initiative in exchange for publicity or advertising. Sponsorships are given according to advertising benefits calculated in advance. The corporate sponsor then judges the performance of the investment in terms of visibility, rapid response awareness, and the vehicle's reach – that is, the number of consumers receiving the message.

Donors, on the other hand, provide disinterested assistance based on personal tastes and preferences. In the case of a foundation, its mission and goals will determine the choice of a cause. Donors are rewarded by some form of recognition, but this does not usually motivate their philanthropic gesture.

The partners' market
Although some companies sell their product directly to the ultimate consumer, many must use the services of an agent or intermediary. The distribution market comprises these agents or intermediaries. In the performing arts, for instance, the presenter is a distribution agent. A touring company uses a presenter to reach consumers in a specific city

or region. There is a distribution market in almost all cultural sectors. Other partners can be found in co-productions whereas two or more entities invest together in one project. Finally, artistic organizations make great efforts to get the media people to help them to reach the audience.

The consumer market

Surveys focusing on the sociodemographic profile of consumers of cultural products have been carried out in nearly every European country (both East and West), as well as in Canada, the USA, Australia and Japan. These surveys have systematically, unequivocally and consistently revealed a strong polarization among audiences and consumers. They show, for example, that cultural products catering to high art attract educated consumers, while, conversely, those catering to popular culture draw upon a less-educated population segment. Other sociodemographic variables are also linked to attendance; these include personal income (high in the first case and low in the second) and the type of occupation (white-collar workers in the first case and blue-collar in the second). Moreover, attendance rates at high-art performances are nearly identical across all industrialized countries, with some variations attributable to the specific cultural heritage of given countries (for example, attendance is higher for opera in Italy and for classical music in Germany).

Audiences in the arts are mainly female (Gainer, 1993). In dance, for example, as many as 70 per cent of the spectators are normally female; halls for performing arts, or museums, are usually filled by 55 per cent to 65 per cent females; in sports, it is the reverse: roughly two-thirds of the spectators are men. The reason for this phenomenon resides in the way boys and girls are raised. Parental attitude (Gainer, 1997) has a major impact on the preferences of children. Arts are high-involvement products and are perceived as a way of expressing one's emotions. Parents see boys as needing activities that will permit them to release their natural aggression, while they see that, by nature, girls are more passive and emotional. These widely shared parental attitudes affect what activities adults will suggest to their children: playing the piano and taking ballet lessons for girls; playing sports for boys. These attitudes then act as social norms and define roles and preferences of the future adults. This does not mean that all parents push this kind of stereotype. Actually, parental attitude towards the arts is one of four elements that affect future consumption of the arts, but it is the main factor as far as gender bias is concerned. The three other documented elements that explain preference for the arts are the attitude of the school system towards the arts, the fact that a child will be exposed to live art or museums when they are young, and the practice of an art form as an amateur. These, with parental attitude, are the four factors that can explain the future consumption of cultural products. However, the gender effect will always be present unless there is a major shift in attitude by parents.

The environment

A marketing strategy cannot be drawn up in a vacuum; many external restrictions affect the market and the firm. The environment is composed of two elements that constantly influence all organizations: competition, over which the company has some control, and macro-environmental variables, also known as 'uncontrollable variables'. There are five main variables in the macro-environment: demographic, cultural, economic, political–

legal and technological; these variables are in constant evolution and affect all firms in the long term and, sometimes, even in the short term.

For example, the economic environment of arts organization has changed compared to the situation in the 1970s. At the beginning of this new century, arts organizations are facing a deeply oversupplied market (Colbert, 2009). Every year, new artists come out of training schools, new companies are created, but the growth of the market is very timid and cannot absorb all those new ventures. Competition is then fierce between the different players in the market. New concepts, such as positioning, quality of service to the clientele or the use of information technology are envisaged by artistic groups to maintain or gain their place on the market.

The marketing information system (MIS)

Marketing information systems rely on three key components: internal data, secondary data published by private firms or government agencies, and the data collected by the company itself. 'Internal data' means all information available from within the firm itself. The firm's accounting system actually provides more than financial analysis; it is a rich source of internal data for the marketing specialist. The term 'secondary data' is used to describe data published by public sector agencies, such as a Statistics Bureau, Arts Councils or Ministries of Culture, and private sector firms that specialize in producing research reports.

If the internal and secondary data together do not provide the information required in the decision-making process, it may be useful to gather primary data. In other words, the consumer must be questioned directly. This is commonly called a market study.

The marketing mix

As mentioned earlier, every marketing strategy is composed of the same four components: price, product, place and promotion. Successful marketing depends on a skilful balance of these components and all firms aim at creating synergy through the combined strengths of all four. Synergy exists when the overall effect of several elements is greater than the sum of the effect of the elements taken separately. The components of the marketing mix are called 'controllable variables'.

Product

The product is the centrepiece of any enterprise. This statement becomes particularly meaningful in the cultural sector, in which the product constitutes the starting point of any marketing activity. We use the term 'product' in its broadest sense to mean a tangible good, a service, a cause or an idea. 'Product' is associated with any result of the creative act – for example, a performance, an exhibition, a record, a book or a television programme.

We define a product as 'the set of benefits as they are perceived by the consumer'. A product may be described by its technical dimension or symbolic value, yet, in the end, what the consumer buys is a set of benefits, real or imaginary. Consumers agree to invest money and effort in obtaining the product according to the importance of their needs and the resources available to them.

The complexity of a product may vary greatly according to the specific features of the product, the consumer's characteristics or the consumer's perception of the product.

Some products are considered more complex because their technical specifications require substantial personal effort on the part of the consumer just to be familiar with their features. Most cultural products, however, may be defined as complex, especially when works produced require specific knowledge or rely on abstract notions that depend on the consumer's ability to appreciate such concepts. Complexity becomes even greater when the consumer is unfamiliar with a particular type of product.

The cultural or artistic sector does, nonetheless, include less complex products, such as work drawing on stereotypes known to most people or using very concrete concepts. These products are often labelled 'popular'.

To be consistent with their missions, most cultural companies must constantly launch new products without being able to pre-test them. The development and launching of a new product always involves a certain amount of risk for the producer – 'risk' in the sense that the possibility of not satisfying the consumer or not meeting marketing objectives or corporate financial goals is ever present. Moreover, once launched, much of a cultural product can no longer be changed. A museum, for instance, launching a new exhibit must sell the product as it is to the potential consumer. No artist or theme can be guaranteed success in advance. Of course, the newer the product, as is the case for modern art, the greater the risk, in terms both of appreciation and of financial loss for the producer. For a classic product that is well known by the public, the risk is still present, but lower.

Commercial success alone does not satisfy the corporate mission of many cultural enterprises, especially if they are product-oriented. In their case, the risk is both financial and artistic.

Price
Every product has a price, which is normally expressed as the monetary value attributed to that product. Price also includes the effort a consumer must expend in the act of buying the product, and the risk perceived by the consumer in buying one's product. But there is another important dimension to price – time; in the leisure sector, this is a commodity that can be very limited. Thus there is always a price to pay for a product, even when it is advertised as being free.

The time dimension of pricing may become a very important element of a marketing strategy. The market for performing arts, for example, is composed of two types of consumers: those who have the means but not the time to go out, and those who have the time but not the means. Seats are thus priced differently to catch the differences in the willingness or capacity to pay. On the other hand, theatres offer enhanced benefits for those who cannot afford to commit themselves ahead of time; they sell flexible subscriptions where the patron can change his pre-paid ticket for a particular night to an alternative evening; of course, there is a premium to pay for this benefit (or privilege). For this kind of patron, money is not the problem; it is the busy life of an executive or of a professional that limits the time available for leisure.

Place
Place is composed of several elements. The main ones are physical distribution, distribution channels and commercial venue. First, the logistics of distributing the product, be it a theatrical tour or a book delivered from the publisher to the reading public, are consid-

ered. Then the focus shifts to the relationships and the various agents within a channel – in an artistic example, the network from artist to producer to broadcaster. Lastly, location is an important factor in the success or failure of companies selling directly to the consumer. The location of a bookshop, cinema, hall, museum or even a traditional business must be carefully selected.

Promotion

Promotion comes last in the first sequence of this definition of the marketing mix. In the pre-preparation stage of a promotional campaign, a company must know which product is offered at which price and where. It must know beforehand the main characteristics of the target consumers and, in particular, the most convincing selling arguments for those consumers.

Since the same consumers are targets of advertising, promotion and marketing campaigns, these three areas are often confused. They are inclusive, since promotion is made up of four distinct components: advertising, personal selling, sales promotions and public relations, and since marketing includes promotion.

Two influential elements

Two other elements must be considered in any marketing analysis: time and the specificity of the firm. All companies must work within a changing environment. Market conditions evolve over time, as do consumer needs and tastes. The variables of the macro-environment may be modified and the competition may adjust its strategies. An excellent marketing strategy may seem outdated after a few years, or even a few months.

Every organization has its own personality and acts as an individual entity. What may be an excellent marketing strategy for firm *A* may prove hopelessly inadequate for firm *B*. Neither their products nor their market shares are necessarily the same. Their corporate images may also vary. It would therefore be risky to try to transplant a strategy from one firm to another.

The company and its marketing management

Decisions on marketing strategies must always conform to the company's mission and objectives. These decisions must also take into account the organization's human, financial and technical resources.

Implementation of a marketing plan requires the skilful coordination of all parties involved and the participation of all corporate sectors. For example, the production, finance and personnel departments must be included to ensure that resources are available. A financial plan must be agreed before financial outlays are made. Personnel must be advised in case additional staff are needed. As soon as a strategy is set up, corporate executives must be kept up to date on the operation. Monitoring allows the company to compare results with objectives and, if need be, to adjust any discrepancies through corrective measures.

Conclusion

Although the various elements of the marketing model have been presented individually, they are interdependent. In fact, they form a whole in which one or a majority may influence the others.

Marketing managers must be well acquainted with the market and the variables likely to influence it. They must correctly determine consumers' needs, measure the level and development of the demand for a particular good, and divide the larger market into submarkets or segments in order to take advantage of opportunities and gain a distinct advantage over the competition. They must also study the different variables within the macro environment. Competition in any form may affect product sales. Demographics, culture, economics, laws and regulations, and technology constantly change the rules of the game. As a result, marketing professionals must use their information system wisely and know how to juggle the variables of the marketing mix.

See also:

Chapter 26: Demand; Chapter 45: Participation; Chapter 49: Pricing the arts.

References

Balnaves, Mark, Tom O'Regan and Jason Sternberg (2002), *Mobilizing the Audience*, St Lucia, Queensland, Australia: University of Queensland Press.
Bennett (2005), 'Factors Encouraging Competitive Myopia in the Performing Arts Sector: An Empirical Investigation', *The Service Industries Journal* 25 (3), 391–401.
Briggs, Sarah (2007), 'Fresh Eyes: Attracting and Sustaining Young Visitors to Tate', *Museum Management and Curatorship*, 22 (1), 5–9.
Carpenter, Gaylene and Doug Blandy (eds) (2008), *Arts and Cultural Programming : A Leisure Perspective*, Champaign, IL: Human Kinetics.
Colbert, François *et al.* (2007), *Marketing Culture and the Arts: An Annotated and Selected Bibliography*, 3rd edn, Montréal: Chair in Arts Management/HEC-Montréal.
Colbert, François (2009), 'Beyond Branding: Contemporary Marketing Challenges for Arts Organizations', *International Journal of Arts Management*, 12 (1), 14–21.
Gainer, Brenda (1993), 'The Importance of Gender to Arts Marketing', *Journal of Arts Management, Law and Society*, 23 (3), 253–60.
Gainer, B. (1997), 'Marketing Arts Education: Parental Attitudes towards Arts Education for Children', *Journal of Arts Management, Law and Society*, 26 (4), 253–68.
Georgie, Vincent and Mariachiara Restuccia under the direction of François Colbert, (2010), 'Marketing Culture and the Arts: An Annotated and Selected Bibliography', Montréal: HEC/Chair in Arts Management, available on www.gestiondesarts.com/english/publications.
Ravanas, Philippe (2008), 'Hitting the High Note: The Chicago Symphony Orchestra Reverses a Decade of Decline With, New Programs, New Services, and New Prices', *International Journal of Arts Management*, 10 (12), 68–87.

Further reading

Balnaves *et al.* (2002), Bennett (2005), Briggs (2007), Carpenter and Blandy (2008), Georgie and Restuccia (2010), and Ravanas (2008).

38 Media economics and regulation
Gillian Doyle

Media economics concerns itself with the economics of making and supplying media content, and covers activities such as film-making, news production, print and online publishing, television and radio broadcasting. The economics of mass media is a lively and diverse area of scholarship that, over a number of years, has developed more or less independently from cultural economics but several areas of shared interest exist between these two subfields, for example, concerning economics of creativity or questions around copyright protection. Throsby (2001, p. 4) has described cultural provision in terms of activities that involve 'some form of creativity in their production' and where symbolic meanings are important and outputs embody intellectual property. Understood in this way, most if not all suppliers of media are involved in cultural industries. But the scope of 'culture' and of cultural economics extends well beyond media and includes, for example, the arts – literature, drama, dance, visual arts and so on – and heritage. In media economics, the focus is on applying economic theories and concepts to all aspects of media and on developing models and paradigms for the advancement of study of this particular subject area. This chapter sets out to give a flavour of the concerns and issues that mark out media economics as a distinctive field and, also, to provide an introductory overview of the overlap between economics and media regulation.

What is special about economics of media?
In many respects the media industry is unique. Unlike that of other sectors, the business of producing and distributing media involves supplying messages and ideas and this, inevitably, involves significant public welfare implications. So research that falls within the ambit of media economics stems not only from traditional economics but also from the perspective called critical political economy. The justification for a broader and more normative approach, as opposed to focusing purely, say, on efficiency, is summarized well by Douglas Gomery (1993, p. 198) who observed that 'studying the economics of mass communications as though one were trying to make toaster companies run leaner and meaner is far too narrow a perspective'.

Generally, the key concern underlying studies in media economics is how best to organize the resources available for media provision. Are firms producing the right sorts of goods and services, and are these being produced efficiently? Answering these questions in the context of media sometimes involves challenges. One problem, as noted by Alan Peacock (1989), whose work on economics of broadcasting has been seminal, is that the welfare impacts associated with communicating with mass audiences are not easily incorporated within the framework of standard quantitative economic analysis. Other challenges stem from the unusual public-good aspects of media content, or from grappling with the uncertainties and irrationalities that characterize production of creative output, or from the problem of trying to analyse an industry that is prone to constant technological upheaval and change.

However, judging by the growth of work in this area, the distinctiveness of media economics is more of a draw than an impediment to scholarly interest. Media economics has advanced in popularity and has flourished internationally over the past two decades within departments of economics, business and media studies. Fuelling this trend has been a growing appetite for understanding the effects of digitalization, convergence and globalization in reshaping media businesses. Deregulation of national media is another key factor shifting the attention of media policy-makers and academics more and more in the direction of economics. So, although media economics is still at a relatively early stage of development as a subject area, its importance for industry, for policy-makers and for scholars is increasingly recognized.

A number of characteristics distinguish media from other commodities. It is sometimes said that media operate in 'dual-product' markets. This refers to the way that media generate two sorts of output: first, media content (that is, programmes, news stories etc.) and, second, media audiences (Picard, 1989, pp. 17–19). This in itself is unusual, but in addition one of these outputs – media content – exhibits a number of interesting peculiarities that, over the years, economists have sought to elucidate.

Early work in the field by Collins, *et al.* (1988, p. 7) flagged up a similarity between broadcast output – for example, a programme broadcast on television – and other cultural goods in so far as that 'the essential quality from which their use-value derives is immaterial'. Many cultural goods share the characteristic that their value for consumers is symbolic and tied up in the messages they convey, rather than with the material carrier of that information (that is, the radio spectrum, the digital file and so on). The 'public-good' characteristic of not being used up or not being destroyed in the act of consumption means that broadcast material and some other forms of media output exhibit the peculiarity that this same output can be supplied over and over again at no extra cost. In this respect, media content seems to transgress the most basic assumption upon which economics is based – scarcity.

The various insights offered by Collins *et al.* about, for example, the non-rivalrous and non-excludable nature of broadcast output were an important early landmark in the development of thinking about how the economic characteristics of mass media differ from those of other industries. More recent work by Richard Caves (2000) again underlines the special characteristics of, in this case, creative activities – such as uncertainty of demand, incentives and motivations guiding artistic and creative 'talent' – and how these shed light on the organization and behaviour of firms in the creative industries (of which media are a part).

One very notable feature of the economics of media is the prevalence of economies of scale. Firms in this sector tend to enjoy increasing marginal returns as consumption of their output expands. This is because of the public-good nature of media output and how it is consumed. The cost of producing a feature film, a music album or a television programme is not affected by the number of people who are going to watch or listen to it. 'First-copy' production costs are usually high but then marginal reproduction or distribution costs are low and, for some media suppliers, zero.

Another feature that is commonly characteristic of media industries is the prevalence of economies of scope. Economies of scope are generally defined as the savings available to firms from multi-product production or distribution. They are common, again because of the public-good nature of media output and the fact that a product created for one market can, at little or no extra cost, be reformatted and sold through another. Because the value of media output is contained in ideas and messages that are intangible and therefore do not get used up or 'consumed' in the traditional sense of the word, the product is still available to the supplier after it has been sold to one set of consumers to then sell over and over again. So, for example, an interview with a celebrity can potentially be packaged into a television documentary, a news item, a radio transmission and so on. The reformatting or altering of the scope of a product intended for one audience into a 'new' one that extends consumption of it releases savings for the firm and therefore generates economies of scope.

Key themes in media economics

Several enduring themes and concerns help define media economics as a distinctive field. One is the role of audiences and advertising in directing and supporting provision of media. Many media goods and services are funded at least partly through advertising, and so patterns of advertising activity tend to exert considerable influence over the fortunes of the industry as a whole. A good deal of work on the economics of advertising was carried out in the 1970s and 1980s, much of which concerned itself with whether the role played by advertising is helpful in making the market system work more effectively (Schmalensee, 1972; Chiplin and Sturgess, 1981). A central concern was the extent to which advertising improves information flows and promotes competition or whether, on the other hand, expenditure on advertising may distort consumer decision-making and have a damaging impact on market access.

Another theme in economics of advertising, whose practical relevance is underlined in periods of economic recession, is that of the relationship between economic wealth (or, more specifically, growth rates for the economy) and cycles in advertising expenditure. In order to make more accurate predictions about future trends in advertising, many media agencies and organizations engage in collecting and analysing data about historic patterns of advertising activity and factors that have influenced these patterns. In the UK, for example, the Advertising Association publishes extensive statistical information about levels of advertising activity each year. An interesting trend that emerges is that, over long periods of time, there appears to be an association between economic wealth and levels of advertising: a stronger economy and greater wealth is generally associated with higher expenditure on advertising (Advertising Association, 2009, p. 5). Historically, advertising expenditure has been 'more volatile than GDP, falling sharply during recessions and rising steeply in booms' (ibid.) But movements in GDP and in advertising expenditure also diverge on occasion (Van der Wurff *et al.* 2008), and ongoing work in this area is concerned with understanding the exact nature, strength and consistency of the relationship between economic wealth and advertising activity.

Related to this, a number of studies have examined the nature of audiences (or of access to audiences) as a commodity, audience ratings, and how demand amongst advertisers for audience access is converted into revenue streams by media enterprises (Webster *et al.*, 2000; Wildman, 2003; Napoli, 2003). Audience fragmentation, although present as an issue in early work about television audiences (Barwise and Ehrenberg, 1989), has become even more pressing as a concern in recent years, as is reflected in much recent literature (Webster, 2005; Lotz, 2007). As Picard (2002, p. 109) puts it, fragmentation of mass audiences is 'the inevitable and unstoppable consequence of increasing the channels available to audiences'.

Turning from audiences towards content, another important set of concerns in media economics is firms and how they produce and supply media content and, also, the markets in which media organizations operate and levels of competition. Media firms come in many different shapes and sizes. The notion spans a variety of entities, from a small and specialist online publisher to a vast international conglomerate such as News International or Time Warner. Many media firms are commercial organizations but some are not and, consequently, standard economic theories about the behaviour of firms have their limits in this context. Nonetheless, the industrial organization model (and associated Structure–Conduct–Performance paradigm) that rests on the theory of firms has frequently provided a useful framework for work carried out by economists interested in media firms and industries (Hoskins, *et al.*, 2004).

Another framework often deployed in economic analyses of media firms and markets is that of the 'value chain'. Definitions of markets and sectors in media economics work are often implicitly or explicitly informed by this concept originally developed by Porter (1998). For media, the key stages in the industry's value chain or vertical supply chain usually include the production or creation of content (which usually, though not always, brings initial entitlement ownership of intellectual property); plus assembling that content into services and products (for example a newspaper or television channel); plus distribution or sale to customers. All of the stages in the vertical supply chain are interdependent and, as much research work in media economics has shown, this has important implications for the kinds of competitive and corporate strategies media firms will pursue.

Two major forces that have brought enormous changes to market structures and boundaries, and have affected media firms, large and small, in recent decades are convergence and globalization. Thanks to the arrival and rapid spread of digital technologies, avenues for distribution of media have been expanding and a greater overlap or convergence in the technologies used across the industry has opened up new opportunities for innovative and more interactive products and services. In addition, numerous factors, including new state policies, have opened up national broadcasting systems and contributed towards growing internationalization of operations by media firms. The economic and strategic implications of these changes have naturally been of central interest for those interested in media economics (Chan-Olmsted, 2006).

At the same time, a number of the business strategies and behaviours of media firms that economists have sought to shed light on reflect distinctive features and circumstances of this industry that are relatively long-standing. For example, strategies of risk-spreading are important in media because of inherent uncertainties surrounding the success of any new product. The hit-or-miss nature of the business of supplying a product such as a feature film or a television programme requires risk mitigation. Hoskins *et al.* (1997) explain how risks and uncertainties associated with generating high-cost audio-visual content can be offset through such tactics as using sequels. Production of sequels and series that build on successful formats and the use of 'stars' helps to build up and capitalize on brand loyalty among audiences and therefore to promote higher and more stable revenue streams.

Many scholars working on economics of media have focused on the success of the Hollywood majors in counteracting risk and dominating international trade (De Vany, 2004). Key to the risk reduction strategies of Hollywood is control over distribution plus the ability to supply copious well-funded product. The ability of the majors to support and replenish a large portfolio of film output is dependent on being able to fully exploit new and old hits but, as with the music industry, this is now potentially under threat from the growth of the Internet and – associated with this – growth of illegal copying.

This steers us back to the fact that, for media firms, the need to understand, participate and capitalize effectively on technological advancements is a constant challenge. Media regulators also need to understand that media markets are constantly evolving due to new technologies. So a great deal of work in media economics is fundamentally about exploring and uncovering the implications of recent technological changes. At present, digitalization and growth of the Internet are the key forces for change. This is reflected in numerous studies that, in one or another, shed light on how organizations have adapted their strategies to deal with these developments (for example, Aris and Bughin, 2009; Chan-Olmsted and Ha, 2003; Dennis *et al.*, 2006; García Avilés and Carvajal, 2008; Küng, 2008; Küng, *et al.*, 2008; Raviola and Gade, 2009). However, in a climate of ongoing upheaval, the task of building a full understanding of the transformative impacts of convergence and of the development of digital distribution infrastructures is likely to remain a key challenge for economists for many years to come.

Economics and media regulation

An important concern underlying much thought and research work related to economics of media is what role the state can or should play in media provision. What forms of state intervention in the media industry are desirable? There is, of course, an important political dimension to such questions, but economic considerations are often vital in guiding media policy decision-making.

Media firms, like those in all other sectors, are subject to the usual economic and industrial concerns (e.g. growth and efficiency) and to the normal laws of the land (such as those on health and safety) wherever they are based. But mass media organizations – and especially those in the broadcasting sector – are also frequently subject to a range of *special* rules and regulations that stem from the fact that their core business activity involves communication with audiences. In recognition of the sociopolitical and cultural importance of mass communications, interventions of one kind or another are generally seen as necessary or desirable and thus regulation is often at the forefront in determining the economic performance of media markets and firms.

Whenever the state is confronted by an industry whose activity happens to have a strong impact on public well-being, two choices are, broadly speaking, available for dealing with this. First, the state itself may take responsibility for being the provider of services in that industry and can organize provision through the *public* sector on a non-commercial basis funded by taxes, as is often done, for example, in defence, education and healthcare. In some countries, media provision is or has in the past been supplied and controlled largely by the state, albeit this raises obvious concerns in relation to freedom of speech and democracy. A second alternative is to allow the forces of demand and supply to determine how resources should be allocated – to leave it to the free market and allow commercial firms to supply whatever consumers express a need or want for through their willingness to pay for it.

The problem with taking this second approach is that there is no guarantee that the way in which resources are allocated and the sort of media that is supplied under free market conditions will match or be in accordance with the best interests of society. For example, there may be a tendency to oversupply the sort of content that is mainstream and popular (perhaps even that is damaging, so long as there is demand for it) and to undersupply, say, the needs of non-affluent minority groups or groups within society that advertisers are not interested in reaching.

Most countries adopt a 'mixed-economy' approach, with commercial firms supplying much media but supplemented by an element of non-market provision. In the UK, the BBC is the main provider of public service content and its activities are funded by a compulsory licence fee imposed on all owners of television-receiving equipment. This *non-market* approach of using public funds for broadcast and other media provision, while retaining considerable support in many countries, has become increasingly controversial as the technologies and avenues for distribution of media have advanced and multiplied.

The broad ideological case in favour of relying on free markets to allocate resources is based on the idea that decentralized decision-making, in which consumers exercise sovereignty, is usually better than decision-making carried out by the government. Even so, state intervention is sometimes called for to counteract problems or deficiencies arising from the free operation of markets. As far as media are concerned, generally speaking the most important economic reasons why intervention may be required are to address market failures, to deal with the problem of 'externalities' and to curb monopoly power. It is worth noting that governments also intervene in media markets for non-economic reasons (such as to protect minors or to achieve impartiality in news provision) but these are not the focus here.

The sector of media that is most evidently prone to market failure happens to be the component of industry that is of greatest significance financially and, arguably, remains supreme in terms of sociocultural influence – that is, broadcasting. One example of failure is that broadcasting would not have taken place at all in the first instance if left entirely up to the market and to profit-seeking firms, because at the emergence stage for radio and television no mechanism existed for earning a return from the activity. In the absence of a means of identifying and charging listeners directly, the conventional mechanism of market funding – that is, consumer payments – was missing.

Advances in broadcasting technology have gone some way towards correcting the initial causes of market failure and, in an era of vastly increased choice of content, some argue that the use of public funds to finance public service content provision is no longer appropriate (Elstein, 2004). But many believe that a completely unregulated market for radio and television will still fail to allocate resources efficiently and, consequently, some form of publicly funded and state-owned broadcasting entity remains a feature in most countries.

The public-good characteristics of broadcasting already mentioned are at the root of many perceived failures. With any good or service that is 'non-excludable' (i.e. you cannot exclude those that do not want to pay) and where customers do not have exclusive rights to consume the good in question, free-rider problems are virtually inevitable. Being a public good, broadcast output also has the characteristic of being 'non-exhaustible' – typically, there are zero marginal costs in supplying the service to one extra viewer. So a persuasive argument can be made that restricting access to media content, where such access can be provided at no additional cost, triggers a welfare loss that is wholly unnecessary and is therefore inefficient (Davies, 1999, p. 203). Another cause of market failure relates to the problem of asymmetric information. Graham and Davies summarize this by explaining that '[p]eople do not know what they are "buying" until they have experienced it, yet once they have experienced it they no longer need to buy it!' (1997, p. 19).

Externalities are another factor that calls for the use of special interventions. Provision of mass media is associated with both positive and negative externalities. The latter are external effects imposed on third parties when the internal or private costs to a firm of engaging in a certain activity (for example, pollution) are out of step with costs that have to be borne by society as a whole. Broadcasting may have negative external effects when, for example, provision of violent content imposes a cost on society (through increasing fear of violence among viewers) that is not borne by the broadcaster. A market failure arises here in that broadcasters may well devote more resources to providing programmes with negative external effects than is socially optimal so long as those programmes are popular. Equally, some forms of media content are generally recognized as conferring positive externalities, for example documentaries, educational and cultural output, but, again, because the benefits to society are out of step with the benefits to the firm, such 'meritorious' output may well be undersupplied under free market conditions. Externalities need to be corrected through some form of intervention, for example content regulations that seek to restrict the supply of output that confers negative societal effects and/or other measures that encourage more production and supply of content seen as collectively desirable.

Special support measures for meritorious content are very common and generally take two forms. Some interventions are essentially protectionist and help domestic producers by restricting the permitted level of imports of competing non-domestic television or feature film content. Much work in media economics has focused on international trade in audiovisual and trade disputes, on the dominance of US suppliers and on the efficacy of policy measures to counter this such as tariffs and quotas (Acheson and Maule, 2001; Hoskins *et al.*, 1997, 2004; Noam and Millonzi, 1993). Aside from imposing trade barriers, the other main approach, adopted in many European states, is to provide grants and subsidies for content producers to boost indigenous production levels. Work in media economics has helped explain how production grants correct the failure of the market system to provide an adequate supply of certain forms of content, but, has also highlighted dangers accompanying promotion of a culture of dependency and deviations from profit-maximizing behaviour among local producers.

One other major concern confronting media policy-makers is the way in which, on account of the prevalence of economies of scale and scope in the sector, there is a natural gravitation towards oligopoly and monopolization. Concentrations of media ownership are a widespread phenomenon (Sánchez-Tabernero and Carvajal, 2002) and, notwithstanding the arrival and growth of the Internet and other ongoing technological advances affecting distribution, questions around how policy-makers should deal with these remain of enduring interest to those working in media economics. If media empires are a problem, how should they be tackled? And what about monopolized control over specific access points and bottlenecks along the vertical supply chain for media?

It is worth noting that the main reason for public intervention to prevent media empire-building is usually not to do with economics but rather is about pluralism – the need, in the interests of democracy and social cohesion, to maintain a diverse and open system of media provision. However, regulation of ownership and of competition in the media industry also involves an important economic dimension.

Corporate strategies of expansion and diversification, which are commonplace and especially characteristic of media, are typically associated with two key incentives related to profit-maximizing behaviour: increased efficiency or increased market power. Efficiency gains imply an improved use of resources and are seen as beneficial to the economy as a whole but, by contrast, increased market power in the hands of individual firms poses a threat to consumers and rivals and is therefore seen as damaging for society and for the operation of markets. A problem for policy-makers is that proposed mergers and expansion strategies in the media and communications industries may often result in both these outcomes (Doyle, 2002, p. 166). Expansion makes possible greater efficiency but, at the same time, it facilitates market dominance and therefore poses risks for competition. Research work carried out by economists focusing on media concentrations is often aimed at shedding light on the 'natural monopoly problem' and on the challenges for policy-makers in finding suitable measures to accommodate the development of media firms while enabling competition.

See also:

Chapter 11: Broadcasting; Chapter 12: Cinema; Chapter 17: Creative industries; Chapter 27: Digitalization; Chapter 58: Television.

References

Acheson, Keith and Christopher Maule (2001), *Much Ado about Culture*, Ann Arbor, MI: University of Michigan Press.
Advertising Association (2009), *The Advertising Statistics Yearbook 2009*, Ad. Assoc./WARC, London: WARC.
Albarran, Alan, Sylvia Chan-Olmsted and Michael Wirth (eds) (2006), *Handbook of Media Management and Economics*, Mahwah, NJ: Lawrence Erlbaum.
Aris, Annet and Jacques Bughin (2009), *Managing Media Companies*, (2nd edn), Chichester: John Wiley & Sons.
Barwise, Patrick and Andrew Ehrenberg (1989), *Television and Its Audience*, London: Sage.
Caves, Richard (2000), *Creative Industries: Contracts between Art and Commerce*, Cambridge, MA: Harvard University Press.
Chan-Olmsted, Sylvia (2006), 'Issues in Media Management and Technology', in Alan Albarran, Sylvia Chan-Olmsted and Michael Wirth (eds), *Handbook of Media Management and Economics*, Mahwah, NJ: Lawrence Erlbaum, pp. 251–73.
Chan-Olmsted, Sylvia and Louise Ha (2003), 'Internet Business Models for Broadcasters: How Television Stations Perceive and Integrate the Internet', *Journal of Broadcasting and Electronic Media*, 47 (4), 597–617.
Chiplin, Brian and Brian Sturgess (1981), *Economics of Advertising*, London: Advertising Association.
Collins, Richard, Nicholas Garnham and Gareth Locksley (1988), *The Economics of Television: The UK Case*, London: Sage Publications.
Davies, Gavyn [Chairman] (1999), *The Future Funding of the BBC; Report of the Independent Review Panel*, DCMS, pp. 202–8.
Dennis, E., S. Warley and J. Sheridan (2006), 'Doing Digital: An Assessment of the Top 25 US Media Companies and their Digital Strategies', *The Journal of Media Business Studies*, 3 (1), 33–63.
De Vany, Arthur (2004), *Hollywood Economics: How Extreme Uncertainty Shapes the Film Industry*, London: Routledge.
Doyle, Gillian (2002), *Understanding Media Economics*, London: Sage Publications.
Doyle, Gillian (ed.) (2006), *The Economics of Mass Media*, Cheltenham, UK and Northampton, MA, USA: Edward Elgar.
Elstein, David (2004), 'Building Public Value: The BBC's New Philosophy', Institute of Economics Affairs (IEA) Current Controversies Paper, London: IEA.
García Avilés, J. and M. Carvajal (2008), 'Integrated and Cross-Media Newsroom Convergence', *Convergence: The International Journal of Research into New Media Technologies*, 14 (2), 221–39.

Gomery, Douglas (1993), 'The Centrality of Media Economics, *Journal of Communication*, 43 (3), 190–98.

Graham, Andrew and Gavyn Davies (1997), *Broadcasting, Society and Policy in the Multimedia Age*, London: John Libbey.

Hoskins, Colin, Stuart McFadyen and Adam Finn (1997), *Global Television and Film: An Introduction to the Economics of the Business*, Oxford: Clarendon Press.

Hoskins, Colin, Stuart McFadyen and Adam Finn (2004), *Media Economics: Applying Economics to New and Traditional Media*, Thousand Oaks, CA: Sage Publications.

Küng, Lucy (2008), *Strategic Management in the Media*, London: Sage.

Küng, Lucy, Robert Picard and Ruth Towse (2008), *The Internet and the Mass Media*, London: Sage.

Lotz, Amanda (2007), *The Television will be Revolutionized*, New York: New York University Press.

Napoli, Philip (2003), *Audience Economics: Media Institutions and the Audience Marketplace*, New York: Columbia University Press.

Noam, Eli and Joel Millonzi (eds) (1993), *The International Market in Film and Television Programs*, Norwood, NJ: Ablex Publishing.

Owen, Bruce and Steve Wildman (1992), *Video Economics*, Cambridge, MA: Harward University Press.

Peacock, Alan (1989), 'Introduction', in G. Hughes, and D. Vines (eds), 'Deregulation and the Future of Commercial Television', David Hume Institute Paper No. 12. Aberdeen: Aberdeen University Press, pp. 1–8.

Picard, Robert (1989), *Media Economics: Concepts and Issues*, Newbury Park, CA: Sage Publications.

Picard, Robert (2002), *The Economics and Financing of Media Companies*, New York: Fordham University Press.

Porter, Michael (1998), *Competitive Strategy: Techniques for Analyzing Industries and Competitors*, New York and London: Free Press.

Raviola, E. and P. Gade (2009), 'Integration of the News and the News of Integration: A Structural Perspective on Media Changes', *Journal of Media Business Studies*, 6 (1), 1–5.

Sánchez-Tabernero, Alfonso and Miguel Carvajal (2002), *Media Concentrations in the European Market, New Trends and Challenges, Media Markets Monograph*, Pamplona, Spain: Servicio de Publiciones de la Universidad de Navarra.

Schmalensee, Richard (1972), *The Economics of Advertising*, Amsterdam North-Holland.

Throsby, David (2001), *Economics and Culture*, Cambridge: Cambridge University Press.

Van der Wurff, Richard, Piet Bakker and Robert Picard (2008), 'Economic Growth and Advertising Expenditures in Different Media in Different Countries', *Journal of Media Economics*, 2, 28–52.

Webster, James (2005), 'Beneath the Veneer of Fragmentation: Television Audience Polarization in a Multichannel World', *Journal of Communication*, 15 (2), 366–82.

Webster, James, Patricia Phelan and Larry Lichty (2000), *Ratings Analysis: The Theory and Practice of Audience Research*, (2nd edn), Mahwah, NJ: LEA Publishing.

Wildman, Steven (2003), 'Modeling the Advertising Revenue Potential of Media Audiences: An Underdeveloped Side of Media Economics', *Journal of Media Economics and Culture*, 1 (2), 7–37.

Further reading

Any of the following introductory textbooks and reference volumes will be helpful for those coming new to media economics: Doyle (2002, 2006); Hoskins *et al.* (1997, 2004); Owen and Wildman (1992); Picard (1989, 2002); Albarran *et al.* (2006).

39 Motion pictures
Darlene C. Chisholm[1]

From an economist's perspective, the history, market structure and production chain characterizing the motion-pictures industry present fascinating puzzles and illustrate central principles of economic theory. The objective of this chapter is to outline some of the key economic phenomena that characterize the motion-pictures industry by examining the economic history of the industry, and by exploring the economics underlying the production, distribution and exhibition of motion pictures.

Industry history

By 1930, the US motion-pictures industry was dominated by five major studios: MGM, Paramount, RKO, Twentieth-Century Fox and Warner Brothers. The production process among these leaders was characterized by full vertical integration, with studios controlling film production, distribution and exhibition.[2] Each studio maintained a roster of actors and actresses who agreed to perform exclusively in films produced by that studio. The long-term contracts into which the actors and studios entered formed the basis of the Studio System. Access to a constant supply of talent guaranteed the studios control over a constant flow of films. The studios' control over distribution, and the preferential treatment the studio-owned movie theatres received in acquiring films, led to a significant degree of industry dominance by the major studios. During the 1930s, studio-owned theatres were granted favourable clearances and other advantageous terms from studio distributors to exhibit studio-produced films.

The extensive vertical integration by the major studios led to allegations of anti-competitive practices. In 1938, the Department of Justice initiated a series of actions against the major studios[3] on behalf of non-studio exhibitors, who claimed that they faced an anti-competitive environment in their attempts to secure a steady supply of motion pictures on favourable terms. In 1948, as a result of *U.S. v. Paramount*, the Supreme Court ordered the major studios to divest themselves of their theatres, to level the playing field for the smaller, non-studio exhibitors.[4]

The economics of the exhibition divestiture are noteworthy. Since the studios no longer faced a guaranteed outlet for the films they produced, films that might have been marginally profitable under the Studio System were no longer produced. Further, as television became a commercially viable entertainment alternative to movies exhibited in theatres, the studios needed to modify the attributes of the product they produced. In order to draw consumers away from their homes and televisions, the studios needed to provide an experience that television could not offer; hence the innovations in 3-D production, Technicolor, and the proliferation of 'epic' films.

During the days of the Studio System, actors specialized in specific characters in films that had a serial quality to them. Actors would play the same characters facing similar circumstances as in their previous films. For example, Bud Abbott and Lou Costello 'defined Universal to the public', appearing in a series of comedies in the 1940s, based on their 'long-prepared routines'.[5] However, by the 1950s, television replaced movies as the preferred medium for repeat appearances of characters facing familiar scenes in familiar settings.

In response to these changes in demand conditions, the studios produced fewer and larger-scale films, offering more variety than the previous serials, which television now provided.[6] It was no longer profitable for the studios to invest in promoting stars, and no longer optimal for actors to allow themselves to be typecast as a particular character, given the greater variety of film genres the studios were producing. Neither the studios nor the actors had an incentive to continue making specific investments in each other. These economic forces led to the demise of the star system. By the end of the 1950s, virtually all long-term contracts between stars and studios expired, leaving a labour market characterized by free agency and negotiation on a film-by-film basis (De Vany and Eckert, 1991; Chisholm, 1993; Caves, 2000).

Production

The film production process can be divided into three stages: development, production and marketing. The development stage includes the acquisition of rights to the story on which the film is based, making the necessary arrangements with talent agents and the production studio, arranging financing, and hiring and working with a writer. The production stage includes a pre-production phase, the actual production of the film, collaboration between the producer and director, and post-production editing and creation of the final 'negative' or print. The marketing stage includes marketing the film, conducting market research, advertising, devising and implementing a foreign distribution strategy, and auditing and accounting for the revenues and costs associated with the three stages of this process.[7]

Casting the film

As a producer enters the first stage of film production, one of his tasks is to line up the cast, particularly the actors who will play the leading roles. Often, producers consult with talent agents, who act on behalf of actors and actresses to negotiate their contracts and who typically receive a percentage of the gross income received by their clients. An agent may approach the 'talent' (the actor) with a firm offer for a film that has already received financing, or with an offer contingent on financing. If a producer seeks to engage a leading actor or actress in his film, the offer will probably be a firm offer. According to Paul N. Lazarus III, Director of the University of Miami's School of Communication's Motion Pictures Program, former film producer and motion-picture agent, 'if you are in hot pursuit of one of the handful of so-called "bankable" stars, the likelihood is that you will be competing with many projects with firm offers attached'.[8]

Economists have examined the various contractual offers made to the talent involved in film production. The lead actors in a film, particularly among the bankable stars, are typically offered a fixed-payment, a profit- or gross-sharing contract, or a combination of the two. Chisholm (1997) examined a data set of contracts for leading actors and actresses and found that an actor was most likely to receive a sharing contract in the cases in which the benefits from providing an incentive for the actor to work harder outweighed the transaction costs of writing and enforcing a sharing contract. The evidence provided weak support for the hypothesis that risk-sharing concerns influenced optimal contract design. Weinstein (1998) explored the historical evolution of producers' contracting terms and concluded that the increase in the number of sharing arrangements for producers was best explained as a response to a more risky contracting environment. De Vany (2004) found that the complexity in directors' contingent pay agreements reflects an attempt to contract in the face of highly uncertain revenue outcomes.

Financing the film

A producer will seek financing from a variety of potential sources. A producer can choose to enter a 'negative pickup deal' with either a major or an independent studio.[9] In such an arrangement, the studio agrees to distribute the film for the producer once it is complete. The studio further pays an advance against the revenues received by the producer once it is released and distributed. The producer can then take this agreement to a bank to try to secure funding for the production of the film. The bank and studio will require a completion guarantee, which historically involved a charge of 6 per cent of the budget to compensate the bank and studio for financial services provided.[10] If the producer incurs costs that are over the budget, the completion guarantee allows the financiers to complete the picture themselves. We shall consider a negative pickup deal from an economic perspective.[11]

When a producer proposes a film project, standard investment theory would suggest that the distributor should formulate an expectation of revenues, R, and determine the expected variance, θ^2, or degree of risk, associated with the project. In principle, the more uncertain the market prospects of the film, the greater the risk a studio faces in agreeing to distribute it. However, De Vany and Walls (1996, 1999, 2004) argue that revenue distributions have effectively infinitely large variances. De Vany (2006) proposes that this extreme uncertainty explains the pervasiveness of contingent contracting in the industry. Despite the highly uncertain environment, producers, studios and bankers will still attempt to assess the risk associated with a film project. The studio will agree to distribute the film without having observed the final product if they expect it to generate sufficient revenues to offset the cost of distribution, which will include the actual distribution and marketing costs, and the opportunity cost of not distributing an alternative film. Given the choice between two film projects, for a given estimated revenue, the distributor will be more likely to pick up the film with the smaller perceived risk. For a given degree of uncertainty, the distributor will be more likely to pick up the film expected to generate larger revenues.

The completion guarantee serves to limit some of the risk exposure to the distributor and to the bank or other lending institution. Further, once a distributor chooses to pick up a film, the bank will take the distributor's choice as a signal about the anticipated risk involved with financing it. Since it is in the interest of the distributor to make as accurate a measure as possible of the risk associated with a new film, the distributor's and bank's incentives are aligned. Thus a profit-maximizing bank will be more likely to finance a film that has received a pickup guarantee from a distributor.[12]

Distribution and exhibition

Following production, a film is distributed for exhibition. Typically, a film is first released in the US domestic theatrical market, then in foreign theatrical markets, although simultaneous domestic and foreign release has become more common, par-

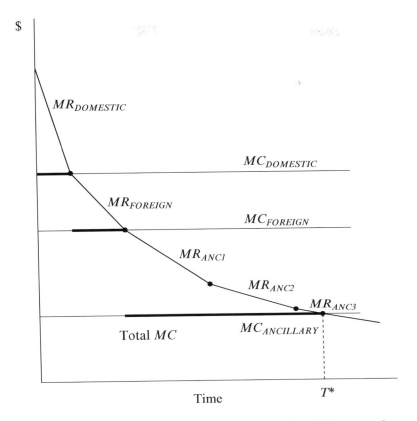

Figure 39.1   Historical optimal timing of film distribution by exhibition medium

ticularly among higher-budget 'event' films. Following the theatrical release, a film will probably be sent to at least one of the following markets, often in the following order: pay-per-view; worldwide home video; pay television; foreign television; network television; and syndication. In 1980, over 50 per cent of a film's revenues came from theatrical sources (domestic and foreign). By 2004, theatrical sources amounted to only 16.5 per cent of a film's revenues.[13]

Distribution strategy

Vogel (2007) presents the economic rationale for a sequential-market distribution strategy. He invokes the basic principles of profit maximization and opportunity cost. He summarizes his argument as follows: '[F]ilms are normally first distributed to the market that generates the highest marginal revenue over the least amount of time. They then "cascade" in order of marginal-revenue contribution down to the markets that return the lowest revenues per unit of time' (Vogel, 2007, p. 118). Figure 39.1 illustrates this profit maximization principle.

The kinked curve in Figure 39.1 represents the historical total marginal revenue curve over time, with the highest marginal revenue generated in the domestic market over a relatively short time horizon. Following a generally quick decline, the marginal revenue from the foreign theatrical markets would exceed that from the domestic market. By a similar logic, eventually the television media would generate higher marginal revenue than the foreign theatrical market, and typically for longer time horizons, as the films moved from home video, to pay television, to foreign television, to network television, and to syndication.[14]

The total marginal cost is a step function, for which each step measures the marginal cost of distribution in that particular market. A film's exhibition will end at time T^*, when the marginal revenue from the television market equals the marginal cost of distribution in that market. As the home-video/DVD market expands, particularly as the quality of home viewing improves with large-screen, high-definition televisions, the potential marginal revenue from this market segment rises, thus reducing the expected length of time between theatrical and home-video release. In addition, as studios face the threat from piracy and illegal distribution of content, the opportunity cost of delaying release in ancillary markets rises. These trends suggest that time lags in sequential releases will probably continue to decline and perhaps lead, in some cases, to more instances of simultaneous release across these markets.[15]

While it is clear that ancillary revenue sources are important to a film's success, we shall limit our remaining discussion of film distribution to the US domestic theatrical market.

Distribution contracts
Distributors are in the business of 'acquiring sufficient prints of [a] film, planning and executing an advertising campaign, and physically distributing [a] film through its network of branch offices'.[16] Distributors agree to make prints available to movie theatres for exhibition. In the US theatrical market, the contract between a distributor and an exhibitor typically involves an agreement on how to split the box-office receipts. The distributor's share of the net box-office receipts can be as high as 70 per cent for the first two weeks of a major release's run, declining to 60 per cent, then stabilizing at a flat rate of 35 or 40 per cent.[17]

As noted above, De Vany and Walls (1996) examined revenue distribution patterns and found evidence of revenue streams having what amounts to infinite variance. However, once a film's run has reached a critical number of weeks, the film is far more likely to sustain a relatively long run or have 'legs'. Given the nature of the typical distributor–exhibitor contract, the exhibitor can benefit if a movie generates a steady audience over a relatively long run.[18]

One interesting question pertaining to theatrical distribution is: given the highly uncertain market in which distributors operate, how do they choose the specific release date for each of their films? The distributor must also decide whether to release a film slowly, in an increasing number of cities, or to engage in a wide national release right from the start of the run. The film's genre, cast, director, plot, seasonal timeliness, among other attributes, play an important role in this decision. Further, the unique degree of product differentiation across films is significant in the determination of an optimal movie release strategy. According to Wyatt (1994), '[T]he marketplace for films is divided not just by different demand functions (or preferences), but also by differences between the many films which appear simultaneously in the market.'[19] Thus a studio will strategically respond to the expected release patterns of the other studios.

Distribution and economies of scale

The nature of distribution costs explains the observed structure of the distribution industry. To establish a distribution system large enough to handle the exhibition of large-scale major theatrical releases, a studio will incur a large annual fixed operating cost. However, once this system is established and maintained, the marginal cost of distributing and advertising a film will be relatively small. Thus we expect the market for distribution to consist of a relatively small number of distributors operating at a relatively large scale. Once the demand is met, that is, once the existing capacity of first-run exhibitors is supplied, no new distributors will enter the market, since a potential entrant would anticipate experiencing losses by doing so.[20]

Conclusion

The economic analysis of the motion-pictures industry is a growing and relatively new addition to the economics literature. Economists have documented patterns of revenue distribution, contracting terms at all levels of the production–distribution–exhibition chain, and the antitrust issues that have historically confronted the industry. Current research is under way to formally examine exit and entry patterns in exhibition, to measure the extent and nature of product differentiation, and to formalize the analysis of financial decision-making in an industry characterized by a high degree of risk. The motion-pictures industry provides a rich source of institutional dynamics and financial evidence for economists to systematically explore central tenets of economic theory.

Notes

1. I am grateful to Denexxel Domingo for his capable research assistance.
2. In addition, Columbia and Universal produced and distributed films, and United Artists provided distribution services. See Vogel (2007, pp. 66–74) and De Vany (2006, pp. 630–37) for histories and discussions of exhibition, production and distribution in the industry.
3. The defendants also included Columbia, United Artists and Universal.
4. See Vogel (2007) and De Vany (2006) for detailed discussions of the Paramount Consent Decrees and their impact on the industry's organization to the present.
5. See Gomery (2005, p. 159).
6. In 1956, the major studios released 48 per cent of the films they released in 1940. See Caves at (2000, p. 94).
7. See Lazarus (1992).
8. According to Lazarus, a 'bankable' star is one whom a picture can be financed around – someone whom bankers would unhesitatingly finance in a feature film (Lazarus, 1992, p. 28). See also De Vany (2006, pp. 649–50).
9. The 'negative' refers to the film produced, not a reversal of ownership.
10. Competitive pressures significantly lowered these rates in the 1990s. See Donahue (1987) and Vogel (2007, pp. 144–5).
11. In two recent papers, Goettler and Leslie (2005) and Palia *et al.* (2008) explore competing hypotheses explaining the co-financing choice, including portfolio risk reduction, internal-capital market factors and resource pooling.
12. A distributor may simply provide an advance to produce the film, in which case the financial terms will be stricter. Typically, the distributor will acquire all rights to the film in such an arrangement. See Donahue (1987, p. 49). Other sources of financing include: industry sources, such as talent agencies, and in-house production arrangements; lenders, such as financial institutions and distributors; and investors, including both public and private sources. See Vogel (2007, pp. 108–14 and pp. 175–94) for detailed discussions of financing and accounting practices in production and distribution deals.
13. See Vogel (2007, pp. 91–2 and 118).
14. See ibid.
15. See Waterman *et al.* (2007) and De Vany and Walls (2007) for further discussion of the impact of piracy on distribution strategies for digital media and on box-office revenue, respectively.

16. See Caves (2000, p. 112).
17. See De Vany (2006, pp. 627–8) for a detailed discussion of exhibitor–distributor contracting terms. Also see Filson *et al.* (2005) for an empirical study of exhibition contracts, which examines the role of risk aversion and transaction costs in optimal contract design.
18. In addition, the contract will include a rental escalation clause. If the film not only sustains a long run, but also generates significant revenue in a given week, the contract will revert to the exhibitor's paying 90 per cent of box-office receipts, less the house nut, which is an allowance for the theatre's operating expenses. The exhibitor pays the distributor the higher of this amount compared to its flat rental fee against box-office receipts. See De Vany (2006) for further details.
19. See Wyatt (1994, p. 97). Einav (2007) finds empirical support for this proposition, particularly as it relates to seasonality.
20. See Caves (2000).

See also:

Chapter 12: Cinema; Chapter 31: Globalization.

References

Caves, Richard E. (2000), *Creative Industries: Contracts between Art and Commerce*, Cambridge, MA: Harvard University Press.
Chisholm, Darlene C. (1993), 'Asset Specificity and Long-Term Contracts: The Case of the Motion-Pictures Industry', *Eastern Economic Journal*, 19 (2), 143–55.
Chisholm, Darlene C. (1997), 'Profit-Sharing versus Fixed-Payment Contracts: Evidence from the Motion Pictures Industry', *Journal of Law, Economics, & Organization*, 13 (1), 169–201.
De Vany, Arthur (2004), 'Contracting with Stars When Nobody Knows Anything', in Arthur De Vany, *Hollywood Economics: How Extreme Uncertainty Shapes the Film Industry*, London: Routledge, pp. 231–54.
De Vany, Arthur (2006), 'The Movies', in Victor A. Ginsburgh and David Throsby (eds), *Handbook of the Economics of Art and Culture*, Vol. 1, Amsterdam: North-Holland, pp. 615–65.
De Vany, Arthur and Ross D. Eckert (1991), 'Motion Picture Antitrust: The Paramount Cases Revisited', *Research in Law and Economics*, 14, 51–112.
De Vany, Arthur and W. David Walls (1996), 'Bose–Einstein Dynamics and Adaptive Contracting in the Motion Picture Industry', *Economic Journal*, 106 (439), 1493–514.
De Vany, Arthur and W. David Walls (1997), 'The Market for Motion Pictures: Rank, Revenue, and Survival', *Economic Inquiry*, 35 (4), 783–97.
De Vany, Arthur and W. David Walls (1999), 'Uncertainty in the Movie Industry: Does Star Power Reduce the Terror of the Box Office?', *Journal of Cultural Economics*, 23 (4), 285–318.
De Vany, Arthur S. and W. David Walls (2004), 'Motion Picture Profit, the Stable Paretian Hypothesis, and the Curse of the Superstar', *Journal of Economic Dynamics and Control*, 28 (6), 1035–57.
De Vany, Arthur S. and W. David Walls (2007), 'Estimating the Effects of Movie Piracy on Box-Office Revenue', *Review of Industrial Organization*, 30 (4), 291–301.
Donahue, Suzanne Mary (1987), *American Film Distribution: The Changing Marketplace*, Ann Arbor, MI: University of Michigan Press.
Einav, Liran (2007), 'Seasonality in the U.S. Motion Picture Industry', *RAND Journal of Economics*, 38 (10), 127–45.
Filson, Darren, David Switzer and Portia Besocke (2005), 'At the Movies: The Economics of Exhibition Contracts', *Economic Inquiry*, 43 (2), 354–69.
Goettler, Ronald L. and Philip Leslie (2005), 'Cofinancing to Manage Risk in the Motion Picture Industry', *Journal of Economics and Management Strategy*, 14 (2), 231–61.
Gomery, Douglas (2005), *The Hollywood Studio System: A History*, London: British Film Institute.
Hanssen, F. Andrew (2000), 'The Block Booking of Films Reexamined', *Journal of Law and Economics*, 43 (2), 395–426.
Kenney, Roy W. and Benjamin Klein (2000), 'How Block Booking Facilitated Self-Enforcing Film Contracts', *Journal of Law and Economics*, 43 (2), 427–35.
Lazarus, Paul N. III. (1992), *The Film Producer: A Handbook for Producing*, New York: St Martin's Press.
Moul, Charles C. (ed.) (2005), *A Concise Handbook of Movie Industry Economics*, New York: Cambridge University Press.
Moul, Charles C. (2007), 'Measuring Word of Mouth's Impact on Theatrical Movie Admissions', *Journal of Economics and Management Strategy*, 16 (4), 859–92.
Nowell-Smith, Geoffrey (ed.) (1996), *The Oxford History of World Cinema*, Oxford: Oxford University Press.

Palia, Darius, S., Abraham Ravid and Natalia Reisel (2008), 'Choosing to Cofinance: Analysis of Project-Specific Alliances in the Movie Industry', *Review of Financial Studies*, 21 (2), 483–511.

Prag, Jay and James Casavant (1994), 'An Empirical Study of the Determinants of Revenues and Marketing Expenditures in the Motion Picture Industry', *Journal of Cultural Economics*, 18 (3), 217–35.

Ravid, S. Abraham (1999), 'Information, Blockbusters, and Stars: A Study of the Film Industry', *Journal of Business*, 72 (4), 463–92.

Sawhney, Mohanbir S. and Jehoshua Eliashberg (1996), 'A Parsimonious Model for Forecasting Gross Box-Office Revenues of Motion Pictures', *Marketing Science*, 15 (2), 113–31.

Squire, Jason E. (ed.) (2004), *The Movie Business Book*, 3rd edn, New York: Simon and Schuster.

Vogel, Harold L. (2007), *Entertainment Industry Economics: A Guide for Financial Analysis*, 7th edn, New York: Cambridge University Press.

Waterman, David (2005), *Hollywood's Road to Riches*, Cambridge, MA: Harvard University Press.

Waterman, David, Sung Wook Ji and Laura R. Rochet (2007), 'Enforcement and Control of Piracy, Copying, and Sharing in the Movie Industry', *Review of Industrial Organization*, 30 (4), 255–89.

Weinstein, Mark (1998), 'Profit-Sharing Contracts in Hollywood: Evolution and Analysis', *Journal of Legal Studies*, 27 (1), 67–112.

Wyatt, Justin (1994), *High Concept: Movies and Marketing in Hollywood*, Austin, TX: University of Texas Press.

Further reading

Analyses of the practice of block booking are presented in Hanssen (2000) and Kenney and Klein (2000). The impact of word of mouth on movie attendance is addressed in Moul (2007). Empirical work on box-office revenue determinants includes Prag and Casavant (1994), Sawhney and Eliashberg (1996), and Ravid (1999). Excellent references on business practices, and economic and historical analyses of the industry, include Nowell-Smith (1996), Caves (2000), De Vany (2004, 2006), Squire (2004), Moul (2005), Waterman (2005), and Vogel (2007).

40 Museums
Víctor Fernández-Blanco and Juan Prieto-Rodríguez

Most people would agree that museums are cultural institutions *par excellence*. However, more questions arise when we want to establish a definition of the museum and explain its economic characteristics.

The museum: an economic definition

There are many definitions regarding the museum as an institution devoted to the collection, storage, display and research of objects, artefacts, or even intangibles. Along these lines, the Statutes of the International Council of Museums (ICOM) offers the following definition: 'a museum is a non-profit, permanent institution in the service of society and its development, open to the public, which acquires, conserves, researches, communicates and exhibits the tangible and intangible heritage of humanity and its environment for the purposes of education, study and enjoyment'.[1] We might categorize this as an institutional definition; note that it is not uncontroversial, since it leaves out for-profit organizations that collect or exhibit any kind of object. Alternatively, although they recognize the importance of the functions defined by ICOM, Ginsburgh and Mairesse (1997) point out that this definition risks neglecting other activities such as leisure, tourism or regional economic development. In the end, it offers a partial, conservative and even biased definition of the museum.

Following an economic point of view, together with the seminal perspectives of Montias (1973) and Peacock and Godfrey (1974), we offer a definition that considers the museum as an economic agent. We posit it as an organization that follows a general path specified by economic behaviour, that is, the maximization of an objective function under a set of economic and institutional restrictions. From this perspective, we allow room for various objectives, including the maximization of attendance and the maximization of profits; as such, our definition acknowledges that such goals require efficient management and that economics can help to achieve them.[2] Considering the museum as an economic agent, our analysis starts by defining its production function to describe technology rather than economic behaviour and shows the relationship between the quantities of production factors used and the maximum amount of product obtainable. The main inputs a museum deploys are labour and capital. Under the first category, we include not only specialized and administrative labour but also volunteers; capital includes financial resources, buildings, equipment and the museum's collection itself.

Nevertheless, any definition of museum must take into account that it has a multi-output production function, including conservation, exhibition, research and so on. If we accept Becker's (1965) procedure, all of these outputs can be considered as market goods, which, when combined with inputs and time, allow visitors to obtain desirable commodities such as knowledge, aesthetic experience and/or simply enjoyment.

We can group museum outputs into three broad categories:

(a) *Collection*: this includes the identification, documentation, expansion and preservation of museum contents.
(b) *Exhibition*: this makes funds available to citizens for use as purely aesthetic enjoyment and/or entertainment experiences as well as for education, training and research.
(c) *Other services*: the content of this category is much broader and more varied; for example, it includes catering and merchandising. Such services emerge and evolve as museums are reoriented towards better serving visitors, and thus these services become increasingly important as a funding source.

In recent decades, museums have been seen as mechanisms or agents of economic development, although a critical perspective might interpret some recent projects in terms of a new kind of social lottery. In a sense, these projects can be understood as a type of political betting game played by politicians who are not concerned about the crowding-out implications of the game. Hence we can add a new type of output, namely, the economic impact of the museum (Mairesse and Vanden Eeckaut, 2002; Plaza, 2010).

Once we have adopted an economic approach, an analysis of the museum can be pursued by utilizing the main instruments of economics. This involves understanding the demand and supply sides of museums and then delineating the logic of their incentives, which may or may not be defined by the market independently if the museum follows a commercial strategy.

The demand side of museums

The demand side includes private and public components. Private demand can be considered the result of an individual utility maximization process, and in this sense, demand is particularly sensitive to an individual's preferences, summed along his or her utility function together with the constraints he or she must fulfil. These constraints may include not only budget constraints that are linked to traditional economic variables such as prices or income, but also (and even more importantly) time constraints.[3] The bulk of empirical research on private demand in the context of museums is focused on visitor characteristics and attendance rates. In general, these studies conclude that an individual's museum attendance increases with the level of income and education and age, at least until the median age and among women (Dickenson, 1992; Peterson, *et al.*, 2000). In terms of ethnic origin, we find mixed results (Lewis and Seaman, 2004). There are also studies that introduce qualitative determinants of museum demand, such as the positive impact of the quality of the collection (Luksetich and Partridge, 1997) or repeated visits (Darnell and Johnson, 2001). Finally, there is another field of research that estimates museum demand functions and discusses price elasticity with the aim of understanding the impact of introducing or increasing admission fees. In general, these studies conclude that demand for museums is price-inelastic (O'Hagan, 1995; Luksetich and Partridge, 1997). Since, in many cases, data on the entire population are not available, and only a sample of museum visitors is available, the results can be biased. Prieto-Rodríguez *et al.* (2005) have used a representative sample of the entire population to estimate a demand system in which museums are aggregated with other cultural products. They have found an elastic demand for cinema, theatre, concert, ballet and museum tickets when considered together.

Regardless of price elasticity, we should bear in mind that visitors are a relatively select part of the entire population; consequently, policy should be oriented to attract people to those museums that are considered 'merit goods', among other legitimate targets. In this sense, it is important that policy-makers recognize that foreign tourists, domestic tourists and local citizens give rise to completely different externalities, and thus it could be difficult or even impossible to define policies that simultaneously fulfil the requirements of all three of these groups. Yet these policies are the basis of public demand for museums, which incorporates components of externalities including values such as the well-known existence, option, bequest, prestige and education values, with effects that can be considered as public goods. We should also highlight the museum as a local or regional development factor. The Guggenheim Museum in Bilbao can be considered the most representative museum in this context, and it has been joined by other franchise museums. For instance, we cite the new Louvre museums that have appeared in different areas, such as Abu Dhabi, a developing area, and Lens (France), an old mining and industrial region that was hardest hit by the industrial crisis. Public demand can be built in through the social valuation of a museum. Some research has tried to measure the social valuation of a given museum, particularly using contingent valuation techniques (Martin, 1994; Bedate *et al.*, 2009). It is remarkable that, as Noonan (2003) has pointed out, willingness to pay is lower in the case of museums than in archeological or historical sites.

The supply side of the museum

When analysing museums as economic agents, we pay special attention to their production and cost functions as well as to the nature of their ownership. We have already suggested that the most accurate approach to a museum is a multi-output production function with a cost structure similar to other cultural firms that have very large fixed costs, while variable costs account for a small percentage of the total costs. Moreover, marginal costs, that is, the change in total cost due to an additional visitor, are close to zero. Consequently, the presence of economies of scale can be verified, although in the largest museums (measured by the number of visitors) the situation can be reversed so that we see diseconomies of scale (Jackson, 1988). Finally, there is empirical evidence of technical and scale inefficiency in museums (Mairesse and Vanden Eeckaut, 2002, in Belgium; Basso and Funari, 2004, in Italy; Barrio *et al.*, 2009, in Spain), although inefficiency is higher when the museum is focused on preservation than when oriented to visitors or external objectives (Mairesse and Vanden Eeckaut, 2002). Alternatively, Bishop and Brand (2003) consider technical inefficiency to be directly related to public grants and volunteer activities.

Museums are open to both public and private ownership. In Europe, since a great portion of museums include collections originally developed by the Church, royalty or nobility, public ownership is more frequent, while in the USA, the majority of museums are privately owned. In both cases, museums tend to be non-profit organizations. Public ownership provides stability to a museum as well as a certain lack of incentive to develop economically efficient management. Private ownership can improve economic efficiency, but it increases risk and uncertainty. Trying to exploit the advantages of both sides while simultaneously avoiding their disadvantages, the hybrid model incorporates a mix of public and private governing authorities and provides more opportunities for the autonomous management of museums (Schuster, 1998; Meier and Frey, 2003).

Financing museums

Present-day museums combine several sources of income that are independent of the nature of the ownership: admission prices, the sale of items besides admission and public grants are undoubtedly the most important sources. As attention to visitors and other potential customers has become more important, new sources of revenue have emerged, especially those linked to merchandising, restoration and selling of ancillary goods. These strategies are oriented towards people who do not necessarily visit the museum itself as well as towards people who are attracted to visit the collection only after they visit the museum café or its shop. There are also other means of finance, such as lending out items from the collection, that are becoming quantitatively more important and fully accepted as an appropriate management practice, especially when financial difficulties arise. This was the case at the Musée National Picasso in Paris, which loaned part of its collection to the Centro de Arte Reina Sofía in Madrid, for a €3.5 million fee; 'I have to pay for the expansion project and I need the money', said Anne Baldassari, director of the Musée. However, revenues from ticket sales and public grants are still the main sources of income for museums.

The presence of admission fees in museums has been the object of some controversy. We find different kinds of arguments against charging fees. First, charging fees may reduce museum attendance, especially among lower socioeconomic classes (Anderson, 1998); however, empirical evidence does not support this hypothesis (Luksetich and Partridge, 1997; Bailey and Falconer, 1998). Second, charging for admission may not be an effective measure for raising revenues, since it could reduce public grants or private donations (Hughes and Luksetich, 1999; Maddison, 2004) or income from ancillary goods, such as sales in museum stores or cafés. Third, the Pareto-optimal pricing rule is to make price equal to marginal costs; due to the typical cost structure of a museum with marginal costs close to zero, the efficient solution is not to charge. This solution is compatible with charging positive fees when congestion increases marginal costs (Maddison and Foster, 2003),[4] and reinforces the idea that in the presence of continuously decreasing average costs, the optimal welfare solution entails public finance.[5] And fourth, museums generate well-known positive external benefits for the entire population, and the theory of market failure suggests that finance by public budgets is an efficient means of financing provision. However, considering that visitors benefit more than other people, the principle of benefit in taxation suggests that public finance should be complemented with fees.

In the end, we conclude that both sources of income (i.e. public grants and ticket prices) may coexist. We can also define an optimal financing schedule using a principal–agent framework under conditions of imperfect information (Prieto-Rodríguez and Fernández-Blanco, 2006). In the case of a museum, the public agency, which is risk-neutral, plays the role of the principal, and the manager of the museum, who is risk-averse, plays the role of the agent. The principal designs a contract with the agent and sets down which payments correspond to each possible scenario under the contract. The agent chooses his/her action among a set of possible actions. The results of this action depend on the agent's efforts, which may or may not be known, as well as on some uncontrollable environmental conditions, which are usually denominated as the 'state of nature', and impose uncertainty on the relationship. The results can be measured in terms of the number of museum visitors, where the probability of achieving a certain number of visitors depends positively on the agent's effort. That is, the better the manager's policy, the higher is the probability of obtaining favourable results.

The principal aims to maximize an objective function that depends positively on the number of visitors and the public agency's valuation of such visitors and negatively on the amount of grants.[6] The agent, the museum's manager, can be considered a bureaucrat *à la* Niskanen, and so his or her utility function depends positively on the museum budget (including both ticket and grants income) and negatively on his or her effort. Therefore there is a conflict of interest between the principal and the agent. On the one hand, greater levels of effort help to ensure a better result for the principal but reduce the agent's utility. On the other hand, larger payments reduce the principal's profit but increase the agent's utility. The signed contract should make compatible the interests of both participants.

Under these conditions, the principal should design a contract that tries to maximize the expected social benefit under the constraint that the agent agrees to sign the contract; that is, he/she obtains his/her reservation utility. The contract can be designed under conditions of symmetric or asymmetric information. In the case of symmetric information, the public sector (that is the principal) knows the effort put in by the museum manager (the agent), and the contract clauses should specify the optimal ticket price and grant level as well as the agent's optimal effort. In the case of asymmetric information, the agent can hide his or her effort, and therefore it cannot be included in the contract clauses. Then the principal must design a payment schedule in the contract that gives the agent sufficient incentive to make the optimal level of effort.

If the public sector knows the manager's effort, the optimal grant policy implies a museum budget constant that is independent of the number of visitors. This means that the public agency must fully insure the manager's museum budget, assigning him or her a subsidy that, given the optimal level of effort, allows the manager to obtain his or her reservation level of utility. Hence the public sector must finance the museum budget deficit if it has not been completely covered by ticket sales. In this case, the public grant decreases with the number of visitors and box-office income. The resulting ticket price is Pareto-optimal since it equalizes expected marginal social benefit (i.e. expected marginal private revenue plus expected marginal social value) with marginal costs. And when there is a social benefit from visits, this optimal price is located at a point at which demand is inelastic, thereby providing a new justification for the inelastic pricing strategy. Finally, the manager's optimal effort level is Pareto-optimal because, at equilibrium, the expected marginal revenue product of effort must be equal to the manager's marginal rate of substitution between budget and effort.

Under conditions of asymmetric information, the public agency faces great difficulty in controlling the manager's effort, and it faces a moral hazard problem that leads the public sector to not use the grants to fully insure the manager. This is because he/she has incentives to be inefficient by reducing his/her effort and, for example, by making inefficient expenditures or not maximizing alternative sources of revenue. The best choice for the public agency is to use grants to provide adequate incentives to the manager in order to improve his or her effort level, thereby achieving more efficient museum management. In this case, the equilibrium is no longer a Pareto-optimal situation with respect to the budget and the grant. In terms of prices, however, the solution is the same as that under symmetric information and therefore Pareto-optimal.

In sum, in the presence of asymmetric information and even with a risk-averse manager and a risk-neutral public agency, grants and budgets depend on results, because higher budgets related to good results provide the main incentives to increase a manager's level of effort. Hence transferring ticket pricing policy to the authority of the manager is not the best way to introduce adequate incentives in any circumstances. In short, the manager of a museum should not be left to decide the ticket price for admission into that museum. Rather, the public agency must regulate these prices in accordance with social valuation and use grants as an incentive mechanism to achieve optimal managerial effort.

Notes

1. This was approved in Vienna, 24 August 2007.
2. This economic point of view has its detractors. For instance, Cannon-Brookes (1996) thinks that this approach defines a museum as a delivery services firm and thereby obscures its traditional and historical mission. However, perhaps now the problem involves defining the objective function rather than considering museums as economic agents in general terms.
3. The general ticket for El Prado is less expensive than a Big Mac meal in Spain.
4. This congestion problem arises, for instance, in the case of special exhibitions, when a museum faces increasing marginal costs and a higher potential attendance that shifts up the demand curve. Hence the optimal behaviour in this case is to charge a positive fee that could eventually generate profits for the museum. In any case, special exhibitions (for example, in superstar museums) are not frequently put on in the majority of museums. In addition, while special exhibitions increase the number of visitors, they can also disturb the display or attendance at permanent collections.
5. In any case, it should be noticed that, when other sectors of the economy are charging prices above their marginal costs, museum ticket prices should be positive (above marginal cost) in order to achieve a Pareto-optimal allocation of resources (Bailey and Falconer, 1998).
6. The public agency's valuation can be considered a constant, but if the public sector has different valuations for different visitors, it varies with visitor characteristics, allowing us to introduce the possibility of price discrimination.

See also:

Chapter 15: Costs of production; Chapter 42: Non-profit organizations; Chapter 45: Participation; Chapter 46: Performance indicators; Chapter 49: Pricing the arts.

References

Anderson, R.G.W. (1998), 'Is Charging Economic?', *Journal of Cultural Economics*, 22 (2–3), 179–87.
Bailey, S. and P. Falconer (1998), 'Charging for Admission to Museums and Galleries', *Journal of Cultural Economics*, 22 (2–3), 167–77.
Barrio, M.J., L.C. Herrero and J.A. Sanz (2009), 'Measuring the Efficiency of Heritage Institutions: A Case Study of a Regional System of Museums in Spain', *Journal of Cultural Heritage*, 10 (2), 258–68.
Basso, A. and S. Funari (2004), 'A Quantitative Approach to Evaluate the Relative Efficiency of Museums', *Journal of Cultural Economics*, 28 (3), 195–216.
Becker, G.S. (1965), 'A Theory of Allocation of Time', *Economic Journal*, 75 (299), 493–517.
Bedate, A.L.C. Herrero and J.A. Sanz (2009), 'Economic Valuation of a Contemporary Art Museum: Correction of Hypothetical Bias Using a Certainty Question', *Journal of Cultural Economics*, 33 (3), 185–99.
Bishop, P. and S. Brand (2003), 'The Efficiency of Museums: A Stochastic Frontier Production Function Approach', *Applied Economics*, 35 (17), 1853–8.
Cannon-Brookes, P. (1996), 'Cultural–Economic Analyses of Art Museums: A British Curator Viewpoint', in V. Ginsburgh and P.M. Menger (eds), *Economics of Arts: Selected Essays*, Amsterdam: North-Holland, pp. 255–74.
Darnell, A. and R. Johnson (2001), 'Repeat Visits to Attractions: A Preliminary Economic Analysis', *Tourism Management*, 22 (2), 119–26.
Dickenson, V. (1992), 'Museum Visitor Survey: An Overview, 1930–1990', in R. Towse (ed.) (1997), *Cultural Economics: The Arts, The Heritage and the Media Industries*, vol. 1, Cheltenham, UK and Lyme, USA: Edward Elgar, pp. 272–81.

Feldstein, M. (ed.) (1991), *The Economics of Art Museums*, Chicago, IL: University of Chicago Press.
Frey, B. (2006), 'The Economics of Museums', in V. Ginsburgh and D. Throsby (eds.), *Handbook of the Economics of Art and Culture*, Amsterdam: North-Holland, pp. 1017–47.
Ginsburgh, V. and F. Mairesse (1997), 'Defining a Museum. Suggestions for an Alternative Approach', *Museum Management and Curatorship*, 16 (1), 15–33.
Hughes, P. and W. Luksetich (1999), 'The Relationship among Funding Sources for Art and History Museums', *Nonprofit Management and Leadership*, 10 (1), 21–38.
Jackson, R. (1988),'A Museum Cost Function', *Journal of Cultural Economics*, 12 (1), 41–50.
Johnson, P.S. (2003), 'Museums', in R. Towse (ed.), *A Handbook of Cultural Economics*, Cheltenham, UK and Northampton, MA, USA: Edward Elgar, pp. 315–20.
Journal of Cultural Economics (1998), 22 (2–3), Special Issue on the Economics of Museums.
Lewis, G. and B.A. Seaman (2004), 'Sexual Orientation and Demand for the Arts', *Social Science Quarterly*, 85 (3), 523–38.
Luksetich, W.A. and M.D. Partridge (1997), 'Demand Functions for Museum Services', *Applied Economics*, 29 (12), 1553–9.
Maddison, D. (2004), 'Causality and Museum Subsidies', *Journal of Cultural Economics*, 28 (2), 89–108.
Maddison, D. and T. Foster (2003), 'Valuing Congestion Costs in the British Museum', *Oxford Economic Papers*, 55, 1, 173–90.
Mairesse, F. and P. Vanden Eeckaut (2002), 'Museums Assessment and FDH Technology: Towards a Global Approach', *Journal of Cultural Economics*, 26 (4), 261–86.
Martin, F. (1994), 'Determining the Size of Museum Subsidies', *Journal of Cultural Economics*, 18 (4), 255–70.
Meier, S. and B. Frey (2003), 'Private Faces in Public Places: The Case of a Private Art Museum in Europe', *Cultural Economics*, 3 (1), 1–16.
Montias, J.M. (1973), 'Are Museums Betraying the Public's Trust?', *Museum News*, 51, May/June, 25–31.
Noonan, D. (2003), 'Contingent Valuation and Cultural Resources: A Meta-Analytic Review of the Literature', *Journal of Cultural Economics*, 27 (3–4), 159–76.
O'Hagan, J.W. (1995), 'National Museums: To Charge or Not To Charge?', *Journal of Cultural Economics*, 19 (1), 33–47.
Peacock, A.T. and C. Godfrey (1974), 'The Economics of Museums and Galleries', *Lloyd Bank Review*, 111, January, 17–28. Reprinted in R. Towse (1997) *Cultural Economics: The Arts, the Heritage and the Media Industries*, Cheltenham, UK and Lyme, USA: Edward Elgar, 364–75.
Peterson, R.A., P.C. Hull and R.M. Kern (2000), 'Age and Arts Participation: 1982–1997', Research Division Report No. 42, Washington, DC: National Endowment for the Arts.
Plaza, B. (2010), Valuing Museums as Economic Engines: Willingness to Pay or Discounting of Cash-flows?, *Journal of Cultural Heritage*, forthcoming.
Prieto-Rodríguez, J. and V. Fernández-Blanco (2006), 'Optimal Pricing and Grant Policies for Museums', *Journal of Cultural Economics*, 30 (3), 169–81.
Prieto-Rodríguez, J., D. Romero-Jordán and J.F. Sanz-Sanz (2005), 'Is a Tax Cut on Cultural Goods Consumption Actually Desirable? A Microsimulation Analysis Applied to Spain', *Fiscal Studies*, 26 (4), 549–75.
Schuster, M. (1998), 'Neither Public Nor Private: The Hybridization of Museums', *Journal of Cultural Economics*, 22 (2–3), 127–50.

Further reading

A general introduction to the economics of museums is to be found in Feldstein (1991), Frey (2006), Johnson (2003), Peacock and Godfrey (1974) and the Special Issue on the Economics of Museums of the *Journal of Cultural Economics* (1998). For a more specialized treatment of the economic impact and the social valuation of museums see Bedate *et al.* (2009), Martin (1994) and Plaza (2010). Demand for museums is discussed in Luksetich and Partridge (1997), Dickenson (1992) and O'Hagan (1995). Production and cost functions are estimated in Barrio *et al.* (2009), Bishop and Brand (2003) and Jackson (1988). For a more specialized treatment of museums financing see Hughes and Luksetich (1999), Maddison and Foster (2003), Meier and Frey (2003) and Prieto-Rodríguez and Fernández-Blanco (2006).

41 The music industry

Andrew E. Burke

This chapter provides a perspective on the changing economics of the music business. It is selective and largely driven by a desire to understand the performance of the recorded music sector (excluding classical music). This sector is, if anything, highly dynamic, with high levels of product differentiation in music titles, high levels of entry and exit among artists, and ongoing technological innovation in audio software and hardware. Thus one would expect enterprise to play a prominent role in any analysis of the industry. Indeed the various forms of entrepreneurship can be found with ease within the music industry including *creative/imaginative* (Shackle, 1979) musicians, *risk-taking* (Knight, 1921) music publishers and record companies who are *alert* (Kirzner, 1979) to new market trends, and *R&D intensive* (Schumpeter, 1942) audio hardware multinationals. Simultaneously, the record industry has also demonstrated features more commonly associated with more static industries with features such as highly concentrated markets and low levels of change in firm ranking (in terms of market share). However, disruptive technology in the form of the Internet and digital distribution has been transforming the core economics that has dominated the industry over the last 50 years. In this chapter we examine the implications of this emerging process for the performance of the recording industry. In the next section we focus on the economics underlying the traditional physical record industry and then we show how these are affected by the digital record music revolution outlining the main implications for performance and policy.

The physical recorded music industry

We begin with the basic economic features of the various markets within the record industry's supply chain in the physical (non-digital distribution) domain. Table 41.1 summarizes two of the intermediate markets (creative artist and record company) as well as the final market (retail) involved.[1] We note that all of these are highly concentrated. Thus, the issue of market power arises along with the concomitant antitrust concerns. However, the degree of dynamism across these persistently concentrated markets varies, with the biggest difference occurring between the two intermediate markets. The creative artist sector is the most highly dynamic, with high levels of entry and exit alongside changes in artist ranking by market share (Burke, 1994, 1995). In stark contrast, record company market share among the dominant firms entails low levels of entry and exit and a slow pace of industry turbulence (see Table 41.2). Apart from Geffen in the USA and Virgin in the UK, virtually no new record company has managed to occupy a lasting independent position among these dominant firms – so dominant, in fact, that they have become known as the Majors.

The relatively static record company market can be explained quite easily with reference to some fundamental industrial economics. In essence, minimum efficient scale (MES) is high in this sector. The economies of scale that cause it to be high include the following:

Table 41.1   Features of key segments of the industry supply chain

Feature / Market	Creative artists	Record companies	Retail record stores
Concentration	High	High	High
Turbulence	High	Low	Low

Table 41.2   Top four and six UK record company album market share, 1985–2005

Albums, % units	1985	1990	1995	2000	2005
Universal (PolyGram pre 2000)	14.5	23.2	20.6	20.5	32.6
EMI	13.4	15.9	13.4	10.7	12.2
CBS–Sony	15.0	10.4	12.0	11.6	22.6
WEA–Warner	12.2	12.1	9.9	11.7	9.9
Total top four	55.1	61.6	55.9	54.5	77.3
Total top six	68.5	73.7	72.3	70.4	81.2

Notes: PolyGram data exclude Universal except for years 2000 and 2005. In 2005 CBS–Sony includes BMG.

Source: BPI *Year Books.*

- *Economies of scale in manufacturing.* However, it should be noted that this advantage has declined as outsourcing opportunities have increased with a proliferation of CD manufacturing plants.
- *Economies of scale in distribution.* Transport costs decline as more CDs are shipped to the same location.
- *Economies of scale in marketing.* This occurs for a number of reasons. First, large firms can negotiate bulk-buying price discounts. Second, incumbent firms with a repertoire of successful artists can provide exclusive access to these artists for particular media in return for media exposure for the record company's lesser-known artists.
- *Economies of scale in finance costs.* Investing in creative artists entails risk. For example, of the total 4892 singles released in the UK in the year 2000, only 926 ever featured in the weekly Top 100 charts – a hit rate of 19 per cent).[2] Large firms are able to reduce exposure to risk by spreading their investment over a wide array of artists. Thus, by reducing risk they reduce the cost of finance over and above that available to a smaller record company.
- *Speed to market.* Running through all of the above factors is the characteristic that being large also allows firms to penetrate markets rapidly, which is important for creative artists who are attempting to sell a service that often simultaneously has a very short product life cycle in a wide array of markets. This allows established record companies to offer more income potential for creative artists than possible through a smaller organization.

Apart from these economies-of-scale factors, the role of record company reputation also gives an advantage to established firms. In general, a record company with a reputation for promoting music with consumer appeal will find it easier to negotiate retail shelf space and media exposure for its new artists than that of a firm new to the market. Cumulatively, these factors imply that large record companies can generate more profits from the sale of a creative work than smaller firms. In turn, this allows large established record companies to offer the highest bids to creative artists compared to those that could be offered by the smaller firms. Thus, apart from exceptional instances when the Majors overlook the consumer appeal of a new creative artist, by and large, new and smaller record companies are only able to compete for artists rejected or overlooked by the dominant record companies (Burke, 1997).

Even when an independent record company does sign an artist whom, with the benefit of hindsight, an established record company should have signed, the Majors' competitive advantages usually cause the artist to be subsequently signed over (or subcontracted) to a Major (for example, Stiff Little Fingers[3]), or indeed the smaller record company itself is acquired by the one of the Majors (as in the case of the independent record company Creation, which originally signed the band Oasis). Burke (1997) showed that over-optimistic artists who started their own record company because they believed this to be the most lucrative approach to market later found this to be an inefficient means of exploiting the value of their work. They soon reverted to a preference to sign a record deal with a major record company. These processes have endured, causing high concentration coupled with low market turbulence. The dominant core is accompanied by a turbulent competitive fringe of firms that operate above MES and presumably can survive because of frequent enough oversights of creative artist talent by major record labels and perhaps a desire by record companies to avoid cannibalization,[4] a willingness on the part of (lifestyle) founders of independent record companies to accept low profits, over-optimism among these founders and perhaps monopolistic pricing of CDs in the final market,[5] which might throw a lifeline for these firms.

The greater the competition between record companies to sign a creative artist, the greater the payoff to the artist. In such a competitive environment we know that the major record companies can consistently bid more than the independent record companies because of the high MES in the industry. However, multi-product record companies face a dilemma in this bidding process in that there is likely to be an element of cannibalization (business stealing or trade diversion effects) from hiring additional artists. In other words, the net increase in record company profits depends on the net increase in sales that it can generate from signing a new artist. However, the more an unsigned artist is a close substitute for artists who are already on the record company's roster, the lower the net increase in sales signing such an artist will generate. In other words, high cannibalization effects can imply that the record company does not generate much, if any, increase in profit from signing the artist. When this occurs, it greatly weakens the record company's ability to bid for unsigned artists with potential consumer appeal. The dilemma for the record company is that if it does not sign them, another company is likely to do so and the cannibalization effects take place anyway. This auction for creative talent in which the record companies indulge gives rise to three predictions:

1. As long as there is a large enough supply of creative talent, the presence of cannibalization effects implies that large established record companies will not be able to bid for all creative talent with market potential. It explains why less efficient small and medium-sized record companies can consistently secure a significant share of the market (historically around 30 per cent) despite being less capable than larger firms due to size inefficiencies and resource constraints (such as lack of finance).

2. If the costs of signing a record deal are only a proportion of the total costs of bringing a creative artist to market, then the greater the cannibalization effects, the higher the incentive for record companies to sign artists but not attempt to commercialize their music.[6] By signing artists, the record company prevents other firms from commercializing the music at the expense of the revenue generated by the record company's existing roster of music. To make this work, there must be a cost saving for the record company from signing an artist and not commercializing his/her music. The record company can ensure this by, for example, underspending on album recording, video and marketing costs. It could also keep the artist in the 'rehearsal/writing' stage and wait until the commercial life of the tunes has subsided. When this occurs, the artist can be dropped by the record company when there is no further threat of cannibalization. As we know, artists frequently complain that record companies perform exactly these activities while record companies deny the allegation, arguing that it has no commercial incentive not to commercialize an artist who has already cost the company in terms of the costs of a record deal. The bidding auction explains why this practice can be the profit-maximizing approach for record companies. The same logic explains why record companies might sometimes resist the repositioning of the genre of an artist when he/she moves from a market segment where the record company has relatively little internal (within its own roster of artists) cannibalization effects to a segment where internal cannibalization is high. Of course, creative artists can attempt to reduce the probability that they will be chosen for 'neglect' if they can reduce the wedge between record deal costs and commercialization costs. One way of ensuring this is to bargain for an advance on royalties rather than a higher royalty rate when negotiating a record deal. The advance on royalties acts as a sunk cost for the record company. Thereafter, it will earn more profits from commercializing artists to whom it has already paid royalties over and above those where low advances imply lower net profit (for the record company) from each unit sale. Thus these forces go some way to explain why apparently risk-prone (evidenced by their willingness to enter the riskiest segment of the music industry) creative artists appear highly risk-averse in demanding advances on royalties rather than more generous royalty rates.

3. The artist auction process, however, can be a self-defeating exercise for record companies. The highest bid a record company can make for any artist is the monopoly profits that creative artists can generate. Thus two effects are unleashed when competition between record companies for artists intensifies. First, record company profits are likely to be squeezed, and second, the likelihood of the record company selling CDs at their monopoly price in the downstream market increases. In fact, in the extreme, all the rents will be passed on to creative artists so that the record company makes minimal profits and the consumer pays a monopoly price. This outcome would be consistent with the evidence unearthed by the UK Monopolies

and Mergers Commission (1994) investigation into the pricing of CDs in the UK when it concluded that record companies were not charging excessive prices for CDs because they were making only normal economic profits. Alternatively, creative artists with market power may use it to secure highly lucrative record deals that then necessitate record companies to charge monopoly prices in order to pay for them.

The digital recorded music industry
The digital music industry resulted from technological advances relating to the compression of digital music files and their electronic distribution by Internet, cable and mobile telecommunications. Digital distribution of music eliminates the need for a supplier to manufacture (press) CDs. It also reduces the per unit cost and the economies of scale involved in distributing music to the end user – shipping a single music title to an isolated region is not much more expensive than shipping 100 titles to the same place. Online marketing can be direct and through the use online networks/communities can be targeted more effectively than offline methods. In sum, in the online environment MES is low and costs are substantially lower than in the physical record industry – the ingredients for greater competition and lower industry concentration.

In addition, the digital market has opened up new points of sale such as mobile phones, computers and digital portable music players. In the UK these markets have grown from a negligible revenue base in 2000 to account for 12 per cent of record industry revenue by the end of 2008 (BPI, 2009). The digital market has also enabled the unbundling of tracks from albums, and this has proved very popular with consumers. Individual digital track downloads accounted for 95 per cent of the singles market in the UK record industry by 2008. Digital album market share has grown less dramatically, from 2.8 per cent of industry album revenue in the UK in 2006 to 10.3 per cent by 2008 (BPI, 2009).

As these trends continue and revenues in the music recording industry move on line, they will cause increased deconcentration in the record industry. The reduction in online record company MES and lower financial requirements of a digital record company compared to a physical record company imply that barriers to entry fall and the market becomes more competitive. Artists do need record companies to reach mass consumer markets and can in effect act as their own record label (as many have effectively done through sites such MySpace and mp3.com). This has led to a vast increase in the number of new track releases – in the UK rising from just under 5000 in 2000 to over 7000 in 2008 (BPI, 2009).

However, whether or not the online market for music does in fact deconcentrate depends very much on how online record companies interact with online retailers. If the online retail market is concentrated, then the aforementioned deconcentration of record companies may not take place if record companies can vertically integrate with online music stores. In other words, since online consumers want choice (i.e. a website that stocks a large variety of music), it follows that if online retailers can secure exclusive supply arrangement with record companies, then the online retail market can be both concentrated and entail monopolistic power. However, a simple form of anti-trust regulation could ensure that this scenario is less likely to occur. If competition regulators enforce a ban on 'refusal to supply' (that is, impose compulsory licensing on record labels/artists) to online retailers as well as record companies, then a much more deconcentrated and competitive online environment will arise. In other words, record companies could not refuse to supply (independent) online retailers, and likewise online retailers with a large customer base could not refuse to 'stock' the content of a particular record company or independent creative artists. This would eliminate the 'content is king' network externality that is a fundamental driver to industry concentration in the online market. Ultimately, it would lead to a greater choice for consumers with associated higher deconcentration and competition.

However, the lure of an online economic welfare Mecca does not eliminate market power altogether. As we know, the physical record industry demonstrates significant skewness of income among creative artists (for example see Burke, 1995; Cox and Felton, 1995; and Towse, 1997). A repeated feature of the record industry is that a small minority of creative artists dominates most of the market at any point in time. A number of explanations have been put forward for this phenomenon. Rosen (1981) suggests that this is due to the high economies of scale in reproduction, which give more talented artists an additional competitive advantage over their less talented counterparts – the market ultimately being dominated by the most talented artists. Rosen's theory assumes that there are no consumer search costs to find talented artists. However, search costs can be a significant part of the cost of purchasing unknown talent (e.g. the risks in buying an album without previously hearing all of the tracks). However, consumers' search costs are lowered substantially when they can sample music for free. Radio and television provide such a service, but the limit on the amount of music that can be exposed on these media, alongside the need for these media to play music that can attract a large audience, lead to inertia in the variety of airplay titles. They also limit the number of total airplay titles that are possible. Avoidance of search costs by consumers can, therefore, result in skewed demand for particular artists. The search cost hypothesis also has empirical support to the extent that it appears that creative artists who can get a relatively high chart position soon after a title release can generate media exposure, which in turn promotes sales (see Burke, 1994, for the interaction between the music and singles charts and Strobl and Tucker, 2000, for snowballing effects).

The implication of these two perspectives on the skewness of artist market share is that their relative importance indicates whether or not the online market is likely to result in the consumption of a wider variety of music, which enhances welfare. If Rosen's model is the true depiction, then one would not expect music consumption to become less skewed in the online environment. In fact, it might become more skewed as reproduction costs fall, disproportionately benefiting more talented artists. On the other hand, if search costs are the main driver of skewness of artists' income, then the online environment may cause a more egalitarian distribution of creative market share because online search costs are reduced significantly as consumers no longer have to pay before listening to music (for example, through sites such as Spotify or Last.fm and the proliferation of online radio and television stations). Thus, in this environment the search costs perspective implies a more even distribution market share (for any given distribution of consumer preferences across varieties). While it is still too early to judge which theory is appropriate for the online record industry, initial evidence seems to support the search cost model as artist income is becoming less skewed. Before to the massive rise in digital music sales in the UK, the annual Top 100 best-selling singles accounted for around 50 per cent of annual single sales. But from 2004 to 2005 this share fell from 53 per cent to 30 per cent, and then continued to fall to 20 per cent by 2008 (BPI, 2009).

Notes

1. Space constraints force us to adopt a narrow analytic scope at the expense of ignoring important sectors such as publishing and artist management.
2. Evident from data published in the BPI *Statistical Handbook 2001*, British Recording Industry, London.
3. Stiff Little Fingers were originally signed by the independent record company Rough Trade but then, following the success of their first album, were passed on to Chrysalis – who earlier had rejected an approach by the band for a record deal.
4. For a theoretical perspective on cannibalization, see, Salop (1979).
5. Monopolistic pricing of records in the final market can arise either because of exertion of market power by any combination of creative artists with strong market appeal, record companies and retail outlets.
6. The logic is akin to the notion of 'sleeping patents' proffered by Gilbert and Newbery (1982).

See also:

Chapter 22: Cultural entrepreneurship; Chapter 27: Digitalization; Chapter 29: Experience goods; Chapter 34 The Internet: culture; Chapter 35: The Internet: economics; Chapter 56: Superstars.

References

BPI (British Phonographic Industry) (1991), *B.P.I. Year Book 1991: A Statistical Description of The British Record Industry*, London: BPI.

BPI (British Recorded Music Industry) (2009), *Statistical Handbook 2009*, London: BPI.

Burke, A.E. (1994), 'The Dynamics of Product Differentiation in the British Record Industry', *Journal of Cultural Economics*, 20 (2), 145–64.

Burke, A.E. (1995), 'Employment Prospects in the Irish Popular Music Industry', *Journal of the Statistical and Social Inquiry Society of Ireland*, XXVII (2), 93–120.

Burke, A.E. (1997), 'Small Firm Start-Up by Composers in the Recording Industry', *Small Business Economics*, 9, 463–71.

Cox, R.A. and J.M. Felton (1995), 'The Concentration of Commercial Success in Popular Music: An Analysis of the Distribution of Gold Records', *Journal of Cultural Economics*, 19, 333–40.

Gilbert, R.J. and M.G. Newbery (1982), 'Preemptive Patenting and the Persistence of Monopoly', *American Economic Review*, 72 (3), 514–26.

Kirzner, I.M. (1979), *Perception, Opportunity and Profit: Studies in the Theory of Entrepreneurship*, Chicago, IL and London: University of Chicago Press.

Knight, F.H. (1921), *Risk, Uncertainty, and Profit*, Chicago, IL and London: University of Chicago Press.

Mol, J.M., N.M. Wijnberg and C. Carroll (2005), 'Value Chain Envy: Explaining New Entry and Vertical Integration in Popular Music', *Journal of Management Studies*, 42 (2), 251–76.

Rosen, S. (1981), 'The Economics of Superstars', *American Economic Review*, 71 (5), 845–58.

Salop, S. (1979), 'Monopolistic Competition with Outside Goods', *Bell Journal of Economics*, 10, 141–56.

Schumpeter, J.A. (1942), *Capitalism, Socialism and Democracy*, New York: Harper and Row.

Shackle, G.L.S. (1979), *Imagination and the Nature of Choice*, Edinburgh: University of Edinburgh Press.

Strobl, E.A. and C. Tucker (2000), 'The Dynamics of Chart Success in the U.K. Pre-Recorded Popular Music Industry', *Journal of Cultural Economics*, 24, 113–34.

Towse, R. (1997), 'Copyright as an Economic Incentive', *Hume Papers on Public Policy*, 5 (3), 32–45.

UK Monopolies and Mergers Commission (1994), *The Supply of Recorded Music*, London: HMSO.

Vogel, H.M. (2007), *Entertainment Industry Economics*, 7th edn, Cambridge and New York: Cambridge University Press.

Further reading

Mol *et al.* (2005) and Vogel (2007).

42 Non-profit organizations
Dick Netzer

In all rich countries, firms organized on a not-for-profit basis produce cultural goods and services, along with for-profit firms (including independent professional artists) and the state. This is also true in many poorer countries. Non-profit firms are defined as organizations that have a formal structure and governance, which differ greatly among countries but share the characteristics that (1) the managers of the organization do not *own* the enterprise or have an economic interest that can be sold to other firms or individuals and (2) any surplus of revenue over expenditure may not be appropriated by the managers of the organization, but must be reinvested in ways that further the stated purposes of the organization. Obviously, such organizations will not be formed and continue to exist unless the organizers and managers expect and realize some economic rewards, including money compensation for their own services and non-financial rewards like consumption benefits (producing cultural goods and services that they want to enjoy but which will not be produced without their efforts) and personal status.

The rules under which non-profit cultural firms are formed and function differ greatly among countries. In some, the rules are highly structured and sharply differentiate non-profit firms from other culture-producing entities, especially in countries like the USA, in which the favoured tax treatment of non-profit firms is central to their success. In others, there is much less formality. For example, in Ireland, non-profit organizations may exist and receive favourable tax treatment without any formal legal status, although the latter is usually acquired by registering as a company in order to limit the liability of members (Donoghue *et al.*, 1999, pp. 4–6).

The extent to which non-profit firms are truly separate from the state can differ considerably within and among countries. Sometimes, ostensibly non-profit firms are very closely connected with and governed by the state and differ little from entities that are formally part of the state, while in other cases state bodies pretend to be non-profit entities (the Corporation for Public Broadcasting in the USA misleadingly advertises itself as 'a private corporation' but is simply the Federal government agency that disburses government grants to local radio and television stations). Moreover, the degree of distinctiveness of the non-profit sector may change over time.

In some countries, some state cultural organizations have substantial autonomy and may raise funds from private sources, so that they function much like entities that are formally private, non-profit organizations. This has increased in Europe in recent years (Boorsma, 1998, pp. 31–2; Klaic, 1998, pp. 171–2; Creigh-Tyte, 1998, pp. 185–90). Even in France, where the state remains the sole provider of the most expensive cultural goods and services, there are some state museums managed by private firms or associations. The Réunion des Musées Nationaux, a state entity for 30 museums that finances acquisitions and exhibitions and manages museum commercial activities, was converted in 1990 to an 'industrial and commercial private establishment', meant to increase flexibility, for example, by employing professionals who do not enjoy lifetime job security. But it appears not to have been successful financially (Benhamou, 1998, pp. 101, 107). Schuster (1998) discusses what he calls the 'hybridization' of American museums in recent years, a process that reduces the distinction between state and private non-profit museums, an extension of Hutter (1997), who discusses the quasi-privatization of state cultural entities in Europe in recent years, which often adds a second set of flexibility-reducing rules to those inherent in state operation and ownership.

A substantial portion of the activities of non-profit organizations in some rich countries is explicitly redistributive in purpose, which can be traced back to the major role of the Church, rather than the state, in succouring the poor. However, redistribution does not play an important role for cultural non-profit organizations, either in declared intent or in actual effect (whatever the declared intent may be). So cultural (and many other) non-profits can be explained by the conventional externality argument: (1) the production of private (excludable and rival) goods and services also generates significant amounts of public goods; (2) profit-maximizing firms are likely to operate at levels of private-goods output that provide rather small quantities of the public goods; (3) democratic governments making budgetary decisions on a median voter basis offer subsidies that generate significantly less public-goods output than many voters prefer and are willing to pay for; and (4) such voters can be identified and persuaded to make gifts of money to that end. Governments are often not trusted to use gifts to such purposes, but instead substitute gift money for funds that otherwise would be provided by ordinary government budgets. The less governments are trusted in this way, the larger the role of non-profits should be. In addition, givers are unlikely to make such gifts to profit-maximizing enterprises, because the managers and owners of such enterprises can readily use the gift money to enhance profits rather than produce more public goods.

This 'trust' argument for the importance of the non-profit form in the arts is largely accepted without comment in the literature, in part because, as Hansmann (1980) asserted, the non-profit form is well suited to deal with situations in which consumers are incapable of evaluating the goods delivered or promised. Non-profit firms will have little incentive to take advantage of consumers, because there is no gain to managers from so doing. However, there is at least one forceful dissent.

West (1987, pp. 37–9) points out that this is a form of the principal–agent problem and markets have generated a variety of solutions, like the use of professional advisers; critics perform this role in the arts. Moreover, the conventional view conflicts with economists' presumption that self-interested behaviour by all parties leads to efficient solutions ordinarily. Next, West (ibid., pp. 39–42) turns to the frequent claim (for example, in Throsby and Withers, 1979) that non-profit firms are likely to produce at a lower price and higher output level than for-profit firms that are monopolies. If the social objective is to expand cultural experiences, then subsidies confined to non-profits seem the right course. West challenges this conclusion; among other points, he shows that this is true only for very simple monopoly situations, with a single price. With perfect price discrimination, only the for-profit firm will have the socially optimum output. Finally, West notes that virtually everything said to be wrong about subsidies to for-profit firms is just as true for non-profits.

In a comment, Heilbrun (1988, pp. 87–9) notes that West's argument rests on his assertion that unit costs are likely to be higher in the non-profit sector than in the profit-making, because of what self-interested behaviour in the latter case will do: keep costs down to ensure that there is more profit to appropriate. Part of that case is the assertion that managers will be paid more in non-profits. West's rejoinder (1988) is that *because* managers cannot appropriate profits, there is an incentive to inflate their salaries. Boards are likely to be amenable to this, rather than a protection against it. Moreover, subsidies from government and private donors surely reduce resistance to high unit costs. Most of these are empirical arguments, but it is difficult to resolve them empirically.

In a much better-known article, Hansmann (1986), as well as other writers, has added a somewhat more direct (and possibly much less altruistic) explanation for non-profit cultural organizations, relating to the cost structure of production in performing arts companies, museums and cultural broadcasting (but not production by independent individual artists). Fixed costs are very high relative to variable costs. Thus it may be impossible to fully recoup costs by charges paid by direct users in most cases. Of course, it would be inefficient to charge would-be customers anything more than the low variable costs.

The exceptional cases ordinarily are those in which the performance or exhibition can have a very long run, during which the fixed costs per performance are modest, and thus admission charges paid by very large numbers of customers can cover costs, as in the commercial theatre in London, New York and other places. Price discrimination can help, but will not solve the problem unless the demand curve has an odd shape. The conventional price discrimination on the basis of the location of seats is limited in effect (unless builders of theatres provide a very large number of really bad seats). Moreover, price discrimination in conventionally designed theatres is restrained by the fact that tickets are transferable.

Hansmann sees gifts by individuals as a form of voluntary price discrimination: it is the donors' way of ensuring that the performance or exhibition or cultural broadcast actually takes place, by surrendering some of their consumer surplus to the producer of the cultural output they strongly prefer. Seaman (1985) examines this argument empirically for US nonprofit performing arts organizations. He finds that ticket price discrimination operates as the standard model would predict and is reasonably effective, while the substitution of donor price discrimination for ticket price discrimination is only partly true. However, the data do show that very large percentages of individual donors are in fact attenders (Frey and Pommerehne, 1989, p. 65), so that the possibility of the substitution is real. In the USA, a very large fraction of private gifts to cultural organizations comes from individuals, rather than companies or foundations (and many of these entities reflect, in their giving, the personal preferences of the individuals who created the foundations or run the companies).

In countries where the state plays a large role in the financing of these types of cultural production, the selfish motives of affluent attenders will be less significant and, indeed, there will be less reason for the cultural enterprise to be a non-profit, rather than state, enterprise. But if the enterprise is a non-governmental one, the state is likely to insist that the producer be a non-profit enterprise. In fact, few governments give significant amounts of subsidy to for-profit cultural enterprises. An exception is cases in which such subsidies have been offered to film exhibitors or producers, to encourage the production and showing of locally made films. The signal lack of success of these cases suggests the difficulty of preventing for-profit enterprises (and their employees) from appropriating the proceeds as extra income.

Thus, as Throsby (2000, pp. 116–18) and others point out, if the cultural enterprise requires grants and gifts in addition to income from sale of services in order to survive and generate the public goods that motivate the organizers, the not-for-profit form is the only practicable corporate structure. But even as the corporate structure is shaped by the goals of the organizers, the non-profit form itself can affect the choices that cultural entrepreneurs make among their multiple objectives.

There is a substantial economic literature on the economic behaviour of the managers of museums, starting with Peacock and Godfrey (1974). Grampp, perhaps the economist who has been the most spirited critic of the economic behaviour of museum keepers, denies that it is the non-profit status of nearly all museums that is the explanation: 'Non-profit does not in principle signify inefficiency even if it does in practice. A prudent use of resources . . . should be as important to an art museum as to a commercial gallery' (Grampp, 1996, p. 221). Instead, he attributes his catalogue of economic sins, notably the failure to utilize much of their capital in the form of the collection at all, by exhibiting little of it at any time, not preserving and protecting it adequately, minimizing opening hours, and so on, to rent seeking by those who run museums. But rent seeking by managers can flourish only if their decisions are seldom if ever overruled by their principals – those who actually own the enterprise – and if their tenure in office is secure. Many museums, large and small, are state museums; in government, security of tenure and insulation of managerial decisions are legendary. In theory, this need not be the case for non-profit enterprises.

But (as Grampp and others note), the proclivities and motivations of non-profit museum managers and their principals – boards of trustees – often are quite similar. Both gain satisfaction from non-economic management of museums, and have no reason to maximize either the utility of museum visitors or financial results: gifts and grants ensure that the latter is satisfactory.

Nonetheless, the economist critics of museum behaviour often see the non-profit form, rather than state auspices, as more conducive to economic management. Peacock (1998, p. 25) views non-profit auspices as an alternative to state auspices that can afford more flexibility in management decisions. Frey (1994) argues that economizing behaviour by museums, such as selling works from the collection to raise money for purchasing other works, better conservation, improved climate control, longer hours and, most of all, actually exhibiting a larger percentage of the collection, requires more independence from the state than is normally the case in Europe, but common in the USA. All his examples of 'good' behaviour are American non-profit museums. However, he recognizes that 'The question of legal ownership is not decisive, but what matters is that the persons responsible for public museums be given the necessary *incentives* and *independence* to employ the resources and possibilities at their disposition more freely' (Frey, 2000, p. 47).

One curator suggests that the problem the critics address may lie in the legal framework, rather than in the organizational form: he points out that, in civil law countries, museums' collections are generally viewed as public property and 'as such inalienable except *in extremis*. In common law countries, trustees are groups of persons to whom care of objects is entrusted for specific purposes, and therefore conceivably can be sold' (Cannon-Brookes, 1996, p. 262). Presumably, in civil law countries, even non-profit museums could not sell works from the collection, while, in common law countries, even state museums might be free to do so.

Although trustees may govern state as well as non-profit museums, and other producers of cultural services and both non-profit and state entities may be subject to similar limits on their discretion under the laws of that country, it seems apparent that non-profit status is likely to provide more opportunity for flexibility in such matters. Moreover, while non-profit auspices obviously do provide scope for much uneconomic behaviour by managers, that scope may be narrower than is the case for state auspices. Uneconomic behaviour often is the very purpose of state provision of the service.

A possibly important consideration in cultural policy is whether the private non-profit form affects the choice of strategies for intervention in art markets by state bodies, such as arts councils. In a 1985 paper, Throsby notes that intervention may occur in either or both of two markets, and on either side of those markets: (1) the market in which artists are the sellers and those who bring the work of artists to consumers (performing arts producers, art dealers, museums of contemporary art) are the buyers, and (2) the market in which those firms interact with final consumers. He concludes that the usual point of intervention – grants to firms, rather than to artists or consumers – is likely to increase quality in the first market and quantity in the second, with some important exceptions. Conceivably, state cultural firms may be under some political pressure to increase quantity, in either or both markets, while non-profit cultural firms that rely heavily on non-state sources of funds may feel more freedom to emphasize quality goals. Moreover, since the personal rewards of non-profit trustees and managers have a large non-monetary component, notably social status, it is to be expected that the non-profit form on balance will encourage emphasis on the quality goal.

Frey and Pommerehne (1990) examine the economic consequences of the basic differences in institutional form in theatres, comparing the commercial theatre and the subsidized theatre, which includes both non-profit theatres and state theatres. While they explicitly deal with state subsidies, the analysis applies to private gifts as well. The predominant form of subsidy for theatre organizations that are non-profit entities and theatres that are not directly part of the 'public administration' is lump-sum subsidy that is not closely related to output, input or prices, essentially meant to ensure the existence of the organization. Such a subsidy eliminates incentives to earn any visible profits, which 'is often accomplished by improving quality above the level desired by the audience, distributing rents to employees, concentrating on the "artistic side" and disregarding other possible sources of revenue' (ibid., p. 180). Less common are ticket subsidies, which may be intended to increase audience size, but which can be diverted readily to quality improvements.

State theatres, in contrast, especially in continental Europe, usually receive subsidies to cover prospective operating deficits. However, 'Achieving a surplus or reducing a deficit does not benefit the theatre; the implicit tax rate is 100%. Moreover, future subsidies are reduced. Therefore, the directors of a public theater have a strong incentive *not* to reduce the deficit, but rather to increase it above the projected level. The sanctions against doing so are low' (ibid., p. 182).

Why does the importance of non-profit organization of cultural production differ among rich democratic countries? Economists should be and are sceptical about explanations for any institutional differences in economic organization on the basis of ancient 'accidents' of history. If culture is a normal good, we would not expect the demand for cultural output to vary inversely with per capita income; instead, we would expect demand to be positively associated with per capita income, probably with considerable variation from the trend line. Thus it is plausible that the aggregate demand (relative to GDP) for the public goods that cultural activities generate is roughly similar among the rich countries. This may be true, but consistent with differential financing of cultural activities by the state in democratic countries, without the need to resort to the political history of the pre-industrial age. A simple explanation is that the views of the median voter on the size and composition of the state budget may be very different from the views of the median among those voters who articulate their positions on the state budget for cultural goods and services. Also, given the differences among countries in the structure of decision making on the state budget (for example, between federal and unitary government countries), the median voter model might work in different ways in different countries, with differential results with respect to state financial support of culture. If, then, the demand for the public goods associated with cultural production is similar among countries, the outcome of the median voter model should be offset by differential funding of cultural activities by non-profit organizations financed by gifts.

The extent to which this is true should be affected by different countries' rules on the organization and functioning of non-profits and the tax treatment of gifts. Thus, in the USA, it is easy to organize tax-favoured nonprofit entities and the after-tax cost (as of 2001) to the donor of most gifts (by dollar value) to non-profit cultural entities in the form of bequests is only about 20 per cent of the value of the gift and that of most gifts during the lifetime of the donor is only about 60 per cent of the value of the gift. It should be no surprise that individual gifts to non-profit organizations of all kinds constitute a much higher percentage of personal income than in most other rich countries, and that the USA (probably – comparative data on this are very limited) is at the extreme upper end of the distribution with respect to the relative role of non-profit organizations in cultural production.

At the end of the twentieth century, non-profit museums accounted for roughly 70 per cent of the receipts of all museums, government museums (which include the very large and lavishly financed Federal government museums in Washington) for about 25 per cent and for-profit museums about 5 per cent. A very small part of the receipts (less than 10 per cent) of the non-profit museums came from government grants, about 25 per cent from 'earned income' (largely admissions payments) and the rest from investment income and current gifts by private parties (American Association of Museums, 2000).

Very few performing arts companies are government entities. In 1997, non-profit entities accounted for nearly all the receipts of opera companies, symphony orchestras and chamber music organizations, and dance companies, and 37 per cent of the receipts of theatre companies; for-profit theatre companies accounted for nearly all the remainder of theatre receipts. About one-fourth of the receipts of promoters of arts events (usually, the owners or operators of performance venues not owned by specific performing companies; Lincoln Center in New York is the largest of these) were in the non-profit sector.

Non-profit organizations accounted for 20 per cent of the receipts of the broadly defined performing arts sector, including mass culture music groups, performing arts companies' promoters, agents and managers, and independent artists and performers (US Census Bureau, 2000). Most of their receipts (62 per cent) came from earned income, 32 per cent from private gifts, past and present, and the remaining 6 per cent from government grants (US Census Bureau, 2001).

Non-commercial broadcasting in the USA (known imprecisely as 'public broadcasting') is devoted to news and public affairs programming, children's programming and cultural programming, the last accounting for as much as 40 per cent of total costs (other than station and network operation). Most of the local stations are operated by state and local governments and their universities and colleges, but nearly all the primary (very-high-frequency) stations in major metropolitan markets are operated by non-profit corporations. Thus most of the receipts and expenditure of the public broadcasting system are the province of non-profit enterprise. However, nearly 40 per cent of the receipts come from government sources, unlike the case for museums and the performing arts (Corporation for Public Broadcasting, 2000).

It is very difficult to piece together comparable data for other countries regarding the importance of non-profit entities in the production of cultural services. However, the Comparative Nonprofit Sector Project of Johns Hopkins University has generated comparative data across countries on the economic importance of non-profit cultural production relative to national economic measures.[1] As Tables 42.1 and 42.2 show, the economic importance of the non-profit cultural sector is relatively small in the USA, although much of the American cultural sector is organized on a non-profit basis. Presumably, it is the relative economic unimportance of the entire cultural sector

Table 42.1   Non-profit culture and recreation operating expenditures, 1990

Country	Percentage of GDP
France	0.59
Germany	0.26
Hungary	0.67
Italy	0.22
Japan	0.04
Sweden	1.03
United Kingdom	0.98
United States	0.20
Average	0.64

Source: Salamon *et al.* (1999, App. B). Tables updated to 20 January 2000 downloaded from www.jhu.edu/~cnp/pdf.

Table 42.2   Employment in non-profit culture and recreation organizations, 1995

Country or area	Percentage of total non-agricultural employment in the country or area
European Union	0.70
Central Europe	0.39
Japan	0.11
Australia	1.15
United States	0.55

Source: As for Table 42.1.

– for-profit and non-profit – in the USA that explains this result. It should be noted that the now-standard international classification scheme for non-profit organizations combines, in one subsector, culture, arts and recreation. The inclusion of recreation may explain what appear to be anomalous results: for example, the high figure for Australia in Table 42.2. Throsby (1996) makes it clear that the non-profit component of the culture sector in Australia is exceedingly small.

Note

1. There is a standard international classification scheme for non-profit economic activity. The sector referred to here is 'Culture and Recreation'.

See also:

Chapter 40: Museums; Chapter 44: Orchestras; Chapter 52: Public support; Chapter 49: Pricing the arts; Chapter 57: Tax concessions.

References

American Association of Museums (2000), *1999 AAM Museum Financial Information, A Report from the National Survey*, Washington, DC: AAM.

Benhamou, Françoise (1998), 'The Contradictions of *Désétatisation:* Museums in France', in Peter B. Boorsma, Annemoon van Hemel and Niki van der Wielen (eds), *Privatization and Culture: Experiences in the Arts, Heritage and Cultural Industries in Europe*, Dordrecht: Kluwer Academic Publishers, pp. 95–110.

Boorsma, Peter B. (1998), 'Privatizing the Muse – and all that Jazz', in Peter B. Boorsma, Annemoon van Hemel and Niki van der Wielen (eds), *Privatization and Culture: Experiences in the Arts, Heritage and Cultural Industries in Europe*, Dordrecht: Kluwer Academic Publishers, pp. 23–45.

Cannon-Brookes, Peter (1996), 'Cultural–Economic Analysis of Art Museums: a British Curator's Viewpoint', in Victor A. Ginsburgh and Pierre-Michel Menger (eds), *Economics of the Arts: Selected Essays*, Amsterdam: Elsevier, pp. 255–74.

Corporation for Public Broadcasting (2000), *Public Broadcasting Revenue, 1999*, Washington, DC: CPB.

Creigh-Tyte, Stephen (1998), 'Mixed Economy and Culture: Britain's Experience', in Peter B. Boorsma, Annemoon van Hemel and Niki van der Wielen (eds), *Privatization and Culture: Experiences in the Arts, Heritage and Cultural Industries in Europe*, Dordrecht: Kluwer Academic Publishers, pp. 183–97.

Donoghue, Freda, Helmut K. Anheier and Lester M. Salamon (1999), *Uncovering the Nonprofit Sector in Ireland: Its Economic Value and Significance*, Baltimore, MD and Dublin: Johns Hopkins University and National College of Ireland.

Frey, Bruno S. (1994), 'Cultural Economics and Museum Behaviour', *Scottish Journal of Political Economy*, 41, 3, 325–55, reprinted as 'For Art's Sake: Open Up the Vaults', in Bruno S. Frey (2000), *Arts & Economics: Analysis & Cultural Policy*, Berlin: Springer, pp. 35–47.

Frey, Bruno S. and Werner W Pommerehne (1989), *Muses and Markets: Explorations in the Economics of the Arts*, Oxford: Basil Blackwell.

Frey, Bruno S. and Werner W. Pommerehne (1990), 'A Comparative Institutional Analysis in the Arts: The Theater', in Michael Hechter, Jarl-Dieter Opp and Reinhard Wippler (eds), *Social Institutions: Their Emergence, Maintenance and Effects*, Berlin: Walter de Gruyter, pp. 171–86, reprinted in Ruth Towse (ed.) (1997), *Cultural Economics: The Arts, the Heritage and the Media Industries*, vol. II, Cheltenham, UK and Lyme, USA: Edward Elgar, pp. 483–98.

Grampp, William (1996), 'A Colloquy about Art Museums: Economics Engages Museology', in Victor A. Ginsburgh and Pierre-Michel Menger (eds), *Economics of the Arts: Selected Essays*, Amsterdam: Elsevier, pp. 221–54.

Hansmann, Henry B. (1980), 'The Role of Nonprofit Enterprises', *Yale Law Journal*, 89 (5), 835–901.

Hansmann, Henry B. (1986), 'Nonprofit Enterprise in the Performing Arts', in Paul J. DiMaggio (ed.), *Nonprofit Enterprise in the Arts: Studies in Mission & Constraint*, New York and Oxford: Oxford University Press, pp. 17–40.

Heilbrun, James (1988), 'Nonprofit versus Profit-making Firms: A Comment', *Journal of Cultural Economics*, 12 (2), 87–92, reprinted in Ruth Towse (ed.) (1997), *Cultural Economics: The Arts, the Heritage and the Media Industries*, vol. II, Cheltenham, UK and Lyme, USA: Edward Elgar, pp. 425–30.

Hutter, Michael (1997), 'From Public to Private Rights in the Arts Sector', *Boekmancahier*, 32, 170–76.

Klaic, Dragan (1998), 'Unlike Airlines and Phone Companies: Performing Arts in Europe', in Peter B. Boorsma, Annemoon van Hemel and Niki van der Wielen (eds), *Privatization and Culture: Experiences in the Arts, Heritage and Cultural Industries in Europe,* Dordrecht: Kluwer Academic Publishers, pp. 170–82.

Netzer, Dick (2006), 'Cultural Policy: An American View', in V. Ginsburgh and D. Throsby (eds), *Handbook of the Economics of Art and Culture,* Amsterdam: North-Holland, pp. 1224–51.

Peacock, Alan (1998), 'The Economist and Heritage Policy: A Review of the Issues', in Alan Peacock (ed.), *Does the Past have a Future? The Political Economy of Heritage,* London: Institute of Economic Affairs, pp. 1–26.

Peacock, Alan and Christine Godfrey (1974), 'The Economics of Museums and Galleries', *Lloyds Bank Review,* 111, 17–28

Salamon, Lester M., Helmut K. Anheier, Regina List, Stefan Toepler, S. Wojciech Sokolowski and Associates (1999), *Global Civil Society: Dimensions of the Profit Sector,* Baltimore, MD: The Johns Hopkins Center for Civil Society Studies.

Schuster, J. Mark (1998), 'Neither Public Nor Private: The Hybridization of Museums', *Journal of Cultural Economics,* 22, (2–3), 127–50.

Seaman, Bruce A. (1985), 'Price Discrimination in the Arts', in Virginia Lee Owen and William S. Hendon (eds), *Managerial Economics for the Arts,* Akron, Ohio: Association for Cultural Economics, pp. 47–60, reprinted in Ruth Towse (ed.) (1997), *Cultural Economics: The Arts, the Heritage and the Media Industries,* vol. II, Cheltenham, UK and Lyme, USA: Edward Elgar, pp. 434–48.

Throsby, C. David and Glenn A. Withers (1979), *The Economics of the Performing Arts,* London and Melbourne: Edward Arnold.

Throsby, David (1985), 'Intervention Strategies in Arts Markets', in C. Richard Waits, William S. Hendon and Harold Horowitz (eds), *Governments and Culture,* Akron, Ohio: Association for Cultural Economics, pp. 16–28.

Throsby, David (1996), 'Government Support for the Arts and Culture: The Australian Model', paper contributed to a Forum on 'Stimulating a Philanthropic Culture for Australia's Creative Future', Museum of Contemporary Art, Sydney, 2 October.

Throsby, David (2000), *Economics and Culture,* Cambridge: Cambridge University Press.

US Census Bureau (2000), *1997 Economic Census, Arts, Recreation, and Entertainment, Geographic Area Series, United States,* EC97S71A-US(RV), Washington, DC: USCB.

US Census Bureau (2001), *1997 Economic Census, Arts, Recreation, and Entertainment, Subject Series, Summary,* EC97S715-0SM, Washington, DC: USCB.

West, Edwin G (1987), 'Nonprofit versus Profit Firms in the Performing Arts', *Journal of Cultural Economics,* 11 (2), 37–47, reprinted in Ruth Towse (ed.) (1997), *Cultural Economics: The Arts, the Heritage and the Media Industries,* vol. II, Cheltenham, UK and Lyme, USA: Edward Elgar, pp. 414–24.

West, Edwin G (1988), 'Government Grants to Nonprofit Firms: Still Searching for the Rationale', *Journal of Cultural Economics,* 12 (2), 93–5, reprinted in Ruth Towse (ed.) (1997), *Cultural Economics: The Arts, the Heritage and the Media Industries,* vol. II, Cheltenham, UK and Lyme, USA: Edward Elgar, pp. 431–3.

Further reading

Netzer (2006).

43 Opera and ballet
Ruth Towse

Opera and ballet have a common history and continue to share many economic features. They are specialized art forms that have developed over the last four centuries, requiring highly skilled performers on stage, an orchestra and a large body of back-stage staff, ranging from *répétiteurs* who rehearse the performers to specialist costume makers. Traditional opera and ballet companies consist of the 'star' principal performers and a large cast of company performers – the opera chorus and the *corps de ballet*. Both art forms make considerable physical demands on the performers and, as a result, the number of performances has to be carefully regulated. Opera and ballet are very often housed in the same theatre, which needs excellent acoustics and sight-lines; these are often old, heritage buildings that not only have limited seating capacity but are costly to maintain. Consequently, the opera house management has to programme both companies' performances and rehearsal time on stage. All these features add up to make opera and ballet the most expensive of the performing arts, with opera taking the lead.

The only study in cultural economics that has analysed opera and ballet together is the study of pricing which Blaug did in 1978 of the Royal Opera House Covent Garden, London's international opera house (hereafter ROH) that is home to the Royal Opera and the Royal Ballet (Blaug, 1997). This still stands out as an exercise in the microeconomics of a performing arts organization. Cultural economists have subsequently tended to concentrate on one particular aspect of present-day opera, the performed repertoire, with the focus on testing for the presence of the 'artistic deficit' predicted by Baumol's cost disease, and have had very little to say about ballet. By coincidence, the only microeconomic treatment of ballet is that by Schimmelpfennig (1997) on the pricing of the summer ballet season at the ROH. Other than that, there is an illuminating literature on the economic history of opera (see, for example, Rosselli, 1984) and of ballet (Schimmelpfennig, 2003). Smith (2003) is a broader study of dance, including ballet, in the USA.

Costs
Opera and ballet often absorb the lion's share of government subsidy to the performing arts, although they are least widely attended. In the UK in 2003, for example, opera received three times the amount of subsidy per attendance and ballet two and a half times compared to other Arts Council supported performing arts organizations, though they were attended by only 7 per cent of the population (Joy and Skinner, 2005).[1]

The costs of opera and ballet can be broken down into those associated with running the opera house or theatre, the fixed costs of maintaining the theatrical facilities and the marginal costs of each performance. Fixed costs of the theatrical facilities, in addition to those of maintaing the fabric of the building, consist of the outlay on lighting, stage management, costume and set construction staff and so on, and of the labour costs of those performers on a regular salary – the orchestra, chorus and company principals and the music staff – that are fixed costs for the duration of their contracts. Each production has its fixed costs (sets and costumes, rehearsal time) and there are marginal costs of each performance, chief among which are the fees to guest artists and other freelance performers. Ballet has other fixed costs: learning the steps of a ballet is an intensive process as the knowledge has to be transferred in person by an experienced choreographer or dancer. Dancers also need daily practice, which requires special rehearsal facilities provided by the ballet company. National ballet companies may also support a ballet school to train young dancers. Schimmelpfennig (2003) points out that ballet, as with other performing arts, has the structure of a natural monopoly, with high fixed costs and low marginal costs. To some extent that relationship is determined by the institutional arrangements for labour contracts, particularly in opera, as explained below.

The underlying causes of high costs are, however, complex and intimately tied to the economic history of opera and ballet, the typical repertoire performed and the economic organization of performance. It is because they are still so closely connected to the grand performance traditions and conventions of the nineteenth century that they are subject to high costs and prices and relatively small audiences.

Economic history of opera

The transition of opera supply from its initial court patronage in various Italian states to a highly developed private market which, in the eighteenth century, spread to London, Vienna and St Petersburg and, in the nineteenth, to New York and Buenos Aires, has been analysed in glorious detail by Rosselli (1984). The 'impresario system' organized and financed the whole chain of operatic production from the commissioning of the libretto and musical composition to box rental in theatres. Most of the operas performed today were first produced under this system in opera houses that were purpose-built for them and that we continue to use. However, this operatic repertoire was created in social and economic conditions of abundant and relatively cheap supply of orchestral musicians and chorus singers, with a few star principals, playing to capacity audiences of between 600 and 1500 who attended frequently. Some of the impresarios even made it pay; nowadays, however, the combination of large labour resources needed for this repertoire and limited seating capacity of the old opera houses conspires to make opera formidably expensive, so that only very high ticket prices could cover costs without some form of subvention.

The comparable economic history of German opera supply would look rather different since theatres and performing companies continue to be owned and managed by state authorities in German-speaking countries without a market developing. Today, Germany, with its 152 publicly owned theatre companies, probably supports more opera companies than any other country (King, 2001). Besides the 'A' houses – Munich, Berlin and Hamburg, for instance – where the company operates in its own house, many opera companies share the city's theatre with ballet, spoken drama and other uses. The typical German opera company tends to offer a broader repertoire than would be found in opera houses in other countries, regularly performing operetta and musicals with their 'classically' trained singers.[2] A major feature of German opera, which is (or was) also to be found in many East European countries, is that all salaried company members, including the performers, are civil servants, either of state or of city, and enjoy the same job protection and conditions of work as other state employees. That includes principal singers, who usually have a 'fixed' contract. This represents a huge fixed cost. By contrast, opera houses in the USA and the UK have developed as private non-profit organizations, which are in receipt of a mixture of public subsidy, private patronage and sponsorship; in these countries there is an active marketplace for singers, conductors, directors and set designers working freelance with contracts that are specific to a particular production and run of performances of an opera. The present-day costs of opera are thus influenced by its institutional economic history. The picture is very similar for ballet as it developed alongside opera until eventually it freed itself in the twentieth century (Schimmelpfennig, 2003).

Organization of performances

An important determinant of the cost of producing opera is the system by which performances are organized – by the *stagione* or in repertory. The *stagione* (meaning literally the 'season') is the classic Italian system whereby one opera is given a certain number of performances (usually six to ten) over several weeks, followed by a rehearsal period for the next opera production, during which the theatre is used for ballet, as well as for orchestral performances and chamber music, after which that opera is performed for its run, and so on.

Over the performing season from late autumn to the end of spring, perhaps six or eight operas are produced sequentially. This system is still followed in most opera houses in Italy, as well as elsewhere. Under the *stagione* system, principal singers are hired by the opera for the rehearsal period and the run of performances; to ensure good-quality performance, the demands made on the singing voice by opera and the need to protect vocal health are met by having only three or four performances of the opera per week. Ballet performances and rehearsals are similarly organized and programmed, alternating with the opera; many operas also require dancers as part of the production.

The repertory system of performance has nightly alternating performances of several operas and ballet in the repertory over the performing season or year. This system is to be found in most German opera houses. It facilitates more performances (of each opera and likely of more operatic works), some portion being revivals from previous performing seasons. It demands either a great deal from the company of performers or a larger company.[3] Many opera houses in practice operate a mixed system of *stagione* and repertory, meaning that an opera or ballet enters the repertoire for a season and is performed alternately with several others over a period of time. This clearly calls for much more careful planning of resource use as well as greater use of guest artists to supplement company principal performers and possibly also a much larger chorus.[4]

There is one other type of performance organization – the opera or ballet festival. Festivals run for a short period of the year, often the summer, and may make use of performers from the other companies in its productions or hire in a whole production with its performers during the summer break (Frey and Vautravers, 2000).

Repertoire

Although thousands of operas have been written, many of which even exist in performing editions, only a very small fraction of them is performed at all and of those there is a canon of the most commonly performed operas that are the mainstay of opera houses. *La Bohème, Madama Butterfly, La Traviata, Carmen, Il Barbiere di Siviglia* and *Le*

Nozze di Figaro are regularly to be found in the performance schedule of every opera house from Stockholm to Sydney. These are the operas that are popular with audiences worldwide and are reliable income-earners. Audiences fall dramatically for modern opera, even at reduced ticket prices, which cannot be performed without extra subsidy. The role of subsidy in encouraging the production of a wider and more risky repertoire has been analysed for the USA by Pierce (2000); however, Heilbrun (2001) found that the repertoire of US opera houses was shrinking. Krebs and Pommerehne (1995) look at this question in the wider context of the incentive structure of German opera houses and argue that managers there can afford to ignore audience tastes and instead put on productions that enhance their professional reputation with their peer group, including the less popular repertoire. The story is rather different with ballet. There are the 'war-horses' – *Swan Lake* and *Nutcracker* – that are ubiquitously performed, but there is also a modern repertoire that has established itself with audiences (Schimmelpfennig, 2003).

Besides its influence on demand and revenues, the choice of performed repertoire also has implications for costs. Some operas and ballets are more expensive to put on than others because they demand more stars (Verdi's *Aida* is an example of an opera that can rarely be made to pay in a conventional opera house because of its casting requirements) and/or a larger chorus or *corps de ballet*, complex sets or lighting, a large orchestra, unusual instrumentation or effects, and suchlike. The management has some freedom to decide on the quality of performers it wishes to hire (and more freedom with the *stagione* system), but certain roles are difficult to cast with 'ordinary' company principals. These roles invite star performance, and uneven casting shows up all too easily. With smaller roles there is some scope for hiring young singers and dancers or casting members of the chorus, allowing cost savings but, by and large, the decision of repertoire dictates 'fixed factors'. Because the demand for performers is a derived demand, the frequency of the performed repertoire determines the demand for principal singers and dancers; freelance principal singers, who have to finance their own learning of the repertoire (company singers/chorus are coached by house *répétiteurs*) tend to supply roles from the standard performed operas, making it more difficult and expensive to hire singers for roles outside the standard repertoire (Towse, 1993).

Pricing policy

All theatres, including opera houses, practise price discrimination according to part of the house, night of the week and so on. In opera and ballet, this is taken somewhat further, with prices being raised for a star singer or dancer or for some operas (for example, those of *Der Ring des Nibelungens*) or reduced to attract audiences to modern opera (Blaug, 1997). A difference arises here between those countries in which the subscription system of payment (*abonnement*) prevails and those where it does not (for example, the UK). When patrons subscribe for a whole season, a mix of repertoire is charged for in the package and this can 'cross-subsidize' less popular repertoires with popular productions. Opera may in part be subsidized by ballet, which tends to generate higher net revenues than opera (Blaug, 1997).

Opera house management

All the points raised above are the subject of management decisions in each opera house. Different approaches have been taken to analysing this topic: a purely management

approach that considers the management structure and its ability to cope with decision making (Auvinen, 2000), a microeconomic approach, looking at the opera house
as a firm (Blaug, 1997), and a political-economy approach that analyses incentives and
agency problems relating to the state subsidy of opera (Krebs and Pommerehne, 1995;
Towse, 2001).

Using case studies of national opera companies in several countries, Auvinen (2000)
shows that, although management structures differ markedly, all have to make the same
decisions and, with an international market for opera, managers face the same set of
prices. Blaug's study of the ROH for the financial year 1974/75 made this point very
strongly: to be an 'international' opera house means paying international prices to international stars (without whom there would be little difference between a 'national' opera
and an international opera company). He concluded that the biggest cost savings could
be made by reducing the number of international stars hired (conductors, producers and
singers). Put another way, maintaining the same 'quality' would mean that costs would
inevitably rise and, unless subsidy were increased, prices would have to rise accordingly.
By the time of my study of the market for singers and the outlay on them by opera companies in the UK (Towse, 1993), though, the proportion of the opera budget spent on
singers had fallen. There are two explanations for this: first, during the 1970s, the rate of
increase in performers' earnings had fallen well behind those in the economy at large, as
the report on inflation in the performed arts in the UK (including data on the ROH) by
Peacock *et al.* (1997) showed; second, the cost of managerial salaries and of items such
as the materials for scenery that had risen with inflation increased, thus reducing the
proportion of the budget on artistic personnel.

Krebs and Pommerehne (1995) have argued that, in Germany, managers have little
incentive to manage their budgets carefully because, as with all publicly controlled
bodies, revenues in excess of costs are not retained by the theatre, and they have every
incentive to squeeze as much out of the state or city administration as possible for 'their'
company. That has also been the case in Italy; Italian opera houses have been 'priva-
tized', meaning turned into non-profit organizations in receipt of subsidy, the typical
model in the USA and the UK, instead of being state-owned and managed. That is
not necessarily a safeguard against special pleading, as the case of the ROH has shown
(Towse, 2001).

Final comments

The literature reviewed here relates to grand opera and Romantic ballet, and does not
consider smaller companies that tour in order to spread the fixed costs of a their productions by taking them to audiences in different locations, or that perform chamber works.
The debundling of the opera and ballet performing companies from the management
of the opera house building and the economics of touring both are interesting topics
for further research. A further question could be the 'make-or-buy' decision whether to
retain a resident ballet company and/or orchestra or to hire it in for performances.

There have been other developments that spread access to opera and ballet both physically and psychologically: education work aims to form tastes and overcome the psychological barrier, but perhaps even more significant is the increased use of 'mass' media
that have vastly increased access, namely producing DVDs, relaying performances to a
screen outside the theatre and now digitalized transmission by satellite to other venues

(usually cinemas) in real time. Information technology is also used to offer far more information about the theatre, the productions, cast, rehearsing and so on. These developments could lead to much wider appreciation of opera and ballet and, in economic terms, they certainly overcome the limitations that make their cost per attendee so high. These are excellent subjects for research.

Notes

1. Few countries appear to report participation in opera and ballet separately; ballet is included with opera or with dance in some places, while in others, especially in Europe, both are reported together with spoken theatre. Even more confusing, opera may also be included with 'music'. According to Eurostat (2007), the overall figure for participation in opera, ballet and dance for the 27 countries in the EU was 18 per cent.
2. In 1998/9, there were 6961 performances of opera, 1854 of operetta, 3296 of musicals and 2692 of ballet in Germany (King, 2001).
3. Singers are protected by their conditions of work, which in Germany even stipulate what roles a singer may be required to sing in his or her *Fach* (literally, 'compartment'); the management, however, has the right to direct the services of principal singers on a long-term contract as it sees fit within those limitations. On some occasions when 'substitute' operas are to be performed, principal singers may find out only a few days beforehand that they are expected to sing a major role in their *Fach* repertory.
4. Opera houses in the UK work on a mixed system; the English National Opera, which performs six opera nights a week from September to June, giving around 200 performances (about twice as many as a major German opera house and four times as many as a provincial Italian one) requires two full-time choruses to supply this performance schedule.

See also:

Chapter 10: Baumol's cost disease; Chapter 15: Costs of production; Chapter 36: Management of the arts; Chapter 44: Orchestras; Chapter 47: Performing arts; Chapter 49: Pricing the arts; Chapter 59: Theatre.

References

Auvinen, Tuomas (2000), 'Policy Equates Resources? Managerial and Financial Structures of Five European Opera Houses', paper presented at the 11th International Conference of the Association for Cultural Economics International, Minneapolis.
Blaug, Mark (1997), 'Why Are Covent Garden Seat Prices So High?', in Ruth Towse (ed.), *Cultural Economics: The Arts, the Heritage and the Media Industries*, vol. I, Cheltenham, UK and Lyme, USA: Edward Elgar, pp. 302–22.
Eurostat (2007), *Cultural Statistics*, Luxembourg: European Communities, http://epp.eurostat.ec.europa.eu/cache/ITY_OFFPUB/KS-77-07-296/EN/KS-77-07-296-EN.PDF.
Frey, Bruno S. and Isabelle Vautravers (2000), 'Special Exhibitions and Festivals: Culture's Booming Path to Glory', in Bruno S. Frey (ed.), *Arts & Economics*, Berlin: Springer, pp. 67–93.
Heilbrun, James (2001), 'Empirical Evidence of a Decline in Repertory Diversity among America Opera Companies 1991/92 to 1997/98', *Journal of Cultural Economics*, 25 (1), 63–72.
Joy, Alan and Megan Skinner (2005), *A Statistical Survey of Regularly Funded Arts Organisations 2002/3*, London: Arts Council of England.
King, Timothy (2001), 'Evaluating Theatrical Subsidies: the Case of German Opera', unpublished MS, timki@attglobal.net.
Krebs, Susanne and Werner Pommerehne (1995), 'Politico-Economic Interactions of German Public Performing Arts Institutions', *Journal of Cultural Economics*, 19 (1), 17–32.
Peacock, Alan, Eddie Shoesmith and Geoffrey Millner (1997), 'Inflation and the Performed Arts', in R. Towse (ed.), *Cultural Economics: The Arts, the Heritage and the Media Industries*, vol. II, Cheltenham, UK and Lyme, USA: Edward Elgar, pp. 319–60.
Pierce, John (2000), 'Programmatic Risk-taking by American Opera Companies', *Journal of Cultural Economics*, 24 (1), 45–63.
Rosselli, John (1984), *The Opera Industry in Italy from Cimarosa to Verdi*, Cambridge: Cambridge University Press.
Rosselli, John (1997), 'From Princely Service to the Open Market: Singers of Italian Opera and their Patrons, 1600–1850', in Ruth Towse (ed.), *Cultural Economics: The Arts, the Heritage and the Media Industries*, vol. I, Cheltenham, UK and Lyme, USA: Edward Elgar, pp. 37–68.

Schimmelpfennig, Jörg (1997) 'Demand for Ballet: a Non-parametric analysis of the Royal Ballet Summer Season', *Journal of Cultural Economics*, 21, 119–27.

Schimmelpfennig, Jörg (2003) 'Ballet', in Ruth Towse (2003), *A Handbook of Cultural Economics*, Cheltenham, UK and Northampton, MA, USA: Edward Elgar, pp. 85–90.

Smith, T. (2003), *Raising the Barre: the Geographical, Financial and Economic, Trends of Non-profit Dance Companies*, Washington, DC National Endowment for the Arts Research Division Report No. 44.

Towse, Ruth (1993), *Singers in the Marketplace*, Oxford: Clarendon Press.

Towse, Ruth (2001), 'Quis custodiet? or Managing the Management: The Case of the Royal Opera House, Covent Garden', *International Journal of Arts Management*, 3 (3), 38–50, reprinted in Ruth Towse (2007), *Recent Developments in Cultural Economics*, Cheltenham, UK and Northampton, MA, USA: Edward Elgar, pp. 219–31.

Towse, Ruth (2010), *A Textbook of Cultural Economics*, Cambridge: Cambridge University Press.

Further reading

I have found the economic history of opera fascinating; Rosselli's (1984) book and a shorter article (Rosselli, 1997) are excellent. Schimmelpfennig (2003) sketches the development of ballet. All the points made in this chapter are developed in my *Textbook of Cultural Economics* (2010).

44 Orchestras
William A. Luksetich

Baumol and Bowen (1966) painted a dismal future for the performing arts in general and symphony orchestras in particular. In their view, costs of staging performances would increase at a faster rate than would their earned income because opportunities for cost reductions are limited. Contributions would probably not increase at a rate sufficient to cover this growing 'income gap'; hence the presence of a 'cost disease' affecting organizations in the performing arts. Consequently, private and government subsidies are inevitable if orchestras are to continue to operate as in the past. They noted subsidies to the arts could be justified: 'If one agrees that the performing arts confer general benefits on the community as a whole . . . the arts are public goods whose benefits demonstrably exceed the receipts one can hope to collect at the box office' (ibid., pp. 385–6).

Hansmann (1981) disagrees, arguing that organizations in the performing arts are not for profit because they face high fixed costs and a relatively small demand. Moreover, their fixed costs have risen faster than their variable costs and revenues. They must rely on a system of price discrimination if they are to cover their costs, because there is no one price that will exceed their average total cost. Consequently, a system of price discrimination has developed whereby the price is set in the inelastic range of demand with the expectation that patrons will voluntarily make a tax-deductible donation to the organization.

Cost disease: empirical tests and evidence

Baumol and Bowen underestimated the ability of non-profit performing arts organizations to adjust. Throsby (1994) cited studies examining organizations in the performing arts and found that

> the combined impacts of production adjustments, increased demand, and generally rising levels of unearned revenue have countered any tendency towards a secular rise in deficits among performance companies, suggesting that although the cost disease will doubtless continue to present the performing arts with difficult problems, it is unlikely to be terminal. (Ibid., p. 16)

Felton (1994–5) addressed the issue of whether symphony orchestras suffered the cost disease and found that, because of productivity lags, orchestras have temporarily suffered budget deficits. By increasing the number of ensemble performances, touring more frequently and offering summer concerts, for example, the orchestras have been able to overcome this problem. Volpe (1991) constructed a growth model to test whether the composition of orchestra output affected the income gap. He found that the income gap was decreasing for all orchestras in his sample, which included orchestras throughout the American Symphony Orchestra League's (ASOL) budget classification. Volpe also found that the deficit for all but the smaller market orchestras was sensitive to the mix of concerts offered, and concluded that there is strong evidence that orchestras to some extent can exert control over their deficits. Brooks (2000) argued that opportunities to overcome any income gap facing orchestras differ according to their relative size. Drawing on empirical research, he concluded that larger orchestras should diversify product lines, use technological innovations and expand audiences through education programmes, whereas smaller orchestras would be served by expanding their philanthropic base.

Economies of scale and scope

Sources of productivity increases can result from scale economies, as research by Baumol and Bowen (1996), Globerman and Book (1974) and Lange *et al.* (1985) has shown. The last-mentioned study found that the number of concerts required to achieve minimum average cost was significantly lower than shown by the other studies and that, while orchestras performing fewer concerts have higher average costs, they may have been at minimum cost given their market size.

Symphony orchestras offer a variety of concerts: regular concerts, summer concerts, concerts on tour, ensemble concerts and other offerings, such as youth and other concerts. Studies that use concerts or attendance as output measures result in an amalgamation variable, which is not homogeneous. The mix of 'outputs' offered by symphony orchestras reveals them to be multi-product non-profit enterprises; consequently, cost studies focusing on economies of scale are misdirected.

Lange and Luksetich (1993) noted that focusing on scale economies directs attention on whether services provided by firms in markets where demand is limited are more expensive. The question therefore arises: should they be combined with other firms producing similar services, resulting in specialization and greater efficiency? The authors argued that, in multi-product firms, the concern is also the interaction between the cost of one service and the amount of other services provided; that is, whether economies of scope exist in the provision of the multitude of services offered. This study revealed that scale economies were not a usual source of efficiency for symphony orchestras. Orchestras serving major markets benefit from scope economies to a far greater extent than those serving smaller markets. Consequently, policies encouraging the diversification of services of the larger orchestras and encouraging the specialization of services offered by smaller orchestras would be efficient if the only concern were costs. Moreover, as Felton (1994–5) noted, the increased diversification of services offered by major orchestras has been a source of increased efficiency, while Volpe (1991) showed that it also results in greater revenues.

Pricing of orchestra services

Hansmann (1981) noted that firms in the performing arts face significantly high fixed costs relative to their marginal costs. Consequently there may be no one price that covers average total costs. Ticket revenues can be increased by price discrimination. Because of the difficulty of identifying demand elasticities of individual patrons or groups of patrons, orchestras may set ticket prices below the revenue-maximizing price in an effort to induce patrons to make a voluntary tax-deductible contribution to the orchestras – a system of voluntary price discrimination.

Attempts to find evidence that symphony orchestras rely on price discrimination to enhance their revenues have taken two routes. One route has been to determine whether orchestras set their price in the inelastic range of demand. Those taking this approach conjectured that if they do so, orchestras are attempting to induce patrons to make a voluntary tax-deductible contribution. In their initial tests of this hypothesis, Lange and Luksetich (1984) estimated price and other demand elasticities for three sets of symphony orchestras as classified by the ASOL as major, metropolitan and urban/regional, based on their budget size.

Using data from the ASOL comparative reports, the authors found that the 30 orchestras classified as major orchestras on average charged prices well below revenue-maximizing prices, that is, in the inelastic range of their demand curve. Prices charged by the other groups of orchestras tended to be in the elastic range of demand. From this and other evidence, it was argued that the price-inelastic demand facing major orchestras was not due to the lack of substitutes but was a deliberate strategy to induce patrons to donate.

Felton (1992) also found that larger orchestras tended to price in the inelastic range of demand and that smaller orchestras had higher price elasticities. She estimated the price elasticity of demand facing individual orchestras and found a wide range, which largely reflected differences in market characteristics and pricing strategies of the individual orchestras. In a second paper (1994–5), Felton's estimates show price elasticities of demand much closer to those reported by Lange and Luksetich (1984) and therefore that orchestras could increase revenues significantly from ticket sales by increasing ticket prices. She did not speculate on whether this strategy would affect donations.

Two studies took a second route and attempted to test directly whether symphony orchestras practise price discrimination to increase donations. Seaman (1987) examined whether firms in the non-profit arts sector offered a greater number of price selections for their performance than those in the for-profit arts sector. He found that non-profit arts firms, including symphony orchestras, charged a greater variety of prices than for-profit arts organizations and that, in the non-profit arts sector, only operatic organizations discriminated in price more than symphony orchestras.

In an effort to tie the number of price categories to donations, Seaman examined whether the number of price categories was correlated with the number of donor categories (each category presumably offered different amenities to donors). Very few of the symphony orchestras tied the purchase of subscription tickets to a particular donor category. He did find that price discrimination is more prevalent among those art forms, specifically opera and symphony orchestras, that have higher fixed costs. Moreover, high fixed cost organizations exhibit a greater correlation between the number of prices charged and the number of donation categories. Seaman concluded that the evidence he presented was largely consistent with Hansmann's argument concerning price discrimination in the arts.

Lange and Luksetich (1995) used time-series data from ASOL's Comparative Reports to examine the behaviour of symphony orchestras. They tested whether prices charged by the various classes of symphony orchestras were in the inelastic range of demand and whether this resulted in increased gifts from private individuals. For the major orchestras, on average, lower than revenue-maximizing prices increase donations. However, revenue losses from the lower prices were not completely offset by the gain in donations: the price was set too low. There was no relationship between price charged and donations for metropolitan orchestras. For orchestras classified as urban/regional (orchestras serving smaller markets), lower prices resulted in lower revenues from donations. It was speculated that, for these orchestras, ticket price was a signal of quality, and higher prices would result in an increased willingness to donate. The results indicated that, on average, all orchestras in all size classifications could increase their net revenues by increasing ticket prices and only the largest would suffer any decrease in revenues from donations.

Goals and fundraising

Economic theory assumes that individuals are maximizers and private for-profit business firms are profit-maximizers. Since non-profits cannot distribute any surplus over costs to the owners or organizers of the institution, it is generally assumed that they are likely to maximize their output, quality, budget or some combination of these goals. Hansmann argued that the goals of non-profit firms in the arts could be ascertained by examining how they spend funds they receive that do not require specific services to be performed (lump-sum grants, in his parlance).

Lange *et al.* (1986) presented results showing that major orchestras spent unrestricted funds in a manner consistent with quality-maximization goals. Although these funds were used to increase administrative expenses, the increased administrative expenses were in turn positively related to quality-enhancing expenditures (as measured by artistic, production, promotion and other expenses per concert). It appeared that budget-maximizing and quality-maximizing were complementary goals in the case of the major orchestras. Estimates showed that both the metropolitan and the smaller market orchestras had output maximization as their major goal. In both cases, the unconditional grants received by orchestras were positively related to the number of concerts, which in turn resulted in greater attendance.

Studies concerned with the fundraising activities of symphony orchestras generally conclude that they do not follow Steinberg's (1986) admonition that they spend up to the point where the marginal benefits from fundraising expenditures equal their marginal costs (for example, see Lange *et al.*, 1987). An examination of the efficiency of symphony orchestra fundraising efforts using data envelopment analysis showed significant inefficiencies. Moreover, it showed that orchestras could learn much about fundraising by examining how orchestras in their 'peer group' conducted their efforts; see Luksetich and Hughes (1997).

Brooks (1999) investigated whether government grants to symphony orchestras 'crowded out' private giving or whether they enhanced private donations. The latter would occur if private donors believed that National Endowment for the Arts grants provided a stamp of excellence on the grantee. His results showed that government grants and private donations were independent of each other. Lange and Luksetich found that, for major orchestras, grants from governments requiring services enhanced private donations, while unconditional grants appeared to replace private giving. They presumed that the former types of grants had a matching provision. Their estimates indicated that both types of grants offset private giving for metropolitan orchestras and that conditional grants crowded out private giving to the small market orchestras.

Recent research, different directions

Recent research on symphony orchestras has taken a different direction. Rather than focusing on determining orchestra goals, the optimal size of orchestras, the cost of producing orchestra services, the demand for their services and so on, the new research has focused on orchestra-hiring procedures, education issues, ownership changes and repertoire determinants.

Goldin and Rouse (2006) examined whether the adoption of 'blind' auditions by symphony orchestras increased the probability of women being hired and advanced in position in orchestras. Their results showed that such auditions increased the probability that a woman would advance from the preliminary round, and by seven times the probability she would be selected in the final round of auditions. Moreover, they report that the adoptions of 'blind' auditions explained 30 per cent of the increase in the proportion of females among newly hired players and 25 per cent of the increase in the percentage of females to succeed in their chosen field and, most probably, they increased the quality of orchestra performances.

In his master's thesis, Ciocoiu (2009) notes that previous research shows a weak effect of human capital on earning differentials and occupational status. Nevertheless, he attempts to determine whether the earnings and employment status of orchestra conductors can be explained by schooling operationalized as social capital. Ciocoiu argues that schooling has social capital effects and finds that it has significant effects on earning and employment status for Conductors Guild Members. The importance of the finding that social capital is a predictor of the economic output of conductors provides a reason and a guide to invest in their education.

Before 1997, symphony orchestras in Australia were structured as a government department. By 2000 all six of the orchestras were individual corporate entities. Boyle (2007) examined how changes in ownership and organizational structure affected orchestral activities and the professional identity of musicians. Using orchestra data and surveys of musicians, Boyle found that orchestras have been able to increase revenues, develop stronger links to their communities and attain some increase in artistic success. Maintaining these higher levels of achievement has been difficult, however. Orchestras in smaller markets have found it difficult to maintain their level of operation under the new structure.

There has been recent debate over whether grants from government or private sources influence music institutions toward particular programmes. Hughes and Luksetich (2009) have extended this research in an attempt to determine whether grants to American symphony orchestras have an effect on orchestra repertoire. They found no systematic causal relation between grants from the various sources and the nature of the repertoire, that is, pieces from various periods, traditional versus contemporary and so on. They did find, however, that federal government grants from the National Endowment for the Arts (NEA) and local plus state grants appear to be strong determinants of expenditures for guest artists. Hughes and Luksetich found that contemporary pieces, music composed in the past 25 years by living composers, as a percentage of total pieces played per orchestras, was positively and significantly related to predicted expenditures for guest artists. These results imply that NEA grants and state and local grants are complementary and are used by orchestras to present works of relatively newer artists to their audiences.

See also:

Chapter 10: Baumol's cost disease; Chapter 15: Costs of production; Chapter 36; Management of the arts; Chapter 42: Non-profit organizations; Chapter 43: Opera and ballet; Chapter 47: Performing arts; Chapter 49: Pricing the arts.

References

Baumol, William and William Bowen (1966), *Performing Arts – The Economic Dilemma*, New York: The Twentieth Century Fund.

Boyle, Stephen (2007), 'Ownership, Efficiency and Identity: The Transition of Australia's Symphony Orchestras from Government Departments to Corporate Entities', unpublished Ph.D. dissertation, Macquarie University, Sydney, Australia.

Brooks, Arthur (1999), 'Do Public Subsidies Leverage Private Philanthropy for the Arts? Empirical Evidence on Symphony Orchestras', *Nonprofit and Voluntary Sector Quarterly*, 28 (1), 32–45.

Brooks, Arthur (2000), 'The "Income Gap" and the Health of Arts Nonprofits: Arguments, Evidence, and Strategies', *Nonprofit Management and Leadership*, 13 (1), 5–15.

Castaner, Xavier and Lorenzo Campos (2002), 'The Determinants of Artistic Innovation: Bringing in the Role of Organizations', *Journal of Cultural Economics*, 26 (1), 29–52.

Ciocoiu, Petru (2009), 'The Effects of Schooling on Earnings and Employment in the Labour Market for Conductors', unpublished MA thesis, Erasmus University, Rotterdam, The Netherlands.

Felton, Marianne V. (1992), 'On the Assumed Inelasticity of Demand for the Performing Arts', *Journal of Cultural Economics*, 16 (1), 1–12.

Felton, Marianne V. (1994–5), 'Evidence of the Existence of the Cost Disease in the Performing Arts', *Journal of Cultural Economics*, 18 (4), 301–12.

Globerman, Steven and Sam Book (1974), 'Statistical Cost Functions for Performing Arts Organizations', *Southern Economic Journal*, 40, 668–71.

Goldin, Claudia and Cecilia Rouse (2006), 'Orchestrating Impartiality: The Impact of "Blind" Auditions on Female Musicians', *American Economic Review*, 90 (4), 715–41.

Hansmann, Henry (1981), 'Nonprofit Firms in the Performing Arts', *Bell Journal of Economics*, 12 (2), 341–61.

Heilbrun, James (2001), 'Empirical Evidence of a Decline in Repertory Diversity among American Opera Companies 1982/83 to 1997/98', *Journal of Cultural Economics*, 25 (1), 63–72.

Hughes, Patricia and William Luksetich (2009), 'Effects of Subsidies on Symphony Orchestra Repertoire'. Working paper 2010-03, http://www.stcloudstate.edu/economics/papers.asp.

Lange, Mark and William Luksetich (1984), 'Demand Elasticities for Symphony Orchestras', *Journal of Cultural Economics*, 8 (1), 29–48.

Lange, Mark and William Luksetich (1993), 'The Cost of Producing Symphony Orchestra Services', *Journal of Cultural Economics*, 17 (1), 1–15.

Lange, Mark and William Luksetich (1995), 'A Simultaneous Model of Symphony Orchestra Behaviour', *Journal of Cultural Economics*, 19 (1), 49–68.

Lange, Mark, William Luksetich and Philip Jacobs (1986), 'Managerial Objectives of Symphony Orchestras', *Managerial and Decision Economics*, 7, 273–8.

Lange, Mark, William Luksetich and Philip Jacobs (1987), 'The Productivity of Symphony Orchestra Campaign Expenditures', in William Hendon and Virginia Owen (eds), *Managerial Economics for the Arts*, Akron, OH: University of Akron Press, pp. 35–42.

Lange, Mark, William Luksetich, Philip Jacobs and James Bullard (1985), 'Cost Functions for Symphony Orchestras', *Journal of Cultural Economics*, 9 (2), 71–85.

Luksetich, William and Patricia Hughes (1997), 'Efficiency of Fund-Raising Activities: An Application of Data Envelopment Analysis', *Nonprofit and Voluntary Sector Quarterly*, 26 (1), 73–84.

O'Hagan, John and Adriana Neligan (2005), 'State Subsidies and Repertoire Conventionality in the Nonprofit English Theater Sector: An Econometric Analysis', *Journal of Cultural Economics*, 29 (1), 35–57.

Pierce, J. Lamar (2000), 'Programmatic Risk Taking by American Opera Companies', *Journal of Cultural Economics*, 24 (1), 45–63.

Seaman, Bruce (1987), 'Price Discrimination in the Arts', in William Hendon and Virginia Owens (eds), *Managerial Economics for the Arts*, Akron, OH: University of Akron Press, pp. 47–60.

Steinberg, Richard (1986), 'Should Donors Care About Fundraising?', in Susan Rose-Ackerman (ed.), *The Economics of Nonprofit Institutions*, New York: Oxford University Press, pp. 347–66.

Throsby, David (1994), 'The Production and Consumption of the Arts: A View of Cultural Economics', *Journal of Economic Literature*, XXXII, 1–29.

Volpe, Joseph (1991), 'The Income Gap and Symphony Orchestras', May, unpublished master's thesis, Department of Economics, University of Nevada, Las Vegas.

Further reading

Work on artistic innovation and programming repertoire over the last decade by Castaner and Campos (2002), by Pierce (2000),and Heilbrun (2001) on opera and by O'Hagan and Neligan (2005) on theatre is followed up by Hughes and Luksetich (2009), who provide similar information for symphony orchestras in the USA.

45 Participation
Charles M. Gray

The arts are complicated phenomena in modern society. They are, among other things, hobbies, means of personal expression, spectator entertainments, social statements, offensive activities and debatable policy issues. But in all of these manifestations, they retain a unifying theme: the arts are economic activities, consuming resources that have alternative uses. As is made amply clear throughout this *Handbook*, production and consumption of the arts constitute supply and demand in more or less well-developed markets. Patterns of participation in the arts, as defined for the purposes of this chapter, provide information on the demand side of the arts marketplace and, in some instances, possible insights into market equilibrium outcomes.

The past three decades have seen a burgeoning interest in public participation in the arts, by which is meant the extent that citizens engage in artistic activities, a few as professional artists of some stripe, but most as either audience or hobbyist. The US National Endowment for the Arts, the chief arts policy-making and implementation body of the federal government, has to date sponsored six national surveys, in 1982, 1985, 1992, 1997, 2002 and 2008, to determine the extent and nature of public participation. Even a cursory search through websites of the cultural ministries of many other nations will yield corresponding results of their own arts participation surveys.

This chapter examines the topic through an economist's lens and offers typical empirical measures based on that perspective. The focus here is on participation as an audience member or visitor, that is, as a consumer of the arts rather than a producer, although the US Surveys of Public Participation in the Arts (SPPAs) also include information on this latter form of participation. Indeed, the SPPAs provide a wealth of information supporting endless analyses by interested researchers.

The chief participation indicator used here is whether or not a survey respondent participated in, or attended, one of several arts activities during the prior 12-month period. A subset of these arts is characterized as 'benchmark' arts, and these, listed in the order of presentation in the survey results, are jazz, classical music, opera, musical theatre, non-musical theatre, ballet, and museums and galleries.

The following section briefly describes results of the 2008 SPPA, with comparisons with earlier surveys. The next section introduces hypotheses drawn from the economics perspective and describes results of empirical tests. The summary and conclusions bring the chapter to a close.

Arts participation in the USA

Table 45.1 displays summary results of selected arts participation surveys in the USA, up to and including the most recent, 2008. It is clear that a minority, and sometimes a very small minority, of the adult population participates in the arts in a given year, and it is also clear that there has been a general decline in arts participation over the years since the initial survey in 1982. We should note that the 2008 survey was conducted during

Table 45.1   *Arts participation: US adults attending an activity at least once in the past 12 months*

	Percentage of adults attending/visiting/reading				Millions of adults, 2008
	1982	1992	2002	2008	
Music					
Jazz*	9.6	10.6	10.8	7.8	17.6
Classical music*	13.0	12.5	11.6	9.3	20.9
Opera*	3.0	3.3	3.2	2.1	4.8
Latin music	n.a.	n.a.	n.a.	4.9	10.9
Performing arts festivals	n.a.	n.a.	n.a.	20.8	46.7
Theatre					
Musical theatre*	18.6	17.4	17.1	16.7	37.6
Non-musical theatre*	11.9	13.5	12.3	9.4	21.2
Dance					
Ballet*	4.2	4.7	3.9	2.9	6.6
Other dance	n.a.	7.1	6.3	5.2	11.7
Visual arts					
Art museums/galleries*	22.1	26.7	26.5	22.7	51.1
Art/crafts fairs and festivals	39.0	40.7	33.4	24.5	55.1
Parks and historic sites	37.0	34.5	31.6	24.9	56.0
Literature	56.9	54.0	46.7	50.2	112.8
Benchmark arts activities	39.0	41.0	39.4	34.6	77.8

Note: *Benchmark arts activity.

Source: National Endowment for the Arts, *2008 Survey of Public Participation in the Arts*, Research report No. 49, November 2009, Figure 1-3, 3.

an economic recession, and this may well account for some of the most recent decline, although the extent is unknown and probably unknowable.

Participation rates range from a high of 50.2 per cent for literature to a low of 2.1 per cent for live attendance at opera, generally regarded as the most complex performing art. Performing arts festivals attract about one-fifth of the adult population in a given year, and arts/crafts festivals draw about one-quarter of the population. Overall, just over one-third of the population attended at least one of the 'benchmark' arts activities in the prior year, but even this was the lowest for any of the reported survey years.

The reported survey results tell us 'how much' but they also imply the question 'Why?' What factors account for arts participation – or, perhaps more interesting, lack of participation? The next section develops a theoretical underpinning and reports general results of several empirical studies.

The economic perspective

The economic approach to understanding and analysing public participation in the arts is based on the assumption that individuals are constrained utility-maximizers. Each person strives to meet his or her wants or needs as fully as possible subject to limited command over resources, inadequate time, cognitive errors and other constraints. When deciding whether or not to attend an orchestral concert, purchase an opera on compact disc, visit a museum, or download a recorded concert, a person will take into account ticket or purchase price, time and effort expenditure, alternative time uses and similar factors. This perspective informs the testable hypotheses that explicitly underlie the economic approach – and implicitly underlie the interpretation of empirical work representing other disciplines.

In a market setting, public participation in the arts is a demand-side phenomenon. Standard utility theory stipulates that any consumer seeks to maximize utility, U: $U = U(A, Z)$; that is, utility is determined by consumption of art goods and services, A, and all other goods, Z.

The consumption of any specific art good or service, A_i, is in turn a function of a 'taste' for that art form, as determined in part by whether an individual has had lessons in that art form, L_i, and other relevant human capital investments, H_i, such as childhood exposure or appreciation classes. This can be represented as

$$A_i = f(L_i, H_i)$$

Consumption of these goods and services is, of course, subject to time and budget constraints, which means that each individual must allocate these scarce resources in their choices among alternatives. It can be demonstrated formally that increases in time and money prices will reduce participation; the task of empirical enquiry is to confirm or disconfirm these expectation. Likewise, we hypothesize that pertinent human capital investments will increase participation, with additional burden on empirical research.

Table 45.2 summarizes several hypotheses related to arts participation, and the following paragraphs enlarge on these.

The impact of place
The existence of economies of agglomeration in the art and culture industry now seems well established (Heilbrun, 1987, 1989; Gray and Heilbrun, 2000; Heilbrun and Gray, 2001, pp. 337–42). Such economies occur when firms are able to share one or more productive factors in a given geographic region. For example, Hollywood's film industry and the theatre industries of both New York and London can draw upon a pool of trained performers. Another factor causing the arts to play a disproportionate role in places with larger populations is the existence of threshold market sizes. Whereas a small community could scarcely support a symphony orchestra or major art museum, most major metropolitan areas are able to support both, and additional cultural organizations as well. Accordingly, one might expect that residents of metropolitan regions would generally exhibit a greater likelihood of attending the live arts if for no other reason than that of their greater availability.

Age
Culture, it is said, is an acquired taste, and acquisition of taste takes time. It would follow that participation would increase with age. The exceptions might be those art forms that, for one reason or another, inherently appeal to younger people, such as jazz among the benchmark arts.

Table 45.2   Summary hypotheses pertaining to arts participation

Determinants	Comment	Expected impact on participation
Explicit price		
Admission fee	The market rationing device	−
Implicit price		
Children at home	Implies child-sitting expenses during parental absence to attend	−
Age	After some peak age, entails additional implicit costs	
Ability to purchase		
Household income	More income implies greater ability to pay	+
Hours worked per week	More hours worked implies greater opportunity costs	−
	More hours worked also implies greater spending power	+
Investment in consumption skills		
Age	Additional consumption skills are acquired with the passage of time	+
Education level	General knowledge acquisition may enhance enjoyment	−
Art/music lessons	Art-specific human capital should enhance enjoyment	−
Sex–male		−
Race	Indeterminate, depending on cultural	
Black	relevance of art form; e.g. jazz is significant	?
Hispanic	for African Americans, and dance is a major	?
Asian	part of American Indian culture	?
American Indian		?

Education

One means by which we acquire a taste for culture and the arts is exposure through education. It has been argued that appreciation of the more complex arts requires investment in 'consumption skills', learning to understand, say, opera. Elementary and secondary school curricula typically offer art and music classes, and most colleges offer – and many require – art or music appreciation courses. Accordingly, we would reasonably expect participation to rise as education level rises. In addition to general education, which can enhance taste for the arts, a more focused education in the form of arts training is intended to have an even greater impact.

Income

The most obvious means by which income would affect arts participation would be ability to pay. Clearly, people with higher incomes are more likely to be able to afford to attend a performing arts activity or to visit a museum.

Gender

There is no obvious or intrinsic reason to expect differential participation rates between men and women, yet the differences are well known: women participate in the arts at higher rates than men. Perhaps this is rooted in early acculturation processes, when boys (certainly in the USA before the 1970s, but probably elsewhere as well) were often channelled into sports, to the exclusion of arts.

Race

As in gender, there is no obvious source of race-based differentials in art participation. Accounting for other factors that are correlated with race, such as income and education, may not eliminate racial differences. Racial or ethnic groups that are not European in origin may not be strongly attracted to such art forms as symphonic music and traditional opera, which are firmly rooted in Western artistic traditions. Minority groups may feel, or even be, excluded from 'mainstream' arts.

The primary question addressed by the most comprehensive studies (Gray, 1995, 1998) is: what is the impact of any one variable on arts participation, controlling for all other influences? Multivariate statistical techniques are most appropriate to address questions of this nature. Such techniques explore relationships among a number of variables simultaneously. The specific technique typically used is logistic regression, which deals more effectively with categorical response variables such as sex (male or female). All of the extant studies find support for the proffered hypotheses, no matter what statistical techniques they use. But while we can say with confidence that a more highly educated or a wealthier population will show a higher arts participation rate, it is not yet clear why the participation rate changes for these groups over time. We can explain arts participation, but we are not yet at the point of being able to predict participation or to implement policies to foster such participation.

Summary and conclusions

This chapter introduced an economic approach to arts participation, reported on recent participation levels and trends in the USA, and presented generally accepted and supported hypotheses pertaining to determinants of participation (attendance) in each of several art forms. Nearly all published studies recognize the need for further research, and additional implications await exploration (Walker *et al.*, 2000; McCarthy *et al.*, 2001; McCarthy and Jinnett, 2001).

See also:

Chapter 26: Demand; Chapter 29: Experience goods; Chapter 37: Marketing the arts.

References

DiMaggio, Paul and Toqir Mukhtar (2004), 'Arts Participation as Cultural Capital in the United States, 1982–2002: Signs of Decline?', *Poetics*, 32, 169–94.

Gray, C.M. (1995), *Turning On and Tuning In: Media Participation in the Arts*. NEA Research Division Report No. 33, Carson, CA: Seven Locks Press.

Gray, C.M. (1998), 'Hope for the Future? Early Exposure to the Arts and Adult Visits to Art Museums', *Journal of Cultural Economics*, 22, 87–98.

Gray, C.M. and James Heilbrun (2000), 'Economics of the Nonprofit Arts: Structure, Scope, and Performance', in M. Wyszomirski and J. Cherbo (eds), *Art and the Public Purpose*, New Brunswick, NJ: Rutgers University Press.

Heilbrun, James and C.M. Gray (2001), *The Economics of Art and Culture*, 2nd edn, Cambridge and New York: Cambridge University Press.

Heilbrun, James (1987), 'Growth and Geographic Distribution of the Arts in the US', in Douglas V. Shaw *et al.* (eds), *Artists and Cultural Consumers*, Akron, OH: Association for Cultural Economics, pp. 24–36.

Heilbrun, James (1989), 'The Distribution of Arts Activity among U.S. Metropolitan areas', in Douglas V. Shaw *et al.* (eds), *Cultural Economics, 88: An American Perspective*, Akron, OH: Association for Cultural Economics, pp. 33–40.

International Federation of Arts Councils and Culture Agencies (2001), *International Comparisons of Arts Participation Data*, report no. 2, available at http://www.ifacca.org/media/files/participationstatsanalysis.pdf.

McCarthy, K.F. and Kimberly Jinnett (2001), *A New Framework for Building Participation in the Arts*, Santa Monica, CA: Rand.

McCarthy, K.F., A. Brooks, J. Lowell and L. Zakaras (2001), *The Performing Arts in a New Era*, Santa Monica, CA: Rand.

National Endowment for the Arts (2009), *2008 Survey of Public Participation in the Arts*, Research report No. 49.

Walker, Christopher *et al.* (2000), *Reggae to Rachmaninoff: How and Why People Participate in Arts and Culture*, Washington, DC: Urban Institute.

Further reading

DiMaggio and Mukhtar (2004) and a report on international comparisons by the International Federation of Arts Councils and Culture Agencies (2001).

46 Performance indicators
Giacomo Pignataro

The use of performance indicators in the arts is quite widespread nowadays.[1] The basic reason for the development of this practice is that the scope for commercial profit-oriented activity is very limited in most sectors of arts production, and the size of public and private contributions can be large. The different stakeholders cannot refer to any market signal, however imperfect it may be, to evaluate different aspects of arts production. Therefore there is a need to define 'virtual' measures of arts organizations' performance so as to provide some empirical support to the judgement on the value of arts production.

Different issues can be considered when analysing performance indicators. The first issue, discussed in the next section, is related to their design. The literature deals with different sets of indicators. The basic questions addressed in all this work are two: what to measure and which methodology is to be used? The second issue, discussed in the third section, refers to the actual use of performance indicators. If these measures respond to the general need for some form of 'objective' reference in the evaluation of the activity of arts organizations, in the absence of other signals like those originating in a market, they are then used for specific purposes and in different contexts. For instance, some indicators are used to monitor the performance of individual organizations, others are employed to determine the size of individual subsidies and still others are implemented to develop rational policies by funding organizations. There are at least three different problems to be examined. First, there needs to be consistency between the purpose of measurement and the choice of indicators to be used. A second important question to be addressed is how to use indicators, with respect to the specific issue of cross-section and temporal comparisons. Finally, there is surely a problem of interpreting the numerical values of indicators, in order to make pertinent judgements.

The design of performance indicators

Different sets of indicators are available in the field of the arts. Usually, these indicators have been developed within the analysis of the performance of a given subsector of the arts and culture, to take account of its specific features. Museums (Ames, 1994; Jackson, 1994) and performing arts (Towse, 2001) are probably among the fields that have mostly been considered for the design of performance indicators. More generally, there are micro indicators that have been developed to measure the performance of individual arts organizations, and macro indicators (Brosio, 1994) that refer to entire sectors or subsectors of the arts.[2] There are indicators that are common to all fields of the arts (for example, attendance) and others that have been specifically designed to capture some peculiar aspect of a given field of the arts (for example, the use of the collection in museums). However, the basic questions remain: what to measure and which methodology is to be used?

As for the first question, we need to make clear what is meant by the word 'performance'. Under the heading of performance indicators, it is possible to find many measures of very different elements of the performance of organizations and sectors. Even if these elements are not totally unrelated, it is possible to identify separate ranges of analysis and empirical application of the different indicators.

First, some measures are a mere quantitative 'description' of some characteristics of arts production and consumption. Examples of this type of indicators are the number of staff in an organization, the costs of the service, the number of attendances, the days open per year and so on. There are other indicators, used instead as a tool for the 'evaluation' of different aspects of the performance of arts organizations or of the functioning of the cultural sector or of its segments. Examples of these other indicators are costs per visitor or attendee, the ratio of public to total income and public subsidy per attendance. The difference between these two classes of indicators[3] lies in the object of measurement. The former indicators measure a single 'real' dimension of arts production and consumption within an institution or a sector and, therefore, they require the identification of this dimension (for example, supply) and of the best way to measure it (for example, number of performances, number of days open per year). It must be noted that, when using these indicators, one must be aware that they represent a single dimension of a phenomenon and possibly a partial view of this dimension. The second class of indicators includes 'constructed' measures, based on the definition of an aspect of performance to be evaluated (efficiency, economy, effectiveness and so on). The main issue here is consistency between the elaborated measure and the object of evaluation, also with respect to the aims pursued in carrying out evaluation (a topic explored in the next section).

Second, the object of measurement indicators is also different with respect to the distinction between the output and the outcome of arts activities. Output is the direct product of the activity of cultural institutions, obtained through the combination of the resources available to those institutions. The outcome is represented by the ultimate goals of arts production, usually in terms of impact on its beneficiaries. For instance, the output of a theatre company subsidized for performing in schools is represented by its performances, while the outcome may be the learning by children and young people.[4] This example shows that outputs of the arts are quite easily identified since they are the specific products of each arts enterprise. They are generally measured by volume and they can also be related to other variables, to build indicators that evaluate how much is produced in relation to the amount of resources employed, the number of attendances and so on. As for the outcomes, their identification is not so straightforward, since they are not connected with the characteristics of each artistic product but with the specific objectives pursued in carrying out arts production. It is not unusual for rather different outcomes to be pursued with the same output. The design of indicators for outcomes is, then, quite complex.

Since most of the conceivable outcomes reflect qualitative aspects of cultural production, it may prove particularly difficult to find measures that can quantify these outcomes. An example comes from the NEA Guidelines for grants. One of the expected outcomes of subsidized projects is that children and young people will use the arts to express their ideas and feelings. A simple descriptive indicator in this case is a measure that quantifies how much use of the arts is made by the children attending a project to express their feelings. It is quite clear that quantification is a rather difficult task in this case, and that the only way to describe or evaluate the impact of arts production on the identified outcomes is to ask the beneficiaries how satisfied they feel about the fulfilment of a project.[5] This raises a further problem. While indicators for outputs are computed from data that are generally collected by any organization in a more or less identical way (costs, attendance, number of performances and so on), the source of data for outcome indicators may be rather 'subjective' since they tend to reflect the perceptions of individuals. This may be a problem because of the well-known information problems existing in the cultural sector. Individual perceptions are in fact idiosyncratic, and therefore the outcome indicators will be computed from data that reflect different ways of measuring the same phenomenon.

The second question about the design of performance indicators relates to the methodology to be employed to compute these indicators. Both the theory and the practice of indicators generally represent them just as simple numbers that measure a phenomenon (number of attendances, number of performances and so on) or, more often, as ratios (cost per attendance, number of custodians per visitor and so on). This type of indicator provides information on single aspects of arts production and consumption.[6] However, when we consider, for instance, the output of many arts organizations, we can see that their production process is generally multidimensional, from both the input and the output side. A general evaluation of the efficiency of production can, then, be obtained only through a multiplicity of indicators,[7] which does not allow a clear-cut evaluation of the efficiency of an organization. Moreover, when comparing the values of the same indicator for different organizations, the relevance of the comparison is limited by the fact that quantities of output, multiples or sub-multiples of that achieved by any given organization, are not necessarily technically attainable employing multiples or sub-multiples of the inputs used by that organization. There is a need, therefore, to use more advanced techniques that take into account the multidimensional nature of arts production and consumption.

There have been now several attempts (Pignataro, 2002; Mairesse and Vanden Eeckaut, 2002; Bishop and Brand, 2003; Basso and Funari, 2004; Finocchiaro Castro *et al.*, 2008; Finocchiaro Castro and Rizzo, 2009; del Barrio *et al.*, 2009) to deal with the efficiency of museums and other cultural institutions using the method of efficiency frontiers.[8] Efficiency frontiers or, as they are sometimes called, *best-practice* frontiers, are the sets of the best production units. The particular advantages of this methodology, with respect to simple productivity indicators, are of different nature. First, by benchmarking the performance of different institutions, it allows to establish a sort of 'best' reference, those institutions that are on the efficiency frontier (that is, they are 100 per cent efficient), so as to compute a single efficiency index, which is the 'distance' of each observation from the frontier. In such a way, it is possible to move from the measure of productivity to that of relative efficiency. Second, this methodology simultaneously takes into account all the relevant inputs and outputs of the production process, developing one single measure of efficiency. Finally, it proves very useful in contexts where comparison of performance is required for management or financing purposes.

The use of performance indicators

As already pointed out, performance indicators are designed not only to satisfy a generic demand for statistical knowledge, but also to provide valuable information for those supporting the arts sector. The information needs that can be satisfied by the use of indicators, however, are heterogeneous and, therefore, there is no 'universal' set of indicators that is consistent with all these needs. Indicators can be used for the purpose of managerial control and, in this case, one would probably concentrate on those measuring the use of the different resources under the control of organizations' managers to produce the different outputs. Another important objective can be accountability in respect of the use of public and private contributions, which mostly requires indicators of outcome. Indicators are also employed within a process of organizational learning, to improve organizations' efficiency and their capacity to achieve their goals. The use of performance indicators thus requires their selection, which is a rather delicate task that can put at risk the usefulness of their application. Schuster (1997) has already argued that 'in the arts and culture the tensions that arise in implementing such indicators have been rooted less in the *theory* than in the *practice* of performance indicators . . . opposition has come not from disagreement in theory but from actual issues arising out of practice' (p. 255, original emphasis). At least three issues arising out of practice need to be mentioned.

A first issue is consistency between the purpose of measurement and the choice of indicators to be used. As already noted, the object of measurement must be identified so as to convey information consistent with the objective of measurement. If, for instance, one wants to evaluate the efficiency of the restoration activity of a museum, one has to select those indicators that relate to the specific inputs and outputs of this activity. Consistency, however, must be interpreted in a broader sense. When used, indicators inevitably affect the behaviour of cultural organizations.[9] Again citing Schuster, 'in the best of all possible worlds, that response would be exactly the behaviour that one wanted to engender' (ibid., p. 257), but he provides evidence that the use of some indicators has eventually achieved results opposite to those aimed at. The implication here is that indicators must be selected not only on the basis of the appropriateness of the object of measurement, but also for predicting the incentives that their use can convey within an institution. Peacock (2003) clearly addresses this issue, stressing the principal–agent nature of the relationship between cultural institutions and the funding bodies, and the difficulties of using performance indicators for control purposes because of the opportunity, for the agent (the cultural institutions), to exert discretionary behaviour.[10]

A second important problem is how to use the measures arising from the application of performance indicators. To value the performance of a cultural institution, is it enough to collect the relevant measures for just this institution? And how should these numbers be judged? The answer comes clearly from Jackson (1994): 'The information content of indicators is only realized if the latter are compared with something' (p. 165). The performance of arts organizations cannot be valued in absolute terms or with reference to some sort of objective or universal standard. This valuation, in other words, is always contingent on the performance of all other institutions operating in similar circumstances, at the same time. Arts organizations should, therefore, try to build up partnerships for the implementation of their performance-monitoring systems.[11] As pointed out earlier, when we compared simple productivity indicators with efficiency frontiers, the different methodologies for the computation of performance indicators may vary in their significance in providing relative measures of performance.

Finally, there is a problem of interpreting the numerical values of indicators, to make pertinent judgements and to derive sound policy implications. The analysis of the scores resulting from the application of performance indicators requires additional information on the factors that may affect the different aspects of performance. This is particularly important when a comparison is carried out among different institutions or countries, to avoid the temptation of a trivial ranking according to the indicators' values. The problem is also relevant to the outcome indicators, since the impact on the ultimate goals of arts production is connected not only with arts outputs but also with a variety of factors outside the control of cultural institutions.

Conclusions

A few remarks can be drawn from this brief survey of the main issues arising from the design and use of performance indicators.

1. There is no such thing as 'the performance' of cultural institutions, or of the whole sector. There are different aspects of performance that can also be evaluated with the help of numerical indicators, but none of these can provide an exhaustive representation of the functioning of arts organizations.
2. Indicators are a way of organizing information on the different aspects of performance and they are characterized by quantification. One must be aware that the significance of this quantification may vary according to the different objects of measurement, and also because of the different 'quality' of data used to compute them.
3. Performance indicators need to be used with great caution, and the actual implementation of a system of indicators must be carefully designed. The quantification allowed by indicators should not induce us to use them in a direct and uncontrolled prescriptive way, as they would be, for instance, if one employed the scores to rank institutions from the best to the worst. Indicators provide only one piece of information, which must be accompanied by other relevant information useful for interpreting the determinants of performance.
4. Once used, indicators are not merely a computation exercise, since they tend to affect the behaviour of institutions according to the incentives arising from the prediction about their possible utilization.

Notes

1. Madden (2005) provides a brief survey of the work done by different institutions and scholars on indicators.
2. Schuster (1997) presents the historical development of the design of performance indicators, with respect to micro and macro indicators.
3. Jackson (1994), addressing the issue of what is measured by performance indicators, makes a distinction between performance measures and performance indicators. The former are precise and unambiguous (p. 163), for example economy, efficiency and effectiveness, while the latter 'are statistics, ratios, costs and other forms of information that illuminate or measure progress in achieving the aims and objectives of an organization' (ibid.) for which it is not possible to obtain a precise measure. The basis of this distinction, measurability, appears, however, to be a bit too vague for many indicators and it does not convey clear implications for the different problems posed by the different indicators.
4. This is one of the five Arts Endowment goals for which funds are available through the National Endowment for Arts (NEA) in the USA. This general outcome is then categorized into 14 more specific outcomes, such as that children and youth will increase and/or strengthen their knowledge and skills in the arts, they will use the arts to express their ideas and feelings, and so on. A complete description of these outcomes is contained in the Grants to Organizations Guidelines provided by NEA on its website (http://www.arts.gov.).
5. As in other fields, there are several attempts to represent consumer satisfaction and the value attributed by users to cultural services. Two recent examples are provided by de Rojas and Camarero (2008), who

also discuss the role of emotions in explaining visitor satisfaction in heritage and cultural expositions, and by Rouwendal and Boter (2009), who use information about destination choice and number of trips to assess the value of museums.

6. While it would be troublesome to list even the most used indicators, Peacock (2003) and Madden (2005) provide a characterization of indicators, in terms of what both they usually are and should be.
7. The potential number of indicators measuring factor productivity, for instance, is equal to the number of inputs multiplied by the number of outputs.
8. All these works, except for Bishop and Brand (2003), employ non-parametric techniques. In contrast to the traditional parametric techniques like regression, non-parametric methods do not need to impose any assumption on the shape of the frontier. Mairesse and Vanden Eeckaut (2002) use the free disposal hull technique while all the others employ data envelopment analysis.
9. Evans (2000) represents some possible ways in which the use of performance indicators may affect the behaviour of cultural institutions: manipulation of data on which performance indicators are computed and attention focused on the selected performance indicators' inputs and outputs.
10. Madden (2005) has a thorough discussion of the problems related to the different uses of performance indicators.
11. There are already experiences in this direction. The Arts Council in England is working in cooperation with other institutions to build up a bank of arts performance indicators. At a more general level, there are resolutions of the EU Council promoting the development of comparable cultural statistics and their alignment within the EU, inviting the member states to exchange information and statistics voluntarily.

See also:

Chapter 15: Costs of production; Chapter 40: Museums; Chapter 49: Principal–agent analysis; Chapter 52: Public support.

References

Ames, P.J. (1994), 'Measuring Museums' Merits', in K. Moore (ed.), *Museum Management*, London: Routledge, pp. 22–30.

Basso, A. and S. Funari (2004), 'A Quantitative Approach to Evaluate the Relative Efficiency of Museums', *Journal of Cultural Economics*, 28, 195–216.

Bishop, P. and S. Brand (2003), 'The Efficiency of Museums: a Stochastic Frontier Production Function Approach', *Applied Economics*, 35, 1853–8.

Brosio, G. (1994), 'The Arts Industry: Problems of Measurement', in A. Peacock and I. Rizzo (eds), *Cultural Economics and Cultural Policies*, Dordrecht: Kluwer Academic Publishers, pp. 17–22.

De Rojas C. and C. Camarero (2008), 'Visitors' Experience, Mood and Satisfaction in a Heritage Context: Evidence from an Interpretation Center', *Tourism Management*, 29, 525–37.

Del Barrio, M.J., L.C. Herrero and J.A. Sanz (2009), 'Measuring the Efficiency of Heritage Institutions: A Case Study of a Regional System of Museums in Spain', *Journal of Cultural Heritage*, 10, 258–68.

Evans, G. (2000), 'Measure for Measure: Evaluating Performance and the Arts Organization', paper presented at the FOKUS–ACEI Joint Symposium, Vienna, 27–9 January.

Finocchiaro Castro, M. and I. Rizzo (2009), 'Performance Measurement of Heritage Conservation Activity in Sicily', *International Journal of Arts Management*, 11, 29–41.

Finocchiaro Castro, M., C. Guccio and I. Rizzo (2008), *Public Intervention on Heritage Conservation: A Semi-parametric Analysis of the Determinants of Regulation Authorities' performance*, Quaderni del Dipartimento di Scienze Storiche, Giuridiche, Economiche e Sociali dell'Università degli Studi 'Mediterranea' di Reggio Calabria.

Jackson, P.M. (1994), 'Performance Indicators: Promises and Pitfalls', in K. Moore (ed.), *Museum Management*, London: Routledge, pp. 155–69.

Madden, C. (2005), 'Indicators for Arts and Cultural Policy: A Global Perspective', *Cultural Trends*, 14, 217–47.

Mairesse, F. and P. Vanden Eeckaut (2002), 'Museum Assessment and FDH Technology: Towards a Global Approach', *Journal of Cultural Economics*, 26, 261–86.

Peacock, A. (2003), 'Performance Indicators and Cultural Policy', *Economia della cultura*, 13, http://www.economiadellacultura.it/english.html.

Pignataro, G. (2002), 'Measuring the Efficiency of Museums: A Case Study in Sicily', in I. Rizzo and R. Towse (eds), *The Economics of Heritage: A Study in the Political Economy of Culture in Sicily*, Cheltenham, UK and Northampton, MA, USA: Edward Elgar, pp. 65–78.

Rouwendal, J. and J. Boter (2009), 'Assessing the Value of Museums with a Combined Discrete Choice/Count Data Model', *Applied Economics*, 41, 1417–36.

Schuster, J.M. (1997), 'The Performance of Performance Indicators', *Nonprofit Management and Leadership*, 7 (3), 253–69.
Towse, R. (2001), '*Quis custodiet?* Or Managing the Management: The Case of the Royal Opera House, Covent Garden', *International Journal of Arts Management*, 3 (3), 38–50.

Further reading

A thorough survey of performance indicators in the arts and of their use is provided in Madden (2005). A good critical discussion of the role of performance indicators in the relationship between cultural institution and their 'principal' is contained in Peacock (2003).

47 Performing arts
Ruth Towse

The term 'performing arts' covers a broad grouping of live art forms, only some of which have been researched in cultural economics. While orchestras, opera, ballet and spoken theatre have all featured in the literature on the subject, circus, puppetry and mime, among other live performance, have not. Popular music typically has been studied in relation to the music business and analysed as a mixture of live and recorded work, and popular musicals have had some mention, but on the whole, work on performed arts in cultural economics has concentrated on building-based, subsidized performance by arts organizations. In some cases, the organization could be that of a festival that brings together many different performances, or that concentrates on one art form, such as a theatre festival, or combines performing arts with other offerings, such as art exhibitions and talks.

The performing arts play a significant part in the development of cultural economics due to the work by Baumol and Bowen (1966), which set the theoretical and empirical framework for research in this subject, initially in relation to the performing arts but later spreading to a broader range of topics. Their focus on rising costs in the performing arts provided the inspiration for much of the subject matter of cultural economics in the subsequent 30 or so years.

Live performance in all art forms has some common features: production requires the input of highly skilled labour of a varied character that is delivered to an audience at a specific moment of time and in a specific place that has been advertised in advance. Once the curtain goes up, the audience is fixed in size and nothing can be done to reduce the cost or to increase the revenue from the sale of tickets for that performance. For the art forms that have been studied, the venue for the performance is most often a theatre or concert hall that has been purpose-built, often a historic building that has limited capacity for audience size and for incorporating technological improvements, and these two features have contributed to rising costs per attendee and per performance. The subsidized performing arts have rarely adopted the sound and visual systems widely used for mass audiences in popular concerts, which may be held in huge stadiums. The development of digitalization of live performances is beginning to alter those features, and it is to be expected this will develop further, with important consequences for the finance of the performing arts. This chapter therefore covers in broad terms the production and finance of the performing arts and aspects of technological change affecting supply and demand.

Production function of performance

A production function relates the output of an activity to the quantity of inputs used to produce it; the greater the quantity of inputs, or factors of production, the greater the quantity of the output. The production function can therefore be used to formalize this relationship in any economic activity, including the performing arts. Every performance requires the input of capital in the form of the venue (theatre, concert hall and so on), the facilities it offers for staging the production, such as the stage, back-stage and front-of-house services and labour, which includes the performers and other staff; the location of the venue may also be important for some purposes. The state of technology in the venue is taken as given in the short run, although it may improve facilities and therefore the productivity of the inputs in the long run. Similarly, the human capital skills of the people working in the venue, including the performers, may also improve productivity over time, for example by reducing the number of rehearsals needed to achieve a specific level of performance quality.

Productivity is the measure of output per unit of input. The labour input is measured in terms of the number of hours worked or of the number of people employed; this can be broken down into different categories, such as artistic and non-artistic labour, performers and stage staff and so on. Capital is usually measured in value terms, although it may be possible to identify specific items in quantity terms. Productivity usually focuses on the value of output per unit of labour.

Capital and labour may be both complements and substitutes for each other: labour is deemed to be more productive when it works with an appropriate amount of capital, in which case they are complementary. They may also be substitutes; for example, digital technology enables lighting systems to be controlled by computer instead of manually and pre-recorded music substitutes for live music by performers. These relationships are crucial to Baumol's prognosis of the 'cost disease' in the performing arts.

Fixed coefficients and Baumol's cost disease
Substitution implies that it is possible technically to choose different combinations of capital and labour to produce a given output, a choice that in economic terms is determined by relative input prices; if wage rates increase, labour gets more expensive and if capital could be substituted, that would offset increasing costs of production. The theory underpinning Baumol's cost disease is that such flexibility does not exist; instead, the combinations of capital and labour, and particularly of specific types of labour, are fixed by the works that are performed. The 'classic' example is the string quartet: it takes four players (with their instruments, of course, although that is not often mentioned) to play a particular work – say a Haydn quartet – and the same amount of time to play it now as when it was first performed. Therefore there are fixed coefficients in the production function of the performance – and the same would apply to a Shakespeare play and an opera by Mozart. Thus productivity cannot be increased.

That led Baumol (1967) to model the performing arts as the 'stagnant' sector in an otherwise dynamic economy that is growing in productivity due the adoption of increasingly capital-intensive methods of production. Greater productivity drives up wages in the economy as a whole, including those of people working in the performing arts, assuming (as Baumol did) that labour markets are integrated. Even if performers' pay did not rise at the same rate as that of others, eventually fewer performers would make even a poor living as the cost of living would rise and they would change occupations. Non-artistic workers who can easily transfer to work in the 'productive' sector would leave the stagnant sector and therefore arts organizations must pay them the going wage to retain them. In order to preserve the quality and quantity of performing arts supply, costs must go up, to be passed on to audiences as price rises. The rate of increase of ticket prices for the performing arts would inevitably be higher than those of goods and services in general for two reasons: first, the increase in wage rates without an accompanying increase in productivity, and second, the labour-intensive nature of the performing arts that causes the wage bill to be disproportionately greater than that in the rest of the economy. Baumol argued that these inevitable forces would lead to an 'income gap' in the finances of arts organizations and, without outside support, they would cause an 'artistic deficit'. Therefore subvention by public finance or private philanthropy was needed to ensure the survival of quantity and quality in the performing arts.

Measurement of output

The question of quantity and quality immediately leads to the matter of how these are to be measured. As far as quality is concerned, Baumol saw it as having to do with sustaining the 'classic' repertoire – performances of the great works for orchestra, string quartet, opera and ballet, the theatre and so on. This raises the question whether smaller-cast plays or chamber orchestras performing a different repertoire (say of Baroque music) are offering a lower-quality supply. That is clearly a subjective matter on which economists are perhaps not sufficiently expert. What is important, though, is to understand that that is what Baumol set as a standard in the theory of the cost disease. Other authors have attempted to measure quality by referring to rating by critics or awards, and funding bodies wishing to monitor the achievement of their objectives in granting subsidy to arts organizations also use some qualitative measures in their performance indicators.

More amenable to 'objective' analysis is the question of how to measure quantity: should it be the number of performances of a given work, the number of works performed (even the number of new works performed) or the number and 'type' of people attending the performances (new audiences, disadvantaged people and so on)? Obviously, each measure of output would yield a different result for productivity. The cost of a production (meaning the presentation of a work) can be calculated per performance or per seat in the venue or per attendee, and each would be different (and funding bodies might also want to calculate the amount of subsidy per attendee). The choice is dictated by circumstances; however, that choice may determine the validity of the cost disease, as demonstrated by the discussion on technology, to which we now turn.

Influence of technology

The last half of the twentieth century saw rapidly increasing changes in technology that have affected all the arts. Initially, they had little impact on the performing arts, for which the capacity of the venue determined the size of the audience. More performances could be put on up to a point, for example, by having two per day that would spread the fixed costs of the production (the set and costumes, rehearsal time and so on), but for some art forms, the same performers could not do both (opera and ballet being notable cases), so extra performers would have to be hired. All this changed, though, with the advent of technologies that enable non-attenders to access the performance, either by sound recording, television or film, and now by digital delivery on line in real time. It is now possible to hear and/or see performances from around the world in one's own home. That means that the number of 'consumers' vastly exceeds the numbers attending live performances and if that is taken as the measure of output, then productivity has certainly risen very considerably. Some critics question whether this dilutes quality, but what is incontrovertible is that this has significant implications for the finance of the performing arts.

Demand and participation

Before turning to finance, this section briefly discusses demand for and participation in the performing arts. From what has been said above, it can be seen that the 1960s view of the cost disease, experienced in many countries during subsequent decades, predicted that audiences would fall as prices rose. Some of the price effect would be tempered by strong, possibly addictive, tastes for the arts that made demand inelastic, and positive income elasticity that with rising incomes would also mitigate the results. Even so, audience data show a reduction in participation. Some performing arts have only ever attracted a small proportion of the population – opera and ballet being the lowest at well below 10 per cent of the adult population in many countries. These data, though, are mostly for ticket-buying audiences; those participating by buying the DVD or listening to the radio have to be identified in other ways that are not included in data on live performance. Interestingly, new digital means of delivery also enable the arts organization to charge: you can pay quite a lot to see the Metropolitan Opera's live performance via satellite in a cinema near you.

Finance of the performing arts

The cost disease, as mentioned earlier, predicted that in order to avoid the 'artistic deficit' of falling quality and quantity of the performing arts, organizations' 'income gaps' would have to be filled by some form of subvention. For many European arts organizations, that simply meant that the state authority that owned and managed performance venues had to spend more of the public budget on them. In the USA, the UK and the other countries with a similar model, though, that meant more public subsidy or private funding to privately owned and managed non-profit performing arts organizations. That was unpalatable to some governments, who saw the performing arts as being enjoyed by only a relatively small elite of above-average income-earners who could pay the higher prices. But even with subsidy, prices could never be so low as to attract all-comers and, even if they were, seating capacity in typical venues would inevitably limit the number who could be accommodated; moreover, there was evidence that however low prices were, many people just would not go though the doors of those venues. Digitalization has now changed that and a generation of young people who have grown up with new technologies seem to be willing to experience the performing arts in new ways that are not only different but also much cheaper. It remains to be seen if this fundamentally increases audiences. If so, the fixed costs of performances can now, as with mass media, be spread over vastly bigger and broader-based audiences with much lower marginal costs. Rising costs can still be present on the supply side but the cost disease can be neutralized by increased demand. The performing arts are not yet in a terminal state.

See also:

Chapter 10: Baumol's cost disease; Chapter 15: Costs of production; Chapter 26: Demand; Chapter 30: Festivals; Chapter 43: Opera and ballet; Chapter 44: Orchestras; Chapter 45: Participation; Chapter 46: Performance indicators; Chapter 49: Pricing the arts; Chapter 52: Public support; Chapter 59: Theatre.

References

Baumol, W. (1967), 'Macroeconomics of Unbalanced Growth: The Anatomy of Urban Crisis', *American Economic Review*, 50 (2), 415–26.

Baumol, W. and W. Bowen (1966), *Performing Arts: the Economic Dilemma*, Hartford, CT: The Twentieth Century Fund.
Journal of Cultural Economics (1996), Vol. 20, No. 3/September. The 30th Anniversary of The Performing Arts: An Economic Dilemma by Baumol and Bowen.
Towse, R. (2010), *A Textbook of Cultural Economics*, Cambridge: Cambridge University Press.

Further reading

All the topics touched on in this chapter are analysed in more depth in my *Textbook of Cultural Economics* (Towse, 2010). The 1996 *Journal of Cultural Economics,* Vol. 20, No. 3 is a special issue devoted to an assessment 30 years on of Baumol's cost disease; recommended are the articles by Tyler Cowen, Alan Peacock and William Baumol himself, with the Introduction and Final Comments by Mark Blaug.

48 Poverty and support for artists
Hans Abbing

In our society the value of art is high and yet the majority of artists are poor. Not only is the symbolic value of art high; often the financial value is high as well. People and institutions are prepared to pay high prices for artworks and performances, and governments and foundations spend huge amounts on prestigious new museums and concert halls. But the typical artist is poor. This sharp and paradoxical contrast can be explained: the low incomes are the consequence of the high symbolic value of art. This implies that poverty in the arts is largely structural. Subsidies intended to raise artists' incomes tend to be futile and can easily be counterproductive.

Poverty and work preference

Many artists have such low overall incomes from work, including non-arts work, that they are likely to be poor. According to research in different countries and in various surveys, between one-third and one-half of the artists in the West and Australia have overall incomes from work that are at or below the so-called poverty line or subsistence level. The definition of who is an artist and who is not differs, but outcomes are not very different; that is, artists are poor. That these artists do not starve is due to support from various sources and income from assets. Looking at income from the arts alone instead of income from work in general, artists earn even less. In most Western countries a majority of artists would not be able to make a living if they worked full time in the arts. The difference with income from work can be explained from the fact that presently many artists have second jobs that pay better than their arts job, and receive social benefits.[1]

Western artists have not always been poor. Before the twentieth century artists' incomes were not particularly low (Frey and Pommerehne, 1989; Montias, 1987; Hoogenboom, 1993; Stolwijk 1998). Especially in the second half of the twentieth century the decrease in income was substantial, while the number of artists grew considerably. At the same time, the number of artists who supplement their income with earnings from second jobs has increased. Depending on the country and the discipline, between 70 and 90 per cent of artists now have second jobs.[2]

Artists have what David Throsby has called a work preference (Throsby, 1994). If the artist earns more from either arts work or non-arts work, he or she typically uses a large part of the extra money to reduce the hours he works in his second job in order to work more hours as artist and/or he uses it to buy materials or equipment, like expensive paints or a special video camera. Throsby (1994) and Rengers (2002) present evidence for the work-preference model with respect to time spent on arts work. Solhjell (2000) presents Norwegian data that suggest an exceptionally strong work preference, including in the form of expenditures on arts work.

Explanations for low incomes

Low incomes in the arts are persistent. Why is this? Why do people become artists when their chance of earning a decent income is very low? And why do they not leave the arts, but instead are prepared to work as artists for many years while earning little? Standard economics cannot explain this phenomenon. However, when the assumptions that people are fully informed or work only for money are dropped, low incomes can perhaps be explained. Artists could be misinformed more than others or interested in other rewards than just money.

Undoubtedly people do not work just for money (Frey, 1997). Anybody earning more than a minimum income wants to have at least some pleasure in working or get some praise from friends or colleagues. The question therefore is whether artists receive more non-monetary rewards than others who earn more. First, in the arts there is the potential for extreme fame and attention, be it only for a few. Therefore artists could be relatively adventurous and have a taste for risk (cf. Towse, 1992). But if this is true it will apply to sports, politics and entertainment as well. Next, recognition by peers and critics is an important reward for artists. However, for scientists recognition is at least as important. Also the joy of working or doing creative work or of working as a self-employed person is likely to matter, but many others like their work, do creative work and enjoy working independently.

What differs is the status of being an artist. Since the eighteenth century art has had an extremely high symbolic value in Western society. Art with a capital 'A' is special. Its specialness shines on the artist. In many ways artists are not like others; they are considered to be better people. Art is good, beautiful and deep; and artists are creative, self-directed, authentic and able to realize themselves. Sometimes characteristics such as being uncommercial or even being poor have a positive value. In a society in which the notion of authenticity and self-realization is so highly rated, these stereotypes are particularly important. Of course, not everyone agrees. The stereotypes make the arts extremely attractive and may well largely explain the low incomes in this sector.[3]

This does not necessarily imply that artists will always be compensated for their low money incomes by non-monetary rewards. They may also be more misinformed than others. Society may well paint too rosy a picture of work in the arts. When society has invested and continues to invest so much value in art, there is bound to be a seamy side as well. The artist who does not live up to expectations threatens people's precious object, Art. As the artist particularly values art and it is not his/her intention to degrade Art, he/she feels shame and may face forms of social exclusion, usually not shown openly. It is not polite to make a person feel ashamed and it is unpleasant to be in situations in which the sacredness of Art is threatened by one of its servants. Therefore the result is a vague awareness of failure and at the same time a collective denial of it. The artist plays the game of the artist who did not fail, who loves his work, who can live with not being successful and poor, or who may still become successful later on in his life.

Do the many poor and failed artists suffer? As far as I know, little research exists in this area; it is not rewarding to do research on the dark side of the arts.[4] Generally people who are poor for a long time tend to become socially isolated, and artists are perhaps no exception. In their case the shame of being poor may well be supplemented by the shame of having failed as an artist.

If artists are not like other professionals, it matters for politicians and policy-makers in which aspect artists differ most. If it is the case that artists receive primarily more non-monetary rewards, they can be said to be willing to work for low incomes because they are compensated. However, if they are foremost misinformed about future hardship, the popular notion of the suffering artist makes some sense. In that case, governments and others have a reason to want to help them.

Support for artists increases poverty
One would expect that when more money flows into the arts, poverty among artists would be reduced. Generally this is not the case. This can best be explained by distinguishing three groups of artists. First, there is the group of *artists who are not poor*. This is a small group. Their overall income from work and other sources is the same or above the minimum income, while a few earn extremely high incomes.

There is a second group of what I call *poor artists for whom poverty is not inevitable*. This is a large group. Their overall income is the same or a little higher than the level required to make a living, but less than the minimum income. If they start to receive more money, they use all or a large part of it to work more hours in their arts job or to spend more money on it. And if they start to earn less, they do the opposite. These artists have room for manoeuvre. But there is a limit to their freedom of movement. If earnings become very low, they run out of choices and poverty is inevitable.

Therefore there is a third group of *artists who are altogether poor*. For them poverty is inevitable and they are in the danger zone. They earn just enough to make a living, but if their overall income goes down only a little or their circumstances change, for example when they have a child, they have to leave the arts. Nevertheless, while never really leaving the danger zone, many of these artists tend to be very inventive. They continually find new solutions just to be able to continue to work as an artist. But of course some do leave, while others enter. After all, most young artists start their career in the arts in the danger zone.

Suppose more money flows into the arts and it does not all go to the group of artists who are not poor. In that case the large group of artists for whom poverty is not inevitable will spend most of the extra money on their arts work. Therefore their overall income stays close to the subsistence level and they remain poor. In the short run the size of the relatively small group of artists who are not poor will increase somewhat, while the group at the other end, the group of altogether poor artists, will become somewhat smaller. But when aspiring artists notice that the group of artists who earn more than a minimum income becomes somewhat larger and the group of altogether poor artists becomes smaller and, most importantly, when they notice that the feeling of well-being of the large group of poor artists who have room to move increases because they need to work fewer hours in second jobs or have more money to spend on their arts job, this will signal to them that prospects in the arts are better than before. And because the arts are so special and therefore extremely attractive, there are always large numbers who are eager to enter when, given their competencies, their prospects improve only a little. Therefore after a while the total population of artists will have grown, but the percentage of poor artists has remained the same. Consequently, due to the extra money flowing into the arts, the absolute number of poor artists has increased.

It follows that if subsidies for artists are intended to raise their overall income, as is often the case in the West, these subsidies are counterproductive.[5] Moreover, in the case of subsidies for artists a vicious circle may arise. Often politicians in prosperous countries feel that they cannot allow a large group of professionals to be poor, especially not artists whose work is so special. Therefore subsidies are granted to raise their income. Next the number of poor artists grows; thus subsidies will be increased, and so on. Of course, in practice this will not go on for ever, but the tendency is clear.

Support for artists in the Netherlands
The hypothesis that subsidies lead to more artists can be tested by a rough diachronic comparison within one country. After a change in subsidy levels there should be a change in the growth rate of the number of artists as well.

In the Netherlands there have been two major changes in the subsidization of visual artists that were accompanied by an unusual development in their number. First, in 1949 the Beeldend Kunstenaars Regeling (Visual Artists Scheme) was established, under which professional visual artists who earned less than a certain minimum income were allowed to sell art to local authorities in order to supplement their income. If their work met certain, rather low, quality criteria, local authorities were obliged to buy it. Between 1949 and 1983 the yearly growth in the number of students in art academies increased much faster than in other arts training and in other post-18 vocational training. The gradual abolition of the scheme between 1983 and 1987, because it had become too expensive, represents a second example. The yearly increase in the number of visual art students dropped below average levels. And in the next ten years more visual artists left the arts than before that time or since.

In 1999 the Netherlands introduced a new scheme, presently called the WWIK (Law for Work and Income Provision of Artists). Poor artists who would otherwise need social benefits can for a maximum of four years receive the WWIK benefits while still being allowed to earn some money in the arts and without an obligation to apply for other jobs. Given the data from the first years of operation, the scheme turned out to be attractive to far more artists than had been expected. Artists not only use it as a replacement for benefits, but also to work fewer hours in second jobs or to spend more money on their arts job. However, since then the scheme has become more restrictive. During the four-year period of the scheme, users have to generate increasing amounts of income from work. Moreover, they are encouraged to take courses to make them more market-oriented or to prepare them for other professions. Whether this will slow down the growth in the number of artists remains to be seen.

One would expect that in prosperous countries there would be few poor artists. The opposite is the case. According to Pierre-Michel Menger, 'the overall picture of artistic labor markets and their growth is however a paradoxical one: employment, underemployment and unemployment have all been increasing steadily and simultaneously' (Menger, 2006, p. 769). Government aid for individual artists adds to the increase in unemployment and number of poor artists. If governments were to reduce their support for artists, this would reduce the number of poor artists and the percentage of poor artists would go down. The latter would also be the case if they used the money they save on more purchases and commissions.

Poverty in the arts is structural. Apart from a reduction in government subsidies for individual artists and the provision of better information to prospective artists on their perspectives, little can be done about it. Many artists in poverty is an inevitable consequence of the specialness of Art. Only when the high symbolic value of Art goes down – and I expect that it will go down in the decades to come[6] – there will be fewer poor artists. Poverty must, however, be put in perspective. First, many artists can be said to be, at least partly, compensated for their poverty. Second, seen from outside, many artists could have avoided being poor. And third, artists come from above-average, well-to-do families. If things go altogether wrong, many poor artists can fall back on families and friends. Nevertheless, older poor artists in particular are likely to suffer.

Notes

1. In most surveys the overall income from work refers to income from arts work, arts-related work, non-arts work and in many surveys social benefits as well, while the income from art refers only to income from arts work including art subsidies.
2. For references and some results of recent surveys on incomes, numbers of artists, multiple jobholding and their development over time in the USA, Australia and France, see Menger (2006) and Alper and Wassall (2006) and for those in five other European countries, see Abbing (2011). Noteworthy in the present context is an older, not undisputed, article by Filer (1986).
3. More about this topic in Abbing (2002) and Abbing (2011).
4. According to research done by Filer (1987) in the USA, earnings of artists who left the arts were not that low.
5. The effect on numbers of different types of subsidies for artists may differ. Abbing (2002) analyses different types of subsidies in more detail, also from the perspective of 'signalling'. Certain schemes give stronger signals to artists than others.
6. Abbing (2011).

See also:

Chapter 3: Art dealers; Chapter 4: Art markets; Chapter 5: Art prices; Chapter 7: Artists' labour markets; Chapter 52: Public support.

References

Abbing, H. (2002), *Why Are Artists Poor? The Exceptional Economy of the Arts*, Amsterdam: Amsterdam University Press.
Abbing, H. (2011), *Social Value of Art. A Sociological Study of Art, Artists and the Arts Economy*, Amsterdam: Amsterdam University Press.
Alper, N.O. and G.H. Wassall (2006), 'Artists' Careers and Their Labor Market', in V.A. Ginsburgh and D. Throsby (eds), *Handbook of the Economics of Art and Culture*, Amsterdam: North-Holland, pp. 813–64.
Filer, R.K. (1986), 'The "Starving Artist" – Myth or Reality? Earnings of Artists in the United States', *Journal of Political Economy*, 94, 56–75.
Filer, R.K. (1987), 'The Price of Failure: Earnings of Former Artists', in D.V. Shaw, W.S. Hendon and R.C. Waits (eds), *Markets for the Arts*, Akron, OH: Akron University Press.
Frey, B.S. (1997), *Not Just for the Money. An Economic Theory of Human Behaviour*, Cheltenham, UK and Brookfield, MA, USA: Edward Elgar.
Frey, B.S. and W. Pommerehne (1989), *Muses and Markets. Explorations in the Economics of the Arts*, Oxford: Basil Blackwell.
Hoogenboom, A. (1993), *De Stand des Kunstenaars. De Positie van Kunstschilders in Nederland in de Eerste Helft van de Negentiende Eeuw*, Leiden: Primavera Pers.
Menger, P.-M. (2006), 'Artistic Labor Markets: Contingent Work, Excess Supply and Occupational Risk Management', in V.A. Ginsburgh and D. Throsby (eds), *Handbook of the Economics of Art and Culture*, Amsterdam: North-Holland, pp. 765–811.
Montias, J.M. (1987), 'Cost and Value in Seventeenth-century Dutch Art', *Art History*, 10, 455–66.
Peacock, A. (2006), 'The Arts and Economic Policy', in V.A. Ginsburgh and D. Throsby (eds), *Handbook of the Economics of Art and Culture*, Amsterdam: North-Holland, pp. 1123–40.
Ploeg, F. van der (2006), 'The Making of Cultural Policy: A European Perspective', in V.A. Ginsburgh and D. Throsby (eds), *Handbook of the Economics of Art and Culture*, Amsterdam: North-Holland, pp. 1183–203.
Rengers, M. (2002), *Economic Lives of Artists*, Utrecht: PhD thesis, University of Utrecht.
Solhjell (2000), 'Poor Artists in a Welfare State: A Study in the Politics and Economics of Symbolic Rewards', *Cultural Policy*, 7 (2), 319–54.

Stolwijk, C. (1998), *Uit de Schilderswereld. Nederlandse Kunstschilders in de Tweede Helft van de Negentiede Eeuw*, Leiden, Primavera Pers.

Throsby, D. (1994), 'A Work-Preference Model of Artist Behaviour', in A. Peacock and I. Rizzo (eds), *Cultural Economics and Cultural Policies*, Dordrecht: Kluwer Academic Publishers, pp. 69–80.

Towse, R. (1992). 'The Earnings of Singers: An Economic Analysis', in R. Towse and A. Khakee (eds), *Cultural Economics*, Berlin and Heidelberg: Springer-Verlag, pp. 209–17.

Further reading

For a discussion of characteristics of artists and their implications: Alper and Wassall (2006), Menger (2006), Abbing (2002, 2011); on legitimization and effects of subsidies, Peacock (2006), van der Ploeg (2006) and Abbing (2002); and on the general importance of non-monetary rewards, Frey (1997).

49 Pricing the arts
Michael Rushton

This survey presents general rules for arts organizations setting menus of prices for live performances, museum exhibitions, festivals and the like. The problem facing arts organizations is how to set prices to capture as much of the surplus generated by the events as possible. In practice, this means finding a way to offer lower prices to 'marginal customers' – those customers highly sensitive to price – while still collecting a higher price from the average customer, who has a relatively inelastic demand for the events. These practices are commonly known as 'price discrimination'. Firms selling goods in perfectly competitive markets must take prices as given, and so price discrimination cannot be used, but such situations are rare in the arts, as each performance, exhibition or festival has some unique characteristics.

Price discrimination can be achieved in two ways. One method is to charge different prices to different groups of customers, where it is easy for the arts organization to identify the group to which each customer belongs. This is known as direct price discrimination, or third-degree price discrimination. A common example is a performance or museum that gives a discount on the ticket price to students or to individuals above a certain age. This practice can be effective only where there is no arbitrage; students must not be able to purchase cheap tickets and resell them to those ineligible for the discount.

Consider for example an arts organization selling tickets for general admission to an event, and that seeks to maximize profits (non-profit firms are dealt with below). Suppose marginal cost is constant at MC, and, for now, that there is no capacity constraint; in this situation MC is nearly zero. There are two groups of consumers. Let MR_i and q_i be the marginal revenue curves and the quantity of tickets purchased by group $i = L, H$, where L is the price-sensitive group, and the H group has low elasticity of demand.

The first rule-of-thumb is that the organization will maximize profits by setting prices P_i such that $MR_i = MC$ for each group. The intuition is clear: if for either group $MR_i > MC$, profits can be increased by lowering the price for that group to sell a few more tickets, and if $MR_i < MC$, profits can be increased by raising the price for that group and selling fewer tickets to them. It is as if the organization is selling two entirely unrelated products.

Now suppose there is in fact a capacity constraint – there are only Q seats in the venue – such that setting prices according to the $MR_i = MC$ rule would entail excess demand. The second rule-of-thumb is that prices P_i should be set such that (1) $MR_L = MR_H$, and (2) $q_L + q_H = Q$. The intuition is that if we were satisfying condition (2), but $MR_i > MR_j$, it would increase profits to lower P_i (and sell to group i a few more tickets) and raise P_j (and sell fewer tickets to group j); what is gained in increased revenue from group i exceeds the loss in revenue from group j.

The second method of price discrimination is called 'indirect' or 'second-degree', and involves offering to all potential customers a menu of prices for different packages of tickets and complementary goods, and allowing customers to effectively sort themselves according to the options they choose. An example is a museum that charges one price for general admission and an additional price for a special exhibit, which customers may or may not choose to see. There are a number of applications.

Two-part pricing

Suppose the organization can charge a general admission price T, and a price P for additional goods that are available once inside, where these additional goods are supplied with a constant marginal cost, MC (suppose there is zero marginal cost associated with general admission). There are many examples in the arts: a museum might have an additional fee for a special exhibit; there might be refreshments or souvenirs available for sale inside a museum or performing arts venue or film theatre; a company might sell hardware for reading digital books or listening to downloaded music recordings, as well as the actual literary or musical content; or, to use the example from the seminal paper in the subject (Oi, 1971), an amusement park may charge an entry fee and a price for each ride.

To get started, imagine a simple case where consumers may differ in their willingness to pay for general admission, but there is no discernible way to classify consumers in terms of their demand for 'rides' (to proceed with the amusement park example). Then the profit-maximizing strategy is (1) set $P = MC$, and (2) set T such that $MR = 0$. In other words, set T to maximize the revenues from general admission, noting that MR and the willingness to pay for general admission is dependent upon P – the higher is the price per ride P, the lower is the willingness to pay for general admission. The intuition is that setting $P > MC$ is inefficient – at the margin there will be some consumers declining to purchase more rides, because of the price, even though their willingness to pay for rides at the margin exceeds MC. If the organization were to lower P, that creates more consumer surplus, which can be extracted by the organization in its subsequent ability to set a higher general admission price T.

This model is amenable to direct price discrimination; the organization might want to set a lower T for students or seniors, following the rule of setting T such that $MR_i = 0$ for each group i. But it would remain the case that all groups would be charged the same price P per ride.

But now suppose a situation where consumer preferences for 'rides' differ between customers, but we have no way of knowing, as we do with direct price discrimination, whether any specific individual is a great fan of rides or quickly tires of them.

In such a situation we should depart from $P = MC$ in the following way: if our marginal, price-sensitive customer has a strong (relative to others) preference for 'rides', then set $P < MC$, and capture the associated increase in consumer surplus by increasing T; and if the marginal customer has a low (relative to others) preference for rides, then set $P > MC$, which will necessitate a lower T.

The intuition is as follows. Suppose the first case, where the price-sensitive visitors have a high preference for rides. Then offering subsidized rides is a way to bring them into the venue. The organization won't need to worry about losing too much of the custom of average customers, since they value general admission highly but have a low demand for rides in any case. When we observe an amusement park offering a high general admission fee but free rides, even though the marginal cost per ride is positive, it is probably the case that marginal consumers have a high preference for lots of rides. Offering rides for free is not all that costly to the firm, since it is only the marginal consumers who will take advantage of the free rides from opening until closing.

Now consider the opposite case, where the typical customer has a greater demand for rides than the marginal customer. Then the organization can entice the marginal consumer into the venue with a low entry fee T, and capture the high surplus of the average customer through charging them for the rides they so enjoy. This provides an explanation of the phenomenon so often remarked upon by laypersons: 'Why is popcorn so expensive in movie theatres?' It turns out that marginal, infrequent attendees of the cinema buy less popcorn than those who attend more often. So it makes sense for the theatre owner to lower the price of admission into the theatre, and earn high profits on popcorn sales (Gil and Hartmann, 2009).

Bundling

Suppose there is some good X, not necessarily an arts-related good, for which there is some demand by price-sensitive, marginal consumers of the arts, but for which there is little interest from the average ticket-buyer for the arts. Then the arts organization might effectively price-discriminate by offering to all ticket-buyers a special discount on good X. This will help lure marginal consumers to the arts venue, but without having to provide any sort of discount in price to the average price-inelastic attendees, who will not be interested in exercising their rights to buy X at a subsidized price. This practice is known as 'bundling'. As an example, consider a theatre in London's West End. It might charge high ticket prices, knowing that average theatre-attendees will pay the high price, and offer a 'bundle' of a pair of theatre tickets, a pair of tickets on a sightseeing bus, and dinner at a good, but not excellent, restaurant, where the price for the bundle is significantly less (although still above cost) than the price of buying all three goods separately. Here, the marginal customers are tourists, probably on a tight budget, and with many different things on offer in the city to compete for their limited time. They might not be willing to pay full price for theatre tickets, but will find the bundle an attractive option. And the theatre is able to attract their business without lowering the price for ordinary, unbundled tickets that would be purchased by London residents.

Differential quality

Arts organizations can charge different prices for customer experiences of different characteristics and quality. For example, preferred seats, or preferred times of performances can command a higher price than lower-quality seats or tickets for performances at low-demand times of day or days of the week. Publishers offer different versions of books: hardcovers have the advantage of more durable binding and being immediately available, while paperbacks have the disadvantages of less durable binding and a delay (usually at least a year) in release. Seats in the upper balcony, and paperback versions of novels, are priced to attract marginal, price-sensitive consumers, while seats in the orchestra, and immediately available hardcover books, are priced higher, with the knowledge that some consumers will be willing to pay the higher price in order to obtain the highest quality.

The challenge for the arts organization is to ensure that the quality difference is high enough relative to the price differential to avoid having too many consumers opting for the lower-quality/lower-priced alternative. Thus, while it makes sense to charge for the lower-quality version a price as close as possible to the marginal customer's willingness to pay, in general the price of the high-quality version is something less than the maximum willingness to pay by high-demand customers, in order to avoid their 'switching' to the lower-priced option. Cheung (1977) adds that high-quality seats might also be 'underpriced' to prevent them from going unsold and, subsequently, occupied by those who bought lower-quality seats and then snuck past the ushers into the vacant high-quality seats.

An interesting empirical study concerns tickets for Broadway theatre, and the half-price day-of-show tickets that can be bought in person at selected outlets in New York. The day-of-show tickets are lower 'quality' in the sense that there is great uncertainty as to whether any will in fact be available on the day of the show, and also in the (deliberate) inconvenience in obtaining them – they cannot be purchased online or by telephone even though such purchases would be easy for theatres to accommodate, since regular tickets can be bought that way. Leslie (2004) used data on sales to find that the theatres were not engaged in profit-maximizing pricing, because the discount for day-of-show tickets was too high – the high price differential combined with the relatively small difference in 'quality' was inducing too much 'switching' by high-demand customers into purchasing the discounted tickets. Leslie suggests a discount on day-of-show tickets of about 30 per cent would have been more profitable for the theatres. See also Courty (2003a, 2003b) on the timing of price discounts.

Quantity discounts
It is commonplace for museums to offer single-day tickets or memberships for families that cost less on a per-person basis than would be charged to a single individual, and this is a fairly obvious recognition of the differential willingness to pay by a single individual and set of two parents with children.

In addition, discounts are given on the number of events attended: festivals offer menus of different numbers of performances to attend, where the cost per event is lower the more events are purchased; performing arts organizations offer season tickets; and museums offer memberships that lower the effective price per visit. For individuals, diminishing marginal benefits work on two levels here. Consider an opera season, where there are options for tickets to individual operas as well as season tickets. The more operas one sees in a season, the lower the marginal benefit for attending one more. But that reasoning applies equally to purchases of oranges or shirts. In addition, however, if one were to purchase tickets for the opera on an individual basis, the person would first choose a ticket to their favourite opera of the season. If they were to buy tickets for a second opera during the season, the second ticket would be for an opera that is less preferred than the first one, and so the reservation price for that ticket will be less.

In general, it is best for the arts organization to ensure that there is a variety of ticket-purchase options, to best capture the surplus from individuals with different willingness to pay not only for a single ticket, but who experience differing rates of decline in marginal benefits.

Pricing when profits are not the only goal
Suppose a museum or orchestra is run by the state or a non-profit. How would pricing depart from the profit-maximizing rules given above?

It might be the case that prices do not change at all; the goals of outreach to under-served communities might best be reached by maximizing profits from museum admissions or concert tickets, and using the proceeds to fund educational programmes.

On the other hand, suppose the goal is simply to increase attendance at the museum or concerts. First note that the means of price discrimination used by profit-maximizing firms already work to the benefit of those with a lower willingness to pay, who can get discounted admission on times and days of the week when demand is typically low, and who can get 'basic' admission at a low rate without paying for special exhibits or prime-location orchestra seats. But a state-owned or non-profit arts organization might discount the basic offering even further to achieve their goals of broad dissemination of the arts.

Would the discount in prices ever extend to charging a basic admission price below marginal cost? We can imagine a few possibilities: the target customer of the deeply discounted price has a willingness to pay above marginal cost, but this is a means of transferring consumer surplus to that person; or, the target customer's willingness to pay is below marginal cost, but (1) there are positive externalities associated with consumption, or (2) consumption now will alter preferences and willingness to pay in the future. If none of these factors is present, it is difficult to justify prices below marginal cost.

New directions in pricing

Arts organizations continue to experiment with new methods of price-setting, owing to the possibilities created by technological change in online transactions and data management. For example, concert tickets can now be sold through online auctions (Halcoussis and Mathews, 2007). And as sports franchises adopt methods of variable pricing through their seasons, where prices adjust according to shifting demand for specific matches, we might also begin to see the same for tickets for live performances in the arts.

See also:

Chapter 1: Application of welfare economics; Chapter 26: Demand; Chapter 37: Marketing the arts; Chapter 40: Museums; Chapter 47: Performing arts.

References

Adams, William James and Janet L. Yellen (1976), 'Commodity Bundling and the Burden of Monopoly', *Quarterly Journal of Economics*, 90, 475–98.
Ansari, Asim, S. Siddarth and Charles B. Weinberg (1996), 'Pricing a Bundle of Products or Services: The Case of Nonprofits', *Journal of Marketing Research*, 33, 86–93.
Cheung, Steven N.S. (1977), 'Why are Better Seats "Underpriced"?', *Economic Inquiry*, 15, 513–22.
Clerides, Sofronis K. (2002), 'Book Value: Intertemporal Pricing and Quality Discrimination in the US Market for Books', *International Journal of Industrial Organization*, 20, 1385–408.
Connolly, Marie and Alan B. Kreuger (2006), 'Rockonomics: The Economics of Popular Music', in V.A. Ginsburgh and D. Throsby (eds), *Handbook of the Economics of Art and Culture*, Amsterdam: North-Holland, pp. 667–719.
Courty, Pascal (2000), 'An Economic Guide to Ticket Pricing in the Entertainment Industry', *Recherches Économiques de Louvain*, 66, 167–92.
Courty, Pascal (2003a), 'Ticket Pricing Under Demand Uncertainty', *Journal of Law and Economics*, 46, 627–52.
Courty, Pascal (2003b), 'Some Economics of Ticket Resale', *Journal of Economic Perspectives*, 17, 85–97.
Courty, Pascal and Mario Pagliero (2009), 'Price Discrimination in the Concert Industry', CEPR Discussion Paper No. 7143.
Cowell, Ben (2007), 'Measuring the Impact of Free Admission', *Cultural Trends*, 16, 203–24.

Currim, Imran S., Charles B. Weinberg and Dick R. Wittink (1981), 'Design of Subscription Programs for a Performing Arts Series', *Journal of Consumer Research*, 8, 67–75.

Gil, Ricard and Wesley R. Hartmann (2009), 'Empirical Analysis of Metering Price Discrimination: Evidence from Concession Sales at Movie Theatres', *Marketing Science*, 28, 1046–62.

Halcoussis, Dennis and Timothy Mathews (2007), 'eBay Auctions for *Third Eye Blind* Concert Tickets', *Journal of Cultural Economics*, 31, 65–78.

Leslie, Phillip (2004), 'Price Discrimination in Broadway Theater', *Rand Journal of Economics*, 35, 520–41.

Leslie, Phillip and Alan Sorenson (2009), 'The Welfare Effects of Ticket Resale', NBER Working Paper No. 15476.

Maddison, David and Terry Foster (2003), 'Valuing Congestion Costs in the British Museum', *Oxford Economic Papers*, 55, 173–90.

Mortimer, Julie Holland (2007), 'Price Discrimination, Copyright Law, and Technological Innovation: Evidence from the Introduction of DVDs', *Quarterly Journal of Economics*, 122, 1307–50.

Oi, Walter Y. (1971), 'A Disneyland Dilemma: Two-part Tariffs for a Mickey Mouse Monopoly', *Quarterly Journal of Economics*, 85, 77–96.

Prieto-Rodríguez, Juan and Víctor Fernández-Blanco (2006), 'Optimal Pricing and Grant Policies for Museums', *Journal of Cultural Economics*, 30, 169–81.

Ravanas, Philippe (2008), 'Hitting a High Note: The Chicago Symphony Orchestra Reverses a Decade of Decline with New Programs, New Services and New Prices', *International Journal of Arts Management*, 10, 68–87.

Rentschler, Ruth, Anne-Marie Hede and Tabitha R. White (2007), 'Museum Pricing: Challenges to Theory Development and Practice', *International Journal of Nonprofit and Voluntary Sector Marketing*, 12, 163–73.

Rosen, Sherwin and Andrew M. Rosenfield (1997), 'Ticket Pricing', *Journal of Law and Economics*, 40, 351–76.

Shiller, Ben and Joel Waldfogel (2009), 'Music for a Song: An Empirical Look at Uniform Song Pricing and its Alternatives', NBER Working Paper No. 15390.

Shy, Oz (2008), *How to Price*, Cambridge, UK: Cambridge University Press.

Steinberg, Richard and Burton A. Weisbrod (1998), 'Pricing and Rationing by Nonprofit Organizations with Distributional Objectives', in B. Weisbrod (ed.), *To Profit or Not to Profit*, Cambridge, UK: Cambridge University Press, pp. 65–82.

Steinberg, Richard and Burton A. Weisbrod (2005), 'Nonprofits with Distributional Objectives: Price Discrimination and Corner Solutions', *Journal of Public Economics*, 89, 2205–30.

Further reading

Shy (2008) is a comprehensive text on pricing, and Courty (2000) provides a survey of ticket pricing. On differential levels of quality and price discrimination see Rosen and Rosenfield (1997) on tickets, Clerides (2002) on books, and Mortimer (2007) on evidence from VHS and DVD versions of movies. On bundling and subscriptions, see Adams and Yellen (1976), Ansari *et al.* (1996), Currim *et al.* (1981), and Ravanas (2008). Connolly and Kreuger (2006) and Courty and Pagliero (2009) consider when popular music performers will use price discrimination. On price discrimination methods for online music downloads, see Shiller and Waldfogel (2009). Leslie and Sorenson (2009) consider pricing strategies when there are secondary markets in tickets. On museum pricing see Cowell (2007), Prieto-Rodríguez and Fernández-Blanco (2006) and Rentschler *et al.* (2007). Maddison and Foster (2003) examine optimal museum pricing when consumers are willing to pay to reduce crowding. On departures from profit-maximizing pricing when there are distributional objectives, see Steinberg and Weisbrod (1998, 2005).

50 Principal–agent analysis
Michele Trimarchi

The cultural sector consists of a complex network of markets in which various flows of exchange occur. These are either monetary or real, in some cases they can be mixed, and often they can be quite difficult to measure in an uncontroversial way: this is due both to the importance of meta-economic profiles (aesthetic, cultural, informational and so on) in the determination of their value and to the influence exerted upon demand, price and other economic variables by subjective evaluation whose reliability is not necessarily related to experience, education or training. Creative artists exchange their works with producers and dealers, with single purchasers or large audiences, central and local governments; funding organizations exchange grants or in-kind subsidies with creators (seldom), producers (normally) and sellers (frequently); private corporations exchange funds with artists and organizations; and individual donors exchange their contributions with theatres and museums. These exchanges can be interpreted as a combination of different principal–agent relationships, both within and between the markets.

A sequence of exchanges also occurs across a number of progressively converging markets involving new technologies: the creative artist produces a text, uploads it on to a blog, then elaborates it as a theatrical script; a director stages it; other artists and technicians transform it into a video; it is seen on YouTube, in a movie theatre, in a home video and so on; somebody will write a novel based upon the subject, and a TV series will be produced. Although the whole sequence may sound extreme, we can observe that a growing proportion of cultural activities are transformed through these various exchanges and markets. This implies a new complexity of contractual relationships, intellectual property rights management, material and financial accessibility, and investment in human capital. Emerging creative artists and cultural managers must be able to deal with such complexities. One issue for cultural economics is whether these changes are altering principal–agent relationships.

Tracking the flows that constitute a whole exchange route is crucial in order to understand that the outcome of each results from the combination of the contractual power of each agent and of the system of incentives (both formal and conventional) that influence strategies, choices and behaviours. Different types of agency can be identified: common agency can be considered typical of the traditional cultural realms, such as the performing arts and the temporary exhibitions in museums, where the selling agent (the arts organization) receives funds from two principals, the public sector giving grants, and the private sector giving donations and sponsorships, each with their particular objectives. A sort of principal–agent chain characterizes the contemporary arts market, where artist, dealer, collector, critic and expert contribute to determine the value of paintings and artists through a system of cross-evaluation and assessment whose main feature is the excess of information. Here the roles of principal and agent are unclear: for instance, is the dealer the agent of the artist or of the collector?

Exchanges between principal and agent in the arts sector are mostly characterized by conflicting goals. Although determined in a generic way (such as diffusion of culture, artistic education of new generations, preservation of cultural heritage and protection of local/national repertoire in the performing arts), goals quite often prove reciprocally conflicting since there may be trade-offs, such as those between preservation of and access to heritage, between innovation and accessibility in the performing arts, and between the appreciation of regular consumers and the expectations of occasional ones.

The distribution of information among agents

Information and, crucially asymmetry of information, where one party to an exhange has more information than the other, is central to principal–agent analysis. Heterogeneity of the relevant information, and its different level of objectivity, makes it the fundamental factor conditioning the relationships between principals and agents in the arts sector. This manifests itself in various ways. First, there is a problem of certification of authenticity, which is quite strong and sometimes contradictory in the visual arts, although it is not irrelevant in the performing arts. Second, evaluation of quality is inherently controversial since it deals with a multidimensional concept covering technical, aesthetic, cultural and social aspects of works of art: not only may expert evaluations differ strongly from each other and upon prevailing convention, but also consumer utility is influenced by the dialogic ability of the arts supply to raise the value of the accumulated stock of knowledge of consumers. Third, consumer choice is based upon largely insufficient information: although consumers seek novelty and uniqueness, the arts are experience goods, and this generates a paradox. Although, on the one hand, unavoidably limited information raises the risk of low hedonistic appreciation and leads to insufficient willingness to pay on the part of the average consumer, on the other hand awareness of the riskiness of novelty generates an increase in the accumulated stock of consumption capital. Only very experienced consumers are able to choose autonomously, being less subject to the informational advantage of cultural agents.

Agents endowed with private information find it convenient to self-assess the relevant aspects of their supply; a great proportion of the value in each exchange is usually generated by information created, processed and distributed by the supplier – the agent (artist, museum curator or theatre director, and so on). Such information is not easily monitored by the principal, the consumer, who may find it very difficult to transform it into objective data. This may lead to so-called 'supplier-induced demand', when the supplier is the main or sole source of information about the product.

Information asymmetry is the cause of adverse selection and moral hazard: the former refers to the 'wrong' choice being made as the agent fails to disclose all the relevant information (the used car is a 'lemon'); and the latter results from faulty incentives to agents to take into full account the consequences of their actions (having insurance encourages greater risk-taking). The problems of adverse selection and moral hazard generated by the asymmetric distribution of information find a partial response in a system of third-party assessment of quality and other such features of cultural products. Expert, critics and consumers themselves produce and exchange a great deal of information about authenticity, quality, reliability and consistency of works of art, as well as the different forms of reproduction (records, pictures, books, digital and audiovisual products) that provide art consumers with additional information that can increase the utility derived from direct experience.

Information and critical assessments produced by these third parties vary in reliability, depending upon their actual independence, and the related risk of collusion or sympathy with the agents leading to biased choices on the part of the principals (consumers, public or private funders). Moreover, agents may be subject to regulatory capture with either public or private principals: this occurs when the agent is the principal's source of information about his conduct. Regulatory capture can be induced either by explicit rules or by the anticipation of the principal's likely expectations. In Italian experience, for instance, although the rules do not establish any preference, opera houses tend to limit their productions to well-known titles so that the state bureaucracy can adopt the conventional view of the operas as a proxy for quality, and so confirm past grants. In this case, the choices of the opera houses can be explained by their extremely high degree of dependence on public subsidies, which induces their risk-averse strategy.

Objectives, strategies and constraints

As noted above, the strategic choices adopted by both principals and agents depend upon their goals and organizational orientation. The formally stated goals of both cultural organizations and cultural public administrations usually cover a wide range of heterogeneous options, implying a very low degree of precision; the imprecise definition of specific objectives is then reflected in the lack of consistent criteria and mechanisms for the determination of public grants (and this quite often holds for corporate sponsorship as well). Accordingly, noble but abstract principles end up supporting weak and uncertain strategies: the absence of a specific 'why' makes it impossible to elaborate any consistent 'how'.

The real goals of cultural organizations, acting as agents both for the principals – funders and consumers – can be inferred from their output and financial structure; this will help us understand the likely outcome of each principal–agent exchange, also considering that such relationships are normally repeated over a long time horizon (implying adaptive and evolutionary strategies on the part of both principal and agent). The heterogeneous nature of activities, the range of material and financial dimensions, the different extent of regional and local competence and many other factors generate a variety of institutional structures in the arts sector.

From a formal perspective, there are several possible organizational forms of arts producers; they normally share the same non-profit constraints but may adopt the label of foundations, institutions or corporations. However, the formal setting does not necessarily ensure any consistent strategy due to the mixed nature of such organizations, since they sell private products that, however, generate wider benefits; they use private, public and corporate funds and progressively expand the range of goods and services offered, acting across a growing number of markets.

Therefore, in order for the organizational orientation to be identified, a few substantial features should be analysed, such as the goals and profiles of price strategies, the selection of inputs, and the length and breadth of product life cycle. In the case of art producers, the organizational orientation normally lies between the extremes of altruistic mission and revenue maximization; a crucial role is played by the degree of utility derived from 'immaterial' satisfaction, that is, utility related to the activity *per se* rather than to its monetary or material implications and effects. As far as public regulators/funders are concerned, they can either be oriented towards social goals such as the diffusion of the arts and culture or equality of access to the arts, on the one hand, or towards typically bureaucratic goals, such as consensus or rent (or some combination of both) on the other. For their part, private companies give funds to the arts either in search of a distinguished reputation or – at the opposite extreme – in order to make their brand name known through indirect publicity (actually, the case may prove much more complex, with exchanges aimed at direct contact with a specific audience of decision-makers rather than the public at large).

There are cases in which the network of exchanges among the various agents operating in the arts sector is more complex, and in which agents of one exchange act as principals in another, forming a sort of principal–agent chain (as in the visual arts market); this makes the analysis of the whole picture more difficult owing to the reciprocal impact exerted by the actual orientation of each agent. Moreover, normative, technological and financial constraints may vary from one exchange to another, especially when such exchanges occur between different markets (for example, between theatre and cinema, or literature and television, and so on).

Also, limiting our analysis to the simple case of a theatre or a museum, we often face a common agency relationship, in which two principals give funds to an arts organization (their common agent) in exchange for a project whose actual nature and cultural value are completely known and evaluated by the agent who receives the funds. The agent therefore has the possibility to provide each of the principals with a false report about the goals actually pursued (and their likely impact upon the principals' goals). It may then prove convenient for the agent to hide some information from one or both principals, according to how one party's orientation combines with the others'. For example, if the agent is revenue-oriented and the principals respectively pursue social goals (public sector) and reputation (private sector), there is a strong incentive for the agent to cheat, overstating the features of his supply that appear to be consistent with these generic and unmeasurable goals. The most efficient response on the part of each principal is then to replace monetary grants with in-kind subsidies: since monitoring of output proves ineffective, the stage of control is 'shifted back' to inputs. This can contribute to the selection of mission-oriented suppliers who are specifically interested not in receiving grants but in having a real opportunity to produce works of art, since in-kind subsidies actually reduce their production costs. Overall, there are various reasons emanating from the presence of asymmetric information that lead to funding organizations favouring existing recipient arts organizations and at the same time raising quite high barriers to entry for new producers, thus freezing the arts.

The existing framework of incentives

An adequate system of incentives can actually reduce – if not offset – the advantages currently enjoyed by the cultural organizations in this complex principal–agent network. Unlike the case in manufacturing, incentives in the arts sector cannot focus upon the price level or other monetary parameters, due to the controversial matter of measuring value, and to the existence of many alternative combinations of inputs needed to produce the artistic outcome.

Therefore we must distinguish between private and public principals. The former may respond adequately to their likely informational gap by identifying specific parameters in order to verify the effectiveness of their choice; in any case, the final goal of a private company is to attain market outcomes, and these can also be tested in the short run. There is growing evidence of a concentration of sponsorships within the restricted realm of blockbuster exhibitions, internationally renowned theatres and one-shot events. By contrast, public institutions suffer from much weaker incentives, due to bureaucratic resistance and the preference for selecting recipients so as to minimize the likely dissent that would be generated by tight controls and actual sanctions, and because institutional cultural goals are loosely identified at the various layers of government. The main obstacle to the establishment of specific incentives is the perception that any mechanism that involves monitoring and consequent sanctions risks impinging upon creative, artistic or cultural freedom. That perception is shared by both arts organizations and public regulators/funders, and is assisted by a very strong and explicit social sanction.

A closer look at the production of the arts and culture should make it clear that cultural choices and managerial strategies can be considered, analysed and evaluated separately. Of course there may be a 'grey area' in between, but certainly many decisions and actions taken by arts organizations can be the object of monitoring and evaluation, according to the prevailing goal of the principal. In fact, while the choice of inputs in a performance or in an exhibition is certainly related to artistic and cultural choices – and therefore responds to subjective and 'untouchable' criteria – there are many other aspects of art production that can be measured through quite precise parameters – the availability of the arts in a certain area, the establishment of an equal-access policy, the educational impact, the offer of side-products that improve the enjoyment of the experience on the part of consumers – whose monitoring does not exert any negative impact upon artistic or cultural choices.

The level and composition of grants can therefore be tailored to the level and composition of art production according to a specified hierarchy of goals and performance indicators. By so doing, public grants could abandon the uncomfortable role of financial lifebelt, becoming instead the explicit reward for the attainment of specific goals. Incentives should therefore be crafted with reference to the actual contribution of each cultural organization to the funder's goals, preferably dividing them into two parts: some aimed at acknowledging the existence value of the facility; that should be determined with reference to past subsidies, in order for the recipient to enjoy a sufficient degree of stability. The remaining part should be determined with reference to a range of parameters connected to the proportion of invested funds, the features of products, the profiles and quality of human resources and the improvements in access and participation.

An effective system of incentives could finally move art production from the false market of grant maximization to its proper market, in which various heterogeneous principals 'buy' different parts (or effects) of the agent's effort, each according to his goals, values and organizational orientation. In this respect each cultural organization appears at the centre of a multiple world of contracts where principals are not hierarchically different, but are too heterogeneous for comparisons to be made; this overcomes the problems generated by the traditional view, according to which the phantom of financial failure requires the acritical intervention on the part of the public sector, and therefore gives importance to the quantity rather than to the quality of public funding. Appropriate incentives, on the contrary, grant the pursuit of publicly relevant goals, and raise the level of responsibility for cultural organizations. This would finally strengthen the importance of consumer choice and expectations, and re-equilibrate the contractual power of principals and agents.

See also:

Chapter 51: Public choice; Chapter 52: Public support; Chapter 54: Regulation.

References

Gimore, A. and R. Rentschler (2002), 'Change in Museum Management: A Custodial or Marketing Emphasis?', *Journal of Management Development*, 2 (10), 745–60.
Hefetz, A. and M. Warner (2004), 'Privatization and its Reverse: Explaining the Dynamics of the Government Contracting Process', *Journal of Pubic Administration Research and Theory*, 14, 171–90.
National Audit Office (2005), *Procurement in the Culture, Media and Sport Sector*, Report for the House of Commons, London: The Stationery Office.
Trimarchi, M. (2004), 'Regulation, Integration and Sustainability in the Cultural Sector', *Journal of Heritage Studies*, 10 (5), 401–15.

Further reading

Suggested further reading: Gimore and Rentschler (2002), Hefetz and Warner (2004), National Audit Office (2005), and Trimarchi (2004).

51 Public choice
Isidoro Mazza

The economic analysis of cultural policy has traditionally focused on its ability to correct market failures, promote cultural progress and preserve and enhance historical heritage. The investigation has devoted relatively little attention to the political decision-making process and institutional issues. This resistance of the discipline to political economic analysis is particularly striking when we consider the prominent role that the government has in the cultural sector, even in those countries where its intervention may be relatively less pervasive (like the USA or UK). Moreover, it sets a sharp contrast with the huge proliferation of political economic studies, now common in virtually every area of economic research. This brief chapter cannot provide a survey of the political economic literature. It rather aims at giving a taste of what can be learnt from the advancements made by public choice theory in order to improve our understanding of cultural policy. Detailed and comprehensive analyses of the field are provided by Mueller (1997, 2003), Persson and Tabellini (2000), Rowley and Schneider (2008), Weingast and Wittman (2006).

The public choice approach
In line with standard welfare economics, a substantial number of studies on cultural policies assume that they are carried out by a fully informed, far-sighted and unelected planner pursuing the public interest. This hypothesis, although reassuring, represents a very strong simplification of reality. It is overly optimistic about information constraints, it does not provide a justification for the benevolence of the planner, and it disregards how politics and institutions may affect the public outcome.

In the broader field of public economics, public choice applies the economic methodology to the analysis of the political – 'non-market' – decision-making process. This research area has contributed in a substantial way to the understanding of fundamental issues: the aggregation of individual preferences in decision rules (social choice theory), the functioning of representative democracies, the role of elections and institutions, the characteristics of collective action, the activity of bureaucracy. In the analysis of policy-making, a strong emphasis is given to the information asymmetries in the public sector. This is depicted as a complex system of principal–agent relationships, where agents enjoy rents from possessing information that is unknown to the principal. On this reasoning, the government is considered as an agent of society and, at the same time, the principal of bureaucratic agents. In this framework, a fairly common tenet is that public agents are (mainly) self-interested. The fulfilment of public interest will then depend on the incentives and constraints that society and institutions impose on those agents.[1]

This chapter discusses some political economic issues that could have particular relevance for the economics of the cultural sector. In the following section, the focus is on the political decision-making process in representative or direct democracy. After that, a brief indication of the relevance of positive and normative analysis of institutions in the investigation of government policies is provided.

Political decision-making

Special interest politics

Public policy results from the composition of conflicting interests. However, we do not expect all interests to be equally represented at the political stage. Since information about the outcome of different policies is a public good and since each individual has a negligible influence on the elections, people have no incentive to be informed about politics: they are 'rationally' ignorant (Downs, 1957). However, when policies produce large selective benefits for narrow specific groups, these have sufficient incentives to be informed about politics and to overcome the transaction costs of organizing for lobbying (Olson, 1965). Lobbies have several instruments to try to influence public decision-makers. They can provide financial resources or valuable information that can be helpful to win an electoral contest. In addition, organized groups may also exert pressure by threatening some politically costly action (such as a strike).

Wealth transfers to interest groups are favoured by the lack of information of the voters about the government activity. On the other hand, these transfers are hardly sufficient to induce taxpayers to bear the costs of information and organization to oppose them, since each individual pays only for a marginal fraction of the total transfers. By similar reasoning, large groups are supposed to have no incentive to organize for pressure activities: benefits are divided among a large number of people and, therefore, 'free-riding' becomes dominant.

There are different views about the effects of lobbying on welfare. The so-called Chicago School argues that competition between lobbies will discipline policy-making and lead to an efficient outcome. According to this view, institutions favour competition and transparency in the political system. To the contrary, the Virginia School emphasizes that private agents waste resources in the activities pursuing wealth transfers and also that policy-makers would choose inefficient forms of redistribution in order to disguise the transfers to powerful interest groups.

Early models of either approach presents several shortcomings (see van Winden, 2008). First, they focus only on the demand side, so that policies are fully determined by the competition of influencing groups. Second, they do not explain what kind of activities determines the influence of lobbies and how. Third, they do not explicitly model information asymmetries; they simply assume that information rents exist, with the voters being unable to fully control their legislators. Fourth, they generally assume that interest groups concentrate to influence only one of the various political and bureaucratic steps of decision-making that contribute to the government outcome (see next section). Recently, an extensive literature has contributed to improving our understanding of the source of political influence of interest groups, addressing the aforementioned shortcomings. A number of theoretical models have shown how the provision of information and/ or contributions by interest groups can positively affect their political influence even in the presence of rational and informed voters.

Cultural goods have peculiarities that may favour the influence of special interest groups. In fact, wealth transfers can be easily disguised in the case of arts. In some cases, it may be difficult for the public to evaluate if and how some forms of public expenditure for the arts contribute to the accumulation of cultural capital. Control by the public on policy-making is then far from easy. Moreover, in the cases of the performing as well as the visual arts, public purchase of cultural services often produces concentrated benefits for the private sellers (and also for a cultural and economic elite), with various costs for society. Therefore we would expect the development of lobbying for the reasons discussed above. There are studies offering some empirical evidence that arts organizations do lobby government for subsidies in the USA and the UK (for example Grampp, 1989). However, we know very little about the channels of influence and the efficacy of lobbying for the arts, that is, the amount and the type of expenditure specifically generated by lobbying. It would also be interesting to make a comparison between lobbying in the USA and the UK and lobbying in continental Europe, where the system of public financing is substantially different. The perception of the existence of lobbying activities should also encourage the diffusion of formal models of endogenous policy, where public transfers depend on the activity of politically influential actors. This theoretical analysis could offer important, empirically verifiable results concerning, for example, the outcome and the efficiency losses of lobbying and the identification of the cultural sectors where lobbying is more likely to develop. In general, although it is often argued that lobbying activities are widespread in the arts, there is a lack of rigorous analysis investigating this phenomenon. In this respect, special attention could be devoted to international trade, which is widely recognized as an area where interest groups show their influence on policy-making more forcefully. This possibility should not be excluded *a priori* for the international trade of cultural goods. Actually, the widespread belief that national culture must be protected against globalization represent a powerful pretext for cultural industries – the audiovisual one, in particular – to ask for special protectionist measures (see Acheson and Maule, 2006). In this context, UNESCO's promotion of cultural diversity could be interpreted as an authoritative support to protectionism of national movie industries against imports from the USA.[2]

Finally, it is important to note that electoral competition may also determine policies favouring specific groups just for the characteristics of the latter, even when they do not attempt to influence policy-making. For example, electoral competition models including groups of voters with different ideological biases show that a rational candidate would choose a policy favourable for the groups having more 'swing' voters, because their votes are less affected by ideology and thus easier to catch than those of strongly ideological voters. If, however, core supporters will be more reactive to political favours than other voters, it can be shown that redistribution will be in favour of groups with more loyal voters. Swing and loyal voters can also be distinguished by their location. Theoretical and empirical studies on the political economy of grants show that general revenue can be used for pork-barrel spending: public resources are allocated to specific districts in order to improve the probability of re-election of the donor government and of the local politicians linked to the latter. Also transfers to local administration for cultural expenditure may be politically influenced (see Guccio and Mazza, 2008). In general, we should expect this phenomenon to be observed more easily when these specific transfers are relatively significant with respect to other earmarked grants, and benefits are sufficiently concentrated.

Direct democracy instruments

The use of referenda has often been suggested as a way to obtain public policies, including cultural policy, that are close to the preferences of collectivity. It is argued that referenda have the clear advantages of reducing the information rents of politicians, public officials and interest groups. Moreover, the questions asked in a referendum can be designed in a way that allows the revelation of the willingness to pay for a specific policy. Although referenda may not necessarily cause low-quality actions, they do not appear to be politically feasible in many countries and there is no clear reason for introducing them just for cultural policy. In fact, the extensive use of this system of collective decision-making would cause a substantial delay in the policy-making and would be rather inconsistent with the existence of a representative democratic process. These problems could be partially avoided by the formation of a sufficiently decentralized federation such that the costs of collective decision-making are substantially reduced.

Nonetheless, we should exert some caution in accepting the advantages of referenda. First, the use of a referendum presents the significant shortcoming of giving a large power to the agenda-setter. By presenting the alternatives to vote in a strategic way, the agenda-setter can pull the voting outcome away from that preferred by the median voter. This power of the agenda-setter is even amplified in a multidimensional policy space. This phenomenon raises more fundamental questions about the choice of the agenda-setter and of the rules for the formation of the agenda, which should probably be settled at a constitutional stage. Second, direct democracy does not avoid definitively the possibility that special interest groups and lobbying will influence the voting outcome. A study by Goldstein (1999) on 'grass-roots' lobbying, or outside lobbying, shows that consultants financed by private associations are able to induce a mass of people to exert pressure on their political representatives in favour of or against a specific bill, notwithstanding the reasonableness of that bill. This observation casts some doubts on the possibility that people could not be manoeuvred in the direction preferred by some elite in a direct democracy system.

Institutions and the supply of government policies

The accountability of political decision-makers depends also on the institutional system determining the powers of the different actors contributing to the outcome of government policies. The analysis of the policy-making process is complicated by the intricate governance system in the public sector. This is characterized by different tiers of decision-making that involve a substantial number of actors at central and local level: political representatives, bureaucrats, voters and organized groups. Therefore, in evaluating a policy outcome, we should not just concentrate on the decisions of the legislator but should pay attention also to the implementation process and to the institutions shaping the relationships between the different actors.

Institutional investigation has proceeded from both a normative and a positive standpoint. A strand of normative analysis assumes that, in a complete contract framework, the judicial system and electoral competition can induce the policy-maker to act as an informed supervisor of private agents and maximize expected social welfare. The main challenge of this complete constitution approach is to design a set of constitutional rules that induce the collective decision-making process to implement policies that maximize collective welfare. Therefore this literature focuses on the problem of selecting the optimal incentive schemes able to reduce information rents and elicit truthful revelation of the agent's private information (incentive-compatible mechanism).[3] In spite of the unrealistic assumption of an unlimited variety of available contracts, this analytical approach offers a very powerful methodology for investigating information rents in political decision-making. Moreover, it sheds a light on the remedies against the inefficiencies caused by information asymmetries and power delegation to agencies. The emphasis on information asymmetries and the principal–agent structure makes this analytical framework highly appropriate for a wide utilization in the domain of cultural policy, although it has not yet received much attention. In particular, this incentive approach could be helpful to investigate multi-principal situations, for example, in the public administration of cultural heritage, as in the case when more regulators and/or institutions have overlapping competence on the same cultural good.[4] Furthermore, the above approach may offer interesting insights into the study of the choice of instruments adopted to correct market failure, and contribute to the debate on the use of public subsidies. In fact the corrective instruments could be interpreted as the implementation of optimal incentive mechanisms in a second-best world with asymmetric information.

Under a positive perspective, a growing literature has investigated how institutions are structured to tackle the agency problems in politics. In this context, political constitutions are interpreted as cases of incomplete contracts that allocate control right over policy-making to different individuals. Therefore, starting from the comparison of different constitutions, numerous studies have investigated, both theoretically and empirically, the effects of alternative institutional frameworks on government policies. This analysis has provided an array of important results. For example, it has shown how electoral rules have a fundamental impact on policy-making, how the separation of powers within the political system may successfully impede the appropriation of political rents, and to what extent fiscal federalism can reduce the inefficiencies of politics. This research area can determine important advancements in the analysis of cultural policies. It can provide useful insights to interpret the differences observed across countries (see van der Ploeg, 2006) and to improve our understanding of the impact of institutions on the definition and implementation of policies.

Regarding the last issue, we observe that the implementation of government policies is generally delegated to bureaucrats. The legislator may have strategic reasons to delegate authority, in addition to the obvious limits of time and expertise required to follow all the stages for the realization of a single policy or project.[5] On the other hand, the delegation of decision power may cause a loss of political control over the outcome of public policies. This could be due to the information advantage of bureaucratic agencies, but it could also happen when the latter simply have the power of initiating the policy-making process, by submitting proposals to the legislator. In these cases, agencies may decide to pursue their personal goals, which may well be in contrast with those of the political principal and produce allocative inefficiencies and overspending. Therefore we can envisage a basic trade-off for the government between the advantages of information and expertise coming from bureaucrats and the risk of bureaucratic drift. Politicians, however, have several institutional devices to limit bureaucratic discretion. The government's control over bureaucracy can be improved, for example, through competition among agencies for acquiring resources; designing a judicial system that allows users to act as watchdogs against abuses of the bureaucracy; and appointing bureaucrats and affecting their career advancements. If full control is successfully exerted, then the bureaucrat is not responsible for a specific policy.

If we then concentrate on the institutional issue of the relationship between government and bureaucracy, the consistency of a policy with the public interest will depend on the combined political accountability of government and bureaucracy. If bureaucracy is under political control, the emergence of special interest policies will depend on the control of voters on government, as discussed earlier. If instead the legislator's oversight over bureaucracy is lacking, the latter may follow private interests and itself be captured by interest groups. In principle, this problem affects any type of governmental policy. Cultural policy is no exception.

Van der Ploeg (2006) suggests that the arm's-length principle applied in the UK represents an institutional mechanism to limit the political influence of the government that would lead to time-inconsistent policies and the imposition of its short-run electoral goals on cultural policy agenda. Although the reasons for this view are well argued, they tend to overlook the problem of accountability of cultural agencies. Actually, with respect to other areas of public intervention, cultural policy presents additional difficulties concerning the identification of the content and the range of intervention. For example, the definition of the genres of visual and performing arts to be supported is barely codified. Consequently the experts play the fundamental role of 'gatekeepers', both in the public sector and in the private sector. The information advantage of public officials in the cultural sector makes their activity difficult to evaluate for the government. Moreover, the absence of free entry makes the art market non-competitive and rents may then be extracted by the experts because of their 'gatekeeping' power.[6] In a similar fashion, the criteria for identifying cultural heritage to be preserved and the type of intervention are not uniquely defined and may differ across time and countries.

Peacock (1998b) and Frey (2000) point out that this difficulty of definition has generated a substantial detachment of public policies from the preference of the community and a dominant role of an elite of experts in the policy-making process. These experts would not have sufficient incentive to take fully into account the interests of the public because they are not elected. Moreover, because of their cultural background, these experts would be biased in favour of conservation paying little attention to the costs caused to the private sphere (see Rizzo and Throsby, 2006). Therefore, in order to reduce the gap between cultural policy and people's preferences, it is suggested that public participation in policy-making be improved. To reach this objective, Peacock suggests allowing the members of cultural organizations to elect their representatives in public agencies implementing cultural policy. The situation envisaged by Peacock implies that political representatives are unable to improve their control on cultural agencies, which then behave discretionally; or, should political control be enforced, this would not guarantee the consistency of cultural policies with the public's interest. But then: would the representatives elected directly to the board of those agencies have better instruments of control of the board than the politicians? And who guarantees that they will produce a policy that is consistent with the preference of the general public? Without further specification, it is unclear whether those elected members of the agencies would be successful in guaranteeing the fulfilment of the public interest.

In conclusion, to further investigate the role of the experts in the policy outcome, we should first investigate how institutions are shaped in order to improve political accountability of politicians and public officials. Institutional analysis suggests that the functions of bureaucracy may be designed so as to keep them under politicians' control. The argument is that, since institutions are shaped by political representatives, they are expected to evolve so as to guarantee the re-election of the latter. This implies restricting bureaucratic discretion that may weaken the constituency's support. More investigation, treating institutions in the cultural sector as endogenous, would be useful to understand why a specific institutional system comes into existence, what effects it has on the policy-making, and who can benefit from its removal.[7]

Concluding remarks

It has been argued here that public choice theory offers a useful analytical methodology to the field of cultural economics. A limit to its application may be the strong dominance of sophisticated game theory models involving hyperrational subjects. This tendency, widespread in economic analysis, represents a strong restriction often invalidated by experiments. This shortcoming is particularly prominent in the case of cultural economics, where emotions, sentiments and irrational behaviour are expected to be more common than in other disciplines. The progressive adoption of behavioural economics and evolutionary games may then facilitate the proliferation of political economic studies applied to cultural policy. The previous literature, in spite of its limited size, has contributed a great deal to spell out several public choice issues and to analyse bureaucracy in the cultural sector. This chapter has provided a few suggestions for future developments in the study of the political decision-making process and of exogenous and endogenous institutions.

Notes

1. In the last two decades, public choice has experienced dramatic analytical progress. This has been interpreted by several scholars as an evolution of the field into a new research area called political economy theory (or 'new' political economy to distinguish it as a specific area of research). The differences between public choice and political economy are not definite or unanimously accepted and, after all, of little relevance for the scope and content of this chapter, which refers to both literatures indistinctly. To provide a partial clarification, from a methodological point of view, political economy analysis would strengthen the microfoundations of the analysis by imposing a higher degree of rationality on all political actors (including voters) than we observe in traditional public choice literature. In terms of outcome, the interpretation of political activity provided by political economic theory seems more trusting than public choice about the effectiveness of institutional and social control over selfish public agents. In fact, the 'right-wing', pro-market bias of part of some public choice studies may have initially hindered its diffusion in academia. On the other hand, public choice insights about political phenomena 'had something going on that got lost when political economy insisted on deriving ever more "optimal" institutions in a reductionist framework including hyper-rationality and equilibrium-*über-Alles*' Lohmann (2006, p. 531).
2. Another example of ambiguous utilization of culture coping with globalization concerns the extension of political rights to immigrants. A multicultural approach may suggest that they should be entitled to import their cultures into their hosting society. However, this view is most fiercely contrasted by those who fear that massive immigration would progressively erode native culture.
3. The analysis relies extensively on the revelation principle. Without limitations on available contracts, an organization with decentralized information is equivalent to a centralized organization where, because of incentive-compatible mechanisms, all the information moves to the centre, which sends commands to be implemented by the agents.
4. Different multi-principal phenomena can be detected also in the private sphere where more artists have a common agent, a gallery, whose promoting activity is fundamental for their success. See also Chapter 50 on principal–agent analysis.
5. For example, delegation of authority may help the legislator to shift the responsibility for a failure to the bureaucrat, or it may represent a commitment device to avoid the inefficiencies of time inconsistency or political logrolling.
6. If gatekeeping is based on some appointment as an expert, then experts may compete for this appointment. This rent-seeking activity may imply a transfer of the expected rents to the agent appointing the experts. For a first attempt of analysis on this kind of rent-seeking problem, see Mossetto (1994).
7. For an application of the theory of endogenous institutions to policy-making on culture in Sicily, see Mazza (2002).

See also:

Chapter 1: Application of welfare economics; Chapter 50: Princpal–agent analysis; Chapter 52: Public support; Chapter 54: Regulation.

References

Acheson K. and C. Maule (2006), 'Culture in International Trade', in V.A. Ginsburgh, and D. Throsby (eds), *Handbook of the Economics of Art and Culture*, Amsterdam: North-Holland, pp. 1141–82.

Downs, A. (1957), *An Economic Theory of Democracy*, New York: Harper & Row.

Frey, B. (2000), *Arts & Economics. Analysis & Cultural Policy*, Berlin: Springer-Verlag.

Goldstein, K.M. (1999), *Interest Groups, Lobbying, and Participation in America*, Cambridge: Cambridge University Press.

Grampp, W.D. (1989), 'Rent-seeking in Arts Policy', *Public Choice*, 60, 113–21.

Guccio, C. and I. Mazza (2008), 'Determinants of Regional Spending for Heritage Conservation and Valorization in Sicily: A Political Economic Approach', Dip. di Economia e Metodi Quantitativi – Università di Catania, Working Paper No. 3.

Lohmann, S. (2006), 'The Non-Politics of Monetary Policy', in B.W. Weingast and D.A. Wittman (eds), *The Oxford Handbook of Political Economy*, New York: Oxford University Press, pp. 523–44.

Mazza, I. (2002), 'Organisation and Decision-making in the Heritage Sector in Sicily', in I. Rizzo and R. Towse (eds), *Economics of Heritage: A Study in the Political Economy of Culture in Sicily*, Cheltenham, UK and Northampton, MA, USA: Edward Elgar, pp. 48–62.

Mossetto, G. (1994), 'Cultural Institutions and Value Formation on the Art Market: A Rent-seeking Approach', *Public Choice*, 81, 125–35.

Mueller, D.C. (1997), *Perspectives on Public Choice. A Handbook*, New York: Cambridge University Press.

Mueller, D.C. (2003), *Public Choice III*, New York: Cambridge University Press.

Olson, M. (1965), *The Logic of Collective Action: Public Goods and the Theory of Groups*, Cambridge, MA: Harvard University Press.

Peacock, A. (ed.) (1998a), *Does the Past have a Future? The Political Economy of Heritage*, London: Institute of Economic Affairs.

Peacock, A. (1998b), 'The Economist and Heritage Policy: A Review of the Issues', in A. Peacock (ed.), *Does the Past have a Future? The Political Economy of Heritage*, London: Institute of Economic Affairs, pp. 1–26.

Persson, T. and G. Tabellini (2000), *Political Economics. Explaining Economic Policy*, Cambridge, MA: MIT Press.

van der Ploeg, F. (2006), 'The Making of Cultural Policy: A European Policy', in V.A. Ginsburgh and D. Throsby (eds), *Handbook of the Economics of Art and Culture*, Amsterdam: North-Holland, pp. 1183–221.

Rizzo, I. and D. Throsby (2006), 'Cultural Heritage: Economic Analysis and Public Policy', in V.A. Ginsburgh and D. Throsby (eds), *Handbook of the Economics of Art and Culture*, Amsterdam: North-Holland, pp. 983–1047.

Rowley, C.K. and F. Schneider (eds) (2008), *Readings in Public Choice and Constitutional Economics*, New York: Springer.

Weingast, B.W. and D.A. Wittman (eds) (2006), *The Oxford Handbook of Political Economy*, New York: Oxford University Press.

van Winden, F. (2008), 'Interest Group Behaviour and Influence' in C.K. Rowley and F. Schneider (eds), *Readings in Public Choice and Constitutional Economics*, New York: Springer, pp. 323–43.

Further reading

Peacock (1998a) offers a political-economic investigation of heritage conservation; Frey (2000), Rizzo and Throsby (2006), and van der Ploeg (2006) address additional political aspects of cultural economics.

For a review of the theoretical models of interest groups and rent-seeking, see Mueller (1997, chs 14 and 23) and van Winden (2008). For the analysis of bureaucratic behaviour, see Mueller (1997, chs 20 and 21), Mueller (2003, ch.16) Weingast and Wittman (2006, ch.14).

52 Public support
Bruno S. Frey

When cultural economists look at public support for the arts, they distinguish between two aspects: the *positive* issue where one analyses the extent of support by the government, and the *normative* issue whether or not the arts should be publicly supported and, if so, to what extent. In the second case, the cultural economist wants to inform the public about an appropriate policy, a welfare-enhancing public policy towards the arts.

How does government support the arts?

Throughout history, governments have been heavily involved in the arts. Table 52.1 provides an overview of direct public spending on the arts in various countries in 2007.

Table 52.1 should be interpreted with great care because what counts as 'arts expenditure', and what falls in the domain of 'government', differs considerably between the countries listed. Nevertheless, the table shows widely different amounts of direct public expenditures for the arts. Russia, Greece and Ireland spend much less, and Norway and Denmark substantially more, than the other countries shown. The source of public support also differs widely. Thus, for example, in Denmark 64 per cent comes from the central government, while in Germany it is only 13 per cent, the bulk coming from the *Länder* and cities.

It is important to realize that a substantial part of the public support for the arts is given in an indirect way, by so-called 'tax deductions'. Individuals' and firms' gifts to the arts may be exempt from tax. Hence the higher the applicable (marginal) tax rate, the less costly it is to give to the arts. It has indeed been observed that a reduction in tax rates led to lower donations to the arts. The extent of tax expenditure for the arts varies greatly between countries, and often depends on a great many conditions. It is therefore impossible to indicate its size, but most cultural economists assume that it is quite substantial, and often larger (for example, for the USA) than direct expenditures.

There is a basic difference between the two types of support. In the case of direct expenditure, the decision about its size and the recipients is taken in the political sector, often by government bureaucracy. In the case of tax expenditures, the support decision is delegated to individuals or firms. This may lead to a different size and type of art being supported.

Many developed economies have constitutional provisions to support art. By necessity, such rules have to be general. The effect on the arts depends to a great extent on how the political actors and the public officials apply them. There is considerable evidence that they prefer to support well-established cultural institutions providing generally accepted art, such as, for instance, opera houses performing popular classical pieces by Verdi, Mozart, Puccini or Rossini. In contrast, more controversial and experimental art has difficulty in getting public support, because the public decision-makers who depend on public opinion and re-election shun scandals, which are more likely to be provoked

Table 52.1　*Government support for the arts in various countries, 2007 or last year available (direct spending in euros per capita)*

Austria	255	Italy	112
Canada	144	Netherlands	183
Denmark	352	Norway	438
Finland	168	Russia	31
France	197	Spain	120
Germany	101	Sweden	220
Greece	32	Switzerland	214
Ireland	52		

Source:　Council of Europe/ERICarts, 'Compendium of Cultural Policies and Trends in Europe, 10th edition' (2009, Table E.2, excerpt).

by this kind of art. Indirect aid via tax expenditures is less subject to such pressures and may bring about the support of a broader range of artistic activities.

Should government support the arts?
Cultural economics has paid much attention to the question of what the rationale for the support of the arts should be. The analysis is based on welfare theory, which focuses on the question of whether the private market misallocates the resources in the domain of the arts, and in particular why too little art is provided for if it is left to the price system. It is useful to distinguish between the demand and the supply side.

Market failures on the demand side
According to welfare economics, too little art is supplied if the markets do not reflect all the preferences of individuals for enjoying art. The following types of demand are not fully, or are only partially, reflected in markets.

1. *External benefits in production and consumption.* The provision of artistic activities may yield benefits, or positive external effects, to individuals and firms not involved in the production process. They reap a benefit for which they do not pay, and which the art producer in a market therefore does not take into account. Similarly, part of the benefits of artistic production may go to individuals and firms that do not pay for such consumption, and that therefore do not influence the production decisions on art markets. In both cases, production is too small compared to what is socially optimal.
2. *Non-market demand.* People may value the *option* of visiting an artistic production although, in fact, they never spend any money to actually attend themselves. People may even know beforehand that they will never themselves attend an artistic production but they value the *existence* of a respective activity. Some people may not themselves value art, but consider it a *bequest* for future generations. In many cases, artistic production is closely identified with *national* identity, prestige and *social cohesion.* Examples are famous opera houses, theatres, orchestras and museums. Artistic production may also contribute to a *liberal* and *broad education* and lead

to *social improvements* among the participants. The experimental nature of (some) artistic endeavours may foster innovation and risk-taking in quite different parts of society. In all these cases, the producers of art are not (fully) compensated in monetary terms for the benefits created. As a result, they are sometimes unable to provide the respective cultural activity at all, or only on a smaller scale than would be socially optimal.

3. *Art as a public good.* Art may be of a collective nature, in the sense that nobody (including those not paying) can be excluded from enjoying it, and that the consumption of one person does not reduce the consumption of other persons. This condition may apply to culture as a whole, or only some parts of it (for example, the beauty of a cultural city may be enjoyed by many people without their having to pay specifically for such a benefit). In contrast, the cultural consumption provided by, say, opera houses or museums is not a public good, because people not paying may be, and generally are, excluded. Moreover, in these cases there is rivalry in consumption: those who occupy a seat, or those who visit a museum, occupy space that is then no longer available to others. But in so far as culture is a public good, the suppliers are incompletely compensated for their efforts, and supply is lower than socially optimal.

Not all spillovers to other sectors induced by the arts constitute market failure. This holds in particular for the multiplier effects generated by expenditures for the arts. They increase the demand for other economic activities, such as hotels, restaurants or travel services, and thus work through the price system. No misallocation of resources is thereby created. The many studies of the so-called 'impact effects' of cultural activities (such as, for example, musical festivals or special exhibitions), which measure the additional economic activity induced, can therefore not be taken as a rationale for government support of the arts. Such studies, moreover, are often misconceived, as they indicate the additional turnover created instead of the added value. They also tend to disregard the alternatives available, that is whether, say, a sports event, rather than the cultural activity considered, would not generate even more economic activity.

On the demand side, further arguments for government support of the arts relating to aspects beyond efficiency may be proposed. Particularly important ones are the following:

1. *Merit goods.* Some cultural activities have, from the point of view of society, been described as desirable to provide larger quantities than the individual consumers would wish to purchase in the market. According to this view, consumer preferences are not to be accepted, but rather the political decision-makers have to decide according to 'inherent' worth or to what the majority of the population wants. Obviously, the idea of merit goods clashes with the basic idea in economics that the consumers know best what suits them. In many cases, 'merit wants' has just been used as another term for externalities and public goods connected with the arts.

2. *Lack of information.* The fact that consumers are often badly informed about the supply of art has often been used to argue for government intervention. While the fact can hardly be disputed, it is necessary to face the question of whether consumers' limited information is a rational consequence of their being little interested in the arts.

3. *Irrationality.* Individuals may be particularly subject to behavioural anomalies and paradoxes when they act in the area of culture, because the area eludes easy and clear definitions or categorizations. It may be argued that individuals therefore underrate the utility provided by culture. The government should therefore support the arts to make up for the lack in demand.

4. *Income distribution.* The consumption of cultural goods should be open to all classes of society and should not be reserved for the rich. Consequently, the government should support the arts in order to make their consumption available to people who are not able to pay much money for consuming them.

Market failure on the supply side

The supply of art may deviate in four major respects from the ideals of a well-functioning market.

1. *Imperfect competition.* The market for many cultural goods and services is characterized by monopolistic actors who offer smaller quantities at prices higher above marginal costs than competitive suppliers would. The government might correct this market failure by supporting additional supply. However, this argument does not apply to all areas of the arts. Thus auctions of art objects are an example of an almost perfectly competitive market.

2. *Declining cost.* Art supply may be subject to increasing returns to scale, which means that additional quantities may be produced at lower average cost. In that case, marginal cost is lower than average cost. The condition of efficient pricing, namely that price equals marginal cost, produces a loss. If the government wants to impose marginal cost pricing, it must support the suppliers by covering the difference between marginal and average cost.

3. *Productivity lag.* Suppliers in the live performing arts are subject to continuous cost pressure. They find it difficult, if not impossible, to increase labour productivity, but they have to pay similar wage increases to those in the rest of the economy. As a result, there is a tendency towards continually increasing deficits. In the long run, the performing arts can only supply if the government makes up for these deficits.

4. *Income distribution.* Artists tend to be, on average, poorer than other members of society. Egalitarian arguments may therefore constitute a reason for government to support persons active in the cultural sector.

Counter-arguments

Some cultural economists committed to free market ideas remain unconvinced that the market failures discussed on the demand and supply side really exist to any relevant extent. The *external effects* are claimed to be small, or even non-existent, or at least not larger than those generated in many other areas of the economy. There is some truth in this argument. It is indeed possible to identify some external effects in most economic activities. However, most cultural economists, on the basis of both theoretical and empirical considerations, are convinced that cultural activities produce more extensive and important positive externalities than in other areas.

The *undesired distributional aspects of cultural demand* have also been thrown into doubt. It has been argued, and also in some instances empirically shown, that government support of the arts often achieves the opposite of what is intended. High-income recipients are the principal consumers of cultural services, so that they are also the main beneficiaries of government support. This has been illustrated by the example of highly subsidized European opera houses, which are mainly attended by persons of above-average incomes, or younger persons (students) who will later in their lives enjoy above-average incomes (that is, people with above-average lifetime incomes). While this argument corresponds to the facts, its relevance should not be overestimated. The consumption of artistic goods and services is certainly not undertaken only by the rich, not least because much cultural consumption requires considerable time (for instance, an opera performance takes a whole evening), which, owing to the opportunity costs of time, is more expensive for high-income recipients. It is in general not the richest part of the population that benefits from publicly supported art but the (upper) middle class, which has sufficient time available for consumption.

As to the *undesired distributional effects on the cultural supply side*, it has been argued that governmental support tends to favour the successful and therefore richer artists. This indeed applies to some forms of government support. In the case of opera houses, for example, the high subsidies given by governments help to raise the already high incomes of the most successful singers and maestros. But it is impossible to generalize this observation. A great part of government support goes to artists with low, and sometimes very low, lifetime income, and thus works in the desired direction.

With respect to *declining costs* and *the productivity lag* of cultural supply, it has been claimed that they exist in many other areas of the economy and that they can be overcome by suitable measures. In particular, revenue can be raised by introducing prices that capture the rents generated to the consumers by the cultural activity. Thus price differentiation enables the setting of high prices for inframarginal cultural consumers with a high consumer rent, while still setting prices equal to cost for the marginal consumers. Cultural suppliers subject to the 'cost disease' have various possibilities for productivity increases. Productivity can be raised, among others, by introducing more capital-intensive production, by seeking the substitution of actors by technological means, by choosing plays with a smaller number of actors, or by having actors play several roles. Clearly, the possibilities for a particular performing arts supplier to do so without lowering the quality of performance are severely limited. Nevertheless, empirical analyses suggest that they do exist. Moreover, productivity in the live performing arts may be on the increase owing to indirect effects. Thus, for example, owing to improved travelling conditions, an actor or a singer may perform at many more venues than was the case in earlier times, which increases his or her overall productivity. It should also be noted that the productivity lag applies only to the *live* performing arts and much less, if at all, to other forms of the performing arts via television, radio, video or film. Indeed, these other forms constitute an enormous productivity increase in the arts, because a given live performance can be extended at very little, and sometimes even zero, cost to large audiences, sometimes even being broadcast to millions of people.

Cultural producers, faced with high costs relative to revenue, have several possibilities for avoiding making a loss. Important ones are to raise revenue by collateral activities, such as running a shop (within the cultural venue and outside), a cafeteria and restaurant, renting out the premises for other activities and seeking support from private and corporate sponsors. Many arts organizations have demonstrated that a great deal of income can be generated in that way. But it should not be overlooked that the possibilities are severely limited, for several reasons. One is that many arts institutions have little scope to engage profitably in such profit-making, most importantly because they are not glamorous enough to attract sufficient visitors and sponsors. This is the case for many local and regional suppliers, who nevertheless produce worthwhile art. Another reason is that such profit-oriented activities may threaten the content and quality of art. Cultural producers should not lose sight of what they stand for, and try to become 'entertainers', not least because they are likely to lose out against the established entertainment industry. This danger is real; some museums, for instance, have gone quite far in this direction by continually trying to feature 'blockbuster' exhibitions of doubtful artistic quality, which, moreover, are in many cases also a failure from the commercial point of view. The profit-making potential is also limited because the cultural suppliers may thereby lose their non-profit status. This most obviously holds for the museum shops run outside their premises, say in large shopping centres. If this status were lost, they would be subject to many additional taxes, and donations would no longer be exempt from tax. Both consequences would threaten the very existence of many, if not most, cultural suppliers and would therefore have counterproductive effects. Clearly, if the 'private' opera houses and museums in the USA were no longer classified as 'non-profit-making', donations would fall drastically and they would hardly be able to survive.

Comparative view
Even if market failures have been theoretically and empirically identified for the arts, they constitute at best a *prima facie* argument for public support. It must be taken into account that government intervention is also subject to failure. The economics of politics (public choice) discusses many reasons why the decisions taken in the political process may systematically deviate from the preferences of the population. Most importantly, politicians are motivated by the need for re-election rather than by any direct incentive to provide welfare-maximizing cultural policies. As elections take place only every fourth or fifth year, they are only insufficiently controlled by the voters. They tend to develop into a political class of their own and to a considerable extent decide according to their own taste to what extent, and how, culture is to be supported. Political failures are also introduced by the behaviour of the public bureaucracy which, because of its informational advantages, has large discretionary power to undertake a cultural policy of its liking. At the same time, both politicians and public officials are exposed to the influence of pressure groups. As a result, they tend to favour those cultural suppliers who are well organized, which in most cases boils down to concentrating the funds on a few large and well-established cultural suppliers (such as opera houses, national theatres and orchestras). In contrast, new, unorthodox and experimental art suppliers find it difficult to get much public aid, which tends to hamper creativity in the arts.

To gain a balanced view, it is necessary to compare the extent of market and political failure with respect to cultural issues.

Constitutional issues for and against public support of the arts
The arguments so far presented in favour of or against publicly supporting the arts are informed by the notion of market and political failure, respectively. But it can be argued

that the world is imperfect. The idea of failure compared to an ideal situation is then of little relevance, because the whole economy and society is dominated by failures. According to this view, it does not make sense to identify the extent to which the cultural sector deviates from ideal market or political conditions, as (nearly) *all* sectors in society do so to a significant extent. A more useful approach is to compare the sectors directly with each other. The question then becomes whether the cultural sector receives more or less public support than other sectors, and whether such support improves the lot of the population. The first part of the question is easy to answer: the cultural sector does receive considerable support from the government but it is tiny compared to that of other sectors, such as agriculture, education, transport or defence. The second part of the question cannot be answered directly, at least as long as it is agreed that there is no such thing as a collective social welfare function that would enable us to evaluate and compare the performance of the various sectors. While such an evaluation is not possible in an empirically relevant way, the issue can be successfully approached by moving to the *constitutional level* of analysis. The support of a sector by the public must be subjected to a generally accepted *decision process*. In a democracy, such support must be approved by the citizens. In a representative democracy, the decisions taken by a duly elected parliament and government are taken as legitimate, even if they are not perfect. In a democracy with direct participation rights of the population via popular referenda (as in various states of the USA, in Australia and Switzerland), the voting outcome to specific propositions, and the corresponding level of support for the arts, is taken as legitimate.

Empirical research indicates that citizens are very willing to support the arts with substantial funds if asked to decide in referenda. The fear sometimes raised that the population is not able to judge issues connected with culture, and will therefore reject the support of the arts by public means, finds no justification at all. In the case of both types of democracy, by implication, whatever has been decided in the political process, with respect to the support of the arts and other sectors, must be assumed to fulfil the wishes of the population. In contrast, when the democratic process is violated, or when the decision process is taken in an authoritarian or dictatorial way, public support for the arts (or for any other sector, for that matter) does not reflect the wishes of the population. In that case, the art supported conforms to what the people in political power consider to be 'art'. Only in the case of highly cultured rulers (an example is the Medici in Italy during the Renaissance) will the art publicly supported be of lasting value. In other cases, the activities of 'artists' who produce for the benefit of the authoritarian rulers are promoted (an example is the socialist realism promoted by Stalin).

An important constitutional decision concerning the public support of art refers to whether decision-making is centralized or takes place in a federal system of government. In the latter case, art suppliers do not depend solely on one public authority but can try out their ideas on several public donors. This raises the possibility and incentives for innovative art.

See also:

Chapter 1: Application of welfare economics; Chapter 50: Principal–agent analysis; Chapter 51: Public choice; Chapter 57: Tax concessions; Chapter 60: Welfare economics.

Further reading

Benhamou, Françoise (2000), *L'Economie de la Culture*, 2nd edn, Paris: La Découverte & Syros.

Blaug, Mark (ed.) (1976), *The Economics of the Arts*, London: Martin Robertson.

Cowen, Tyler (1998), *In Praise of Commercial Culture*, Cambridge, MA: Harvard University Press.

Cwi, David (1979), 'Public Support of the Arts: Three Arguments Examined', *Journal of Behavioral Economics*, 8, 39–68.

Dupuis, Xavier and Xavier Greffe (1985), 'Subsidies to Cultural Employment: The French Experiment', in Richard Waits, William S. Hendon and Harold Horowitz (eds), *Governments and Culture*, Akron, OH: Akron University Press, pp. 164–73.

Frey, Bruno S. (2000), *Arts and Economics*, Heidelberg and New York: Springer-Verlag.

Frey, Bruno S. and Werner W. Pommerehne (1989), *Muses and Markets: Explorations in the Economics of the Arts*, 1990 reprint, Oxford: Blackwell.

Grampp,William D. (1989), *Pricing the Priceless. Art, Artists and Economics*, New York: Basic Books.

Heilbrun, James and Charles M. Gray (2001), *The Economics of Art and Culture*, 2nd edn, Cambridge: Cambridge University Press.

O'Hagan, John W. (1998), *The State and the Arts: An Analysis of Key Economic Policy Issues in Europe and the United States*, Cheltenham, UK and Lyme, USA: Edward Elgar.

Peacock, Alan T. and Ilde Rizzo (1994), *Cultural Economics and Cultural Politics*, Dordrecht: Kluwer Academic Publishers.

Schuster, J. Mark (1998), 'Neither Public Nor Private: The Hybridization of Museums', *Journal of Cultural Economics*, 22, 127–50.

Throsby, David C. (2001), *Economics and Culture*, Cambridge: Cambridge University Press.

Towse, Ruth (1997a), *Baumol's Cost Disease: The Arts and Other Victims*, Cheltenham, UK and Lyme, USA: Edward Elgar.

Towse, Ruth (ed.) (1997b), *Cultural Economics: The Arts, the Heritage and the Media Industries*, Cheltenham, UK and Lyme, USA: Edward Elgar.

Trimarchi, Michele (1985), 'Il Finanziamento pubblico degli Spettacoli', *Economia delle Scelte Pubbliche*, 1, 37–54.

West, Edwin G. (1985), *Subsidizing the Performing Arts*, Toronto: Ontario Economic Council.

53 Publishing
Christian Hjorth-Andersen

The publishing business has the distinction of providing the first known example of the average cost curve, showing the dependence of average total costs on volume. These cost curves were first presented by the German publisher Gottfried Christoph Härtel in about 1800, antedating other authors by almost a century. They were even put to practical use in negotiations with authors and composers including Ludwig van Beethoven; see the amusing account by Scherer (2001).

However, this glorious past has not turned into a present of equal distinction. The knowledge about publishing is very scattered and comes almost entirely from outside the academic world, with Caves (2000) as an exception. The material relating to publishing is enormous, including official reports from various countries, memoirs, biographies and a large amount of anecdotal evidence, but solid knowledge based on research published in academic journals is scarce. Good data on the publishing industry are not very easy to come by as many publishing companies have other businesses besides publishing books, for example publication of magazines, and they publish their accounts for the company rather than for the book division. And data on the economics of the individual book are unavailable on a systematic basis.

The basic functions of a publishing company consist of three parts: acquisition of manuscripts, editing and layout, and sales. The actual printing of the books may very well be outsourced, and so a publishing company need not be a very large company in the sense of employing many people, and quite often it is not. Basically, there are two types of manuscript, the solicited and the unsolicited. A publishing company may get an idea for a new book ('A Guide to Investment in European Bonds') and contact a potential author. This is frequently the case in non-fiction.

The unsolicited manuscript is much more interesting from an economic point of view. The prototype is the young author writing a novel in his spare time, and sending it to some publishing company. Many scientific journals announce that they will only review manuscripts on an exclusive basis. It is not known if the practice of sending the manuscript to many publishing companies simultaneously is widespread or not.

The company will evaluate not only the artistic content but also, and perhaps especially, the possibilities of commercial success, and so rejection does not imply denial of artistic merit. Basically, the publishing company has a classical choice between type I and type II errors, accepting manuscripts that should have been rejected or rejecting manuscripts that should have been accepted. Consequently, the attitude towards risk will matter, and one may speculate that large companies should be in a stronger position to take risks.

If the publishing company opts for a rejection, the author is free to send the manuscript to some other publishing company, and there is no doubt that there is a constant stock of unpublishable manuscripts circulating between companies. The rejection rates of the publishing companies are not known, however. This of course imposes costs on the publishing companies, but the practice from the academic world of requiring a submission fee for an evaluation of the manuscript does not seem to be common in the book world.

If the publishing company decides that the manuscript is acceptable, negotiations between the author and the company begin. It is essential to understand that it is very hard to forecast the success of a particular manuscript, and so the division of risk is an integral part of the negotiations. No study of the contracts between authors and publishing companies has been published but we know that the outcome varies greatly. At the one extreme, we have the very famous people – former presidents and famous actors with juicy memoirs – that auction their manuscript, though it may not even have been written yet, and thus the publishing company essentially takes all the risk. Krieg (1953) reports that Wolfgang von Goethe used the idea of an auction in 1825 to substantially better his terms from the publisher.

At the other extreme, we have the young would-be authors who have a very poor bargaining position. Not only have they already invested their own time in their work, but also quite often the authors have to pay the publishing company to publish the work. This is probably often the case for scientific works with very specialized markets. In Denmark, it was reported in 1983 that one-third of the authors had to partly finance the publication in order to promote their future career. It is an interesting fact that it is the act of publication rather than the number of copies sold that matters for the reputation of many authors.

Contracts in between these two extremes may take many forms. For well-known authors with good prospects the publishing company may be willing to give an advance and a royalty on each copy sold; for others the terms are not so generous. Very often, the royalty will increase if the book comes in many editions, and usually it will be lower for paperback and translated editions. Other things that should concern the author, but probably quite often do not, are the eventual selling price of the book, the promotional expenditure on the book, the television rights and so on. In fact, the contracts between the author and the publishing company may be so complicated that the author may hire a literary agent to act on his or her behalf in commercial matters, but this is a grey area where we have only anecdotal evidence. But it seems safe to conclude that in most cases we have an asymmetrical bargaining situation where the publishing company is much more knowledgeable than the author, and relations between the parties may sometimes be strained. As Goethe once wrote, 'Die Buchhändler sind alle des Teufels, für sie muss eine eigene Hölle geben' (Krieg, 1953, p. 93).

Does the present market system that dominates in most Western countries give the proper incentives to publish new books? By and large, the answer is yes, with some qualifications. One is the financial condition of (young) authors, a subject that will be left to others. Another is the copyright question. The formal copyright is adequate for the protection of publishers and authors in all Western countries, and books are not as easily copied as digital material such as records or films. Some illicit photocopying does take place, however, and this would seem to be a problem in particular for non-fiction. But the library system poses a problem. In some countries authors are compensated to some degree when their work is available free of charge at the public library. Whether the authors are adequately compensated is a moot question, but the publishing companies usually are not.

The publishing companies
There are four features that should be noticed in the publishing business: the market conditions, the cost structure, the aim of the publishing firm, and the evolution of technology.

The market conditions
When a publishing company publishes a book it has of course a monopoly with respect to that book, secured by copyright conventions. However, this book is very often in direct competition with many other books. For example, if a company publishes a thriller, this thriller has to compete with hundreds of other thrillers available to the public. Thus the market conditions can usually be characterized as monopolistic competition. Occasionally, with very specialized work ('An advanced exposition of Albanian grammar') the book may compete only with one other book, or none at all, but in general the assumption of monopolistic competition in the Chamberlinian sense would seem justified.

It is also important to understand that each book is essentially a new commodity. In the standard model of monopoly, the monopoly is taken for granted and emphasis is on how much to produce. In this setting, all economists have learned that fixed costs are irrelevant. This is not the case in publishing. The emphasis is mainly on whether or not to publish the book, and so the fixed costs are crucial.

The cost conditions
There are two types of fixed costs in a publishing company. One type of fixed costs, F, is associated with the firm as such in the usual sense of the fixed costs of a firm. Another is the fixed cost f_i associated with the introduction of each particular book i. Assuming constant variable costs c_i, the cost function of the publishing company may be written:

$$TC(x_1, \ldots, x_i, \ldots, x_n) = F + \sum_{i=1}^{n} f_i + c_i x_i$$

Very little has been published with respect to this cost function (for the special example concerning costs of publishing economic journals, see Bergstrom, 2001), but undoubtedly both fixed cost elements are quite important. The variable cost component, consisting mainly of paper and binding, is only a minor percentage of total costs. This is the main reason why publishing is a risky business. The publishing company has to commit itself to substantial fixed costs with only uncertain sales prospects. As the publishing company usually publishes many books, it may trust the law of large numbers to some extent to even out variations in sales of the individual books, and it may be expected to have a very thorough knowledge of the cost function.

The aim of the company
A profit-maximizing company would try to maximize

$$\Pi = \sum_{i=1}^{n} p_i x_i - TC_i - F$$

The p_is may be thought to be independent as the firm would not want to introduce two books in direct competition with each other ('Two advanced expositions of Albanian

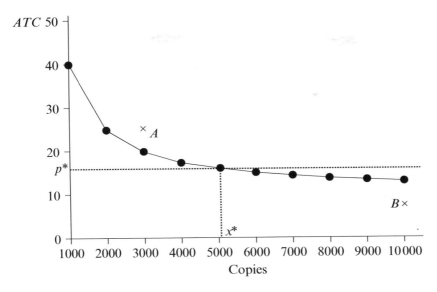

Figure 53.1   Average total costs (ATC) as a function of copies

grammar') but with ordinary books there would be many competitors, each with a negligible influence on the book in question. In Figure 53.1, the stylized cost function is shown. If the firm can sell X^* copies at the price p^* (= 16), the firm will break even. If the firm can sell X^* at the price of 20, the firm will make a profit of $4^* X^*$.

The firm may form an idea of the demand curve. If it believes A to be a point on the demand curve, it may charge a high price of 25 and expect 3000 copies to be sold. The point B, on the other hand, will imply 10 000 copies to be sold at the price of 8. The point B implies a loss, however, as $ATC(10 000) > 8$.

This exposition of the pricing procedure is very much at odds with the usual description of a monopoly equating MR and MC. The standard description, however, assumes that the monopoly already exists and assumes knowledge of the demand curve. This is quite unrealistic, however. The problem is whether or not the firm should introduce a new monopoly, a new book. And the practical problem is the strength of the demand, not the elasticity of the demand curve. This does not mean that prices are exclusively based on cost considerations, as the publisher may consider various combinations such as A and B, and thus in an informal way the notion of demand is introduced.

Thus the very business of the publishing industry is the introduction of new books in an uncertain world. And quite often their estimates turn out to be too optimistic. We do not know the exact percentage of books that are published at a loss, but the fraction is quite large. But in this respect the market for books is not different from the market for films or records.

We have assumed so far that the publishing company had profit maximizing as an aim. Many publishing companies, for example companies associated with a university, do not have that aim. The problem of cross-subsidization thus becomes important. Even idealistic companies have to cover costs, however. Let us consider a company publishing two

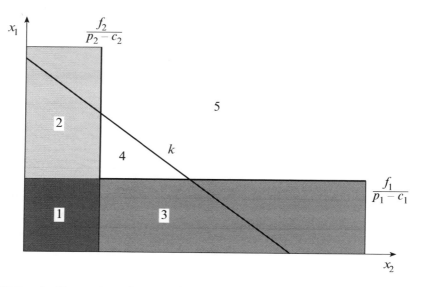

Figure 53.2   An illustration of cross-subsidization

books at prices p_1 and p_2 but where demand is uncertain at these prices. Total revenue $p_1x_1 + p_2x_2$ must be larger than total costs:

$$p_1x_1 + p_2x_2 \geq F + f_1 + c_1x_1 + f_2 + c_2x_2$$

$$x_1 \geq \frac{F + f_1 + f_2}{p_1 - c_1} + \frac{p_2 - c_2}{p_1 - c_1} * x_2$$

In Figure 53.2, all combinations of (x_1, x_2) below the line k are unprofitable; all combinations above the line are profitable. For each individual book to cover costs, we have

$$x_i \geq \frac{f_i}{p_i - c_i} \quad i = 1,2$$

We can thus divide the contemplated policy into a number of areas. In area 1, none of the books is profitable. In area 2 book 2 is individually profitable, and in area 3 book 1 is individually profitable. In area 4, the books are individually profitable but they do not cover the fixed costs of the publishing company, and in area 5 the company shows a profit.

Obviously, and much to the chagrin of many authors, the company will have to safeguard against the possibility of publishing in area 4, and so usually they insist that each book should pay a fraction α of the fixed company costs. We thus get the individual profit conditions:

$$x_1 \geq \frac{f_1 + \alpha F}{p_1 - c_1} \quad \text{and} \quad x_2 \geq \frac{f_2 + (1 - \alpha)F}{p_2 - c_2}$$

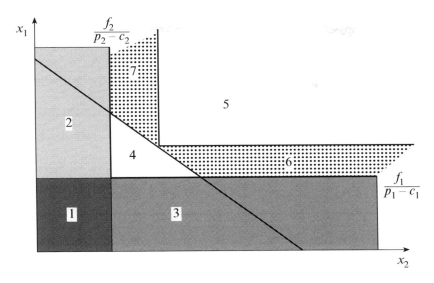

Figure 53.3   An illustration of cross-subsidization with a distribution of company fixed costs

Figure 53.3 is identical to Figure 53.2 except that area 5 in Figure 53.2 is decomposed into areas 6 and 7. These areas are profitable in the sense that they cover their own costs and also make a contribution to cover the fixed costs F, but the publishing company does not judge this contribution adequate.

The lesson of this exercise is that *the question of cross-subsidization and in effect the plight of much minority literature is very dependent upon the firm's cost conditions and its cost allocation.* It should also be remembered that we are talking about purposeful cross-subsidization. Undoubtedly, very often firms publish books that turn out to be failures in the market-place, and as firms like to promote themselves as guardians of the literature,they frequently claim to cross-subsidize minority literature. But, though these claims should be viewed with some scepticism, there is no doubt that sometimes firms do publish books that are not considered *a priori* to be profitable.

The evolution of technology

The technology of printing has seen some remarkable progress. The costs of editing and printing a book have fallen dramatically, as many authors provide manuscripts that are ready to be printed. This has affected the fixed costs f_p, making the break-even point of printing a book much lower. The consequence has been that in most countries there has in the past decades been a marked increase in the number of titles that are introduced every year. Thus, as the total number of books sold has not increased very much, if at all, the average number of copies per book has decreased, tending in some countries to increase the average book price.

The demand for books

In the eyes of the consumer, books display a number of characteristics. They are *experience goods*: you do not know the quality of a book before you have read it. Most books, especially fiction, are characterized by *horizontal quality* rather than vertical quality. It makes no sense to say that this work of fiction is objectively better than another work but rather that you like this book better. And finally, the supply of books is enormous. In large countries, more than 50 000 different titles are introduced each year, and as the titles of previous years are also available, the consumer has a very substantial *information problem*.

These facts would seem to explain many phenomena in the marketing of books. Traditional advertising plays a part, but much more attention has been given to the impact of reviews. Undoubtedly, the publishing industry obtains a lot of free advertising from newspapers and magazines. Favourable reviews are considered important in the marketing process in spite of the fact that books have horizontal quality. But this is an area where research would be most welcome; we have very little knowledge of the impact of book reviews. In interviews, people often state that they bought a book on the recommendation of friends and family, but this begs the question of why the friend bought the book in the first place. What would seem to be certain is that consumers often interact and have dependent preferences. Therefore, once a book gets a good start for some reason it may become a 'must' for culturally inclined people to buy the book. This may even be the case internationally, but our knowledge of the mechanisms of translation is very limited (Hjorth-Andersen, 2001). These processes are not very well researched but they are obviously of the utmost importance to the publishing companies.

Also, an investigation into the nature of book clubs would be most welcome. In a book club people deliberately limit their own choice and trust the book club to select some books for them. Presumably, book clubs cut down on the consumers' information costs and the consumers get cheaper books. For the book club, the risk concerning sales is much reduced, and large print runs may be planned.

Another issue that has not been explored so far is the function of public libraries. From the point of view of the individual publisher, the libraries on the one hand sometimes provide a secure market, but on the other hand sales to the libraries will tend to diminish the market, as some people will abstain from buying a book and borrow it at the library – *the crowding-out effect*. The net outcome of the library system on book sales is simply not known but presumably the crowding-out effect outweighs the sales effect.

The future of publishing
Digitalization and the Internet have had a considerable impact on book publishing: although a few years ago it seemed that it had become possible for authors to avoid a publishing company altogether and publish directly on the Internet for a fee, as was tried by Stephen King, that now seems to be the solution for authors with no prospects of getting a commercial contract. What has probably had the greatest impact so far is the online sale of books via Amazon and other online distributors; Amazon also enables 'self-publishers' to sell their works. E-books have been slow to develop but electronic reading devices such as Kindle and the increasing availability of books in digital form are encouraging readers to change their habits. Despite these developments, the basic functions of the publishing company in selecting and editing manuscripts would seem to be as important as ever.

See also:

Chapter 15: Costs of production; Chapter 17: Creative industries.

References

Bergstrom, Theodore C. (2001), 'Free Labor for Costly Journals?', *Journal of Economic Perspectives*, 15 (4), 183–98.

Canoy, M., J. van Ours and F. van der Ploeg (2006), 'The Economics of Books', in V.A. Ginsburgh and D. Throsby (2006) (eds) *Handbook of the Economics of Art and Culture*, Amsterdam: North-Holland, pp. 721–61.

Caves, Richard E. (2000), *Creative Industries: Contracts between Art and Commerce*, Cambridge, MA: Harvard University Press.

Hjorth-Andersen, C. (2001), 'A Model of Translations', *Journal of Cultural Economics*, 25, 203–17.

Krieg, Walter (1953), *Materialien zu einer Entwicklungsgeschichte der Bücherpreise und des Autoren-Honorars vom 15. bis zum 19. Jahrhundert*, Vienna and Zurich: Herbert Stubenrauch.

Scherer, F.M. (2001), 'An Early Application of the Average Total Cost Concept', *Journal of Economic Literature*, 39 (3), 897–901.

Further reading

Canoy *et al.* (2006) treats in detail many of the topics in this chapter.

54 Regulation
Ilde Rizzo

This chapter explores some of the main issues related to the regulation of the cultural sector, with specific reference to heritage. As the range of activities in the cultural field raises so many different economic questions, not all of them can be dealt with in the space available. Therefore the analysis is restricted mainly to issues connected with built heritage.

In the heritage field, the economic rationale for government intervention relies on the presence of market failure. Different mixes of government policy instruments – public expenditure, taxation and regulation – can be adopted according to prevailing economic and institutional settings; however, 'regulation, in the sense of specific constraints or directives affecting behaviour, is possibly the most widely used tool in heritage conservation, despite the fact that in most circumstances it is the instrument least favoured by economists' (Throsby, 1997, p. 19). Regulation may be used as an independent tool as well as a complement to or a substitute for other government policies (Giardina and Rizzo, 1994).

The chapter focuses on the regulation of the built heritage, trying to address some basic questions – What should be regulated? Why? How? Who should regulate? What are the effects of regulation? – and to point out some policy implications. Attention will be devoted to the positive analysis[1] of heritage regulation and to the features of the collective decision-making process.

Regulatory tools

Broadly speaking, regulation can be defined as non-monetary government intervention usually aimed at restricting or modifying the activities of economic agents in line with government policy objectives. According to Throsby (1997), we can distinguish *hard* and *soft* regulation; the former involves enforceable acts and penalties for non-compliance while the latter consists of non-enforceable directives implemented by agreement and not involving penalties.

In the heritage case, regulation is aimed at controlling the stock of heritage, from both the quantitative and the qualitative point of view, in order to ensure the conservation of those buildings or areas with a social value higher than the private one, to enhance the sense of community and identity, to improve the quality of life and to promote local development. A peculiar feature of heritage is that its deterioration or destruction cannot be compensated by the creation of new cultural capital, as is the case with contemporary artistic items; therefore conservation is needed to meet present needs without compromising the satisfaction of future needs (Rizzo and Throsby, 2006).

Regulation consists of different types of action: the identification of the buildings, sites or areas of historical importance; the assignment of a grade of significance; the imposition of limitations on the use of land affecting heritage and the definition, sometimes by both central and local government, of rules to discipline the various methods of conservation (Peacock and Rizzo, 2008).

Listing is a major regulatory tool in the heritage field. According to Schuster (2004), it is a term with a very broad meaning, referring to several forms of designation – for example, schedules, inventories, lists, classifications, surveys, registers, records, inscriptions and others – varying across national and local contexts.[2] A common feature of most countries is the considerable share of designated buildings in private ownership (Schuster, 1998).

Listing implies that information is collected, organized and communicated to identify and certify heritage and, therefore, it can be a relevant source of information on the social value of cultural heritage. In practice, lists are also connected with other policy actions. The owners of designated buildings are usually subjected to various restrictions and prescriptions: on the use of buildings, on their appearance, on the way maintenance or restoration is carried out, on the use of land affecting the buildings, on the transfer or the demolition of the buildings as well as on public access. Regulation, therefore, constrains the exercise of property rights: owners are obliged to comply with prescriptions, and penalties are imposed for non-compliance. On the other hand, the designation may also bring about eligibility for various forms of government support, such as subsidies or tax incentives, to compensate owners for restrictions and preservation efforts, their extent varying across countries.

From the operational point of view, in the heritage field regulation has certain advantages compared to other government tools. Its adoption or removal takes less time than is required for other forms of public intervention and, therefore, it allows for a greater timeliness of public action. Flexibility, in fact, can be extremely useful in heritage to cope with the necessity of quick decisions, such as preventing the demolition of a building. At the same time, there are some peculiar features related to the regulatory decision-making process that are worth noting.

Decision-making process

The size of the regulated sector is not well defined *ex ante*, especially when minor heritage is involved, but it is a matter for the discretion of the regulator, who enjoys an informational advantage because of the specific knowledge involved in heritage decisions. This is due to the fact that the identification of what is heritage is not unambiguous, being based to a large extent on the evaluation of experts hired by the government who may have contrasting views on the order of priorities concerning the extent and the type of intervention (Peacock, 1994). At the same time, the designation of a building or of an area can also be the result of rent-seeking behaviours of individuals and communities, to the extent that listing brings about not only negative effects – such as constraints and prescriptions – but also benefits – such as subsidies, tax incentives or other forms of government support (Noonan and Krupka, 2010).

Since the identification of heritage is not straightforward, the type of expert (archaeologist, art historian, architect, urban planner and so on) involved in this kind of decision is important in determining the size and the composition of the stock of cultural heritage, as well as the type of conservation that can take place (Peacock and Rizzo, 2008).

Conservation itself is, in fact, a wide concept that

> encompasses all aspects of protecting a site or remains so as to retain its cultural significance. It includes maintenance and may, depending on the importance of the cultural artefact and

related circumstances, involve preservation, restoration, reconstruction or adaptation or any combination of these. (World Bank, 1994)

The terms included in this definition are not straightforward. Moreover, the adoption of technical standards of conservation is usually contested by practitioners because it is agreed that each piece of heritage is unique and, therefore, conservation should be carried out case by case.

On the grounds of the above considerations, the range and intensity of regulation appear to be more the endogenous product of the public decision-making process than just a policy instrument in the heritage field. In this perspective, it is not without significance that in many countries the discretionary power enjoyed by regulators is coupled with the tendency to extend the concept of heritage and the fact that heritage lists are large and keep growing worldwide,[3] while delisting rarely occurs.

The awareness of the importance of regulation and of the shortcomings related to the functioning of the decision-making process calls for strengthening the efforts for measuring and evaluating heritage regulatory activities to reduce the asymmetrical information enjoyed by the regulator. Measurement problems usually arising in the cultural field (van der Ploeg, 2006) are enhanced in the heritage regulation case. The concept of regulation is elusive when one wants to measure it (it is not accounted for in public budgets, regardless which level of government is involved, and output is differentiated); moreover, data are less reliable and comparable since they are affected by the institutional context. In the literature, apart from a few contributions,[4] little attention has been paid to the definition, measurement and evaluation of the output of heritage regulatory activities.

At the operational level, however, there is evidence of appraisal activities, through the extension of a well-established procedure such as the Regulatory Impact Assessment (RIA) to the heritage field, the UK offering a good example of such a practice (DCMS, 2007).

Economic effects

Heritage regulation cannot be considered only a technical matter since it affects the property rights and the possibility of using cultural heritage for private and collective purposes.

The empirical literature has paid attention to the effects of listing on the values of designated buildings as well as of the surrounding properties;[5] the results are mixed as far as the USA is concerned (Netzer, 2006) and remain unconvincing because of endogeneity problems (Noonan, 2009). Within a European perspective, Benhamou (2004) reports that listed buildings score higher values in France than in the UK because they are subjected to fewer constraints, while also enjoying financial benefits.

Moreover, it is useful to recall that heritage is increasingly recognized as a strategic factor in the promotion of local development – urban regeneration and tourism being usually advocated as the most important factors – but its economic impact is affected by the strength of regulation, that is, by the extension of the concept of heritage to artefacts of minor importance as well and by the range of compatible uses allowed for archaeological sites or historical buildings.

The stance adopted by the regulator affects the costs regulation imposes on the regulated as well as on society as a whole. Costs include the administrative and bureaucratic costs related to the issue of regulatory acts (permissions, authorizations, demolition orders, standards and so on) and the monitoring of their effective implementation, as well as the compliance costs imposed on all the regulated subjects (regardless whether private or public). Some of these costs can be foreseen because they are closely connected to conservation itself; for example, the requirement to use special materials, qualified operators and the like to ensure quality. Others are subject to a high degree of uncertainty, as a consequence of the discretional decisions of the regulator; for instance, an adaptation (involving interior modifications for compatible uses) allowed by urban planning might not be permitted by the heritage regulator, with the consequence that a substantial amount of the potential benefits is lost and the public–private mix is likely to be adversely affected (Pignataro and Rizzo, 1997).[6] Moreover, the indirect costs imposed on any activity that interfere with heritage regulation might be significant; for instance, planning regulations may require the diversion of roads to protect archaeological sites (Peacock, 1994) or may prevent construction near to archaeological areas.

The size of the overall costs involved in heritage regulation raises some doubts about the sustainability of the related conservation programmes: a conservationist stance of regulation may 'crowd out' private investments, causing a deterioration of heritage and a considerable pressure on public expenditure. Thus the objective of conserving heritage may not be fulfilled.

Similar results might occur because of the reaction of heritage owners to regulation. The threat of restrictions and of the related costs might induce owners to speed redevelopment, with negative effects on the stock of heritage (Turnbull, 2002). On the other hand, owners might decide not to comply with rules if they are too costly, provided that the risk of being detected is low; this is likely to happen in the presence of a very extensive regulation requiring considerable resources to be allocated in monitoring activities.

As a consequence, the objective of the regulatory policy, that is, conservation of heritage, can actually be endangered by the excessive expansion of the regulation itself. The need to introduce the opportunity cost concept to drive the decision-making process is, therefore, called for.

Some policy implications

In the light of the above considerations, it is useful to sketch very briefly some possible institutional mechanisms available to society to restrain the discretionary scope of regulators and to improve public participation in the political decision-making process. The issue is crucial and controversial at the same time: while it is widely agreed that taxpayers have a legitimate claim to influence public decisions about heritage as with other policies, it is also true that specific knowledge and expertise are involved, so that these decisions cannot be left entirely to taxpayers' choices.

The problem we face – the need for a governance structure to restrain the discretionary scope of the regulator – is common to regulation in general and no unique solution can be provided since the choice is constrained by the 'country's institutional endowment' (Levy and Spiller, 1996). Institutions also matter in the heritage field, and various means can be envisaged to restrain the discretionary scope of the regulator.

Devolution is usually indicated as a means of increasing government accountability; in the heritage field its positive effects would seem even stronger because of the close links between regional/local communities and heritage (Rizzo, 2004). Devolution also favours the use of direct democracy tools, such as referenda, although their costs should not be underestimated. However, devolution as such is not enough if no adequate incentives are introduced in the regulatory decision-making process (Rizzo and Towse, 2002).

Different incentives are generated by different institutional features. In state-driven systems, such as that in Italy, where policy decisions are implemented by bureaucracies, the decision-making process is less 'demand-oriented' than in arm's-length systems, such as UK, where independent agencies operate (Peacock and Rizzo, 2008). Indeed, in the latter system, consultation and review procedures[7] as well as regulatory assessment, which are useful means for reducing information asymmetries and improving the efficiency of the regulatory process, are more likely to take place. As a consequence, participation of citizens and voluntary associations is likely to be enhanced, and the public scrutiny of the regulators' decisions can be improved.

Finally, it might be useful at the local level to adopt codes of practice or guidelines agreed between the regulator and those involved in conservation activities (architects, building firms, engineers and so on) in order to make prior commitments and reduce the uncertainty related to investment in conservation.

The international dimension
Heritage regulation is also widespread at the international level and, *mutatis mutandis*, raises issues similar to those arising within a national context.

Regulation of built heritage at this level mainly consists of non-enforceable directives (charters, codes of practice, guidelines and so on) implemented by agreement and not involving penalties, as well as of listing, such as the UNESCO World Heritage List (WHL).[8] As Peacock and Rizzo (2008) show, heritage experts are widely involved and the list of conventions, charters and recommendations, mainly issued on the same topics, has grown considerably in the last 15 years; each organization seems mainly interested in pursuing its own objectives without paying much attention to the coordination of the various actions.

The WHL also keeps growing; however, this enlargement does not ensure that the aim of preserving cultural heritage, considered as a global public good, is fulfilled, the inclusion in the list being more representative of national interests than of global interests (Frey and Pamini, 2010). Sustainability issues may also arise in poor countries because of the high opportunity costs of preserving global heritage, which is not compensated by any significant support from UNESCO. Whether the WHL is effective in promoting tourism and, therefore, economic local development is an open and controversial question (Cellini, 2011). At the same time, by focusing attention on designated buildings or areas, the WHL is likely to generate a 'displacement effect' to the disadvantage of other heritage (Gamboni, 2001).

Regulation is also adopted to restrict the international circulation of works of art, with the aim of preserving national identity and prestige and to protect future generations' interests. However, the effectiveness of such a policy tool is an open question (Rizzo and Throsby, 2006). If the scope of the restrictions preventing the exports of works of arts is very wide, collectors and/or dealers might be induced to leave the official economy and to undertake their exchanges in an illicit way with a very low risk of being detected and punished, since effective monitoring would be too costly. As a consequence, restrictions tend to be ineffective while they are likely to produce negative economic effects on the dimension of the art market.

Concluding remarks

A general argument stems from this analysis: the range and intensity of heritage regulation cannot be justified in all the cases on normative grounds since they often appear to be the endogenous product of the public decision-making process. If heritage regulators adopt a 'conservationist' stance; that is, the list of buildings or areas claiming historical importance is enlarged and preservation orders prevent modifications for compatible uses, the conservation of heritage could actually be endangered. Extensive regulation would discourage private investment in heritage and would impose an unsustainable pressure on public funds. The need to introduce the opportunity cost concept to drive the decision-making process is, therefore, called for.

There is no unique solution to meeting the need for a governance structure to restrain the discretionary scope of the heritage regulator, with the solution being constrained by the specific institutional framework in which regulation takes place: forms of greater public participation in decision-making and the improvement of information – through consultation and review procedures as well as regulatory assessment – are some of the means suggested here. Arm's-length regulation seems to be more effective either way.

Notes

1. Positive analysis criticizes the normative theory of regulation based on the welfare economics approach to market failure: a classic reference is Noll (1989). An overview of different theories of regulation is provided by den Hertog (2000).
2. An overview of heritage legislation in European countries is offered by Compendium, an information system on cultural policies and trends (http://www.culturalpolicies.net/web/index.php).
3. Schuster (2004) reports evidence on the increase in the number of listed buildings and conservation areas in France, the UK and the USA.
4. Rizzo (2002) and, more recently, Finocchiaro and Rizzo (2009).
5. A review of the literature is provided by Mason (2005).
6. *Façadism* is a suitable compromise: the owners cannot change the *façade* but can alter the interiors according to their needs (Benhamou, 2004).
7. A good example is provided by *Conservation Principles, Policies and Guidance* launched by English Heritage in 2008 after extensive debate and consultation on line.
8. International regulation also protects intangible cultural heritage; in 2003 UNESCO adopted a Convention establishing a Representative List of Intangible Cultural Heritage: http://www.unesco.org/culture/ich/index.php?lg=en&pg=00022.

See also:

Chapter 32: Heritage; Chapter 38: Media economics and regulation; Chapter 50: Principal–agent analysis; Chapter 51: Public choice.

References

Avrami, Erica C., Randall Mason and Marta de la Torre (2000), *Values and Heritage Conservation*, Los Angeles, CA: The Getty Conservation Institute (http://www.getty.edu/conservation/publications/pdf_publications/valuesrpt.pdf).

Benhamou, Françoise (2004), 'Who Owns Cultural Goods? The Case of Built Heritage', in Victor A. Ginsburgh (ed.), *Economics of Art and Culture*, Amsterdam: Elsevier, pp. 187–202.

Cellini, Roberto (2011), 'Is Unesco Recognition Effective in Fostering Tourism? A Comment on Yang, Lin and Han', *Tourism Management*, 32 (2), April, 452–4.

Den Hertog, Johan (2000), 'General Theories of Regulation', in Boudewijn Bouckaert and Gerrit de Geest (eds), *Encyclopedia of Law and Economics*, vol. III, Cheltenham, UK and Northampton, MA, USA: Edward Elgar, pp. 223–70.

Department of Culture, Media and Sports (2007), *Heritage Protection for the 21st Century: Regulatory Impact Assessment*, London; DCMS (http://www.culture.gov.uk/images/consultations/hrp_ria.pdf).

Finocchiaro Castro, Massimo and Ilde Rizzo (2009), 'Performance Measurement of Heritage Conservation Activity in Sicily', *International Journal of Arts Management*, 11 (2), 29–41.

Frey, Bruno and Paolo Pamini (2010), 'World Heritage: Where are we? An Empirical Analysis', Institute for Empirical Research in Economics, University of Zurich, Working Paper No. 462 (http://www.iew.uzh.ch/wp/iewwp462.pdf).

Gamboni, Dario. (2001), 'World Heritage: Shield or Target?', *Conservation. The GCI Newsletter*, 16, 5–11.

Giardina, Emilio and Ilde Rizzo (1994), 'Regulation in the Cultural Sector', in Alan Peacock and Ilde Rizzo (eds), *Cultural Economics and Cultural Policies*, Dordrecht: Kluwer, pp. 125–42.

Levy, Brian and Pablo T. Spiller (eds) (1996), *Regulations, Institutions and Commitment*, Cambridge: Cambridge University Press.

Lichfield, Nathaniel (1988), *Economics in Urban Conservation*, Cambridge: Cambridge University Press.

Mason, Randall (2005), 'Economics and Historic Preservation: A Guide and Review of the Literature', Brookings Institution Discussion Paper (www.brookings.edu/~/media/Files/rc/. . .mason/20050926_preservation.pdf).

Netzer, Dick (2006), 'Cultural Policy: An American View', in Victor A. Ginsburgh and David Throsby (eds), *Handbook of the Economics of the Arts and Culture*, Amsterdam: North-Holland, pp. 1223–51.

Noll, Roger G. (1989), 'Economic Perspectives on the Politics of Regulation', in Richard Schmalensee and Robert D. Willig (eds), *Handbook of Industrial Organization*, vol. II, Amsterdam: Elsevier, pp. 1254–87.

Noonan, Douglas S. (2009), 'Evaluating Price Effects of Historic Preservation Policies: Landmark Preservation in Chicago, 1990–1999', in Fusco Girard Luigi and Peter Nijkamp (eds), *Cultural Tourism and Sustainable Local Development*, Farnham, UK: Ashgate, pp. 289–314.

Noonan, Douglas S. and Douglas J. Krupka (2010), 'Determinants of Historic and Cultural Landmark Designation: Why We Preserve What We Preserve', *Journal of Cultural Economics*, 34 (1), 1–26.

Peacock, Alan (1994), *A Future for the Past: The Political Economy of Heritage*, Edinburgh: The David Hume Institute.

Peacock, Alan and Ilde Rizzo (2008), *The Heritage Game. Economics, Policy and Practice*, Oxford: Oxford University Press.

Pignataro, Giacomo and Ilde Rizzo (1997), 'The Political Economy of Rehabilitation: The Case of the Benedettini Monastery', in Michael Hutter and Ilde Rizzo (eds), *Economic Perspectives of Cultural Heritage*, London: Macmillan, pp. 91–106.

van der Ploeg, Rick (2006), 'The Making of Cultural Policy: A European Perspective', in Victor A. Ginsburgh and David Throsby (eds), *Handbook of the Economics of Art and Culture*, Amsterdam: North-Holland, pp.1183–224.

Rizzo, Ilde (2002), 'Heritage Conservation: the Role of Heritage Authorities', in Ilde Rizzo and Ruth Towse (eds), *The Economics of Heritage: A Study in the Political Economy of Culture in Sicily*, Cheltenham, UK and Northampton, MA, USA: Edward Elgar, pp. 31–47.

Rizzo, Ilde (2004), 'The Relationship between Regional and National Policies in the Arts', in Victor A. Ginsburgh (ed.), *Economics of the Art and Culture*, Amsterdam: Elsevier, pp. 203–19.

Rizzo, Ilde and David Throsby (2006), 'Cultural Heritage: Economic Analysis and Public Policy', in Victor A. Ginsburgh and David Throsby (eds), *Handbook of the Economics of Art and Culture*, Amsterdam: North-Holland, pp. 983–1016.

Rizzo, Ilde and Ruth Towse (eds) (2002), *The Economics of the Heritage: A Study in the Political Economy of Culture in Sicily*, Cheltenham, UK and Northampton, MA, USA: Edward Elgar.

Schuster, Mark (1998), 'Beyond Privatization. The Hybridization of Museums and the Built Heritage', in Peter B. Boorsma, Annemoon van Hemel and Niki van der Wielen (eds), *Privatisation and Culture*, Dordrecht: Kluwer, pp. 58–82.

Schuster, Mark J. (2004), 'Making a List: Information as a Tool of Historic Preservation', in Victor A. Ginsburgh (ed.), *Economics of Art and Cultur*, Amsterdam: Elsevier, pp. 221–40.

Throsby, David (1997), 'Seven Questions in the Economics of Cultural Heritage', in Michael Hutter and Ilde Rizzo (eds), *Economic Perspectives of Cultural Heritage*, London: Macmillan, pp. 13–30.

Turnbull, Geoffrey K. (2002), 'Land Development under the Threat of Taking', *Southern Economic Journal*, 69 (2), 290–308.

World Bank (1994), *Cultural Heritage in Environmental Assessment*, EA Sourcebook Update, No. 8 (http://siteresources.worldbank.org/INTSAFEPOL/1142947-1116497775013/20507410/Update8CulturalHeritageInEA September1994.pdf).

Further reading

Heritage regulation raises interdisciplinary issues, because of the technical, artistic and architectural aspects of conservation. A 'classical' reference to explore the meaning as well as the economic and technical implications of the different types of 'conservation' is Lichfield (1988). The values and benefits of heritage conservation practices and policies have been the subject of a multidisciplinary research undertaken at the Getty Conservation Institute and the results are presented in Avrami *et al.* (2000). The Getty Conservation Institute (http://www. getty.edu/conservation/) also provides the list of international conventions, charters and recommendations.

From a more operational perspective, the issues of the design and implementation of heritage conservation are well represented in the Reports of English Heritage (www.english-heritage.org.uk): 'Heritage Counts 2009' provides an overview of data and indicators on conservation of historic environment as well as qualitative information on the links between heritage and social capital (http://www.english-heritage.org.uk/hc/upload/ pdf/HC09_England_Acc.pdf?1265113794); *Conservation Principles, Policies and Guidance* (2008) (http:// www.english-heritage.org.uk/upload/pdf/Conservation_Principles_Policies_and_Guidance_April08_Web. pdf?1265123076) offers an example of regulation, developed through extensive debate and consultation, to provide support for conservation decisions and for the sustainable management of the historic environment.

55 Resale rights[1]
Victor Ginsburgh

The resale right (RR) is the right enjoyed by the author (and his/her heirs, since the right runs for 70 years after the author's death) of an original work of art to an economic interest in its successive sales. According to the Directive of the European Parliament,[2] the right is supposed to ensure that artists benefit from successive 'exploitations'[3] of their work. All EU countries had to comply with the Directive before 1 January 2006, although derogations were possible.[4]

In principle, the right extends to all resales, with the exception of transactions between persons acting in their private capacity. The royalty is calculated as a percentage of the sale price, and not of the increase (or decrease) in value of works.

Economists (and lawyers) who analyse the economic consequences of RR generally reach the conclusion that it is inefficient. Those who are in favour of its introduction tend to concentrate upon the uneven bargaining position between the artist and the art dealer, and condemn the profits that dealers and auction houses supposedly reap from the artist's labour. Whether or not these injustices can be corrected by introducing RR is dealt with from a protectionist perspective and, consequently, the deeper implications of the right are not usually analysed.[5] It is suggested here that not only would RR worsen the position for the contemporary artist, but it would also have a detrimental effect on international art trade for the states in which it is introduced. As I shall show, it also happens to be severely anti-redistributive.

Effect on prices

It is at the time when the artist is likely to value the marginal increases of income most highly that he or she is placed in a position of forgoing a percentage of earnings, since in principle the initial price will adjust to a lower level. The rationale behind this is that rather than the full bundle of property rights passing over to the new owner at the first sale, the artist still retains certain rights, and this is likely to lower the value of the work to the buyer. The decrease will obviously depend on the amount of the resale right, on the expectations the artist and his or her client have about future resale values, on the way they both value risk, and on their time preference, but the resulting effect is clear. In competitive markets, the rebate on the price of the new artwork will exactly represent the expected discounted value of the future RR.

Although many artists start with the hope of becoming famous, those who find their works being sought among the auction houses in centres such as London, New York and Paris are the exception rather than the rule. Singer (1990) suggests that an estimate would put the figure of such a possibility at one in every 3000, or even lower. It is from these few success stories that the image of the exploited artist in his/her younger days is drawn. For the majority, any increase in the value of the work will be relatively small and will entail little real gain for the artist in terms of future royalty income. The effect of RR for the exceptional artist is thus to distribute his/her income from a period of greater necessity (the first years as an artist) to a time when money has lower utility.

One can wonder how large the decrease on the price of the first sale would be. To give a back-of-the-envelope calculation, let us assume that the RR is 3 per cent, that the probability that a work gets sold at auction is 5 per cent, that the discount rate is 4 per cent and, finally, that the average period of time after which a painting is sold again is 20 years. Then, the order of the expected discounted value of the future RR should be $(0.03 \times 0.05)/(1.04)\exp(20) = 0.00068$. This is a very small effect on the first price that would probably be impossible to detect in practice.

Still, it is reasonable to think that a rational, risk-averse artist would choose to take the full and certain price of the work immediately, rather than investing in the hope that the work will be resold in the future. It is remarkable that some artists, including Appel, Baselitz, Hockney and Polke, are even opposed to RR, and see it as a violation of their human rights.[6]

The seller's perspective
The seller is also carrying the risk that the artist may lose favour.[7] Yet it has never been suggested that compensation should exist for this, nor for the opportunity cost that could maybe have had a higher rate of return. The introduction of RR will add to the overall costs of selling a work, the more so because it is levied on the value of the work at the time of the sale, and not on the profit (or the loss!) that the seller has made.

Effect on the quantity of art produced
If artists are faced with an even slightly lower present income, this will be the turning-point for a number of them to leave the industry and the deciding factor for others not to enter. Those who remain will face lower earnings, and this will have two consequences. First, through a mechanism that is too long to describe here,[8] fewer works may be produced. It is fair to presume that the effect on production will be small, but there is certainly little reason to hope, as was claimed a few years ago by EU Commissioner Mario Monti, that 'the Directive [on resale rights] will contribute decisively to the development of modern art in the European Union'.[9]

Inalienability and retroactivity
Under the Commission's proposals, the right is inalienable. Those who promote an inalienable right follow the belief that artists are in an inferior bargaining position. What makes a painter's position so different from that of actors or novelists who are free to waive their rights? Note also that the right cannot be transferred (it is unassignable), an additional restriction.

Retroactivity is also at issue since, in many legal systems, including the English, non-retroactivity of law is the rule. Here the RR will affect those sellers who bought the work of art while there was no RR, but therefore at a higher price. They will lose when selling, since the price will take into account the newly introduced levy.

Tepper (2007) analyses the legal effects of introducing RR into the USA. He concludes that 'most importantly, the [right] neither promotes the creation of art, nor adds to the public domain, and thus fails to meet the dual purposes prescribed by the Constitution.

For these reasons, the US should not implement [the right]' (ibid., p. 41). See also the very thorough legal analysis by Stokes (2006).

Transaction costs and collecting societies
According to the Directive, member states are responsible for the exercise and the management of the right. Collecting societies are one possibility, but member states should ensure that these 'operate in a transparent and efficient manner'. This was far from being the case a couple of years ago. The Danish society in charge of RR charges 40 per cent of the royalty to cover its administrative costs. ADAGP, the French collecting agency, levies 20 per cent.[10] In some cases, especially in France during recent years, very little is left for the artists, and both Belgian and French collecting societies had and still have a hard time with their respective Departments of Justice.

Redistributive effects
A memo issued by the Commission on 14 December, 1999[11] claims that RR will benefit 'approximately 250 000 artists [and] any suggestion that the resale right would benefit only eight rich families (for example, Picasso heirs) is therefore inaccurate'.

In other words, RR is redistributive. When young, the artist sells at low prices, in the belief that he/she will be compensated when older, since RR will compensate for past misfortunes, because of the large prices obtained on early paintings when resold. This assumption is wrong for two reasons. First, as we have already seen, RR detracts from the price of a work when sold for the first time. If an artist ever becomes entitled to RR, he/she will only receive, on average, and if collecting societies become honest, the benefit forfeited when he/she was young, minus the levy charged by the collecting society. Second, as can be expected, the proceeds of resale rights are very unevenly redistributed.

Kusin and McAndrew (2005) show that the number of living artists whose works are sold in the secondary market is much smaller than the '250 000' claimed by the European Commission. During the four-and-a-half-year period analysed (2000 to June 2004), only 3876 artists' works were sold at auction throughout the whole world. Many of these artists would not qualify to receive RR, since they fall outside the scope of the Directive. The work of 9987 deceased artists was sold during the same period. Even allowing for the fact that the Kusin and McAndrew study focuses on auctions only, the figure of 250 000 clearly represents a wild exaggeration.

How much does RR represent for living artists and their heirs? Table 55.1 considers the situation in France, Germany, Italy and the UK.[12] RR that is highlighted in bold is calculated as a 3 per cent share of the value of sales per artist. This takes into account that 4 per cent is the highest levy, and that some 10 to 20 per cent is kept by collecting societies to administer the right.

The uneven redistribution that results from the calculations can be summarized by four numbers. Heirs of dead artists cash some 85 per cent (88.5 per cent in France) of RR. In the group of those who are most sold (top 50), 95.2 per cent goes to heirs. So, essentially, RR is collected for heirs of dead artists. Those who live received €1000 in 2003, and often much less, while each heir received ten to 50 times more. The top 50 artists collect over 55 per cent of the proceeds in France and Germany and as much as 69 per cent in Italy.

Table 55.1   *Who benefits from RR (works auctioned in 2003: France, Germany, Italy and the UK)*

	Living artists		Heirs	
	Top 50	All other	Top 50	All other
France				
Total sales	3.5	7.7	51.1	34.3
Number of artists	5	204	45	996
Value/artist	700.0	37.7	1135.6	34.4
Droit de suite/artist	**21.0**	**1.1**	**34.1**	**1.0**
Germany				
Total sales	1.8	2.2	16.7	12.3
Number of artists	7	108	43	660
Value/artist	257.1	20.4	388.4	18.6
Droit de suite/artist	**7.7**	**0.6**	**11.6**	**0.6**
Italy				
Total sales	1.7	4.1	24.8	8.1
Number of artists	7	152	43	413
Value/artist	242.8	27.0	576.7	19.6
Droit de suite/artist	**7.3**	**0.8**	**17.3**	**0.6**
UK				
Total sales	23.1	25.1	128.7	100.1
Number of artists	9	299	41	1385
Value/artist	2566.7	83.9	3139.0	72.2
Droit de suite/artist	**77.0**	**2.5**	**94.2**	**2.2**

Note: Calculations are based on Kusin and McAndrew (2005). Total sales are in millions of euros; value/artist and RR are in thousand euros. Top 50 relates to artists who are ranked first according to the value of their sales in 2003. For Italy and the UK the numbers are illustrative, since no RR was collected in 2003.

This, one can claim, concerns salesrooms. But the situation is not much different in general. In Germany, for instance, in 1998, a living artist, whether sold at auction or by a gallery, collected less than DM 2000 (some €1000), while each heir collected DM 17000, and out of the 7400 artists represented by collecting agencies only 480 collected RR.[13] This is again far from the 250000 announced by the European Commission.

This would be fine, though unreasonably small, if artists or their heirs received the proceeds. In some countries, Germany for example, a share of the RR is paid to a fund that supports needy or elderly artists. In Finland and Sweden, it is used to support young artists. The levy may be socially desirable and its implementation loaded with good intentions, but it is no longer an intellectual right, which is a poor excuse for social security contributions, or compensations for past immoral acts.[14] It is useful to add that the Directive is quite lenient in imposing changes to such drifts. It merely suggests that 'Member States which do not, at the time of the adoption of this Directive, apply a resale right for the benefit of the artist [. . .] should be allowed a limited transitional period' to fully adapt to the Directive.

*Table 55.2   Works auctioned in 2003: breakdown by location of sale (€ millions,
             numbers and shares)*

Value of the works (€ million)	Number of works	Number of artists	Value (millions)	RR6 %	UK %	USA %
3000–200 000	34 641	7929	586.9	22.3	11.0	31.2
200 000–2 million	769	465	369.7	8.8	31.5	53.3
Over 2 million	42	29	184.3	4.5	17.6	77.9

Note: RR6 represents the six EU countries in which RR was already implemented in 2003.

Source: Kusin and McAndrew (2005).

Effects on the place of transaction

The Directive's intention is to smooth out distortions of competition, as well as displacement of sales within the Union, but very little is said about displacements to the rest of the world. And this is forgetting what was already realized in 1958 by Jean Cassou, director of the Musée National d'Art Moderne in Paris, who in a letter addressed to the President du Comité Professionnel des Galeries d'Art, dated 13 November 1958, writes: 'I am aware that Paris does no longer host important sales, and I am afraid that RR will impose a new threat [on the Paris art market].'[15] There are many unpublicized examples of dislocations. The £50 million French Gaffé collection was sold in New York in 2001, because UNICEF, the beneficiary of the sale, publicly recognized that they wanted to avoid paying RR.[16]

How many paintings would be involved, and how much would this represent for European salesrooms? Nobody can provide definitive answers to these questions, but it is possible to examine some data on which answers could be based. My guess is based on Table 55.2, which provides illuminating figures concerning sales of modern and contemporary art (subject to RR) in 2003. The table shows that over 97 per cent of the works are priced below €200 000, and that the 811 works that fetch more than €200 000 account for 50 per cent of the value of sales. These are precisely the works for which New York already captures over 50 per cent of the trade (78 per cent for works worth over €2 million). The UK is left with 31 per cent, even before the arrival of RR. The six EU countries where RR is levied count for a lean 8.8 per cent. The introduction of RR in the UK would move a substantial part of the most profitable UK trade to New York, the more so given that some 40 per cent of the turnover of UK auctions consist of works imported from non EU countries.[17] This would leave European salerooms with a large number of only marginally profitable works, and it is questionable whether salesrooms and galleries can live in handling a large number of less valuable works, given that it takes probably as much time to market a work under €200 000 (and there are over 34 000) than it takes for expensive works (811), while the total value of both types is almost identical (€587 versus €554 million).

It is, moreover, slightly vexing to see that Europe may be encouraging a system that could lead to incentives to export its cultural heritage to countries such as the USA.[18] This would also increase the risk of the works to remain there, as European collectors may be discouraged to pay customs in order to reimport them.

But, there is a but . . .

In a recent paper, Graddy and Banternghansa (2009) study what happened in the UK between July 2006 (RR was implemented in February 2006, and collected for living artists only) and July 2007. They run a very careful econometric analysis, and find no evidence of a reduction in price growth in the UK relative to other countries and no evidence of paintings being moved from the UK to countries where there is no RR. On the contrary, they find that over the period 1996 to 2007, the total price growth in the UK market segment subject to RR increased significantly relative to other countries and relative to the segment of the market that is not subject to RR. This may, according to the authors, be due to econometric identification problems, in particular that the market for living artists in the UK behaved differently than elsewhere, or that buyers and sellers are happy and 'treat the payment to living artists as a donation to the arts'. They also suggest that their 'current findings are not necessarily a good indication of the effects from a further coverage [to dead artists], and the UK authorities should proceed with caution'. It may be fair to add that the authors themselves are somewhat puzzled by their own results.

Conclusions

To me, RR appears to lack any appeal, both in theory, and because it solves no practical problem. The disadvantages weigh heavily while the positive proposals of the Commission lack the guidance of long-term efficiency considerations. A no-RR world would seem to be the most efficient solution. There is a danger of over-regulation that the Commission is not willing to recognize. Simple economic analysis shows how even a well-intentioned law could bring about exactly the opposite effect to its original purpose. The RR would appear to be a law that illustrates this pitfall and requires urgent reassessment.

Notes

1. This chapter draws on Bogle and Ginsburgh (1998) and Ginsburgh (1997, 2005).
2. Directive 2001/84/EC of 27 September 2001 on the resale right for the benefit of the author of an original work of art.
3. This is the word used in the Directive. According to the *Oxford Advanced Learner's Dictionary*, 'to exploit' means 'to use or treat sb/sth in an unfair and selfish manner for one's own advantage or profit'. I found it important to quote this word, since it gives an idea of the tone of discussions at the time the decision to implement RR was made!
4. In the UK, for example, RR is collected for the benefit of living artists only. It will be extended to heirs in 2012.
5. See, however, Solow (1998) who shows that RR may have positive welfare effects for artists.
6. *The Art Newspaper*, December 2000, p. 75.
7. The Directive suggests that 'the person by whom the royalty is payable should, in principle, be the seller'. In fact, the result holds no matter who pays the RR.
8. For details, see Filer (1984).
9. Suzanne Perry, 'Artists should benefit when works sold, EU says', Reuters REU2348 3 OVR 365 (ECR EEC GB LIF NEWS) F1301225, 13 March 1996.
10. *The Art Newspaper*, October 2004. See also Hummel *et al.* (1995).
11. Memo/99/68.
12. Note that Italy and the UK did not, at the time, collect RR. The numbers are given as examples of what may happen.
13. Declaration of Norbert Lammert, member of the German Parliament, and culture and media spokesman of the CDU/CSU parties.
14. Australia proposed to introduce RR to compensate aboriginal painters who have, in the past, sold at very low prices, while their works command very high prices today. See *The Art Newspaper*, July–August 2004, p. 27.

15. See Comité des Galeries d'Art (1997), p. 127.
16. *The Art Newspaper*, April 2001, p. 67.
17. This figure has been kindly communicated to me by Christie's and Sotheby's.
18. And Switzerland, a market that is often overseen, since it is dominated by art galleries for which data are difficult to access to, and not by salesrooms.

See also:

Chapter 4: Art markets; Chapter 14: Copyright; Chapter 48: Poverty and support of artists.

References

Bogle, C. and V. Ginsburgh (1998), 'Introducing Droit de Suite into the EU. An Economic Viewpoint', *Temas de Integracao*, 3, 115–37.
Comité des Galeries d'Art (1997), *Les Galeries d'Art en France Aujourd'hui*, Paris: L'Harmattan.
Filer, R. (1984), 'A Theoretical Analysis of the Economic Impact of Artists' Resale Royalties Legislation', *Journal of Cultural Economics*, 8, 1–28.
Ginsburgh, V. (1997), 'Le Droit de Suite: Principe et Réalité', in Comité des Galeries d'Art, *Les Galeries d'Art en France Aujourd'hui*, Paris: L'Harmattan.
Ginsburgh, V. (2005), 'Droit de Suite. An Economic Viewpoint', in *The Modern and Contemporary Art Market*, Maastricht: The European Fine Art Foundation.
Graddy, K. and C. Banternghansa (2009), 'The Impact of Droit de Suite in the UK. An Empirical Analysis', CEPR Discussion Paper No. 8136.
Hummel, M., L. Becker and P. Huber (1995), *The Droit de Suite*, Report commissioned by the French authors' society ADAGP, the German authors' society BILD-KUNST and the Groupement Européen des Sociétés d'Auteurs et Compositeurs (GESAC), München: IFO-Institute.
Kusin, D. and C. McAndrew (2005), 'A Study of the Global Resale Market', in *The Modern and Contemporary Art Market*, Maastricht: The European Fine Art Foundation.
Singer, L. (1990), 'The Utility of Art Versus Fair Bets in the Investment Market', *Journal of Cultural Economics*, 14, 1–13.
Solow, J. (1998), 'An Economic Analysis of the Droit de Suite', *Journal of Cultural Economics*, 22, 209–26.
Stokes, S. (2006), *Artist's Resale Right*, Leicester: Institute of Art and Law.
Tepper, J. (2007), 'Le Droit de Suite. An Unartistic Approach to American Law', available at http://works.bepress.com/cgi/viewcontent.cgi?article=1000&context=jonathan_tepper.

Further reading

Filer (1984) spells out the economic principles that support the case against the resale right.

56 Superstars
Günther G. Schulze

What makes a star a star? Why are Madonna, Luciano Pavarotti or Tom Cruise so immensely rich? The competitive model in its simple version tells us that people are remunerated according to their (marginal) productivity. This would imply that, given the enormous differences in income between the average writer or actor and, say, Stephen King or Sean Connery, there would have to be a huge gap between the talent of the stars and of those that come next but do not enjoy a star status. If you agree with me that Britney Spears's talent is not hugely different from that of your local music club's singer, there must be more to the superstar phenomenon than the simple competitive model would be able to portray.

This is what we investigate in three steps. The next section presents theoretical arguments for the existence of superstars, the third section discusses the empirical evidence for the arts, and the last section points to selected further issues. Although the superstar phenomenon is not limited to the cultural sector – there are superstar law firms, doctors, managers, professors and of course athletes – the focus here is on superstars in the arts.

Theoretical concepts

In his seminal paper on 'The Economics of Superstars', Sherwin Rosen explains how small differences in talent translate into large differences in earnings. The underlying reason for that is the concurrence of imperfect substitutability of different qualities (of the otherwise 'same' service) on the demand side and a production technology that allows for joint consumption. He starts by acknowledging that different qualities of a narrowly defined service (for example, the performance of a particular Beethoven concert) are imperfect substitutes in consumption: people rationally favour fewer high-quality services rather than more of the same service at mediocre levels.[1] That might be true for a number of services (such as medical services) and this higher willingness to pay alone would lead to a difference in pay. It already explains the convexity of the function that translates quality into income. As Rosen (1981, p. 846) writes: 'Hearing a succession of mediocre singers does not add up to a single outstanding performance. If a surgeon is 10 percent more successful in saving lives than his fellows, most people would be willing to pay more than 10 percent premium for his services.' The enormous income differentials between superstars and their colleagues of lesser talent, however, are explained only if the consumption technology is taken into consideration. Public performances of, say, a classical concert exhibit the characteristics of a club good – unit costs decrease with rising audience size. At some point congestion costs will occur as a classical live concert is more enjoyable in a medium-sized concert hall than in a football stadium. These congestion costs put a limit on the optimal size of audiences and therefore lead to non-degenerate market equilibria (more than one supplier). Still, artists of higher quality command higher prices *and* a greater audience, and thus a larger income. Congestion is absent for 'canned performances' such as CD productions, TV performances, books, videos or movies. In Rosen's set-up, this leads to a single artist (or single group of artists) – the best – to serve the whole market. Potential market entry limits the market power of the artist, but since he/she is perceptibly better than the next one he/she enjoys an economic rent that leads to a higher price than his/her closest competitor would need to charge to enter the market. This quality difference can be small, although it needs to be perceptible; it is leveraged through the scale economies in production and can make total rent very large.

Rosen has put forward a powerful idea in a simple model; given the beautiful simplicity of his arguments, he has left many important aspects for others to explore. He deliberately disregarded product differentiation as he defined his competitive market very narrowly and did not adopt a monopolistic competition model *à la* Lancaster or Dixit–Stiglitz.[2] There are far more than only two or three movie superstars of each gender or a handful of superstar rock'n'roll bands, as his model would predict: heterogeneous tastes or a love of variety become an important limitation to star power, in addition to the threat of entry of close competitors. Moreover, he did not explain why people prefer a single superstar performance to a series of performances of lesser quality, but rather assumed it. Lastly, he did not explain the emergence of superstars, but rather assumed a given and observable distribution in quality among artists. Adler (1985) and MacDonald (1988) filled some of the gaps.

MacDonald (1988) provides a dynamic version of Rosen's model. In a two-period stochastic model, performers decide whether to perform, and if they do, the quality of their performance (either good or bad) is observable to all interested. Since outcomes are serially correlated for each artist, first-period reviews have predictive power for the second period's performance. This accumulation of knowledge leads to a separation of market segments in the steady state: those with bad first-period reviews leave the business for an exogenous alternative occupation, while those with a good first-period performance command a larger crowd and a higher price than the newcomers, because consumers face a much smaller risk with regard to the performance quality and are willing to pay for this. These artists experience a vast income growth compared to their first-period income – they rise to become stars.

In his article, 'Stardom and Talent', Moshe Adler describes a learning process as the key to understanding the superstar phenomenon. Learning about art is so important because art consumption is positively addictive in that marginal utility from art consumption increases with the ability to appreciate art, which is a function of past art consumption (Stigler and Becker, 1977): the more you know, the more you appreciate it. In the course of consuming art, 'consumption capital' is accumulated and thus marginal utility from art consumption rises over time. The idea goes back to Alfred Marshall, who wrote, 'It is therefore no exception to the law [of diminishing marginal utility] that the more good music a man hears, the stronger is his taste for it likely to become' (Marshall, [1891] 1962, p. 94). There is substantial empirical evidence for such an addictive effect; see, for example, Smith (1998). This learning process does not refer to art in general but to specific art forms and even artists. Artist-specific consumption capital is built up by consuming the art service provided by the artist in question and by discussing it with others likewise knowledgeable about this artist. The latter effect creates positive network externalities as it is costly to search for someone to interact with about a specific artist.[3] This explains the existence of stars: stars may be born because initially (slightly) more people happen to know one artist than any other artists of possibly equal talent and communicate about him or her more with others. Artist-specific consumption capital is built up more rapidly, and this artist will snowball into a star. However, Terviö (2009) shows that if it is costly to reveal talent, firms will refrain from searching for talent, settling for – mediocre – talent of incumbents who are paid excessive salaries. 'Superstars' are created by the talent revelation process rather than by the underlying scarcity of talent.

Empirical evidence

Hamlen (1991, 1994) tries to single out a superstar effect in the US record industry using a sample of 115 singers for the years 1955–87. Since the superstar phenomenon in the Rosen (1981) sense requires that 'small differences in talent become magnified in large earnings differences, with greater magnification of the earnings–talent gradient increasing sharply near the top of the scale' (p. 846), an empirical analysis requires a quantifiable concept of 'talent'. Hamlen uses data on the *harmonic content of voice*, a concept taken from the technical literature on voice, which measures 'depth' and 'richness' (for details, see Hamlen, 1991, p. 731). He runs the total record sales (Hamlen, 1991) and number of hit singles and hit albums (Hamlen, 1994) on the measure of quality and other singers' attributes such as the year in which the singer first released a single or album, dummies for sex, race (black/non-black), whether the artists write their own songs, whether they have appeared in a movie, and whether they have a recognized band. In his second paper he incorporates the fact that success in the 'low-end' singles market may serve as a signalling device for quality that feeds into consumers' choices in the 'top-end' albums market.[4]

Although talent, measured by voice quality, increases sales, Hamlen (1991, 1994) fails to find a magnification effect. Rewards for talent are far less than proportional to differences in talent. Hence he cannot identify a superstar phenomenon in the Rosen sense. Furthermore, the low-end singles market functions as a quality filter for the albums market, which is in line with MacDonald's idea of a multi-period information accumulation process. While voice quality is important in the singles market, it is less so in the albums market, in which success in the singles market serves as a quality indicator. Other singers' attributes apart from voice quality, such as sex, race, appearances in movies and a good band, influence success as well. That already indicates that there is more to success than just talent.

Chung and Cox (1994) show that the distribution of gold records in the period 1958–89 follows the specific Yule distribution $f(i) = 1/i(i + 1)$, $\Sigma f(i) = 1$ where $f(i)$ is the share of performers which have earned i gold records ($i = 1, \ldots, \infty$). Yule distributions in general have been shown to describe a variety of sociological, biological and economic phenomena such as the distribution of incomes by size, of cities by population, of scientists by the number of papers and so on. The underlying probability process can be described as a sequential buying process: one consumer after the other buys one record first, then in the second round each consumer buys a different record and so forth. The choice of records in each round follows two assumptions: (i) the probability that consumer $k + 1$ buys a record that has been chosen by exactly i of the k previous consumers is proportional to i; (ii) there is a constant small probability that consumer $k + 1$ chooses a record that has not been chosen previously. Assumption (ii) represents a snowball effect in the sense of Adler (1985). The fact that the observed distribution of gold records coincides with a pattern that results from a stochastic process incorporating such a snowball effect leads the authors to conclude that the superstardom phenomenon is merely the result of a probability mechanism that predicts that 'artistic outputs will be concentrated among a few *lucky* individuals' (Chung and Cox, 1994, p. 771, emphasis in original). In their interpretation, difference in talent is not necessary for superstars to emerge, but rather luck that initially increases the user base and reinforces itself. This supports Adler's idea of the emergence of superstars. Giles (2006) measures the distribution of the lifetime of Number 1 hits in the US charts and the number of Number 1 hits per artists for the period 1955–2003. Contrary to Chung and Cox, he fails to find that his two measures of success are distributed according to the Yule–Simon distribution. Spierdijk and Voorneveld (2009) argue that both aforementioned contributions test only a specific Yule distribution (with $\rho = 1$) that is economically implausible and that the test they use (χ^2 goodness-of-fit) is inappropriate for the superstar phenomenon. Using the three data sets of Chung and Cox and of Giles and applying parametric bootstrap, better estimation techniques and more powerful tests,[5] they find that the Yule distribution approximates the empirical distribution well only for the lower quantiles; overall they reject the Yule distribution as its upper tail is too heavy. A generalized Yule distribution results in a much better fit.

Both empirical approaches fail to provide conclusive evidence for the superstar phenomenon. In the Hamlen approach it is by no means clear that the harmonic content of voice is the relevant measure for artistic quality for singers of non-classical music (rock, folk and so on). Charm, sex appeal, the contents of the lyrics and the show on the stage are also very important factors for success for singers, yet they are very difficult to measure. The success of Bob Dylan, who is not renowned for his harmonic voice, or that of Britney Spears, The Spice Girls or AC/DC, and many others are evidence that there is more to a singer's success than just a beautiful voice. Thus Hamlen's approach suffers from an omitted-variable bias. Chung and Cox's – moot – coincidence result does not tell us anything about the underlying *reason* for the selection of consumers; the fact that the outcome may be consistent with a pure reinforcing probability mechanism would not strictly prove that it is at work. The observed outcome could also be explained by a preference for what consumers regard as the highest quality coupled with a certain preference for variety and somewhat heterogeneous tastes.

Crain and Tollison (2002) argue that switching consumption from a non-star to a star is more likely if the acquired consumption capital (for the non-star) is lower and the time horizon is longer as individuals can enjoy easier communication with their peers about stars than non-stars for a longer time and the write-off of acquired consumption capital for the non-star is smaller. In other words, switching to a star is more likely if the consumers are younger. Switching is less likely if time preference rates are higher. Crain and Tollison show that star concentration is higher for a younger population, but the proxies for time preference result in mixed evidence. They show determinants for the skewedness of the earnings distribution, but do not test the superstar theory (which they claim to be untestable due to the difficulties of measuring artistic quality). Their observation is consistent with other explanations as well, such as a larger desire for conformity among younger consumers.

Krueger (2005) analyses the reasons behind soaring ticket prices for rock concerts.[6] *Inter alia*, he tests whether the returns to superstar status have increased as consumer electronics (discman, mp3 players and the like) have become ubiquitous and the Internet,

NAPSTER and so on have gained importance, thereby increasing the effective audience size. He measures superstar power by the space devoted to the artist/band in *The Rolling Stones Encyclopaedia of Rock & Roll*. He finds that superstar effects are large and increasing, but that they cannot explain the surge in ticket prices. Rather, the increased illegal downloading of music decouples concert attendance from record sales and thus it no longer makes sense to keep ticket prices low in order to increase attendance and thus record sales.

Further issues

Measurement

The main difficulty in testing Rosen's theory is measuring artistic quality correctly. Yet superstars are not limited to the arts, but play an important role in sports and other areas. In sports these empirical problems are not as serious, since quality is easier to measure. 'Soft skills' like charm, looks or lyrics play a lesser role; performance is measurable in inches, milliseconds or goals, and comprehensive statistics are readily available. Therefore empirical analyses of the superstar phenomenon in sports are more promising (for example, Lucifora and Simmons, 2003).

In their analysis of salaries in the German soccer league, Lehmann and Schulze (2008) test Rosen's theory by including a host of performance parameters, as well as the Adler–MacDonald theory, by including variables for that part of players' media presence that is not explained by their performance on the field. Adler's idea of the importance of individuals' interaction for the acquisition of artist-specific consumption capital and MacDonald's idea of an information accumulation process point towards the important role of the mass media in the acquisition of information and thus consumption capital. Media presence should thus be included in empirical analyses of superstars. These authors also use a quantile regression approach as convexity of the talent-earning gradient, and the role of media presence is particularly important for the upper tail of the income distribution.

Efficiency considerations

In Rosen's model, markets with superstars are efficient as equally or more highly talented artists can enter the market and establish themselves as stars. In Adler's model, artists of higher talent may not attract consumers away from the incumbents as the incumbents enjoy higher popularity, which serves as a barrier to entry to superstardom (Adler, 2006).

Borghans and Groot (1998) argue that superstars earn more than their marginal contribution to welfare because they have monopolistic power due to their position as 'the best' at the expense of the other artists. Inefficiency may result also from rent-seeking activities of potential superstars trying to capture the superstar rent resulting in rent dissipation. Frank and Cook (1995) argue that superstar salaries trigger stardom-seeking behaviour of artists that disregard alternative education and occupations and end up underpaid compared to alternative occupations. Adler (2006) notes that artists also receive psychic income from being an artist, which makes purely monetary comparisons between being an artist and alternative occupations incomplete. Richter and Schneider (1999) argue that inefficiencies may arise because superstars enjoy an externality in consumption – popularity – which has an economic value (for example in the form of commercials contracts) and that organization of performances has features of a natural monopoly.[7]

Other issues

Ruth Towse (1992) analyses the role that intermediaries play for superstar singers in classical music by reducing search and information costs of opera houses. In this market, the honorarium serves as a signal for quality and popularity, and thus its reduction would not increase the demand for the singer. Lastly, superstars may be culture-specific, raising the question how star power is affected by globalization (Adler, 2006, p. 905).

Notes

1. As a convenient modelling trick he assumes that utility derived from this particular service y is the product of quantity n and quality per unit of output z, $y = n z$, thereby adopting a smooth quantity–quality substitution technology (comparable to the concept of labour in efficiency units). This allows him to use a competitive framework for the single market for y instead of modelling monopolistic competition in products of different quality. Imperfect substitutability is introduced through a fixed cost of consumption per unit of *quantity*, which gives rise to a preference of cost-minimizing consumers for fewer services of high quality (instead of more services of lesser quality) as this reduces the fixed costs. See Hamlen (1994) for a Dixit–Stiglitz model of artistic variety.
2. See also Rosen (1983) on this.
3. The mechanism is very similar to positive network externalities for the usage of word processors and other computer programs, which are more valuable the larger the user base – exchange of files, recommendations and troubleshooting become easier the larger the group of people that shares the same software.
4. Publication of singles typically precedes publication in the album market (although established stars sometimes go back to the singles market).
5. They use the discrete Anderson–Darling and discrete Kolmogorov–Smirnov tests with ML and MM estimates.
6. Between 1996 and 2003 ticket prices in the USA have risen by 82 per cent while the consumer price index (CPI) has increased by 17 per cent.
7. See also Bonus and Ronte (1997).

See also:

Chapter 7: Artists' labour markets; Chapter 26: Demand; Chapter 29: Experience goods.

References

Adler, Moshe (1985), 'Stardom and Talent', *American Economic Review*, 75, 208–12.
Adler, Moshe (2006), 'Stardom and Talent', in Victor Ginsburgh and David Throsby (eds), *Handbook of the Economics of Art and Culture*, Amsterdam: North-Holland, pp. 895–906.
Bonus, Holger and Dieter Ronte (1997), 'Credibility and Economic Value in the Visual Arts', *Journal of Cultural Economics*, 21, 103–18.
Borghans, Lex and Loek Groot (1998), 'Superstardom and Monopolistic Power: Why Media Stars Earn More Than Their Marginal Contribution to Welfare', *Journal of Institutional and Theoretical Economics/ Zeitschrift für die gesamte Staatswissenschaft*, 154 (3), 546–71.
Chung, Kee and Raymond Cox (1994), 'A Stochastic Model of Superstardom: An Application of the Yule Distribution', *Review of Economics and Statistics*, 76, 771–5.
Crain, Mark and Robert Tollison (2002,) 'Consumer Choice and the Popular Music Industry: A Test of the Superstar Theory', *Empirica*, 29, 1–9.
Frank, Robert and P. Cook (1995) *The Winner-Take-All Society*, New York: The Free Press.
Giles, David (2006), 'Superstardom in the US Popular Music Industry Revisited', *Economics Letters*, 92, 68–74.
Hamlen, William (1991), 'Superstardom in Popular Music: Empirical Evidence', *Review of Economics and Statistics*, 73, 729–33.
Hamlen, William (1994), 'Variety and Superstardom in Popular Music', *Economic Inquiry*, 32, 395–406.
Krueger, Alan (2005), 'The Economics of Real Superstars: The Market for Rock Concerts in the Material World', *Journal of Labor Economics*, 23 (1), 1–30.

Lehmann, Erik and Günther Schulze (2008), 'What Does it Take to be a Star? The Role of Performance and the Media for German Soccer Players', *Applied Economics Quarterly*, 54 (1), 59–70.

Lucifora, C. and R. Simmons (2003), 'Superstar Effects in Sports: Evidence from Italian Soccer', *Journal of Sports Economics* 4, 35–55.

MacDonald, Glenn (1988), 'The Economics of Rising Stars', *American Economic Review*, 78, 155–66.

Marshall, Alfred ([1891] 1962), *Principles of Economics*, 8th edn, London: Macmillan.

Richter, Wolfram and Kerstin Schneider (1999), 'Competition for Stars and Audiences: An Analysis of Alternative Institutional Settings', *European Journal of Political Economy*, 15, 101–21.

Rosen, Sherwin (1981), 'The Economics of Superstars', *American Economic Review*, 71, 845–58.

Rosen, Sherwin (1983), 'The Economics of Superstars: Reply', *American Economic Review*, 73, 460–62.

Smith, Thomas (1998), 'The Addiction to Culture', paper presented on the biannual meeting of the Association for Cultural Economics International in Barcelona, 14–17 June 1998; also part of 'Two Essays on the Economics of The Arts: The Demand for Culture and the Occupational Mobility of Artists', unpublished doctoral dissertation, University of Chicago, IL.

Spierdijk, Laura and Mark Voorneveld (2009), 'Superstars Without Talent? The Yule Distribution Controversy', *Review of Economics and Statistics*, 91 (3), 648–52.

Stigler, George and Gary Becker (1977), 'De Gustibus Non Est Disputandum', *American Economic Review*, 67, 76–90.

Terviö, Marko (2009), 'Superstars and Mediocrities: Market Failure in the Discovery of Talent', *Review of Economic Studies*, 76, 829–50.

Towse, Ruth (1992), 'The Earnings of Singers: An Economic Analysis', in R. Towse and A. Khakee (eds), *Cultural Economics*, Heidelberg: Springer; reprinted in Ruth Towse (2001), *Creativity, Incentive and Reward*, Cheltenham, UK and Northampton, MA, USA: Edward Elgar, pp. 79–89.

Further reading

Rosen (1981) and Adler (1985) are recommended.

57 Tax concessions
John O'Hagan

Introduction

Taxation measures aiding the donation of gifts or bequests to the arts are applied on a major scale in the USA (see O'Hagan, 1996, and Schuster, 2006). Some of these measures have formed the cornerstone of government policy towards the arts in the USA since the beginning of the twentieth century and they are defended vehemently to this day. In contrast, while such measures exist in some countries in Europe they have rarely been used on any significant scale. Despite this, there are many who call for more of a US-type tax policy in Europe, and such calls appear to have increased in number and volume in recent years. There have, however, been trenchant criticisms of the US tax policy measures in relation to charitable contributions as they apply to the arts, the most authoritative and comprehensive of these being that by Feld *et al.* (1983).[1] Despite the force of the arguments in this book, few involved in the arts or policy-making in the USA appear today to question this tax policy as a means of channelling public money to the arts. Weil (1991) in particular, in an elegantly argued piece, defends these tax policies over direct government grants and bemoans the diminution of the scale of the tax incentive resulting from tax changes in the USA. Simon (1987) also defends tax concessions over government grants in a very comprehensive review of the tax treatment of non-profit organizations in the USA.

It must be noted, however, that there are tax expenditures on the arts in Europe that, although much smaller than those for charitable contributions in the USA, and more elusive, are fiercely defended by the arts communities there and apparently matter greatly. In particular the concessions in relation to value added tax (VAT) have been subjected to considerable public debate. Besides this, the important property tax exemption is prevalent in both Europe and the USA.

Key policy questions

What precisely are these tax measures? What is the cost of these measures to the taxpayer? What are the effects of these measures on arts institutions? What are their effects on the level and composition of arts inputs and output? These are the questions that matter in relation to tax expenditures, and some of these will be examined briefly here.

In deciding which of the measures deserve most examination, we could choose those measures that incur the greatest tax expenditure in practice or we could choose the tax measure that has the greatest impact on arts institutions and artists. Alternatively, we could choose some other criterion, such as the tax concession for which there is the most information in terms of data, or that with the most interesting analytical features. The latter considerations predominate in discussions of tax policy in general, despite the fact that, from a policy point of view, the tax has no practical significance. The criterion that will most influence the discussion here is the one that places emphasis on tax revenue forgone, although other considerations will also be considered.

Main tax expenditures

In the USA the charitable contribution deduction is by far the most important in terms of tax forgone, and it is followed by the property tax exemption and the capital gains tax remission of gifts to arts institutions in this regard: for example, Feld *et al.* (1983) estimate that the individual charitable deduction concession is, in terms of tax forgone, around twice that of the property tax exemption, and almost three times that both of the corporate charitable deduction and of the capital gains tax and gift/estate tax concession combined (see Feld, 2008, for recent data). Most of the tax measures in the USA have particular relevance for art museums and as a result they appear to be the most favoured arts institutions in this regard.

In Europe the picture is very different, although one must be careful not to over-generalize because of the large number of independent states involved. A related problem in commenting on the European experience is that it is very difficult to obtain up-to-date descriptions of the tax situations that actually apply in relation to the arts: much of the discussion in relation to Europe must therefore refer to work that is quite dated.

Tax expenditures associated with charitable contribution deductions appear to be small, judging from the available evidence; one of the reasons for this is perhaps that similarly favourable tax exemptions do not appear to apply to gifts or bequests of property. The main reason, however, is probably that, independent of tax concessions, Europeans with their much higher general tax rates see support of arts organizations as the role of the state, not as something meriting charitable contributions that they are expected to pay in addition to their taxes.[2] The major effective tax concession in fact is the preferential VAT treatment of the consumption of the output of the arts sector, but no estimates appear to have been made of the cost of this tax concession. This is a tax concession that would favour in particular the performing arts, as it usually applies to the output of all performing arts organizations, not just the publicly funded institutions, which already in addition receive high levels of direct public assistance. Property tax exemption for arts institutions is also widespread in Europe, but again there has been remarkably little discussion, at least in the English-language literature, of this aspect of arts policy. In contrast, the tax concessions that apply in some large European countries in relation to relief from estate duty/capital transfer taxes have been analysed in detail despite the fact that the tax expenditures associated with these concessions are small: the reason appears to be more to do with the interesting analytical and practical issues that the policy entails, as well as the very high level of public controversy that has accompanied the sale of artefacts that are seen as part of the national patrimony, situations that these taxes are sometimes designed to address.[3]

Lack of recognition of cost to the state of tax breaks

It appears odd that so many people still do not associate a cost (that is, a tax expenditure) with a tax break in relation to the arts and that so many governments have still so few data relating to the precise cost of various tax concessions to the arts. Why is this? The first reason is that tax expenditure analysis in general, especially its inclusion in the budget process, is of recent origin and is still not formally included in budget accounts for many countries. Part of this has to do with the fact that many different tax expenditures are extremely difficult to estimate, both for data reasons and because the estimation depends on what behavioural assumptions about the key players are made by the analyst.[4] Second, in relation to the arts, some have argued that the main tax break, the charitable contribution deduction, does not involve a tax expenditure at all, on the grounds that income devoted to a charitable cause (which is how a contribution to the arts is classified) is not available to the person for his or her own consumption, but for the consumption of all, and should not be taxed to him or her.[5] There are very few, though, in the economics or legal profession who appear to support this argument. Third, tax expenditures are rarely designed for the arts specifically, but are established in relation to some much wider target group, such as charities in the USA, of which sector the arts is only a tiny component. Even if estimates of the tax expenditure for the sector were available, it is unlikely that they would be available for every small subcomponent. Fourth, it may be that the very obscurity of a tax expenditure removes the pressure to quantify it. The state's contribution to a local wealthy individual's gift to his or her local museum is never identified as such by the individual or the museum. The donor is treated in every official version of this transaction, and by the media, as the sole source of the funds. Likewise, what local government computes the value of a property tax exemption to a local theatre? If its value is unknown it appears as a costless subsidy, especially since no money actually changes hands. Yet this exemption is in many respects equivalent in financial terms to the local government providing a tied direct grant to the local theatre, the value of which would of course be known and debated in public.[6]

It is this very obscurity that provided the driving force for the Feld *et al.* treatise, as they see it as the principal defect of the tax break system to the arts, preventing it from looming in the consciousness of arts administrators, scholars and the public alike. Whatever the controversy may be over the tax expenditure associated with taxation policy, it is clear that these tax breaks are highly valued by the arts community (judging at least from the reaction when there is a proposal to abolish them), as each and every one of them bestows favours on the arts sector, even though it may be very difficult to quantify the exact magnitude of the implicit subsidy involved. A related point is that, even if the implicit subsidy could be accurately calculated, proposals to replace it with a direct and explicit subsidy are mostly rejected by the arts community on the understandable grounds that there is no guarantee that, once the tax concession is abolished, governments will not subsequently renege on their promise to replace it fully with a direct subsidy.

An examination of specific tax breaks illustrates most clearly the nature of the tax expenditure involved. Nowhere is this truer than in relation to the deductions that can be claimed against income tax in the USA, the most important and significant tax that applies to the arts anywhere, and the VAT concessions applying in Europe.

Individual charitable contribution deductions in the USA

The federal income tax code in the USA accounts for three significant income tax expenditures for the arts: individual charitable income tax deductions; corporate income tax deductions; and capital gains tax forgone on gifts of property. The charitable contribution deduction, as seen earlier, accounts for the vast bulk of the tax expenditure under this heading, however and is, as mentioned, the cornerstone of indirect federal aid to the arts in the USA (for a discussion of the other two, see O'Hagan, 1998).

Since 1917, individual taxpayers in the USA have been allowed to deduct contributions to non-profit, charitable institutions, including arts institutions, when computing their income taxes, at both federal and state level (see Fullerton, 1991). Although the basic principles of the charitable contribution deduction are in operation in several European countries, the charitable contribution system in practice is of minimal significance, in terms of take-up, to the arts in Europe, although this may be changing.

The tax deduction clearly changes the price to the donor of a charitable gift to the arts. Specifically, the deduction reduces the net cost to him or her of channelling a fixed sum to an arts institution and thereby could induce donors to provide even more than they would in the absence of the tax concession. Thus, for example, if a donor wanted to give $500 to a museum before the tax concession and the marginal tax rate of this donor was 50 per cent, the effect of the tax concession would be, first, to reduce the after-tax cost to the donor to $250 and, second, to induce some response to this by the donor, in particular to increase the initial gift. If the donor increased the gift to $1000, the net cost would be $500, the same as the individual was prepared to donate before the tax concession. The magnitude of this induced giving, that is the price elasticity with respect to charitable giving to the arts, is central to the economics of the charitable contribution deduction.

One key feature of the charitable contribution deduction to note is that the tax expenditure depends on the marginal tax rate of the donor, ranging from zero for those who are not liable for income tax, to the top rate times the value of the gift for those in the highest income bracket (for illustrative purposes, assume that the top rate is 50 per cent: the top marginal rate at the federal level has in fact varied very considerably in the USA over the last 70 years). Thus, the higher a person's marginal tax rate, the more the gift will be subsidized by the state: a gift of $500 from those on the zero rate will cost the state nothing, and the donor the full $500, whereas a gift from a donor on a marginal rate of 50 per cent will cost the donor only $250, the state paying the rest of the bill of $250. This feature of the charitable contribution deduction has come in for the most criticism.

Value-added tax (VAT) concessions in Europe

The VAT concession on the consumption of the output of the arts applies only in Europe and, as mentioned previously, may involve a large tax expenditure in relation to the arts, both in absolute terms and in relation to direct funding to such institutions.

In principle, the VAT is a pure revenue-raising tax, the intention being that a uniform rate would apply to all goods and services, thereby leaving relative prices and, as such, the choices of individuals in the marketplace unchanged. This, and its administrative simplicity, at least in a computerized economy, were seen as the major advantages of the tax. The practice is rather different. In particular, different rates of VAT now apply to different goods, thereby providing a tax incentive to the sectors with the lower rates.

Practice varies considerably between the countries of the European Union (EU), with regard both to the standard rate and to the rates that apply to outputs of the arts sector. The level of the standard rate is important, as it is in relation to this that the tax expenditure associated with the lower rates would be calculated.[7] It is clear that in Europe the intention is to have a lower rate of VAT for the arts sector, as the Sixth European Council Directive of 1977 committed the member states eventually to exempt theatre, concerts and other cultural events, the reason being the interest.

The tax forgone associated with the concession is likely to be very sizeable, as it would amount to 15 to 20 per cent of box-office income of all performing arts companies, not just the non-profit institutions. This assumes, though, that attendance would not drop significantly if VAT were imposed on the performing arts sector, thus raising the price of a ticket, in other words, that the demand for tickets is price-inelastic. As mentioned, reduced VAT rates apply to all arts institutions, which makes this tax concession a very unfocused funding device for the government. There is no reason, though, why tax expenditures cannot be designed to be more targeted (see Rushton, 2008) and hence comply more with government policy towards the arts.

Notes

1. See Feld (2008) and Rushton (2008) marking the 25th anniversary of the publication of this book.
2. A further reason may be related to the more unequal distribution of income in the USA, and the higher per capita incomes there, which, together, would mean many more very wealthy people than in Europe
3. See O'Hagan and McAndrew (2001) for a discussion of these.
4. For example, if the tax concession of a zero VAT rate on theatre admissions were abolished, what assumption would be made about the level of attendance resulting from the higher price? If, say, it dropped by 50 per cent, is the tax forgone calculated on the basis of attendance after or before the tax is imposed?
5. Simon (1987) provides a very useful discussion of this issue. The essence of the argument is that 'an item of revenue received by a taxpayer and then given away to charity during the same period does not increase the taxpayer's net worth' (p. 73). It applies also, Simon argues, to the estate tax charitable deduction, in that the definition of wealth for estate tax purposes should refer to those assets available only for private accumulation or consumption of private goods (and not public or semi-public goods such as the output of an art museum). While Simon argues that these points should not be rejected, he does appear to recognize that the general view, in both legal and in economic circles, is that such deductions do constitute a tax expenditure or indirect subsidy.
6. Simon argues that the property tax exemption may not be an exemption at all, in that property tax should not apply anyway to many arts institutions since they do not form part of a correctly defined property tax base (Simon, 1987). However, this is a view that is difficult to sustain.
7. Or more correctly, perhaps, the rate that would apply if there were a single rate applied to all goods and services.

See also:

Chapter 42: Non-profit organizations; Chapter 52: Public support.

References

Feld, A., M. O'Hare and M. Schuster (1983), *Patrons Despite Themselves: Taxpayers and Tax Policy*, New York: New York University Press.
Feld, A. (2008), 'Revisiting Tax Subsidies for Cultural Institutions', *Journal of Cultural Economics*, 32 (4), 275–9.
Fullerton, D. (1991), 'Tax Policy Toward Art Museums', in M. Feldstein (ed.), *The Economics of Art Museums*, Chicago, IL: University of Chicago Press, pp. 195–234.
O'Hagan, J. (1998), *The State and the Arts: An Analysis of Key Economic Policy Issues in Europe and the United States*, Cheltenham, UK and Lyme, USA: Edward Elgar.
O'Hagan, J. and C. McAndrew (2001), 'Restricting International Trade in the National Artistic Patrimony: Economic Rationale and Policy Instruments', *International Journal of Cultural Property*, 10 (1), 32–54.
Rushton, M. (2008), 'Who Pays? Who Benefits? Who Decides?', *Journal of Cultural Economics*, 32 (4), 293–300.
Schuster, M. (2006), 'Tax Incentives in Cultural Policy', in V. Ginsburgh and D. Throsby (eds), *Handbook of the Economics of the Art and Culture*, Vol. 1, Amsterdam: Elsevier, pp. 1254–98.
Simon, J. (1987), 'The Tax Treatment of Non-profit Organizations: A Review of Federal and State Policies', in W. Powell (ed.), *The Non-profit Sector*, New Haven, CT: Yale University Press, pp. 67–98.
Weil, S. (1991), 'Tax Policy and Private Giving', in S. Benedict (ed.), *Public Money and the Muse: Essays on Government Funding for the Arts*, New York: W.W. Norton, pp. 153–81.

Further reading

The key general readings on this topic include: Feld *et al.* (1978), O'Hagan (1998), ch. 5; Schuster (2006) and Simon (1987).

58 Television
Christopher Maule

The production and transmission of pictures electronically was invented in the USSR and the USA in the 1920s. By the 1950s, television content and carriage had become a commercial mass medium competing for audiences with radio and other media. Since then developments have included the introduction of colour, cable, the videocassette and personal video recorder, the remote control, satellites, digitalization and compression technology, and currently the Internet and interactive television. Each technological development has altered the economic organization of the industry, moving it from the traditional broadcast one-way medium to a narrowcast and interactive medium, with viewers having greater control over what and when to watch.

There are two dimensions to consider – content and carriage. Television content now includes both television programmes and other forms of video content transmitted in non-traditional ways such as via the Internet. The website YouTube is an example of how all types of video content are available on demand via the Internet, as well as complete commercially produced television programmes and excerpts from these programmes that have already been broadcast. In October 2009, YouTube served over one billion videos a day. Other examples of hybrid forms of delivery include electronic editions of newspapers that include a video window.

As viewers gain greater control over what and when they watch, and what they choose to pay for, changes are occurring to the way video content is produced, financed and delivered. These and future developments will allow viewers to control a wealth of content but will need their more active participation and different forms of payment.

The main industry players are broadcasters, cablecasters, satellite and Internet service providers, content producers, advertisers, networks and viewers. Others include equipment manufacturers for the production, sending, receiving, storage and replay of audiovisual signals. Surrounding this cast is government, which is involved in numerous ways, at times to the detriment of the industry and its viewers, by restricting competition. In Europe, it was some time before private broadcasters were allowed to compete with public ones. Aside from assigning frequencies, governments regulate the type and nationality of content, its time of showing, the length and type of advertising, and the intellectual property rights of content owners. Many aspects of regulation become complex, with Internet delivery of video as opposed to transmission by government-assigned frequencies. Financing of video content and delivery requires experimentation with the combination of revenue streams from advertising, licensing, taxation and viewer-pay business models.

Economic characteristics

A principal economic feature of video content is non-exhaustibility. Once produced, the content can be used repeatedly without additional expenditure of resources. With few incremental costs, the content can be translated into other languages and reach wider markets. These public-good features encourage commercial content producers to sell in international as well as domestic markets. Programmes are also sold over time, so that new and old programmes compete with each other.

Non-exhaustibility applies to some extent to video distribution. A signal broadcast from a transmitter can reach anyone within range of the signal for no added cost on the part of the broadcaster. Each additional viewer has either to acquire a receiving device such as a television set or computer, or share a receiver with someone else. Reaching a larger audience requires expenditures for a stronger terrestrial transmitter or use of some more powerful means of communication, such as satellites. Internet delivery requires the receiver having Internet access by cable, satellite or wireless.

A second economic feature of video content is non-excludability. It is costly to charge viewers for free traditional television content. If some agreed to pay for these signals, free-riders could not be excluded. Public-good dimensions of television become converted to private goods when signals are packaged so that non-payers are excluded. Delivery of programmes by cable companies to subscribers, scrambling satellite signals and renting or selling videocassettes are methods of excluding non-payers. None is perfect.

The combination of non-exhaustibility and non-excludability makes protection of intellectual property an important issue. Content is protected by copyright and distributors obtain the rights for programme distribution in a given format, language and region. However, current methods of delivery also allow video signals to be altered, manipulated and borrowed, thus weakening the protection provided.

A further economic aspect of video content results from two forms of personal interaction. Word of mouth spreads information about a programme, such as a posting on YouTube or Twitter, which can lead to an informational cascade promoting the video in ways that lead producers to spend resources on stimulating favourable reports. Second, consumption of video content is both a personal and a social phenomenon. Discussion of the content with others is part of the satisfaction obtained by viewers. Its use as a political and instructional tool in recruiting and rallying for a particular cause has become significant.

Finding the money

There are three main sources of funding for traditional television programmes: advertisers, taxpayers and viewers. These may be used individually or in combination. Video produced for distribution by broadcasters, cablecasters and satellite service providers may appear in whole or in part on the Internet, perhaps accompanied by advertising. When original video content on the Internet is posted and paid for by individuals or organizations, it becomes a form of advertising in addition to Internet banner advertising.

Conventional commercial television broadcasting

Traditional television programmes are received over wireless, satellite and cable and by renting or buying videocassettes and digital video discs (DVDs). In the conventional television broadcast industry, viewers receive so-called 'free' commercial television by wireless, often described as broadcasters delivering eyeballs to advertisers. To succeed, they must entice audiences to watch the programmes in which their commercials are embedded. The viewers' commitment is to their time and to the purchase of a television set. Competition for their time comes mainly from other leisure-time activities including surfing the web and playing video games.

Broadcast stations may produce some of their own programmes, such as news and local current affairs, or purchase programmes from independent producers. They are paid to broadcast programmes acquired and distributed by the networks that may reward their affiliates with funding or shares of advertising revenues. Stations may deal with advertisers directly for the programmes they produce themselves or acquire independently. The advertisers' hope is that viewers will buy the products seen as commercials. Ultimately, customers for the advertised products, whether viewers or not, pay for the commercials and help to fund the television industry.

The establishment of networks is an organizational response to conditions facing the industry. Governments often license several stations in a given area and permit the same frequency to be used in different locations. By affiliating with a network, broadcasters can share programming costs with other stations and gain access to better-quality programmes since larger budgets tend to produce more hits. Advertising sold to national advertisers reduces transaction costs. The network collects revenue from advertisers rather than advertisers selling to each station. The funds are spent to acquire programmes and pay individual broadcasters to carry them. As intermediaries, networks act as wholesalers.

Syndication is another form of wholesaling where a firm obtains the rights to existing programmes, such as reruns of *Coronation Street* or *Baywatch*, and sells them to broadcasters who in turn sell advertising to be combined with the programmes. Barter syndication refers to programmes supplied to broadcasters with some commercials already embedded in the programmes, allowing the broadcaster to pay less.

Public broadcasters

In many countries, but excluding the USA, television began with state-owned and -controlled public broadcasters funded out of government revenues. Variants of this model have evolved. The British Broadcasting Corporation (BBC) has no commercials at home and is paid for by a licence fee for the ownership of a television set. The international service of the BBC contains advertising; the government-funded Australian Broadcasting Corporation is commercial-free for television programmes; the Canadian Broadcasting Corporation has two funding sources, commercials and government, including access to government subsidies; and the Public Broadcasting System in the USA receives a combination of government funding, money from voluntary support drives, video sales and corporate sponsorships, which are akin to advertising.

Despite attempts to make public broadcasters independent of the political process, this seldom happens. Those responsible for funding have a direct or indirect influence on programme content, especially when it can affect political outcomes. Private broadcasters are affected by governments through regulation.

Technology

Successive technological developments alter relationships between the players. Colour television made the medium more competitive. The videocassette recorder allowed the viewer to record and store programmes for watching when desired and skip commercials. Pre-recorded programmes can either be rented or purchased as videocassettes or DVDs, leading to competition with the broadcaster's schedule.

The remote control allows viewers an easy means to control what they watch. They can readily switch between programmes and exclude commercials. The impact on advertisers can be substantial and broadcasters can no longer expect that viewers will stay with a particular station. Programmes are often scheduled sequentially in the hope that a popular offering will attract an audience to the previous and following programmes. The remote control weakens this strategy.

Cable television came into being because some viewers were unable to receive wireless signals. An entrepreneur would pick up the signals and for a fee transmit them by cable to the excluded viewers. Television then had two sources of funding, advertisers and subscribers. Cable technology also gave the companies the capacity to deliver more signals and remove the spectrum scarcity that had limited the number of channels and provided a rationale for governments to license stations. Cable companies received distant broadcast signals by satellite for delivery to local audiences. Specialist channels were developed later, producing content such as sports, films, weather, history and children's programmes, as well as classified advertising and shopping channels. Cable companies pay the specialty channels for their content on a per-subscriber basis. In the case of a shopping channel, where sales can generate a separate source of revenue, the channel pays the cable company to be carried. In turn, the cable company charges subscribers according to the package of signals received. Wireless cable and streaming television signals through the Internet further increase distribution capacity and viewer choice.

Viewers gain more choice with cable, but it is not yet a pick-and-pay or video-on-demand system for individual programmes or channels as cablecasters, often responding to government regulations, are only allowed to offer packages of channels. For example, a cable company is usually required to carry local wireless channels. Webcasting of video content provides the viewer with more choice, requiring only high-speed Internet access.

Cable companies are typically licensed as monopoly suppliers in a given region. Competition arises when satellite delivery covers the same area, but the extent depends on whether satellite providers have programme rights that allow them to compete and can effectively scramble the signals. Competition policy problems arise with vertical integration, when cable companies own programme channels and favour delivery of their own content.

Production risks

Technological developments have fragmented mass into niche audiences, altering their importance to advertisers. Smaller audiences with focused interests may have greater appeal to advertisers. A wide range of programmes is produced in different genres – news, public affairs, sports, drama, movies, 'soaps' and children's programmes. Each appeals to a particular aspect of viewers' preferences and to selected advertisers. Toy manufacturers will tend to advertise on children's programmes and sports equipment manufacturers on sports programmes. The problem for advertisers is to know the number and demographic profile of viewers. This is especially difficult for free television, while subscription television reveals some information about subscribers even if it is not known who is actually watching at any particular moment.

The economics of programme production, especially for drama and entertainment programming, is beset by uncertainty. No one knows if a movie or programme will be successful or not, and yet expenditure has to be made to complete the programme before it can be shown. All production expenditures are sunk costs and, if the programme fails, few if any costs may be recovered. A second type of risk stems from productions where artistic and technical teams must develop the project within tight schedules. Costs escalate with production delays. Opportunistic behaviour by key players choosing not to cooperate after some of the programme has been shot may strain the budget. The ability to protect intellectual property rights is a third type of uncertainty. Once broadcast, the programme can be easily captured on DVDs and copies made inexpensively. Owned or rented material can also be copied cheaply. For each of these risks, the industry has developed contractual, organizational and technical responses.

Piracy is probably the biggest problem facing the traditional television industry, but more so for some programmes than others. News and current affairs programmes have a short time value that discourages piracy. Entertainment such as films or popular series and children's programmes, which are viewed repeatedly, are more likely to be stolen. This problem has become more acute with the Internet, where file-sharing makes it cheap to exchange digital files.

The distribution of programmes takes place in 'windows' or a series of markets, each of which generates revenues (for the owners of programme rights) by allowing price discrimination to occur. Windows vary by timing, format and geographical market according to the programme content. Films, for example, are typically released first in theatres and then on videocassettes and DVDs, pay-per-view cable, pay cable, basic cable, satellite dish, broadcast network television and syndication cable. International distribution is carefully timed with domestic release. Some films, such as *Casablanca* (1942), *Citizen Kane* (1941) and *The Wizard of Oz* (1939), continue to generate television revenues long after their initial release.

Role of government

Governments have been intimately involved with the television industry from the outset because of its effect on the political process. Democratic as well as authoritarian governments are concerned over the ways public opinion can be influenced at the ballot box by television. Licensing of private broadcasters allows governments to reward their supporters. Public broadcasters can be influenced more easily than those that are commercially financed. Governments have used licensing of the spectrum as a way to control entry into television broadcasting and programme content. Instead of auctioning the spectrum, governments have until recently used a 'beauty contest' format to select the winners. They have often stipulated conditions such as advertising time per hour, amount of children's programming per week, timing of adult entertainment, and required national content per day or week.

Broadcasters and cablecasters receive a licence for a set period and apply for licence renewal, at which time further demands can be made on them. Governments' concerns have been universality – that signals be equally available to all; fairness – that opposing viewpoints receive equal time, especially during elections; and appropriate content – that material dealing with violence, hate, bad language and pornography should meet social standards, issues for which a broadcasting standards council is often established to help the regulators uphold community norms.

The future

The Internet and the replacement of analogue by digital signals have disturbed current economic relationships. Traditional television broadcasters establish websites as an extension of their traditional forms of programme delivery. Radio stations stream audio signals including advertising over the Internet to be received by audiences using computers. In the same way, video signals are streamed, providing alternatives to the television set as a means of watching programmes. As yet, the picture quality is not as good on a computer terminal or on other handheld electronic devices as on a television set, but this will certainly change. Exploiting streaming video via websites requires more active participation by audiences than has typically been the case for the 'couch potato-type' viewer, but the range of choice has expanded enormously, to include not only existing television stations but available websites. There were an estimated 21 billion web pages posted in 2009, up from 3 billion in 2000. While the majority are in English, many languages are used.

Advertising revenue is migrating slowly from traditional broadcast television to the Internet. While the latter still attracts a much smaller percentage of advertising revenue than traditional television, the rate of growth of Internet advertising is much higher. In the USA, broadcast television advertising was virtually unchanged between 2000 and 2007, while its share of total advertising fell from 18 per cent to 16 per cent; for Internet advertising total expenditure rose 62 per cent and its share increased from 2.6 per cent to 3.8 per cent.[1] Advertising expenditure on the Internet in the UK now exceeds television advertising.[2] In 2009, Google searches generated $21 billion of advertising revenue from Internet advertising, an amount equal to all advertising in US consumer magazines and two-thirds of advertising revenue in US newspapers.[3] Where these revenue streams go in the future and the business models developed will determine the nature and extent of video delivery by broadcast television and the Internet.

Television viewership is decreasing, especially among the young, the same people spending more time on the Internet for e-mail, chat, games, homework or downloading music, as well as for content traditionally provided by television. YouTube, Twitter, Flickr and other arenas are used for social networking, especially by the young. Other use of leisure time is to buy and sell goods and services, access news and entertainment from and do research on the Internet. As the availability of high-speed broadband increases, more people will be drawn to these alternatives, with implications for traditional programme viewership and advertising expenditures. Consumers will acquire even greater control over programming with the introduction of personal VCRs using digital technology, where users can access a programming guide and record up to 20 hours of high-definition and 90 hours of regular digital programming. Viewers can then create their own programme schedule with the ability to bypass commercials.

As storage devices become cheaper and capable of storing more information, there will be increased competition for the electronic transmission of many types of programmes. Traditional television may then be limited to real-time news and sports programmes, which will have difficulty covering the high fixed costs of broadcasting. Even here, live-action sports such as Wimbledon tennis is available on pay Internet. Another development will be interactive television, where, for example, the viewer can answer game show questions by using a button on the remote control, vote for competing contestants or bid on and buy merchandise. How these developments play out will determine the future shape of the industry (Shirky, 2008). Two indicators of ongoing developments in television are trends in audience and advertising data. In order to keep abreast of these developments, the author has found trade publications to be useful sources such as *Wired* magazine, *Broadcast and Cable News*, the *Economist* and financial newspapers as well as Internet searches using related key words.

Notes

1. http://www.census.gov/compendia/statab/tables/09s1239.pdf (accessed 1 November 2009).
2. http://news.bbc.co.uk/2/hi/business/8280557.stm (accessed 10 December 2009)
3. http://www.charlierose.com/download/transcript/10700 (accessed 15 November 2009)

See also:

Chapter 11: Broadcasting; Chapter 17: Creative industries; Chapter 27: Digitalization; Chapter 38: Media economics and regulation.

References

Acheson, Keith and Christopher Maule (2006), 'Culture in International Trade,' in V.A. Ginsburgh and David Throsby (eds), *Handbook of the Economics of Art and Cultures*, Sydney: Elsevier, pp. 1141–82.
Auletta, Ken (2009), *Googled: The End of the World as We Know It*, New York: Penguin.
Caves, Richard E. (2006), 'Organization of Arts and Entertainment Industries', in V.A. Ginsburgh and David Throsby (eds), *Handbook of the Economics of Art and Cultures*, Sydney, Elsevier, pp. 553–6.
Legros, Patrick (2006), 'Copyright, Art and Internet', in V.A. Ginsburgh and David Throsby (eds), *Handbook of the Economics of Art and Cultures*, Sydney: Elsevier, pp. 285–308.
McKinsey and Company (1999), 'Public Service Broadcasters Around the World: A McKinsey Report for the BBC' (online at: http://www/bbc.co.uk/info/bbc/pdf/McKinsey.pdf).
Owen, Bruce M. (1999), *The Internet Challenge to Television*, Cambridge, MA: Harvard University Press.
Shirky, Clay (2008), *Here Comes Everybody: The Power of Organizing Without Organizations*, New York: Penguin.

Further reading

Developments are taking place rapidly both with the technology and the ways in which attempts are made to commercialize television content and carriage. Hard-copy publications are not always the best source for keeping abreast of developments. The following online resources are useful for remaining up to date: http://www.broadcastingcable.com/; http://www.wired.com/ and http://www.economist.com/. Television issues related to copyright are found in Legros (2006), to the organization of cultural industries in general in Caves (2006) and to international trade in Acheson and Maule (2006). See also Auletta (2009), McKinsey and Company (1999) and Owen (1999).

59 Theatre
Daniel Urrutiaguer

In Ancient Greece, the state controlled and financed theatrical activities in order to celebrate Dionysus. In Western Europe, the dependence of the arts on the Church has weakened since the Renaissance with the professionalization of companies. Royal court patronage promoted an academic production of tragedies whereas an interest for comedies or bourgeois dramas grew in the eighteenth century. The development of a private market is related to the social recognition of the playwrights' originality. The popular taste for spectacular and stars' ham acting drove highbrow directors to develop naturalistic or symbolic forms on stage at the end of the nineteenth century, while modern authors broke the psychological unity of characters. Following Bernheim (1932), Leroy (1990) distinguishes the 'stock system', where a 'director-*cum*-manager' heads a permanent company, from the 'combination system', where directors assemble artists for each production on an *ad hoc* basis. Because of the 'industrial revolution' on the stage, the combination system has grown since 1875 in the USA and since the early twentieth century in France. French subsidies for new staging of an existing work or the creation of new theatrical works and indirect grants with specific unemployment benefit for 'intermittent' artists and technicians stimulate the splitting up of theatrical production within an economic system of short-run shows. Germany or Russia is closer to the 'stock system' with permanent companies in state-owned and -managed theatres. The proportion of public subsidies in the total income contrasts with the North American and UK systems where private contributions have more weight. Compared to profit-making privately owned proprietary companies, private and publicly owned non-profit-making firms are prevalent everywhere.

In most countries, the number of shows and theatre companies is growing much faster than private demand, while decreasing public budgets are a common experience. Since the 1970s, fringe companies expanded from the official institutions by mixing experimental shows and shows with appeal for local low-income people. Consequently, the main problems of regulation nowadays come from excess supply of theatrical productions, an unequal stratification of the distribution networks, and tension between the public objectives of artistic excellence and equality of access in increasingly multicultural societies.

Demand for theatre

International surveys of theatre participation show a positive correlation with academic qualifications, income and town size. The distribution is more unequal for opera, jazz or classical music, and more balanced for other performances (see Heilbrun and Gray, 2001; Eurostat, 2007). The hypothesis of 'rational addiction' justifies a deterministic framework with the accumulation of consumption capital that reduces the implicit price of arts (Becker and Murphy, 1988). 'Learning by consuming' models the discovery of taste with positive or unpleasant surprises from past experiences (Lévy-Garboua and Montmarquette, 1996). Their econometric study shows that French theatre attendance in 1987 was greater for people who know a lot about actors and directors and talk about theatre in their social circles; furthermore, the substitution effects of reading and cinema attendance on the demand for theatre are important too. Abbé-Decarroux and Grin (1992) have related the perception of risk of potential disappointment on the part of older people to account for the younger attendance rate at spoken theatre, compared to opera and symphony concerts. Whereas most econometric studies analyse the global demand for theatre as being price-inelastic (Heilbrun and Gray, 2001), Abbé-Decarroux (1994) estimates the demand is price-elastic for reduced seat price at the Geneva Theatre for the period 1982–89. For the 26 Turkish public theatres in 2002–03, Akdebe and King (2006) estimate that the price elasticity is smaller in Ankara, Izmir and Istanbul than in less developed cities. For 178 German public theatres over the period 1965–2004, the full-income elasticity, when including leisure time income in the consumer's budget, is much greater than the disposable income elasticity (Zieba, 2009).

A main line of research concerns the analysis of the heterogeneous demand for theatre. In the USA, Ateca-Amestoy's latent class model (2008) distinguishes, among non-theatregoers in 2002, the people who will never attend from those who might go later. Income and being single reduce the probability of never participating more than parental education. The probability of attending a performance increases more significantly with age and theatrical education than with income, and is greater for women. Throsby (1983, 1990) introduced quality variables with the standards of source material, production, acting and design, which he appraised by a condensation of press reviews into the demand function for individual theatres, finding that estimates varied according to the specific image of the theatres. In contrast with Abbé-Decarroux (1994), Corning and Levy (2002) highlight the insignificance of the critics' impact upon audiences, except in one theatre. Just as the positive impact of income on demand for performing arts is offset to some extent by the negative effect of the opportunity cost for highly time-intensive leisure (Moore, 1968), Urrutiaguer (2002) assumes a contrasting influence between critics' comments and nationally approved directors' reputation upon attendance of French theatrical institutions in 1995 and 1996. Both coefficients are significant with opposite signs when he splits the sample into two subsets, while they are insignificant for the overall sample. Tobias (2004) proposes a non-cardinal aggregation measure of expert opinions and infers their judgements on public theatres in Germany are less connected to economic variables than is the case for ballet or opera.

Costs of production and firm strategy

Baumol and Bowen's (1966) 'cost disease' is based on a view of quality as the capacity to reproduce standard classical plays, whereas demand is assumed to be rather price-elastic and income-inelastic. Baumol and Baumol (1985) interpreted the decreasing average cast size of Broadway non-musical plays for the period 1946–79 as an 'artistic deficit'. Hence they adopt a questionable view of the quantity of work as a main criterion of quality. As fixed costs of production are significantly higher than marginal costs of distribution, scale economies are possible by increasing the number of performances if there is a demand for them. Translog cost functions show an inefficient allocation of capital and labour inputs for theatres in Finland (Taalas, 1997) or in Emilia Romagna in Italy (Fazioli and Filippini, 1997). Touring more frequently can raise revenues that partially offset fixed costs, and price discrimination according to attendees' willingness to pay may increase box-office sales. Whereas the proportion of revivals in Broadway theatre productions grew significantly, Maddison (2005) shows that this risk-averse strategy does not stochastically dominate original productions from a financial perspective.

Economies of scope occur when the joint production of a group of products is cheaper than separate productions. Multi-product production breaks down into programmed shows and other cultural offerings. As most attendees rate sociability highly when they go out, meeting spaces within the theatre like halls, restaurants or bookshops, and the capacity of the management team to give convivial signs are important to enhance the social value of the consumers' experience. A cultural gap between artistic excellence and the local population's interest may increase Baumol and Bowen's 'earnings gap'. The sophistication of technical norms, as a response to competition from cinema and television, increases the costs of production of theatrical performances. More and more theatres are trying to attract regular attendees with short-term events like mini-festivals. Artistic education may above all reproduce the social composition of audiences because parents transfer their culture to children, and school education cannot provide a counterweight to this process without a large amount of subsidy. To make the average person aware of the benefits of theatrical performances primarily requires taking into account their cultural habits. The composition of repertoire may therefore be a crucial question.

Repertoire and theatre management

Following DiMaggio and Stenberg (1985), O'Hagan and Neligan (2005) propose a 'conventionality index' to record the number of productions of works by a playwright in the sample of theatres under consideration. Using this index as the dependent variable, their cross-sectional regression analysis of 40 English subsidized non-profit repertory theatres for the seasons 1996/97 to 1998/99 shows that repertoire is less conventional when venue capacity and budgets are smaller. In accordance with DiMaggio and Stenberg' s results for New York City, location in London reduces the conventionality index because of competition in wealthier markets. However, a higher proportion of public subsidies in a theatre's total income is connected with less conventional choices.

In France, a 'director-*cum*-manager' heads national theatres and national drama centres (NDC). He directs theatrical shows and buys in outside programming. The manager of '*scènes nationales*' (SN) is not usually a director. He is responsible for the theatre's entire programme covering a range of performing arts and events. For the period 1995–97, managers of the biggest NDC and the smallest SN were more open to programming French contemporary shows and SN managers showed a greater interest in contemporary plays than NDC 'director-*cum*-managers' (Urrutiaguer, 2004). Unlike the assumption that artists prefer innovation (DiMaggio and Stenberg, 1985; Castañer and Campos, 2002), the risk of producing theatrical shows compared with buying in performances is hence a key factor.

As classical plays are less risky than contemporary ones, the relationship between the proportion of them in both repertoire and in attendance is expected to be positive. However, the coefficient is weak or insignificant in regression models of demand. For 59 Flemish subsidized theatres over the period 1980–2000, Werck and Heyndels (2007) estimate that cast size, plays by Dutch-speaking playwrights and revivals have a more positive effect on demand. Zieba (2009) estimates that the expenses for décor and costumes and the number of guest performances of the German public theatres are positively related to demand. Artists and theatres' fame may therefore have more influence than the type of repertoire.

Repertoire choice enhances the management's reputation for programming and the viability of theatre. Except for some 'managers-*cum*-directors' who support innovative playwrights, profit-making privately owned theatres focus on light comedies or musicals to increase the probability of commercial success. The trade-off for managers of non-profit organizations is that between the maximization of audience, budget and quality. Principal–agent analysis usually focuses on agents that manipulate information to maximize their public budget. The strategies of managers' theatres are more complex when we consider that they are both the agents of public authorities and the managers of programmed artists.

Krebs and Pommerehne (1995) initiated a psycho-economic approach to the trade-off between lowbrow and highbrow productions for German regional theatre directors. It is a way to refine the analysis of managers' economic motivations in grant-aided theatres. Their reputation comes from a trade-off between box-office revenues, critics' comments and peer groups' judgements on quality. Tension is mounting between a state's requirement of international recognition and the local authorities' expectations of more convivial services in their territories. The necessity to raise their own resources is increasing competition within the sector. Shorter-term productions accentuate artistic excessive offer and the skew distribution of performances per theatre. Hence, as stated by Throsby (1994), progress in quality measurement should be useful to better understand the theatre utility according to the goals of managers, artists and public or private patrons.

See also:

Chapter 15: Costs of production; Chapter 26: Demand; Chapter 47: Performing arts; Chapter 49: Pricing the arts.

References

Abbé-Decarroux, François (1994), 'The Perception of Quality and the Demand for Services. Empirical Application to the Performing Arts', *Journal of Economic Behavior and Organization*, 23, 99–107.

Abbé-Decarroux, François and François Grin (1992), 'Risk, Risk Aversion and the Demand for Performing Arts', in Ruth Towse and Abdul Khakee (eds), *Cultural Economics*, Berlin: Springer-Verlag, pp. 125–40.

Akdebe, Sacit H. and John T. King (2006), 'Demand for and Productivity Analysis of Turkish Public Theater', *Journal of Cultural Economics*, 30, 219–321.

Ateca-Amestoy, Victoria (2008), 'Determining Heterogeneous Behavior for Theater Attendance', *Journal of Cultural Economics*, 32, 127–51.

Baumol, William J. and William G. Bowen (1966), *Performing Arts – The Economic Dilemma*, Cambridge, MA: Twentieth Century Fox.

Baumol, Hilda and William J. Baumol (1985), 'The Future of the Theatre and the Cost Disease of the Arts', in Mary A.,Hendon, James F. Richardson and William B. Hendon (eds), *Bach and the Box*, Akron, OH: Association of Cultural Economics, pp. 7–31.

Becker, Gary S. and Kevin M. Murphy (1988), 'A Theory of Rational Addiction', *Journal of Political Economy*, 96, 675–700.

Bernheim, Alfred L. (1932), *The Business of the Theater – An Economic History of the American Theater, 1750–1932*, New York: Actors Equity Association.

Castañer, Xavier and L. Campos (2002), 'The Determinants of Artistic Innovation: Bringing in the Role of Organizations', *Journal of Cultural Economics*, 26, 29–52.

Corning, Jonathan and Armando Levy (2002), 'Demand for Live Theater with Market Segmentation and Seasonality', *Journal of Cultural Economics*, 26, 217–35.

Di Maggio, Paul and Kristen Stenberg (1985), 'Why do Some Theatres Innovate More than Others?', *Poetics*, 14, 107–22.

Eurostat (2007), *Cultural Statistics*, Brussels: European Commission.

Fazioli, Roberto and Massimo Filippini (1997), 'Cost Structure and Product Mix of Local Public Theatres', *Journal of Cultural Economics*, 21, 77–86.

Krebs, Suzanne and Werner Pommerehne (1995), 'Politico-economic Interactions of German Performing Arts Institutions', *Journal of Cultural Economics*, 19, 17–32.

Heilbrun, James and Charles M. Gray (2001), *The Economics of Art and Culture*, Cambridge: Cambridge University Press.

Leroy, Dominique (1990), *Histoire des arts du spectacle en France*, Paris: L'Harmattan.

Lévy-Garboua, Louis and Claude Montmarquette (1996), 'A Microeconomic Study of Theatre Demand', *Journal of Cultural Economics*, 20, 25–50.

Maddison, David (2005), 'Are There Too Many Revivals on Broadway? A Stochastic Dominance Approach', *Journal of Cultural Economics*, 29 (4), 325–34.

Moore, Thomas G. (1968), *The Economics of American Theater*, Durham, NC: Duke University Press.

O'Hagan, John and Adriana Neligan (2005), 'State Subsidies and Repertoire Conventionality in the Non-Profit English Theatre Sector: An Economic Analysis', *Journal of Cultural Economics*, 29, 35–57.

Taalas, Mervi (1997), 'Generalised Cost Functions for Producers of Performing Arts – Allocative Inefficiencies and Scale Economies in Theatres', *Journal of Cultural Economics*, 21, 335–53.

Throsby, David C. (1983), 'Perception of Quality in Demand for the Theater', in James L. Shanahan (ed.), *Markets for the Arts*, Akron, OH: University of Akron Press, pp. 162–76.

Throsby, David C. (1990), 'Perception of Quality in Demand for the Theatre', *Journal of Cultural Economics*, 14, 34–55.

Throsby, David C. (1994), 'The Production and Consumption of the Arts: A View of Cultural Economics', *Journal of Economic Literature*, 32, 1–29.

Tobias, Stefan (2004), 'Quality in the Performing Arts: Aggregating and Rationalizing Expert Opinion', *Journal of Cultural Economics*, 28, 109–24.

Urrutiaguer, Daniel (2002), 'Quality Judgments and Demand for French Public Theatre', *Journal of Cultural Economics*, 26, 185–202.

Urrutiaguer, Daniel (2004), 'Programme Innovations and Networks of French Public Theatres', *The Service Industries Journal*, 24, 37–55.

Werck, Kristin and Bruno Heyndels (2007), 'Programmatic Choices and the Demand for Theatre; the Case of Flemish Theatres', *Journal of Cultural Economics*, 31, 25–41.

Zieba, Marta (2009), 'Full Income and Price Elasticities of Demand for German Public Theatre', *Journal of Cultural Economics*, 33, 82–108.

Further reading

Regression models of demand are provided in Krebs and Pommerehne (1995), Lévy-Garboua and Montmarquette (1996), O'Hagan and Neligan (2005), Akdebe and King (2006), Werck and Heyndels (2007) and Zieba (2009), whereas Throsby (1983, 1990), Abbé-Decarroux (1994), Corning and Levy (2002), Urrutiaguer (2002) and Tobias (2004) take into account subjective judgements on quality. Non-theatregoers' behaviours are the subject of Ateca-Amestoy (2008). Cost inefficiencies are discussed in Taalas (1997), Fazioli and Filippini (1997) and Maddison (2005). For the cost disease see Baumol and Bowen (1966), Throsby (1994) and Heilbrun and Gray (2001).

60 Welfare economics
Mark Blaug

The arts are subsidized to some extent in every country in the world and yet the standard tools of welfare economics do not readily provide convincing arguments for public funding of the arts. Typically, economists base a case for public subsidies of a sector or industry on the existence of 'market failure', meaning a violation of one or more of the conditions for competitive efficiency. The most frequently cited examples of market failure are (1) 'externalities' or 'spillovers', whether of production or of consumption; (2) 'economies of scale', such that unit costs fall as output increases; (3) 'public goods', that is goods that are non-rivalrous in consumption and non-excludable in their benefits; and (4) endemic consumer ignorance about technically complex goods as, for example, the demand for healthcare.

When it comes to the arts, however, these are frequently supplemented by special arguments about (1) 'equality of opportunity', according to which cultural goods are necessarily 'experience goods', that is, goods that are demanded only by those who have inadvertently experienced them; and (2) the 'option value' of a cultural heritage maintained at public expense across the generations; and (3) the straightforward, self-demonstrable 'merit' of the arts independent of any instrumental value (see Baumol, Chapter 1 in the present volume). It does appear, therefore, that we need something more than standard welfare economics if we are going to talk meaningfully about an economic rationale for public funding of the arts. I label this 'something more' Pigovian welfare economics to distinguish it from standard Paretian welfare economics. Pigovian welfare economics is steeped in partial equilibrium analysis, the type of thinking that Alfred Marshall bequeathed to his leading disciple, A.C. Pigou. Paretian welfare economics, on the other hand, is steeped in general equilibrium theory, which descended from Leon Walras to his principal disciple, Vilfredo Pareto. Paretian welfare economics is orthodox welfare economics expounded in every modern textbook and is marked above all by its claim to analyse economic welfare without appealing in any way to the equality or inequality of the distribution of income among individuals.

Pareto optimality
Walras virtually invented general equilibrium (GE) theory in 1871. Its object was to demonstrate the possibility and even the likelihood of simultaneous multi-market equilibrium in a capitalist economy. Of course, Walras hoped to show not just that GE is possible, but that it is good. But he never got much beyond the idea that voluntary exchange between two traders improves the welfare of both of them – otherwise, why would they have traded? What is true of bilateral exchange, Walras thought, will also be true of competitive exchange between a large number of traders if individual producers cannot themselves set prices, so that all consumers face identical prices for identical homogeneous goods. This is precisely what happens in a state of perfect competition. Thus, QED: perfect competition maximizes social welfare.

Pareto carried on where Walras left off. He too was convinced that GE is good for everyone but, as a follower of Ernst Mach in philosophy, he hated such behavioural assumptions as maximizing happiness, utility, welfare, or call it what you will, and he strenuously objected to interpersonal comparisons of utility (ICU) on the grounds that such comparisons cannot be made operational. Pondering these issues, he realized that the one circumstance that avoids ICU is a social state that meets with unanimous approval or at least with the absence of conflict in which one person is made better off only at the expense of another person. In other words, we want a state that is so efficient that there is no surplus, no waste, no slack, 'no such thing as a free lunch', that can be handed to one person without taking it away from someone else. But is not perfect competition just such a state? Yes and no! Of course, it may leave some people rich and some people poor, but that will be the consequence of the fact that we started with unequal endowments of the individuals in our economy – some people are born clever and some people have rich parents – but, given those endowments that are not themselves explained by GE theory (after all, no theory ever explains everything), the GE model will grind out the rental prices of all the services of land, labour and capital as well as the prices of all goods produced with those services. Once we have somehow arrived at the end state of perfectly competitive equilibrium, it will be impossible to make one person better off without making another person worse off, except by interfering with the initial endowments of agents, say, by giving some people more inherited wealth. In this way, Pareto thought that he had finally found an admittedly narrow definition of the beneficial effects of competition that was totally free of those inherently objectionable ICUs, objectionable because there appears to be no objective way of resolving disagreements about such comparisons.

The idea, only later called 'Pareto optimality', fell into oblivion as soon as it was announced, but was resuscitated along with Walrasian GE theory in the 1930s by John Hicks and Nicholas Kaldor. They extended the scope of Pareto optimality by arguing that any economic change, whether from a position of competitive equilibrium or not, was welfare-improving if the gains to beneficiaries of that change were large enough to enable them, at least in principle, to bribe the losers voluntarily to accept the change. The existence of such potential Pareto improvements (PPI), as they are nowadays called, still involves no ICU because it is grounded in the voluntariness of market exchange: only the judgements of gainers and losers themselves are involved in describing it as an improvement. In short, Hicks and Kaldor (with a prodding from Lionel Robbins), remained faithful to the Paretian conception of how an economist should study welfare economics.

At first glance, the Hicks–Kaldor compensation test does seem virtually to pull a rabbit out of a hat, but further reflection soon shows that the achievement is semantic, not substantive. Why a potential and not an actual PI? The moment we try to implement PPI by encouraging gainers and losers to negotiate a compensation payment between themselves, they will engage in strategic bargaining and, even without fancy game theory, it is easy to see that they may never reach an agreement. If the change has political significance, the state may then intervene to force the parties to agree – in which case we have said goodbye to our taboo on ICU. No matter how we slice it, in the end we cannot avoid (1) a qualitative judgement from on high of the size of the PPI – remember that there is no objective way short of a voluntary transaction to measure the magnitude of a gain or a loss to the parties concerned – and (2) an interpersonal comparison of that gain and loss to the respective parties. But all that brings us back to Pigou, whose *Economics of Welfare* (1921) contained none of Pareto's compunctions about ICU and who was perfectly content to declare that a pound sterling taken from a rich man or woman by a progressive income tax hurts him or her less than the pleasure it gave the recipient of government expenditures.

We have not quite reached the end of this story. Paretian welfare economics was furnished in the 1950s with Kenneth Arrow's proof of what he labelled the First and Second Fundamental Theorems of welfare economics. The first theorem demonstrates that every competitive equilibrium in a decentralized economy is Pareto optimal, which we have already discussed, and the second theorem demonstrates that a Pareto optimum can always be achieved via perfect competition if lump-sum taxes and transfers are feasible, so that, whatever are the original endowments of agents, we can still make everyone better off with a perfectly competitive economy. Immense pains are taken in every textbook of microeconomics to persuade readers of the validity of those two theorems. And they are valid – as mathematical exercises. Lump-sum taxes and transfers are changes that do not affect economic behaviour and even the most ingenious modern welfare economists have never been able to provide convincing examples of such things: for example, in order for them to be unanticipated and therefore not to affect behaviour, they would have to be randomly assigned to individuals or else made to reflect some personal non-economic characteristic, such as more consonants than vowels in one's last name.

I think we may safely conclude that the First and Second Fundamental Theorems of welfare economics are just mental exercises without the slightest possibility of ever being practically relevant. They are what Ronald Coase called 'blackboard economics', an economics that is easy to write on a blackboard in a classroom but that bears no resemblance to the real world outside the classroom.

Why is competition good?

I contend that perfect competition is a grossly misleading concept whose only real value is to generate examination questions for students of economics. It is misleading because it breeds the view that economics is a subject like Euclidean geometry, whose conclusion may be rigorously deduced from fundamental axioms of individual behaviour plus some hard facts about technology. But of course this does not imply that competition is bad. I believe, along with most economists, that competition is good, and the more competition, the better. But if perfect competition is misleading and Pareto optimality almost impossible, what is the basis of this belief in the desirability of competition? It is based on a concept of dynamic efficiency, the results of market operations, and not the static efficiency of Walras, Pareto and the First and Second Fundamental Theorems of welfare economics.

The economy is never in a state of general equilibrium and is riddled with second-best departures from first-best perfect competition in the form of taxes, tariffs, monopolies, regulatory constraints and so on. We call such departures 'second-best', but really they might as well be called tenth-best or hundredth-best because once we are not in a first-best state, being near or far from first-best has no meaning. That was precisely the point of Richard Lipsey and Kevin Lancaster's 'general theory of the second-best'. Given the existence of governments that levy taxes and collect revenues, it follows that we are never at first-best. We know from Lipsey and Lancaster that we cannot prove that, say, the removal of a tax that prevents some business enterprise from pricing its products in accordance with their marginal costs of production – as they should in first-best competitive equilibrium – would improve social welfare. But that is 'prove' mathematically in the language of Paretian welfare economics, in the light of the maxims of static efficiency. It does not mean 'prove' in terms of dynamic efficiency: a particular tax might be statically inefficient but dynamically efficient in that it promoted the process of economic growth over time. Whatever the limitations of Paretian welfare economics, we are constantly faced with the problem of evaluating concrete proposals for taxing or subsidizing specific activities, including of course the visual and performing arts.

Pigovian welfare economics
I label the welfare economics we employ for those purposes 'Pigovian welfare economics' because it owes to Pigou the willingness and even the eagerness to engage in rough-and-ready comparisons of the welfare of individuals endowed with unequal incomes. This is particularly pertinent in respect of arguments for public support of the arts because, as has been amply documented, the typical consumer of the arts is most always richer and wealthier as well as better educated than the average taxpayer.

If we stick to Pareto and avoid any and all ICU, we should, if we are honest, maintain a studious silence about subsidies to the arts. Pigou, on the other hand, emphasized, indeed overemphasized, the first of our four 'market failures', namely, external economies and diseconomies in production and consumption. In all such cases where the various production functions are interdependent rather than independent, the Pareto optimum welfare conditions must be replaced by Pigou's golden rule of welfare maximization: equalization of marginal private and marginal social costs and benefits of all resources and all alternative uses; the national income is maximized if and only if this equalization is obtained. The touchstone of all Pigou's many policy prescriptions to deal with externalities is 'the transference of wealth from the rich to the poor'; if such a transfer does not diminish the growth of national income, it must, Pigou argued, improve social welfare. The reliance of such an assertion on ICU is too obvious to call for discussion.

The stress on the growth rather than on the level of income reminds us of the inherently dynamic flavour of many of Pigou's policy recommendations. By eschewing the very name of Paretian welfare economics with its debt to static GE theory, we are more liable to pay attention to intertemporal welfare arguments for, say, subsidizing arts education in schools or supporting heritage maintenance expenditure for future generations. Paretian welfare economics is grounded in the principle of consumer sovereignty: every individual is the best judge, and indeed, the only judge, of his or her welfare. Without abandoning that principle entirely, it must be emphasized that the arts can be appreciated only by those who have experienced their consumption; in other words, consumer sovereignty must be the sovereignty of the experienced consumer. If that is a value judgement, so are ICUs, and of course, the very notion of *welfare* economics without value judgements is an absurdity. No doubt, labels are only labels and not arguments, but by adhering to the label of Pigovian welfare economics we advertise a distinct heterodox approach to the evaluation of arts spending.

Recent developments in welfare economics

Even Pigovian welfare economics, however, remains indebted to Jeremy Bentham and John Stuart Mill rather than to Aristotle and Kant, in short to the eighteenth-century philosophy of ethics known as utilitarianism. As Amartya Sen has famously argued (Sen and Williams, 1982), utilitarian reasoning is grounded on three axioms: (1) welfarism, namely that every social state must be evaluated only in terms of 'utility' interpreted as personal happiness or the fulfilment of desires; (2) consequentalism, namely that alternative social states must be appraised in terms of their consequences for utility rather than their moral imperatives like duty or obligation; and (3) the summing of utilities, that is, that the utilities of different persons must be appraised by simply adding them up arithmetically regardless of their distribution. These axioms ruled the roost and dominated traditional welfare economics until the last decade or so.

Recently, a different approach to social evaluation has appeared under the umbrella term of eudaimonism. Eudaimonism takes its name from 'daimon', the Greek word for 'nature' and it denotes the belief that individual well-being or welfare consists, not in the maximization of personal satisfaction *à la* Bentham, but in fulfilling one's 'nature'. Eudaimonism, most famously expressed in Aristotle's somewhat opaque words, is less an end-state definition of what it means to be happy than a definition of the active process of flourishing, a striving for perfection, a series of activities that culminate in the realization of one's true potential.

Nussbaum and Sen (1993), in a book about the quality of life, suggest that there is really no conflict between utilitarianism and eudaimonism, so that we can, so to speak, have our cake and eat it too. But it seems to me that these two strands of ethics are actually very difficult to reconcile and in terms of arguments for subsidizing the arts, eudaimonism is deeply subversive of the traditional scepticism of utilitarianism to any state intervention in the arts that is not grounded in clearly expressed market demand.

According to eudaimonism, the very process of experiencing the arts is welfare-enhancing and you cannot really have too much of it. It is difficult to see how this approach would provide an arts administrator with a quantitative guide to a subsidy policy.

The open-ended quality of eudaimonism is highlighted when we link it to Sen's capability approach. The capability approach stemmed originally, not from Aristotle, but from Sen's concern with Third World poverty and the desire to provide the poor with basic needs, such as food, housing, medical care and schooling. But Aristotle's conception of welfare suggest that well-being requires much more than the provision of such essentials, calling in addition for personal autonomy, control of one's environment, access to social groups, family life, participation in political activity and so forth. Some have questioned whether the capability approach is actually operational and have insisted on the need to spell out a list of the capabilities that the state ought to support. However, Sen has resisted spelling out a precise list of essential functionings, arguing that such a list would infringe the very freedom of agents that is central to the capability approach.

On the one hand, Sen insists that individuals themselves should decide what is good for them. On the other hand, he is highly critical of utilitarianism, which derives its idea of social good precisely from what is good for the individual. Moreover, he underlines his conviction that capabilities are both intrinsically heterogeneous and incommensurable, so that the maximization of well-being is an activity rather like Herbert Simon's concept of 'satisficing'; that is, it is achievable only relative to constantly shifting levels of aspirations. In other words, welfare economics in this approach does not achieve a complete ordering or ranking of different possible social states, and even if it does achieve a partial ordering, it is a fuzzy ordering and nothing like the precise quantitative ordering provided in the Benthamite tradition.

Perhaps I have now said enough to suggest that it is by no means obvious how one would answer the mundane questions of arts policy with the aid of the philosophy of eudaimonism. Suffice it to say that it points the way in almost direct opposition to standard welfare economics. It remains to be seen what policy implications follow from this approach.

See also:

Chapter 1: Application of welfare economics; Chapter 52: Public support.

References

Baumol, W.J. and C. Wilson (eds) (2001), *Welfare Economics*, Cheltenham, UK and Northampton, MA, USA: Edward Elgar, vol. 1, pp. xv–xliv.
Blaug, M. (1997), *Economic Theory in Retrospect*, 5th edn, Cambridge: Cambridge University Press, pp. 570–95.
Hennipman, P. (1995), 'Hicks, Robbins and the Demise of Pigovian Welfare Economics', in D.A. Walker, A. Heertje and H. van den Doel (eds), *Welfare Economics and the Theory of Economic Policy*, Aldershot, UK and Brookfield, USA: Edward Elgar, pp. 272–90.
Pigou, A.C. (1921), *Economics of Welfare*, London: Macmillan.
Nussbaum, M. and A. Sen (eds) (1993), *The Quality of Life*, Oxford: Clarendon Press.
Sen, A.K. and A.B. Williams (eds) (1982), *Utilitarianism and Beyond*, Cambridge: Cambridge University Press.
Sloman, J. (1997), *Economics*, London: Prentice-Hall, 3rd edn, ch. 1, pp. 316–57.

Further reading

For a comprehensive survey of the 'old' and the 'new' welfare economics, see the Introduction to Baumol and Wilson (2001). For a less demanding journey over the same territory, see Blaug (1997) and for a really introductory textbook review of welfare economics as economists see it, consult Sloman (1997). Pieter Hennipman's (1995) chapter attempts to purge welfare economics of all its subjective aspects. Whether successful or not, this introduces students to the classical Aristotelian conception of welfare, which throws a radical new light on the old question of state support for the arts.

Index